TO END ALL WARS

TO END ALL WARS

Woodrow Wilson and the Quest for a New World Order

THOMAS J. KNOCK

New York   Oxford
OXFORD UNIVERSITY PRESS
1992

Oxford University Press

Oxford   New York   Toronto
Delhi   Bombay   Calcutta   Madras   Karachi
Kuala Lumpur   Singapore   Hong Kong   Tokyo
Nairobi   Dar es Salaam   Cape Town
Melbourne   Auckland   Madrid

and associated companies in
Berlin   Ibadan

Published by Oxford University Press, Inc.,
200 Madison Avenue, New York, New York 10016

Oxford is a registered trademark of Oxford University Press

Library of Congress Cataloging-in-Publication Data
Knock, Thomas J.
To end all wars : Woodrow Wilson and the quest
for a new world order /
Thomas J. Knock.
p.   cm. Includes bibliographical references and index.
ISBN 0-19-507501-3
1. Wilson, Woodrow, 1856–1924.   2. League of Nations—History.
3. World War, 1914–1918—Peace.
4. United States—Foreign relations—1913–1921.
I. Title.   E767.1.K56 1992   973.91'3—dc20   92-5054

2 4 6 8 9 7 5 3 1
Printed in the United States of America
on acid-free paper

For
my mother and father,
Evelyn T. Moorman and Jack A. Knock
my aunt, Dorothea M. Drischel
and Arthur S. Link

Preface

This volume is a study of the impact of ideas and events upon a statesman who, for weal or for woe, attempted to shape the course of the history of the modern epoch. It is not, however, a monograph about the Paris Peace Conference and the battle over ratification of the Treaty of Versailles, per se. Those two subjects—with the exception of perhaps a single chapter devoted to events before November 1918—have been the exclusive focus of practically every book ever written about Woodrow Wilson and the League of Nations. This study substantially reverses that emphasis—although the creation of the League at Paris and the ratification fight (from an interpretive perspective) receive considerable attention.

In the course of my research it seemed to me that many of the most interesting and decisive developments in the evolution of the League of Nations idea took place well before Wilson went to the peace conference, and that greater light might be shed on the struggle by going back to its inception—some four or five years before those months of superheated debate upon which the historiography tends to dwell. I have, therefore, endeavored to describe and analyze the American origins of the League in a way that has not been done before. It is, to begin, a highly dramatic story in which domestic politics and foreign policy are inextricably inter-twined, turning on the pivot of what I have called "progressive internationalism." The meaning of this term, as a particular approach to international relations, will become apparent in the chapters that follow; suffice it to say here that progressive internationalism was distinctly different from the "conservative internationalism" of the sort espoused by William Howard Taft and the League to Enforce Peace (the most influential of all pro-League organizations); nor does "progressive internationalism" necessarily fit neatly into the New Left classification of "liberal-capitalist internationalism," an interpretation that has prevailed since the 1960s.

Progressive internationalism evolved within the context of American neutrality, during the first two-and-a-half years of the Great War—coincidentally, an extended interlude in American political history when many liberal reformers and socialists (especially the respective left and center-right wings of their movements) seemed to agree on more things than they disagreed on. Frederick Jackson Turner once called the Progressive Era "the age of socialistic inquiry." It was an apt description. Beginning in 1914 and continuing roughly into the first months after the United States entered the war, Wilson regularly sought the counsel and support not only of progressives outside the Democratic party, but also of individuals and groups of relatively pronounced leftist tendencies, including key residents of the socialist left. Many of the latter, like John Reed and Max Eastman, became fascinated with Wilson at an early stage in his presidency because of their singular understanding (and approval) of his intervention in the Mexican Revolution.

Although its consequences have never been closely scrutinized, Wilson carried on a communion of profound significance with the American left along with the liberal-left. In many respects, this exchange of ideas influenced his thinking at least as much as, say, his relationship (amply investigated by historians) with the liberals of the *New Republic* or the British radicals. I refer here, for example, to organizations such as the Woman's Peace party, the American Union Against Militarism, and various elements of the Socialist Party of America. These groups made up the most intellectually vital part of the short-lived, but no less historically crucial, left-of-center coalition that helped elect Wilson to a second term in 1916.

Wilson frequently corresponded and held innumerable conferences with leading members of the foregoing groups—including Jane Addams, Eastman and Reed, Amos Pinchot, Upton Sinclair, John Spargo, Oswald Garrison Villard, Lillian Wald, Rabbi Stephen S. Wise, Morris Hillquit, and James H. Maurer, among others. They were at once the advance guard of the so-called New Diplomacy in the United States and the impassioned proponents of an Americanized version of social democracy. From them emanated most of the components of Wilson's formula for a new world order as well as a program for social and economic justice at home. They also helped Wilson grasp the fact, particularly as he grappled with the issue of military preparedness in 1915–16, that the reactionary opponents of domestic reform and the advocates of militarism, imperialism, and balance-of-power politics were twins born of the same womb.

Wilson won the political support of most liberals, a large bloc of socialists, and many in between when, on the eve of his re-election campaign, he finally pushed through Congress an impressive list of social justice reforms. He secured the genuine allegiance of those groups by drawing together the strands of their thought on foreign policy and by focusing world attention on the idea of a league of nations; but he began to do so long before the famous Fourteen Points address of January 1918. In fact, Wilson made the League an issue as early as 1916, and it was during his re-election campaign, not in 1918, that the League first began to take on a partisan and strongly ideological complexion. If any doubts about him lingered in the minds of progressive internationalists, they surely evaporated when he issued his peace note of December 1916 and followed it up with the climactic "Peace Without Victory" address to the Senate, on January 22, 1917. It was in this manifesto (delivered before the onset of the Russian Revolution) that he first launched his critique of European imperialism, militarism, and balance-of-power politics—the root causes of the war and related disturbances, he said. In their stead he called for a "community of nations"—a new world order sustained by procedures for the arbitration of disputes between nations, general disarmament, self-determination, and collective security. The chief instrument of this sweeping program to supersede the old order was to be, of course, a "League of Peace." Thus Wilson began his ascent to a position of central importance in the history of international relations in the twentieth century.

These were stirring days for most American liberals and socialists. Through the touchstone of Wilson's reform legislation of 1916 and his synthesis of the tenets of the New Diplomacy, the progressive internationalists were able to seize the initiative and claim title to the League, at least until the spring of 1917 (and perhaps somewhat beyond). Once the United States entered the war, however, Wilson's immediate priorities soon shifted to the exigencies of mobilization. And, in part owing to stinging Republican criticism of "Peace Without Victory" as the basis for the postwar settlement, he refused to discuss the League in any detail throughout the period of American belligerency and neglected to lay essential political groundwork for it at home.

By the autumn of 1918, important segments among conservative and progressive internationalists alike had grown disenchanted with Wilson, albeit for entirely different reasons. This development would prove to be as unfortunate as the overt, partisan opposition to his league idea led by Theodore Roosevelt and Henry Cabot Lodge. On one hand, Wilson repeatedly frustrated the wartime efforts of conservative internationalists (the Taftites of the League to Enforce Peace) who wanted to make formal plans for the League in cooperation with the British government. (There were, of course, serious ideological differences between his and William Howard Taft's approach to the League.) On the other hand, Wilson failed to nurture the coalition of 1916—a dynamic political force that, if it had remained intact, might have made it possible for him to prevail in the critical mid-term elections of 1918 and to secure and validate American leadership in a peacekeeping organization intended to serve progressive purposes in world politics. But he began to lose his grip on much of his former base of support in his acquiescence in the suppression of civil liberties at home. (American participation in the Allied intervention in the Russian Revolution, reluctant though Wilson was about it, contributed to the unraveling as well.) He also failed to take advantage of opportunities to rekindle the coalition just as the bitter parliamentary contest was getting under way. Ultimately, after he had already lost the active support of most socialists and left-wing progressives, many liberal supporters turned their backs on him after reading the Treaty of Versailles.

Thus the die was cast but not alone for the reasons conventionally cited in the literature on the subject (including Wilson's physical collapse). On one level, the struggle over ratification represents no more (and no less) than a dénouement. For this entire sequence of events was set in motion at the birth of the progressive internationalist movement in 1915–16 and in the forging of Wilson's victory coalition of 1916. The circumstances surrounding the dissolution of progressive internationalism at length sealed the fate of a *Wilsonian* League. Perhaps of greater significance, it also cut the pattern for American politics and foreign policy for the rest of the century: to wit, the disinclination of most liberals ever afterward to seek support from even the "domesticated" left; and, concomitantly, the proclivity among conservatives to brand liberals as incipient socialists, which the Republicans did for the first time (and with penetrating effect) from 1918 to 1920.

Decades later, Wilson would be designated by historians and political scientists (both admirers and critics) as the father of modern American "globalism," but with virtually no distinctions drawn between a foreign policy based on the national security state and one based on the concept of internationalism (progressive or otherwise). Despite their occasional appropriation of certain forms of his rhetoric, I suggest in my conclusion that, in light of all that has attended Cold War globalism since 1945, there are reasons to doubt whether its architects were the bona fide legatees of Wilsonian progressive internationalism; and that even upon the liquidation of the Cold War (accompanied, as it has been, by new pronouncements about a "new world order") Wilson's message still awaits sorting out by the makers of American foreign policy.

Acknowledgments

In writing this book I have incurred many personal and professional debts I would like to acknowledge here. Anyone who has ever worked in the field will understand why I must begin with Arthur S. Link. As honors and tributes continue to come his way (particularly upon the completion of the monumental sixty-eight-volume series, *The Papers of Woodrow Wilson*), it would be futile for me to try to surpass what so many others have said about the foremost scholar of the Wilson era and his work. But since my first semester of graduate school at Princeton, he has been my friend, critic, and mentor, and his influence on my life has been no less than fundamental. If there is one that is beyond valuation it is the debt that I owe him.

The folks at the Wilson Papers project assisted me in my research on countless occasions; my sincere thanks go to my dear friend Manfred Boemeke as well as to David W. Hirst, John E. Little, Frederick Aandahl, Denise Thompson, and L. Kathleen Amon (who, among other things, helped me locate and select the photographs). As for other Princeton friends, I am grateful to Margaret Douglas Link, Richard D. Challener, and Nancy Weiss Malkiel for their interest and support during and since my years as a graduate student. For his kindness and encouragement, I also wish to express my appreciation to Arno J. Mayer, whose work has always been a source of inspiration to me.

Among those who read and commented on the manuscript in whole or in part, I will always be obliged, for their wise counsel and many kindnesses, to John Milton Cooper, Jr., of the University of Wisconsin, and Charles E. Neu of Brown University. Over the past few years I have profited enormously also from conversations with Lloyd C. Gardner of Rutgers University, Lloyd E. Ambrosius of the University of Nebraska, Betty Miller Unterberger of Texas A & M University, and George W. Egerton of the University of British Columbia. John Whiteclay Chambers II of Rutgers and Kendrick A. Clements of the University of South Carolina each read about ten chapters of an early draft; the time and thoughtful effort they put into their lengthy commentaries far exceeded any reasonable expectations I might have had in anticipating critical feedback. At Oxford University Press, Sheldon Meyer and Karen Wolny cheerfully and expertly guided me through the shoals of publishing a first book, and Gail Cooper edited the manuscript with exceptional care and intelligence. Laura Moss Gottlieb of Madison, Wisconsin, compiled the index.

The American Philosophical Society, the National Endowment for the Humanities, and the University Research Council of Southern Methodist University provided essential financial assistance for my research and writing. The faculty of SMU's Department of History, in a variety of ways, have always been challenging colleagues; in light of their recent recommendation of my tenure and promotion I have learned never to underestimate their wisdom or their sense of humor. I have felt especially strengthened by the unstinting support and friendship of Jennifer Tolbert Roberts, Kathleen A. Wellman, James K. Hopkins, David J. Weber, and Daniel T. Orlovsky (whose example as departmental chair I have always admired). James O. Breeden, Luis Martín, and Donald L. Niewyk (each in his inimitable way) helped me to keep a balanced perspective on things in general. My thanks go also to our excellent administrative staff (past and present), Mona Wildman, Judy Bland, Mildred Pinkston, and to Susie Meyn.

A considerable number of friends and colleagues have rendered services at different stages of my work, and I am grateful to them all: James E. Reynolds, Christine A. Lunardini, Jeffrey R. Wells, Maureen Callahan, David F. Schmitz, Peter S. Onuf, Kristen Onuf, Catherine Clinton, Perry K. Blatz, Elizabeth Craven, Ronald L. Kalin, Kathryn Bernhardt, Kevin Chandler, Olga Boemeke, Tom Fitzsimmons, Ronn Cummings, D. Fred Foster, David M. Kemme, Jack T. Kirby, Andrew Buni, James Timothy Eaton, Mark Schlifer, Grace Hallett Brackin, Robert Szychowski, Louis P. Masur, Gary Kohn, Joseph A. Chrostowski, Patricia Sullivan, M. Francesca Nudo, Diana Page, Rick Maguire, Sheila Brogan Howardton, Michael A. Bernstein, Gary Gerstle, and Fran Walsh, Gail Walsh, Mark Walsh, and James Cosgrove Walsh.

Several members of my family warrant acknowledgment at this time. The dedication page speaks for itself, but, in addition to my parents and my aunt, I would like to express my gratitude and love to my extraordinary sister Betty Jane Mori, of Charlottesville, Virginia, who remains my best friend and most unsparing critic; my younger brother and sister, Joseph A. Knock and Tammy K. Knock; my nieces, Olivia Mori and Adele Mori, and their father, Ken; my uncle, Willard Drischel; and my stepfather, Edward Moorman. I should also like to mention four beloved persons now deceased—my stepmother Donna Myers Knock, John E. Walsh, Michael S. Cole, and Professor Janet Wilson James; it pains me deeply that I will never have the pleasure of putting a copy of this book into their hands. Finally, I wish to thank three exceptional people. The friendship of Alan S. Corcoran has meant more to me than I could ever adequately express. My associaation with James S. Amelang and Louis H. Rose, since we began graduate school together, has been the most edifying part of my experience in becoming a historian.

In closing, I would like to state that, notwithstanding the significant contribution of many friends and colleagues, this book is solely my own creation, and for whatever merit it may possess I am at least ninety-five per cent responsible; all the aforementioned persons are welcome to divide up the remaining five per cent as they see fit. Needless to say, I reserve the right to reverse the proportions as events may require.

Dallas, Texas   T. J. K.
February 1992

Contents

Preface, vii

1. A Political Autobiography, **3**

2. Wilson and the Age of Socialist Inquiry, **15**

3. Searching for a New Diplomacy, **31**

4. The Political Origins of Progressive and Conservative
   Internationalism, **48**

5. The Turning Point, **70**

6. Raising a New Flag: The League and the Coalition of 1916, **85**

7. "All the Texts of the Rights of Man":
   Manifestoes for Peace and War, **105**

8. "If the War Is Too Strong": The Travail of Progressive
   Internationalism and the Fourteen Points, **123**

9. Waiting for Wilson: The Wages of Delay and Repression, **148**

10. "The War Thus Comes to an End," **167**

11. The Stern Covenanter, **194**

12. "A Practical Document and a Humane Document," **210**

13. "The Thing Reaches the Depths of Tragedy," **227**

14. Wilson's Fate, **246**

Epilogue, Echoes from Pueblo, **271**
Abbreviations, **277**
Notes, **279**
Bibliography, **341**
Index, **359**

TO END ALL WARS

"For a brief interval Wilson stood alone for mankind. Or at least he seemed to stand for mankind. And in that brief interval there was a very extraordinary and significant wave of response to him throughout the earth. So eager was the situation that humanity leapt to accept and glorify Wilson—for a phrase, for a gesture. It seized upon him as its symbol. He was transfigured in the eyes of men. He ceased to be a common statesman; he became a Messiah. Millions believed him as the bringer of untold blessings; thousands would gladly have died for him. That response was one of the most illuminating events in the early twentieth century. Manifestly the World-State had been conceived then, and now it stirred in the womb. It was alive.

"And then for some anxious decades it ceased to stir."

—H. G. WELLS
The Shape of Things to Come

1

A Political Autobiography

Thomas Woodrow Wilson's earliest memory was of hearing, at the age of four, that Abraham Lincoln had been elected President and that there would soon be a war.[1] His father, the Reverend Dr. Joseph Ruggles Wilson, was one of Georgia's most prominent Presbyterian ministers and, despite his Yankee heritage, an ardent Southern sympathizer.[2] Both of Wilson's parents were Northerners; in the 1850s, they had moved from Ohio to Staunton, Virginia (where Wilson was born in 1856), and eventually to Augusta, Georgia, where the Civil War overshadowed Wilson's childhood. As his eighth birthday approached, he witnessed the solemn march of thousands of Confederate troops on their way to defend the city against Sherman's invasion. He watched wounded soldiers die inside his father's church and pondered the fate of the ragged Union prisoners confined in the churchyard outside. Soon he would see Jefferson Davis paraded under Union guard through the streets and would recall standing "for a moment at General Lee's side and looking up into his face."[3]

Wilson once commented, "A boy never gets over his boyhood, and never can change those subtle influences which have become a part of him."[4] It is an important fact that he experienced, at an impressionable age, the effects of a great war and its aftermath. It may also be that the

3

foregoing incidents later exerted "subtle influences" on his sense of purpose in the creation of the League of Nations.

Yet undoubtedly the central influence on Wilson's early personal development was his upbringing in a Presbyterian household. "The stern
Covenanter tradition that is behind me sends many an echo down the
years," he told an English audience in December 1918.[5] Indeed, in most
of Wilson's pre-presidential writings and speeches, Christian doctrine played
an essential, though not exclusive, role in his political thought. John M.
Mulder has argued that the key to understanding Wilson's "years of preparation" is the Presbyterian covenantal religious tradition, the spiritual
curriculum that the elder Wilson imparted to his son.[6]

The covenantal tradition itself harked back to the story of Abraham's
sacrifice of Isaac and the agreement between God and his people, who, in
exchange for their obedience and faith, would receive his blessings and
protection. Dr. Wilson taught young "Tommy" that even individual success inhered in obedience to divine law. Moreover, in a world filled with
struggle between good and evil, service to God was that much more imperative.[7] Wilson venerated his "incomparable" father and dutifully appropriated the lessons. For example, shortly before graduating from
Princeton, he wrote in his journal, *"If God will give me the grace I will try
to serve him . . . to perfection."* [8]

Since the early national period, American Presbyterians had expanded the idea of the covenant to account for their perception of a special relationship between the United States and Providence; the new nation, they believed, would prosper as long as it remained righteous. Dr.
Wilson embraced this concept, along with another—one that held that the
nations of the world also were administered in harmony with God's moral
law. This "theology of politics" constituted a comprehensive scheme in
which the individual, the church, society, and the nations of the world
were all properly juxtaposed in the firmament. Mulder's thesis—that Wilson wove covenant theology into practically every aspect of his existence—
is instructive.[9] In his father's well-ordered philosophy of life and politics,
Wilson apparently found both emotional and intellectual self-assurance.
With his Princeton classmate Charles A. Talcott, for instance, he formed
a "solemn covenant" in a joint quest to "acquire knowledge that we might
have power."[10] He portrayed his forthcoming marriage to Ellen Louise
Axson in 1885 as "a compact," and suggested that they create "an Inter-
state Love League (of two members only that it may be of manageable
size)," complete with a constitution. "Then," he added, "we can make by-
laws at our leisure as they become necessary."[11]

Wilson exhibited a penchant for constitutional order in other realms
as well. At the rather advanced age of seventeen, he founded the imag-
inary "Royal United Kingdom Yacht Club," with "Lord Thomas W. Wil-

son" as commodore, and went so far as to stipulate punishments for breaches of conduct, divisions of command, and regulations for regattas.[12] Three years later, at Princeton, he wrote the constitution for the Liberal Debating Club, "founded upon the fundamental principles of *Justice, Morality, and Friendship.*"[13] Throughout most of his academic career, he founded or revamped debating societies—as a law student at the University of Virginia, as an attorney in Atlanta, as a political science graduate student at Johns Hopkins University, and as a professor at Wesleyan University.[14] Although too much should not be inferred from them, these exercises do provide certain insights into Wilson's creation of the League of Nations. Writing constitutions, or covenants, served a number of functions: they brought order and rationality to anarchic conditions; they promoted the cause of democracy through political debate and emphasized the Christian duty to perform good works; and they could be applied to virtually any sphere of human endeavor—even to affairs of the heart or to the setting of goals for a career in politics.

The main intellectual activity of Wilson's academic career was the pursuit of more perfect government at all levels. *Congressional Government* (1885), his doctoral dissertation at Johns Hopkins, is the best-known of such works. Inspired by Walter Bagehot's *The English Constitution* (1867), Wilson argued that the American Constitution was inferior to its cousin. He singled out for special censure the diffuse congressional committee system, which he described as chaotic and irresponsible. *Congressional Government* represents Wilson's first step toward the kind of critical understanding and mastery of the American political system that in part accounted for his early legislative successes as President. The book received lavish reviews and established his professional reputation.[15] (It is also epigraphically rich in irony. "The treaty-*marring* power of the Senate," he wrote, ". . . made the comparative weakness of the executive very conspicuous." With the upper house, the President could never deal "upon a ground of real equality," he lamented. "The Senate always has the last word."[16])

The most mature work of Wilson's early career was probably "The Modern Democratic State" (1885), a little-known benchmark—and a prospectus for many of his subsequent essays—in his lifelong reflections on the nature of democracy, political leadership, relations among nations, and the future of the United States.[17] "Democracy," he wrote, "is the fullest form of state life . . . for a whole people"—chiefly because it made politics "a sphere of moral action" and strode inexorably toward "the universal emancipation and brotherhood of man."[18] The United States had been able to practice democracy to a relatively full degree, Wilson believed, because it possessed none of the traditions and institutions—such as entangling foreign alliances and standing armies—that hindered "the free action of social and political forces."[19] Yet democracy was both means and end—"It is a stage of development . . . built by slow habit. Its process is experience." In order to put down firm roots, democracy required a well-educated and enlightened people, wide public debate, a citizenry with a common purpose, and "not the habit of revolution, but the habit of resolution." Other countries, therefore, could attain democracy only by steps, "through a period of political tutelage," before their people would be ready to take "entire control of their affairs."[20]

From such a conservative perspective, Wilson was expansively optimistic about the future. He attributed the apparent recession of autocracies and monarchies in the late nineteenth century to the proliferation of public education and democratic institutions; therein beamed the promise of "the establishment of the most humane results of the world's peace and progress."[21] In a "covenantal" conclusion, he equated the supreme objective of both the nation and the individual: "The goal of political development is identical with the goal of individual development. Both singly and collectively man's nature draws him . . . towards a fuller realization of his kinship with God."[22]

Most studies of his political career emphasize that Wilson entered public life virtually an unreconstructed Jeffersonian who clung to the concept of the negative state even as he sought the presidential nomination as a progressive Democrat.[23] Yet his intellectual life did not always hew a straight and predictable path. The political and economic upheavals of the final two decades of the century posed unsettling challenges to Wilson's serenity. The trend toward concentration of enormous wealth and power in the hands of a few "Captains of Industry" mocked his perception of political reality. Moreover, the two major parties responded uncomprehendingly to the fitful growth of organized labor and agrarian insurgency. These developments caused Wilson to rethink his views on the proper role of government in constructing a modern political economy. His ruminations in the late 1880s and early 1890s are quite compelling; they entertained the possibilities of an American commonwealth that would at once preserve individual liberties, serve as the guardian of the public interest, and harmonize conservative and radical values.

In August 1887, Wilson read Richard T. Ely's pioneering study, *The Labor Movement in America* (1886). Within a few days, he composed an essay (buried in his papers until 1968) entitled "Socialism and Democracy."[24] The central idea behind state socialism, he wrote, "is that no line can be drawn between private and public affairs which the State may not cross at will. . . . Applied to a democratic state, such doctrine sounds radical, but not revolutionary. It is only a[n] acceptance of the extremest logical conclusions deducible from democratic principles long ago received as respectable. *For it is very clear that in fundamental theory socialism and democracy are almost if not quite one and the same.* They both rest at bottom upon the absolute right of the community to determine its own destiny and that of its members."[25] Wilson's meditations on the conditions of social and economic life in the United States grew mainly out of his concern over "a monstrously changed aspect of the social world"—the aggrandizement of giant corporations that threatened to swallow up, not only individuals and small businesses, but democratic government itself. "In the face of such circumstances," he asked, "must not government lay aside all timid scruple and boldly make itself an agency for social reform as well as political control?"[26] Indeed it should, he concluded. But democracy had yet to undertake "the tasks which socialists clamour to have undertaken."[27]

Two years later, in *The State,* a comparative study of government in Europe and the United States, he went a step further. "The modern industrial organization has so distorted competition as to put it into the power of some to tyrannize over many, as to enable the rich and strong to combine against the poor and weak."[28] On one level, "we ought all to regard ourselves as *socialists,"* he went on. For they were right to condemn "selfish, misguided individualism; and certainly modern individualism has much about it that is hateful, too hateful to last."[29] Thus, because of "the power of unscrupulous or heartless men," it was necessary for the state to regulate monopolies, to establish maximum hours and standards for safe working conditions, and to put an end to child labor.[30] (In the first advanced course in political economy he taught at Princeton, in 1891, he considered, along the same lines of argument, the salutary role socialism might play in the United States.[31])

Wilson would enter the White House at the beginning of a new epoch in world history, one characterized by profound revolutionary movements—in particular, in Mexico and Russia. These revolutions were informed by the socialist critique of industrial capitalism and presented fundamental challenges to the prevailing political and economic systems of the great powers. Wilson, of course, fell far short of the intellectual coherence that Eugene V. Debs eventually achieved in integrating socialist principles with Christianity and the American democratic and revolutionary traditions. But it is nonetheless significant that, unlike any other chief executive, he had ascribed a considerable degree of legitimacy and had devoted serious thought to socialist theory long before he became president.

During the Great Depression of the early 1890s, Wilson searched for a compass. He found it in Edmund Burke, his new philosophical "master." Populist victories in 1892 and the violence surrounding the Pullman strike in the summer of 1894 had apparently increased his appreciation

for Burke's famous condemnation of the excesses of the French Revolution.[32] At the same time, he abhorred the unwillingness of the political
leadership of the Gilded Age to tear off the blindfolds of laissez faire and
respond to the demands of a new day. To be sure, the center of gravity
of his political thought remained relatively conservative, as his statement
in a lecture on Burke, "It is both better and easier to reform than to tear
down and reconstruct," would suggest.[33] Yet he also admitted that revolutions were sometimes both necessary and productive of good.[34]

Revolution or no, Wilson preferred Burke as a general guide to lasting political change—Burke and his emphasis on the process of law.[35] As
he refined his thinking on the proper role of the state, he began to apply
to international society his conception of the process of change and social
improvement.[36] From 1892 to 1894, Wilson taught courses in international
law at Princeton. In these lectures—arguably one of the most important
sources on his ideas about international relations before 1913—he synthe-
sized his thought about the nature of democracy, public debate, reform,
the state, sovereignty, and man's responsibility to God.[37]

As he had done in his interpretation of democracy, Wilson emphasized that international law actually was "not made," as such. Rather, it
was the result of organic development—"a body of abstract principles
founded upon long established custom." Quoting Johann Kaspar Bluntschli,
he equated the law of nations with the law of Nature, "which binds different states together in a humane jural society, and which also secures to
the members of different states a common protection of law for their
general human and international rights."[38] In the second lecture of the
series, Wilson asked, "Do the nations of the world constitute a community?" He answered himself in the affirmative, stating that three things
had brought into being a community, of sorts, among nations. The first
was the recognition of Roman law as the basis of all Western legal systems. The second was the simple fact of commerce—in ideas as well as
in goods. The third and most vital component was Christianity.[39] According to Wilson, Christianity had prepared the way for international law by
establishing standards of morality and common principles of "civilization"
and education. In another lecture, he also maintained that Christianity
promoted the growth of international law because the concept of the fa-
therhood of God implied the brotherhood of man, which, in turn, created
natural bonds between nations.[40] "Regardless of race or religion," there
existed "fundamental, vital principles of right" proceeding from God and
human reason that all enlightened people held in common; this, he said,
constituted "the universal conscience of mankind." Hence, any nation could
be admitted into the community if it recognized the "common principles
of right."[41]

Wilson had thus reduced the objective of international law to a moral and legal system somewhat akin to his father's theological world order, altered now in subtle ways by his reading of Burke (and perhaps by his tentative understanding of socialism). In this instance, the objective was to substitute "disorder and invasion of right which provoked war" with "ordered relationships and recognized obligations" that promoted "a moral sense of community among states."[42] Moreover, girding this community were the "imperative forces of popular thought and the concrete institutions of popular representation," or, to put it another way, the promise of democracy—"the rule of counsel, the catholic spirit of free debate . . . [and] the ascendency of reason over passion."[43]

By the winter of 1894, then, Wilson had established, at least in a general sense, a theoretical rationale for a genuine community of nations. None of this is to insist on absolute linearity; but on the whole his academic strivings suggest, if not a final destination, then surely an indication of direction—the subterranean intellectual context of the Wilsonian origins of the New Diplomacy.

As much as the domestic social and political upheavals of the late nineteenth century altered Wilson's thinking about the state, so, too, did the pulse of events beyond American shores. The period from the late 'nineties to his entrance into politics in 1910 afforded him many opportunities to speak and write about American foreign policy, particularly after Admiral Dewey's portentous victory at Manila Bay.

"A brief season of war has deeply charged our thought and has altered, it may be permanently, the conditions of our national life," Wilson observed in a memorandum entitled "What Ought We to Do?" in August 1898. Like most citizens, he had accepted President McKinley's rationalization that the purpose of the war with Spain was to give Cuba self-government.[44] The subsequent annexation of the Philippines, however, nettled him for a time. (In his forthcoming *History of the American People,* he would underscore the "inexcusable aggression" of the United States in the Mexican War and condemn the seizure of territory to which it could claim "no conceivable right except that of conquest."[45])

The Treaty of Paris set off an intense national debate. Many Republicans justified their advocacy of imperialism as a corollary to reform of domestic life. Overseas expansion—"spreading the American dream," one historian has described it—suddenly became an integral part of the "historical mission" of the United States. More decisively, it proffered the likely cure for a stagnant economy burdened by huge surpluses. But Americans could also bring to the Filipinos democracy and constitutional order, along with the benefits of capitalist development. Then, too, a toehold in the Far East had already been established by hundreds of Christian missionaries, whose reports back home stimulated other agendas. To celebrated advocates of an expanded navy, such as Theodore Roosevelt and Alfred Thayer Mahan, the Philippines seemed the perfect agent to advance the interests of the United States against great powers already on the scene in Asia. Thus, the retention of the archipelago would provide a permanent base for an American naval presence in the Pacific, as well as a way station for Christian and capitalist pilgrims alike, en route to their respective China markets.[46]

Not a few Democrats saw the same things. Even Eugene Debs, in 1894 (the year of his conversion to socialism), had written that the "heathens" of Asia must "open their ports and admit the civilizing influence of commercial nations." Though he opposed the Philippines annexation on racial grounds, Debs deemed Hawaii "a coaling station for the United States, and this government must needs protect itself in this regard."[47] For its part, the Democratic party demanded independence for the Philippines in its national platform of 1900 when, for a second time, William Jennings Bryan was nominated for President.[48]

Wilson, however, did not subscribe completely to the party line. "It was my personal wish at the time that we should not take the Philippines," he told a Connecticut audience the year before. But the important question now was, "what are we going to do with them?"[49] The acquisition of a small empire in the Caribbean and the Pacific would "make the politics of the twentieth century radically unlike the politics of the nineteenth," he wrote in the *Atlantic Monthly* after Bryan's defeat. "It is only just now that we have awakened to our real relationship to the rest of mankind." The American form of self-government was "by no means the one necessary and inevitable form,"[50] but Providence had nonetheless chosen the United States to nurture the conditions precedent to self-government, to enter into a small-scale international covenant under the aegis of imperialism, and "make the government in our new possessions the best it can be."[51]

Wilson was not inattentive to the prospects of expanding American trade. Even in his initial contemplation of the Philippines, he rhetorically asked himself, "Which nations shall possess the world?"[52] He agreed with the views of his friend and former student Frederick Jackson Turner, whose "frontier thesis" of American history implied that the United States required greater foreign markets in order to sustain its prosperity.[53] "Our frontier disappeared less than fourteen years ago and now a new one has been given us in the Philippines," he said in an address on the Constitution in 1904.[54] And to numerous audiences he rehearsed a theme that he first struck in the *Atlantic:* "The East is to be opened and transformed, whether we will or no; the standards of the West are to be imposed upon it; nations and peoples which have stood still the centuries through are to be quickened, and made part of the universal world of commerce and of ideas which has so steadily been a-making by the advance of European power from age to age."[55]

Wilson actually referred to himself as an imperialist on two occasions and once disparaged "the anti-imperialist weepings that came out of Boston."[56] Even so, in the *Atlantic* article, he admitted that things were not in such fine shape at home "that we might . . . divert our energies [solely] to tasks beyond our borders." The main task of the United States was "to moderate the process in the interests of liberty."[57] Indeed, for every sentence he uttered on commerce, he spoke two on the moral responsibility of the United States to sustain its historic idealism and render the service of its democracy. In this way, Wilson attempted to distinguish his own set of imperialist assumptions from the colonialism practiced by the European powers and implicitly endorsed by many Americans during the first decade of the century. Typically, he said it was the country's duty "to keep faith also with the people of the Philippines . . . by showing them the way to liberty without plundering them or making them our tools for a selfish end."[58] On the eve of his entrance into public life, he said: "We have come out upon the stage of international responsibility from which we cannot retire. . . . [A]nd in proportion as we discover the means for translating our material force into moral force shall we recover the traditions and glories of American history."[59] During his campaign for the Democratic presidential nomination in 1912, he made no pretense of where he assumed the dialectical charge reposed: "I believe that God planted in us visions of liberty . . . that we are chosen and prominently chosen to show the way to the nations of the world how they shall walk in the paths of liberty."[60]

Yet Wilson still had not explained how all of this would come to pass or pointed to the instrumentalities that might give coherence and form to his conception. He found provisional answers to that question—how the mission might be accomplished—in the work of organized peace-seekers of the early twentieth century. Since the founding of the American Peace Society in Boston in 1828, this movement had developed as a collective reform impulse based on the principle that war was inconsistent with Christianity. By 1900, its ranks were filled by inchoate groups of religious pacifists, imperialists and anti-imperialists, free-trade liberals, and so-called conservative legalists. Together, they exerted their energies on behalf of Anglo-American friendship, arbitration treaties, and, most conspicuously, American participation in the Permanent Court of International Arbitration, established by the First Hague Convention in 1899.[61]

Because of the nature of its composition, the loose coalition almost completely unraveled during the controversy over self-determination and overseas expansion in 1900. Two main factors contributed to a renascence during the next decade—anxiety over the growing rivalry among the great powers of Europe, and, especially, faith in the idea of human progress rekindled by the gathering momentum of reform at home. By 1912, the peace movement had undertaken programs of public education that stressed Christian morality as the primary ingredient of progress and had made specific proposals for multilateral arbitration agreements and international courts, disarmament, and world federation.[62] Like Wilson, many proponents of this crusade had become imbued with the notion that every problem in society could be solved through education, enlightened reason, and democratic efficiency. They were convinced that the United States was unique among nations, and that it possessed the exceptional capabilities to bring peace and progress to the world.[63]

Wilson himself had first written about world federation in 1887. In "The Study of Administration," he had contemplated "the confederation of parts of empires like the British, and finally of great states themselves," which would constitute "a wide union . . . of governments joined with governments for the pursuit of common purpose."[64] In 1908, he joined the American Peace Society, appeared regularly at peace gatherings, and later lent his support to President Taft's arbitration treaties with England and France.[65] Peace-seekers played a measurable role in the development of Wilson's internationalism. Their influence on him was not altogether decisive; but they helped prepare the soil that he was soon to till. He breathed deeply of the same heady atmosphere that they breathed and shared their confident vision of the future. He also maintained a steady correspondence with the leaders of the movement and supported many of their specific aims. As President of the United States he would incorporate into his own program their proposals for arbitration of international disputes and disarmament, and others pertaining to world federation. At length, however, Wilson's impact on the peace movement would prove greater than its impact on him.

Henry Kissinger once observed that "the convictions that leaders have formed before reaching high office are the intellectual capital they will consume as long as they continue in office."[66] However knowing, Kissinger's comment does not assay the potential for growth and change, or for regression, in significant historical actors; nor does it reckon with personal ambition. Perhaps more perceptively than any other politician at any time, Abraham Lincoln explained how history compensates biography. "It is to deny what the history of the world tells us is true to suppose that men of ambitions and talents will not continue to spring up amongst us," Lincoln said in an address at the Young Men's Lyceum in Springfield, Illinois, in 1838. "And when they do, they will as naturally seek the gratification of their ruling passions as others have done before them. Towering genius disdains a beaten path. . . . It thirsts and burns for distinction; and, if possible, it will have it, whether at the expense of emancipating slaves or enslaving free men."[67]

Woodrow Wilson may or may not have been a towering genius. But he surely scorned roads traveled by illustrious predecessors and thirsted for distinction—ultimately, at a considerable expense to himself and, his harsher critics would say, to the United States as well. On his thirty-third birthday, he wrote in his "Confidential Journal" the stunning question: "Why may not the present generation write, through me, its political *autobiography?*"[68] Since adolescence, he had wanted to become "a leader of men." As a law student at the University of Virginia, he inscribed calling cards with "Thomas Woodrow Wilson, Senator From Virginia." Throughout his academic career he wrote many pieces about the charismatic personalities—Burke, Bismarck, Gladstone, Washington, and Lincoln—whom he admired.[69] Real statesmen, he averred, were those "who stood alone at the inception of a movement and whose voices . . . [were] the more sensitive organs of society—the parts first awakened to consciousness of a situation."[70] To his fiancée, Ellen Axson, he wrote the most premonitory lines of all, in 1885: "I have a strong instinct of leadership, an unmistakably oratorical temperament, and the keenest possible delight in affairs. . . . I have a passion for interpreting great thoughts to the world; I should be complete if I could inspire a great movement of opinion, if I could read the experiences of the past into the practical life of the men of to-day and so communicate the thought to the minds of the great mass of the people as to impel them to great political achievements."[71]

Wilson did not have much hope for personal fulfillment as he came to his majority during the Gilded Age.[72] Once the Spanish-American War raised critical questions of foreign policy to a new prominence, however, his contempt for the office of president changed markedly. In a new edition (1900) of *Congressional Government,* he wrote that President McKinley was now "at the front of affairs, as no president, except Lincoln, has been since the first quarter of the nineteenth century, when the foreign relations of the new nation had first to be adjusted."[73] In his final scholarly work, *Constitutional Government in the United States* (1908), he predicted that "the office will be as big and as influential as the man who occupies it."[74]

In Theodore Roosevelt's ascension, Wilson could not have found a brighter illustration of this. But vicarious experience could not satisfy him much longer. Great missions, he stated in 1904, were made by "the drawing of individuals together into a net formed by the conceptions of a single mind, and the greater the organization, the more certain you are to find a great individuality at its origin and center."[75] Suffice it to say that, in

1912, a unique and profound intersection occurred in the history of the United States and the life of Woodrow Wilson when, on the forty-sixth ballot, the Democratic party nominated him for President. For he had already committed himself to the pursuit of perfecting democratic constitutional order as he understood it—not only within the United States, but also, where practicable, in places where it did not exist. He had already set out, at least intellectually, upon a quest for a community of nations—through the proliferation of democracy and appropriate amendments to international law as well as through an emphasis on the concept of Christian fellowship. Eventually, with the League of Nations, he would attempt to strike, in a sense, the supreme covenant between God and the United States.

In 1901, Wilson agreed to write the preface for *Harper's Encyclopedia of the United States*. The final sentences of the essay, entitled "The Significance of American History," revealed at once the disposition of a discerning historian and that of a victorious politician and captured the perilous assumptions and aspirations of the "American Century" to come: "The life of the new world grows as complex as the life of the old. A nation hitherto wholly devoted to domestic development now finds its first task roughly finished and turns about to look curiously into the tasks of the great world at large, seeking its special part and place of power. A new age has come which no man may forecast. But the past is the key to it; and the past of America lies at the center of modern history."[76] If Wilson had consciously tried to do so, he could not have composed a more fitting epigraph for his own and the nation's ensuing "political autobiography."

2

Wilson and the Age
of Socialist Inquiry

A s Eugene Debs once remarked during the great campaign, 1912 was "a year with supreme possibilities."[1] The four candidates for President that season constituted arguably the best field since the generation of the Founding Fathers and, thus far, the most impressive of the twentieth century. Of all the contenders, Theodore Roosevelt was the country's most electrifying politician and Progressivism's greatest publicist. Although he had fulfilled only a limited reform agenda while in office, the former chief executive had moved noticeably to the left since turning over the White House to his protégé, William Howard Taft, in 1909. When, after nearly four years, Taft revealed himself as a stand-patter incapable of ever appreciating Debs's observation, Roosevelt felt betrayed. Despite the odds, he tried, but found it impossible to loosen his former friend's control over the party machinery and win the Republican presidential nomination for himself. Believing that the cause of reform had been thwarted by corrupt reactionaries, Roosevelt and his followers gathered in Chicago to chart a new course.[2]

The Progressive party convention displayed all the characteristics of a religious revival meeting. When Roosevelt stepped onstage, pandemonium broke out. In his "Confession of Faith," he called for sweeping legislation to make the nation's vast corporate structure accountable to the

public through a new system of federal supervision and regulation. Social
and industrial justice, the candidate also said, could be had only by the
establishment of the minimum wage, one day's rest in seven for all, compensation for death or injury in the workplace, the prohibition of child
labor, and protective legislation for women. These measures, along with
others aimed at reforming the political process, constituted TR's "New
Nationalism." When he declared, "We stand at Armageddon, and we do
battle for the Lord," the fifteen thousand delegates could no longer contain their exhilaration. Out into the city streets they poured, waving red
bandanas and singing "Onward Christian Soldiers."[3]

Meanwhile, the party of Bryan, too, was in the grip of progressive
metamorphosis. None of the Democratic aspirants was either as conservative as Taft or as liberal as Roosevelt; but their personalities and qualifications ran the spectrum from Champ Clark of Missouri, the alcoholic
Speaker of the House of Representatives, to Governor Woodrow Wilson
of New Jersey, the "Princeton Schoolmaster." Wilson's background provided excellent (and unusual) campaign material. As he was a scholar of
the first rank, his books and articles on how to run a government were
standard reading at universities on both sides of the Atlantic. He had
transformed Princeton from a genteel college for wealthy young men into
a place of higher learning rivaled by few others in the world. Then, after
fate intervened to give him the governorship in 1910, he had boldly pushed
through the New Jersey legislature a comprehensive package of timely
reforms—including a workmen's compensation act, laws to regulate public utilities and railroads, the direct primary, and corrupt-practices legislation. Suddenly, Wilson had become the new hope of national progressivism within the Democracy.[4] In June 1912, in sweltering Baltimore, the
party experienced one of the most riotous conventions in its history. Days
of inconclusive balloting and intensive infighting at last ended in the
triumph of the party's progressive forces and the nomination of Governor
Wilson.[5]

Because of the breach in the Republican party, it was virtually a
foregone conclusion that the Democrats would capture the White House.
Even so, as John Milton Cooper, Jr., has written, "for the only time except
perhaps for Jefferson's first election in 1800, a presidential campaign aired
questions that verged on political philosophy."[6] Roosevelt's program—to
use the power of the federal government both to regulate monopolies
(instead of doing away with them) and to safeguard the rights of working
people—defined the terms of this debate.[7]

Wilson responded to the New Nationalism by attacking it as governmental paternalism. With most of the goals embodied in the Progressive
party platform he did not disagree; but he dissented quite warmly over
the means of achieving them. "[O]nce the government regulates monop-

oly, then monopoly will see to it that it regulates the government," he warned. Whereas his opponent offered "a program of regulation," he offered "a program of liberty," or a "New Freedom."[8] His thinking sharpened by the ideas of Louis D. Brandeis, the "People's Lawyer" of Boston, Wilson intended to rehabilitate democracy and the political economy by restoring competition. This task could be accomplished by destroying the very process of monopoly, or "special privilege," through strong antitrust legislation as well as by reducing the tariff and creating a new and more elastic currency system.[9] Yet, notwithstanding the rather traditional approach of his New Freedom, Wilson also said several times during the campaign that the "organization of business on a great scale of cooperation is, up to a certain point, inevitable." He even had words of praise for Alexander Hamilton and indicated that he had disowned at least one of Thomas Jefferson's principles—"that the best government is that which . . . exercises its power as little as possible."[10]

Where, precisely, Wilson was heading was not altogether clear, even as the opportunity to write his generation's "political autobiography" beckoned. But, perhaps owing as much to Roosevelt as to Brandeis, his understanding of progressivism had deepened by election day. His inaugural address suggested that he was prepared to go beyond the New Freedom and place social reform high on the national agenda. Indeed, he dwelt upon the fact that, in its rush toward industrial achievements, the nation had not stopped to count "the cost of lives snuffed out, of energies overtaxed and broken, the fearful physical and spiritual cost to the men and women and children upon whom the dead weight and burden of it all has fallen pitilessly the years through." The firm basis of government was justice, not pity, he said. "There can be no equality of opportunity, the essential of justice in the body politic, if men and women and children be not shielded in their lives . . . from the consequences of great industrial and social processes which they can not alter, control, or singly cope with."[11]

The disruption of the Republican party and the debate between Roosevelt and Wilson were not the sole factors that made 1912 a remarkable year. What gave the campaign a truly extraordinary complexion was the appeal of the fourth candidate, Eugene Debs. By 1912, the Socialist Party of America and its quadrennial standard-bearer had attained respectability and legitimacy.[12] The party's official membership exceeded 115,000, and approximately 1,200 Socialists held public office in 340 municipalities in twenty-four states.[13] As many as three million Americans read socialist newspapers on a regular basis. Julius Wayland's *Appeal to Reason,* with 760,000 weekly subscribers, ranked among the most widely read publications in the world.[14] As Frederick Jackson Turner once declared, the age

of reform was "also the age of socialistic inquiry," and the general cast of
Roosevelt's and Wilson's campaigns, alongside Debs's, gave ample proof
that this was so.[15]

Like the establishment parties, the Socialist party experienced the
strains of internal division. Right-wing Socialists, such as Congressman
Victor Berger of Milwaukee, worked primarily in movements for municipal ownership of public utilities, safety regulations in the workplace, and
the minimum wage.[16] Left-wing Socialists argued that "gas and water
socialism" failed to distinguish itself from Republican and Democratic
progressivism; Debs maintained that the paramount task was "to teach
social consciousness" and to seek a "majority of Socialists, not of votes."[17]
Centrists, such as Morris Hillquit, shared Debs's outlook, but believed that
the country's acceptance of so many Socialist-led reforms meant that America
was "already living at least on the outskirts of the 'socialist state.'"[18]

Whatever serious differences might divide them, virtually all American Socialists exalted the American democratic and revolutionary traditions. They spoke most effectively through the granite voice of Debs, the
cement that held the party together.[19] His share of the popular vote in
1912—a historic record of six per cent, or 901,255 votes in all—was not
unexpected and would have been larger but for Roosevelt's candidacy.
Even so, he outpolled President Taft in seven states and Roosevelt in
another. In twenty-one states he exceeded his own national average, with
a high of almost seventeen percent in Oklahoma.[20]

The ferment of progressivism and the success of the Socialist party
caused a certain blurring of political lines in 1912. To millions of voters,
a ballot cast for either Roosevelt, Wilson, or Debs amounted to a protest
against the status quo. That protest, from top to bottom, sanctioned an
unfolding communion between liberals and socialists practically unique in
American history.[21] Governor Wilson, for example, had occasionally shared
the speaker's platform with such well-known socialists as John Spargo,
Max Eastman, and Florence Kelley, who themselves traveled calmly with
liberal reformers and socialists alike.[22] In campaigning for the presidential
nomination, Wilson routinely spoke of his admiration for his minority
rivals. "When you do socialism justice," he told an audience in Buffalo
(to cite but one instance), "it is hardly different from the heart of Christianity itself."[23] *The Call,* New York's leading socialist newspaper, recorded satisfaction with his statement to the city's Press Club that he had
"a great deal of respect for the Socialist party . . . [because he knew] how
many serious and honest men" belonged to it.[24] And in *The Masses,* the
era's most exuberant journal of radical opinion, Allan L. Benson, who
would replace Debs as the party's nominee in 1916, pronounced the new
President "a breath of fresh air" and his inaugural "the finest . . . since
Lincoln's second one."[25] Over the next four to five years, fewer and fewer

socialists and progressives would feel the need to guard the border that seemed only tenuously to separate the respective right and left wings of their movements. The mutual respect that began to manifest itself between Wilson and many socialists in the year of "supreme possibilities" was potentially the most important consequence of that development.

The election of 1912, like almost all the others of the preceding century, did not hinge on foreign policy. President Taft now and then reflected upon his futile exertions for reciprocal trade with Canada and arbitration treaties with the European powers.[26] Debs viewed foreign policy as irrelevant to working-class interests, just as he had during the debate over imperialism in 1900.[27] The Progressive platform advocated free passage through the Panama Canal for American coastwise shippers and recommended the construction of two battleships per year, while the Democratic platform called for independence for the Philippines.[28] But none of the candidates said much about even these rather innocuous issues.

At the start of his campaign for the nomination, Wilson did attempt to establish a connection between domestic reform and foreign policy. "The same exploitation and injustice within our borders applies to international questions," he told the Universal Peace Union in Philadelphia. "Just as soon as we are just to the people of the United States, justice and equity in China and Manchuria will follow. . . . How are we going to do justice to other nations if we don't know justice?"[29] Three days before the election, he gave out his strongest statement—a shot aimed at the "special interests" behind Taft's "Dollar Diplomacy": "The nations look to us for standards and policies worthy of America. We must shape our course of action by the maxims of justice and liberality and good will, and think of the progress of mankind rather than of the progress of this or that investment. . . ."[30] Such critical allusions, however, were rare. Wilson confined himself mainly to exhorting business groups about the advantages of the new Panama Canal and the importance of a merchant marine. "America is straining at the leash to capture the markets of the world," was a typical declamation.[31]

Shortly before his inauguration, the President-elect remarked to a friend, "It would be the irony of fate if my administration had to deal chiefly with foreign affairs."[32] Many historians have used this quotation to suggest that Wilson entered the White House uninterested in, or ill-equipped to manage, the foreign relations of the United States. But Wilson was commenting on the nature of the recent campaign; he had, of course, been a commentator on foreign policy since the 1890s and had already composed—albeit in the circumstance of academic quietude—a full standard of principles and ideas that governed his outlook on how nations properly should interrelate with one another. From the intellectual standpoint, the body of Wilson's written work in the fields of comparative government, contemporary history, and international law constituted a preparation unrivaled by any incoming president since John Quincy Adams.[33]

As chief executive, Wilson never really worried that someday he might be confounded by fate. He approached the administration of foreign affairs, like most other things, with unshakable certitude.[34] As Arthur S. Link has shown, Wilson the diplomatist made all final decisions himself, routinely composed important diplomatic notes on his own typewriter, and, in many instances, conducted diplomacy without informing the State Department of his actions.[35] With the possible exception of Franklin D. Roosevelt, no other president in American history exerted more personal control over foreign policy.

As the nation's sovereign diplomatist, Wilson intended that the United States should serve the world in no less a capacity than as "the light which shall shine unto all generations and guide the feet of mankind to the goal of justice and liberty and peace."[36] Two political friendships, in particular, abetted these great expectations. In November 1911, Wilson met "Colonel" Edward Mandell House, one of the first "kingmakers" in modern American politics.[37] "Almost from the first," the Colonel later recalled, "our minds vibrated in unison." Wilson concurred: "Mr. House is my second personality. . . . His thoughts and mine are one."[38] A politician of independent wealth and for years a major power broker in Texas, House desired neither official position nor the public spotlight; he thereby cultivated a silent partnership and became the President's most trusted counselor.

Although he gave Wilson fairly constant emotional and intellectual support, House thought of himself as the *éminence grise* and often tried to manipulate his chief. In *Philip Dru: Administrator,* published anonymously in late 1912, he illuminated the full expanse of his designs. The improbable protagonist of this grandiose work of fiction is a recent West Point graduate from Kentucky who leads a revolution against America's plutocratic government and imposes upon the nation a program of far-reaching reforms—the single tax, the nationalization of public utilities, old-age pensions, the eight-hour day, and a role for labor in the councils of industry. The "Administrator of the Republic" then voluntarily relinquishes power and uses his prestige to persuade the great powers of Europe to eliminate trade barriers and armaments. Thus does Dru help to usher in a new epoch, crowned by an international league of peace![39]

Despite its many unintentionally ludicrous passages, *Philip Dru* deserves serious attention if only for the prophetic self-exposition of its author. Clearly, House's driving ambition in life was to influence the course of history. To an extent, he succeeded. Although he was never quite so ventriloqual as he supposed, he was right on the mark when he wrote: "I was like a disembodied spirit seeking a corporeal form. I found my opportunity in Woodrow Wilson."[40]

Wilson's relationship with his first Secretary of State is also instructive.[41] Ray Stannard Baker once wrote that William Jennings Bryan was perhaps the "statesman of largest caliber among Wilson's advisers."[42] As the indefatigable veteran of three frustrated presidential campaigns, Bryan was the second most powerful and the single most beloved figure in the Democratic party in 1912. Wilson chose him to preside over the State Department primarily because Democratic public opinion demanded it.

Bryan came closer to embracing Christian pacifism than any other Secretary of State in American history. He believed devoutly that universal peace could be brought about through the spread of democracy and the teachings of Jesus. In these matters, he stood on common ground with Wilson. Yet Wilson, like many others, regarded the Nebraskan's fundamentalism as naïve and his thought processes as unsophisticated; he doubted Bryan's skill as a diplomatist and relied instead on Colonel House to carry out delicate missions abroad. But, until he resigned in June 1915, no one exerted a stronger influence on Wilson's foreign policy. He also served as the major link between the administration and the American peace movement, then in the prime of its life. Bryan championed arbitration and conciliation with particular effectiveness and therein contributed one of the main components of Wilson's own program.

In Bryan's appointment, peace-seekers could not have found a gladder omen of great things to come. Since the beginning of the century, their priority had been to establish intrumentalities that would lessen the possibility of war between the United States and any other nation—a goal the Secretary of State held dear. Bryan regarded as the supreme accomplishment of his career his negotiation, in 1913–14, of a series of "cooling off" treaties with some twenty nations, including Great Britain, France, and all but two of the countries of Latin America. These bilateral agreements required signatories to submit any dispute between them (failing of conventional diplomacy) to investigation by an international commission, and to forego hostilities until the commission had filed its report; thereafter they could do as they pleased.[43]

Bryan's endeavor to bring a form of the New Freedom to international relations initially encountered an unfriendly reception. The New York *Sun* suggested that he try out a treaty on the Moros. And the Carabao Club, an élite society of American army and naval officers, toasted the "Hon. Wm. Jenny Bryan" and the "piffle" he had served up. (Wilson publicly reprimanded the members of the Club for this act of insubordination.)[44] By the autumn of 1914, however, the *New York Times* was calling the undertaking a "solid contribution to the welfare of the world," while the *Times* of London declared the treaties "eminently practical." After the first Battle of the Marne, Sir Cecil Arthur Spring Rice, the perpetually irritable British ambassador to the United States, conceded to Bryan: "No one . . . can ever speak lightly of your idea again."[45]

The signing of the cooling-off treaties is frequently portrayed as an episode of little consequence in the history of international relations. Wilson's endorsement of them, also, is often viewed either as evidence of "the general inadequacy of New Freedom diplomacy," or as personal indulgence of a well-intentioned Secretary of State.[46] But what is frequently overlooked is the fact that Wilson became as serious about the treaties as Bryan once the war in Europe broke out.[47] Moreover, from Bryan, he received an idea that would reappear as one of the cardinal provisions of the Covenant of the League of Nations. In 1919, Wilson often asserted that the war might have been averted if such agreements had had multilateral sanction in August 1914—if "nations [had]solemnly covenant[ed] not to go to war for nine months after a controversy becomes acute."[48] The Bryan treaties constituted Wilson's first step toward the formulation of an internationalist foreign policy.

As the cooling-off negotiations proceeded, the President began to heed other voices within the peace movement—those that called for general disarmament of the great powers. Ever since the administration had taken office, Colonel House himself had coveted the role of negotiator (or, rather, secret agent) who would lay the groundwork for international disarmament. Much like Philip Dru had done, he envisioned some kind of four-power *entente* (with Britain, France, and Germany) to subdue the alarming proliferation of European militarism and navalism. With Wilson's "warm approval," he began the first leg of what he called his "Great Adventure," arriving in Berlin on May 26, 1914.[49]

House was sobered by what he initially heard and saw. He described to Wilson the self-destructive capacity of the European balance of power, poised like a house of cards waiting for a gust of wind to bring the whole structure crashing down. "It is jingoism run stark mad," he wrote from the German capital. "Unless someone acting for you can bring about an understanding, there is someday to be an awful cataclysm."[50] Conversations with the leading statesmen of Europe, however, soothed House's anxieties. Wilhelm II, though steadfast in his ambition to build a navy equal to Great Britain's, evidently welcomed the plan for an American *démarche*.[51] Prime Minister Herbert Henry Asquith asked House to convey to Wilson his personal approval of holding a disarmament conference as well as his country's peaceful intentions toward Germany.[52]

These reassurances motivated House to go beyond the specific charge of his mission. Like Wilson, he believed that the tensions within the present international system could be substantially reduced, and the foundations of peace strengthened, by the establishment of universal liberal trade practices. This, along with disarmament, would help redirect potential conflict among the major powers into safer, more prudent forms of rivalry. His idea was for the United States, Great Britain, France, and Germany to reach an agreement under which their respective investors would lend money to developing nations at uniformly low rates. Such an arrangement would rescue small, usury-bound nations from foreign exploitation and help them achieve constitutional democracy. Not incidentally, it would also insure stable conditions for investment and trade and engender cooperation among the lending nations.[53] House discussed his scheme only with the British, who seemed favorably disposed. "It was the general consensus of opinion," he told Wilson, "that it would do as much as any other one thing to insure international peace."[54]

The Colonel's maiden voyage into high diplomacy would have won (measured) plaudits from Philip Dru. He had secured pledges from the Germans, the French, and the British to begin in the near future talks on disarmament under American auspices. And he had received assurances from the British (and had every reason to expect them from the Germans) that they would subscribe to his plans for economic cooperation. From London, he wrote to Wilson: "A long stride has been made in the direction of international amity."[55]

Taken together, Bryan's and House's independent activity on behalf of conciliation and disarmament constituted a modest but illuminating program to repair the defects of the international system of 1914. Theirs were neither comprehensive nor coordinated enterprises; but the connection between the two projects was clear in the mind of their supervisor— parallel paths toward complementary goals and, in retrospect, substantial strides toward Wilson's own larger plan, as yet unconceived.

Throughout his first eighteen months in office, Wilson's priority was to bring the New Freedom to fruition. In October 1913, he achieved a historic breakthrough when Congress enacted the Underwood-Simmons bill, the first downward revision of the tariff since the Civil War. This was the New Freedom's initial assault on the special interests. Wilson aided its passage by lashing out publicly against Capitol Hill lobbyists—the "insidious" minions of the protected industries who, according to the President, conspired to subvert the public interest for their own gain. The tariff victory was followed up in December with a restructuring of the nation's currency system. The Federal Reserve Act curbed Wall Street's dominance over the nation's finances, balanced the concerns of small and large banking interests by creating a network of twelve regional Federal Reserve banks, and applied the principle of public control through the creation of the Federal Reserve Board, which imposed federal supervision over the entire complex. It is generally regarded as Wilson's single great-est legislative accomplishment.[56]

The President's leadership in the enactment of these two measures elicited handsome praise from nearly every quarter. But the triumph of New Freedom ideology *per se* was not long-lived. As he confronted the problem of the trusts in the following year, he began to respond to those progressives who argued that the remedy to economic concentration did not lie in antitrust legislation alone. Soon Wilson shifted emphasis away from the Clayton Act (an antitrust law of only moderate scope, passed in October 1914) and toward the creation of a federal trade commission. This body would exercise continuous governmental supervisory authority over big business; it amounted to the Rooseveltian solution.[57]

Most historians maintain that the signing of the Federal Trade Com-mission Act in September 1914 indicated that Wilson had abandoned the New Freedom in favor of the New Nationalism; perhaps it would be more accurate to say that it anticipated the merging of the two. At any rate, Wilson had yet to satisfy the demands of an array of progressive groups devoted to the cause of social justice. He withheld his support for legislation to abolish child labor and for a federal woman suffrage amend-ment; he did not respond to pleas from farm state progressives for a rural credits program; and only under extreme pressure in late 1914 did he countermand his subordinates' introduction of racial segregation in the Treasury and Post Office departments.[58] Even so, Wilson thus far had achieved much in areas where his predecessors had failed. And, in some cases, he did affirm advanced social justice positions. For instance, he agreed to renegotiate numerous commercial treaties in order to facilitate passage of the Seamen's Act, a bill (sponsored by Senator Robert M. La Follette, progressive Republican of Wisconsin) that dramatically improved contrac-tual rights and safety conditions for tens of thousands of merchant mari-ners.[59] If social justice reformers sustained some heavy disappointments, most of them believed that the President possessed the right instincts and the capacity to become their champion. Not until 1916 would his actions fully justify their faith; by then, he was prepared to go beyond even the New Nationalism.

If, as early as 1913–14, Wilson's progressivism was in flux, it was so also on account of events that caused him to focus more sharply on the rela-tionship between domestic reform and foreign policy. In no instance was this more apparent than in his response to the most complicated diplo-matic crisis of the prewar period—the Mexican Revolution. For Wilson, the Mexican Revolution raised two broad but fundamental issues. First, it challenged his belief that democratic political processes alone could compose any situation and bring about necessary social and economic change. Second, the revolution demonstrated to his satisfaction that the "special interests"—be they American, Mexican, or British—would employ any means at their disposal to hold back the future. Wilson's involvement in this struggle, like the explorations into the possibilities of conciliation agreements and disarmament, contributed in both conclusive and subtle ways to his formulation of a new diplomacy; it also impelled the manner of politics that suffused the entire evolution of the League of Nations.[60]

By 1910, Mexico's feudal sovereigns—the landed aristocracy, the army, the Catholic Church, and reactionary business interests—had encumbered the vast proportion of the country's wealth with debilitating concessions to foreign investors. American and British firms together controlled ninety per cent of the oil industry and virtually all of Mexico's railroads.[61] The revolution led by Francisco I. Madero, in 1911, against the aging dictator Porfirio Díaz was closely watched from afar. Once Madero proved unable to satisfy his disparate coalition of urban middle classes and agrarians, a clique of foreigners in Mexico City, led by Ambassador Henry Lane Wilson of the United States, encouraged and assisted counterrevolution. In February 1913, General Victoriano Huerta, on behalf of the old régime, staged a *coup d'état,* ordered the execution of Madero, and declared himself provisional ruler of Mexico. The great powers of Europe extended Huerta diplomatic recognition with unseemly alacrity. In a matter of days, elements of the shaken Madero coalition, calling themselves the "Constitutionalists," took up arms against the junta.

It was indeed "an irony of fate" that Huerta had violently seized power just as the author of several books on constitutional government entered the White House. Indignant that the Europeans had accorded the general any legitimacy at all, Wilson refused to grant recognition to "a government of butchers."[62] He held to this course over the protests of Ambassador Wilson and other Americans who believed that only a strongman like Huerta could safeguard American property and investments. Operating on extremely limited information, the President, during the summer of 1913, fired the ambassador, imposed an arms embargo, and devised a fairly simple plan of pacification. The United States would mediate between the Huertistas and the Constitutionalists and help to facilitate a free election.[63] But even Huerta's opponents wondered how the good doctor could prescribe a mere patent medicine for a revolution as profound as theirs, and they resented his presumption. Then, on October 10, 1913, Huerta arrested the entire Chamber of Deputies and proclaimed a dictatorship. To make matters worse, the general had apparently acted with the approval of the British Foreign Office.[64] Wilson thereupon decided the time was ripe for a major address on foreign policy, his first, to the Southern Commercial Congress in Mobile, Alabama, on October 27.

Wilson's main theme was imperialism in Latin America. The real problem for weaker countries, he said, grew out of the depredations of foreign financial interests, which undermined the political independence of the countries in which their capital was employed. In this regard the United States had yet to prove itself the friend of Latin Americans—"by comprehending their interest, whether it squares with our own interest or not." Then he made his most important statement: "We have seen material interests threaten constitutional freedom in the United States. Therefore, we will now know how to sympathize with those in the rest of America who have to contend with such powers, not only from within their borders but from outside their borders also." A new policy was needed, one based on "terms of equality" and "sympathy and friendship"; only this could rectify the "degrading" policies of the past and help establish a "family of mankind devoted to the development of true constitutional liberty."[65]

Wilson's critique of European imperialism and its American variations, the "Big Stick" and "Dollar Diplomacy," was hailed in liberal circles up and down the hemisphere. The address was all the more striking because it implied that the forces that resisted political and economic regeneration at home and the forces that exploited an intolerable status quo in other countries were one and the same. The Mobile address, then, was the first indication that Wilson might seek a potentially radical departure in American foreign policy; however, he had yet to shed the Burkean panacea of "fair and honest elections."

By January 1914, the Constitutionalists informed the administration that they required only three things: recognition as the legitimate government of Mexico, the right to purchase arms in the United States, and a minimum of advice from Wilson. Both the "First Chief," Venustiana Carranza, and his more radical lieutenant, Francisco ("Pancho") Villa, insisted that an election would not redress Mexico's desperate social and economic conditions.[66] Wilson's frustrations over the persistence of the old régime caused him to reflect long and hard on what Carranza and Villa were trying to teach him. Although he decided to hold diplomatic recognition in abeyance, he lifted the arms embargo in early February. According to one worried British official, this act on behalf of the Constitutionalists meant that the President "was irrevocably committed to their cause."[67]

But there was more. Wilson not only preferred a group of revolutionaries whom most people in the United States and Europe regarded as bandits, he had also concluded, as he told British officials, that "the real cause of the trouble in Mexico was not political but economic," and that an election would not address "the prime cause of all political difficulties" in Mexico—that the mass of the people did not own the land to which their lives were bound.[68]

Ambassador Spring Rice could hardly believe his ears. The President of the United States had declared that "a radical revolution was the only cure." He was demanding that His Majesty's government withdraw support from Huerta and that Mexico "be left to find her own salvation in *a fight to the finish*."[69] And, when an aide to Spring Rice asserted that only foreign intervention could restore order, the President rejoined that he "knew of no instance in history in which political advance had been made by benefits granted from above; they all had to be gained by the efforts and the blood of the elements from below. . . ."[70] From this dramatic pass onward, Wilson's thoughts and motivations followed a somewhat consistent line; but his next move nearly led to disaster.

On April 9, 1914, Huerta's troops detained several American sailors who had landed a small craft attached to the naval squadron anchored off the port of Tampico. The horrified local commander immediately released the sailors and issued an apology, but Admiral Mayo of the American squadron demanded a twenty-one gun salute. Huerta refused to comply. Wilson, seizing this trivial incident as a chance to bring Huerta to heel, stood behind his admiral. Then the news arrived that a German steamer, carrying a huge cache of machine guns and ammunition, was fast approaching Veracruz. On April 21, Wilson ordered the occupation of the coastal city to prevent delivery of the weapons. By the next morning, 126 Mexicans and nineteen American marines lay dead.[71]

The reaction in Mexico was explosive. Even if Carranza understood Wilson's motivations, he could hardly condone the offensive action, especially now that Huerta was posing as the defender of Mexican honor. As Mark Gilderhus has written, "Mexicans had not identified with Wilson as much as he with them."[72] Further conflict was averted only by Pancho Villa's decision not to protest Wilson's conduct and by a timely offer of mediation from Argentina, Brazil, and Chile. Huerta's downfall had begun, but his abdication in July 1914 carried a heavy penalty. Although the revolution could now resume course where it had been halted, the Veracruz incident made Carranza openly hostile to Wilson's ministrations. Moreover, when Villa broke with Carranza in September, Wilson vacillated for months over whom to recognize.[73] To most contemporaries and historians, his entire approach was arrogant, contradictory, and imperialistic.[74]

The record of the deeper impact of the Mexican Revolution on Wilson's thinking about politics and foreign policy is complex, but unambiguous; not until the 1980s did any historian plumb it fully.[75] The professor who had set out "to teach the South American Republics to elect good men"[76] ended up the wiser pupil. His private correspondence after Veracruz reveals a chastened view of military intervention as well as a discernment of the similarities between the forces of reaction in both the United States and Mexico. When, for example, in August 1914 the Secretary of

War pressed for a full-scale invasion to protect American property, Wilson replied: "There are in my judgement no conceivable circumstances which would make it right for us to direct by force or by threat of force the internal processes of . . . a revolution as profound as that which occurred in France. All the world has been shocked ever since the time of the revolution in France that Europe should have undertaken to nullify what was done there, no matter what the excesses then committed."[77] A year later, when the American Catholic Church launched a propaganda campaign against Carranza, Wilson explained to Edith Bolling Galt: "Every revolution in Mexico which has had popular support has had as part of its programme the curbing and subordination of the church. Therefore the alliance of the church is necessarily with the 'cientifico' class, the educated, privileged, and propertied class, who are, as with us, owning and running everything, the reactionary class. Hence the wedge in our own domestic politics."[78]

Wilson's most eloquent attempt to explain himself occurred in the course of his oration on the Fourth of July, 1914, in Philadelphia: "If American enterprise in foreign countries, particularly in those foreign countries which are not strong enough to resist us, takes the shape of imposing upon and exploiting the mass of the people of that country, it ought to be checked and not encouraged. I am willing to get anything for an American that money and enterprise can obtain, except the suppression of the rights of other men. I will not help any man buy a power which he ought not to exercise over his fellow human beings." It was regrettable if some Americans lost their property or even their lives in Mexico, "but back of it all is the struggle of a people to come into its own."[79]

Such sentiments were scarcely appreciated by domestic critics, especially Republicans. Senator Henry Cabot Lodge of Massachusetts, for example, did not object to intervention to protect American lives and property; but Wilson, it turned out, had gone into Veracruz to rekindle the revolution "in an attitude of an ally of Pancho Villa." Furthermore, because of his lack of resolve with regard to Carranza, he was "directly responsible" for the ensuing civil war.[80] In general, Lodge judged the chief executive "singularly ignorant" in the realm of foreign policy. Mexico, as William C. Widenor has written, "prompted the virtually inevitable contrast between [Wilson's] behavior and conduct of the nation's foreign relations and those of Roosevelt."[81]

The Bull Moose, of course, could speak for himself on the subject. Only when Wilson offered financial compensation and apologies to Colombia for the forced acquisition of the Panama Canal Zone did Roosevelt soar to greater heights of apoplexy.[82] On December 6, 1914, the former president published a merciless attack in the New York Times, in which he blamed the administration for the civil war and said that the United

States should have either recognized Huerta or established a protectorate over Mexico. So strong were Roosevelt's feelings that he ended his friendship with the editors of the *New Republic,* who censured him for assailing the President so "blindly and unfairly."[83] Mexico became the turning point in relations between the Wilson administration and the Republican leadership and set the tone for every issue of foreign policy thereafter.

Of equal importance to future developments, however, were those instances of emphatic praise for Wilson's approach to Mexico, and these came almost exclusively from quarters to the left of progressivism. Many leading American socialists acknowledged Wilson's pains much differently than even his more reliable editorial patrons;[84] their comprehension, moreover, is at wide variance with the historical interpretations of their counterparts among scholars of the late twentieth century. For instance, William English Walling, left-wing Socialist and prolific writer for the *Masses,* defended Wilson against attacks in the *New Statesman* and ridiculed Sidney Webb's and George Bernard Shaw's assertion that "Huerta is a 'capable' and 'honest' old soldier, Carranza a mere brigand, while Wilson's fight for constitutional government is 'dollar diplomacy.'"[85]

Then there was John Reed, the poet-journalist on the "Lyrical Left," who rode with Pancho Villa, later sat in the councils of Lenin, and wrote the classic eyewitness account of the Russian Revolution, *Ten Days That Shook the World.* Reed first enjoyed celebrity as a chronicler of the Mexican Revolution.[86] His writings on Villa and agrarian reform played an important role in Wilson's education. Reed never knew that the President clipped his articles and sent them to Ambassador Walter Hines Page in London;[87] but he had apparently intuited that Wilson was tracking a "well-thought-out plan" based on the conviction that "the social and economic freedom of a people is more important than property." On June 15, 1914, Wilson granted Reed an "extraordinary interview."[88]

Neither friends nor enemies entirely understood the President, Reed wrote, because he "has been more interested in principles than policies." In foreign policy, he believed that American sympathy should always be "on the side of a people in revolt"—an outlook that contradicted Roosevelt's support of "the bloody dictatorship of Díaz." Wilson "had not interfered [in Mexico], paradoxical as it may seem," Reed concluded. On one hand, Huerta had snuffed out the revolution; on the other, the pressure on the administration to impose a protectorate was still enormous. "The Tampico incident was the President's opportunity to check this tendency without harm to the Mexican people and with comparatively little bloodshed." "The Mexicans can restore the land as they see fit," Wilson said to Reed. "If they want to confiscate the great estates, that is their business." His aim was to see "that no one shall take advantage of Mexico,—in any way; neither military dictators, citizens of this country, citi-

zens of foreign countries, nor foreign governments." Alas, the situation
was full of dangerous possibilities.[89]

Wilson admired Reed and his work and opened his mind to him
completely. Still, he decided not to permit the young journalist to print
his account of their meeting.[90] Before the year was out, however, Max
Eastman, editor of the *Masses,* an acquaintance of Wilson's, and Reed's
good friend, published "a tribute" to the President. Using arguments closely
corresponding to Reed's position, Eastman praised the intervention against
Huerta. "I give unreserved admiration to President Wilson for his statesmanship in the Mexican situation," he wrote, "and for his unswerving
purpose to let the Mexican people govern, or not govern, themselves."
Americans should be grateful, he added, that Wilson, and not Roosevelt,
was in the White House at this moment.[91]

Many Americans, of course, would have disagreed with Eastman's opinion
of Wilson's apprenticeship in foreign policy, which the ordeal in Mexico,
along with the initiatives on behalf of arbitration agreements and disarmament, constituted. Yet, by the end of his first two years in the White
House, he had demonstrated the capacity to become an extraordinary
president, exclusive of the accomplishment the New Freedom represented.
Eastman's commentary was much more than a palm extended from an
unlikely source. The left-wing editor, like Reed and Walling, had discerned certain qualities of Wilson's mind and leadership that few liberal
editors had as yet discerned and no conservative could ever esteem. Among
other things, it hinted at the potentialities for significant realignments in
American politics. The cordiality that had prevailed between Wilson and
many leading Socialists during the presidential campaign appeared to have
some staying power.

In the new age of progressive reform and socialistic inquiry, it would
be Wilson's opportunity and challenge to attempt not only to shape, but
also to harmonize domestic and foreign concerns in ways that no other
previous chief executive had ever contemplated. While he became a mas-
terful practitioner of party government, Wilson, with growing frequency
and considerable equanimity, would seek the counsel and support not only
of progressives outside the Democratic party, but also of individuals and
groups of the socialist left. The result, as we shall see, was a period of
singular distinction and creativity in the history of American politics and
foreign policy.

3

Searching for a New Diplomacy

In 1914, only the last of the aging survivors of the American holocaust of 1861–1865 could recall firsthand the experience of total war. In that conflict, armies marched in numbers as strong as 100,000, and in some battles, casualties ran as high as thirty-three per cent. In one suicidal assault against Confederate trenches and earthworks at Cold Harbor, Ulysses S. Grant spent the lives of 7,000 soldiers before noon. Three days at Gettysburg cost Robert E. Lee's legion of 80,000 at least 28,000 dead, wounded, or missing. In all, approximately 620,000 men in blue and grey went to their deaths in the Civil War, theretofore the most destructive four years of warfare in the history of Western civilization.

Even so, until the autumn of 1914, no person living anywhere in the world could imagine the insensate spectacle of modern armies of *millions* of soldiers amassing in Eastern and Western Europe to inflict upon each other sometimes tens of thousands of casualties in a single engagement. The magnitude of Europe's grief strained human comprehension. In September, during the first Battle of the Marne, each side sustained more than half a million casualties. By the end of 1914, France alone buried or carried off to hospitals 900,000 of her sons. In 1915, 330,000 French soldiers fell in battle and another million were wounded; for Germany the figures were 170,000 and 680,000; for Great Britain, 73,000 and 240,000.

Losses in the following year reached even more horrendous levels. Between dawn and dusk on the first day of July 1916, machine-gun fire cut down 20,000 British conscripts on the Somme, a campaign that ultimately claimed 400,000 British casualties. The carnage of the titanic struggle between the Germans and the French around Verdun, in five months' time, nearly equalled that of the entire American Civil War. Russia, by the end of 1916, had suffered some 3.6 million dead or otherwise incapacitated, while losing another two million in prisoners to the Central Powers.

By the onset of the winter of 1914–15, as the belligerents constructed barriers of barbed wire and concrete and bored into the ground to escape each other's enormous firepower, it became obvious to participants and observers alike that the duration of this war would be calculated, not in months, but in years. The weight of these grotesque facts, during the opening phase, brought only a few Americans to a full awareness of the potential consequences of the conflict; most Americans refused to believe that their country had any stake in the outcome.

Colonel House was still in London on June 28, 1914, tending to the proposal for the disarmament conference, when a young Serbian nationalist shot the Archduke Franz Ferdinand, heir to the Hapsburg throne, and his wife Sophie, at Sarajevo, in the Balkan province of Bosnia. In his diary, House made only two brief notations about the assassination, on July 11 and 20.[1] It was, of course, the event that would precipitate the "awful cataclysm" that he had pondered just a few weeks before. Back in Washington, the eight press conferences that Wilson held between the end of June and the end of July reflected the indifference with which the country as a whole responded. Not until the seventh of these press conferences did any reporter so much as raise the subject; at the next one, on July 30, following Austria-Hungary's declaration of war on Serbia, only three out of eighteen queries addressed the proliferating crisis.[2] Nor could one tell from these transcripts that Wilson, coincidentally, was about to withstand the most rending personal trial of his life—the death of his wife, Ellen. In the final days of July, Mrs. Wilson's failing condition was the cause of the President's most intense anxiety. By then, events in Europe, too, had taken on tragic dimensions. On August 1, Germany declared war on Russia, and on France two days later. At midnight on August 4, Great Britain declared war on Germany. Wilson thereupon issued a proclamation of neutrality.[3] He spent most of the following day at Ellen's bedside. She died late in the afternoon on August 6. "Oh, my God," the President whispered, "what am I to do?"[4]

The beginning of the Great War marked the beginning of the historically crucial period in Wilson's life. He conveyed his first reactions in a letter to Colonel House on August 3: "I know how deep a sorrow must have come to you out of this dreadful European conflict in view of what we had hoped the European world was going to turn to," he wrote, "but we must face the situation in the confidence that Providence has deeper plans than we could possibly have laid for ourselves."[5] The deeper plans of Providence would reveal themselves in an objective toward which, it seems in retrospect, Wilson had already begun to move. The outbreak of the war accelerated the process.

Thus far, even allowing for the impact of the Mexican Revolution upon his thinking, Wilson had usually attempted to base his foreign policies on philosophical assumptions drawn together in the years before he entered politics. If disorder and invasion of right provoked war, then ordered relationships and obligations promoted a moral sense of community among nations; if Christianity evidenced the brotherhood of man, then union among nations existed, however imperfectly, in nature; and, if the weight of popular opinion and institutions of free debate and representation were allowed to prevail, then human progress and reason would triumph over atavistic passions and regression. For Wilson, these precepts took on greater meaning in the autumn of 1914.

The rules of international behavior he would seek to establish in order to bring about progress, stability, and a moral sense of community among nations certainly flowed from his religious faith and his convictions about political democracy; they were also implicitly manifest in those prewar diplomatic initiatives he had formulated himself or had closely supervised. Wilson was not, however, an original thinker. The salient ideas with which he is identified historically, almost without exception, he derived from other groups and individuals in the United States and Europe. Even the term "League of Nations" was not of Wilson's coining. The broad concept of a community of nations had long been espoused by a disparate constellation of activists in (primarily, but not exclusively) the labor, peace, and socialist movements on both sides of the Atlantic. They acted upon a wide variety of motivations and differed, often vehemently, on means as well as ends. Wilson's essential contribution to this ferment was propagation and grand synthesis—a synthesis that would take shape in the final months of his first administration. It would amount to nothing less than a new international political ideology.

In the immediate circumstance of the war, Wilson found himself beset by innumerable complex problems for which there existed few guiding precedents in American history. The vicissitudes of neutrality have been thoroughly treated elsewhere; a brief compass will suffice here.

The administration's chief difficulties in the early months were twofold. They centered around the restrictions Great Britain imposed on American commerce when the Royal Navy blockaded the North Sea and the Atlantic in order to deprive the Central Powers of vital war materials.

Anglo-American relations grew strained when the British began to seize American merchantmen suspected of carrying contraband, and when, in March 1915, an Order in Council authorized the interdiction of all neutral commerce bound for Germany. This policy provoked from the United States the famous cry of "freedom of the seas." The severity of Allied economic warfare, however, was eclipsed in the eyes of most Americans by the German government's novel method of retribution. On February 4, 1915, Berlin commenced submarine warfare against all enemy vessels—which ultimately might threaten American lives and commerce. Yet neither the Central Powers nor the Allies wanted to rashly pursue policies that would arouse the world's most powerful neutral to retaliation. Each side made well-calculated concessions to Wilson at critical moments. As crises ebbed and flowed, the administration alternately protested against, and sought ways to accommodate, the conduct of both hostile alliances, at the same time striving to preserve American neutral rights and public sensibilities. For thirty months, Wilson scored a considerable success on all counts.[6]

Wilson's paramount objective in all of this was to keep the United States out of war. His decision to ply the course of neutrality—as far as it was practicable—easily won the support of the vast majority of Americans. As he urged his constituency to be "impartial in thought as well as in action," he also contended that such disinterestedness would eventually permit the government the opportunity "to play a part of impartial mediation and speak the counsels of peace."[7] It was in this context—the pursuit of mediation—that the objective of a multifaceted system of collective security emerged as a critical factor in Wilson's foreign policy.

As Wilson attempted to set the actual process of mediation in motion, other strata of context began to form. They consisted of several components—on his part, two remarkable private reflections on the war, the beginning of an exchange of ideas between the President and a small group of British radicals, and an effort to lay the cornerstone of a community of nations in the Western Hemisphere. Together, they help clarify the origins of Wilson's commitment to some sort of peacekeeping organization.

Near the end of 1914, Wilson worked out a provisional analysis of the causes and potential consequences of the conflict, to the point where he could isolate some of the conditions that he considered requisite to "the counsels of peace." He disclosed these thoughts confidentially, on December 14, 1914, in an interview with H. B. Brougham of the *New York Times*.[8] The best outcome, from the standpoint of neutrals and belligerents alike, would be a deadlock that "will show to them the futility of employing force in the attempt to resolve their differences," he stated. "The Powers are making the most tremendous display of force in history. If the result of it all is merely to w[e]ar each other down without coming to a decision, the point will be at length reached when they will be glad to say . . . there remains this alternative of trying to reason out our differences according to the principles of right and justice. So I think that the chance of a just and equitable peace . . . will be happiest if no nation gets the decision by arms; and the danger of an unjust peace, one that will be sure to invite future calamities, will be if some one nation, or group of nations succeeds in enforcing its will upon the others.

"It may be found before long that Germany is not alone responsible for the war, and that other nations will have to bear a portion of the blame in our eyes. The others may be blamed, and it might be well if there were no exemplary triumph and punishment. I believe thoroughly that the settlement should be for the advantage of the European nations regarded as Peoples and not for any nation imposing its governmental will upon alien people."[9]

Wilson's comments suggested a fairly critical attitude toward all the belligerents, notwithstanding his carefully controlled personal sympathy for the British.[10] Whereas he reaffirmed his confidence in disarmament and conciliation and, significantly, vented the principle of self-determination, he did not specify what a "Peoples" settlement might consist of. But apparently he had provided a partial answer to that question somewhat earlier—again, in private. In 1925 Wilson's brother-in-law, Stockton Axson, recalled for Ray Stannard Baker a conversation with the President that took place just after the family had returned from Mrs. Wilson's funeral. According to Axson, Wilson articulated for the first time a four-point program for a league of nations:

1. No nation shall ever again be permitted to acquire an inch of land by conquest.
2. There must be a recognition of the reality of equal rights between small nations and great.
3. Munitions of war must hereafter be manufactured entirely by the nations and not by private enterprise.
4. There must be an association of nations, all bound together for the protection of the integrity of each, so that any one nation breaking from this bond will bring upon herself war; that is to say, punishment, automatically.[11]

Axson's recollection is quite Wilsonian in both tone and substance. It is doubtful, however, that the President would have propounded such a position on collective security at this time, especially given his state of mind just after the death of his wife. But we can be certain that he enumerated the propositions at a significantly early date—probably during the first week of February 1915, as Axson's personal papers indicate.[12]

In any case, the Brougham and Axson documents together constitute

Wilson's earliest assessment of the dysfunctional features of the international system as he (like many other progressives at the time[13]) understood them. First, his condemnation of national conquest and his assertion of the equality of states in Axson's presence (unmistakable echoes of the Mobile address) along with his general comment to Brougham about a "Peoples" settlement, reflected a judgment that imperialism was one of the root causes of the war. Second, Axson's listing of the item on governmental control of munitions as well as the veiled references to the Bryan treaties in the Brougham interview pointed directly to the race for military and naval supremacy among the great powers as another primary factor in the war equation. And finally, Wilson's preference for a stalemate in tandem with the proposal for an association of nations composed perhaps his most important systemic criticism—that the balance of power was a fatally flawed arrangement that somehow must be supplanted by a concert of power within the framework of a new community of nations.

Not until early in 1915 did any political organization in the United States bring forth a proposal that resembled a possible solution to the world crisis. The first important petition that more or less adopted the ideas of collective security, the peaceful settlement of disputes among nations, and a negotiated settlement of the war, emanated from an heir to the British peace movement. This was the Union of Democratic Control (UDC), founded in London during the second week of August 1914.[14]

In the prewar years, increasing numbers of Quakers and other pacifists, activists in the burgeoning labor movement, and disaffected Liberals filled the ranks of the British peace movement. Beginning in the 1910s, they publicly condemned, albeit with little appreciable effect, the Liberal government's traditional conduct of foreign policy based on a strong navy, secret diplomacy, and the balance of power, and commended the virtues of arbitration, disarmament, parliamentary control of foreign policy, and free trade. Even so, the movement's adherents could not conceive of a truly great war and, ironically, exhibited a certain complacency—a function, in part, of their very faith in progress. One of the most notable examples of this conflicted attitude was Norman Angell's *The Great Illusion* (1910), which had sold over one million copies in twenty-five languages before the war. Angell had argued that, because the great powers had become so economically dependent upon one another, a great war would prove disastrous to victor and vanquished alike; the implication was that no government would plunge headlong into such obvious folly.[15]

Germany's invasion of Belgium threw the movement into confusion. Peace-seekers in the main forsook their antiwar philosophy in the face of the unenviable choice between supporting or opposing their country's war effort. The Union of Democratic Control, however, was born of precisely this dilemma. The UDC's founders upheld and expanded the much-calumniated tradition of radical dissent in British politics. The small organization's stand seemed all the more impressive when it mustered an executive board from Oxford, Cambridge, and Parliament. Prominent members included Norman Angell, H. N. Brailsford, Goldsworthy Lowes Dickinson, J. Ramsay MacDonald, E. D. Morel, Bertrand Russell, and Charles P. Trevelyan. Unlike nearly all their Liberal and Labourite brethren, they blamed not only Germany, but also their own Foreign Office (along with the French and Russian ministries) for the "drift into war." The UDC demanded a negotiated settlement and drew up "four cardinal points" (and later a fifth) for the construction of an enduring peace. Published in November 1914, their manifesto was the first important synthesis of the so-called New Diplomacy in any form:

1. No territory shall come under the control of any government unless it be with the consent of the population of the territory in question.
2. The Government of Great Britain shall enter into no treaty without the consent of Parliament; machinery shall be created to thus insure the democratic control of foreign policy.
3. The foreign policy of Great Britain shall eschew alliances for the purpose of maintaining the "Balance of Power"; rather, it shall be directed toward concerted action between the Powers determined by public deliberations in an International Court.
4. As part of the peace settlement, Great Britain shall propose drastic reductions in armaments and the general nationalization of the manufacture of armaments by all the nations of the world.
5. Economic warfare cannot continue after the present military conflict has ceased; the British Government shall promote free commercial intercourse among all nations by expanding the principle of the Open Door.[16]

Wilson became acquainted with this statement of principles through one of the UDC's most distinguished fellows—Goldsworthy Lowes Dickinson, the Cambridge classicist who contributed to the lexicon of diplomatic history the term "League of Nations." Lowes Dickinson presented his case in "The War and the Way Out," published in the *Atlantic Monthly* in December 1914. He contended that the war was the inevitable culmination of the intrigue and connivance of the governments, not the peoples, of the belligerent countries. The *sine qua non* of the peace to come, he therefore reasoned, was the rehabilitation and proliferation of democracy—specifically, the establishment of democratic control of foreign policy throughout Europe, the recognition of the rights of small states, and the application of self-determination in the disposition of colonial possessions. And, because the war had so obscenely demonstrated the gross futility of the resort to arms, three comprehensive changes in the prevailing rules of international behavior had to be set down: the submission of all

disputes between nations to a council of arbitration; an end to the waste
of resources on armaments; and the relinquishment of existing armaments
to an international authority. Such a compact would permit a "League of
Europe" to flourish and rekindle the light of civilization. "For the moment, the voice is mine and the listener that one person who at any moment, in any place, may peruse these lines," he concluded. "I appeal to
his common sense, his reason, his conscience, and his heart."[17]

One is tempted to wonder whether Lowes Dickinson (who realized
that his own government abjured the UDC's position) had in mind
Woodrow Wilson as "that one person who at any moment . . . may peruse these lines." For if he did, his hope was soon gratified when Newton
D. Baker, the progressive mayor of Cleveland and Wilson's good friend,
brought the *Atlantic* article to the President's attention. "The use of armed
force as an international police is, of course, not new," Baker wrote, "but
it is put rather more persuasively than I have seen elsewhere." Wilson
looked it up at once.[18] We do not know what his reaction was, but we
can be confident that both Lowes Dickinson's entreaty and the platform
of the UDC had enormous intellectual and emotional appeal. The President had previously advocated the principles behind each of their proposals and had already attempted to apply some of them in his own foreign
policy.

It is interesting to note that Lowes Dickinson did not stress the economic causes of the conflict in his impassioned analysis. (The fifth point,
about prohibiting commercial warfare, written by J. A. Hobson, the author of *Imperialism,* was not added until May 1916.) Nor had Wilson done
so in his conversations with Brougham and Axson. Wilson (and Lowes
Dickinson) was fully aware of this dimension, however—that the sun,
indubitably, never set on the British Empire, stretching as it did over
twelve million square miles of the earth's surface and incorporating a
quarter of its population; and that Germany's ambition to rival the British
rendered her a menace to the security of all of her neighbors. To a small
degree, Wilson also perceived the fact—and his perceptions in this regard
would sharpen during the next two years—that virtually the whole of the
Continent, despite extraordinarily rapid industrialization, was chained to
a feudal past. European governments, he believed, were fundamentally
conservative, élitist, imperialist, militaristic, and undemocratic. (The British government might not be guilty of all of these iniquities, but it was
absolutely dominated by imperialist interests resistant to democratic control of foreign policy.) Moreover, the old régimes, in their haste to apoc-
alypse, had demonstrated once again that they would undertake any measures necessary to maintain their hegemonic positions within their respective
societies against the internal challenges of liberal and socialist minorities,
just as they had tried to do in Mexico.[19]

It was not entirely coincidental, then, that Wilson turned to Latin America itself, in late 1914, as the arena for his first important, practical experiment to give life to a league of nations, just at the moment when he and Colonel House seriously began to take soundings of the depth of peace sentiment in Europe. This endeavor to attach wings to the phoenix, the Pan-American Pact, has been long overlooked in studies of Wilson's League; yet, for a while it became the confluence of many of the administration's intentions—to launch a new era in hemispheric relations, to promote disarmament and the practice of arbitration and conciliation, and to impress upon the belligerents the urgency of mediation.[20]

The idea for the Pact originally came across Wilson's desk in November 1913, in a letter from Representative James Slayden, a Texas Democrat and veteran of the peace movement. Wilson called it "very striking" and told Bryan he would like to pursue it after the Mexican situation was resolved.[21] Once the war broke out, other prominent figures in the peace movement revived Slayden's motion. For instance, Andrew Carnegie, upon his return from a personal survey of the war, wrote the following lines to Wilson in September 1914: "There is no service American Republics can render the civilized world equal to setting them such an example as proposed. Twenty-one Republics welded into a peace of brotherhood would be such an example to the rest of the world as could not fail to impress it."[22] Colonel House, too, placed the issue before Wilson, in December. The President could "play a great and beneficent part in the European tragedy," House told him, by formulating "a plan to be agreed upon by the Republics of the two continents which, in itself, would serve as a model for the European Nations when peace is at last brought about."[23]

Wilson became very enthusiastic and immediately typed out two basic articles similar to those he had outlined to his brother-in-law:

1st. Mutual guarantee of political independence under republican forms of government and mutual guarantees of territorial integrity.

2nd. Mutual agreement that the government of each of the contracting parties acquire complete control within its jurisdiction of the manufacture and sale of munitions of war.[24]

The first article was the heart of the proposal. It constituted (on paper) a kind of mutualization of the Monroe Doctrine among hemispheric states.[25] Of more importance, it was Wilson's first composition on collective security, and it would become the seed of Article X of the Covenant of the League of Nations.[26] In Wilson's view a Pan-American Pact could serve two salutary functions. First, in conjunction with Bryan's cooling-off treaties, the guarantees could seal the elusive covenant of friendship and cooperation with Latin America Wilson had been striving for since his Mobile address. Second, he and House (as well as Bryan) believed that a successful negotiation might craft a powerful lever to move the European belligerents toward mediation.

The first step in diplomacy belonged to House—to contact the ambassadors of the three great South American republics, Argentina, Brazil, and Chile. On December 19, he showed the two-point memorandum to Rómulo Sebastian Naón, the Argentine ambassador, who asked to keep the document as a historical memento upon learning that Wilson had typed it himself. That afternoon House visited Domicio da Gama and Eduardo Suárez-Mujica, the ambassadors from Brazil and Chile, respectively. "Da Gama was of easy conquest," House wrote; Suárez-Mujica was not. But all three had assured him that they would commend the proposal to their governments. In the evening House reported to Wilson that he hoped to "button up" the matter within a few weeks.[27]

Good news arrived on Christmas Eve. Da Gama informed the Colonel that Brazil was "agreeable" in principle to the "epoch-making negotiation." Shortly afterward House called on Ambassador Naón at his home. Argentina, also, received the Pact "with sympathy," and Naón added that it would transform "the one side[d] character of the Monroe Doctrine into a common policy for all the American countries." With this, House wanted to give the treaty priority over his imminent peace mission to Europe (see below), "for the reason that if brought to a successful conclusion, the one might have a decided influence upon the other."[28]

House had neglected, however, to read all the signals. Suárez-Mujica was not forthcoming. Because of a long-standing boundary dispute with Peru over the nitrate fields in the provinces of Tacna and Arica, the Chilean government blanched at Article I of the Pact. After some delay, the ambassador conveyed the impression that his government was "favorable in principle," which triggered another burst of (as it turned out) misplaced optimism on House's part. "Everything now seems to be in shape for you to go ahead," he wrote Wilson on the eve of his departure for Europe. "I believe the country will receive this policy with enthusiasm and it will make your Administration notable, even had you done but little else."[29]

Confident of the prospects, Bryan and Wilson now took the reins. At the Secretary's request, the covenant presently acquired two more articles, prescribing arbitration as the means of settling pending and future disputes among the signatories.[30] These very Bryanesque additions proved maladroit. Whereas Naón seemed to welcome the change—he was also eager, like the Wilson administration, to move quickly "in order to produce an effect upon the European belligerents"—the Chileans' apprehensions over the Tacna-Arica dispute only increased. Santiago raised objections not only to arbitration, but also to the arms control feature and to the guarantee of territorial integrity under republican forms of government—the latter because it verged on interference in the internal affairs of states.[31] Wilson could not understand this challenge. Naturally, he replied, it was the inviolate right of a people to choose their leaders as they saw fit, but "the trend of the world" was "toward the idea of popular government," was it not? Likewise, "nothing would seem to go further to insure peace among the nations of the western hemisphere" than the mutual guarantee of territorial integrity. In any event, Wilson and Bryan appreciated Chile's overriding interest and informally exempted the controversy with Peru; no boundary would be recognized until the disputants, within one year's time, had reached a settlement.[32]

The Chileans still harbored suspicions. In reality, Suárez-Mujica opposed the Pact and secretly advised his government to reject it. Tacna-Arica aside, he argued, Chile should not "tie its hands and condemn itself to any limitation of sovereignty for reasons of an altruistic nature." Enrique Villegas, the foreign minister, agreed for other reasons: "The treaty, if skillfully exploited, would tend to erect a United States tutelage over Latin-America and might lead to commercial and political absorption by the United States of smaller, weaker Latin-America countries."[33] Throughout most of 1915 the Pact hung in limbo because Chile was slow to respond formally and because German-American tensions over submarine warfare diverted Wilson's attention.

For Wilson, the European connection was the one constant *leitmotif* evident at every stage of the negotiations. Yet, whereas his central motivation remained decidedly political, there was another dimension to the Pan-American policy. So often when he spoke about the future, Wilson predicted economic as well as political preeminence for the United States in world affairs. Moreover, despite the almost instinctive aversion to the reform impulse felt by perhaps a majority of the business community, Wilson's New Freedom had served to give overseas trade a substantial boost. For example, the Federal Reserve system provided American bankers with the machinery to establish branches abroad. William Gibbs McAdoo, the Secretary of the Treasury, engineered comprehensive legislation (passed in 1916) to create a United States Shipping Board and empower the government to purchase or lease a great merchant fleet. And, finally, the Underwood tariff in many cases yielded reciprocity, another stimulant to the economy.[34]

The upheaval in Europe, however, initially threw American trade into a tailspin. It practically paralyzed Latin America. Consequently, by the middle of 1915, expectations for a new intra-hemispheric trade relationship had become a major topic within business and governmental circles, from New York to Rio de Janiero.[35] Thus, the British blockade and German submarine warfare (and the coincidental opening of the Panama Canal) had the effect of bringing about closer commercial ties between the United States and Latin America—or, as Wilson was wont to put it, of creating "new instrumentalities of acquaintance, intercourse, and mutual service."[36]

No one was more alive to the new opportunities than the Treasury secretary. In October 1914, he proposed that the United States sponsor a Pan-American Financial Conference to promote "more intimate and effective relations" with her neighbors. The President called McAdoo's plan "a splendid idea," and, in May 1915, businessmen and politicians from eighteen Central and South American countries traveled to Washington to attend the highly publicized convention. The delegates, acting out of mutual interests, unanimously passed two resolutions which called for the granting of ample credits to Latin America by businesses and banks in the United States and the prompt establishment of steamship lines between the two continents.[37]

Wilson motored to the Pan-American Union building to welcome the delegates personally. In his remarks he wove together a number of themes. The purpose of the conference, he said, was "to draw the American republics together by bonds of common interest and mutual understanding." But there could be "no sort of union of interest if there is a purpose of exploitation by any one of the parties to a great conference of this sort. The basis of successful commercial intercourse is common interest, not selfish interest." Then he turned to the war. If any good result had possibly accrued from Europe's distress, it was that it had revealed the American nations to one another: "[I]t has shown us what it means to be neighbors." In an allusion to the Pan-American Pact (which only four or five people present were aware of), he added: "I cannot help harboring the hope, the very high hope that, by this commerce of minds with one another, as well as commerce in goods, we may show the world in part the path to peace."[38]

By the final session, McAdoo had scored a great public-relations triumph. The *Washington Post* accorded the financial congress front-page coverage and called it "the most important [of its kind] ever held from both a national and international viewpoint." The *New York Times* made it the subject of a main editorial, under the banner "The Nation's Turning Point," and read Wilson's speech closely enough to include within the text the subheading "May Show Path to Peace."[39] In Latin America, however, the reviews were somewhat mixed. Whereas *La Prensa* of Buenos Aires acknowledged that Pan-Americanism was "a moral force, useful and advantageous," it also stressed the potential perils of too much commercial dependence on the United States. One Brazilian polemicist warned that "on the basis of commercial interchange with the southern countries" the United States would engage in conduct akin to imperialism, "in spite of Wilson's tranquilizing expressions." In Santiago, *El Mercurio* touted the conference as the prelude to "a new epoch in commercial relations"; but this opinion did not assuage the government's wariness of Wilson's treaty.[40]

It is important to emphasize at this juncture that Chilean fears of Yankee imperialism—well-founded apprehensions about the potential economic ramifications of an essentially political conception—resembled the broader analysis that many New Left historians of the 1960s advanced with regard to Wilson's "liberal-capitalist-internationalist" outlook on world politics.[41] The saga of the Pan-American Pact illustrates certain aspects of what the late William Appleman Williams, for example, has called "the tragedy of American diplomacy." In this classic study, Williams proffered the "Open Door thesis" of American foreign policy. "Combined with the ideology of an industrial Manifest Destiny," the Open Door policy, devised by John Hay in the aftermath of the Spanish-American War, supplied the basic tactics and strategy the United States has employed ever since to achieve its primary goal in foreign policy—"the enlargement of American trade."

Wilson, on one hand, was trying to construct a new regional political system theoretically based on the principles of the equality and sovereignty of states, for the sake of peace and security. On the other hand, in the economic components of both early New Freedom diplomacy and Pan-Americanism, he was vigorously promoting a program obviously advantageous to the United States, which, presumably, would improve the political economies of Latin America. If one employs Williams' phraseology to describe this particular Wilsonian countenance, then one might conclude that "the policy of the open door"—Foreign Minister Villegas would have said "Pan-Americanism"—"was designed to clear the way and establish conditions under which America's preponderant economic power would extend the American system throughout the world without the embarrassment and inefficiency of traditional colonialism."[42]

For all its cogency, this interpretation does not fully measure the breadth of Wilson's endeavors and intentions, his emphasis on the primacy of politics over economics (Mexico notwithstanding), or, even at that, his consciousness of the conflict between his own best ideals and capitalism itself. Since the early days of his exposure to the conundrum of Mexico, Wilson, more earnestly and on a profounder level than any other president to date, had begun to grapple with the circumstances that arrayed the imperatives of an international capitalist economy against the American commitment to political self-determination. As he averred in his July Fourth address of 1914, in reference to Mexico, he was "willing to get anything for an American that money and enterprise can obtain, except the suppression of the rights of other men." From his perspective, the war in Europe presented a unique opportunity. Together, the Americas somehow might transcend the dilemma—by offering one another the collective political guarantees of a new diplomacy and all that it entailed, by encouraging necessary social change through the process of reform, and (in some exceptional instances, if one included Mexico) by even accommodating revolution when reform had failed. Thus Wilson's ambition for the Western Hemisphere, which by his own admission came from both the head and the heart, was "to set an example to the world in freedom of institutions, freedom of trade, and intelligence of mutual service"—an exemplary structure of peace, grounded in collective security, that Europe might find worthy of adoption.[43]

Wilson's incontrovertibly herculean labor, of course, awaited him in Europe. It was one thing to formulate such categorical objectives as those embodied in the Brougham interview, the Axson memoir, and the Pan-American Pact; to win over belligerents enmeshed in history's ultimate war—indeed, to bring the Europeans to the task of peace on any terms—was quite another. In October 1914, the President and Colonel House (perhaps somewhat naïvely at this pass) commenced their mediatorial work in overtures to Sir Cecil Arthur Spring Rice, the British ambassador, and Count Johann von Bernstorff, the German ambassador. At the same time, to London and Berlin, House conveyed Wilson's general plan for ensuring peace once the war was over: a mutual guarantee of the territorial integrity of all the nations of Europe, at least partial disarmament on land and sea, state control of munitions and weapons construction, and machinery for the arbitration of future disputes.[44]

The common attitude of all the belligerent governments towards Wilson's proposals is well represented in a letter of November 23, 1914, from Theobald von Bethmann Hollweg, the German chancellor, to Foreign Secretary Gottlieb von Jagow: "We have to avoid the appearance of favoring, in principle, the continuation of the war," Bethmann Hollweg wrote. "Furthermore, I see a certain danger in an American mediation move because it would probably lead to an international congress, and . . . we would have to expect Mr. Wilson's and Mr. Bryan's known do-good tendencies and the injection of a lot of questions (disarmament, arbitration, and world peace) which, the more utopian they are, the more they make practical negotiations difficult."[45] (One simple fact crippled Wilson's mediatorial diplomacy throughout the entire period of American neutrality. Neither the Central Powers nor the Allies ever responded to him forthrightly; both sides were dedicated to expansive war aims, which required military victory and a dictated peace.[46])

The British and German foreign offices were masterfully evasive. Wilson and House soon realized that diplomatic correspondence was unavailing. By mid-January 1915 they had decided that their only alternative was for House to go to Europe for face-to-face talks with the belligerents.[47] Bryan, who had coveted the assignment for himself, was deeply hurt by this first overt indication that Wilson had greater confidence in House than in him. But the Secretary of State acceded gracefully and even suggested a tactic to facilitate House's mission. This was the idea of holding a second peace convention after a first convention, of belligerents only, had taken place. Bryan's approach, among other things, would spare Wilson the indignity of being rejected if he otherwise demanded a role in the actual negotiations of the final terms. Instead, he could summon a subsequent, or simultaneous, gathering of both belligerents and neutrals. With military operations suspended, they could recast international law in order to secure a permanent peace along the lines that the President had previously recommended.[48]

Wilson charged House, then, not to define peace terms for anyone; rather, he was to bear the President's good wishes and profound hope that the war could be ended quickly, to get all of the belligerents' reactions to a second convention, and to try to be of service in bringing about preliminary parleys.[49] His mission would constitute the first stage in the evolution of the League of Nations in transatlantic diplomacy.[50]

The Colonel crossed the Atlantic onboard the *Lusitania* (one of that majestic liner's last voyages) and arrived in London on February 6, 1915. He met with Sir Edward Grey on the next day. Their first topic was the problem of armaments. House recommended that the United States as well as the belligerents agree to halt the construction of warships and the manufacture of munitions for ten years. This, along with the general guarantee of territorial integrity, would fairly accomplish what he and Wilson had in mind. Somewhat to House's surprise, the Foreign Secretary assented to the proposals, and especially to the territorial guarantee. Indeed, he practically insisted that the United States become a party to such an arrangement. House, however, retreated at this point. Wilson was not prepared to offer an *official* pledge which, for all practical purposes, would shatter the century-long American tradition of noninvolvement in European affairs. (He had yet to explain his position to Congress and the public; the administration's Pan-American plan was still held in confidence as well.) At any rate, House hastened to another subject—the second convention. Grey apparently saw no obstacle to it, but, as House told Wilson, "He did not accept this as our full duty."[51]

In a later meeting, Grey again pressed House on the matter of the territorial guarantee. The Colonel stated that he presently could promise only that the United States would sign a postwar recodification of international law.[52] This being the case, the Foreign Secretary replied, the Allies could not consider peace until they had won some decisive victory in the field; moreover, he doubted whether Germany was sincere about mediation. Then House suddenly unburdened himself in such a way as to relieve his host of his anxieties about American mediation. "I told Sir Edward that I had no intention of pushing the question of peace," he wrote in his diary, but he never disclosed this to Wilson. "I could see the necessity for the Allies to try out their new armies in the Spring, and . . . for Germany not to be in such an advantageous position as now."[53]

House once wrote of his working relationship with Wilson: "Nine times out of ten we reached the same conclusions. When we did, neither he nor I felt it necessary to counsel with the other."[54] The exchange with Grey no doubt was one of those "tenth" times. Theretofore, House had usually followed Wilson's instruction without much deviation; but in certain critical instances, "Phillip Dru" seemed to overpower the Colonel. His statement to Grey hardly reflected Wilson's position. To the contrary, House often expressed unabashedly pro-Allied sentiments, desired a limited Allied victory over Germany, and firmly believed that the basis for future peace lay in an Anglo-American *entente*.[55] He never accurately informed Wilson about this part of his conversation with Grey; while thus gaining the Foreign Secretary's trust, he obviously did not serve his own chief very well. (Bryan, it must be said, would have followed Wilson's instructions to the letter.) Whatever slim chance for mediation might have existed at this time had now vanished.[56] Over the next few weeks, House nonetheless continued to seek the support of British leaders, in and out of government, for the second convention, which he regarded as of "more far reaching [consequence] in fact than the peace conference itself."[57]

House traveled to the Continent and arrived in Berlin on March 19 for talks with Bethmann Hollweg, von Jagow, and Arthur Zimmermann, the Undersecretary of State for Foreign Affairs. Evidently unmindful of the futility of the mission, he hoped to facilitate mediation by persuading the Germans of the wisdom of evacuating northern France and restoring Belgium if, in turn, he could get the British to consent to freedom of the seas. As ever, Bethmann was equivocal; however, he and his colleagues favored the notion of the second convention. In spite of Germany's expansive war aims, Zimmermann said that the main thing that his countrymen desired was "a settlement which would guarantee permanent peace." "It is the same cry in each of the belligerent states," the Colonel wrote to Wilson.[58]

In the weeks that followed, House was alternately optimistic and pessimistic about mediation. He repeatedly emphasized the virtues of holding a second convention in all of his discussions with the Germans and the French and took special pains to inform the American ambassadors at Bern, Madrid, and Rome about it.[59] But the mystery behind all of this activity was how House could possibly have expected a second convention of neutrals and belligerents to take place. Although officials in London, Berlin, and Paris received the idea cordially, none of them welcomed a first convention to begin with, and all of them had, in fact, indicated that peace discussions were out of the question! When House returned to London at the end of April to consult about an agenda for the second convention, Sir Edward was frankly bewildered.[60] A week later, on May 7, the *Lusitania* was sunk and, with her, all hope for mediation. "Peace talk is yet mere moonshine," Walter Hines Page scratched in his diary. "House has been to Berlin, from London, thence to Paris, thence back to London again—from Nowhere (as far as peace is concerned) to Nowhere again."[61]

In part because of the ensuing crisis between the United States and Germany over the *Lusitania,* Wilson never caught on that House was responsible for the failure of his own mission. But Wilson had at least learned conclusively that the belligerents were far more interested in victory than in a negotiated settlement. Then, too, he could assume, owing to House's faithful promotion of the second convention, that they were all amenable to some kind of treaty to establish international security after peace itself was achieved, whenever that might come. If nothing else, this information, conflicting though it was, reaffirmed in the President's mind the wisdom of neutrality. It also demonstrated, paradoxically, that traditional American isolation from European politics (which neutrality only abetted) was quickly growing dangerously obsolete. Whether or not Grey had merely been testing the Americans on the issue of collective security, one can only wonder about the results if House, speaking for Wilson, had been able thus to commit the United States during the first year of the war. Such a commitment was obviously a political impossibility.

Perhaps most important of all, then, House's mission illustrated the absolute necessity of laying a foundation of domestic support for the kind of international structure that Wilson was beginning to envision, and of educating his fellow citizens about the new facts of international life and about their probable future role in world affairs. These requirements were as exigent as gaining the cooperation of the belligerents; and they could not be met in the sterile vacuum of diplomacy alone. It is to this subject— the critically formative domestic political environment in which Wilson's League of Nations was conceived—that we now turn.

4

The Political Origins of
Progressive and Conservative
Internationalism

Theodore Roosevelt was a man often ahead of his times. Within weeks of the outbreak of the European war, the former president became the first prominent American politician publicly to advocate the creation of some kind of league of nations. The general idea was not new for Roosevelt. In 1910, he had made an international league his main focus when he formally accepted the Nobel Peace Prize (for having mediated the Russo-Japanese War), at Christiania, Norway. During the fall of 1914, a series of thoughtful articles on the subject, in the context of the war, flowed from his pen. Of Belgium, he wrote in the *Outlook* in late September, "We have not the smallest responsibility for what has befallen her." Yet Germany's trampling of that country in the drive toward Paris raised serious issues for a neutral like the United States. Americans would not find their future well-being secure in disarmament or in milk-and-water "cooling-off" treaties, he was keen to say; rather, they would need to strengthen the country's military capabilities and put force behind arbitration (if that approach were to have any real worth). "Surely the time ought to be ripe for the nations to consider a great world agreement among all the civilized military powers to *back righteousness by force,*" he concluded. "Such an agreement would establish an efficient world league for the peace of righteousness."[1]

In November, in a piece for the *New York Times,* Roosevelt came as close as he ever would to condemning the concept of the balance of power (and to anticipating President Wilson). The alliance system, he declared, was "shifty and uncertain" and "based on self-interest." The kind of world league he dreamed of would show its true temper through "conduct and not merely selfish interest." The United States must brace itself "to take some chance for the sake of internationalism, that is of international morality."[2]

Roosevelt's mood and frame of mind underwent a dramatic change in late autumn. He soon became the country's most obstreperous pro-Allied extremist and the administration's most wrathful (some observers said "crazed") critic. His personal correspondence seethed with vituperation of the President and Secretary of State. Bryan was "a professional yodeler, a human trombone," and a "prize idiot," and Wilson was "a prime jackass" who had mastered the "hypocritical ability to deceive plain people." How could it be that destiny had placed these "preposterous little fools" in such positions of power at the very moment "when that great black tornado trembles on the edge of Europe?" he asked an intimate.[3] The administration's failure to protest Belgium's fate—sheer partisanship, the Colombian treaty, and Wilson's handling of Mexico played large roles, too—ostensibly provoked Roosevelt's increasingly shrill public denunciations from November 1914 onward. His criticism of American neutrality had a consistent logic to it, and by his lights he had the country's interests at heart; but the manner and proportions of his antagonism, the public at large and even his friends knew, were inappropriate in the circumstances and unbecoming of someone of Roosevelt's stature.[4] A man who had once revered him summed it up best: "The truth is," President Taft told a friend, "he believes in war and wishes to be a Napolean and to die on the battlefield. He has the spirit of the old berserkers."[5] Had Roosevelt, in 1914–15, put his immense prestige behind a movement for a league, the final chapter of his life and a part of American history would have been substantially different. Instead he let the opportunity pass. After 1914, he ceased any longer to exert a salutary influence in American politics.

One of the chief responsibilities of the President of the United States, Wilson believed, was to give purpose and direction to public opinion, particularly during times of stress and change.[6] Throughout the first eighteen months of the war, however, most of Wilson's public utterances on foreign policy were aimed at justifying and maintaining neutrality, as public reaction to both the British blockade and German submarine warfare seemed to demand. His private deliberations and confidential diplomatic overtures notwithstanding, Wilson had done less than Roosevelt—which was not much—to cultivate public opinion on the question of an international league.

The great issue, though, had already begun to stir in American politics. Beginning in early 1915, several small but influential groups of new internationalists began to seek Wilson out, rather than the other way around. Theretofore, the American peace societies had demonstrated little more than intellectual bankruptcy in the war crisis. They had not begun to fathom the causes of the conflict, to define any goals for peace, to agitate for mediation, or to make contact with potential European allies, such as the Union of Democratic Control.[7] A new American internationalist movement, however, soon came into being. It would transform American politics and diplomacy. Accommodating far more diverse perspectives than the long-established peace organizations, this movement was loosely composed of two divergent aggregations of activists—"progressive internationalists" and "conservative internationalists." Wilson's relationship with both of them was of fundamental importance.[8]

Feminists, liberals, pacifists, socialists, and social reformers of varying kinds, in the main, filled the ranks of the progressive internationalists. Their leaders included many of the era's authentic heroes and heroines, both the celebrated and the unsung: Jane Addams, the "Beloved Lady" of Hull House; Emily Greene Balch, Wellesley's controversial sociology professor whose future (like Addams') held the Nobel Peace Prize; Crystal Eastman, the industrial reformer and radical suffragist; her brother, Max Eastman, of the *Masses;* David Starr Jordan, president of Stanford University; Oswald Garrison Villard, crusader in the fledgling civil rights movement and editor of the *New York Evening Post* and, later, of the *Nation;* Paul Kellogg, the nonpartisan conscience of the *Survey;* Lillian Wald, founder of New York's Henry Street Settlement; and Louis Paul Lochner, secretary of the Chicago Peace Society.

The quest for peace provided a new frontier and logical common ground for many liberal reformers, pacifists, and socialists. For them, domestic politics and foreign policy had suddenly become symbiotic: Peace was essential to change—to the survival of the labor movement and of their campaigns on behalf of women's rights, the abolition of child labor, and social justice legislation in general. If the war in Europe were permitted to rage on much longer, then the United States could not help but get sucked into it; and not only their great causes, but also the very moral fiber of the nation would be destroyed. Thus the *raison d'être* of the progressive internationalists was to bring about a negotiated settlement of the war.

Jane Addams played a pivotal role in this wing of the internationalist movement; indeed, she personified its purposes and values perhaps better than anyone else. Dismayed by the failure of the established peace societies to show any muscle, Addams, with the help of Paul Kellogg and Lillian Wald, organized the Woman's Peace party in January 1915. The Wom-

an's Peace party distinguished itself as the first organization of its kind—
unlike the Carnegie Endowment for International Peace or the World
Peace Foundation—to engage in direct political action (and on a variety
of fronts) in order to achieve its goals.[9]

Three thousand delegates attended the WPP's inaugural convention
on January 10, 1915, in Washington, D.C. Guided by the principle of "the
sacredness of human life," the platform committee produced the earliest,
and what must be acknowledged as the most comprehensive, manifesto
on internationalism advanced by any American organization throughout
the entire war. Their "program for constructive peace" somewhat resembled the platform of the UDC. It called for an immediate armistice, international agreements to limit armaments and to nationalize their manufacture, removal of the economic causes of the war (that is, a reduction of
trade barriers), democratic control of foreign policy, self-determination,
machinery for arbitration, freedom of the seas, and, finally, a "Concert of
Nations" to supersede the balance-of-power system and rival armies and
navies. Significantly (and without extended debate), the party also assumed a strictly neutral position toward the belligerents and planned to
agitate for "continuous mediation" by neutral nations as the best means
of bringing about a cessation of hostilities. The party made sure that President Wilson received copies of all their recommendations.[10]

The ideas of the Woman's Peace party cut a wide swath among
progressives and radicals. Within a year the WPP had an active membership of 40,000, while several kindred organizations sprang up and adopted
its platform. Addams displayed a determination to press hard for the New
Diplomacy in Europe as well. She became the dominating figure at the
International Congress of Women, which met at The Hague during the
last week of April 1915. After The Hague Congress endorsed the WPP
platform and continuous mediation, she received authorization to plead
the case before the leaders of every major European country. So esteemed
was Addams in the eyes of world opinion that she and her associates were
granted audiences with Asquith, Grey, Bethmann Hollweg, von Jagow,
and Pope Benedict XV.[11] In mid-summer, however, she returned to the
United States, not only to thunderous acclaim at Carnegie Hall, but also
to opprobrium, owing in part to the impasse with Germany over submarine warfare. When Roosevelt was invited to welcome home the entou-
rage of the woman who had seconded his nomination in 1912, he fairly
spat, "They have not shown the smallest particle of courage; and all their
work has been done to advance the cause of international cowardice; and
anyone who greets them or applauds them is actively engaged in advancing that cause."[12]

But they were welcome at the White House. On several occasions
after the women's congress at The Hague, Addams and Emily Balch met

with Wilson, Colonel House, and Robert Lansing, Bryan's successor as
Secretary of State. On July 19, Addams appealed to House on behalf of
continuous mediation but failed to persuade him. Balch had what she
believed was a more productive session with Wilson a month later when
she presented him with additional material on mediation. He assured her
that he would seize "any opportunity to be of use" if it presented itself.
Wilson, of course, could not divulge to Balch the nature of Colonel House's
recent mission to Europe; nor did he care to be pressured on the subject.[13]
Hence, his polite evasions perplexed these progressive internationalists as
they continued to advise him on the matter of continuous mediation. Their
campaign nonetheless generated an extended correspondence within the
administration. Wilson and his advisers regarded their interlocutors as
well-intentioned, but impractical and naïve. As Robert Lansing put it,
"The perversity and selfishness of human nature are factors which they
have left out of the problem."[14]

Yet, if Wilson and progressive internationalists like Addams and Balch
sometimes felt frustrated with each other, their relationship was rather
well-tempered by mutual comprehension and admiration. "I have unlimited faith in President Wilson," Addams told a London reporter in the
summer of 1915, and Wilson fully reciprocated in his personal regard for
her.[15] Moreover, although he doubted the wisdom of their approach to
mediation, Wilson was deeply impressed with the other proposals of the
Woman's Peace party's, especially their "program for constructive peace."
Addams' personal record of one of her many interviews with Wilson is
particularly enlightening: "He drew out the papers I had given him, and
they seem[ed] to have been much handled and read. 'You see I have
studied these resolutions,' he said; 'I consider them by far the best formulation which up to the moment has been put out by anybody.' "[16] This
was an important admission. The fact was that the Woman's Peace party
had furnished Wilson with a pioneering American synthesis of the New
Diplomacy during the critical year in which his own thinking acquired a
definite shape.

The Woman's Peace party was not, of course, the only organization that
made a potent contribution to early progressive internationalism. The Socialist Party of America, too, formulated a momentous program for a
"democratic peace." It also motivated a sizeable constituency to think about
foreign policy in new ways and, significantly, enjoyed access to the White
House.

No group suffered greater despair over the events of August 1914
than American socialists. For them, the most troubling thing of all was
that every leading socialist party of Europe had put its own nation before
the International. One by one, those parties had voted in favor of war

credits and mass human slaughter in their respective parliaments. Most American socialists found it extremely difficult to swallow the rationalizations, for example, of both the French Socialist party and the German Social Democratic party (however sincere the French and Germans' perceptions) that the actions of their incipient foes constituted wanton aggression, when they had all failed even to try to stop the war.[17]

Reeling under such blows to the cause of international worker solidarity, the American party scarcely knew which way to turn. In the circumstances, Eugene Debs, like the vast majority of his followers, advocated strict neutrality. The party leader also took it upon himself to prepare Americans for "the impending social revolution" by explaining why the war had happened.[18] "Despotism in Russia, monarchic Germany and republican America is substantially the same in its effect upon the working class," he wrote in the *New Review* in October 1914. From the stump he thundered against capitalism, which monstrously and climactically had proved itself irredeemable. He denounced the ruling classes for having driven the workers into the hell of the Marne and Tannenburg in order "to extend the domination of their exploitation, to increase their capacity for robbery, and to multiply their ill-gotten riches."[19] Yet Debs' assessment hardly explained his European comrades' defense of nationalism or their encouragement of army enlistees.

Clearly, the Socialist party could not afford to indulge any longer its historic indifference to foreign policy issues. The stakes had grown too high. Morris Hillquit and William English Walling, among others, saw the urgent need to take, not only "a leading place in the anti-war movement," but also a position distinguished by socialist principles as opposed to the simple "bourgeois pacifism" of liberal-reformist peace societies. In December 1914, the National Executive Committee drafted a "Proposed Manifesto and Program of the Socialist Party of America on Disarmament and World Peace." After heated debate the party revised and finally adopted the document the following May: although the chief author was Hillquit, its contents—in particular, unequivocal statements on disarmament and indemnities—reflected the ascendent influence of the left wing. The "manifesto" portion contained a sweeping analysis of the political and economic causes of the war. Specific peace terms included the following:

1. No indemnities.
2. No transfer of territories except upon the consent and by the vote of their people.
3. All countries under foreign rule to be given political independence if demanded by their inhabitants.
4. An international parliament with legislative and administrative powers over international affairs and with permanent committees, in place of present secret diplomacy.

5. Universal disarmament as speedily as possible.
6. Political and industrial democracy [that is, the nationalization of basic industries and improvement of working conditions].[20]

The manifesto was accorded ample space in the pages of the country's major socialist publications, which meant that at least two million Americans read it. If they happened to place it alongside the platform of the Woman's Peace party, however, discerning readers could see that the Socialist party's official stand on the war presented few stark contrasts with that of America's foremost "bourgeois pacifist" organization (in which, it should be mentioned, many individual Socialist party members held leadership positions).[21] The Socialist peace formula further echoed the WPP by calling on the President to convoke a congress of neutral nations and offer mediation to the belligerents. Morris Hillquit justifiably boasted in his memoirs that the plank on "no indemnities" anticipated by more than two years the comparable slogan of the Russian Council of Workers and Soldiers.[22] But this was the party's sole (not to say, by any means, unimportant) radical supplement to the progressive internationalist program. Even bearing the patent of the party's left wing, almost all of the proclamation might have been written—though, as of May 1915, not for publication—in the seclusion of the Oval Office.

None of these observations is meant either to suggest that the work of Hillquit, Walling, and company lacked originality, or to diminish its significance. The Socialist party was second only to the Woman's Peace party in its impact upon both radicals and reformers (Wilson included) during the progressive internationalist movement's crucial formative stage. Then, too, it is impossible to gauge who exerted the greater influence on whom. Whereas the Socialist party officially kept its distance from groups like the WPP, many prominent Socialists (left, right, and center) worked closely on an informal basis with their otherwise radical friends, who earnestly believed that the endeavor to reform capitalism was meaningful and worthwhile.

The Socialist program came to Wilson's personal attention through official delegations commissioned to lobby the White House. Although the party propagated its peace terms with vigor, keeping the United States out of the war received the stronger emphasis throughout 1915. The National Executive Committee regarded continuous mediation (of the sort advocated by the WPP) as the best means of accomplishing that object. Meyer London of New York, the lone Socialist member of the House of Representatives, introduced a resolution in Congress that proposed that the President take the initiative for mediation now endorsed by several organizations.[23]

Wilson received Meyer London, Morris Hillquit, and James Hudson Maurer, president of the Pennsylvania State Federation of Labor, on January 25, 1916. According to Hillquit's account, their host looked preoccupied and tired when they arrived but became deeply interested and animated once the conversation got under way. (Maurer, who interviewed Wilson on two other occasions, described him as "a good listener.") Congressman London read his resolution aloud, and the four men then proceeded for the next hour to discuss the other provisions of the Socialist party manifesto. Hillquit was somewhat surprised when Wilson, in confidence, "informed us that he had had a similar plan under consideration" and also "hinted at the possibility of a direct offer of mediation by the government of the United States." (This was privileged information he had not chosen to divulge to representatives of the WPP.) The meeting proved to be more encouraging and productive than London, Hillquit, and Maurer might have hoped. "[H]is sympathies were entirely with us," Hillquit told the *Appeal to Reason*. As the committee rose to take its leave, however, Maurer turned and said, "Your promises sound good, Mr. President, but the trouble with you is that you are surrounded by capitalist and militarist interests who want the war to continue; and I fear you will succumb to their influence." Placing a hand on Maurer's shoulder, Wilson smiled and replied, "If the truth be known, I am more often accused of being influenced by radical and pacifist elements than by the capitalist and militarist interest."[24]

From their point of view, it remained to be seen whether Wilson's visitors could rest assured in his perception of which elements of the polity exerted the greatest influence on him—for progressive internationalists confronted formidable rivals. Indeed, conservative internationalists made up the largest and, generally speaking, the most influential segment of the broad American league movement. Unlike their liberal and left-wing counterparts, most leading conservative internationalists had helped found peace organizations—such as the Carnegie Endowment for International Peace and the American Society for the Judicial Settlement of International Disputes—in the prewar years. They therefore benefitted from a financially secure base of operations and from the kind of respectability and power that came with membership in the establishment. Almost all of them had been ardent imperialists and champions of Anglo-American *entente* since the 1890s.

Many conservative internationalists—like Senator Elihu Root of New York, the first president of the Carnegie Endowment (formerly Secretary of War under McKinley and Secretary of State under Roosevelt) and Nicholas Murray Butler, president of Columbia University—were so-called legalists. Seeking stability rather than change in international relations, legalists viewed the concept of world peace primarily through the prism of international law. Conflicts between major powers, Root argued throughout the 1910s, could best be ameliorated through the steady growth of international legal precedents established by a world court. Other conservatives, such as William Howard Taft, while not denying the value of strictly juridical procedures, put greater faith in compulsory arbitration of certain kinds of disputes sustained by coercive sanctions to compel the submission of a dispute to a tribunal (though not compliance with the arbitration decision itself). This approach suggested a form of collective security, an alternative that legalists like Root considered too extreme.[25]

Conservative internationalists became a force to be reckoned with in the summer of 1915. Under the auspices of the New York Peace Society and Hamilton Holt, the editor of the *Independent* (and an internationalist who also traveled in progressive circles), some 120 conservatives prominent in the fields of business, education, law, and politics gathered in Philadelphia at Independence Hall and, on June 17, founded the League to Enforce Peace (LEP).[26] The executive board of the new organization included Taft; Theodore Marburg, who had served as minister to Belgium under Taft; and Abbot Lawrence Lowell, president of Harvard University. Their platform, entitled "Warrant from History," corresponded to the ideas of the Bryce Group, a British conservative internationalist roundtable that had been meeting quietly in London since late 1914.[27] The LEP's platform called for American participation in a postwar league in which representatives from all nations would assemble periodically to make appropriate changes in international law. Member nations would also be bound to submit "justiciable" disputes (questions pertaining to treaty obligations and international law) to a judicial tribunal or council of arbitration, and "non-justiciable" disputes (questions of national honor or vital national self-interest) to a board of conciliation. Finally, the plan would require signatories to bring economic and military force to bear against any state that made war on another signatory before submitting its grievance to the foregoing process.[28]

Because of its prestigious charter membership, the League to Enforce Peace enjoyed considerable public attention and favorable editorial comment. Soon the LEP began to formally consult and coordinate activities with the Bryce Group as well as with the League of Nations Society, founded in Great Britain in May. By the end of 1916, it had established some four thousand branches in forty-seven states and had published thousands of pamphlets explaining its "Warrant from History." Although the LEP was not a Wilsonian enterprise, it nonetheless ultimately became the most influential pro-league organization in the United States and perhaps in the world.[29]

When reporters asked Wilson about the conclave in Philadelphia, his response was noncommittal, almost to the point of indifference.[30] From the start, Wilson kept the conservative internationalists at arm's length.

He did so in part because of their connections with the Republican party—Taft was elected president of the LEP—and because he did not want to commit himself to a definite program that might later restrict his freedom of action. But, for now, the fairly limited recommendations and personal discretion of conservative internationalist leaders averted potential friction between them. Cordiality prevailed throughout the early stages of the relationship, mainly because the LEP's directors demanded nothing of the President.[31]

The influence of the conservative internationalists on Wilson would never be decisive in any case, but not only on account of partisan considerations or Wilson's desire to protect his options. Wilson surely realized that on certain points their platform converged with his own prescriptions, as well as with those of the Woman's Peace party, the Socialist party, and the Union of Democratic Control. But what the LEP omitted was as important as what it prescribed. On one hand, its recommendations for settling disputes squared with Bryan's cooling-off treaties, and its position on sanctions was roughly similar to Wilson's own thoughts about mutual guarantees of territorial integrity and political independence (which the progressive internationalists had yet to endorse explicitly). On the other hand, the LEP did not concern itself much with the economic causes of the war, with disarmament or self-determination, and certainly not with "democratic control" of foreign policy. Thus, even though the two wings of the American internationalist movement were very broadly constituted, the differences between them were substantial; in most respects, fundamental.

It is important to emphasize that, whereas they were absolutely vital, Wilson did not regard collective security and arbitration as adequate by themselves to prevent future wars. Self-determination, reduction of armaments, and free trade were equally important to the community of nations to come. Moreover, he and the progressive internationalists sought to mediate an end to the war and believed a fair peace settlement to be one based on a stand-off in Europe. In contrast, most conservative internationalists made no bones about their wish to see the Allies win a clear-cut victory. Significantly, the slogan, "The LEP does *not* seek to end the present war," appeared on their letterhead in the autumn of 1916.[32] Finally, for progressive internationalists, a league of nations symbolized the confluence of other dreams and purposes. The ultimate objective of Wilson and the progressive internationalists was a lasting peace that would accommodate change and advance democratic institutions and social and economic justice; and a just peace was dependent on the synchronous proliferation of political democracy and social and economic justice around the world.

Few conservative internationalists could identify with the exalted as-

pirations of liberals, pacifists, and socialists. Leading conservative intellectuals like Taft, Lowell, and Root rarely entertained doubts about their
Social-Darwinist views of human relations. Some were fit to rule; the vast
majority were not; the poor were poor because they were poor. Worst of
all, liberal reformers and socialists abetted each other's causes: together,
they threatened to overturn the natural order of things by appealing, either
inadvertently or overtly, to class differences. They strove toward a welfare
state that would destroy basic constitutional rights of individual liberty
and property.[33] Furthermore, conservative internationalists regarded diplomacy as unquestionably the province of an educated élite. Wilson might
fit into the latter category, but they could take little comfort in reading
newspaper stories about the regular flow into the White House of counselors committed to mob rule.

Neither could conservative internationalists see much good coming
from a military stalemate in Europe. Because they considered the defeat
of Germany as essential to peace, they often regarded Wilson's policies of
neutrality as either wrongheaded or morally reprehensible. Then, too,
whereas they advocated American participation in a league to enforce peace,
they remained committed nationalists and resisted any diminution of
American sovereignty or military strength. They believed that the United
States should pursue international stability through the power of deter-
rence inherent in collective security, yet reserve to itself the right to improve its capacity to undertake independent coercive action against the
forces of disorder that threatened the national interest.

Such divergent viewpoints within the burgeoning American league
movement held serious implications for the subsequent course of the new
crusade as well as for virtually every other major issue related to the war,
including the climatic domestic debate over the Treaty of Versailles. For
the time being, however, Wilson and the progressive and conservative
internationalists seemed inclined to perceive their differences as more apparent than real. Throughout 1915, on the broad proposition of a league
of nations, they observed an unstated political truce in deference to the
greater common task of exploring the possibilities for a domestic consensus to underwrite such a basic change in American foreign policy.

From mid-1915 to mid-1916, the single most divisive issue in American
politics was neither the league idea, nor the New Freedom, nor neutrality;
it was, rather, the state of the nation's military preparedness. Not since
the days of the early Republic had the question of the role of the military
in American life driven so sharp a wedge into American politics. The
Progressive era witnessed the opening phase of a larger controversy that
would persist in various manifestations through the twentieth century to
the present day. In its own immediate context, the preparedness contro-

versy would, among other things, reveal a subtle moldering within the American internationalist movement before it had reached its apogee.

During the autumn of 1914, the relentless advocates of a large navy and standing army had gained some momentum in Congress. Even before Germany had raised the specter of submarine warfare, Representative Augustus Peabody Gardner of Massachusetts, encouraged by his senior colleague and father-in-law, Henry Cabot Lodge, introduced a measure calling for an investigation into the nation's preparedness for war.[34] Wilson responded forcefully in his annual message to Congress, on December 8. "From the first we have had a clear and settled policy with regard to military establishments. We never have had, and while we retain our present principles and ideals, we never shall have a large standing army," he declared. "We shall not ask our young men to spend the best years of their lives making soldiers of themselves." He reminded the Congress that the country had a National Guard. The citizen soldier, a tradition compatible with democratic institutions, would suffice in the present circumstances. "More than this," he went on, "would mean merely that we had lost our self-possession." Then, looking directly at Senator Lodge, the President added, "We shall not alter our attitude toward it because some amongst us are nervous and excited."[35]

This was not the first time that antimilitarists had heard such sweet music from the administration. The year before, William Jennings Bryan had caused a commotion when he spoke at a military camp in Texas and confessed that he could not understand how the men could prefer service in the Army to "a respectable civilian profession." Secretary of the Navy Josephus Daniels, likewise, had raised some hackles. While casually talking with a couple of stokers during an inspection of a battleship, he upbraided the admiral escorting him for not following his example. "Do you think that you are too good to shake the hand of a sailor?" Daniels wanted to know. Then, too, there was the Carabao Affair, which had earned for the officers responsible for the notorious anti-Bryan theatricale a severe public reprimand from the President. "In military circles there is great astonishment and dismay over the proceedings of the Democratic regime," the Austrian naval attaché in Washington reported to Vienna. "Up till now the Democrats have done nothing to raise the esteem of officers. Indeed they have damaged the officers' own conception of their place in society."[36]

Whether or not the Austrian attaché's judgment was accurate, Wilson's summoning of Congress to uphold America's venerable antimilitarist tradition won overwhelming public approval, and the Republican drive to expand the armed forces was easily quashed. Within a year, however, the incessant abuses of the Allied blockade, and, especially, German submarine warfare brought about a gradual shift in public opinion as well as

within the administration. The shift rapidly evolved into a marked conversion soon after May 7, 1915. On that day a German submarine had
perpetrated one of the biggest public-relations disasters of all time when
it torpedoed without warning the great British passenger liner *Lusitania,*
which took down with her 1,198 men, women, and children—among them
124 Americans. In the United States the shock of this seemingly wanton
murder of so many innocent civilians was so great that ten years later
people remembered exactly where they were and what they were doing
when they had heard the news, according to the findings of journalist
Mark Sullivan.[37]

Americans barely had the chance to digest this assault on their sensibilities when, during the next week, the British government released an
official report on German atrocities, bearing the name and validation of
Viscount James Bryce, the esteemed former Ambassador to the United
States. The crescendo of a systematic propaganda campaign to overcome
American neutrality, this document catalogued in the most lurid detail
some 1,200 alleged acts of barbarism and cruelty committed by German
soldiers, primarily against Belgians—including the crucifixion and decap-
itation of prisoners of war, the gang rape and sexual mutilation of women,
the hacking off of children's fingers for souvenirs, and the bayoneting of
infants.[38] Although much of it was later proved to be fictional, the Bryce
Report created a sensation. Germany would never fully recover from the
revulsion that swept the United States during these seven days in May.[39]

Because it raised the distinct possibility of war, the *Lusitania* incident
presented the real crisis. Yet cries for intervention, though loud as they
could be, represented the voice of extremists. The vast majority of Americans, including the Congress, expected their president to keep his head
and save them from Europe's awful mess. Three days after the tragedy,
Wilson addressed an audience of newly naturalized citizens in Philadelphia. "The example of America must be a special example," he said. "The
example not merely of peace because it will not fight, but of peace because
peace is the healing and elevating influence of the world and strife is not.
There is such a thing as a man being too proud to fight. There is such a
thing as a nation being so right that it does not need to convince others
by force that it is right."[40]

Such eloquent convictions notwithstanding, Wilson's subsequent demands that Germany cease submarine warfare against unarmed merchantmen were stern enough to compel the Secretary of State to resign in
protest from the Cabinet in June. Bryan believed that the President's second note to Berlin, in particular, would lead to war. The outcome of these
negotiations was still in doubt when, on the morning of August 19, 1915,
two Americans were killed in the sinking of another British liner, the
Arabic. "The worst worst [*sic*] thing that could possibly *happen to the*

world," Wilson wrote that evening to Mrs. Galt, "would be for the United States to be drawn actively into this contest,—to become one of the belligerents and lose all chance of moderating the results of the war by counsel as an outsider."[41] In any case, he took firm action, threatening to sever diplomatic relations if Berlin refused henceforth to cease attacks on unarmed passenger liners without warning and without providing for the safety of those on board. The German government met Wilson's demands, and kept American neutrality alive, in the *"Arabic* pledge" of September 1, 1915. Consequently, tensions between the United States and Germany abated until the following spring.[42]

Wilson's consistent example of self-possession and restraint throughout these protracted early crises made him something of a hero in the eyes of most progressive internationalists. The conclusion to the *Arabic* negotiations moved Oswald Garrison Villard, for instance, to break all precedents by running the President's portrait on the front page of the *New York Evening Post,* above the caption "The man who, without rattling a sword, won for civilization."[43] Yet if Wilson had "won for civilization," his stern notes, in the opinion of most Republicans, had not wrung enough meaningful concessions from Berlin. The Germans never admitted the illegality of undersea attacks on nonmilitary vessels, and the administration's demands did not require them to forego submarine warfare against Allied armed merchantmen. This ambiguity, along with the resounding impact of the *Lusitania* calamity, supplied preparedness advocates with all the ammunition they needed. Fortified by such organizations as the National Security League, the American Defense Society, and, eventually, the League to Enforce Peace, the movement now shifted into high gear.

Theodore Roosevelt had no peer in the preparedness crusade, and he beat the drum with both conviction and relish. Enraged by Wilson's comment about being "too proud to fight," he virtually called the President a coward and went so far as to hold him and Bryan personally responsible for the *Lusitania's* and the *Arabic's* misfortune. "It is our own attitude of culpable weakness and timidity—an attitude assumed under pressure of the ultra-pacifists—which is primarily responsible for this dreadful loss of life and for our national humiliation," he was still saying well into 1916.[44] The Colonel also called for a standing army of two million men, as well as for universal military training for adult males and drills and instruction for high school students. Soon the Governor of New York signed into law five preparedness bills, two of which provided for Roosevelt's training program in private and public schools. Huge preparedness parades marched down the avenues of all the nation's big Eastern cities. And a series of popular books and motion pictures, pandering to fears of invasion, flooded the nations bookstores and theaters.[45]

Although the issue cut across party lines, the most vocal proponents of preparedness and universal military training—Roosevelt, senators Lodge and Root, General Leonard Wood, and Taft—happened also to be Republicans. Lodge was no doubt sincere in the argument (one of infinite resilience in this century) that "there is no such incentive to war as a rich, undefended, and helpless country, which by its condition invites aggression."[46] But politics informed conviction. Republicans portrayed themselves as the true patriots and the Democrats as the party of submission—the party that was "too proud to fight." Preparedness seemed an altogether splendid charger upon which to ride to victory in 1916.

From the standpoint of politics, the President met the challenge masterfully. Most Americans had reluctantly concluded that the changed circumstances of the war required some degree of rearmament. By developing a measured response, the Democrats posed as something better than patriots—patriots with cool heads. On December 7, 1915, Wilson presented to Congress a program of national defense to increase substantially the size of the Army and the Navy. He then embarked upon a speaking tour of the Middle West to counter the Republicans and build support for "reasonable" preparedness among the many doubters within his own party.[47]

The Republicans hoped to exploit the troubles that Wilson initially encountered within Democratic and progressive ranks (see below) and to make his alleged lack of leadership the keynote of their campaign in the forthcoming national election. But eventually Wilson marshaled both public opinion and a bipartisan congressional majority behind the administration's program. Many Republicans—and many prominent conservative internationalists, including Taft, Root, and Lowell—regarded Wilson's recommendations both as inadequate and as a characteristic example of the basest political opportunism.[48] Even harder to abide was the fact that, in the end, Wilson beat his opponents at their own game. Compromise and moderation robbed the Republicans of one of their most potent political issues. These were portentous complications in light of the Republican identity of the League to Enforce Peace, which had come into existence just as the preparedness controversy burst forth. Although Wilson managed to sustain a respectful correspondence with them, an important element of the conservative internationalists experienced the first stirrings of partisan bitterness toward the President.

Preparedness cut into the issue of a league of nations from another, potentially more acute, angle. Many progressive internationalists watched with alarm as their old collective nemesis—big-navy advocates, munitions makers, imperialists, big business, and all other manner of reactionaries—mounted what they viewed as an insidious offensive to thwart social and economic progress at home as well as disarmament, international cooperation, and the repudiation of war as an instrument of foreign policy. But opponents of preparedness suffered the greatest blow to their morale when Wilson appeared to have surrendered to the enemy.

"The war in Europe is due to industrial strife, and the efforts of capitalists to further enslave the workingmen," Socialist Helen Keller declared to the Labor Forum of New York. "If President Wilson had supported the policy of military preparedness which he recently sent to Congress, in 1913, the people would have demanded his removal to an insane asylum."[49] In despair, Jane Addams, on behalf of the Woman's Peace party, reminded her friend in the White House of his own noble expressions "that the United States might be granted the unique privilege not only of helping the war-torn world to a lasting peace, but of aiding toward a gradual and proportional lessening of that vast burden of armament which has crushed to poverty the peoples of the world." She ended with a warning: increased war preparations would "tend to disqualify our National Executive from rendering the epochal service which this world crisis offers for the establishment of permanent peace."[50] Shortly after the administration introduced its national defense bill, Lillian Wald's Henry Street Group organized an "Anti-Militarism Committee." It became the American Union Against Militarism (AUAM) in April 1916.[51]

The American Union Against Militarism represented one of the outstanding collaborations of liberal reformers and socialists of the Progressive Era. Its leaders and sympathizers included Addams and Wald, Paul Kellogg, Amos Pinchot, Frederick C. Howe, Crystal and Max Eastman, Rabbi Stephen Wise, Louis Lochner, Florence Kelley, Helen Keller, Oswald Garrison Villard, James Maurer, Hamilton Holt of the LEP, and many other friends and acquaintances of Wilson's. Their movement was augmented by a cluster of Southern and Western Democratic congressmen and senators (some of whom considered the issue from an isolationist perspective), led by William Jennings Bryan; Claude Kitchin of North Carolina, the House Majority Leader; and William J. Stone of Missouri, the Chairman of the Senate Foreign Relations Committee.[52]

Within the year, the AUAM had established branches in every major city in the country. Members disseminated some 600,000 pieces of antipreparedness literature through a variety of publications and lobbied extensively on Capitol Hill and at the White House. To match Wilson's swing around the circle, they hired the largest halls they could find and filled them to overflowing in New York, Buffalo, Pittsburgh, Cleveland, Cincinnati, Chicago, Detroit, Minneapolis, Des Moines, Kansas City, and St. Louis. "Jingo," the papier-mâché dinosaur (who wore a collar bearing the label "ALL ARMOR PLATE—NO BRAINS") won national fame as the AUAM's mascot, while "I Didn't Raise My Boy to Be a Soldier" became a hit song.[53] Notable figures outside the AUAM—Bryan being the most prominent and effective—also went out on the hustings to drive the an-

tipreparedness message home. Eugene Debs, speaking for the majority of
Socialists, did not mince words. If citizens succumbed to the current hysteria, he declared, the ultranationalists would "transform the American
nation into the most powerful and odious military despotism on the face
of the earth."[54] John Reed, too, devoted his talents to exposing widespread
collusion between the National Security League and the munitions industry and to rebutting arguments that the United States was vulnerable to
invasion by a European foe.[55] In almost all cases, the AUAM itself was
careful to strike, not at Wilson personally, but rather at the dangers of
militarism.

Not all liberals or socialists who advocated an internationalist foreign
policy, however, contested increased military and naval appropriations. For
instance, the editors of the *New Republic*—Herbert Croly, Walter Lippmann,
and Walter Weyl—followed an interesting, and rather tortuous, middle
path. For them, the question was not preparedness, but "Preparedness for
What?" Their point of departure was the complacency that they perceived
in Wilsonian reformers once the New Freedom had been consummated
by 1915. The influential voice of "pragmatic liberalism" searched for a
way to overcome the nation's stultifying drift. Preparedness had the potential to restore the lost sense of national purpose, according to the *New
Republic,* because it would at once strengthen the federal government's
direction of the economy and advance the cause of social welfare. Properly
bridled, the editors suggested, preparedness was a Trojan horse that carried within it the means to undermine special privilege and to restructure
American society along democratic, collectivist lines.[56] Wilson, thus far,
had failed to place the issue in this vital context. Nor could they depend
on their favorite Bull Moose to set the tone. As William Allen White later
observed, "social and industrial justice no longer interested Colonel Roosevelt. He had a war, a war greater than even he realized it would be, to
engage his talents. He made a tremendous clamor for preparedness. He
won back many of his old enemies, the big businessmen, who now saw
eye to eye with him and applauded as the Colonel raged at Wilson."[57]

Moreover (and ironically so, from the point of view of the *New Republic*), both Roosevelt's militant nationalism and the AUAM's militant
pacifism, albeit from opposite poles, contributed to isolationist torpor. Since
its first number, in November 1914, the *New Republic* had attempted to
explain to its 15,000 readers (the President among them) that Jeffersonian
drift and complacency made poor substitutes for Hamiltonian mastery
over both domestic and foreign policy. The United States could not afford
to float aimlessly in the isolationist backwaters of the nineteenth century—
not if democratic institutions were to survive. The quality of Wilson's
neutrality, then, was considerably strained. The United States had an *active* role to play in the service of international peace—perhaps through a

league of peace, they began to say in March 1915.[58] And for that task something more than a provincial constabulary was required to impress the great powers.

The editors of the *New Republic* probably had gotten to the pith with respect to foreign policy. Yet, as Christopher Lasch once pointed out, their analysis still "left the most important question of all, the question of war or peace, to the decision of the European powers."[59] Whereas, after the *Lusitania,* Croly and Lippmann in particular considered a German victory over the Allies a threat to American national interests, they would continue to balk at intervention until other related issues further clarified themselves. But if Wilson was adrift, they surely had not supplied much of a rudder. Then, too, their other criticisms—that the "pacifists" preferred to let the country go unprepared in an emergency and encouraged isolationism as well—utterly ignored the clear distinctions the AUAM made between militarism and "sane" preparedness. Even more important, the *New Republic* also overlooked the distinctly internationalist principles of the AUAM and the Woman's Peace party, not to mention those of the Socialist party. (One could make the case that these groups by 1915 had worked out far more advanced, coherent, and comprehensive proposals for addressing the general world crisis than the editors of the *New Republic* ever would.)

The *New Republic* nonetheless justifiably reproached Wilson in at least two areas. Was there a coherent relationship between neutrality (or, for that matter, his domestic agenda) and his advocacy of preparedness, or was he merely reacting to events? And what of the future, beyond his vague and platitudinous hopes of offering the services of the United States in the cause of peaceful counsel? Colonel House had not yet begun his famous courtship of the *New Republic* crowd, so no one there seemed to have a clue.[60]

As we have seen, Wilson actually had, very early on, mapped out a rudimentary peace plan on his own. He also had closely studied the proposals of the Woman's Peace party and the Socialist party, and was familiar with those of the Union of Democratic Control and the League to Enforce Peace. Secretly, he pursued the Pan-American Pact, a model organization for the Western Hemisphere; and he and House, in late 1915, embarked on yet another undisclosed mediatorial exploration in Europe. (Either endeavor would have mitigated the concerns emanating from various progressive internationalist quarters.) But as late as January 1916, the President had not so much as dropped a hint, publicly, about the real direction of his thoughts. As the preparedness controversy reached its climax, he at last began cautiously to remedy the situation—though, again, not in an arena designed to gain a lot of attention. Rather provocatively, he chose to do so for the benefit of those to his left.

In the spring of 1916, the AUAM sent a distinguished delegation to the White House.[61] The representatives included Lillian Wald, Paul Kellogg, Crystal and Max Eastman, Adolf Berle, Jr., Amos Pinchot, and Rabbi Wise. The delegation emphasized that the AUAM stood neither for "peace at any price" nor against "sane and reasonable" preparedness.[62] But they were anxious about those numerous agents of militarism who were "frankly hostile to our institutions of democracy." Their deepest fear, Lillian Wald said to the President, was that "the acceptance by the American people of a big army or big navy would simply neutralize and annul the moral power which our nation ought, through you, to exercise when the day of peace negotiations has come."[63] Significantly, Wilson contended that some measure of military force was, in fact, essential to the vindication of moral force. "I am just as much opposed to militarism as any man living," he said, and he had a record to substantiate that claim. He went on at some length to explain how his program actually conformed to Wald's criteria—that it would provide adequate security "without changing the spirit of the country."[64] Then he addressed her observation about moral force and peace. "When you go into a conference to establish the foundations of the peace of the world, you have got to go in on a basis intelligible to the people you are dealing with. . . . And that means that, if the world undertakes, as we all hope it will undertake, a joint effort to keep the peace, it will expect us to play our proportional part in manifesting the force which is going to rest back of that. Now, in the last analysis the peace of society is obtained by force."[65]

He continued: "Now, let us suppose that we have formed a family of nations, and that family says, 'The world is not going to have any more wars of this sort without at least the duty at first, though, to go through certain processes to show whether there is anything in the case or not.' And if you say we shall not have any war, you have got to make that 'shall' bite. The rest of the world, if America takes part in this thing, will have the right to expect from her that she contributes her element of force to the general understanding. Surely that is not a militaristic ideal. That is a very practical, possible ideal."[66]

"Would that not, Mr. President, logically lead to a limitless expansion of our contribution?" Wald inquired. Wilson did not think so: "Now, quite the opposite to anything you fear, I believe that, if the world ever comes to combine its force for the purpose of maintaining peace, the individual contributions of each nation will be much less, necessarily, naturally less, than they would be in other circumstances, and that all they will have to do will be to contribute moderately and not indefinitely."[67]

After the meeting, the members of the delegation adjourned to a nearby hotel. According to an account by Max Eastman, they agreed unanimously that "the President had taken us into his intellectual bosom."

The *Masses* editor was especially pleased that throughout the interview Wilson had "always referred to the Union Against Militarism as though he were a member of it," and had talked "of how 'we' could meet the difficulties of national defense without the risks of militarism." Speaking for himself, Eastman wrote, "I believe that he sincerely hates his preparedness policies."[68] Although the *New York Times* would miss the point in its brief account of the meeting, Eastman emphasized in the *Masses* the explicit connection between preparedness and "the idea of world-federation and the international enforcement of peace."

Moreover, during the colloquy, Amos Pinchot had asserted that the United States, in time, could become more aggressive than any other nation (in part because of its enormous economic might); and Wilson had said, "I quite see your point. It might very easily, unless some check was placed upon it by some international arrangement which we hope for." These comments, Eastman concluded for the consideration of the readers of his socialist monthly, placed Wilson "far above and beyond" his peers, especially Roosevelt. He could not help but wish "that the President might point the way to all as boldly as he did to our committee."[69]

There is no evidence that Wilson ever read Eastman's appraisal in the *Masses,* a publication that boasted a readership more than thrice that of the *New Republic.*[70] But this conference at the White House was at least a minor historic occasion. In making a plausible case for stronger national defense to the AUAM, Wilson, for the first time, had not only discussed the role of force in the modern world; he had also articulated to persons other than absolute confidants his idea for "a family of nations." Not incidentally, as the tenor of Eastman's article suggests, Wilson had inadvertently scored several points with a number of doubting progressive internationalists who represented liberal and socialist constituencies of key political importance.

Throughout the preparedness controversy Wilson received countless other peace delegations. In November 1915, Jane Addams brought a group of women from The Hague to see him and had arranged to flood the White House with over twelve thousand telegrams from women's organizations across the country demanding mediation of the war.[71] Earlier that month Louis Lochner of the Chicago Peace Society and President David Starr Jordan of Stanford University (progressive internationalists who occasionally worked in conservative internationalist circles) again presented arguments for continuous mediation and a conference of neutrals. Lochner related his experiences in Europe during the previous winter and made Wilson wince when he described how nurses in the field had accidentally snapped off the limbs of frozen soldiers while trying to remove them to burial sites. Three million men had already perished. Struggling coalitions of liberals within the belligerent countries, Lochner and Jordan told him, were awaiting his summons. The President must act before another gruesome winter passed.[72] By the end of the session Wilson was visibly moved. Jordan later reflected, "[N]ever have I seen him so human, so deferential, and so ready to listen. Usually he was difficult to talk to and rather haughty." Even so, Lochner found him inscrutable, and was convinced that he was "playing a lone hand."[73]

Jordan and Lochner—indeed, all progressive internationalists, but particularly those who agitated for mediation and against preparedness— might have been slightly more sanguine had they been privy to recent conversations between Wilson and House. A few weeks before, Wilson— his hopes raised by the temporary resolution of the submarine issue—had begun anew to explore the possibilities for mediation.[74] On September 3, House wrote to Sir Edward Grey: "Do you think the President could make peace proposals to the belligerents at this time upon the broad basis of the elimination of militarism and navalism and a return, as nearly as possible, to the status quo [ante bellum]?" Grey wanted some specifics. "How much," he cabled back on September 22, "are the United States prepared to do in this direction? Would the President propose that there should be a League of Nations binding themselves against any Power which broke a treaty . . . or which refused, in case of dispute, to adopt some other method of settlement than that of war?"[75]

Wilson could not have wished for more appropriately tailored questions. For a number of reasons, the moment seemed propitious for House to return to Europe, not only because of the relaxation of German-American tensions and the presumed tractability of Grey. Secretary of State Lansing and Ambassador Naón of Argentina were working on a revision of the Pan-American Pact, apparently to the satisfaction of everyone involved. Anticipating a breakthrough, Wilson now contemplated going public with the treaty—in part to prove to the British that the United States was serious about joining a larger postwar peacekeeping organization. But, perhaps most important of all, Grey's questions could be answered in the affirmative because of the activities of both wings of the new American internationalist movement. Their ongoing campaigns had begun to create a fairly substantial body of opinion—which had not existed at the time of House's previous mission—to support an American pledge to join a league of nations.

Wilson gave House instructions for his assignment on Christmas Eve, 1915. The United States should have nothing to do with the actual settlement; it was concerned only with the maintenance of the peace after the war. "The only guarantees that any rational man could accept are (a) military and naval disarmament and (b) a league of nations to secure each nation against aggression and maintain the absolute freedom of the seas,"

Wilson wrote. "If either party to the present war will let us say to the other that they are willing to discuss peace on such terms, it will clearly be our duty to use our utmost moral force to oblige the other party to parley, and I do not see how they could stand in the opinion of the world if they refused."[76] Thus the establishment of a postwar league of nations had at last become embedded as the central fact in Wilson's mediatorial diplomacy.

Yet if any of the progressive or conservative internationalists had known the range of Wilson's initiatives, they still might have asked him to act on the thoughts that he had once conveyed in an intimate letter to Ellen Axson some thirty years before—a confession of his ambition to so "communicate the thoughts of the great mass of the people as to impel them to great political achievements."[77] Since the beginning, Wilson had exhibited an extraordinarily broad understanding of the war and had entertained bold ideas and worthy plans that might avert another. But he had permitted caution to overcome his natural propensities to lead, to the extent that neither wing of the internationalist movement yet regarded him as their obvious leader. All of this was about to change, however, commencing in the first week of 1916—"a year of madness," as Wilson later called it, "a year of excitement, more profound than the world has ever known before."[78] And, from that point onward, the issue of a league of nations would become the suture of American politics and foreign policy.

5

The Turning Point

O nly weeks before his resignation, William Jennings Bryan conveyed to Wilson his personal sense of urgency about the Pan-American Pact: "The sooner we can get this before the public the better, for the influence it may have across the Atlantic."[1] But, due to a combination of unfavorable circumstances—Chile's persistent doubts about the treaty and Wilson's preoccupation with the submarine crises after May 1915—a public announcement remained for some months highly problematical. In the autumn, Robert Lansing and Ambassador Naón of Argentina finally overcame Chile's objections (or so it seemed) by removing the cumbrous one-year time limit for the settlement of pending disputes. Their draft also satisfied Wilson's concern that the collective security guarantees be kept intact, if, as he put it, "these articles are indeed to serve as any sort of model for the action of any other nations."[2] Wilson's subsequent decision to unveil the Pact at the Second Pan-American Scientific Congress in early January was but the first indication that 1916 would be a crucial year in the history of the creation of the League of Nations.

Wilson was positively buoyant as he walked onto the stage to address the Scientific Congress on the evening of January 6. He and Edith Bolling Galt of Washington, D.C., had been married only three weeks before, and this was her first public event as First Lady. Since New Year's Day, rumors had spread among the delegates that something big was in the offing. The President did not disappoint them. Before alluding to the Pan-American Pact, he offered some prefatory comments that riveted the attention of his audience. He had chosen to speak critically (perhaps even self-deprecatingly) about one of the shibboleths of American foreign policy. "The Monroe Doctrine was proclaimed by the United States on her own authority." he said. "[I]t has been fears and suspicions on this score which have hitherto prevented the greater intimacy and confidence and trust between the Americas. The states of America have not been certain what the United States would do with her power. That doubt must be removed." The removal of that doubt, he continued, "will be accomplished, in the first place, by the states of America uniting in guaranteeing to each other, absolutely, political independence and territorial integrity." Upon highlighting its other features, he announced that negotiations for the Pan-American Pact were under way and imparted his views of the higher historical imperative of these "very practical" proposals: "They are based on the principles of absolute equality among states, equality of right, not equality of indulgence. They are based, in short, upon the solid, eternal foundations of justice and humanity. No man can turn away from these things without turning away from the hope of the world. God grant that it may be given to America to light this light on high for the illumination of the world."[3]

The address was probably the most encouraging moment, for Wilson, in the entire mercurial evolution of the Pact. The delegates responded with a thunderous ovation. Editorial opinion was extremely generous. The *New York Times* endorsed the Pact on the front page and added, "The President's appearance before the congress was a great personal triumph." The *New Republic* also suggested that the administration had cause to rejoice: "Mr. Wilson's method of dealing with the other American states . . . has had the great merit of disarming their suspicions and winning their confidence. Our southern neighbors seem finally convinced of the good faith of the United States. The Monroe Doctrine no longer looks to them like . . . an imperialist policy."[4] A. G. Gardiner, the English essayist and journalist, submitted the most ebullient and prescient review in late February. "Is it not possible," Gardiner asked in the London *Daily News,* "that in the President's scheme we have the seed of that larger peace that shall encompass the world?" Time and the experience of the war would eventually pull, not only the Americas, but also a reconstructed British Empire, France, Italy, Russia, and even Germany and the Hapsburg Empire "within the orbit of a common deliverance." Such was the mission of the New World, he wrote—"to help the old find the way out of the wilderness."[5]

It was no coincidence that A. G. Gardiner should have so vividly conjured. Colonel House had arrived at Falmouth on the day before Wilson's address. His specific task, it will be recalled, was to work out terms among the belligerents for possible mediation based on the *status quo ante,* disarmament, and the establishment of a league of nations. After making the rounds in Paris and Berlin, however, he decided on his own to broach the subject of Pan-Americanism upon his return to London in February. His intention was to gain official British approval of the Pact, and he started his campaign by taking a number of London newspaper editors into his confidence.[6] Then, on February 21, House told Sir Edward Grey about the treaty and asked whether he would be willing to express his support for it in Parliament, provided that Sir Robert Borden, the Canadian Prime Minister, approved. When Grey agreed to do so, a second thought occurred to House. Great Britain should actually enter into the Pact by virtue of its New World territorial possessions! In House's opinion, this was "an opportunity not to be disregarded and its tendency would be to bring together an influence which could control the peace of the world."[7]

Virtually all scholarship on House's mediatorial diplomacy of 1916 overlooks this bold and unauthorized formulation of foreign policy. The mission is best known for a document which he and the Foreign Secretary initialed on February 22, the famous House-Grey Memorandum. It, too, ultimately played a part in the fortunes of the league issue in transatlantic diplomacy, as we shall see.

House had come away from his conferences in Berlin with the distinct impression that the pro-submarine faction within the German High Command was ascendant and therefore very likely to drive the United States into the war before long. For their part, the French were hardly more receptive to peace talk than the Germans, until such time as their foes were beaten back beyond the Rhine. Indeed, both Jules Cambon, the French Foreign Minister, and Grey had told him flatly that the President's terms were unacceptable. The Colonel now felt compelled to assure the French of American sympathy. Circumventing Wilson's instructions, he went so far as to tell Cambon that the United States would intervene against Germany before the end of the year, if the Allies could avoid stirring up American resentment over their commercial blockade. (House deliberately misled Wilson about the astonishing surety he had given the French. Instead, he sent back optimistic reports about the chances for mediation, which would have stood as the historical record to this day had Cambon not preserved his own account of the conversations.[8]) Even so, when he returned to Britain from the Continent in mid-February, House continued in earnest to discuss mediation with Grey and Asquith. As a kind of inducement to gain their cooperation, House, on the day after he raised the subject of British membership in the Pan-American

Pact, devised an agreement embodied in the controversial memorandum. The document stipulated that if the British and French asked him to, Wilson would summon a peace conference. If Germany refused to attend, then the United States would "probably" enter the war on the side of the Allies; if Germany agreed to attend but otherwise proved unreasonable about the terms of peace, then the United States also would "probably" enter war on the side of the Allies.[9]

The Colonel obviously had a lot of ground to cover when he briefed Wilson at the White House on March 6. Wilson accepted his Pan-American overture with little trepidation; his one concern was how Great Britain, technically, could sign a treaty that referred to guarantees under *republican* forms of government, since the Empire was not a republic. He considered the matter, however, not in terms of whether, but of how and when, Britain should become a party to the Pact. In any case, it is clear that, by this juncture, Wilson and House conceived of the Pact as both a potential foundation league from which to build outward and a model to show the Europeans in conjunction with their peace moves.[10]

The House-Grey Memorandum was a more hazardous proposition. For one thing, everybody concerned interpreted it to suit their own purposes. The British conceived of it as partial insurance against disaster; they would use it only as an alternative to abject defeat.[11] House privately believed that the memorandum would facilitate American intervention once the Germans resumed submarine warfare. Wilson himself realized that the terms carried the high risk of war. But, if, as House explained, Germany was bound sooner or later to renege on the *Arabic* pledge and the Allies only required the assurances stipulated, then the gamble was worthwhile; moreover, Wilson could not conceive of the peoples of Europe permitting the renewal of hostilities once they had ceased. Therefore, after inserting the "probablys," Wilson approved the memorandum because it seemed to be the best available means of bringing the war to an end, short of belligerency, and of moving forward with work on some kind of league. Unfortunately, Wilson's strategy for achieving these objectives was based on misinformation from House and an erroneous assumption of the good faith of the British. Nonetheless, other events had unexpectedly begun to set the stage for the long-overdue public declaration on behalf of American membership in a league nations. The first of these events was the resolution of the submarine issue in the spring of 1916; the second, ironically, was the concurrent refusal of the Allies to activate the House-Grey Memorandum at Wilson's urgent request.

On March 24, a German submarine torpedoed the unarmed French steamer *Sussex* in the English Channel. Four Americans were among the eighty casualties.[12] On April 6, the President, Colonel House, and Secretary Lansing held a long session to determine what course of action to take in the face of impending war. They discussed the *Sussex* crisis, the prospects for getting Grey to execute the agreement of February 22 (in the hope of setting the process of mediation in motion), and the status of the Pan-American negotiations, which had settled into another bog, again, owing to Chile's uneasiness about the Tacna-Arica dispute.[13] Within a matter of days, House received several messages from Grey. The Canadian Prime Minister had approved of Britain's joining the Pan-American league; but, Grey also reported, it would be best to delay an endorsement in Parliament until the United States and Argentina, Brazil, and Chile had reached a solid understanding among themselves.[14] As for the House-Grey Memorandum, the French could not consider a peace conference while the outcome of the titanic struggle then raging around Verdun was still in doubt. "There must be more German failure and some Allied success before anything but an inconclusive peace could be obtained," the Foreign Secretary added.[15]

This was not encouraging news. In the meantime, Wilson weighed the potential consequences of holding Germany to strict accountability, a decision he was obliged to make if he expected the British to take him seriously as a mediator. In a very real sense, Wilson placed the choice between peace and war in the lap of the Germans. On April 18, 1916, he demanded that they restrict their undersea operations in accordance with the rules of cruiser warfare, or "visit and search"; he did not, however, insist that they abandon the submarine altogether. This concession, along with the fact that Germany's fleet of U-boats was not large enough to justify the risk of irrevocably offending the United States, probably prevented war between the two countries in 1916. On May 4, the German government accepted Wilson's conditions. The so-called *Sussex* pledge was the greatest diplomatic triumph of Wilson's first administration, and it seemed to vindicate the counsels of patience and forbearance. Sheer luck, however, had intervened as well.[16]

The happy resolution of German-American tensions caused many commentators in the United States to speculate that peace through Wilsonian offices was imminent.[17] It also contributed to the President's belief that both peace in Europe and the establishment of a league of nations were now attainable, if only the Allies would cooperate. Just two days before the arrival of the German note, Brazilian and Chilean representatives had submitted a new draft of the Pan-American Pact; because the Chileans had participated agreeably, the administration awaited in high anticipation the official responses of the three principal South American governments.[18] In the meantime, Wilson concentrated his attention on the British and mediation. Accordingly, he directed House to send Grey yet another entreaty, on May 10, to stress the growing public demand for action to end the war, and that the President was now willing to *publicly* commit the United States to postwar collective security and to propose a conference to discuss peace.[19]

Grey responded with unadorned frankness on May 12. If the President acted on his stated intentions, the Allies would construe it as a plot "instigated by Germany to secure peace on terms unfavorable to the Allies."[20] House was mortified. "Sir Edward has been talking to me for two years concerning the necessity of the United States doing what you now propose," the Colonel (attempting, in part, to cover his own tracks) wrote to Wilson; "and yet when you are ready to do it, he hesitates."[21] Wilson was not exactly overjoyed, either. The administration must "get down to hard pan," he told House, and either insist on the rights of trade as against the Allied blockade, or make a decided move for peace. He proposed a course of action on May 16: the United States would have nothing to do with the terms of peace the belligerents might agree on; it would, however, join "a universal alliance to maintain freedom of the seas and to prevent any war begun either a) contrary to treaty covenants or b) without warning and full inquiry,—a virtual guarantee of territorial integrity and political independence."[22] House drafted a cable that embodied Wilson's thoughts and dispatched it to Grey on May 19. Thus Wilson had met the Foreign Secretary's previous conditions for mediation and, in no uncertain terms, had conveyed to London his position on a league of nations. The time had come to make his position explicit to the American people as well.

During the height of the *Sussex* crisis, Wilson had declined an invitation from William Howard Taft to address the first anniversary meeting of the League to Enforce Peace, to be held in Washington. When Taft renewed the request on May 9, the day after Wilson outlined his ideas about a league to the American Union Against Militarism, he accepted.[23] The President's decision had all the characteristics of good politics and good statesmanship, and demonstrated how closely yoked domestic politics and foreign policy had become.

Domestic considerations were varied. Setting aside his own diplomatic initiatives, Wilson's sensibilities had surely been sharpened by the almost constant, impassioned pleas of the progressive internationalists. He also deemed it appropriate that, as head of the government, he should provide leadership and guidance for a movement that had captured the imagination of so many people. But why employ the Republican-dominated League to Enforce Peace as the forum? Wilson realized that he commanded the allegiance of probably most progressive internationalists, but not that of the conservative internationalists. By making his first public declaration before the LEP—the most influential of all pro-league organizations—he might bring some conservatives around to his own position and lay the foundation for broad-based, if not quite bipartisan, support for the movement. Even so, it was general knowledge that Wilson conferred much more often with left-wing progressives and socialists about the subject than with conservatives. There existed, then, the greater likelihood, as the electoral season approached, that the distance between Wilson's views and those of the conservatives would widen, thus fanning the embers of partisanship, especially if the public began to identify the league idea with Wilson and the Democratic party.

The Europeans—and, in particular, the British—were a consideration as well. If Wilson came out strongly for a league and perhaps called for a peace conference, he not only would make it clear that the United States intended to guarantee the peace settlement; his declaration would also focus the attention of the world on a peace league, invigorate all the elements of the British movement, and thus exert tremendous pressure on the Allies to consent to mediation.

"I am thinking a great deal about the speech I am to make on the twenty-seventh," Wilson wrote to House, "because I realize that it may be the most important I shall ever be called upon to make." He had, of course, voluminous material to draw upon. He kept a large file that contained reports and memoranda from the Woman's Peace party, the AUAM, the LEP, and the Union of Democratic Control, a collection of quotations from the speeches of Asquith, Grey, Viscount Bryce, and clippings from the *New Republic,* Hamilton Holt's *Independent,* and other publications.[24] As usual, House was the chief consultant; since Sir Edward had not yet responded to his latest message (the cable of May 19), he advised Wilson to treat only the subject of the league and to do no more than hint at mediation. "Whether you succeed in starting a peace movement at this time or not," he wrote after reading Wilson's final draft, "you are making, I think, a good record to go before the world with."[25]

At 7:20 P.M., on the evening of May 27, some two thousand people greeted the President as he entered the main dining room of the New Willard Hotel and sat down at the speakers' table with former president Taft, A. Lawrence Lowell, and Senator Henry Cabot Lodge.[26] He was, by choice, the last speaker on the agenda, after Lodge.

Wilson began by talking about the war. "With its causes and objects we are not concerned," he said, although the American people "were as much concerned as the nations at war to see peace assume an aspect of permanence." The United States, he observed, had reached a point in its history when it could no longer be guided by the timeworn precepts of George Washington's valedictory: "We are participants, whether we would or not, in the life of the world. The interests of all nations are our own also. We are partners with the rest. What affects mankind is inevitably our affair as well as the affair of the nations of Europe and of Asia.

"The peace of the world must henceforth depend upon a new and more wholesome diplomacy," he continued. "Only when the nations of the world have reached some sort of agreement . . . as to some feasible method of acting in concert when any nation or group of nations seeks to disturb those fundamental things, can we feel that civilization is at last in a way of justifying itself." He thereupon proclaimed that the American people believed in the following things: "First, that every people has a right to choose the sovereignty under which they shall live. . . . Second, that the small states of the world have a right to enjoy the same respect for their sovereignty and for their territorial integrity. . . . And, third, that the world has a right to be free from every disturbance of its peace that has its origins in aggression and disregard of the rights of peoples and nations.

"So sincerely do I believe in these things that I am sure that I speak the mind and wish of the people of America when I say that the United States is willing to become a partner in any feasible association of nations formed in order to realize these objects and make them secure against violation." This would involve (once the belligerents had come to a peace settlement on their own) "an universal association of the nations to maintain the inviolate security of the highway of the seas for the common and unhindered use of all the nations of the world, and to prevent any war begun either contrary to treaty covenants or without warning and full submission of the causes to the opinion of the world—a virtual guarantee of territorial integrity and political independence.

"But I did not come here, let me repeat, to discuss a program," he said in conclusion. "I came only to avow a creed and give expression to the confidence I feel that the world is even now upon the eve of a great consummation, when some common force will be brought into existence which shall safeguard rights as the first and most fundamental interest of all peoples and all governments, when coercion shall be summoned not to the service of political ambition or selfish hostility, but to the service of a common order, a common justice, and a common peace. God grant that the dawn of that day of frank dealing and of settled peace, concord, and cooperation may be near at hand!"[27]

The tumultuous applause that shook the New Willard Hotel was but the first indication that Wilson's momentous pronouncement would be received, as Colonel House described it, as "a land mark in history." The president of Williams College, for instance, compared it to the Gettysburg Address. Walter Lippmann, using the Monroe Doctrine as his point of reference, wrote: "In historic significance it is easily the most important diplomatic event that our generation has known." Hamilton Holt proclaimed that the address "cannot fail to rank in political importance with the Declaration of Independence." In an editorial entitled "Mr.

Wilson's Great Utterance," the *New Republic* suggested that the President might have engineered "a decisive turning point in the history of the modern world." Because he had given new meaning to preparedness and had broken with isolationism, Wilson's stand represented "one of the greatest advances ever made in the development of international morality."[28]

While the preponderance of American opinion was overwhelmingly favorable—literally hundreds of editorials characterized the speech as "the voice of America"[29]—Wilson had also incensed many observers. The New York *Tribune,* for example, condemned as "fantastic" the idea of self-determination and described the performance as "another flagrant illustration of Mr. Wilson's instability as a statesman, his fluid sentimentalism, his servitude to winged phrases."[30] Theodore Roosevelt's organ, the *Outlook,* castigated the President for not taking sides with the Allies.[31]

The *Outlook* was practically alone in discerning that the League to Enforce Peace might have less cause for celebration than the first flush of exhilaration seemed to warrant. Hamilton Holt considered the speech an "almost official endorsement" of the LEP's position; Taft, usually a shrewd analyst, believed simply that Wilson's appearance evidenced "sympathy with our general purposes." But they both had failed to note Wilson's comment "I did not come here, let me repeat, to discuss a program." Indeed, he had not endorsed the LEP's platform. Even in its generalities, the address implicitly testified to the unreconciled differences between the progressives and conservatives over several important questions, including self-determination, national sovereignty, and whether the war itself should end in favor of the Allies or in a draw. If anything, Wilson had articulated the position of the American progressive-left and the British radicals. As Philip Snowden correctly observed, "Every one of the principles of the U.D.C. was stated and approved in the speech by the American President."[32] In any case, Wilson clearly had achieved two important objectives: he had elevated the general proposition of postwar collective security to a position of preeminence in American politics, and, virtually overnight, he had secured for himself the leadership of the American league movement.

This much could also be said about the effect of the address in Europe. A. G. Gardiner, in the London *Daily News,* claimed that Wilson had opened "a new chapter in the history of civilization." Sir Horace Plunkett added that the League had now been raised "to a high place among the prophetic visions of international statesmanship."[33] Commenting on the UDC's plans to disseminate the speech, Kate Courtney wrote that Wilson had "filled us with hope," while Noel Buxton, a Liberal member of Parliament, told House that his party would now begin active propaganda.[34] Viscount James Bryce, whose views more closely approximated Taft's than Wilson's, informed House that all groups in the British movement were "greatly cheered and encouraged by the President's recent deliverances."[35]

The majority of European commentators, however, were decidedly not cheered and encouraged. The most prevalent interpretation was that Wilson was about to intervene independently to try to end the war, chiefly to impress the American electorate.[36] Both the French press and Foreign Office fairly scoffed at Wilson's alleged presumptions as mediator. Jean Jules Jusserand, the ambassador to the United States, warned House that his countrymen believed that the appeal was "clearly inspired by German interest."[37] For its part, the German press also dismissed the speech as Wilson's opening petition for reelection (an opinion not without some basis).[38] The response of the Foreign Office was subtler. Since the war then appeared to be moving in their favor, the Germans did not welcome a Wilsonian settlement. In the event that a serious peace move materialized, they hoped to remain equivocal and to shift to the Allies the onus of rejecting Wilson's hand.[39] In Great Britain, the political right and center were stung by Wilson's professed unconcern with the war's causes and objects. Lord Cromer, in a letter to the London *Times,* claimed that the remark disqualified the President from exercising "any decisive influence on the terms of peace." This opinion was shared by many publications, including the *Times* itself.[40]

The British Cabinet was probably Wilson's most important foreign audience—not only because of the messages that were traveling back and forth between Washington and London at the time, but also because the Cabinet had just had an intense internal debate over the league idea. In May 1915, Lord Chancellor Haldane had prepared a memorandum on the subject. His study reflected the influence of the Bryce Group (the British equivalent of the LEP) and suggested that a league would serve Britain's security interests, but only if the United States became a dedicated member. Two days before Wilson's LEP address, Maurice Hankey, secretary of the War Committee, rejoined that security through a league was illusory. He feared that the Allies and other presumably peace-loving nations would fall prey to the "enthusiasts for social reform and the anti-war and disarmament people," while the Germans (and perhaps the Russians) would exploit the postwar craving for peace, rearm themselves, and attack the democracies at the appropriate moment. The United States, he further argued, could not be counted on. Its tradition of isolationism and its allegiance to the almighty dollar offered proof of his assertions. Any international scheme was doomed to failure, Hankey concluded. Arthur James Balfour, First Lord of the Admiralty, had earlier staked out the middle ground. In reply to the Haldane memorandum, Balfour had suggested that periodic, informal conferences between nations, which brought disputants together without forcing a judgment on them, would do more good than compulsory arbitration and ironclad guarantees of territorial integrity. In any case, he was now advising that the government inform Wilson that the league idea would best be furthered by American intervention against Germany.[41]

On the general question of a league of nations, then, there was divided counsel within the British government. On the question of a peace conference, however, there was unanimity. And in this respect, the timing of both House's request of May 19 for action on the House-Grey Memorandum and Wilson's celebrated preachment could not have been worse. Germany was in a vastly superior position vis-à-vis the Allies, and the War Office was just then eager to unleash a new British army on the Somme and deal the enemy the crushing blow. The government would never consider mediation as long as some hope of victory remained. Wilson would be called in only if Allied defeat appeared certain.[42]

Consequently, Grey's formal response to House on May 29 explicitly ruled out American mediation. It also demonstrated the fundamental differences, in this instance, between the British government's qualified view of the league predicated upon victory and a postwar *Pax Atlantica,* and Wilson's view of the league begat by self-determination and a peace short of victory. "The best chance for the great scheme," Grey wrote, "is the President's willingness that it should be proposed by the United States in convention [with] a peace favorable to the Allies obtainable with American aid. The worst chance would be that it should be proposed in connection with an inconclusive peace. . . . No such peace could secure a reliable and enduring international organization of the kind he contemplates."[43] Thus was Wilson at last confronted with reality; or, as he later put it to House, with "the stupidity of English opinion."[44] Yet no one in the Cabinet had altered his attitude since the initialing of the agreement of February 22; Grey had said nothing that he had not previously said to House. Although he failed to grasp it, Wilson had finally reaped what the Colonel had sown.

The ensuing summer witnessed the lowest ebb in Anglo-American public and official relations since the British burned Washington in 1814. The British government's ruthless suppression of the Irish Rebellion in April and the subsequent execution of its leaders disturbed even the staunchest Anglophiles, including Theodore Roosevelt. The tensions soon heightened when the Allies began to seize American mails on the high seas. Then, on July 19, the British government published a "blacklist" and forbade its subjects to do business with some 347 American and Latin American firms suspected of carrying on trade with the Central Powers. This action generated another swell of indignation in the United States. By September, Wilson's attitude toward the British had so hardened that

Secretary Lansing feared that the United States would soon find itself aligned with Germany.[45]

Meanwhile, House's and Grey's correspondence tapered off. "I am not sure that there is anything further that the President can do for the moment, for he gets little support or encouragement outside of America," House lamented to the Foreign Secretary. "We are standing it seems at the roads of destiny, waiting to see which way to turn." Grey did not answer for six weeks. "There is nothing more that *I* can do at the moment," he retorted on August 28, and reminded House that he, Grey, had publicly advocated a league on three occasions. It was too bad if the President was disappointed "at the want of response to his speech." But both Wilson and the American people were apparently hell-bent on avoiding war, even at the cost of national honor. He now wondered whether Americans really understood what was at stake in the war and whether "even with a League of Nations the United States could be depended upon to uphold treaties and agreements by force."[46] The situation had reached an utter stalemate.

For about three weeks after Wilson's address to the League to Enforce Peace, events seemed to auger extremely well for the Pan-American Pact, despite the fact that Grey had all but disposed of House's overture to include Great Britain in it. On June 3, the government of Brazil, following the example of Argentina, accepted the Wilson-emended, Lansing-Naón draft treaty. Although Chile had not responded, Ambassador da Gama launched a new drive to persuade her to come along. The Foreign Minister of Brazil announced that he would travel to Washington personally to affix his signature, and Ambassador Naón began preparations for a gala ceremony in which some thirteen Latin American countries were expected to sign the Pact. "I think it is safe to say," Henry P. Fletcher said in a letter to House on June 15, "we have arrived."[47]

Even as Fletcher wrote, however, untoward developments in the Mexican Revolution conspired to ruin the credibility of the United States in the eyes of practically every Latin American government and dealt the Pan-American Pact a mortal blow. In October 1915, Wilson had granted Venustiano Carranza's Constitutionalists recognition as the *de facto* government of Mexico. On March 9, 1916, Pancho Villa, Carranza's opponent, led a mounted attack on the little town of Columbus, New Mexico, killing nineteen Americans. A substantial historiography has since grown up around the question of Villa's motivations. For years, the most prevalent interpretation held that Villa, encouraged by German intrigues, sought to further his own ambitions by provoking war between the United States and Mexico. New documentary evidence, brought to light by Friedrich

Katz, suggests that the raid sprang from the general's firm (but unfounded) belief that Carranza and Wilson had reached an agreement that would have made Mexico a virtual protectorate of the United States.[48]

The killing of American citizens put the Wilson administration in an extremely difficult position. Although few individuals of influence demanded war, many Republican critics of his Mexican policy blamed the President for creating the circumstances that incited the raid. Perilous as any sort of retaliation promised to be, Wilson, in this situation, could not cry "too proud to fight"—and certainly not in an election year. On March 15, he ordered Brigadier General John J. Pershing, with a force of approximately 7,000 soldiers, to pursue Villa into Mexico. (Wilson took special pains to keep a tight rein on Pershing in order to avoid a clash with Carranza's troops; he also cautioned several news services not to put a dramatic construction on the intrusion.[49]) Initially, Carranza tacitly sanctioned the so-called Punitive Expedition; by late spring, however, it had penetrated 350 miles into the interior without even catching sight of Villa. Then on April 12, a detachment of Pershing's command clashed with *Carranzistas* at Parral, leaving from forty to one hundred Mexicans dead. At Carrizal, another incident occurred on June 21. Carranza now demanded that Pershing's forces withdraw to the border. Wilson would not comply.[50]

At this point, the situation quickly went from bad to worse. The first reports from Carrizal, on June 22, characterized the incident as a treacherous ambush by Mexican soldiers. Upon learning that Carranza refused to release the prisoners taken in the engagement, Wilson seriously considered asking Congress to authorize him to clear northern Mexico of forces that placed American citizens of the border states in harm's way.[51] Clearly, the President was losing control of events that now threatened to bring on full-scale hostilities between the United States and Mexico and, short of that, to wreck not only the Pan-American Pact but also his standing among progressive internationalists.

Although the evidence is not altogether conclusive, it appears that the crucial factor in averting war was a series of extraordinary steps taken by the American Union Against Militarism and the Woman's Peace party. During the last week of June 1916, the AUAM publicly called upon William Jennings Bryan, David Starr Jordan, and Frank P. Walsh to meet with three Mexican representatives at El Paso, Texas, "in an effort to get at the difficulties which have arisen between the two governments."[52] Then, to disprove the sensationalized accounts of the clash at Carrizal, the AUAM, on June 26, published in several major newspapers an eye-witness account of an American captain, which revealed that his troops, and not the Mexicans, had been the aggressors.[53] Within twenty-four hours, the AUAM's advertisements precipitated a flood of telegrams to the White

House and editorials imploring the President not to take any belligerent action. "My heart is for peace," Wilson assured Jane Addams on June 28, in response to a petition from the Woman's Peace party.[54] When, later that evening, word arrived that the Mexicans had released their prisoners, the crisis began to recede.

On June 30, Wilson, obviously with an enormous sense of relief, addressed the New York Press Club and obliquely acknowledged the salutary results of the good offices of the AUAM and the WPP. "Do you think the glory of America would be enhanced by a war of conquest in Mexico?" he asked his audience. "Do you think that any act of violence by a powerful nation like this against a weak and distracted neighbor would reflect distinction upon the annals of the United States?" With one voice, the seven hundred diners shouted "No!"[55]

From the point of view of the AUAM and the WPP, these developments, coming on the heels of the former group's colloquy at the White House, furnished new proof that they wielded influence where it counted most.[56] For his part, Wilson realized that the AUAM and the WPP had helped save him from a disaster. The unusual circumstances surrounding the resolution of the crisis with Mexico had strengthened the bonds between Wilson and the progressive internationalists.

This was definitely not the case for the bonds of Pan-Americanism. To an extent, the initial American military operation was a legitimate retaliatory response to Villa's attack. But by June it had become a blatant violation of Wilson's verbal commitment against interventionism, notwithstanding his very limited goal in the incursion and the political pressures he was subject to. The Punitive Expedition aroused anti-American feeling in most of the prospective members of the Pan-American family.

Both Lansing and Fletcher informed the President that the imbroglio would have a very bad effect on the Pact. Somewhat cryptically, Wilson replied that the situation constituted "an additional reason for signing rather than otherwise."[57] Argentina, Brazil, and Chile did not share his opinion. *La Prensa* of Buenos Aires remarked, "The triumph of the Pan-America policy is preferable to any advantage that could be gained by war."[58] But by this point, not even.Ambassador Naón, the staunchest Latin American champion of the Pact, could recommend proceeding. "It is difficult to sign treaties which tend to impose concord and union on the continent," he wrote Fletcher on June 27, "while threats of war are passing between two of the most important nations of America."[59] This was the heaviest blow of all. Da Gama, too, believed that it would be a mistake to sign, in view of the likelihood of war between Mexico and the United States, and also because Chile was now "decidedly opposed to the treaty." Although the war crisis abated by mid-July, neither Argentina nor Brazil found Wilson's attempt to rekindle the courtship beguiling as long as Pershing remained in Mexico. In early August, Frank L. Polk, Counselor at the State Department, told Colonel House that the Pact "seems dead for the moment." At length, the grand endeavor became a closed incident.[60]

Chile's unremitting reluctance to commit herself to the Pact's guarantees, when Argentina and Brazil (and several other sister republics) were willing to do so, was one of two chief reasons for the project's failure. The second reason was the Mexican incursion, especially after the bloodletting at Carrizal. With that, Wilson extinguished the light of all his earnest work—the good faith and confidence which many Latin Americans had temporarily come to repose in the United States. There is some irony in the fact that Wilson interfered in the internal affairs of neighboring states (Nicaragua, Haiti, the Dominican Republic, as well as Mexico) on a scale to rival Roosevelt and Taft. He was not unconscious of those "blind spots"—of the contradictions between his pronouncements and his actions. The President's response to Argentina's and Brazil's decisive alarm over the Punitive Expedition—that the situation was "an additional reason for signing rather than otherwise"—was not disingenuous; rather, it reflected his conception of the Pact as a means of removing the causes of those problems that, in his thinking, compelled him to do violence to his own words.

Two years later, Wilson was still trying to explain himself. The trouble was that the Monroe Doctrine "was adopted without your consent," he said to a group of Mexican newspaper editors. "We did not ask whether it was agreeable to you that we should be your big brother." Whereas the Monroe Doctrine was ostensibly intended to check European aggression in Latin America, there was nothing in it to restrain the United States. The Pan-American Pact was, alas, "an arrangement by which you would be protected from us." The whole family of nations someday would have to do this—to guarantee that none should violate another's political independence and territorial integrity. "That is the basis, the only conceivable basis, for the future peace of the world, and I must admit that I was anxious to have the states of the two continents of America show the way to the rest of world as to how to make a basis of peace."[61]

In any event, by the late spring of 1916, Wilson had brought the United States closer to a commitment to join some kind of postwar league of nations—as much by the failure of the Pan-American Pact as by the ringing success of his address to the League to Enforce Peace. Now a new campaign season approached. The precise cast of his bid for re-election, with respect to both domestic and foreign policy, remained to be seen. Yet, as his convictions about progressive internationalism continued to grow, one thing was sure: there could be no turning back.

6

Raising a New Flag

The League and the Coalition of 1916

C olonel House was the first administration insider to realize that Wilson's attendance at the meeting of the League to Enforce Peace held one of the keys to his re-election. As we have seen, many European critics, fearing that he was about to intervene on behalf of mediation, sought to dismiss the President's address as a transparent attempt to solicit votes. The address was not conceived for that purpose, however. Taft certainly did not invite Wilson to speak in order to help a Democrat renew the lease on the executive mansion. And House originally considered the belligerents Wilson's primary audience. But, because of the unprecedented outpouring of acclaim, a very bright idea occurred to the Colonel. "Do you not think that your speech . . . should be endorsed by the St. Louis convention?" he asked Wilson on May 29. "Many people with whom I have talked today regard it as the real democratic platform. Some of them say it leaves the republican leaders without a single issue either foreign or domestic."[1]

Other sources, for somewhat different reasons, confirmed House's judgment. At the New Willard Hotel, Wilson had administered a large dose of adrenaline to American and European friends of the league. Now they clamored for more. Sir Horace Plunkett urged the President to restate his case as often as possible and in greater detail. Such efforts, Lord

Loreburn added, would "render priceless service to the cause of common sense." Noel Buxton wrote to House that the people, in general, needed more education on the subject. "The President's prestige as a statesman and speaker is immense," the Liberal Member of Parliament also told the Secretary of the Interior. "A great public following exists potentially if he shows that he means to push the League of Peace."[2]

Well-nigh all scholarly accounts of the subject cite the wartime congressional elections of 1918 as the point of no return in infusing an intense degree of partisanship into the debate over American membership in the League of Nations. That interpretation must be revised. For it was during the presidential campaign of 1916 that the league idea first became an issue of national importance; and therein the partisan element had its origins. That fact necessitates, as well, a reevaluation of the nature and significance of Wilson's bid for re-election.

Wilson appealed to the electorate by emphasizing his achievements in domestic reform and his success in having kept the country out of war—a "campaign for progressivism and peace," as Arthur S. Link aptly characterized it in the fifth volume of his biography of the President. Yet, as he set out to win votes, Wilson could actually boast of deeds which went beyond even the New Nationalism—if the spectrum of progressive and socialist opinion were any guide. Moreover, Wilson, persuaded by the counsel of House, Buxton, and others, would defend his foreign policy record and speak of things to come in terms that were much stronger than a defense of neutral rights and the wish simply to remain at peace with Europe. His first step in this regard was to fashion a party platform that stressed progressive internationalism. For example, he built into a plank on preparedness an explanation based on the one that he had made to the American Union Against Militarism—the requirement of an army and navy "equal to the international tasks which the United States hopes and expects to take a part in performing." He also wrote a separate, major plank on international relations (lifted from his speech to the LEP) that affirmed the right of every people to self-determination and the duty of the United States to join a league of nations. The fact that he had embedded these ideas in the Democratic platform, Wilson told House, would "give them immensely increased importance. That ought to soak in on the other side, with all parties to the war."[3]

Wilson could not have made a truly plausible case for a new diplomacy and a league—nor, as the election returns bear out, would he have been continued in office—if, at the same time, he had not been both willing and intellectually able to move plainly to the left of the center of American politics. Indeed, the impressive array of (primarily) social-justice legislation that he pushed through Congress on the eve of the campaign gave legitimacy and magnetism to his aspirations in foreign policy like nothing else could have. Never was the relationship between reform and foreign policy more decisive than during the campaign of 1916. It was no mere coincidence that leading conservative internationalists lined up as Wilson's chief domestic critics, while progressive internationalists (socialists as well as liberals) enthusiastically applauded his work and cheered him on. These parallel alignments framed practically every important issue pertaining to domestic affairs that arose throughout the whole of 1916. In fact, if a gulf separated the internationalist movement's two wings, it seemed to grow wider, not simply because of competing views on the proper role that the United States should play in world affairs, but because of their respective visions of the future of American society.

The response to Wilson's two additions to the Supreme Court in 1916 is an illuminating example. Wilson created an almost unprecedented sensation when, in January, he nominated Louis D. Brandeis for Associate Justice. Not until Ronald Reagan attempted to elevate Robert Bork to the high bench in 1987 would such an acrimonious battle over confirmation take place in American politics. Progressives were extremely impressed with what Wilson had done. "It took courage & sense to make this appointment," said Amos Pinchot of the American Union Against Militarism, "& I take off my chapeau to the President."[4] Because Brandeis was so closely identified with the social-justice movement and so hated by powerful corporate interests, conservatives could not have been more upset if Eugene Debs had been recommended. That "a socialist" could be put on the Court, the president of the League to Enforce Peace told a friend, "is one of the deepest wounds that I have had as an American and lover of the Constitution." Taft also joined with other prominent conservative internationalists, including Elihu Root and A. Lawrence Lowell, to organize a national campaign to discredit Brandeis; along with five other former presidents of the American Bar Association, Taft and Root signed a statement declaring him "not fit" to be a Supreme Court Justice.[5] Brandeis was confirmed, on June 1, in large measure because Wilson went to the mat for him.[6]

The "People's Lawyer" was no sooner sworn in, however, than Wilson proffered "Another Supreme Court Radical," John Hessin Clarke of Ohio.[7] Clarke, a protégé of Cleveland's mayor, Tom Johnson, and Mark Hanna's opponent in the senatorial race of 1903, was then a federal district judge noted for his decisions on behalf of organized labor. According to the *New York Times,* his nomination, coming so close on the heels of Brandeis', was "likely to be viewed with some doubt and misgiving by the conservative part of the public." The liberal and socialist press, on the other hand, was almost as pleased as it had been by the tapping of Brandeis. The New York *World,* a staunch supporter of the Wilson administration, underscored Clarke's "sympathies and activities for the causes of political and social justice." The *Call,* New York's leading socialist daily, quoted a statement that Clarke had made during the preparedness controversy, "If we expect labor to fight our nation's battles we must give labor a nation worth fighting for," and focused attention on a recent court decision in which Clarke had saved the jobs of the wage-earners of Brewster, Ohio. "There will be another radical on the bench," the *Call* proclaimed. "Not as radical as Justice Brandeis, but something of a near-radical."[8]

Wilson appointed Clarke and Brandeis because, he said, they believed in a "liberal and enlightened interpretation" of the Constitution.[9] Although their membership on the great tribunal gratified progressive internationalists, it was a source of resentment among most conservative internationalists. By autumn, Taft had come to regard the approaching election as the most critical one of his career, and worried that Wilson might have additional opportunities to select "men who are radical in their views, who have no idea of preserving the rights of property. . . ."[10]

In retrospect, it is somewhat ironic that historians frequently cite the nomination of Brandeis—who was the principal architect of the New Freedom—as the beginning of Wilson's transition to the New Nationalism. The signs of at least a merger of the New Freedom and the New Nationalism had been gathering since early 1915. They were manifest in, among other things, the flexibility that Wilson had demonstrated in the evolution of federal trade and antitrust legislation; in the assistance he had lent to certain social-justice measures of limited scope, such as the La Follette Seamen's Act; and in his sympathetic approach to the grievances of the miners of Ludlow, Colorado, who had been murderously victimized by John D. Rockefeller's private army in the notorious massacre of 1914. Nor can one discount in Wilson's metamorphosis the cumulative impact of his regular exposure, from 1915 onward, to the eclectic ministrations of socialists and liberals who spearheaded the progressive internationalist movement. Then, too, the connections that he perceived between domestic politics and foreign policy, as well as the very nature and development of his internationalist thought, suggested a predisposition to advanced positions on social issues, once a political environment conducive to them had materialized.

There was a comparative dimension to all of this, too. It centered upon the devolution of Theodore Roosevelt, the politician who had once stood as the incarnation of progressivism.[11] Since 1913, the Republican party had begun pulling itself back together under the aegis of the Old Guard; by the following year, conservatives had completely consolidated their control. In the mid-term elections of 1914, the former Bull Moose, conflicted and frustrated, declined to campaign for most Progressive party candidates. While the Democratic majority in the House of Representatives fell from seventy-three to twenty-five, the Progressive party succeeded in electing only a single member to Congress. "The fundamental trouble was that the country was sick and tired of reform," Roosevelt wrote to William Allen White. "Not only did the people wish to beat all the reform leaders but they wished to beat the reform legislation." As for the Republican party, he said, "the dog has returned to its vomit."[12]

After 1914, Roosevelt's real political passions were restricted to the war, to preparedness, and to the hated Wilson. As many of his erstwhile adherents became increasingly identified with antimilitarists, socialists, and other assorted miscreants, he distanced himself from them even further. In 1915, he began to make peace with the chieftains of the GOP. This was proof enough for many critics that the Progressive party, now only a brittle husk of its former self, had been created to vent the spleen of one man.

It was, therefore, almost inevitable that Progressives should turn for leadership in 1916 to someone who seemed as sincere and inspired as the Roosevelt of 1912, to someone who already possessed a record of significant accomplishment as well as a capacity to expand his concept of the role of government in order to confront the social problems born of industrial capitalism. Wilson needed the Progressives as much as they needed him. The Democrats, still the country's minority party, had gained power because of the rupture within Republican ranks, which was now on the mend. Simple political arithmetic dictated an expansion of the Democrats' present electoral base if the party intended to remain in power. Certain aspects of the President's performance were thus shaped by expedience.

For instance, until 1916, Wilson had opposed a system of federal rural credits that would gradually lower the discount on farm mortgages. By the time a new Federal Farm Loan Act was introduced in Congress in January, however, he had become more conversant with agrarian problems, specifically those generated by usurious interest rates that burdened farmers in many regions. He also knew that the Democratic party stood to lose the Middle West in November, as a Nebraska farmers' organization warned, if he failed "to give suitable legislation on this subject." In March, Wilson declared the Federal Farm Loan Act an administration measure, worked to enlarge its provisions, and signed it into law in July. By late summer, its beneficiaries were hailing the bill as the "Magna Carta of American farm finance."[13]

Wilson's political instincts undoubtedly motivated a pre-campaign decision to follow the lead of progressives in Congress in another critical matter, one that concerned both domestic and foreign policy and registered a "radical" postscript to the preparedness controversy. Near the end of summer, the administration had secured compromise legislation to expand the size of the Army and Navy (though not enough to satisfy Roosevelt, who pronounced the bill's supporters guilty of "moral treason to the American commonwealth").[14] The question of the hour, though, was who was going to foot the bill. Representative Warren Worth Bailey, an ardent antipreparedness Democrat from Pennsylvania, had an answer: "If the forces of big business are to plunge this country into a saturnalia of extravagance for war purposes in time of peace, it is my notion that the forces of big business should put up the money." Socialist James Maurer agreed. "We are sick and tired of being turned into fodder for cannons and then [sic] have to pay for 'preparedness,'" he said to the Senate Committee on Military Affairs. "If it's right to take a poor man's life, it's right to take the rich man's fortune."[15]

The coalition of antimilitarists and progressives wrested more than modest indemnities. The Revenue Act of 1916, signed by Wilson on September 8, levied a surtax, ranging from six to thirteen per cent, on incomes over $20,000; an estate tax, from one to a maximum of ten per cent, on amounts over $50,000; a two per cent tax on annual net corporate income; and a tax of twelve-and-a-half per cent on gross income of all munitions manufacturers. Designed to shift virtually the entire financial burden for preparedness—some $300,000,000—onto the country's wealthiest classes, this bill established the first and one of the few truly progressive tax schedules of the twentieth century. Few presidential signatures ever gave radicals greater satisfaction, or conservatives greater apprehension.[16]

Where Wilson really proved himself worthy of the support of liberals as well as of potentially large numbers of socialists was in the realm of social welfare, particularly as it affected the lives of everyday working people. During the first week of June, Wilson sat down to write the national party platform, a manifesto in the spirit of "Progressive Democracy." The document could be distinguished in two important respects from the one that the Republicans would adopt. First, Wilson's synthesis of progressive internationalist intentions, as concise as it was, represented a position far in advance of the foreign policy planks contained in, not only the Republican, but also the Socialist, party platform. Second, Wilson catalogued his administration's proudest deeds and endorsed the sections of the Progressive party program of 1912 that the Democrats had not yet brought to legislative fruition—the enactment of federal laws to restrict child labor, to provide workers with adequate compensation for industrial accidents, and to establish the eight-hour day.[17] These three measures had for years engaged the energies of progressives and of both left-wing and "gas and water" socialists.

Unannounced, on July 18, Wilson traveled up to Capitol Hill to confer with Democratic leaders about the Keating-Owen child labor bill and the Kern-McGillicuddy bill for federal workmen's compensation, both of which had already passed the House. Commending the justice of the laws and stressing that they constituted solemn platform pledges, he enjoined his colleagues to see them through before the Senate adjourned. His personal appearance on the Hill, then considered an extraordinary step for any president to take on behalf of pending legislation, did the trick. The action "may have been extremely good politics," remarked the Brooklyn *Eagle*, "but it was also a use of party leadership in the interests of humanity." The bills arrived on Wilson's desk on September 1, a day of celebration for the nation's labor leaders and for the folks at Hull House and the Henry Street Settlement.[18]

To be sure, Wilson was a distinctly political animal. Yet his dramatic exercise of power on behalf of children and adult workers also represented genuine convictions and reflected the historian's sensitivity to the changing world around him. In foreign policy, Wilson had first demonstrated a growing awareness and appreciation of the fact that the problems of the Industrial Age were as much social as political; they could not be adequately addressed (as, for instance, he had learned in Mexico in 1914) by recourse to old nostrums or by clinging to narrowly conceived constitutional scruples. So also with the conditions of life and work at home. Times had changed. "The pressure of low wages, the agony of obscure and unremunerated toil did not exist in America in anything like the same proportions that they exist now," he said to a convention of woman suffragists on September 8. "As the populations have assembled in the cities, . . . the whole nature of our political questions has been altered. They have ceased to be legal questions; they have more and more become social questions, questions with regard to the relations of human beings to one another."[19] And, on the Fourth of July, he had declared to some ten thousand people assembled for the dedication of the American Federation of Labor building in Washington: "The great difficulty about the relationship between capital and labor is this: Labor is in immediate contact with the task itself—with the work, with the conditions of the work, with the tools with which it's done, and the circumstances under which they are used; whereas, capital, in too many instances, is at a great remove."[20]

Wilson gave climactic proof of his conviction in an unforeseen series of events that flared up just as the presidential campaign was getting under way. Since the spring, the country's major railroad brotherhoods had been struggling to obtain the eight-hour day (reduced from ten hours), without a cut in pay and with time and a half for overtime. When twenty railroad presidents rejected these demands and mediation failed in June, ninety-four per cent of all the railroad workers voted to call a nationwide strike.[21]

The situation was easily the gravest domestic crisis that Wilson had

yet confronted. Throughout August he invited to the White House delegation after delegation of representatives from management and the
brotherhoods to try to work out a settlement. He assured the brotherhoods he favored the eight-hour day because, he said, it was right, and,
on August 18, persuaded them to compromise on the issue of punitive
overtime pay. During the next three days, forty-three railroad presidents
entered the Green Room to hear what Wilson had to say. They did not
like a word of it. When they refused to budge, he reportedly said, "I pray
God to forgive you. I never can."[22] Capital had demonstrated to his satisfaction that it was, indeed, "at a great remove."

Wilson had pleaded with the railroad presidents to help him to untie
the Gordian knot. With the shutdown of the nation's transportation system set for September 4, he would now undertake to cut it with the
stroke of a pen. Between August 28 and 31, he ventured up to the halls
of Congress four times—three times to hammer out legislation with the
Democratic leadership, once to address a joint session of Congress—on
behalf of the railroad workers. On the latter occasion he portrayed management as unreasonable and the eight-hour day as "a thing upon which
society is justified in insisting."[23] The Adamson Act passed the House
by a vote of 239 to 56 on September 1, and the Senate by 43 to 28 the
next day. When Wilson placed this final jewel in the crown of "Progressive Democracy," the most hotly debated subject of the campaign was
born.

The Adamson Act, perhaps more than any other domestic issue, separated the progressives from the conservatives among internationalists. "[T]he
most humiliating thing in the recent history of the United States" was
how William Howard Taft characterized the settlement, in a letter published in the *New York Times.* Charles Evans Hughes, the Republican
nominee for President, heartily agreed. "I am opposed to being dictated
to either in the executive department or in Congress by any power on
earth," he said in a hard-hitting campaign speech at Nashville. Attacking
both Wilson and the brotherhoods, Hughes declared at Beverly, Massachusetts: "This country must never know the rule of force. It must never
know legislation under oppression." The *New York Times,* usually sympathetic toward the administration, also condemned the settlement for
"reduc[ing] 100,000,000 people to a condition of vassalage."[24]

The vast majority of progressives and socialists, however, saw the
matter differently. If nothing else, Wilson should be honored for having
averted what was potentially the worst strike of the century, argued most
Democratic newspapers. Although its editorial board was still undecided
about whose candidacy to endorse, the *New Republic* could not have been
more impressed with the "high statesmanship" that Wilson exhibited: "In
a very real and accurate sense the President has made himself the spokes-

man of a whole people . . . [and] has shown how to turn an emergency to constructive purposes."[25]

Such handsome praise was a welcome contribution to Wilson's uphill re-election campaign; but, in view of Hughes' attempt to exploit the Adamson Act in the context of the Republican party's swerve to the right, it might have been expected that the *New Republic* and the presidents of the American Federation of Labor and the United Mine Workers, as well as Democratic and progressive Republican newspapers, would issue strong statements commending Wilson's attitude toward labor. What really exceeded all expectations, though, was the way leading Socialist party members acknowledged Wilson's accomplishment—despite the fact that any palm extended to him was bound to hurt their own presidential candidate, Allan Benson.[26]

For instance, Max Eastman startled many of his fellows by addressing the Woodrow Wilson Independent League. There were several reasons why the President had earned Socialist support, he suggested, among them "his announcement that the best judgment of mankind accepts the principle of the eight-hour day." This was compelling evidence—in contrast to Hughes' "petty and indiscriminate scolding,"—that Wilson "has vision and sympathy with human progress." The *Weekly People,* a socialist publication in New York, while giving the brotherhoods the greater share of credit, also exulted because Wilson had conceded the "power of the working class when consolidated upon the field of industry."[27] Mary Harris ("Mother") Jones, the beloved, eighty-two-year-old radical and inveterate crusader for the rights of working people, declared that Wilson was the first chief executive ever to "demand that the toilers be given an even break in the world."[28] Frank Bohn of the *Masses* wrote that the President, coming "face to face with the social problems of the new industrialism," had established himself "the ablest progressive yet produced by our politics."[29]

Out of the heady welter of American progressive and socialist politics, then, a left-of-center coalition was becoming an increasingly distinct and practical possibility, with Wilson as its pivot. For Wilson could boast, not only of the Underwood tariff, the Clayton Act, the Federal Reserve System, and the Federal Trade Commission; he had also put "radicals" on the Supreme Court, and had secured enactment of an unprecedented program of legislation to improve the lives of all working men, women, and children. Moreover, he had defused the conservatives' appeal to militarism with his moderate approach to preparedness, which, not incidentally, had yielded the first real tax on wealth in American history. And he had kept the country out of war.

Throughout the United States, growing numbers of Roosevelt's former followers as well as independents representing every shade of pro-

gressivism came out for Wilson.[30] Walter Weyl of the *New Republic* and
Amos Pinchot and Rabbi Wise of the American Union Against Militarism
presented the President with a resolution (signed also by John Dewey,
Ray Stannard Baker, and Walter Lippmann) expressing their regret for
having earlier opposed him; they now averred their unified support and
admiration for his battle against "privilege" as the "reactionaries of all
parties have watched this with dismay."[31] Paul Kellogg and Lillian Wald
organized "Social Workers for Wilson," which claimed that the President's driving purpose was "the social welfare of the whole people." On
October 14, the Democratic National Committee proudly announced that
Jane Addams planned to vote for Wilson. In explaining her decision to
one activist in the internationalist movement, she confessed to having been
"quite unprepared for the distinctive period in American politics developed under the brilliant Party leadership of President Wilson."[32]

Socialist luminaries admitted as much, too. John Reed, Jack London,
Charles Edward Russell, Helen Keller, Upton Sinclair, John Spargo, William English Walling, Florence Kelley, Algie M. Simons, and Gus Myers,
among others, forsook the party's candidate for Wilson. For some, a practical consideration figured prominently; in the current world situation a
Socialist vote was too great a luxury when the race between Wilson and
Hughes promised to be so close.[33] Others, like Frank Bohn, Max Eastman,
and John Reed, put their endorsements in wholly positive terms. Un-
grudgingly, they recognized that great advancements had been made and
they did not quarrel over the instrument (a capitalist party) employed.
Indeed, Mother Jones doubted whether a Socialist president could have
improved upon Wilson's record on behalf of children, railroad workers,
and farmers. "I am a Socialist," she explained. "But I admire Wilson for
the things he has done. . . . And when a man or woman does something
for humanity I say go to him and shake him by the hand . . . and say,
'I'm for you.' "[34] Bohn and Eastman made similar arguments. "The old-
fashioned, impossible attitude on the part of some Socialists—that of hat-
ing every radical because 'he steals our thunder,' and so on—has no place
in the minds of intelligent persons in 1916," Bohn admonished dissenters.
"Let us try to use our brains freely; love progress more than party," Eastman wrote, "and see if we can get ready to play a human part in the
actual complex flow of events."[35]

According to the *Literary Digest,* the rank and file was of the same
mind. In certain parts of the country, union labor was divided between
Wilson and Benson, rather than between Wilson and Hughes. Socialists
frequently said that they preferred the President "because in the way of
actual accomplishment he can do more for the Socialists." An official of
the Western Federation of Miners reported that Wilson's labor legislation
"will cause many members to vote the Democratic ticket who would oth-

erwise vote for Benson." A member of a local of the Ladies' Garment-
Cutters' Union in Boston put it this way: "Nearest related to the workers
are the Socialists and next to the Socialists are the Democrats. Because the
Socialists are too extreme and the Republicans are too slow," most of them
were supporting the Wilson ticket. In the pivotal state of Ohio, where the
Socialist party was strong, an official of the International Association of
Machinists reported to the *Literary Digest:* "Everywhere . . . the machine-
shop workers give Wilson credit for doing more than any other President
has done." Citing the child labor bill and the Adamson Act, the inter-
viewer said "the shopmen seem to think Wilson is the best President we
ever had. . . ."[36]

All of this, of course, was only the half of it. A brother of the Painters Union of Tennessee also emphasized that Wilson should be re-elected
because he kept the country out of war—for "labor as well as all other
units of society know full well that war is only wanted by the people who
reap special dividends from their munitions and shipyard-holdings."[37] The
left-wing *Internationalist Socialist Review* struck the same note. Responding to Victor Berger's attacks on Wilson's preparedness program, that
publication told its 150,000 readers: "To howl of militarism against a president who has kept the working class of America out of war during a
hair-trigger period is a species of treachery to the working class that does
no good."[38] Max Eastman carried the argument a step further in an editorial that corresponded to House's thoughts about the implications of
Wilson's address to the League to Enforce Peace. The President would be
re-elected, Eastman predicted in late summer, but not just because "he
kept us out of war." He would win because *"he has attacked the problem
of eliminating war,* and he has not succumbed to the epidemic of militarism in its extremest forms."[39]

That point has never been established either in biographies or in
more specialized studies of Wilson's foreign policy. But Wilson made
American membership in a league of nations one of the themes of his
campaign. As he set out to win votes, he also had other goals in mind: to
persuade the belligerents that the guarantee of collective security rebutted
every reason for fighting on; and to continue, personally, what he had
begun at the New Willard Hotel—the education of the American people
on the subject of progressive internationalism.

Wilson introduced the message at the very start, in his acceptance
speech at Long Branch, New Jersey, on September 2. The speech was
quite unlike any that either Hughes or Benson would deliver. Marking
off the distance that the Democracy had traveled since 1912, Wilson argued that the party had surpassed itself and the Progressives of that time.
"An age of revolutionary change," he said, "needs new purposes and new
ideas." The United States now faced searching problems born of both the

nineteenth and the twentieth centuries. "They will require for their solution new thinking, fresh courage and resourcefulness, and in some matters
radical reconsideration." Even though Americans had not been forced to
take sides in the present awesome war, its effects could no longer be
confined to Europe. "[A] new atmosphere of justice and friendship must
be generated by means the world has never tried before. The nations of
the world must unite in joint guarantees that whatever is done to disturb
the whole world's life must first be tested in the whole world's opinion
before it is attempted. These are the new foundations the world must
build for itself, and we must play our part in the reconstruction, gener-
ously and without too much thought of our separate interests."[40]

Wilson gave his first full-fledged campaign speech about a league of
nations at Omaha, Nebraska, on October 5. Ever since 1898, he said, "we
have been caught inevitably in the net of the politics of the world." Whereas
there was now "a program for America in respect of its domestic life . . .
we have never sufficiently formulated our program for America with regard to the part she is going to play in the world. And it is imperative
that she should formulate it at once." The world was no longer divided
into little circles of interest. "The world is linked together in a common
life and interest such as humanity never saw before, and the starting of
wars can never again be a private and individual matter for the nations.
What disturbs the life of the whole world is the concern of the whole
world. And it is our duty to lend the full force of this nation—moral and
physical—to a league of nations."[41]

On October 12, in Indianapolis, Wilson attempted to relate his domestic reforms to his aspirations in foreign policy. The United States, he
said, was in the throes of rebirth. "We have been making America in
pieces for the sake of the pieces. Now, we have got to construct her entire,
for the sake of the whole and for the sake of the world, because, ladies
and gentlemen, there is a task ahead of us for which we must be very
soberly prepared. I have said, and shall say again, that, when the great
present war is over, it will be the duty of America to join with the other
nations in some kind of league for the maintenance of peace. . . . It is
now up to us to say whether we are going to play, in the world at large,
the role which the makers of this great nation boasted and predicted we
should always play among the nations of the world."[42]

Two days later, at Shadow Lawn, New Jersey, Wilson defended
American neutrality in the following terms: "What Europe is beginning
to realize is that we are saving ourselves for something greater that is to
come. We are saving ourselves in order that we may unite in that final
league of nations in which it shall be understood that there is no neutrality
where any nation is doing wrong, in that final league of nations which
must, in the Providence of God, come into the world, where nation shall

be leagued with nation in order to show all mankind that no man may lead any nation into acts of aggression without having all the other nations of the world leagued against it."[43]

Society was struggling to understand itself, he continued at Chicago on October 19, so that it could create a new instrument of civilization. And the United States could facilitate this great endeavor by infusing in international relations the qualities of mercy and sympathy, and by demonstrating to the family of nations its disinterestedness—the regenerative influence that sprang, not from the power of arms, but from "the great invisible powers that well up in the human heart." He also publicly expressed an opinion, for the first time, on a fundamentally important aspect of collective security. "There is coming a time, unless I am very much mistaken," he said, "when nation shall agree with nation that the rights of humanity are greater than the rights of sovereignty."[44]

As election day drew near, Wilson pressed his case for a league again, on October 26, in two major addresses in the great river city of Cincinnati, the home of William Howard Taft. After briefly describing the European balance-of-power system, he said: "Now, revive that after this war is over, and, sooner or later, you will have just such another war. And this is the last war of the kind, or of any kind that involves the world, that the United States can keep out of." Neutrality, then, would be impossible to maintain. "We must have a society of nations. Not suddenly, not by insistence, not by any hostile emphasis upon demand, but, by the demonstration of the needs of the time, the nations of the world must get together and say, 'Nobody can hereafter be neutral as respects the disturbance of the world's peace for an object which the world's opinion cannot sanction."[45] Later that day he reiterated the same points, with a reference to the Declaration of Independence: "Other nations owe it to a decent respect for the opinion of mankind to submit their cases to mankind before they go to war. And I believe that America is going to take pride in the days to come in offering every dollar of her wealth, every drop of her blood, every energy of her people, to the maintenance of the peace of the world upon that foundation."[46]

In his penultimate speech of the campaign, at Madison Square Garden, he spoke of his vision of international relations in the context of domestic politics and social justice. "In proportion as we defend the children, as we defend the women, as we see that the men are safe in the mines . . . will the country be triumphant in all its affairs," he told the forty thousand people assembled in the Garden. "We have formed, for the first time in recent years in this country a party of the people. We have set up government in response to the opinion of the people. . . . And as America feels her unity, she is gathering her force to play a part among the nations such as she was never able to play before. When America has found herself, then she will be able to play the part which it was destined she should play."[47]

Wilson brought his two-point message to a climax in his final campaign address, at Shadow Lawn, New Jersey. He characterized the conditions of work in many regions of the United States as "a disgrace to our civilization." He had not *given* working people anything; he had simply gone "into the fight shoulder to shoulder with them to get the rights which no man has a right to give them." He questioned whether the Republicans even wanted "to expound the real heart of the social necessities and the political exigencies of America." Wilson's coalition, in contrast, was "trying to reconstruct America along the lines of justice and equity, which cut very much deeper than any party lines." The crisis of change at home was all the more exigent, he suggested, because it had a bearing upon and mirrored the life of the world. "We have seen that, unless we could unite and direct and purify the forces of this country, we could not do what it was necessary to do for the world through the instrumentality of America." Then, he declared: "The United States will never again be what it has been." For all time, America was caught "in the great drift of humanity which is to determine the politics of every country in the world." Thus so for the decision on Tuesday next, he said in a closing peroration. The great forces of humanity were growing stronger and stronger. "In the days to come, men will no long wonder how America is going to work out her destiny, for she will have proclaimed to them that her destiny is not divided from the destiny of the world, that her purpose is justice and love of humanity."[48]

To Colonel House, Wilson's sponsorship of the league idea had an emphatic meaning. Even before the campaign had commenced, he warned Sir Edward Grey in a letter on July 15, "If the President is re-elected the people will have endorsed his position on this question and the country will stand committed to it."[49] This view was not restricted to partisan Democrats. Wilson's utterances on the league (as the epiphenomenon of his advanced progressivism) had a significant impact on progressive internationalists and, ultimately, on the election. Max Eastman's controversial remarks to the Woodrow Wilson Independent League in mid-October— about why Socialists could in good conscience vote for the administration—are a good example. Eastman had discussed, not only the President's labor policy, but also his foreign policy. "Wilson aggressively believes not only in keeping out of war, but in organizing the nations of the world to prevent war," he had said. "His official endorsement of propaganda for international federation in the interest of peace is the most important step that any President of the United States has taken towards civilizing the world since Lincoln."[50]

Two weeks later, Herbert Croly, after agonizing (by all accounts) over whom to support, finally came out for Wilson, but not solely on the grounds of Wilson's domestic record, as it is always implied in scholarly discussions of that influential editor's decision.[51] The President, Croly wrote in the October 21st issue of the *New Republic,* had "committed himself and his party to a revolutionary doctrine"—that is, to "ardent and intelligent support of the plan of international organization which has the best chance of substituting security for insecurity as the basis of international relationships." He described Wilson's campaign as "educative": "He has been gradually domesticating in the minds of the plain American people some sense of international responsibility. . . . In its net result his leadership has helped to bind the nation together, because it has been gradually squaring popular ideas about foreign policy with the facts of the American international situation. Public opinion . . . is better prepared for action than it was two years ago." Croly also attributed this apparent fact in part to "the bracing and healing effect of the administration's domestic policy." In the following issue of the *New Republic,* he added that "enormous progress" had been made in arousing American sentiment for the league, "chiefly as a consequence of President Wilson's assistance."[52]

Because of the kind of re-election campaign that Wilson waged, the proposition of American membership in a league of nations had begun to put down roots. But the young plant grew in rocky, highly politicized soil. The contest between Wilson and Hughes turned into one of the bitterest and most rancorous in American political history; and rarely have the two major parties exhibited such strong ideological differences as they did in 1916. That the league issue would acquire a vexatious partisan dimension probably became unavoidable, however, when, just as the parties launched their campaigns, conservative internationalists failed to secure even a vague endorsement of their position in the Republican party platform.

Taft had lobbied strenuously for a plank based on the ideas of the League to Enforce Peace. But Roosevelt, still personally estranged from Taft, regarded the LEP's propaganda as an "education of evil." As Taft once noted, the fact that he was president of the LEP "is like a red flag to a bull to Roosevelt."[53] Republican opinion was therefore very much divided on the question. It fell to Henry Cabot Lodge to bridge the gap. Previously, Lodge himself had expressed general approval of the LEP, or so it seemed, inasmuch as he had shared the dais with Wilson on May 27. But as William C. Widenor has demonstrated, Lodge had always harbored suspicions. Ever the vigorous proponent of the Allies and of preparedness, he believed that the future peace could be maintained only by a large army and navy, and, perhaps, by Allied-American cooperation in a "league of victors." To the extent that the LEP matched these views, he had endorsed its aims. (It should be added that Wilson's coupling of progressive internationalism with neutrality during the campaign only served to increase the senator's doubts about the desirability of a league—be it Taft's or Wilson's.)[54]

In any case, Lodge's chief concern was the presidential campaign. "My one, overwhelming desire is to beat the Wilson administration," he told Roosevelt. "I shudder to think what four years more of that crowd would mean."[55] On this score, Taft was in complete accord; he realized that any disruption provoked by the party's two titular leaders—especially a battle over foreign policy—could only damage the party's chance to recapture the White House. Hence, at Lodge's insistence and with Taft's acquiescence, the Republican platform would contain only a general statement on behalf of the principle of arbitration.[56]

Wilson's campaign, as House had predicted, deprived the Republicans of any completely serviceable issue. From child labor, rural credits, and preparedness, to Mexico, the European war, and the league idea in general, the President made the causes of advanced progressivism and, especially, peace and internationalism, his own. The situation was exacerbated by the campaign that the Republican mounted. Charles Evans Hughes, the former governor of New York and an Associate Justice of the Supreme Court, possessed impressive credentials—one wag referred to him as "Wilson with Whiskers"—and a few progressives initially applauded his nomination.[57] But Hughes proved to be a listless campaigner. Roosevelt privately dubbed him "the bearded iceberg," and William Allen White characterized the Republican ticket as "two estimable mutes . . . who could conduct nothing but a funeral."[58] More often than not, Hughes was on the defensive. Of crucial importance, his doubts about the virtues of the eight-hour day (or, rather, his hostility to it) and related domestic issues drove away probably tens of thousands of voters who feared that the Adamson Act, along with other social-justice measures, would be repealed by a Republican President and Congress.[59]

On foreign policy, it was equally difficult to determine Hughes' position. Despite occasional references to the LEP and an innocuous declaration that the United States could no longer maintain its old policy of isolation, neither he nor his supporters gave the league idea the attention that Wilson did. The one indelible impression that Hughes made on the voters—mainly because he permitted Roosevelt to campaign for him, while the Democrats chanted their peace slogan everywhere they went—was that the country was more likely to get into the war under the Republicans than under the Democrats.[60] Moreover, as the contest heated up, contempt for Wilson among Republicans grew apace. Lodge characterized the administration as "the worst Presidency this country has ever had, and I do not except Buchanan."[61] Taft, a Republican first and a sincere internationalist second, regarded Wilson as "a ruthless hypocrite . . . who has no convictions that he would not barter at once for votes."[62] What perhaps should have been more regrettable to the president of the League to Enforce Peace was the fact that, for a number of reasons, his party (and the LEP) had handed the issue of the league to Wilson and the Democrats virtually on a silver platter.

It is almost superfluous to say that the Republicans considered the outcome of the election something of a national disaster. Hughes swept the Northeast and the upper Middle West, with the exception of New Hampshire and Ohio. On election night, the *New York Times* conceded the race to the challenger and Wilson went to bed thinking about his imminent release from enormous responsibilities. But two days later, the official returns showed that Wilson had won not only the Democratic stronghold of the South, but also all the Western states, save South Dakota and Oregon. The final tally went as follows: Wilson, 9,131,511 popular votes and 277 electoral votes; Hughes, 8,548,935 popular votes and 254 electoral votes; Benson, 585,974 popular votes. The returns revealed an important personal victory for Wilson; he polled approximately 2,830,000 more votes than he had in 1912. His plurality over Hughes, however, came to only some 582,000 out of the 18,536,000 votes cast for all candidates.[63]

So close was the race in several states that any single factor could have tipped the balance one way or the other. By all estimates, labor and the farm vote proved vital to the winning coalition, particularly in Ohio, the Plains states, and the Far West.[64] As a bloc, women also were a decisive factor. Wilson carried ten (all west of the Mississippi) of the twelve woman-suffrage states; women voted for him in disproportionately large numbers because of the peace issue.[65] Contemporary analysts and historians generally agree that the key to the dramatic victory was Wilson's appeal to voters who had supported Roosevelt in 1912. Across the board, he drew at least twenty per cent of the former Progressive vote.

Significantly, however, Wilson's proportionate share of the Socialist party vote was probably far greater. Slightly over thirty-three percent of it shifted to him, or some 315,000 of the 901,000 who had supported Debs four years earlier—a figure that represented well over half of his overall margin of victory. At the local and state level, the Socialists improved their showing over 1912 by approximately 250,000. Reports of ticket-splitting at the top were common, however; and the fact that Wilson did well in states with a sizeable distribution of Socialists was crucial. For example, a switch of 1,983 votes in California (.01 per cent of all votes cast for Wilson and Hughes) would have given Hughes that state's thirteen electoral votes and thus the presidency. Wilson prevailed by attracting almost half of those 79,000 Californians who had favored Debs in 1912.[66] The

Golden State notwithstanding, if he had not made comparable inroads in New Hampshire, North Dakota, and Washington, Wilson would have lost those states' combined sixteen electoral votes as well as the national election. Literally all of Debs' 7,000 supporters of 1912 cast their ballots for Wilson in North Dakota, which gave him a plurality of 1,735; he squeaked through by fifty-six votes in New Hampshire where about a third of Debs' small bloc switched to the President; and some 17,000 of the 40,000 Socialist votes of 1912 moved to Wilson's column in Washington, where he bested Hughes by 16,000 out of approximately 380,000 votes cast.[67]

There were similar trends in other parts of the country as well. According to Charles P. Taft, the ex-President's brother and owner of the Cincinnati *Times-Star,* Wilson owed his victory in Ohio (an electoral college prize of twenty-four) to the Socialist vote: "The President was radical enough to catch the extreme radical vote without being so radical as to drive away many moderates who on general lines favored his policies," Mr. Taft explained. Wilson won about 52,000 of those Ohioans (sixty per cent of his edge over Hughes) who had previously gone for Debs. The current ran in the same direction in Missouri, where Socialists made up about half of Wilson's margin.[68] Two independent reports—one by William English Walling and another by the New York *Evening Sun*—confirmed massive ticket-splitting in New York City; Socialists supported local party candidates but voted in the thousands for Wilson (albeit not enough for him to carry the state).[69] J. A. H. Hopkins, a leader of the Progressive party and a good friend of Wilson's, reported an identical pattern in New Jersey, at the rate of thirty per cent.[70] In Minneapolis, both Wilson and the Socialist candidate for mayor split an unexpectedly large number of ballots. Statewide, Wilson reduced the Debs bloc of 27,505 votes by 7,388. Had he succeeded in attracting another 196 Socialists, he would have carried Minnesota.[71]

In the context of the politics and diplomacy of the previous two years as well as of the nature of the campaign itself, we can assume that the implications of the returns were too awful for all Republicans and many conservative internationalists to contemplate. For their part, advanced progressives, socialists, and certainly all progressive internationalists had as much reason to rejoice as the right had to grieve. They and their triumphant, like-minded President had not merely checked the reactionaries; they had presided over the creation of a left-of-center coalition that now seemed to hold the balance of political power in the United States. At the very least, as so many pundits noted, Wilson had fulfilled William Jennings Bryan's dream of uniting the West and the South.[72] Eastman acknowledged the birth of "the state capitalistic social reform party"; it was hardly a revolutionary party, but "its attack on the plutocracy was genuine and important," he said. "It was the clearest line-up we have had in

American politics."[73] One of Wilson's colleagues in the moribund Progressive party suggested that he had built the foundations for an entirely new party "to sweep the country clean"—a Progressive Democracy augmented by elements of the Socialist party.[74]

Precisely what such conclusions portended for future domestic struggles could hardly be predicted. As for foreign policy, however, the election had surely sharpened the conflict imbedded in the diverse political configurations of the American internationalist movement. The participation of the United States in a league of nations now seemed a much greater likelihood; yet, in retrospect, the most compelling fact was that circumstances surrounding the election had, if anything, dimmed the prospects for bipartisan support for a league some two years before actual membership impended. Likewise, with regard to Europe, Wilson's electoral success had emboldened the league movement in Great Britain; but that movement, too, was far from united in purpose. Moreover, the Allied governments remained implacable in their opposition to ending the war on Wilson's terms.

Even so, the campaign of 1916 was the prelude to a new era in the history of international relations. By election day, Wilson had thrust the proposition of a league of nations into the vortex of political debate on both sides of the Atlantic. The American electorate had reconfirmed the new leader of the internationalist movement, who, in the course of his campaign, had implicitly committed his administration to pursuing the concept and cause of collective security. In this fact alone, Wilson's reelection marked the first important culmination in the quest for a new world order based on the League of Nations.

The American people had traveled a great distance since 1912. The legislative record the Wilson administration had achieved by the late summer of 1916 represented a watershed in American social and political history. Those four years also heralded the primacy of foreign affairs in the life of the nation. The United States, unlike any other major power, now had begun to weigh and to champion the New Diplomacy. The origins of this profound conjunction of events were manifold. From the strictly Wilsonian standpoint, they lay in his administration's prewar efforts on behalf of arbitration and conciliation, disarmament, and economic cooperation among nations. These aims further crystalized as Wilson gained experience in hemispheric diplomacy and as the magnitude and significance of the Great War became clearer to him. In his mind, the European conflict illustrated the utter necessity of establishing instrumentalities that, in addition to securing peace, would also insure the right of self-determination for all peoples and "a decent respect for the opinion of mankind" by the major governments of the world.

In all of this, it would be misleading to portray a solitary Wilson, imperturbably rolling over in his mind political systems and possible solutions to the world crisis. As several historians have pointed out, he was indebted to the formulations of the British radicals;[75] but the British radical influence has perhaps been exaggerated. Wilson owed his greatest debt to the American progressive internationalists—the advance guard of the New Diplomacy in the United States and the impassioned proponents of a fledgling, Americanized version of social democracy. The American political origins of the New Diplomacy lay in the intellectual communion that Wilson and the American left and liberal-left had carried on together, and that was now manifested in the unusual political coalition that had just elected him to a second term. Out of the hybrid of liberal and socialist perspectives had blossomed Wilson's formula for a community of nations as well as a program for social and economic justice at home. Perhaps more important than anything else, the progressive internationalists had helped Wilson to grasp the fact—which his own experience and independent thinking corroborated—that the opponents of domestic reform and the advocates of militarism, imperialism, and balance-of-power politics were twins born of the same womb.

At the same time, Wilson's distinctive contribution should not be underestimated. He had become the touchstone by which progressive internationalist ideas acquired force and legitimacy. Because of him, conservative proponents of the league as well as the center-right opposition in both America and Europe would have to reckon with potentially revolutionary concepts in international relations. No one, then, who had voted either for or against Wilson, or who had watched the proceedings from afar, could fail to see the deeper meaning of the politics of 1916. "[I]f public education is equal to the strain of understanding what the President is trying to do, he may accomplish a service perhaps larger than any other president," Amos Pinchot submitted. "For the President we re-elected has raised a new flag, or, at all events, a flag that no other president has thought or perhaps dared to raise. It is the flag of internationalism."[76] The United States, as Wilson himself had declared on the eve of his victory, would never again be what it had been.

7

"All the Texts of the Rights of Man"

Manifestoes for Peace and War

A few days after Wilson's re-election, his greatest admirer among British journalists declared that in the next few years the United States would become "the single greatest political potentiality on earth." This was so, wrote A. G. Gardiner, because the President was struggling toward a conception of a society of nations. Gardiner praised Wilson's unrewarded efforts to construct such a community in the Western Hemisphere and even went so far as to defend American neutrality. If the great powers of Europe could only be brought to see their own self-interest, those policies might, in the end, "bring all the nations into this world society, regulated by law and backed by force which alone can make the rule of law valid." This was "the only vision that makes the future thinkable."[1]

Gardiner's praise of Wilson's higher purpose, however, overlooked the absence of any concrete achievements on behalf of that purpose. By November 1916, the Pan-American Pact had slipped beyond resuscitation, and the belligerents stood no closer to peace than they had two years before. Yet Wilson—imbued with the ideas of progressive internationalism, in the grip of intellectual metamorphosis, and acutely aware of the historical moment—was the first major statesman to commit his government to the pursuit of a league of nations; soon, while the United States remained a neutral, he would become the first statesman to articulate a

comprehensive synthesis of progressive internationalism—a New Diplomacy based upon the principles of the equality of nations, self-determination, the peaceful settlement of disputes, freedom of the seas, disarmament, and collective security.

Wilson's re-election meant different things to different people. To A.
G. Gardiner, it represented something akin to the salvation of Europe. To
Theodore Roosevelt and Henry Cabot Lodge, it signaled the diminution
of the character of the American people and perhaps (through Wilson's
spineless neutrality) the destruction of Western European civilization, if
the United States acquiesced in a German victory. Wilson himself could
interpret the election as a referendum on neutrality and, by reasonable
inference, on the desirability of both a negotiated settlement of the war
and the establishment of a league of nations to maintain that settlement.
At the same time, Wilson fully realized that Germany shared the bouquet
for the happy circumstance that had facilitated the slogan, "He Kept Us
Out of War." Although he was content to have his managers run with it,
Wilson, personally, never felt comfortable with such prating; any little
German lieutenant, he knew, at any moment could throw the country
into an irremediable crisis by some unexpected outrage on the high seas.
Thus, strengthened by the electoral mandate for peace, he was now determined to force a compromise in Europe. As before, he believed that the
most alluring inducement he could offer the belligerents was the promise
of postwar collective security. Conversely, he was no less resolute in the
conviction that a military standoff was essential to the creation of a peacekeeping organization. During the few remaining months before the war
would engulf the United States, in Wilson's thought and diplomacy the
quest for a negotiated peace and a league of nations became symbiotically
linked.

On November 10, 1916, Theobald von Bethmann Hollweg, the German
Chancellor, addressed the Reichstag and pledged that Germany would
cooperate to establish a peace league after the war in order to prevent the
recurrence of another monstrous catastrophe. "Germany is at all times
ready to join a league of nations," he said; "yes, even to place herself at
the head of such a league—to keep in check the disturbers of the peace."[2]
Bethmann's declaration may have been, as the *New Republic* asserted, "the
most momentous and encouraging utterance" made by any belligerent
spokesman since the beginning of the war.[3] But the speech was motivated
by a number of considerations. Bethmann was responding in part to growing
restiveness among Social Democrats in the Reichstag and, it was said, to
Wilson's campaign speeches about the league (in particular, the ones he
had made in Cincinnati).[4] Bethmann's appearance before the Reichstag
amounted to a public invitation to Wilson to resume his mediatorial efforts.

The German government was receptive to a negotiated settlement for the same reasons that the Allies opposed it—that is, because the Central Powers now commanded the Continent from northern France to Eastern Europe. Bethmann also sought Wilson's help because he did not know how much longer he would be able to withstand renewed pressure from within the German High Command to reinstitute unrestricted submarine warfare; this, he feared, would mean war with the United States. Already he had instructed Count von Bernstorff to explore the possibilities with Colonel House, and to indicate that Germany would be willing to evacuate Belgium and France as a first step.[5]

The Allies, meanwhile, once again had indicated their unchanging view of mediation even as Wilson was making his campaign speeches on the League. On September 28, David Lloyd George, Great Britain's war minister, told the press that, until Prussian despotism was crushed, outside interference would not be tolerated. "Peace now or at any time before the final and complete elimination of this menace is unthinkable," he avowed. "The fight must be to the finish—to a knockout."[6] Since that time, nothing had passed between London and Washington to indicate a change of heart.

In the circumstances, Wilson told House, on November 14, that he was prepared to send a note to all of the belligerents and demand that the war cease. He must act soon if the United States were to avoid drifting into war over the submarine issue, and in such a way as to persuade the Allies that, through his offices, they could obtain everything that they claimed to be fighting for.[7]

Before writing the note itself, Wilson composed a lengthy prolegomenon, an eloquent indictment of the balance-of-power system, which he never sent and never showed to anyone. "War before this one used to be a sort of national excursion . . . with brilliant battles lost and won, national heroes decorated, and all sharing in the glory accruing to the state," he wrote. "But can this vast, gruesome contest of systematized destruction . . . be pictured in that light . . . wherein the big, striking thing for the imagination to respond to was untold human suffering? . . . Where is any longer the glory commensurate with the sacrifice of the millions of men required in modern warfare to carry and defend Verdun?"[8]

The actual draft of the peace note was more restrained; but it, too, revealed the progressive's despair over a holocaust that humankind never previously imagined possible.[9] After reading it, both Colonel House and Secretary Lansing argued that the introduction—which placed the war aims of all the belligerents on the same plane—would enrage the Allies. House recommended that Wilson explicitly state that he was not attempting to impose mediation and later suggested that the House-Grey Memorandum be activated instead.[10] Wilson spurned that idea as obsolete. If necessary, he would use coercion to compel the Allies to come to the peace table. Shortly after he finished the draft of his peace note, he instigated a formal warning from the Federal Reserve Board to American bankers against making any further unsecured loans to the Allies.[11] During the next weeks, the troubled, chain-smoking Lansing fretted openly—House was far subtler—over the possibility of Germany's acceptance and England's rejection of the President's overture. "Would it not be a calamity for the nation, and for all mankind?" he asked Wilson.[12]

There were, however, other voices to counter Lansing's. On December 2, Wilson received an advance copy of "An Open Letter to Americans" by Charles P. Trevelyan, radical pacifist of the Union of Democratic Control and a Member of Parliament. "My countrymen do not see that your approval of the League of Peace amounts to an American cooperation in the objects for which they profess to be fighting—a secure civilization," Trevelyan wrote. "Sooner or later your espousal of that plan will affect the course of the war. It will shorten it." Trevelyan also appealed personally to Wilson to remind him of his standing in world opinion. "However much you try to influence Prime Ministers and Chancellors, it is far more important that your great, sane policy should be heard and understood by peoples," he wrote. "I am certain you can evoke the spirit that will make mediation possible."[13] These were welcome words. "That was a most impressive letter from Mr. Trevelyan," Wilson wrote to House. "The time is near at hand for *something!*"[14]

As Wilson polished his peace note, new political developments in Great Britain brought about the downfall of the Asquith-Grey government and the formation of a center-right coalition, on December 7. Lloyd George was now Prime Minister, and Arthur James Balfour became Foreign Secretary; neither was enthusiastic about a league of nations.[15] On the following day, in Germany, Kaiser Wilhelm listened to his advisers debate the potential advantages of a negotiated peace versus victory through expanded undersea operations. The outcome was that Bethmann Hollweg would be permitted one final peace initiative—which he took on December 12—while the Navy was to prepare for submarine warfare against all vessels in the event that the Chancellor's move failed.[16]

Wilson dispatched his own peace note on December 18, the first instance in which he directly thrust himself into the politics of the war. It began by calling attention to the fact that the *apparent* objects of the belligerent governments were "virtually the same." His review of their stated objects emphasized that each side was "ready to consider the formation of a league of nations to ensure peace and justice throughout the world." But, he beseeched them, the war had to be ended now so that "millions upon millions of lives will not continue to be sacrificed . . . and lest, more than all, an injury be done civilization itself which can never be atoned for or repaired." The President was not proposing peace, or even offering to mediate. He was simply requesting a direct statement of terms—earnest soundings that might reveal "how near the haven of peace we may be for which all mankind longs with an intense and increasing longing."[17]

Because it was the first official, public statement that suggested that the United States was willing to join a postwar peacekeeping organization, Wilson's note set off the first important debate on the league issue to take place on the floor of the Senate. On December 21, the day that Wilson's peace note was published, Senator Gilbert M. Hitchcock, Democrat of Nebraska, introduced a resolution endorsing the President's action.[18] Over the next few days, several Republican senators—including Henry Cabot Lodge, Jacob H. Gallinger of New Hampshire, and the progressive William E. Borah of Idaho—rose to speak against the measure. While they did not necessarily object to Wilson's request for a statement of terms, Lodge, in particular, accused the White House of partiality toward Germany and indicated that he did not want to find the United States suddenly ranged against the side that he personally believed was "fighting the battle of freedom and democracy as against military autocracy."[19] The senator and his fellow Republicans were also alarmed in this instance by the implied commitment to membership in a league of nations. This commitment constituted an irrevocable break with tradition, Lodge said. It meant the abandonment of the venerable policy "of confining ourselves to our own hemisphere, and makes us part of the political system of another hemisphere." How much, he wanted to know, would such a sweeping change interfere with the security and sovereignty of the United States? Would it not shatter the Monroe Doctrine, the bulwark that had repelled European encroachments for nearly a century?[20] These were all important and legitimate questions that Wilson had yet to answer satisfactorily.

Lodge's arguments were not based on isolationist sentiments. Intellectually, his objections stemmed from his own unilateralist approach to internationalism, which countenanced few of the restrictions on American freedom of action that Wilson's references to the league seemed to entail; but, perhaps more important at this juncture, he took exception to the league because Wilson had attached the proposal to an "inconclusive peace." In any event, the Senate passed an amended version of Hitchcock's resolution by a vote of forty-eight to seventeen (with Lodge among the latter) and thirty-one abstentions. The resolution simply endorsed Wilson's call for a statement of peace terms.[21]

Although the senatorial discord was a portent of what lay beyond the horizon, it was drowned out by acclaim for the peace note.[22] In official European circles, however, it was quite another matter. Again, as in the case of his address to the League to Enforce Peace, Wilson's assimilation

of the belligerents' motives incensed the Allied governments and most of
the Allied press. Ambassador Page used the words "sorrow," "anger," and
"disappointment" to describe the mood in London. James Bryce was "pro-
foundly depressed" when he sought out the ambassador. Asquith could
not bring himself to discuss Wilson's note with anyone. The King, reportedly, wept. The UDC, Page wrote, was the "only section of opinion
that is pleased."[23]

Much like the great majority of the Allied press—which accused
Wilson of working hand-in-glove with the Central Powers—the Pan-Ger-
man press asserted that the President was seeking to rob the Fatherland
of deserved victory. Many leaders within the German High Command,
including the Kaiser, shared this view. Nonetheless, Germany avowed its
willingness both to confer with the enemy and to cooperate with the United
States in the "sublime task" of establishing a peace league.[24]

The German response was less important for what it said than for
what it did not say; that is, it did not indicate specific terms under which
the Central Powers would agree to negotiate. This evasiveness allowed
the Allied governments to reject Bethmann's peace note of December 12
as insincere. To enter into a conference without knowing exactly what
Germany was proposing "is to put our heads into a noose with the rope
end in the hands of Germany," Lloyd George assured the House of Commons.[25] Of course, the Allies could not so easily dismiss Wilson's request
for terms. They would, indeed, respond with a list of specifics—and with
some assistance from the American Secretary of State.

On the day that Wilson's note was published, Lansing was almost
prostrate with worry that the President would permanently alienate the
Allies. "When we go into the war," he had written in his diary on December 3, "we *must* go in on the side of the Allies."[26] Suddenly he took
it upon himself to tell the press that the note was not, in fact, a peace
note; it was merely an effort to learn exactly what the belligerents' aims
were because the United States was "drawing nearer the verge of war
itself."[27]

Lansing's statement set off an explosion that reverberated from
Washington to Wall Street. When Wilson first learned of it, he considered
firing Lansing on the spot. He relented, however, at this delicate juncture,
and simply ordered him to issue a public retraction on the following day.[28]
But this was not the only nail that Lansing had driven into the coffin. On
December 20 and 21, he had conferred with the British and French ambassadors and recommended that the Allies respond to the note by demanding the return of Alsace-Lorraine to France, an indemnity for France,
Belgium, and Serbia, and the democratization of Germany—in short, terms
that only the victor could impose on the vanquished.[29]

Arthur S. Link has characterized this attempted sabotage as "one of the most egregious acts of treachery in American history."[30] Be that as it may, the Allies were capable of framing a reply—without instructions from Lansing—calculated to thwart Wilson and to encourage Germany to revert to unrestricted submarine warfare (which is what the Secretary of State hoped would happen). In any event, when the Allies responded on January 10, 1917, their terms included all of Lansing's suggestions, as well as a obligatory expression on behalf of a postwar league of nations.[31]

In the meantime, Colonel House had prevailed upon Count von Bernstorff to find out whether Berlin would be willing to reveal to Wilson, in strictest confidence, its specific terms, thus enabling the President to begin mediation.[32] This breakthrough caused Wilson to believe that the elusive goal was within reach. While awaiting Bethmann's reply to von Bernstorff, as well as the Allies' response to his own note of December 18, he came to a momentous decision. After twenty-nine months of neutrality, he would finally explain to the peoples of the world what he believed the general terms of the settlement ought to be—the kind of peace which the United States would be willing to uphold. This, Wilson's climactic attempt to end the war, would beget the most important American pronouncement on international relations since the Monroe Doctrine—the supreme progressive internationalist synthesis and the basis of all of Wilson's state papers thereafter.

Wilson discussed his idea with House on January 3. "We thought that the main principle he should lay down was the right of nations to determine under what governments they should continue to live," the Colonel recorded in his diary. "The keystone to the settlement arch," they agreed, should be "the future security of the world against wars and letting territorial adjustments be subordinate to the main purpose." "You are now playing with what the poker players term 'the blue chips,'" House said.[33]

Most senators were taken by surprise on January 22 when Vice President Marshall announced at noon that, within the hour, the President would make a personal communication to them concerning foreign affairs. Not since George Washington had any president addressed a formal session of that body. Senators rushed to take their seats and members of the lower house packed the gallery and the back of the chamber. According to the *New York Times,* as Wilson spoke, the entire audience leaned forward in solemn, strained attention so as not to miss a word.[34]

Since the parties to the Great War had replied to his recent request for a statement of terms, he began, they were all that much closer to peace discussions. It was, therefore, his duty to disclose to the council associated with him in the final determination of foreign policy his thoughts and purposes in regard to the foundations of the anticipated settlement.

The creation of a league of nations, he declared, was the one essential element of the peace to come: "In every discussion of the peace that must end this war it is taken for granted that peace must be followed by some definite concert of power which will make it virtually impossible that any such catastrophe should ever overwhelm us again." It was "inconceivable that the people of the United States should play no part in that great enterprise." This was the destiny they had sought to prepare themselves for since the Founding Fathers. He then went a step further, in an expansion of his previous comment, which was informed by the Pan-American Pact: "No covenant of cooperative peace that does not include the peoples of the New World can suffice to keep the future safe against war." Together, the Americas would lend "their power to the authority and force of other nations to guarantee peace and justice throughout the world." To this he added a vigorous brief on behalf of collective security, reminiscent of his justification of preparedness to the American Union Against Militarism: "It will be absolutely necessary that a force be created as guarantor of the permanency of the settlement so much greater than the force of any nation now engaged or any alliance hitherto formed . . . that no nation, no probable combination of nations could face or withstand it." The peace must be made secure "by the organized major force of mankind."

Wilson then turned to an analysis of the basic structural causes of the European conflict. "Is the present war a struggle for a just and secure peace, or only for a new balance of power? If it be only for a new balance of power, who will guarantee, who can guarantee, the stable equilibrium of the new arrangement?" he asked. "There must be, not a balance of power, but a community of power; not organized rivalries, but an organized common peace." If, as the belligerents had repeatedly claimed, neither side wished to crush the other, then the peace must be "a peace without victory." A decision by arms would mean peace forced on the loser, "accepted in humiliation, under duress, at an intolerable sacrifice, and would leave a sting, a resentment, a bitter memory upon which terms of peace would rest, not permanently, but only as upon quicksand. Only a peace between equals can last."

He then outlined the basic principles upon which both the peace and a league must stand. They constituted his version of the New Diplomacy. First, "the equality of nations . . . must be an equality of rights; the guarantees exchanged must neither recognize nor imply a difference between big nations and small, between those that are powerful and those that are weak." Second, no peace could last "which does not recognize and accept the principle that governments derive all their just powers from the consent of the governed, and that no right anywhere exists to hand peoples from sovereignty to sovereignty as if they were property. . . . Any peace which does not recognize and accept this principle will inevitably be upset." Third, every people, so far as practicable, should be assured an outlet to the sea. "Freedom of the seas is the *sine qua non* of peace, equality and cooperation." Fourth, "there can be no sense of safety and of equality among nations if great and preponderating armaments are henceforth to continue here and there to be built up and maintained." The question of armaments, he said, was "the most immediately and intensely practical question connected with the future fortunes of nations and of mankind."

As if to answer some of his Republican critics, Wilson characterized his proposals as the logical culmination of, rather than a departure from, American diplomatic tradition. "I am proposing, as it were, that the nations should with one accord adopt the doctrine of President Monroe as the doctrine of the world: that no nation should seek to extend its polity over any other nation or people, but that every people should be left free to determine its own polity, its own way of development, unhindered, unthreatened, unafraid, the little along with the great and powerful. . . . There is no entangling alliance in a concert of power. . . .

"These are American principles, American policies," he said in conclusion. "We could stand for no other. And they are also the principles and policies of forward-looking men and women everywhere, of every modern nation, of every enlightened community. They are the principles of mankind and must prevail."[35]

A sharp round of applause broke the momentary silence after Wilson finished speaking. Virtually every Democrat and a significant number of Republicans gave the President unstinting praise. "It was the greatest message of the century," exclaimed Senator John F. Shafroth of Colorado, on behalf of the Democrats. "We have just passed through a very important hour in the life of the world," said Senator La Follette, who led the applause from the other side of the aisle.[36] William Howard Taft stated that adherents of the League to Enforce Peace could "rejoice sincerely."[37] Several senators who previously held doubts about the league admitted that they were now completely won over. Others, however, described Wilson's proposals as utopian, presumptuous, and impracticable. One Republican remarked, "The President thinks he is President of the whole world"; while another quipped that the address "will make Don Quixote wish he hadn't died so soon." Senator Lodge declined immediate comment. "Peace without victory," Roosevelt said a week later, "is the natural ideal of the man who is too proud to fight."[38]

Partisan critics notwithstanding, Wilson's "Peace Without Victory" address met with the same response from every quarter as did his address to the League to Enforce Peace and his peace note. This time, however, in the United States, the superlatives and comparisons with the Declaration of Independence were all the more excessive. "The President's great-

est utterance," the *New York Times* said, served notice to all the world
that "in the great adjustments at the end of the war our views must be
consulted, our interests must have representation."[39] Herbert Croly told
Colonel House that "it was the greatest event in his own life" and wrote
to Wilson to say that the address "will reverberate throughout history."
The *New Republic*'s editorials were only slightly less fulsome.[40]

On behalf of the American Union Against Militarism, Lillian Wald,
Oswald Garrison Villard, Paul Kellogg, and Amos Pinchot stated that
Wilson had rendered "a service to all humanity which it is impossible to
exaggerate." To their minds, the address was "destined to an immortality
as glorious as that of the Gettysburg Address." Wilson's pronouncements
on the league and his call for peace without victory, they continued, would
penetrate "every American town and hamlet" as well as the "silent mass
of mankind."[41] Max Eastman, upon reflection, was not to be outdone by
his liberal friends in the AUAM. "I believe that the histories of the nations of the world will hold a venerated record of President Wilson's
address to the Senate," he said in the *Masses*. As one of the few commentators to point out that it was significantly different from the program of
the League to Enforce Peace, Eastman added (in perhaps the most amazing assessment of all) that Wilson's formulation was "the one hope of
preserving that struggle for a new civilization which we call Socialism, or
Syndicalism, or the Social Revolution, or the Labor Struggle, from the
continual corruption of militarism, and the ravaging set-back of patriotic
war."[42] If any doubts had lingered in their minds, Wilson had surely
vindicated and even enhanced the faith that progressive internationalists
of all persuasions had reposed in him in November.

Since Wilson's address was not a formal diplomatic communication,
none of the belligerent governments gave out a formal response. But the
British government's attitude was well represented by Viscount Bryce.
Wilson's goals were admirable, he wrote to Colonel House, but unattain-
able so long as Germany remained a militarist autocracy. In the Allied
press, the opinion was the same, though much less friendly in tone. Likewise, in Germany, many commentators noted the impartiality of Wilson's
statements, but doubted their practicability, especially in view of the Allies' announcement of uncompromising war aims on January 10. Others
more critical were rankled by Wilson's presumption that he could parcel
out the whole of Europe, and wondered who had asked him for his views
in the first place.[43]

How Wilson could have expected, at this time, to achieve the kind
of peace he had outlined is difficult to fathom in light of the previous
succession of rebuffs that he had met with, and considering what he knew
about the belligerents' ambitions. But, as he wrote to John Palmer Gavit,
"the real people I was speaking to was *[sic]* neither the Senate nor foreign
governments, as you will realize, but the *people* of the countries now at

war."[44] From this perspective, in Europe (and, as we have seen, in the United States), he had achieved a great deal. On January 26, the French Socialist party registered "with joy the admirable message of President Wilson" and asked that the French Government "instantly and clearly declare its agreement with Wilson's noble words of reason." When the "Peace Without Victory" address was read aloud to the annual conference of the British Labour party, the delegates stood and cheered Wilson's name for five minutes. Previously, this important group, unfaltering in its support for the war, had repudiated the goals of the Union of Democratic Control and the radical Independent Labour party; but now, Labour joined with the radicals and unanimously passed a resolution calling for "the formation of an international League to enforce the Maintenance of Peace on the plan advocated by the President of the United States."[45] And from the foreign ministry in Petrograd came word, on January 26, that Russia, reeling after two and a half years of savage blows from the German and Austrian armies, embraced Wilson's program in its entirety.[46] (All of these developments transpired within two days.) Thus Wilson's address had opened the floodgates of an ensuing international debate on war aims— in spite of the obduracy of the belligerent governments themselves—and caused the first cracks in the political truces within and among the Allied countries.

As a peace move, "Peace Without Victory" failed. Nonetheless, Wilson had drawn the attention of practically the entire world to the fact that the warring nations, in their responses to his peace note, had joined the United States in a commitment to the proposition of collective security. The creation of some kind of league of nations at the conclusion of the war now seemed a virtual certainty. Most significant of all, however, the address marked the first time that any statesman of stature had launched such a penetrating critique of European imperialism, militarism, and balance-of-power politics. In their stead, Wilson had called for a "community of nations," sustained by general disarmament, self-determination, freedom of the seas, and collective security. The chief instrumentality of this new world order to supersede the old system was to be a "League of Nations." Thus, Wilson had spoken to every major issue and had offered an answer to every important question the war had raised, or would raise. With this grand synthesis of progressive internationalism, forged in the struggle for neutrality, Wilson began his ascent to a position of central importance in the history of international relations in the twentieth century. The "Peace Without Victory" address was *the* Wilsonian manifesto of the Great War.

Even as Wilson digested the voluminous commentary on his address, the irony of fate was overtaking his exertions with cruel indifference. On January 9, the pro-submarine faction within the German High Command had become a majority. Wilhelm's advisers argued that the Allies had demonstrated their true intentions in their responses to both Wilson's and Bethmann Hollweg's peace notes; only by making war on ships of every flag could victory be Germany's, and the war would be over before the United States would have a chance to affect the outcome.

Count von Bernstorff received word of this drastic change of policy on January 20, but kept it to himself. On January 26, Colonel House told the ambassador of a letter Wilson had written him just two days before: "If Germany really wants peace she can get it, and get it soon, *if she will but confide in me and let me have a chance.*"[47] Bernstorff apparently was moved, and made a last, vain attempt to convince his superiors in Berlin of the wisdom of mediation. By then, however, Germany's sizable fleet of long-range submarines had already steamed to their positions, beyond the point of recall. Moreover, British intelligence had intercepted the Foreign Office's previous instructions to Bernstorff; the Allies had only to pay lip service to Wilson and wait for an incident to occur that would bring on war between the United States and Germany. Bernstorff's attempt to blunt the effect of the new submarine policy was all for naught: when, at the designated time, he was to inform the American government of the new conditions of war, he was told that he could also tell Wilson, in confidence, of the terms under which Germany would have been willing to enter into negotiations if the Allies had accepted Bethmann's peace proposal of December 12. In addition, the ambassador should encourage Wilson to continue his efforts, but the President should know—and, in this, Wilhelm was adamant—that he would not be welcome to participate even if he were able to bring a peace conference about. Bernstorff delivered the grim message to Lansing on January 31.[48]

Wilson paced the floor and rearranged his books as he and House discussed the situation on the following day. House openly advocated a policy that had been in the back of his mind for so long—the severance of diplomatic relations with Germany. On February 2, the Cabinet concurred in House's judgment: Germany's unqualified decision left him no choice. Yet, when he announced the diplomatic break before Congress on February 3, Wilson expressed the hope that Germany would not actually sink American ships. While pursuing a policy of "armed neutrality," Wilson continued to work for a negotiated peace in the belief that justice could be done only if the conflict ended in a draw.[49]

Events in February and March did not bode well for Wilson or armed neutrality. On February 25, a German U-boat sank the British passenger liner *Laconia* without warning and with the loss of two American lives. On the following day, Wilson learned of a fantastic secret plot in which Arthur Zimmermann, the German Secretary of State for Foreign Affairs, had attempted to induce Mexico to declare war on the United States in the event of war between Germany and the United States, with the "lost provinces" of Arizona, New Mexico, and Texas as bait. In light of the recent history of Mexican-American relations, the Germans could not have made a more unfortunate choice of countries with which to conspire. Not even the resumption of unrestricted submarine warfare disturbed Wilson as much; the Zimmermann Note virtually shattered his confidence in Germany's good intentions. When the plot was made public under blazing headlines on March 1, the reaction rivaled the uproar that had accompanied the sinking of the *Lusitania.* Then, in mid-March, German submarines, after having sunk hundreds of thousands of tons of Allied vessels, demonstrated the frailty of armed neutrality by sending to the bottom three American merchant ships—the *City of Memphis,* the *Illinois,* and the *Vigilancia.* On March 20, the Cabinet unanimously recommended full-fledged belligerency.[50] "He is to be for recognizing war and taking hold of the situation in such a fashion as will eventually lead to an Allies' victory over Germany," the Secretary of the Interior wrote of the President on April 1. "But he goes unwillingly."[51]

Although Wilson had not abandoned his cherished goals, from the moment that he announced the break with Germany on February 3, the progressive internationalist movement was hurled onto the horns of a dilemma and suffered wounds from which it would never completely recover. It was one thing for Theodore Roosevelt's organ, the *Outlook* (along with countless other publications), to demand war during the week of March 14.[52] It was quite another for the *New Republic,* a month earlier, to have characterized Germany's war against the Allies as "a war against the civilization of which we are a part." With an almost mystical faith that the means would not alter the ends, that fount of progressivism asserted that, by joining in the "the defense of the Atlantic world," the United States "would weight it immeasurably in favor of liberalism and make the organization of a league of peace an immediately practical object of statesmanship."[53]

Yet, until at least the end of February—before intrigue in Mexico and the sinking of American ships changed public attitudes—it was the more radical and pacifistic elements of the progressive internationalist movement who seemed to speak for the majority of Americans. As if to counter the *New Republic,* Paul Kellogg coincidentally wrote in the *Survey's* issue of February 17 that the United States was now "the world's only great reservoir of good will and resource for the generous purposes of reconstruction." Go in now, he warned, and that, and much more, would be lost forever.[54] Leading members of the AUAM, the Women's Peace party, the Socialist party, and not a few Democrats marshaled their collective energies to prevent "ignominious eleventh-hour participation in a struggle for mastery that is not our own." On February 12, they staged a march on Washington. Other great antiwar rallies (matched by equally well subscribed pro-interventionist congregations) were held in major cities throughout the country. In Philadelphia, James Maurer called for a general strike in the event of a declaration of war. The AUAM took out full-page ads in major newspapers on behalf of continued armed neutrality and democracy at home.[55] On February 28, Wilson received 150 delegates of the newly formed Emergency Peace Federation, headed by Louis Lochner, Jane Addams, and Emily Balch. That same afternoon he met with a delegation from the AUAM, led by Lillian Wald and Amos Pinchot, and listened to a moving memorial on behalf of forbearance by Max Eastman.[56]

Leaders of the AUAM probably realized that they could not indefinitely hold back the surging interventionist tide when principled colleagues in their ranks struggled with their own souls. In late February, Rabbi Stephen Wise, sweat streaming down his face, told the AUAM's executive committee that triumphant Prussianism posed a greater threat to democratic and progressive internationalist values than any possible consequences of American belligerency. By the end of March, many prominent Socialist party members, including William English Walling, Charles Edward Russell, and Upton Sinclair, had come to the same conclusion. It is no wonder that Lillian Wald was moved to write to Wilson's private secretary: "Our anxieties are with the President. His friends hardly sleep at night or rest by day in their ardent desire to help him sustain his high moral plane and to keep out of the war."[57]

There is no direct evidence that reveals why Wilson decided to lead the country into war. To be sure, a number of cumulative influences weighed upon him. Arthur S. Link has suggested that the *immediate* factors that shaped his decision were twofold: Germany's flagrant assault upon American lives and property, and the Zimmermann Note. Together they caused him to lose all faith in the intentions of the German government. Link further concludes that Wilson chose war because he believed that the European conflict was in its final stages and that American intervention would hasten its end; but that he did not chose war because he regarded the Allied cause as altogether just and Central Powers' cause as altogether unjust. Rather, he believed that American belligerency would insure his place at the peace conference at the end of the war and thereby guarantee a liberal settlement and American participation in a league of nations.[58] In the opinion of this writer, the latter considerations—and especially the promise of a league of nations—were the crucial factors in Wilson's decision, once Germany demonstrated its intention to prosecute submarine warfare without quarter.

On February 11, long before Wilson had made up his mind, Lloyd

George conveyed a personal message to the President through Ambassador Page. The Prime Minister wanted the United States to enter the war, not simply to help in the fighting, but to help in the peace-making. "The President's presence at the peace conference is necessary for the proper organization of the world," he insisted. "Nobody therefore can have so commanding a voice. . . . Convey to him this deep conviction of mine. He must help make peace if the peace made at the conference is to be worth keeping. American participation would enable him to be there and the mere effect of his participation would shorten the war, might even end it very quickly."[59]

Wilson well understood the underlying motive behind the Prime Minister's plea; he had no illusions about the purported virtues of Allied war aims. (In fact, Lloyd George had not even begun to think seriously about a league of nations.) But others in Great Britain who genuinely shared Wilson's outlook—including the leaders of the UDC—cultivated the nobler idea quite persuasively. For instance, as early as November 1916, Norman Angell sent the President a lengthy memorandum on the subject. Wilson's professions of unconcern with the causes and objects of the war were illogical, he argued, for they contradicted his other avowed convictions. The United States *was* involved in the war by sheer force of circumstance, and it should not permit itself to drift into hostilities simply as a result of some humiliation inflicted by a belligerent. Theoretically, Wilson's neutrality was unsound—it had been all along, if he truly believed in collective security—in its protests against violations of American rights alone: "Only by directing efforts first to the establishment of rights which are common to all can particular rights be safeguarded." In a community of nations, no one was secure against aggression unless all were secure; and, Angell concluded, unless the United States entered the war for that purpose, then a punitive peace—a peace that would sow the seeds of another war—was inevitable.[60]

Charles P. Trevelyan had put it more succinctly, in a somewhat different context, in his "Open Letter to Americans." "Sooner or later," he had written in reference to Wilson and the league, "your espousal of that plan will affect the course of the war. It will shorten it." Noel Buxton, another leader of the UDC, added in late February that, whereas he had previously supported American neutrality, he now believed that Wilson "could do more good by 'coming in' as a check on the Entente jingoes."[61]

Walter Lippmann effectively assimilated these views (in consultation with Colonel House) and sent them to Wilson in a memorandum on March 11. Lippmann knew that, despite Germany's deplorable course, Wilson's long-range objectives had not changed; the point now was that the German government posed the greatest obstacle to their realization.

Whenever Germany was ready to abandon its present policies it would be welcome in a league of nations. In the meantime, the United States faced a terrible dilemma. The solution to it lay in Wilson's principles and the quality of his leadership. Under Wilson, belligerency would always remain subordinate to liberal policy and to the goal of establishing a league of nations. Indeed, Lippmann concluded, "the only victory in this war that could compensate mankind for its horrors is the victory of international order over national aggression."[62]

Perhaps the best evidence that these kinds of invocations penetrated Wilson's thought and provided the solution to his dilemma comes from Jane Addams' poignant account of the Emergency Peace Federation's visit to the White House on February 28. "The President's mood was stern and far from the scholar's detachment," she later recalled. "He still spoke to us, however, as to fellow pacifists to whom he was forced to confess that war had become inevitable. He used one phrase which I had heard Colonel House use so recently that it still stuck firmly in my memory. The phrase was to the effect that, as head of a nation participating in the war, the President of the United States would have a seat at the Peace Table, but that if he remained the representative of a neutral country he could at best only 'call through a crack in the door.' The appeal he made was, in substance, that the foreign policies which we so extravagantly admired could have a chance if he were there to push and to defend them, but not otherwise."[63]

One is tempted to make a final comment about Wilson's decision that, in a sense, is implicit in all of the foregoing. In January 1916, Robert Bridges, England's poet laureate, published a small volume entitled *The Spirit of Man*. The war, he wrote, had made it increasingly necessary to affirm that "man is a spiritual being and the proper work of his mind is to interpret the world according to his higher nature." For Europeans, such an outlook was now all the more essential because it lent "distraction from a grief that is intolerable constantly to face, nay impossible to face without the trust in God which makes all things possible."[64] Bridges might have said much the same about Wilson. For Wilson was a deeply religious man, the son and grandson of Presbyterian ministers, and the statesman who had called for peace without victory. He was intensely aware of the fact that perhaps thousands of young Americans might go to their deaths upon his command. Once, during a campaign address in October, he had said in defense of neutrality, "When you are asked, 'Aren't you willing to fight?' reply, yes, you are waiting for something worth fighting for; that you are not looking about for petty quarrels, but that you are looking about for that sort of quarrel within whose intricacies are written all the texts of the rights of man."[65] Only the reasonable prospect of redemption—the hope of a league of nations and lasting peace, attainable, now, apparently only through the crucible of war—could permit someone such as Wilson, in whom fate had so mixed the elements, to pronounce the words for belligerency.

Thus, on the evening of April 2, 1917, Wilson asked Congress to recognize that a state of war existed between their country and the German empire. He began by indicting submarine warfare as "a warfare against humanity" and recounted the events of the previous two months. Because armed neutrality had proved impracticable, he said, the United States was compelled to accept the status of belligerent that had thus been thrust upon it.

After outlining the measures necessary for getting the country's war effort underway, he turned to more transcendent matters. His thoughts, he said, were still the same as when he had addressed the Senate on January 22: "Our object now, as then, is to vindicate the principles of peace and justice in the life of the world as against selfish and autocratic power and set up amongst the really free and self-governed peoples of the world such a concert of purpose and of action as will henceforth insure the observance of those principles." Yet he emphasized several times, in all of this, the United States had no quarrel with the German people themselves; it was not they, but their military masters, who had brought on the war. "A steadfast concert of peace can never be maintained except by a partnership of democratic nations. No autocratic government could be trusted to keep faith within it or observe its covenants."

He continued: "The world must be made safe for democracy. Its peace must be planted upon the tested foundations of political liberty. We have no selfish ends to serve. We desire no conquest, no dominion. We seek no indemnities for ourselves, no material compensation for the sacrifices we shall freely make. We are but one of the champions of the rights of mankind. We shall be satisfied when those rights have been made as secure as the faith and the freedom of nations can make them."

Then, in words that one observer compared to Shakespeare's for their rhetorical grace and power, Wilson compressed into a final peroration his vision of the American historical mission, in all its arrogance and innocence—a summons to the New World to return to the Old to vindicate the creed for which it had broken away a hundred and forty years before:

> It is a distressing and oppressive duty, Gentlemen of the Congress, which I have performed in thus addressing you. There are, it may be, many months of fiery trial and sacrifice ahead of us. It is a fearful thing to lead this great peaceful people into war, into the most terrible and disastrous of all wars, civilization itself seeming to be in the balance. But the right is more precious than peace, and we shall fight for the things which we have always carried nearest our hearts,—for democracy, for the right of those who submit to authority to have a voice in their own governments, for the

rights and liberties of small nations, for a universal dominion of right by such a concert of free peoples as shall bring peace and safety to all nations and make the world itself at last free. To such a task we can dedicate our lives and our fortunes, everything that we are and everything that we have, with the pride of those who know that the day has come when America is privileged to spend her blood and her might for the principles that gave her birth and happiness and the peace which she has treasured. God helping her, she can do no other.[66]

In the thirty-six minutes that it took to deliver the address, Wilson had seemingly united behind him the preponderance of the American people. Even Lodge and Roosevelt admitted being impressed by the President's words and performance. Of all the outpouring of public commentary, none better captured the thoughts and emotions of Wilson's admirers and critics at that moment than the *New Republic*. "Our debt and the world's debt to Woodrow Wilson is immeasurable," the editors wrote. "Only a statesman who will be called great could have made American intervention mean so much to the generous forces of the world, could have lifted the inevitable horror of war into a deed so full of meaning. . . . Through the force of circumstance and through his own genius he has made it a practical possibility that he is to be the first great statesman to begin the better organization of the world."[67]

Thirty years later, another of Wilson's disciples, from a different corner of the progressive internationalist movement, reflected on his high speech to Congress and on the exhilarating few years that had preceded it: "As I look back, my whole life up to that point seems to have been introduction—a too tender introduction, politically, to the hard, fierce, bloody thing that man's life on this planet has been and is. Like all my radical friends, I had mistaken for final reality the brief paradise of America at the turn of the century. . . . It was, comparatively, a protected little historic moment of peace and progress that we grew up in. We were children reared in a kindergarten, and now the real thing was coming."[68]

8

"If the War Is Too Strong"

The Travail of Progressive Internationalism and the Fourteen Points

The evolution of the League of Nations entered a new and decisive stage in American and world politics after April 1917. Whereas all of the potential obstacles to its creation had their genesis in the neutrality period, the issue took on an entirely new complexion once the United States became an active belligerent. Wilson's problems, needless to say, were numerous and complex. They included, first, an indeterminate measure of opposition, both ideological and partisan, which was clustered in the Senate and had first begun to stir in reaction to his peace note of December 1916. Second, the ideas and the growing influence of conservative internationalists of the League to Enforce Peace, with whom Wilson enjoyed neither a good working relationship nor ideological affinity, complicated the senatorial challenge. Third, and just as important, the exigencies of war imposed a fearful toll on progressive internationalists, Wilson's most important source of political strength outside the Democratic party. Finally, the wide divergence between the United States and the Allies over objectives for peace constituted virtually an insoluble problem from beginning to end.

The outstanding ideological and partisan parameters of the American debate over the League bared themselves during the presidential campaign of 1916; in some respects, they gained greater clarity in the final

months of neutrality. On January 23, 1917, a number of Republican senators publicly challenged the assumptions behind Wilson's "Peace Without Victory" address—"the stump speech from the throne," as Lawrence
Y. Sherman of Illinois characterized it.[1] During the extended floor debate,
Senator Borah introduced a resolution, on January 25, that reaffirmed the
verities of Washington's Farewell Address and the Monroe Doctrine, while
Porter J. McCumber of North Dakota asked whether Wilson really represented the views of most Americans "when he leaves the realm of generalities."[2]

On February 1, the chamber listened to a well constructed speech by
Senator Lodge. It contained some of the most trenchant criticisms that he
had theretofore raised. In the first place, Lodge questioned the desirability
of the kind of settlement that Wilson advocated, and defended Great Britain against those who would hinder her righteous cause. He then turned
to the subject of the future peace and the role of the United States in
preserving it. If self-determination was the essential condition upon which
the peace must rest—and he did not contest the justice of that notion—
what steps, Lodge asked, was the United States prepared to take in order
to secure the adoption of the principle by other governments? The Senator also acknowledged the salutary function of voluntary arbitration in
settling international disputes; but as for compulsory arbitration and collective security, he noted, these were matters that could not be determined
"by verbal adherence to general principle; everything here depends on
details." What, exactly, was a league of nations supposed to do if a member went to war after arbitration had taken place? How large an armed
force was the United States expected to contribute to the international
force that, presumably, the league must maintain? Then, too, in such a
league, would not the smaller nations, by virtue of their numerical majority, be able to compel the United States to go to war without any action
by the Congress?

"You can not make effective a league of peace, 'supported by the
organized force of mankind,' by language or high-sounding phrases," he
said in conclusion. The United States must first preserve its own peace
with the world. It should enter into only those agreements that were
possible to uphold, build a strong national defense, and work to recodify
international law. Only then should Americans consider whether they
wanted to consign their vital interests to a league of nations, and then
only with "a full appreciation of just what it involves."[3]

As William C. Widenor has pointed out, Lodge's remarks were motivated, not only by second thoughts about collective security, but also by
Wilson's coupling of the league with an "indecisive" peace.[4] He apparently felt so strongly about the latter point that he had formally disasso-
ciated himself from the League to Enforce Peace two days before, in a

letter to A. Lawrence Lowell. Since addressing that organization, the LEP had "become involved in one way or another in the popular mind, and now definitely by the President's action [his peace note and the "Peace Without Victory" address], with the peace which is to end the present war. To me this is most unfortunate and so far as I am concerned I do not feel that [the LEP] any longer represents my opinion."[5] Lodge may have been concerned (for any number of reasons) about the public's identification of the league idea with Wilson; but he had grossly misinterpreted the LEP's views on the war, which had never included a peace short of Allied victory. He had only to observe the LEP's letterhead to comprehend that fact.

The debate in the Senate probably would have generated a major controversy if it had not been for Germany's resumption of unrestricted submarine warfare on the same day. When events finally compelled Wilson to call for war, Lodge joined in the cacophony of praise for the President. The war address, after all, was a tacit admission that the administration's pro-Allied critics had been right all along, and, for a while, it dissipated a certain amount of Republican ire. Lodge believed that American entry into the war symbolized the formation of the kind of peace league that he could support.

Not all Republican opponents of Wilson's internationalism, however, were of the same mind as Lodge. For instance, Senator Borah, a progressive Republican from Idaho, had come to conclusions similar to Lodge's during the Senate debates in first week of February; but Borah's approach was significantly different. When the time came to vote on the war resolution, he did so from the distinctly isolationist perspective (unlike Lodge) that he had articulated on at least two previous occasions. "I join no crusade," he declared in explaining his vote. "I seek or accept no alliances; I obligate this Government to no other power. I make war alone for my countrymen and their rights, for my country and its honor."[6] Between Wilson and many Senate Republicans, substantial and varied differences over both the league and the nature of the peace in general remained unresolved as the United States entered the war.

Even as the wave of international acclaim began to wash over the White House, Wilson confessed to a close friend, "I have been a little low in my mind the last forty-eight hours because of the absolute lack of any power to see what I am driving at, which has been exhibited by the men who are looked upon as the leading Republican members of the Senate. After all, it is upon the Senate that I have to depend."[7] Herbert Croly shared the concern. "There seems to be a tendency among Republicans," he told Wilson on January 23, "to oppose the participation of the United States in a League of Nations under any conditions. They seem to have decided to try to make party capital out of it." Although he did not think that the League was in danger, he recommended a presidential speaking tour for the league.[8] (In the main editorial of the *New Republic*'s next issue, Croly berated the Republican party for its unbecoming capacity "to crouch at its own fireside, build a high tariff wall, arm against the whole world, cultivate no friendships, take no steps to forestall another great war, and then let things rip."[9])

Republican animadversion had a far more important impact on Wilson. It aggravated his disinclination to talk about the league in very specific terms. The Senate Republicans' interpretations of his address, he believed, constituted a deliberate misrepresentation. They "had read all sorts of things into his speech he never said," he told Louis Lochner on February 1. He shuddered to think what would happen "if an elaborate, detailed program were to be submitted for discussion."[10] During a press conference, on January 10, reporters dropped the subject after the following exchange took place:

A reporter: "Mr. President, your world peace league plan you unfolded to the Senate seems to give the United States a certain interest in the possible future quarrels of Europe. It occurred to me that if the European nations would be given a reciprocal interest—"

Wilson: "My dear boy, do you suppose I am going to tell you an answer? If you want to find out, attend the conference that brings this thing about. I don't know anything about it."[11]

Wilson was considerably more courteous in responding to an inquiry from Edward A. Filene, a Boston Democrat, and the LEP's most successful fund-raiser. "I have carefully put forth only the idea, . . . feeling that it could be best achieved by leaving the whole question of organization and detail to the [peace] conference," Wilson wrote. "At present the opponents of the measure are rejoicing in setting up men of straw and knocking them down, and all the men of straw are particular plans and details."[12]

Personal distemper and his own partisan anxieties were not the sole factors behind Wilson's position. His silence on the details was also attributable to the very nature of his conception of the structure of the league. And that conception did not conform to the picture of unlimited diplomatic entanglements and military commitments that opponents conjured up from the start. In early February 1917, Wilson set down some essentials for the league in a document entitled "Bases of Peace." These included guarantees of territorial integrity and political independence, equal trade opportunities, and a provision for the limitation of armaments. The document also stressed that no administrative agency or permanent tribunal was necessary in order to uphold such a settlement: "It would in all likelihood be best to await the developments and suggestions of experience before attempting to set up any common intrumentality of international action." [13] Wilson had no illusions about the difficulties involved, he assured Ambassador Jusserand confidentially in March 1917, but he was convinced that the league should evolve, rather than be created by formal convention. One should begin with simple covenants, he explained in a subsequent communication to Jusserand—for instance, with the obligation to submit disputes to arbitration. Then, "in the very process of carrying these covenants into execution from time to time a machinery and practice of cooperation would naturally spring up which would in the end produce . . . a regularly constituted and employed concert of nations." [14] " 'The establishment of a league of nations,' " he told William E. Rappard, a Swiss authority on international organization, in November 1917, " 'is in my view a matter of moral persuasion more than a problem of juridical organization.' " [15]

Within Wilson's rationale lay an important proviso to what would become Article X of the Covenant of the League of Nations as well as a cogent response to one of the penetrating issues that Lodge, among others, had raised—but that Wilson never clarified in any public forum before it was too late to do any good. A mutual guarantee of political independence and territorial integrity would *not* oblige every member of the League automatically to throw an army into the field every time the peace was disturbed; nor would it empower the League itself to compel a member to do so. Whether the United States would employ military force would depend entirely on all the circumstances surrounding a particular incident. Then, too, Wilson (unlike conservative internationalists) also laid great stress on disarmament as a crucial component of collective security. Disarmament would eliminate many potential problems from the start. By itself, the League could not prevent conflict in every instance. But it could provide, as Walter Lippmann pointed out for him in 1917, "a temporary shelter after the storm." The best strategy for peace after the war was "to establish enough order for a few decades in order to release some of the more generous forces of mankind." [16] For Wilson, then, the League of Nations was a compass rather than the final destination. Could such a league, formed under specific covenants and subject to a broad construction, really work in actual practice? That, Wilson admitted, was a very good question. But, as he said to Jusserand, "It would be an experience to try it." [17]

Wilson's considered opinions were not unsound. After the United States entered the war, however, he courted trouble by not taking any leading internationalists, conservative or progressive, into his confidence. Until the autumn of 1918, the major strain between the administration and the conservative internationalists did not grow out of differences pertaining to the League's responsibilities. Rather, frustration and bad feelings developed owing to the pains Wilson took to preserve, almost jealously, his freedom of action. This problem became especially acute when the LEP began to recommend the establishment of a commission to formulate a constitution for the League.[18]

Early on, Wilson took things more or less in stride. The LEP's activities were "based upon a very much too definite programme," he wrote to an old friend in May 1917, "but in view of my concurrence with the general idea they have advocated, I have never felt at liberty to criticize them."[19] As they continued to press him, however, Wilson began to reveal some hostility. To Colonel House he complained about "the folly of the League to Enforce Peace butters-in" and worried that he would not be able to head off Taft because "Mr. T. never stays put." Theodore Marburg, Wilson's most loyal supporter in the LEP, was dubbed "one of the principal woolgatherers." As for A. Lawrence Lowell, House wrote in his diary, "The President dislikes [him] as much as he could."[20]

Wilson's indisposition toward the leaders of the LEP was no doubt nourished by their Republican affiliations, by their commitment to a particular program for the league, and by the bitter residue of the recent presidential campaign. Although he refrained from public criticism, rarely did he consult with them personally. That assignment fell to Colonel House, whom the LEP regularly sought out; and House occasionally showed them materials he and Wilson were working with. But the main result was simply to protect Wilson, Taft, and Lowell from one another's scrutiny.[21] Ultimately, this would not prove sufficient. By 1918, the LEP would become the single most assiduous propagator of the league idea, reaching millions of Americans through its cohort of public speakers and by disseminating some four million pieces of literature.[22] Meanwhile, in part (but only in part) because he was absorbed by the enormous task of running the nation's war effort, Wilson did not carry on with the impressive program of public education that he had mounted from May 1916 to January 1917. With the exception of Colonel House, Wilson's ideas about the League remained a mystery to all. We shall return to these subjects in the next chapter; suffice it to say at this point that that omission, along with Wilson's failure to extend a friendly hand to the LEP leadership (especially to Taft) would have extremely unfortunate repercussions.

To an extent, Wilson was justified in distancing himself from the LEP's program. By and large, it was advanced by very conservative people who, on one hand, advocated for the United States a sort of garrison-state internationalism, and, on the other, had serious doubts about domestic reforms as basic as the eight-hour day. The conservative internationalists were not Wilson's natural constituency; the progressive internationalists were. Let us, then, turn to the wartime relationship between Wilson and those groups who constituted the left-of-center coalition that had sustained him in November 1916 and who had appreciated and contributed so much to the "Peace Without Victory" manifesto of January 1917.

Wilson's legislative accomplishments, his synthesis of the anti-imperialist New Diplomacy, and a war message as inspiring as the oration of Henry V on St. Crispin's Day settled most things for most progressives. "The war liberals," Christopher Lasch once observed, "now began to argue that a national emergency of such scope would unify the country behind a program of socialized democracy, . . . putting an end to years of aimless drift."[23] Indeed, during the week preceding the declaration of war, the *New Republic* had outlined "A War Program for Liberals," one that not only liberals, but also many socialists could endorse.

First and foremost, this program echoed the rationalization for war that Walter Lippmann had presented to Wilson in March—that is, "the need for constant subordination of strategy to political aims. . . . [U]nless the world emerges from this war a more liberal and more peaceful world America is beaten no matter how badly Germany is crushed." The substance of the war program flowed logically from the Wilsonian reforms of 1916, under the general category of "administrative efficiency"—of the sort that would "keep the conduct of the war out of the hands of the jingoes." This would require nationalization of all the country's important economic resources, progressive taxation of wealth and war profits, the encouragement of the unionization of labor, the expansion of educational opportunities, and, finally, universal military training, short of conscription. Through such a program, the *New Republic* concluded, the United States "may be able to maintain democracy at home and contribute to the internationalism of the world."[24]

So confident was Walter Lippmann of the progressive uses the war could be put to that he told a leading pro-war Socialist, in May 1917, that the country stood "at the threshold of a collectivism which is greater than any as yet planned by the Socialist party."[25] To the *New Republic*'s benefactor, Herbert Croly wrote that "under the stimulus of the war & its consequences there will be a chance to focus the thought & will of the country on high and fruitful purposes such as occurs only once in many hundred years."[26] These were exceedingly extravagant claims, but not entirely without justification. At least on some levels, the changes that occurred in America during the First World War could be characterized, as Allen F. Davis once suggested, as "the flowering of progressivism."[27]

For instance, the newly created War Industries Board, though it shied away from full-scale state control, exercised unprecedented centralized powers in coordinating industrial production.[28] Under the United States Railroad Administration, the federal government took over and modernized the nation's transportation system, increased wage scales, and gave impetus to plans (supported by both the American Federation of Labor and the brotherhoods) for permanent nationalization of the railroads. "Not even the Declaration of Independence nor the Emancipation Proclamation would equal for liberty and democracy your act in taking the operation of the railroads out of private hands," one overwhelmed progressive told Wilson.[29] Whereas war bonds ("Liberty Loans") supplied about two-thirds of the $33.5 billion that the war cost the United States, the remaining third was raised through new taxes. And, with some vengeance, wartime tax legislation picked up where the Revenue Act of 1916 had left off. The Revenue Act of 1917 (denounced by Senator Lodge as "perfectly exorbitant taxation") placed some seventy-five percent of the burden on corporate profits and on individuals with high incomes. Then the Revenue Act of 1918 increased the previous rates by nearly two-and-a-half times, eighty percent of which was imposed on the same well-heeled groups. Together, these bills represented one of the real triumphs achieved by progressives and radicals during the war.[30]

Finally, as Frederick C. Howe noted at the time, "the consideration . . . shown for the workers in the midst of the war that commanded all our energies, exceeds anything the most optimistic reformer felt could be achieved in a quarter of a century."[31] Howe was commenting on the fact that for the first time the federal government had recognized labor's right to organize and bargain collectively. The National War Labor Board also established a minimum wage and the eight-hour day in most industries, and settled labor disputes almost always in favor of the workers. By the end of the war, membership in the AFL had increased from slightly over two million to some 3,260,000, and real income for all of labor had increased by twenty percent over the prewar level. In addition, other notable progressive initiatives included the beginnings of federal public housing, social insurance, federal programs to improve public health, and an abortive venture (personally initiated by Wilson) to build a government-owned munitions plant in order to deprive Pierre S. Du Pont of immoderate profits.[32]

By any reasonable standards, one had to conclude that the total mobilization effort reflected certain traditional American liberal and socialist values. But to infuse a progressive character into the wartime political economy was not without its political costs. Although some Republicans and Democrats liked to maintain the fiction that "politics is adjourned" (a phrase coined by Wilson), the enactment of virtually all of the foregoing measures was accompanied by partisan bitterness, by accusations that sectional interests were at work, and by administrative and legislative confusion.[33] Moreover, the Wilson administration endured incessant criticism of its conduct of the war and incurred the deep resentment of the business community. "They dread government control of the railroads and the mines: they chafe under taxation: they fear the growing power of labor in the councils of the nation," Ray Stannard Baker wrote in his journal in January 1918. "They recognize in Wilson, clearly, a truly progressive if not radical leadership and they fear and despise him."[34]

Skepticism, and even fear, about the nature of Wilson's domestic war policies was not confined to Republicans and conservative businessmen. The criticism and opposition that was the most unsettling for Wilson and the progressives emanated from within—from vital elements within the progressive internationalist movement itself. The outcome was by no means inevitable, but the constituent parts that made up the American left had a potential every bit as great as that of the American right to undermine essential support for the League. And, as in the past, domestic and foreign policy could not be separated.

The events of the four days between Wilson's address on April 2 and the vote on the war resolution were a portent of the broader problem. During that time one of the most intense dramas in the history of the United States Congress was played out. "Treason! Treason!" Senator Norris's colleagues shouted when he said, "We are going to war upon the command of gold" and "I feel that we are about to put the dollar sign on the American flag." In all, six senators (including Norris and Robert La Follette) and fifty representatives, mainly from the West and South, voted no. Impressive as those numbers were, they probably did not reflect the full extent of the opposition to the war, or at least the misgivings, in either the Congress or the country as a whole. Yet, Senator Norris, after voicing his convictions, had vowed that, should war be declared, "all of my energy and all of my power will be behind our flag in carrying it to victory."[35]

No such reassuring qualification, however, was given out by the Socialist party at its emergency convention in St. Louis during the second week of April. Denouncing American participation in the war as "a crime against the people of the United States," its proclamation also promised to oppose conscription and the sale of war bonds and to resist any restrictions on First Amendment rights. (A minority report, drafted by John Spargo, urged support for the war as the best means of advancing socialistic reforms as well as an anti-imperialist peace, which required the defeat of German militarism.) The uncompromising majority document was approved overwhelmingly by both the Socialist press and the party membership in a national mail referendum.[36]

The principled stand of the Socialist party intensified the protracted crisis that had overwhelmed the pacifist and radical elements of the progressive internationalist movement from the moment the United States entered the war. Within the American Union Against Militarism, younger members, such as Roger Baldwin and Norman Thomas, proposed a campaign against conscription and another to defend conscientious objectors.

Jane Addams, Lillian Wald, and Paul Kellogg, however, saw the need to "distinguish between opposition to militarism and war and active opposition to this war" and, especially, to preserve the lines of communication with the White House. Should they attempt to interfere with the prosecution of the war (which Baldwin and Thomas' proposals seemed to entail), the AUAM would be perceived as a "party of opposition" and lose all respectability and influence. Within four months, irreconcilable differences over these issues paralyzed the organization. When Addams, Wald, and Kellogg stepped down from the executive board, the AUAM all but disintegrated.[37]

That the war was a giant wrecking machine with the potential to batter the progressive wing of the American internationalist movement to ruins was foreshadowed by the travail of the Socialist party. Upon the adoption of the St. Louis Proclamation, many prominent members resigned from the party. By no means were all of the "deserters" right-wing socialists. They included, from the left, William English Walling and Frank Bohn; and from the center, Spargo, Charles Edward Russell, Upton Sinclair, Algie M. Simons, Gus Myers, and Allen Benson. Although even better-known lights—Debs, Eastman, Reed, Hillquit, Berger—endorsed the St. Louis Proclamation, the party was badly hurt, especially when publications like the *New York Times* delighted in reporting resignations (for instance, Spargo's) on page one.[38] The defections proved detrimental to progressive internationalism as well, for they signaled the beginning of the end of the intellectual communion and joint political activities between American liberals and socialists, the great hallmark of the pre-1917 period that had given progressive internationalism and the reform movement in general so much of its vitality.

Some pro-war socialists were not content merely to sever party affiliations and let it go at that. Spargo denounced the St. Louis proclamation as "essentially un-neutral, un-American, and pro-German."[39] Gus Myers wrote to the President that the party's "dangerous and insidious propaganda [must] be exposed."[40] And Walling, only one month into the war, informed Secretary of Labor William B. Wilson: "None of the official leaders of the Majority now in control of the American Party can be trusted. On the contrary, all of them are in bitter opposition to the American government and the American people."[41]

Walling's intolerance, however, was mild compared to other manifestations of "One Hundred Percent Americanism" that soon coursed though the country. On March 19, 1917, while he was still weighing his fateful decision, President Wilson told Frank Cobb of the *World:* "Once lead this people into war . . . and they'll soon forget there ever was such a thing as tolerance."[42] But, by April 2, Wilson had emerged from his torment singleminded in his conviction to prosecute with as much dispatch and efficiency as possible a war to end all wars. "If there should be disloyalty," he noted briefly in his address to Congress, "it will be dealt with with the firm hand of stern repression."[43] In his next public address, on Flag Day in 1917, while making the case for a war against German militarism, he concluded with a warning: "Woe be to the man or group of men that seeks to stand in our way in this day of high resolution. . . ."[44]

To help sustain the high resolution and vindicate principles held dear, Wilson created the Committee on Public Information (CPI), headed by the energetic progressive publicist George Creel. In "the fight for the *minds* of men, for the conquest of their convictions," as Creel called it, the CPI launched a propaganda campaign of unprecedented proportions. An estimated seventy-five million pieces of pamphlet literature spread the official line on the war to all parts of the country. Stirring poster art, to encourage enlistments and the purchase of war bonds, appeared everywhere. Famous movie stars lent their celebrity to national Liberty Loan drives. And, not only to sing the virtues of democracy and "Americanism," but also to discredit all things German, the CPI coordinated 75,000 so-called Four-Minute Men to make speeches that were heard by tens of millions of people.[45]

As early as the summer of 1917, it was clear to many observers that the CPI was doing its work all too well. Citizens of German ancestry, of socialist inclination, and of dissident mind in general bore the brunt of the national campaign for patriotic conformity. Some aspects of the campaign at the local and state level were merely ludicrous—for instance, the removal of pretzels from saloon counters in Cincinnati and the renaming of German measles, sauerkraut, and German shepherds to "Liberty measles," "Liberty cabbage," and "police dogs." But from there it was a short step to local ordinances that banned Brahms and Beethoven from major concert halls, to the removal (and burning) of works of German literature from small-town schools and public libraries, and to demands by Theodore Roosevelt to prohibit the teaching of the German language—a "barbarous tongue," according to one noted scholar at Johns Hopkins.[46]

Inspired by federal legislation, encouraged by national organizations such as the American Protective League and the National Security League, and frequently instigated by local committees on public safety, acts of political repression and violence were committed in almost every region of the United States. In July 1917, thousands of soldiers and sailors attacked a parade of Socialists on Boston Common and sacked the local party headquarters while the police stood by and watched. That same month some 1,200 miners peaceably walked off the job in the copper fields of Bisbee, Arizona, in protest against substandard wages and working conditions. A small army of thugs, equipped by the Phelps-Dodge Corporation, rounded them up at gunpoint, loaded them into cattle cars, and transported them miles into the desert where they were abandoned without food, water, or shelter. (Federal authorities rescued the workers three days later.)[47] In August, Frank Little, a physically handicapped union organizer in Butte, Montana, made the mistake of speaking out against strike breakers and the war of the capitalist class. In the middle of the night, he was taken from his bed by vigilantes, chained behind an automobile, and dragged until his kneecaps were worn away. His patriotic assailants then sexually mutilated him and hanged him from a railroad trestle.[48] Around Cincinnati, it was well known that the Justice Department monitored the pacifistic sermons of Herbert Bigelow, a leading minister of the city and a former associate of Secretary of War Newton D. Baker. In October, a mob seized Bigelow, stripped him to the waist, and cut his back to ribbons with a horsewhip.[49]

Thousands of citizens suffered less brutal forms of chastisement as rumors of espionage spread like plague. German-Americans frequently were forced to kiss the flag in retribution for a casual remark that smacked of disloyalty. Municipal judges issued countless fines to individuals who failed to stand up when the national anthem was played at public events. A movie producer received a three-year prison sentence for having made *The Spirit of '76,* a film about the American Revolution that portrayed the British in an unfavorable light. Teachers routinely lost their jobs if they betrayed any objectivity about the causes of the war or discussed the possibility of an early armistice. Perhaps the crowning blow came when the Los Angeles Board of Education ordered teachers to cancel a student debate on the subject of William Howard Taft's League to Enforce Peace.[50]

From the start, many progressive internationalists feared for the overall health of the body politic. Only two weeks after Congress adopted the war resolution, Lillian Wald, Herbert Croly, Jane Addams, Amos Pinchot, Paul Kellogg, Norman Thomas, and Oswald Garrison Villard sent Wilson a letter of caution: "It is possible that the moral damage to our democracy in this war may become more serious than the physical or national losses incurred." So that "the spirit of democracy will not be broken," they urged the President to make "an impressive statement" to curb local and state officials who might exploit the wartime circumstances to serve their own agendas.[51] "Surely you can find a way for us to pull together," Wald wrote in a separate note to Wilson. "You will not drive your natural allies from you. You will not banish us from the Democratic party which you promised to make the home of all liberal spirits."[52]

Wald's letter anticipated a broader issue—the preservation of civil liberties in wartime—which held the gravest implications for the success or failure of the league from the standpoint of progressive internationalism. Wilson was not insensitive to the problem. However, he not only never came forth with "an impressive statement"; he permitted Attorney

General Thomas Watt Gregory and Postmaster General Albert Sidney Burleson virtually to become the arbiters of the First Amendment. In the long run, their activities would prove to be the main source of disruption within the progressive internationalist movement.

On July 15, 1917, Congress passed the Espionage Act.[53] Title I imposed stiff fines and up to twenty years' imprisonment for any one who attempted to cause insubordination or disloyalty in the armed services or to obstruct recruitment. The Justice Department prosecuted more than 2,000 cases under this provision. Title XII gave the Postmaster General power to exclude from the mails any material that could be construed to be in violation of the strictures of Title I, or that advocated or urged "treason, insurrection, or forcible resistance to any law of the United States."[54]

Postmaster General Burleson was not a man of broad political or social vision. Any day laborer in America, he once told a reporter, could become "a railroad president as J. P. Morgan"; if he did not, it was due to "the shape of the brain." Burleson also held that the work of Jane Addams, Lillian Wald, and the AUAM had done "great harm" to the country and that Max Eastman was "no better than a traitor."[55] According to the Postmaster General, "papers may not say that the Government is controlled by Wall Street or munitions manufacturers," nor could they indulge in "attacking improperly our allies."[56] As Upton Sinclair observed in a letter to Wilson, Burleson was "a person of such pitiful and childish ignorance concerning modern movements that it is simply a calamity that . . . he should be the person to decide what may or may not be uttered by our radical press."[57]

Burleson exercised his new powers to the fullest against socialists and, on occasion, liberals. In July 1917, he excluded from the mails the *American Socialist,* the *Appeal to Reason,* the *International Socialist Review,* the *Masses,* and *Social Revolution* (formerly the *National Rip-Saw*), along with several weeklies in Chicago, Philadelphia, Detroit, and St. Louis. Together, these publications had a circulation of more than one million.[58]

Burleson struck at the August 1917 issue of the *Masses* because of its "general tenor." (The issue contained an editorial that defended Emma Goldman and Alexander Berkman, both recently convicted of conspiracy to obstruct Army recruitment.) Eastman, Amos Pinchot, and John Reed protested directly to Wilson on behalf of all of Burleson's victims. "Can it be necessary, even in war time, for the majority of a republic to throttle the voice of a sincere minority?" they asked. "As friends of yours, and knowing how dear to you is the Anglo-Saxon tradition of intellectual freedom, we would like to feel that you do not sanction the exercise."[59] Wilson promised to "go to the bottom of the matter" and wrote to Burleson, "These are very sincere men and I should like to please them."[60]

Burleson claimed that he had excluded only particular issues that "have gone far beyond what might properly be termed criticism."[61] But he continued to impose the ban on the *Masses,* arguing that, since the publication had skipped an issue, it no longer fitted the category of "periodical." This maneuver compelled Eastman to seek redress in the United States Court of Appeals and to petition the White House both in person and by letter. Reactionary forces had seized on the war "to kill the propaganda of socialism," he told Wilson on September 8, and "you also know that this propaganda will surely play a great part in the further democratizing of the world." Eastman's anxiety thus extended to foreign policy. "I believe that the support which your administration will receive from radical-minded people the country over, depends greatly on its final stand on these two critical matters of free speech and assemblage and freedom of the Press."[62]

Wilson confessed to Eastman that he had little confidence about how to proceed in the matter of censorship: "I can only say that a line must be drawn and that we are trying, it may be clumsily, but genuinely, to draw it without fear or favor or prejudice."[63] He was no doubt sincere; but, as of September 1917, only timidity and deference marked his efforts to restrain his subordinate. In early September, he wrote to Burleson, "[Y]ou know that I am willing to trust your judgment after I have once called your attention to a suggestion."[64]

The controversy over the *Masses* was still hanging fire when, in October, the *Milwaukee Leader,* the New York *Call,* and the *Jewish Daily Forward*—with a combined readership in excess of 200,000—were denied second-class mailing privileges. Censorship now became the object of serious concern, not only for the journalists directly affected, but also for pro-war socialists and straight-line liberals.[65] Colonel House advised Wilson "to err on the side of leniency" and take the matter out of Burleson's hands.[66] Walter Lippmann attempted to explain to the President that "the feeling on this issue is at white heat," not only for the radicals, but also for the liberals and the labor movement. If he permitted the Postmaster General to persist, he would "divide the country's articulate opinion into fanatical jingoism and fanatical pacifism." Lippmann emphasized the importance of the relationship between coalition politics and foreign policy. "[T]he overwhelming number of radicals can be won to the support of the war simply by conserving the spirit of the President's own utterances."[67] In reply to a similar letter from Herbert Croly, Wilson said the Postmaster General was "misunderstood," and "inclined to be most conservative in the exercise of these great and dangerous powers."[68] Yet, when he informed Burleson—"I am afraid you will be shocked," he began—that he did not think that the *Milwaukee Leader* "ought to be regarded as unmailable," Burleson simply ignored him.[69]

Soon, even pro-war Socialists pressed the vital point. Upton Sinclair, who had agonized over his decision to break with his party, practically pleaded with the President. He had tried to stay out of it, but the measures taken against the *Masses* could "only be described as disgraceful," and he now had to speak his mind. "I voice the sentiments of millions throughout America, who will give their sincere support to a war for democracy, but who will feel weakened in their enthusiasm if they see any signs that while helping to win democracy abroad, we are losing it at home."[70]

If any doubts remained about the implications of censorship for progressive internationalists, they should have been laid to rest by the warnings of the ardent pro-war Socialist John Spargo, whose own previous public statements had helped undermine the respectability of the Socialist party's anti-war position. "In common with a very large number of radicals, I have rejoiced to acknowledge your leadership," he wrote to the President. But he knew personally scores of men and women who found themselves constant critics of the administration because of "the unwarranted and unnecessary suppression of criticism." Wilson *must* find a way— and it could be done, perhaps, by inviting "a group of leading radicals of various schools" to help formulate a new policy to replace Burleson's— "to overcome opposition and remove misunderstanding, and to secure the support of by far the greater number of those liberals and radicals who are now distrustful of our part in the war and more or less active opponents of the Administration."[71]

Wilson's attitude toward civil liberties would remain an unresolved problem throughout the war. After the autumn of 1917, however, the issue seemed to abate somewhat. Indeed, by the early spring of 1918, Wilson had regained his standing among progressive internationalists of virtually all persuasions, chiefly because the editors of socialist publications, like their liberal counterparts, found themselves on common ground with the President in the ensuing international debate over war aims. Nonetheless, the controversy would have a most untimely revival, during the summer and fall of 1918.

In most of his wartime reflections on the subject, Wilson emphasized that the proper application of the League's guarantees would depend on whether the territorial agreements at the peace conference *"ought* to be perpetuated"—whether the final settlement conformed "with the general principles of right and comity" as set forth in his "Peace Without Victory" address.[72] Yet the last time that the Allies had made a statement on war aims was on January 10, in their response to Wilson's peace note of December 1916. That declaration hardly conformed to the precepts of the New Diplomacy. In a sense, Germany's resumption of submarine warfare had temporarily rescued the Allies from Wilson. Moreover, Wilson had not imposed any conditions on the Allies in exchange for American belligerency; thus, divergence in avowed purposes remained unreconciled as Congress voted on the war resolution.[73]

Both Wilson and the Allied governments knew full well that a day of reckoning was inevitable. In the first months after the United States entered the war, however, Wilson avoided a direct confrontation. Otherwise, as House said, the Americans and the Allies would have soon hated "one another more than they do Germany."[74] Shortly after he visited Washington in late April, Foreign Secretary Arthur Balfour sent Wilson copies of the secret treaties the Allies had earlier negotiated among themselves to divide enemy territories as the spoils of victory.[75] In Wilson's eyes, such egregious violations of the principle of self-determination justified his designation of the United States as a wartime *associate,* rather than as an ally, of the powers arrayed against Germany. "England and France *have not the same views with regard to peace that we have* by any means," he told House. Alas, not much could be done about it so long as Germany was undefeated; he took solace in the optimistic assumption that, after the war, "we can force them to our way of thinking, because by that time they will, among other things, be financially in our hands."[76]

The great question of war aims acquired a new urgency, however, not just because the entrance of the United States into the war meant that the Allies would eventually have to contend with Wilson. In March 1917, the repressive autocracy of Tsar Nicholas II had been overthrown, to the gratification of liberals, socialists, and not a few conservatives around the world. When Wilson went before Congress on April 2, the revolutionary transformation of the government of Russia had made it possible for him rhetorically to portray the world conflict as a struggle between the forces of democracy and the forces of autocracy. The United States also became the first power to recognize the Provisional Government of Alexander Kerensky.[77]

From the start, Kerensky, vowing to continue the war (but now for democratic socialist purposes), was besieged from within and without. Week by week, the Russian army, starving and poorly equipped, staggered under the relentless blows of the German and Austrian armies. In April and May, the soldiers' and workers' councils in Petrograd challenged the Provisional Government's authority and issued dramatic proclamations that might easily have been passages from the "Peace Without Victory" address. These proclamations appealed to all the belligerents for a peace based on self-determination and prevailed upon the peoples involved in the war to press their respective governments to repudiate plans for conquest.[78]

Wilson's series of anti-imperialist pronouncements before April 1917, in tandem with the Petrograd formula, stood in stark contrast to Allied war aims. In light of both Russia's precarious internal situation and the existence of a formidable anti-war minority in the United States, pro-war liberals and socialists on both sides of the Atlantic began to put new demands on Wilson. "Something needs to be done at once," the *New Republic* said on May 19. "The thing which is needed is a powerful reaffirmation of the international purposes for which the war is waged."[79] The executive committee of the Union of Democratic Control also pressed Wilson to give his public endorsement to the Petrograd formula—"so in accord with your own pronouncements"—and thereby remove the suspicions hanging over the Allied cause.[80]

In his Flag Day address, Wilson had characterized the war as a "Peoples' War." At the same time, however, his exhortations to crush Prussian militarism tended primarily to fortify super-patriotism and anti-German hysteria and concomitantly obscured the objectives of a just peace and a league of nations.[81] The tone alarmed not only progressive internationalists at home; the British radicals as well sought reassurance that Wilson had not forsaken his higher goals.[82] Although Wilson naturally sympathized with the Petrograd formula, his first priority would always be the prosecution of the war. He preferred to agitate for the revision of Allied war aims, initially, through the quiet channels of diplomacy.

Before the end of summer, however, Wilson was compelled to make a public declaration. On August 13, Pope Benedict XV (who sympathized with the German and Austrian governments) published an appeal to all the belligerents to end the war on the basis of the *status quo ante bellum*.[83] Such a challenge from the Holy See could not go unanswered. Before releasing his reply, Wilson told House, "I have tried to indicate the attitude of this country on the points most discussed in the socialistic and other camps."[84] In the document, Wilson suggested that the peace initiative was premature, particularly if the object of the war were in fact "to deliver the free peoples of the world from the menace and the actual power of a vast military establishment." He also implied that the Russian Revolution would fall prey to "the certain counter-revolution which would be attempted by all the malign influence to which the German Government has of late accustomed the world." The note continued: "Punitive damages, the dismemberment of empires, the establishment of selfish and exclusive economic leagues, we deem . . . no proper basis for a peace of any kind, least of all for an enduring peace. That must be based upon justice and fairness and the common rights of mankind."[85]

Wilson's forthright reply to the papal gambit accomplished a number of things. In recapitulating his "peace without victory" formula, he had publicly registered his displeasure with the Allies' prevarication on war aims, provided a more satisfactory response to the Petrograd soviet, and

had also relieved the British radicals[86] and American progressive internationalists of much of their anxiety. The *Appeal to Reason* described the
message to the Pope as "not only a step toward the ending of the war,
but also a blow to the imperialist schemers."[87] Max Eastman, even while
under attack from Burleson, wrote to Wilson: "Now that you have declared for substantially the Russian terms—no 'punitive damages,' no 'dismemberment of empires,' 'vindication of sovereignties,' and by making a
responsible ministry in Germany one condition of your entering negotiations, you have given a concrete meaning to the statement that this is a
war for democracy. The manner in which you have accomplished this—
and apparently bound the allies to it into the bargain—has my profound
admiration."[88]

Eastman's understanding, while representative of the responses of
American liberals and socialists, was erroneous on at least one count. The
Allies had not been bound to the bargain, as Wilson well knew. And to
prepare for the day when he would have to make the American case for
the peace settlement and the League of Nations, he instructed Colonel
House to gather a group of experts in the fields of economics, geography,
history, and political science. This group, the first "Brain Trust" in American history, subsequently became known as "The Inquiry"; it put together detailed, scholarly studies on social, economic, and political conditions in Europe and Asia, which helped Wilson immensely throughout
the war and during the peace conference as well.[89] In October, Wilson
also decided to send House to the forthcoming Inter-Allied Conference in
Paris where he was to try to obtain a joint statement on war aims.[90]

Before House arrived in Paris, the Provisional Government of Russia
had met with disaster. Under the leadership of V. I. Lenin and Leon
Trotsky, and armed with the irresistible slogan "Peace, Land, and Bread,"
the Petrograd soviet overthrew Kerensky on November 7, and intended
to turn the stirring words of the "International" into reality. On November 8, the new Bolshevik government issued a peace decree, strikingly
Wilsonian in tenor, calling for "the immediate opening of negotiations for
a just and democratic peace." Two weeks later, to tell the unholy lie on
Allied war aims, the Bolsheviks published most of the Allies' secret treaties.[91]

Russia's virtual (or incipient) withdrawal from the war, in conjunction with a coincidental military disaster in October—the defeat of the
Italian Army at Caporetto—dealt the Allied position a potentially mortal
blow. When the Inter-Allied Conference convened on November 29, Lloyd
George, Georges Clemenceau, and Baron Sidney Sonnino of Italy showed
far more interest in getting American soldiers and matériel to the western
front than in countering the enormous psychological advantage that the
Central Powers had gained by the Bolsheviks' publication of the secret

treaties. Repeatedly, Colonel House tried get them to designate terms, and he even presented the conclave with a vague resolution on war aims before returning home. Clemenceau and Sonnino, however, would have no part of it. This being the case, House reproved them, the President would have to act unilaterally.[92]

Wilson had already decided to do just that. In his annual message to Congress, on December 4, he made his most unambiguous statement since the "Peace Without Victory" address. It was his duty, he told the Congress, to add "specific interpretations" to what he had said to the Senate in January. Whereas he assailed the German autocracy for its exploitation of the Bolsheviks, he also asserted that the damage was as much the fault of the Allies themselves for not having purged their cause of suspicion before world opinion. Had they cleared the air, then "the sympathy and enthusiasm of the Russian people might have been once and for all enlisted on the side of the Allies." In any case, Wilson now promised the German *people* an impartial settlement if they would but rid themselves of the encumbrance of the Kaiser's government. With German militarism defeated, "an unprecedented thing" would be possible: "We shall be free to base peace on generosity and justice, to the exclusion of all selfish claims to advantage even on the part of the victors," and Germany itself could be admitted "to the partnership of nations which must henceforth guarantee the world's peace."[93]

Wilson's message to Congress did not make the slightest dent in the leaders of the Allied governments; they chose to interpret it mainly as a reaffirmation of American commitment to victory. The British radicals, however, regarded the remarks as a most timely addendum to the "Peace Without Victory" address.[94] Significantly, in the United States, the message appeared to have brought a halt to the dissolution of the progressive internationalist coalition. The faithful and the doubters alike were greatly encouraged by Wilson's analysis of the events of November. "I rejoice exceedingly to have you remind the Congress as well as the statesmen of the world of that immortal January address to the Senate," George Foster Peabody wrote the President. In the Philadelphia *Public Ledger,* the progressive publicist Lincoln Colcord praised the Bolsheviks for bringing order out of chaos and described the "magnificent liberalism of President Wilson's address" as a "gift" to the Russian people that would also "uplift the failing hearts of the whole world." Grenville Mcfarland, who had prevailed upon Wilson on behalf of the socialist press, wrote in the New York *American* that the message to Congress "breathes the spirit of Lincoln's second inaugural and will take its place beside that great document."[95] And Louis Kopelin, editor of the *Appeal to Reason,* wrote: "Your open-hearted espousal of a democratic peace after the central European peoples have been freed from the yoke of Prussian militarism removes the last possible suspicion against the cause of the entente allies." From December 1917 onward, the *Appeal*—"the oldest and largest American socialist publication," Kopelin had reminded Wilson—reversed its anti-war position and for the next year became one of the President's most faithful editorial patrons.[96]

As word of Wilson's pronouncement reached Europe, the Bolsheviks had begun to consider a bold initiative for a separate peace. In part to consolidate their own power in Russia, in part because the Allies (not to say Wilson) had studiously maintained silence about their régime, the Bolsheviks at last signed an armistice with Germany at Brest-Litovsk, on December 15. One week later, Adolf Joffe, the leader of the Russian delegation, laid down six points as the basis for the negotiations, which the Germans accepted on December 25. In broad strokes, the program constituted a model "peace without victory"—no forcible annexations, the application of self-determination for all national groups, no indemnities, no economic boycotts or restrictions on freedom of trade.[97] This extraordinary new set of circumstances—the Bolsheviks' appropriation of most of the New Diplomacy, coupled with the specter of a separate peace in the East that would enable Germany to bring new might to bear in the West—rendered Wilson's recent utterances inadequate.

Colonel House's diary entry of December 18 offers a succinct explanation of the immediate genesis of what was to become the most celebrated diplomatic statement of Wilson's career: "I never knew a man who did things so casually. We did not discuss the matter more than ten or fifteen minutes when he decided he would take the action I told the Interallied Conference he would take as soon as I returned to America."[98] Wilson then instructed House to put The Inquiry to work. Over the next two weeks the team of experts labored day and night, drawing up specific recommendations on a wide variety of economic, political, and territorial matters.[99] On their own, the President and House hammered into shape a series of (as it turned out, fourteen) concise, categorical paragraphs on war aims, on January 5. "We actually got down to work at half past ten," House recorded, "and finished remaking the map of the world, as we would have it, at half past twelve o-clock" (It had been a remarkably productive morning!)[100]

Unexpectedly, on the same day, Lloyd George had abandoned the ancient Foreign Office custom of sitting on the fence and had managed to upstage Wilson, or so it seemed for a short while. On December 28, the British Labour party had published a "Memorandum on War Aims." It declared that the war could no longer be justified, except "that the world may henceforth be made safe for democracy," and that a league of nations would be established so "that there should be henceforth on earth no more war." Labour thus served notice that its continued support hinged on a satisfactory answer from the government. The negotiations at Brest-Litovsk and the weary prospect of yet another year of senseless slaughter had obviously triggered the memorandum. Its substance, however, was determined by the previous pronouncements of Wilson and the British radicals. The war cabinet concluded that it had no choice but to reply.[101]

Accordingly, on January 5, Lloyd George addressed the British Trades Union League at Caxton Hall, in order to remove all "misgivings and doubts" about British war aims. Great Britain longed only for a democratic peace, the Prime Minister said; she harbored no ambitions to destroy the Central Powers, even though Germany was presently perpetrating the conquest of Russia. He then went on to pay obeisance to the New Diplomacy and assuage British Labour with a declaration of moderate terms: "First, the sanctity of treaties must be re-established; secondly, a territorial settlement must be secured based on the right of self-determination or the consent of the governed; and, lastsome, we must seek by the creation of some international organization to limit the burden of armaments and diminish the probability of war."[102]

When Wilson learned of the address, he momentarily hesitated to go forward with his own plans. House, however, persuaded him that Lloyd George had merely primed the pump, and that the President's "would so smother the Lloyd George speech that it would be forgotten."[103]

Wilson delivered his address to a joint session of Congress on January 8. He began by acknowledging that the Russian representatives at Brest-Litovsk had recently engaged the Central Powers in parlays for a peace based on democratic principles. The Central Empire, he pointed out, was merely exploiting the precepts of the New Diplomacy in order to absorb part of Russia. Even so, there was no good reason not to respond to the Bolsheviks' earnest invitation to the Western powers to state their terms. The conception of the Russian people "of what is right, of what is humane and honorable for them to accept, has been stated with a frankness . . . and a universal human sympathy which must challenge the admiration of every friend of mankind," he said. "Whether their present leaders believe it or not, it is our heartfelt desire and hope that some way may be opened whereby we may be privileged to assist the people of Russia to attain their utmost hope of liberty and ordered peace." The American people saw clearly that unless justice be done to others it would not be done to them. "The programme of the world's peace, therefore, is our programme; and that programme, the only possible programme, as we see it, is this. . . ."

The first five of the fourteen points were familiar to all progressive internationalists: open covenants openly arrived at and the abolition of secret treaties; absolute freedom of the seas, "except as the seas may be closed . . . by international action for the enforcement of international covenants"; the removal of all economic trade barriers and the establishment of the equality of trade conditions; the reduction of all national armaments to the lowest point consistent with domestic safety; and the impartial adjustment of all colonial claims in observance of the principle of self-determination.

The sixth point demanded the evacuation of all Russian territory and the "unembarrassed opportunity for the independent determination of her own political institutions." The way other nations treated Russia in the months to come, Wilson said, "will be the acid test of their good will." Points seven through thirteen specified the evacuation of Belgium; the return of Alsace-Lorraine to France; the readjustment of Italian frontiers along clearly recognizable lines of nationality; autonomous development for the peoples of Austria-Hungary, the Balkans, and the Turkish portions of the Ottoman Empire; and the creation of a Polish state assured of free and secure access to the sea.

According to Colonel House, Wilson thought that the subject embodied in the fourteenth point "should come last because it would round out the message properly." For Wilson, it was the most important one of all: "A general association of nations must be formed under specific covenants for the purpose of affording mutual guarantees of political independence and territorial integrity to great and small states alike."

It was for these things that the United States and its associates were fighting. "We have no jealousy of German greatness, and there is nothing in this program that impairs it. . . . We wish her only to accept a place of equality among the peoples of the world." Before serious discussions could begin, however, the United States must know for whom Germany's representatives spoke—whether for the Reichstag majority or for the military party whose creed was imperial domination. The single thread that ran through the whole program, he said in conclusion (as he had said many times before), was "the principle of justice to all peoples and nationalities and the right to live on equal terms of liberty and safety with one another, whether they be strong or weak." This was the only principle upon which the American people could act. "The moral climax of this the culminating and final war for human liberty has come, and they are ready to put their own strength, their own highest purpose, their own integrity and devotion to the test."[104]

The Fourteen Points address, as the New York *Herald* described it at the time, continues to stand as "one of the great documents in American history."[105] Since the height of the Cold War in the late 1950s and 1960s, the preponderance of historical interpretations—most notably those of Arno J. Mayer, William Appleman Williams, N. Gordon Levin, and Lloyd C. Gardner—have emphasized the degree to which Wilson's program was formulated in response to, and the degree to which its provisions were influenced by, the revolution in Russia. Yet, save the very one on Russia, Wilson did not define a single point that was in any way inspired by the Bolsheviks. The seven proposals for territorial adjustments (principally the work of Walter Lippmann and The Inquiry) would have been advised in any circumstances. The remaining six, a sermon on progressive internationalism, were fundamentally a reprise of Wilson's pronouncements before the United States had even entered the war, and long before revolutionary upheaval in Russia appeared imminent.

To be sure, but for the events that culminated at Brest-Litovsk, Wilson would not have delivered such an address just when he did. Two of his purposes were to diminish the impact of the publication of the secret Allied treaties and to try to bring the Bolsheviks back into the war against Germany through an appeal to common principles. Another purpose was to rally all groups at home and abroad behind a peace settlement grounded in a league of nations and other new principles of international conduct, and to induce the Allied governments to embrace that cause—an object Wilson had been striving for since the spring of 1916. Finally, Wilson hoped to foment political dissension within Germany and Austria-Hungary by indicating upon what terms they could obtain peace. Yet, in all of this, the Bolsheviks played a primary role only insofar as the timing of the Fourteen Points was concerned.

Neither was the address the opening salvo of a counterrevolutionary campaign. Not until the spring of 1918, when a German victory became a distinct possibility, did Wilson's historical appreciation of the Russian upheaval begin to show signs of real hostility toward Lenin.[106] For one thing, the President was far too self-assured to regard Lenin as any sort of challenge or threat to his own preeminence as a world statesman. (Lenin was, after all, a comparatively obscure politician at the head of a very shaky government, and Wilson knew very little about him.) Moreover, one of the most striking aspects of the Fourteen Points, in its restatement of the "Peace Without Victory" address, was its uncompromising anti-imperialism. As he had done in the case of Mexico, and thus in Russia, he fully accepted revolution as a legitimate, if undesirable, agent of change. And, as he had palpably demonstrated in American domestic politics, he did not consider liberalism and socialism, practically speaking, as irreconcilable—and certainly not in the sort of community of nations he envisioned, in which such contending forces would naturally audit and regulate one another.

In any event, Lenin himself reportedly hailed the address as "a great step ahead towards the peace of the world" and arranged for its publication in *Izvestiya*. American representatives and Bolsheviks worked together to circulate millions of copies in Petrograd and Moscow and among German soldiers inside Russia.[107] The entire French left, along with most of the French press, greeted the Fourteen Points with unqualified approval—despite the circumspect attitude of Clemenceau's government.[108] In Great Britain, the UDC regarded the President's reiteration of the progressive internationalist synthesis as the vindication of its own platform. Whereas the London *Times* commented that the speech presumed "that the reign of righteousness upon earth is already within our reach," the London *Star* implored British politicians "to emulate . . . the greatest American president since Abraham Lincoln." Without actually endorsing its contents, Balfour called the address a "magnificent pronouncement." Lloyd George sent word informally that he was "grateful" that his and President Wilson's peace policies were "so entirely in harmony."[109]

In the United States, the most important impact that the Fourteen Points had was to engender a fresh environment for progressive internationalism and the League. The approbation heaped upon the address approached phenomenal proportions. Although a few Republicans took sharp exception to the point on free trade, praise from both parties was generous. Many congressmen and senators expressed the opinion that the address marked the moral turning point of the war.[110] The headline that the *New York Times* ran above its main editorial—"The President's Triumph"—was indicative of the general reaction across the country. Wilson had articulated "the very conscience of the American people," said Hamilton Holt in the *Independent*.[111] "We think that your message to Congress expresses the broadest understanding and profoundest insight and that your program would bring about the possibility of nations harmonized in their relationship with each other," Lillian Wald wrote to the President. Jane Addams transmitted to Wilson a resolution passed by the Woman's Peace party which acclaimed the address "the most profound and brilliant formulation as yet put forth by any responsible statesman of the program of international reorganization." John Spargo deemed it "a great inspiration to the believers in democracy in all lands, including the enemy nations."[112]

It was not, perhaps, surprising that leading members of the coalition of 1916 like Holt, Wald, and Addams, or a pro-war Socialist like Spargo, should lavish such praise. But indications that progressive internationalism was on the road to recovery extended further than that. Max Eastman's initial reflection, "A World's Peace," emphasized the fourteenth point, upon which rested all the others. "If the world falls into peace, exhausted, without having accomplished this," he wrote, "it will be a sad peace—a peace without victory indeed."[113] The *Appeal to Reason* ran a front-page banner headline, "World League to Preserve Peace Is Now Vital Issue" and subsequently called upon the Socialist party to revise the St. Louis Proclamation.[114] Eugene Debs pronounced the Fourteen Points "thoroughly democratic," deserving of "the unqualified approval of everyone believing in the rule of the people, Socialists included." There were even bigger surprises coming. "I am not in the habit of paying tribute to public officials," Mother Jones told the West Virginia Federation of Labor, "[but] I pay my respects to President Wilson." She even announced that working people now could in good conscience buy Liberty Bonds. Meyer London followed suit, expressing the hope that soon "the world will be at peace, based on the principles formulated by President Wilson."[115]

Later, in the spring, Eastman offered an additional, 6,000-word meditation entitled "Wilson and the World's Future," published in the *Liberator,* the new incarnation of the *Masses.* Through his efforts to advance the New Diplomacy and the League, the President had brought to statesmanship "some of the same thing that Bergson and William James and John Dewey have brought into philosophy—a sense of reality of time, and the creative character of change. . . . It is the expression of a wisdom which is new and peculiar to our age." Eastman also commented on Upton Sinclair's recent statement that, in light of the Fourteen Points, the Socialist party should formally declare its support of President Wilson. It might be better, Eastman noted wryly, if Wilson joined the Socialist party. "I should be willing to take the risk of accepting him as a member."[116]

In October 1917, the brilliant young radical Randolph Bourne published in *The Seven Arts* what was to become his most famous essay—"Twilight of Idols." Disillusioned by his mentor, John Dewey, who had embraced the war because of its "plasticity," Bourne had asked all pro-war socialists and liberals the haunting question: "If the war is too strong for you to prevent, how is it going to be weak enough for you to control and mould to your liberal purposes?"[117] In the autumn of 1917, it appeared that Bourne had surely struck home. By the early months of 1918, however, most progressive internationalists could claim that his question was no longer necessarily relevant, or they could turn to Wilson for an emphatic answer. For, if the response of progressive internationalists to the Fourteen Points was any guide, then it seemed that at last the war *was* being molded to serve the good purposes of, not only liberals, but also socialists. The President had forsaken neither after all. Even in the suffocating atmosphere of "One Hundred Percent Americanism," he had administered a most comforting balm to those important constituents who had been battered and betrayed. His championship of progressive internationalist values, like a cure endowed with miraculous properties, had also breathed new life into the hope that a better world could come of the violent and complicated spectacle humanity was passing through. If this was in fact "the culminating and final war for human liberty," as Wilson had said, then was it not worthwhile to see the struggle through to the bitter end? Was it not possible that Wilson could be right? There no longer seemed to be any serious reason to doubt it.

9

Waiting for Wilson
The Wages of Delay and Repression

I t gives me peculiar gratification that you and your associates should
feel as you do about my recent address to the Congress," Wilson
wrote to Jane Addams after receiving the resolutions passed by the Woman's Peace party.[1] Yet if the Fourteen Points had helped mend fences with
progressive internationalists, the address had other consequences not entirely to the Wilson's liking. On both sides of the Atlantic, his pronouncement on war aims set in motion new agitation on behalf of the League.
This was all well and good, of course, except for the fact that the activity
was accompanied by renewed entreaties that the President formulate specific proposals for the League—and that was something to which he was
implacably opposed. His attitude was not likely to facilitate mutual understanding between the administration and British internationalists or to
improve his relationship with the League to Enforce Peace; nor, for that
matter, did it nurture progressive internationalism.

The strength of Wilson's appeal in Europe, especially among British
Labour, helped swell the ranks of Great Britain's expanding league movement in 1918. The League of Nations Society established new branches
throughout the country, held large public meetings, and circulated thousands of pamphlets about world organization.[2] Within the British government, Lord Robert Cecil became the heir to Edward Grey's mantle as the

leading Cabinet-level advocate of the League. As early as September 1917, Cecil had proposed to Colonel House the creation of "some Commission of learned and distinguished men" to study the League. But, as he learned from the Colonel, Wilson "felt it was best not to have a cut and dried agreement."[3] Undaunted, Cecil prevailed upon Balfour to appoint the British government's own committee. Under the chairmanship of Sir Walter G. F. Phillimore, a distinguished jurist, this committee worked in secret to develop some concrete ideas on the League. Cecil informed Colonel House of the Phillimore group's existence in mid-February.[4]

Within the United States, as well, the league movement entered a new phase. In the wake of the Fourteen Points address, groups such as the National Committee on the Moral Aims of the War began to enlist thousands of clergymen in the cause and to distribute pamphlet literature. The American School Peace League sponsored essay contests in which children wrote compositions on "How Should the World Be Organized so as to Prevent Wars in the Future?"[5] During the spring of 1918 the League to Enforce Peace drew up a "Tentative Draft" of a constitution for the League and began to press hard for some leadership from Wilson.[6] Theodore Marburg became the LEP's chief presidential correspondent. But with each communication Wilson only grew more worried that he would be unable to keep the LEP reined in, especially when he learned of Marburg's extensive correspondence with Viscount Bryce.[7]

Wilson's objections were not without substance. He expressed them most succinctly in an important letter to House on March 22: "My own conviction, as you know, is that the administrative constitution of the League must *grow* and not be made; that we must *begin* with solemn covenants, covering mutual guarantees of political independence and territorial integrity . . . but that the method of carrying those mutual pledges out should be left to develop of itself, case by case. . . . To take one thing, and only one, but quite sufficient in itself:

"The United States Senate would never ratify any treaty which put the force of the United States at the disposal of any such group or body. Why begin at the impossible end when there is a possible end and it is feasible to plant a system which will slowly but surely ripen into fruition?"[8]

Wilson's annoyance with the LEP was also petty. In the foregoing letter to House, he wrote: "Yes, indeed, I think your lunch with Taft, Lowell, and Root is most wise and should be most helpful, if they have any sense among them,—which I sometimes seriously doubt."[9] Wilson was never more exercised with the LEP than when that organization scheduled a three-day convention to be held in Philadelphia, in May 1918. If prominent individuals announced detailed plans for the League it would put him in a very difficult position. This was his chronic fear.

To head them off, Wilson invited Taft and Lowell to the White House for a meeting on March 28.[10] According to Taft's account, Wilson offered cautious views on how a league could prudently respond to violations of members' territorial integrity and political independence. "He said he knew this would be slow, but that the common law was built up that way," Taft wrote. "He gave it as his opinion that the Senate . . . would be unwilling to enter into an agreement by which the majority of the other nations could tell the United States when they must go to war." When Lowell raised the subject of a brain trust, Wilson said that any kind of transatlantic, or strictly American, commission would create more problems than it could solve. Taft and Lowell seemed to understand his position and assured him that the purpose of the LEP's gathering in May was to promote the war effort, not to draw up a constitution for the League. Wilson thereupon withdrew his objections. Taft and Lowell then gave him a copy of the LEP's "Tentative Draft" and took their leave.[11]

Almost a year later, Wilson told his physician, Dr. Cary T. Grayson, about "a strange coincidence" that had occurred during the session with Lowell and Taft—a sudden, loud crash out in the hallway adjoining the Green Room. The source of the distraction, Wilson later found out, was a huge portrait of President Taft, which had fallen from its wall-hanging.[12] As Wilson remarked, the coincidence was rather strange; it was also a symbolic portent. Whereas Taft and Lowell had soothed some of the President's anxieties, Wilson had failed to soothe theirs; in fact, he had completely confused Taft about the degree of his commitment. The main impression that Taft came away with, he wrote in a second account of the meeting, was that "Wilson does not favor our League to Enforce Peace."[13]

By summer, the nature of Wilson's relationship with the LEP was sealed. The organization had by then been apprised (by Colonel House) of the work of the Phillimore committee, whence the ill-advised Lowell informed the President of the need for a committee to coordinate plans with the British—and urged him to appoint one immediately, "if," he wrote, "you desire to maintain the leading part in directing the movement." Wilson matched Lowell's indiscretion by practically telling him to mind his own business: The enterprise was a question of *governmental* policy, not to mention a "part of the intricate web of counsel now being woven between the associated governments." He would "consider it very embarrassing" if the LEP undertook to establish "connections with committees of a different origin abroad."[14]

Lowell's views, however, were shared by others. The Inquiry had earlier suggested holding a conference in Washington to formulate plans.[15] Colonel House, as much as Wilson the object of the importunings of both the British and the LEP, had come to the same conclusion by late spring.

The President, he believed, was dragging his feet and ought to put some of his own ideas down on paper, if not discuss them with other interested parties. Upon receiving a copy of the Phillimore Report in June, House knew, even if Wilson did not, that the issue could no longer be put off.[16]

The Phillimore Report, submitted to the British Cabinet on March 3, constituted the closest thing to a "policy" on the League that any government had thus far put together. Referring to the League as the "alliance," the Report combined the recommendations of the Bryce Group and the LEP. It proposed, first, that members should agree not to go to war against another member without having previously yielded to arbitration or conciliation. If a signatory broke this pledge, then it would be *"ipso facto"* at war with all the others; they, in turn, would be obliged to restrain the violator through joint economic and military sanctions. Second, the report outlined procedures for arbitration and conciliation and, in phrases reminiscent of Bryan's, emphasized the utility of delaying hostilities so that "passions will have cooled." The authors made no recommendation for possible action in the event that disputants took up arms after having awaited the arbitration decision. The third section provided for invitations to nonmembers to submit their disputes to the foregoing process.[17]

The Phillimore Report was not a comprehensive plan. Its authors advanced it as "a possible solution," not as an endorsement of collective security, let alone of the New Diplomacy. The document said nothing about disarmament or about who, beyond the members of the wartime alliance, should be invited to subscribe. A nation could still go to war against another nation, presumably with impunity, once arbitration was completed; there were no provisions for the enforcement of decisions. In practically all respects, it was as one with the LEP's "Tentative Draft." As George Egerton has written, the Phillimore Report "involved only minor departures from conventional diplomatic practice."[18]

Even so, the Imperial War Cabinet gave the report a mixed reception, notwithstanding Cecil's enthusiasm for it. The chief stumbling block was the use of sanctions of any kind. Lloyd George wondered whether it would be best simply to have a forum for heads of state to confer with one another on a regular basis. The cabinet failed to arrive at a consensus on exactly what burdens the League ought to shoulder and on what role it should play in British foreign policy. Lord Robert was given permission, however, to send the study on to Washington.[19]

After reading the Phillimore Report, House decided to lay before Wilson the present state of affairs. The League of Nations "will not wait for the peace conference," he wrote on June 25, and he was worried that the British, the French, or some American group would put out a plan that would capture public opinion in spite of the President's views. "The whole world look upon you as the champion of the idea, but there is a feeling . . . that you are reluctant to take the initiative."[20]

Coming from House, this was pretty strong language, and it had the desired effect. Wilson immediately authorized House to send Cecil a letter outlining the functions and responsibilities the League might fulfill.[21] Then, on July 3, Wilson received a copy of the Phillimore Report. "It has no teeth," he later said to Sir William Wiseman. "I read it to the last page hoping to find something definite, but I could not."[22] Wilson now saw the utility of coming up with some details of his own and asked House to rewrite the Phillimore Report along the lines of the letter to Cecil. This, he said, would provide him with a basis for his own plan and for comment on the British recommendations.[23]

During the second week of July, House and David Hunter Miller, The Inquiry's specialist on international law, drafted a constitution.[24] Consisting of a preamble and twenty-three articles, it incorporated many features of the Phillimore Report,[25] along with House's and Wilson's views on arbitration and the mutual guarantee of territorial integrity. House modified the territorial guarantee, however, so that the League accommodated future territorial adjustments "pursuant to the principle of self-determination." At the same time, he limited sanctions to diplomatic and economic coercion; therein he adopted the language of the Phillimore Report—that the contracting powers "*may* come to the assistance" of a threatened country. In addition, the document contained a strong article on disarmament and the prohibition of the manufacture of munitions by private enterprise, and another providing for an International Court.[26]

The draft was "written with a view of not hurting the sensibilities of . . . the Entente or the Central Powers," House explained to Wilson. He also suggested that the League be confined to the great powers, "giving the smaller powers every benefit that may be derived therefrom." This would take account of the fears (voiced by Senator Lodge, for instance, and now shared by House) of superior numbers of small nations outvoting the powers that would have to shoulder larger responsibilities. House advised Wilson to release the document "as quickly as possible in order to let thought crystallize around your plan instead of some other."[27]

Wilson was not entirely satisfied. He readily embraced the corollary on self-determination, which would infuse into the territorial guarantee the element of flexibility, in observance of "the welfare and manifest interest of the peoples concerned" as well as of "the principle that the peace of the world is superior in importance to every question of political jurisdiction or boundary." He struck out the provision on the International Court and slightly modified the one on disarmament. His most significant change was to strengthen House's article on sanctions. Wilson intended to rectify the Phillimore Report's toothlessness. Should any power begin hostilities against another, either before or after arbitration, the contracting powers would be bound not only to cease commercial and diplomatic intercourse, but also to unite in closing the frontiers of the aggressor, using "any force that may be necessary to accomplish that object."

In sum, Wilson thus would have a league of nations that, in at least four respects, differed markedly from that of both the Phillimore Report and the LEP's "Tentative Draft." First, his League would make the arbitration process compulsory and the decisions binding. Second, it would hold out an absolute guarantee of territorial integrity and political independence while also compelling the recognition of the principle of self-determination. Third, disarmament would be a serious priority—not a mere afterthought—integral to the success of the whole system. And, finally, by omitting any discriminatory reference to representatives in the Body of Delegates or to their assigned responsibilities, the League would recognize the principle of the equality of states. This, then, was the "COVENANT"—a supremely ambitious conception, compressed into thirteen articles, with roots in Wilson's youth and academic career and more proximate ones in the formulations of progressive internationalism as embodied in the Bryan treaties, the Pan-American Pact, the "Peace Without Victory" address, and the Fourteen Points. It was the most important document that he would take with him to the Paris Peace Conference.[28]

On August 15, Wilson traveled to Magnolia, Massachusetts, to visit Colonel House. "This is what I have done with your constitution of a league of nations," he said as he proceeded to read it aloud. House objected to the omission of the International Court, but did not press the issue, contenting himself with the thought that it would be restored at the peace conference. Their strongest disagreement came over the question of representation of small and great states. House argued that equal representation was impractical because the major powers presumably would have to carry out the enforcement of sanctions and pay the League's bills. Wilson understood House's apprehensions, but "dissented quite warmly." To deny the smaller states equal status, he said, would contradict all of his previous declarations. For the time being, they let the issue rest, with House again believing that his own position would prevail at the peace conference.

In one other important matter, House decided not to persist. The President was irrevocably set against publishing either his own or the Phillimore recommendations. "It would cause so much criticism in this country," he said, "particularly by Senators of the Lodge type . . . [and] increase the difficulties of getting a proper measure through at the Peace Conference." House agreed, but wrote in his diary, "if the President had taken the lead earlier and had pushed the matter vigorously, he might have given out his own conception of what a league of nations should be, and have rallied the world around it."[29]

On the day after their working session, Sir William Wiseman joined Wilson and House at Magnolia. On this occasion, Wilson rejected Wiseman's request (emanating from Cecil) that he consent to the publication of the Phillimore Report. He also said that he had no intention of creating an American version of the Phillimore committee. "How then are we ever to exchange views?" Wiseman asked, and Wilson at last conceded that he would be glad to discuss the League, in private, with a representative of the British government. As it turned out, however, by the time the Imperial War Cabinet was able to authorize Lord Reading to return to Washington to get these talks underway, unforeseen developments in the war aborted the mission.[30]

In the Magnolia Covenant Wilson had fashioned a fine document distinguished by the salient principles of progressive internationalism. But, with the single exception of Colonel House, until the Paris Peace Conference convened, absolutely no one—American, European, progressive, or conservative—would know precisely what he had in mind for this, his most cherished objective. In the case of the Allies, it was doubly unfortunate that Wilson had not let his views be known. One of the results of the Fourteen Points address had been to create the public impression of Allied-American conformity on war aims. Although he remained at heart distrustful of British motives, Wilson was eager to believe that their policy, by virtue of Lloyd George's Trades Union speech, mirrored his own. Yet Vittorio Orlando of Italy had protested against *both* speeches. Clemenceau had seen fit to congratulate Lloyd George on his speech, but not Wilson on the Fourteen Points. Moreover, none of the Allied governments had as yet officially endorsed the President's edition of the New Diplomacy. Here, then, he might have done well to seize the opportunity that Cecil and others had repeatedly held out, if for no other reason than to explore one area of potential, mutual understanding on the coming peace settlement. Then, too, in the event that such explorations gave vent to cross purposes, Wilson would have had greater leverage in compelling the Allies to accept his terms while the war still continued rather than after Germany had ceased to pose a threat.

One arena in which Wilson did consent to cooperate with the Allies in the summer of 1918 concerned a woeful postscript to the Brest-Litovsk negotiations. In the context of others, this development would at length have an adverse impact on many progressive internationalist supporters of the League and undo much of the good work accomplished by the Fourteen Points.

In late January 1918, the governments at Berlin and Vienna sent out a series of peace feelers to Wilson; these came in response to the Fourteen Points as well as to a consequent movement within the Reichstag for the democratization of Germany.[31] The ensuing diplomatic exchange was terminated, however, when the Central Powers decided instead to exploit Russia's prostration and impose upon her a Carthaginian peace. In the Treaty of Brest-Litovsk the Bolsheviks surrendered about one third of Russia's territory, thus permitting Germany to mount a ferocious spring offensive against the western front. Together, these harrowing setbacks loosed anti-Bolshevik tirades in both the United States and Western Europe; they also appreciably undermined, in the eyes of the Allies and many Americans, Wilson's arguments for the measure of peace without victory that was implicit in the Fourteen Points.

No less inauspiciously, Brest-Litovsk also revived a series of ill-conceived Allied schemes to reopen the eastern front by way of northern Russia and to authorize the Japanese to secure control of the Trans-Siberian railroad terminus at Vladivostok. As early as December 1917, the British, French, and Japanese governments had launched a campaign to gain Wilson's consent to these proposals.[32]

From the start, Wilson smelled imperialist rats within the Allied coalition. His thoughts now went back to Mexico. Among other things, such encroachments on Russian territory would violate the principle of self-determination. This skepticism was also reinforced by the opinions of his chief military advisers, who doubted both the feasibility of the venture and the military advantages that supposedly would accrue.[33] "The wisdom of intervention seems . . . most questionable," Wilson informed the Japanese government on March 5. There were other factors to consider, but the whole action "might play into the hands . . . of the enemies of the Russian Revolution, for which the Government of the United States entertains the greatest sympathy. . . ."[34] Because Wilson refused to go along, intervention in Siberia had been quashed—for the time being.

After Brest-Litovsk the situation quickly changed. The Supreme War Council became convinced of the need to interrupt Germany's transference of some forty divisions from Eastern to Western Europe. They reopened the question of intervening, not only in Siberia, but also at Murmansk and Archangel, where German troops apparently threatened caches of Allied munitions. In April, Wilson learned that Leon Trotsky had indicated that he might consent to an Allied military presence in those two ports, ostensibly to keep them from falling to the Germans; and at Vladivostok, if the Japanese were accompanied (and thereby restrained) by other Allied forces.[35] Throughout May and June of 1918, the Allies kept up practically a daily barrage of notes to Wilson. By then they had the help of a wavering Colonel House and the virulently anti-Bolshevik Lansing. The Japanese now threatened to take unilateral action. Marshal

Ferdinand Foch, the supreme Allied commander, sent the following message to the President in late June: "More than ever . . . I consider the expedition to Siberia as a very important factor for victory." A week later Wilson wrote to House, "I have been sweating blood over the question of what is right and feasible *(possible)* to do in Russia. It goes to pieces like quicksilver under my touch."[36]

Finally, by July, when it appeared that a legion of abandoned Czechs had clashed with German and Austrian ex–prisoners of war in Siberia and were in need of rescue, Wilson became the object of intense pressure from all sides.[37] Ambassador Reading reported to Lloyd George that the President feared "the interventionist movement would be controlled by friends of the old Imperial regime and . . . [would] be converted into an anti-Soviet movement and an interference with the right of Russians to choose their own form of government."[38] But, apparently because he worried about Japanese expansion through unilateral intervention (as well as about the likely fate of the Czechs), Wilson at last yielded. In August, with great misgivings, he dispatched some 5,000 soldiers to Murmansk, where the British already had stationed forces. Another 10,000 joined the Japanese at Vladivostok.

Wilson's trepidations were soon borne out in full. Within two months, the Japanese increased their contingent to 70,000, thus extending their military presence well into Russian territory; a threat to the Allied stores at Murmansk and Archangel never materialized; the Czechs themselves started moving east, instead of west, just as Wilson announced that he was sending American troops to facilitate their egress; and the British commander who superintended the forces at Murmansk eventually involved Americans in several minor battles with Bolshevik troops. In such circumstances, Wilson would find it more difficult to get out of Russia than it had been, even for him, to get in. Whereas by the autumn of 1918 he had developed considerable hostility toward the Bolsheviks and was convinced that their leaders were doing Germany's bidding, he still felt resentful toward the Allies about the intervention. "My policy regarding Russia is very similar to my Mexican policy," he said to Wiseman in October. "I believe in letting them work out their own salvation, even though they wallow in anarchy for a while."[39]

In virtually all aspects, the Russian intervention was a dismal failure. After more than seven decades, Wilson's intentions continue to be the subject of extended historical debate. But perhaps the most revealing commentary on his participation came from Lloyd George, during a meeting of the War Cabinet in July 1919. As his colleagues remonstrated over Allied policy toward the Soviets, the Prime Minister said that he "did not think that we should blame the Americans, as they had always been very much against undertaking operations against the Bolsheviks, and what they had done up to date was only on account of the pressure which had been brought to bear on President Wilson."[40]

"[T]he strongest supporters of intervention have been men with conservative views and some of its strongest opponents the more advanced liberals," Ambassador Reading informed Whitehall just as Wilson was on the verge of making his decision.[41] Indeed, so-called advanced liberals, from Lillian Wald to Max Eastman, had, in their estimations of the Fourteen Points, singled out for special tribute Wilson's understanding of the Russian Revolution. In early March, Norman Thomas had confided to Wald: "Frankly, my own feeling with regard to the war is undergoing something of a change. . . . [T]he Russian situation and the progressive abandonment of imperialistic aims by the Allies under pressure from the President and British Labour remove the reproach of hypocrisy from us."[42] In May, Eastman had cited the league of nations idea as an example of "the essence of the President's strength" and had applauded his initial thwarting of Japanese imperialism in Russia, comparing it to his earlier efforts to help the Mexican Revolution: "Wilson did the biggest thing—of a negative nature—that could be done to comfort the soldiers of the world that they are fighting for some principle higher than national prestige."[43]

From late summer onward, however, the question that Randolph Bourne had asked in "Twilight of Idols" took on a new resonance. On August 7, Wilson confessed to the Czech leader, Thomas Masaryk, that he "felt no confidence in [his own] personal judgment about the complicated situation in Russia."[44] This being the case, then leading progressive internationalists could hardly have been expected to feel confident. In its first editorial on the subject, the *New Republic,* like the majority of the American press, accepted the rescue of the Czechs as a legitimate rationale; but by autumn, the publication began to raise serious questions about the purposes of the intervention. (Eventually, it would denounce the American role as counterrevolutionary.[45]) Oswald Garrison Villard, condemning the venture as a repudiation of Wilson's stand against secret diplomacy, wrote facetiously in the *Nation,* "The President has assured us that it is only to be a little intervention, and we are to forgive it or approve it on the grounds of its littleness."[46] Colonel House found it impossible to convince Lincoln Colcord, one of his protégés, that Wilson had not "gone over to the reactionaries."[47] In September, Norman Thomas wrote "The Acid Test of Our Democracy," a scathing editorial about American and Allied activity in northern Russia and Siberia, in his new periodical, the *World Tomorrow.*[48] Eastman was dismayed as well. For a while, Wilson had stood "alone among all the bourgeois powers, an eccentric, obdurate idealist, resisting their logical and entirely economical determination to crush the Soviet republic." Eastman wondered whether the

President was any longer the hope of the progressive internationalists and the farmers and workers.[49]

The disillusioning effects of the Russian intervention and its potential to damage Wilson's standing with progressive internationalists might have been blunted had it not also been for the fact that Burleson and Gregory, in the late spring and early summer of 1918, got their second wind. In April, Max Eastman and John Reed were tried in the Federal District Court of New York on charges of violating the Espionage Act. (By this time, the *Masses* had ceased to exist.) Although the trial ended in a hung jury, the prosecutor announced that he would seek a second trial.[50] Wilson possessed the power to order his Attorney General to discontinue the case against the journalist, who, in the May issue of the *Liberator,* had warranted that the President was to statesmanship what William James was to philosophy. Liberals, radicals, and socialists alike saw in the prospect of a second *Masses* trial, not only an example of persecution, but also a more critical issue impinging on foreign policy.

Amos Pinchot appealed to the White House on May 24. That "this sort of thing" was going on at all was "infinitely horrible," but that "men of the finest social feeling"—such as Max Eastman and John Reed—should be prosecuted under the Espionage Act was simply "outrageous." Reed had "antagonized his employers and took his future in his hands by campaigning for you," Pinchot reminded the President, and Max Eastman had secured untold numbers of indispensable votes in 1916 when "he pointed out the reasons why socialists should vote for you."[51] Upton Sinclair also emphasized that the travail of the *Masses* troubled more people than those under indictment and had implications that went far beyond the issue of censorship. "These men are ready to give real support to your policies, & and they have a large and very active following," he told Wilson.[52] There was "no question," Edward P. Costigan wrote, "that Eastman, Reed and the rest are in accord with the present overwhelming national mind and purpose."[53] In June, William Kent attempted to make what was at stake as clear to the President as anyone could: "Every thoughtful Socialist is driven into our camp in the contest now on, and I do not believe that we can afford to throw away the opportunity of reclaiming for constructive work men like Max Eastman."[54]

In response to these appeals to the spirit of 1916 (and to political common sense), Wilson took up the matter with his Attorney General. Gregory, however, persuaded him that the Justice Department should be permitted to proceed with the prosecution. (The second *Masses* trial, like the first, ended in a hung jury.[55]) Nor was this all. Other friends and erstwhile compatriots of leading progressive internationalists felt "the firm hand of stern repression" in the summer and fall of 1918. And Wilson was not in every instance exactly distressed by it. In June, the Socialist

Rose Pastor Stokes was convicted in Kansas City under the Espionage Act and sentenced to ten years' imprisonment for making several speeches against the war. Wilson considered the conviction (presumably not the sentence) "very just."[56]

The most famous indictment of all occurred shortly afterward. On June 29, the United States Attorney for northern Ohio charged Eugene Debs with ten violations of the Espionage Act for a rousing speech at Canton in which he had railed against the capitalist war and federal violations of the First Amendment. His trial in September was the occasion of his most memorable line: "While there is a lower class, I am in it; while there is a criminal element, I am of it; while there is a soul in prison, I am not free." Socialists were electrified by the heroic closing speech, and many liberals suffered heavy pangs of conscience. For the high crime of critical thought, Judge D. C. Westenhaver sentenced Citizen Debs—aged sixty-two and in failing health—to ten years in prison. Although the indictment had been sought contrary to the advice of Attorney General Gregory, the entire proceeding spoke volumes about the selective limits to democratic freedoms at home during the war for those freedoms abroad. Debs' and Wilson's paths would cross again, at a more critical time.[57]

The administration's policies continued to erode confidence in the President and the possibilities for a united progressive internationalist front as the fall elections approached. In September, the *World Tomorrow* lost its second-class mailing privileges because it condemned the Russian intervention. "If I had my way," Burleson told Norman Thomas, "I'd not only kill your magazine but send you to prison for life." John Nevin Sayre, Thomas's good friend and the brother of Wilson's son-in-law (Francis B. Sayre), rushed to the White House. When Sayre told him the story, Wilson fondly remembered Thomas, a former Princeton student, and read through the article in question; he did not find its contents particularly objectionable. "I would not like to see this publication held up unless there is a very clear case indeed," he wrote to Burleson, adding that the young man was "absolutely sincere." But Wilson's good offices in September did not prevent Burleson from seizing the magazine again in October. Having struggled for life for nine issues, the *World Tomorrow* expired.[58]

The real *coup de grâce* came close on the heels of the *World Tomorrow* case. On September 13, the Post Office Department withheld the next day's issue of the *Nation,* presumably on account of an editorial, "Civil Liberty Dead."[59] Wilson, obviously embarrassed and mindful of the consequences, moved quickly to countermand Burleson in this instance, too.[60] Nonetheless, the suppression of even a single issue of the venerable paper edited by Oswald Garrison Villard raised the greatest furor yet. The New York *World,* Wilson's most loyal editorial supporter, declared the recent action of the administration nothing less than an attempt "to undertake the Prussianization of American public opinion."[61]

After the very first wave of federal repression, Villard himself had warned Colonel House of the harvest that was being sown. Whether Wilson wanted to own up to it or not, "the administration has been antagonizing, by the stupidity of Burleson and Gregory in their prosecutions of newspapers and periodicals, the very liberals who will be so important to him," he had written in February 1918. "The President will be completely unable to put through his peace program in America unless he can rally behind him the liberal and radical opinion of the country."[62] With withering sarcasm, Amos Pinchot compressed into a single quip his frustration with Wilson: "He puts his enemies in office and his friends in jail."[63]

This, then, it appeared, was what the Post Office and Justice Departments had wrought—and with Wilson's acquiescence—on the eve of a mid-term congressional election that would turn out to be more important than most presidential elections in American history.

The straits progressive internationalists found themselves in had become increasingly difficult to navigate as well, because, notwithstanding the Fourteen Points, Wilson had declined to provide specific bearings with respect to the League of Nations, either privately or publicly. The President may or may not have had sound reasons for refusing to cooperate with the League to Enforce Peace and with Robert Cecil. But conservative internationalists, in both the United States and Great Britain, had drawn up charts of their own anyway.

In the spring of 1918, Paul Kellogg had begun to worry about the fact that the only "lay body" dedicated to planning for world organization was the League to Enforce Peace, "which is mostly absorbed in the machinery of international control rather than the democratic principles which must shoot through all such arrangements to make them tolerable, and whose leaders . . . were lined up against the Brandeis appointment to the supreme court."[64] Kellogg's observation underscored an acute shortcoming in Wilson's wartime leadership: there was no progressive internationalist counterpart to the conservative LEP, and he had not encouraged the formation of one. And in all the months of American belligerency, the President had not made a single speech that dealt expressly with the League.

In order to fill this void, Kellogg summoned to New York a number of leading progressive internationalists for a series of seminars, held from April through the end of the year. The participants included such reliables as Lillian Wald, Hamilton Holt, Herbert Croly, Norman Angell, John Dewey, Charles A. Beard, and Norman Hapgood. They soon were joined by representatives from the *Nation,* the *New Republic,* the *Independent,* the *Survey,* the *Public,* and the *Dial,* and by other, individual progressives—

Jane Addams, Frederic C. Howe, John Palmer Gavit, Felix Frankfurter, Learned Hand, and Thomas W. Lamont. Initially calling themselves the "Committee on Nothing at All," by autumn the group had become the "League of Free Nations Association."[65]

After months of study, the LFNA put out a "Statement of Principles." Unlike the LEP, but much like Wilson, the LFNA did not lay great stress on international machinery for its own sake. Rather, it emphasized a "sounder future international order," guided by a league of nations "open to any nation . . . whose government is responsible to the people." The principle functions of the league, the document stated, must be to maintain "security: the due protection of national existence" and to bring about "equality of economic opportunity." The failure of the system of the balance of power to provide either of these things had resulted in "that competition for political power which . . . has been so large an element in the causation of war and the subjugation of weaker peoples."[66] Thus, the LFNA was essentially as one with Wilson.

Yet the LFNA did not achieve its main purpose—public education. Not until after the armistice did the study group begin to mount vigorous propaganda; nor did its members actively seek out Wilson until after that time—primarily because they knew, through Hamilton Holt's contacts with the LEP, that he did not want to talk about, or publicize, "cut and dried" plans.

The immediate catalyst behind Kellogg's decision to organize the LFNA was an extended visit to Great Britain during the spring of 1918. He had observed that the chief source of support for the league was British Labour, in addition to many left-leaning Liberals. They were "the only force in western Europe," Kellogg wrote to Felix Frankfurter in June, "competent and desirous of throwing its strength alongside President Wilson's in securing a democratic outcome in the settlement of the war."[67] By the summer, information of this nature had made its way to Wilson, too. In July, Oscar T. Crosby of the Treasury Department, who had attended the Inter-Allied Conference, told Wilson that the league of nations idea was not taken seriously by European heads of state. "Mr. Lloyd George has laughed at the proposed League in my presence," he said, "and M. Clemenceau has sneered at it."[68] In August, Ray Stannard Baker reported to Colonel House from London that although the Allied governments often paid lip service to Wilson's pronouncements, it was Labour, most Liberals, and the radicals who staunchly advocated his program; and they needed Wilson's help if they were to brook the potentially dangerous political consequences that were bound to flow from a crushing defeat of Germany.[69]

Out of these concerns, as well as those pertaining to the general state of domestic affairs, House, just before receiving his final copy of the Covenant, urged Wilson to obtain from the Allies a definite commitment to his peace program and to rally the nation around the banner of the League before victory overwhelmed everyone. The support the President was presently enjoying "in the nature of things, is uncertain and erratic." Therefore, Wilson ought to persuade the Allied governments to agree to the publication of the American covenant. This would make the inclusion of the League in the peace treaty more certain, and, with that guarantee from the Allies, "there would be no opposition in this country worth mentioning." Then, too, "it could not have any but a good effect in the Central Powers and should shorten the war."[70]

When Oscar Crosby reported the unpleasant truth about the attitudes of British and French officials, Wilson had replied, "Yes, I know that Europe is still governed by the same reactionary forces which controlled this country until a few years ago. But I am satisfied that if necessary I can reach the peoples of Europe over the heads of their Rulers."[71] This was his answer to House as well. The appeal to "the people" was his greatest strength. It had proved decisive throughout his presidency—in the passage of important legislation, in creating the coalition of 1916, and, at crucial passes, in uniting divided groups behind the war. He had written a speech that he thought "would cover the case," he told House. The opening of the Fourth Liberty Loan in New York, they decided, would be the appropriate occasion to address both his American and his European constituencies (including the Germans) and compel the approval of the Allied governments.[72]

Great throngs of people turned out to welcome the President and Mrs. Wilson as they motored through the streets of Manhattan on the evening of September 27. Only the week before, the American First Army, in its first independent action of the war, had wiped out the German salient at St. Mihiel. By September 26, General Pershing had amassed some 1,200,000 men and hundreds of heavy guns and tanks along the front in preparation for a titanic, cooperative Allied exertion to consume the enemy. Victory might come early in 1919, and speculation abounded as to what the President would say to the crowd of 6,000 persons packed inside the Metropolitan Opera House.

"It is my mission here to-night to try to make it clear once more what the war really means," he began once the cheers died down. If the common object of the governments arrayed against Germany was to achieve "a *secure* and *lasting* peace," the Allied and Associated powers must realize that there was but one price to pay. "That price is impartial justice in every item of the settlement, no matter whose interest is crossed; and not only impartial justice but also *the satisfaction of the several peoples whose fortunes are dealt with."* The one "indispensable instrumentality" of the future peace was a league of nations. And, as he saw it, "the constitution of that League . . . must be a part, in a sense the most essential part, of the peace settlement itself." It could not be formed now, lest it become merely an alliance of victors; and it could not be formed after the settlement, if the people really meant to have it.

Wilson then outlined five "particulars" as practical guidelines for the program. He intended them as much for the instruction of Allied officials as for the gratification of the converted. First, impartial justice must have no standard but the equal rights of both the victors and the vanquished. Second, no special interest of any single nation could supersede the common interest of all. Third, there could be no special understandings within the new family of nations. Fourth, there could be no selfish economic combinations within the League, nor any economic boycotts except as they might be imposed as a collective sanction. Fifth, all international agreements must be made known in their entirety to the rest of the world.

Wilson addressed his next comment directly to American critics who invoked George Washington's warning against entangling alliances. Only special, limited alliances "entangled," he explained; a general alliance for universal rights would eliminate the danger of entanglement. By assuming "its full share of responsibility for the maintenance of common covenants," the United States would demonstrate a new comprehension of the Farewell Address.

Finally, he turned once more to the peoples of Europe. It was "the peculiarity of this great war that while statesmen have seemed to cast about for definitions of their purpose, . . . the thoughts of the mass of men . . . have grown more and more unclouded." The "people" now demanded that their leaders declare *"exactly what it is"* that they were seeking in the war. The people had a right to know. He then threw down a challenge to the Allied governments: if they did not agree with his interpretation of the issues, he hoped they would say so now. Silence on their part, he implied, would signal agreement. At this critical moment in history, "unity of purpose and of counsel" were as imperative as "unity of command in the battlefield." Complete victory—"the final triumph of justice and fair dealing"—could be had in no other way. " 'Peace drives' can be effectively neutralized and silenced only by showing that every victory of the nations associated against Germany brings the whole world nearer the sort of peace which will bring security and reassurance to all peoples and make the recurrence of another such struggle of pitiless force and bloodshed forever impossible, *and that nothing else can."* [73]

The Fourth Liberty Loan address was the last of Wilson's public utterances to meet with nearly unanimous acclaim in the United States. Although it rarely receives more than passing reference in writings on the war aims debate, it was regarded as an exceptional address at the time. David Lawrence, in the *New York Evening Post,* characterized it as by far the most important speech that Wilson had made during the war. Of all of the President's wartime statements, this one, said the *New Republic,* "will probably rank as the most timely . . . and the most triumphant." The *New York Times* saw fit to fill its entire front page with the text.[74]

Significantly, a major section of opinion gave evidence that nothing Wilson had said had diminished the pervasive war fever in the country. For example, the Indianapolis *Star* said that the President's position could not be mistaken—the United States and the Allies "shall push on until Prussian militarism and all that it means has been blotted forever from the face of the earth." The *Knickerbocker Press* of Albany also equated peace with "wiping Potsdam off the map" and suggested that Wilson had "not made himself wholly plain in his analysis of the future."[75]

The majority of the nation's press, however, was apparently comprehending as well as laudatory. "The President goes into details with fearless frankness," the Pittsburgh *Dispatch* observed. According to the *St. Louis Republic,* Wilson was right to tell, not only the enemy, but also the Allies that "they must purge themselves of any hopes of self-aggrandizement." The Cincinnati *Commercial Tribune* concurred: "In taking a position against a merely vengeful economic exclusion, he rises to new heights of statesmanship." Like many others, the Richmond *Times-Dispatch* agreed that the League must be "the most essential part of the peace settlement itself."[76] The *New York Times* hailed the League as "the beginning of a new era in the history of the world, a wonderful reversal of the intentions and policies that led to the Holy Alliance."[77]

On Capitol Hill, leading Democrats were effusive, while most Republicans were circumspect amidst the hail of kudos. Theodore Roosevelt, who had just finished a speaking tour for the Fourth Liberty Loan, declined direct comment.[78] William Howard Taft, however, spoke forthrightly: "The President has admirably . . . demonstrated the absolute necessity of a League of Nations to maintain a just and permanent peace."[79] In light of such assessments, the *New York Times* seemed to be on fairly solid ground in asserting: "When Woodrow Wilson speaks to the American people he speaks for them; their wish, their purpose, their innermost thoughts are expressed in his words, for he has an instinctive understanding of their will."[80]

As for European opinion, Wilson's natural constituency was well pleased. The Union of Democratic Control passed a resolution of endorsement, and the London *Nation* and the *Daily News* acknowledged that the President had grandly met the needs of the hour.[81] Robert Cecil wrote to House in praise of "the finest description of our war aims yet uttered."[82] On October 10, Viscount Grey spoke before a huge gathering at Westminster and declared that Wilson's address must serve as the Allies' guide and that the League must be created at the peace conference.[83] The Archbishop of Canterbury declared in the London *Times:* "We mean that this thing shall come to pass."[84]

Even so, the preponderance of opinion in both the British and French press was simply polite. Few quarreled any longer with the general idea of the League, but the Paris *Journal des Débats* also noted, "In truth this program is neither very clear nor very practical." Likewise, the London *Outlook* had no trouble in coming to terms with the imminence of the League, while expressing concern about the President's "magnanimity towards the Germans."[85] And, again, as in the case of the Fourteen Points, none of the Allied governments issued an official endorsement, or ever answered Wilson's questions about "unity of purpose." Although the Italian and French foreign offices indicated their agreement "in principle," the British and French governments imposed a two-week blackout on editorial commentary on the speech.[86]

If the Fourth Liberty Loan address was not altogether successful in the ministries of the Allied nations, American editorial opinion nonetheless seemed to demonstrate that the League of Nations enjoyed wide support in the United States. Just how deep that support ran, however, and how long it could be sustained (even in the absence of an organized opposition) were another set of questions. Without a doubt, Wilson had thoroughly identified himself with the League and had made it his own. Yet his effort was much too little, much too late. It was his only speech on the subject since the United States had entered the war. And still, despite some claims to the contrary in the press, he had given out precious few details. Moreover, no preparatory groundwork had been systematically laid—for he had not permitted any—to provide a full and proper context; and, because of the way subsequent events unfolded, he would not be afforded the opportunity to follow up. Finally, the Fourth Liberty Loan address obviously had not assuaged those who were out to quench their thirst for German blood. Progressive internationalists might not have any trouble understanding what kind of league and peace settlement Wilson was determined to get. But their faith in Wilson—not to mention their political cohesion and sense of common purpose—was nearly exhausted; only the week before, his staunchest champion in the liberal press had practically accused his administration of conducting an intellectual reign of terror. It was a heavy burden that Wilson had expected this solitary speech to carry—and an unreasonably severe hardship that he was imposing on himself as well.

There was, however, one conclusive and momentous reward. More so than any other audience, the Germans had listened carefully to Wilson.

During the following week, the combined Allied and American armies pounded the Hindenburg Line with irresistible force and began to push the enemy back toward Belgium and Germany. On September 29, the German High Command began to consider the grave implications of their present military situation. On October 6, Chancellor Max von Baden appealed to Wilson to take steps for the restoration of peace. Germany accepted as the basis of the negotiations the program laid down by the President in the Fourteen Points and in his subsequent pronouncements, "particularly in his address of September 27, 1918."[87] In the ensuing diplomatic exchanges, the Germans would refer to the latter as often as to Wilson's more celebrated statement on war aims. Thus, the Fourth Liberty Loan address helped bring the fighting to an end and probably averted the sacrifice of additional thousands of lives. Wilson's long-overdue speech on the League of Nations, then, turned out to be the rhetorical climax to the Great War, and a most fitting one at that.

10

"The War Thus Comes to an End"

Fate and the American political calendar rendered the timing of the German request for an armistice exceedingly inauspicious. Although the main issues in the congressional campaign had been firmly established by October 1918, the unexpected overture by Prince Max elevated those issues to a level of ideological and partisan intensity they might otherwise not have reached. As a result, the biennial event suddenly acquired all the urgent qualities of a presidential election. The sense of high stakes, excessive partisanship on both sides, and (there is simply no other term for it) extremist behavior by leading Republicans, in most respects, surpassed even that of the campaign of 1916.

Historically, the congressional election endures primarily because of the consequences of Wilson's attempt, near the end of the campaign, to turn it into a vote of confidence in his leadership. It is important to note, however, that the Republican party made a direct appeal of its own three months earlier. On July 19, Roosevelt, Lodge, Root, and, significantly, Taft publicly called for the election of a Republican majority. They justified their petition mainly by arguing that the GOP had supported Wilson's measures to prosecute the war with greater devotion than his own party had done.[1]

But there was more to it than this. In 1916, the Republicans had permitted Wilson to defuse their own best issues and to set the terms of debate for others. They had misread the depth of anti-interventionist sentiment throughout the country and had underestimated the popularity of Wilson's domestic reforms and his early promotion of a league of nations. Moreover, party strategists had failed to seize upon the relatively radical ecumenism of the "Progressive Democracy," which was far more palpable in 1916 than in 1918. They would not repeat those mistakes. To Republican propagandists it did not matter that, this time around, public endorsements on behalf of the administration by leading Socialists and advanced progressives hardly matched those of the previous contest; or that Wilson had acquiesced in the suppression of the civil liberties of many of his former supporters. The centralization of the wartime economy and, especially, the core of Wilson's foreign policy still placed the administration sufficiently left of center to make all Democrats vulnerable to charges that they were "un-American." By September, Lodge had begun to subsume all the issues under the single one of "Wilsonism," particularly by asserting that the President advocated "peace at any price," in accordance with "the socialists and Bolsheviks among his advisers."[2] Even the *New York Times* occasionally commented that a "certain socialist coterie" exerted an unsavory influence within the White House.[3]

Yet, to a significant extent, Wilson himself shared responsibility for the reactionary onslaught. The nature of the campaign (and its results) would provide ample evidence of the perspicacity of those friends who had repeatedly warned the President that his administration's policy on censorship and sedition would give free rein to "the very people who subsequently will make the task of realizing the constructive purposes which lie behind American fighting excessively and unnecessarily difficult."[4]

The chief architects of the Republican campaign were Roosevelt, Lodge, and Will H. Hays, the indefatigable national party chairman from Indiana. In the future, Hays would become more famous as the Hollywood censor who "timed the kisses" and required Walt Disney to excise the udders on his animated cows; but, in 1918, he came as close to achieving the status of household name as any party chairman ever has. The Republican strategy included the shrewd exploitation of local controversies in certain states—for example, the price of wheat in the Plains states (see below). But the Republicans concentrated mainly on two broad national issues, both of which enabled them to impugn the patriotism of the Democrats and to launch a frontal assault against the President's peace program.

The first major issue was designed to play upon businessmen's fears about the future of the domestic economy. Republican propaganda emphasized the alleged threat to American free enterprise manifest in the Democrats' imposition, under the pretense of wartime exigency, of "widespread state ownership" and other "bolshevik principles." Hays framed this issue in August in an exposition of the party's platform, and later credited it with having produced the Republican victory. "Every thinking man and woman has noted the socialistic tendencies of the present government," the exposition stated. "The Republican party from its inception has stood against undue federalization of industries." Its mission, Hays said, was the "just restriction of the present socialistic tendency in our government. . . ."[5]

Big business was quite responsive to this sort of contrivance—because of high taxation and because the administration had responded sympathetically to the demands of labor and had abetted unionization as well. Hays also adroitly linked domestic economic issues, such as the tariff, to Wilson's foreign policy. In particular, he highlighted the third of the Fourteen Points—the reduction of trade barriers—with the Democratic party's commitment to a low tariff in the Underwood Act of 1913. The *American Economist* argued that a Wilsonian peace would "saddle upon America a policy of Free-Trade or 'new freedom,'" which would result in economic disaster. The Republican Congressional Committee asserted that it was necessary, therefore, to elect a protectionist Republican Senate to defeat the free-trade League of Nations and save America from the waves of European goods that would soon crash upon her shores.[6]

On August 23, Senator Lodge struck the keynote for the other major issue. Because Germany faced almost certain defeat, the time had come to state precisely the kind of peace that all patriotic Americans desired. "It cannot be a peace of bargain," Lodge declared on the floor of the Senate. "The only peace for us is one that rests on . . . unconditional surrender. No peace that satisfies Germany in any degree can ever satisfy us. . . . [We] must go to Berlin and there dictate peace."[7]

Roosevelt, who sometimes likened Wilson's leadership to "fighting the Civil War under Buchanan," echoed Lodge's theme at every opportunity.[8] In a series of speeches ostensibly on behalf of the Fourth Liberty Loan, he equated advocacy of the League of Nations with pro-Germanism. "We are not internationalists. We are American nationalists," he protested to 100,000 Chicagoans in late summer. "We intend to do justice to all other nations. But in the last four years the professional internationalists like the profound pacifists have played the game of brutal German autocracy."[9] A few days later he told New Yorkers: "To substitute internationalism for nationalism means to do away with patriotism. The professional pacifist and the professional internationalist are equally undesirable citizens."[10] Thus had the Republicans set the tone of their campaign as Germany's request arrived in Washington.

Wilson approached the proposition of an armistice with the reserve of both a victorious leader and a would-be mediator. What he was still striving to achieve was some practicable measure of "peace without victory"— a settlement that "would prevent a renewal of hostilities by Germany yet which will be as moderate and reasonable as possible."[11] Yet, as he stepped upon this narrow crossing, Wilson was at last confronted head-on by the contradictions of fighting a common enemy for reasons significantly different from those for which the Allies were fighting. His speeches of January 8 and September 27, 1918—in many ways, as much arraignments of the Allies as of the Central Powers—surely had a penetrating, if delicate logic to them; but, until now, the implications of that logic had been sedulously avoided by all diplomatists concerned.

Moreover, to arrive at the point where his speeches might have practical application had required "force without stint or measure," as Wilson himself had declared during the war. The very act of girding on the sword had sanctioned for some nineteen months the incessant portrayal of the enemy as the most evil and autocratic power the world had ever known and had created a political environment that allowed no variance. If he hoped to achieve a settlement based on the Fourteen Points and a league of nations, Wilson had also somehow to quell, or satisfy, the demands of the American public and the Allied governments that Germany acknowledge military defeat and political bankruptcy. That this was the case was made abundantly clear after October 6, both in the debates that took place in the Senate and in the numerous diplomatic communications that flashed between Washington and the Allied capitols.

Republican Senator Miles Poindexter of Washington, inspired by fears of a "compromise peace," initiated debate in the upper house on October 7. "The only condition of an armistice ought to be an allied victory," he said. "Anything else would be approaching in a degree the betrayal of the great cause for which we are fighting, and would be action along the line of what the Bolsheviki of Russia perpetrated in a larger degree." Poindexter also said he counted on Clemenceau and Lloyd George "to protect their countries and ours from the results of any such unwise step." He commended, not fourteen terms, but one, for an armistice—"unconditional surrender."[12]

No one was surprised that Lodge, too, rose at this time to demand a peace of retribution. More illuminating for Wilson, however, were the comments of several Democrats. "A wide pathway of fire and blood from the Rhine to Berlin should be the course our Army should take," declared Henry F. Ashurst of Arizona, "and when our armies have reached Berlin, . . . the German Government will be told what the peace terms will be." After other Democrats expressed similar views, Senator Hitchcock, Chairman of the Committee on Foreign Relations, acknowledged that a suspension of hostilities just now was "absolutely abhorrent" to the sensibilities of the entire chamber.[13]

Wilson read portions of this debate aloud to Colonel House on the following day. "He did not realize how war mad our people have become," House noted, nor the extent to which the country was "against anything but unconditional surrender."[14] Yet Germany had turned to Wilson—not to the Allies—precisely because he appeared to promise some degree of fairness. On one hand, he could not dismiss the possibility that Germany's ongoing transition to parliamentary government and the request for an armistice was a devious feint, after which the German High Command would reassert control and resume defensive efforts; on the other hand, he could not responsibly let pass the opportunity to end the war without testing the enemy's sincerity.

Thus, in a noncommittal reply on October 8, he sought to ferret out Germany's true intentions. Before entering into actual negotiations, his note said, the President first must have assurances that the German Government accepted the terms of his Fourteen Points and subsequent addresses. Second, he could not propose a cessation of arms until the German armies had evacuated Allied territory. And, finally, by asking whether the Imperial Chancellor was speaking "merely" for those who had conducted the war, Wilson implied that he would deal only with a civilian ministry.[15]

Initial Republican reaction could almost be predicted. Lodge cited Ulysses S. Grant as the example whom Wilson should emulate in dealing with a defeated foe. Roosevelt dismissed the diplomatic exchange as "an invitation to further note-writing" apt to hamper the advance to Berlin. Senator Poindexter said that any peace based on the Fourteen Points would be tantamount to the Allies' losing the war. Taft, only slightly less intemperate, now aired his doubts about the Fourteen Points. "[A]re not many of them so phrased that a formal acceptance of them would leave many issues open for dispute and easily lead to a renewal of hostilities?" he asked.[16]

The open attacks rallied the Democrats to Wilson's defense. On October 10, Key Pittman of Nevada said that the people had the right to know whether Senate Republicans would attempt to block a treaty incorporating the President's program should they become the majority. The forthcoming elections, he asserted, represented a struggle "between the policies of Woodrow Wilson and the policies of Senator Henry Cabot Lodge."[17] Senator Ashurst then demanded to know why Republicans had chosen this moment to voice their objections to the Fourteen Points when they had kept silent on them since January 1918.[18]

Wilson's detractors were temporarily countered by sober journalistic commentary, particularly in some Republican newspapers, and by the absence of criticism in the Allied press. For instance, the *Chicago Tribune* (no admirer of Wilson) praised the "masterly skill with which he parried the German thrust."[19] Even so, the administration's most dependable editorial supporters—the *New York Times,* the *World,* the *Springfield Republican*—believed that Wilson must tear German autocracy out by the roots and demand the Kaiser's abdication as the minimum conditions of peace. In all, the note was received as something less than a stirring battle cry, yet as a shrewd diplomatic maneuver, worthy of the benefit of the doubt.

As for Allied opinion, the London *Westminster Gazette* affirmed that Wilson "fulfills the hopes and expectations of the Allies in Europe." In Paris, the *Journal des Débats* emphasized that Wilson's question about who spoke for Germany was "a blow in the Kaiser's face."[20] On the golf links outside Paris, Lloyd George and Robert Cecil read the note apparently with such equanimity that they saw no reason not to finish their game.[21] From the British Foreign Office, Lord Reading sent the following communication to Washington: "The President's message in answer to Germany has been extremely well received here."[22]

Political calculation did not alone motivate the Republicans. When, on October 12, the Germans professed unqualified acceptance of the Fourteen Points and agreed to evacuate occupied Allied territory under the supervision of "a mixed commission," the Republicans earnestly worried that the President might not possess the resolve to press beyond the endeavor to clarify the picture.[23] This consideration became a source of apprehension for many Democrats, especially for those who upheld the Fourteen Points and insisted on unconditional surrender as well.

On October 14, Senator Ashurst requested an audience at the White House. The Senate, the press, and the people all expected "that you demand an 'unconditional surrender' of the German armies," he said to the President. "If your reply should fail to come up to the American spirit, you are destroyed." Could it be, Wilson rejoined, that the people did not remember the Fourteen Points, the League, and his recent Liberty Loan address? "I am thinking now only of putting the U.S. into a position of strength and justice. I am now playing for 100 years hence." As for his being destroyed, he said, "I am willing if I can serve the country to go into the cellar and read poetry for the remainder of my life." Wilson's assurances—that the people need not have any anxiety over his next move—failed to comfort. If he came up short of unconditional surrender, Ashurst warned, "the cyclone of the people's wrath" would indeed force him into the cellar.[24]

By this juncture, Wilson realized that he could no longer hold all the cards in his own hand. For one thing, despite Lord Reading's agreeable message, the Allies were voicing legitimate concerns. Before he answered the German response of October 12, the prime ministers of Great Britain, France, and Italy conveyed to him their unanimous judgment: measures must be taken to prevent Germany from fortifying her defensive position; the terms of the armistice must square with the recommendations of Allied and American military and naval experts—and, in this, the Germans could have no say.[25] Wilson personally vouchsafed to Ambassador Jusserand that he understood these concerns perfectly well. A German evacuation was "only a condition to be met, so that one could *speak* of an armistice," he said.[26] All the same, the Allies remained uneasy, for Wilson also told Sir Eric Geddes that "undue humiliation [of Germany] would be inexcusable."[27]

Wilson sent a second note to Berlin on October 14. Though far from a demand for abject surrender, it conformed to the wishes of the Allies and reflected the mood of American public opinion. The conditions of an armistice were matters to be determined exclusively by Allied military advisers, and neither the Allies nor the United States could accept any arrangement that did not guarantee the military supremacy of their armies in the field. The note closed by implying that the whole process of peace would depend on the further democratization of Germany.[28]

Wilson's sharper tone received nearly unanimous approval on both sides of the Atlantic. As one his advisers commented, when the text was read in the Senate, "it spoiled everything that had been said all day long by everybody." Even Lodge hesitated to criticize it.[29] For the same reasons, the note fell heavily in Berlin. Wilson had not only rejected the "mixed commission" to supervise the evacuation of Belgium and France; he was also presuming to interfere in Germany's internal affairs. The Kaiser and the Supreme Command initially proposed a defiant response. The civilians in the Cabinet, however, did not regard that as a practical alternative. Germany's military position had further disintegrated, and internal political conditions teetered precariously on the brink of revolution. Moreover, Max von Baden took some solace in the first sentence of Wilson's note, which had finally acknowledged the sincerity of his government's acceptance of the Fourteen Points. Furthermore, reports on the political situation both in the United States and in the Allied countries suggested that a rejection of the President's terms would only undercut the possibilities for a Wilsonian settlement—the one thing that stood between Germany and a dictated peace.

Thus a third German note, dispatched on October 20, capitulated to Wilson, trusting that he would "approve of no demand which would be irreconcilable with the honor of the German people." In addition, the Germans gave assurances that fundamental constitutional reforms were underway—the choosing of a Reichstag through universal franchise. The request for an armistice, then, came from a government "free from arbi-

trary and irresponsible influence . . . [and supported by] the overwhelming majority of the German people."[30]

Germany's latest affirmations only made Democrats more nervous.
Homer S. Cummings, the party's national vice-chairman, wrote to Wilson
on October 22 that the public regarded the German pledge as scarcely any
"guarantee that arbitrary and autocratic power has been destroyed." So
much hinged on the President's next communication: "It is of the highest
consequence . . . that we should be successful in the November elections,"
Cummings emphasized. "Unless we win that success the whole peace program is imperiled, and the greatest conception as to the destiny of humanity which ever sprang from a human brain may come to naught."[31]

On the same day, the British Foreign Secretary also conveyed an
admonitory message to Wilson. The German note still assumed "an un-
disturbed retreat," Balfour wrote, which would give the enemy the opportunity to reorganize defenses should some diplomatic impasse arise.
The evacuation of France and Belgium was not enough. Any armistice
must contain absolute guarantees against a resumption of hostilities, and
that end could be attained only by providing for Allied occupation of
some enemy territory and preventive measures against German naval warfare.[32]

In the circumstances, on the afternoon of October 22, Wilson called
his cabinet together. According to Franklin K. Lane, the Secretary of the
Interior, the President appeared "manifestly disturbed" as he described
Senator Ashurst's visit and alluded to his second note to Germany, pointing out that it "had no pacifism in it." Now he had not only to respond
again, but also to decide whether to recommend to the Allies the commencement of formal negotiations. "I do not know what to do," he said.
"I may have made a mistake in not properly safe-guarding what I said
before."[33]

Only Burleson counseled unconditional surrender. McAdoo countered by saying that the United States could not finance the war indefinitely; it would be a terrible responsibility to carry on if the war could be
ended on the President's terms and the Allies made secure by ironclad
guarantees against a renewal of hostilities. William B. Wilson, the Secretary of Labor, observed that the press clamored for "all kinds of punishment for the Germans, including the hanging of the Kaiser"; but, in his
opinion, labor "opposed war for what imperialistic England desired." Secretary Lane then emphasized the risk of calling for an armistice over
Allied objections; this would amount to coercion, he said. The President
replied that the Allies "needed to be coerced, that they were getting to a
point where they were reaching out for more than they should have in
justice."[34] David F. Houston, the Secretary of Agriculture, agreed. As

WOODROW WILSON OF PRINCETON
*June 1910, shortly before his campaign for Governor of New Jersey. (Princeton
University Library)*

COLONEL EDWARD M. HOUSE OF TEXAS
Confidant and chief adviser to the President. (Princeton University Library)

WILLIAM JENNINGS BRYAN
Three-time Democratic presidential candidate, peace seeker, and Secretary of State, 1913–1915. (Library of Congress)

ROBERT LANSING
Secretary of State, 1915–1920. (Library of Congress)

HERBERT CROLY
Editor of The New Republic.
(Courtesy of David W. Levy)

WALTER LIPPMANN
Progressive journalist and presidential adviser. (Pirie MacDonald)

MAX EASTMAN
Socialist editor of The Masses *and* The Liberator. *(Princeton University Library)*

JANE ADDAMS OF HULL HOUSE
*Co-founder of the Woman's
Peace Party and winner of the
Nobel Peace Prize. (Swarth-
more College Peace Collection)*

LILLIAN WALD
*Progressive internationalist, peace seeker,
and founder of the Henry Street Settlement. (Swarthmore College Peace
Collection)*

THE SINKING OF THE LUSITANIA, MAY 7, 1915

An event that helped to spark the Preparedness controversy. (New York Times)

PREPAREDNESS CONTROVERSY

"President Wilson: 'But I don't want them—there isn't any enemy to fight.' Morgan, Schwab & Co.: 'You buy these guns and we'll get you an enemy.'" (From The Masses, *January 1916; National Archives*)

PRESIDENT WILSON AND THE FIRST LADY, EDITH BOLLING GALT WILSON
(Library of Congress)

THEODORE ROOSEVELT
President of the United States, 1901–1909, and Wilson's arch-critic. (Theodore Roosevelt Collection of Lawrence H. and Doris A. Budner, Dallas, Texas)

WILSON DELIVERING HIS WAR MESSAGE
To a Joint Session of Congress, April 2, 1917. (Princeton University Library)

WILLIAM HOWARD TAFT
President of the United States, 1909–1913, president of the League to Enforce Peace, and Chief Justice of the Supreme Court, 1921–1930. (Library of Congress)

EUGENE V. DEBS

Five-time Socialist presidential candidate, speaking on the war at Canton, Ohio, June 16, 1918. (Debs Foundation, Terre Haute, Indiana)

PARIS GREETS WILSON
(Credit: Princeton University Library)

WILSON WITH PRESIDENT RAY-
MOND POINCARÉ OF FRANCE
(Credit: National Archives)

THE BIG FOUR
(Left to right) *David Lloyd George, Vittorio Orlando, Georges Clemenceau, and Woodrow Wilson. (Library of Congress)*

Lord Robert Cecil
Co-author of the Covenant of the League of Nations. (National Archives)

General Jan Christiaan Smuts of the Union of South Africa *(National Archives)*

SENATOR HENRY CABOT LODGE OF MASSACHUSETTS
Conservative internationalist, bitter foe of Wilson's, and chairman of the Senate Committee on Foreign Relations, 1919–1924. (National Archives)

"Going to Talk to the Boss."
The Chicago Daily News *on Wilson's campaign for the League. (The Warder Collection)*

"Refusing to Give a Lady a Seat."
Joseph Pulitzer's New York World *on the Senate's rejection of the League. (Library of Congress)*

WILSON ARRIVING AT ST. PAUL,
MINNESOTA
*On the Western tour. (Library
of Congress)*

WILSON SPEAKING AT TACOMA STADIUM
On the Western tour. (Library of Congress)

WILSON ADDRESSING THOUSANDS
At Berkeley's Greek Theater, on behalf of American membership in the League of Nations. (Library of Congress)

THE FORMER PRESIDENT IN RETIREMENT
At his house on S Street. (Library of Congress)

Germany's collapse appeared to be imminent, the Allies simply would "have to be held in check."[35]

Two hours of discussion seemed to confirm Wilson's misgivings about unconditional surrender. Of course, American public opinion was "as much a fact as a mountain and must be considered," he said to Josephus Daniels on the following day.[36] But, if his next note embodied Balfour's latest communication, then no one could accuse him of not being alive to the security concerns of the Allies. At the same time, by endorsing the German request for soundings leading to an armistice—that is, the commencement of negotiations to discuss the application of the Fourteen Points—the Allies could then be "held in check." If Wilson accepted the Allies' basic *military* terms, then, would they not at last have to accept his political terms, especially if Germany accepted a Wilsonian compound of both sets of conditions?

Wilson cabled Berlin on October 23. His note reiterated the German government's previous assurances about the terms of peace he had enunciated on January 8 and September 27. It also contained Balfour's proviso that the armistice must leave the Allies "in a position to enforce any arrangements that may be entered into and to make a renewal of hostilities on the part of Germany impossible." Finally, Wilson required further guarantees that he was dealing with "the veritable representatives of the German people who have been assured of a genuine constitutional standing." It was his duty to say that if the United States must continue to deal with Germany's military masters, "it must demand, not peace negotiations, but surrender."[37]

Simultaneously, Wilson transmitted to the Allies all of his correspondence with the Germans, along with his recommendation that formal negotiations with the enemy begin at once. Germany would not respond to the third American note for almost a week; already, however, Colonel House was on his way to Paris for direct talks with Lloyd George, Clemenceau, and Orlando. The question remained as to whether the President had gained the essential and irreducible leverage that would give him the opportunity to resolve the monumental political conundrums of the war to end war. The key seemed to lie in an armistice itself, or, to put it another way, in removing the serpent's fangs without actually destroying the beast. Keeping the German state intact (even as it underwent fundamental political reform) would prolong the Allies' material reliance on the United States throughout the entire process of peace. Moreover, an armistice based on the Fourteen Points would invigorate European liberals and the moderate left. That, too, could provide leverage. An unconditional "peace without victory" was perhaps no longer a possibility, but then, neither was unconditional surrender.

Meanwhile, the congressional campaign had entered its most rebarbative phase. Two days before Wilson's third dispatch to Berlin, the *Rocky Mountain News* attempted to define the central issue. "[T]here should be a curb on the Bolsheviks in the Democratic party when the peace terms are framed," it declared. "A Congress in obedience to the nod of the White House at such a time would be a positive danger to the country."[38] On the same day, Senator Poindexter submitted a resolution to make it "unlawful" for the President to enter into negotiations "before such time as the German armed forces shall have surrendered to the allied nations." If the President did not observe this stricture, said the Senator, "I think he should be impeached."[39] Then, on October 24, Theodore Roosevelt at last publicly unburdened himself on the subject of the Fourteen Points, in a momentous telegram to Lodge, Poindexter, and Hiram Johnson. Printed in major newspapers across the country, the telegram urged the Senate to demand Germany's unconditional surrender and to "declare against the adoption in their entirety" of the Fourteen Points. "Let us dictate peace by the hammering of guns," he inveighed, "and not chat about peace to the accompaniment of the clicking of typewriters." So "thoroly mischievous" were the Fourteen Points that they held the potential to bring about "the conditional surrender of the United States."[40]

Notwithstanding the razor-sharp edge of Roosevelt's missive, the most cutting blows to Wilson's program by this stage were being struck by none other than the president of the League to Enforce Peace. Whereas, in July, Taft had joined in the call for the election of a Republican Congress, Chairman Hays had prevailed upon him to go yet an extra mile. By the time Roosevelt had published his letter, Taft had already denounced the Fourteen Points and, in the Philadelphia *Public Ledger,* had asked, "Do we need during the life of the next Congress an absolute dictator?" His general behavior seemed to imply that a Republican victory was the best hope for the League, despite the fact that Roosevelt, Lodge, and Hays continued to malign virtually all internationalists as "anti-American." Most leading members of the LEP had refrained from partisanship in the campaign; they could only wonder whether Taft had taken leave of his senses or had simply placed the fortunes of party above those of the League.[41]

On October 25, Governor Thomas W. Bickett of North Carolina, chairman of the state's chapter of the LEP, demanded an explanation. Bickett characterized Roosevelt's war upon the Fourteen Points as "Prussianism to the bone"—an assault not only on the President, but also against the principles of the League to Enforce Peace. The Governor wrote that Taft must "defend the life of the League" and issue a "withering condemnation of the utterances of Mr. Roosevelt."[42] Taft replied a week later: "Those fourteen points cannot be made the safe basis of a treaty of peace.

They are too vague and indefinite." Furthermore, he went on, "Mr. Roosevelt has come around to favoring the League to Enforce Peace, provided it does not mean universal disarmament. I find myself in general agreement with [him] on this subject, indeed more than I would with President Wilson."[43]

Bickett was incredulous. "I would have gone on the witness stand and testified that the greatest enemy of the League to Enforce Peace is Mr. Roosevelt," he shot back, citing the latter's public commentaries.[44] What the Governor did not know, however, was that Taft and Roosevelt, after eight years of silence between them, had recently consummated a rapprochement—the careful work of Will Hays.[45] Addressing each other as "Dear Will" and "My Dear Theodore" in correspondence since the summer, Taft was determined to compose their differences over the League. For his part, Roosevelt, nursing ambitions to run for president in 1920, realized that his political well-being necessitated some tactical concessions. When Taft explained that his conception of the League envisioned neither disarmament nor the abandonment of universal military training, Roosevelt found a *modus vivendi*. "I will back it as an *addition to,* but not as *a substitute for,* our preparing our own strength for our own defense," he granted Taft. "Don't you think this is the right way to handle it?"[46]

This sudden change of heart was at least partially affected. When Albert J. Beveridge inquired about his apparent wavering, Roosevelt nimbly acquitted himself. "I am for saying with a bland smile whatever Nationalism demands," he told the former senator. "Mine is merely a platonic expression, designed to let Taft and his followers get over without too much trouble, and also to prevent any accusation that we are ourselves Prussian militarists."[47] Unaware of this duplicity, Taft was able credulously to brush off Bickett's cross-examination.

Yet Taft's insistence that the GOP was the party of the League was as much the consequence of other factors. In his rationalization, he also referred to his and Lowell's visit to the White House back in March. "The truth is that the President does not favor our League to Enforce Peace," he apprised Bickett. Even though Wilson had previously "announced his complete acquiescence in the principles of the League [he] advised us . . . that he had changed his mind."[48] Thus Wilson's studied reticence toward the LEP and his consistent lack of good will toward Taft had culminated in a cosmic misunderstanding. The country's leading conservative internationalist had come to the conclusion that the President was an unreliable friend to the cause.

That Wilson was virtually demanding Germany's submission to Allied military terms as the first condition in granting an armistice impressed few Republicans. For all practical purposes, they had declared themselves opposed to his peace program *in toto*. The big question now was whether Wilson could afford any longer to suffer their slings and arrows, or risk taking arms against them.

Historically, presidents have better served their own and their parties' interests by limiting their involvement in mid-term elections.[49] In exceptional years, however, circumstances have compelled partisans to remind voters that their choice of local representatives holds extraordinary implications for larger issues and for their regard for the chief executive. President McKinley and Senator Lodge, for instance, had done so during the congressional campaign of 1898, while the negotiations ending the Spanish-American War were taking place in Paris. Roosevelt himself had put the matter to the electorate this way: "[Y]our vote this year will be viewed by the nations of Europe from one standpoint only. They will draw no fine distinctions. A refusal to sustain the President . . . [will] be read as a refusal to sustain the war and to sustain the efforts of our peace commission to secure the fruits of war."[50]

For the same reasons, Vance McCormick, the Democratic party chairman, Vice-Chairman Cummings, most of the Cabinet, and leading Wilson supporters in the press encouraged the unfurling of the colors in 1918. Should he fail to express himself, wrote David Lawrence in the Chicago *Daily News,* "[i]t will be construed as indifference on his part to the outcome." The President was *entitled* to "go before the country with the same request for a vote of confidence that Lloyd George is shortly to ask in Great Britain. . . ."[51] Joseph Pulitzer personally composed "No Divided Government" for the New York *World's* Sunday editorial of October 6. "The election of a Republican House or a Republican Senate," he asserted, "might readily work more injury to the United States than Germany itself is capable of inflicting."[52] The *New Republic* stated that the President had "earned the allegiance of every American voter who proposes to fight to the bitter end against any restoration of the status quo ante." Victory consisted not only in beating Germany, but also in American participation in the League of Nations.[53]

According to Franklin K. Lane, the entire Cabinet, with the exception of Secretary of War Baker, believed that the Democrats "would win because the President had made a personal appeal for a vote of confidence." During a Cabinet meeting a few weeks earlier, however, Lane had expressed reservations. Burleson (who later claimed that he had been against the appeal) had interrupted to say that both the party and the nation wanted "a leader with *guts.*" Those were the Postmaster General's exact words, Lane emphasized—"a challenge to his (the President's) virility, that was at once manifest."[54]

Notwithstanding Lane's curious interpretation of Burleson's influence, Wilson really did not need to be challenged or coaxed. In late September he had told Colonel House that he intended to ask the voters to return a Democratic Congress.[55] "I believe it essential to the maintenance of my prestige abroad," he explained to Thomas Lamont a few days later.[56] Around October 11, Tumulty sketched the first in a series of drafts, reviewed by Wilson, Vance McCormick, Homer Cummings, and Key Pittman.[57] If Wilson entertained serious doubts about a direct appeal, then Senator Poindexter's threat of impeachment, Roosevelt's repudiation of the Fourteen Points, and Taft's wild claims must have settled the matter for him.[58] He wrote the final version himself. It was released on Friday, October 25, and published in most newspapers on the twenty-sixth.

The President was compelled to ask his fellow citizens to return a Democratic majority, the appeal began, if they approved of his leadership and wished him to continue to be their "unembarrassed spokesman in affairs at home and abroad." It was not a matter of patriotism, for the Republicans had been "unquestionably been pro-war." The problem was that they were not in sympathy with the administration. The return of a Republican majority, Wilson said in the most important passage, would "certainly be interpreted on the other side of the water as a repudiation of my leadership." In ordinary times, he would not feel at liberty to make such a plea. But, he concluded, "[i]f in these critical days it is your wish to sustain me with undivided minds I beg that you will say so in a way which it will not be possible to misunderstand either at home or among our associates on the other side of the sea. I submit my difficulties and my hopes to you."[59]

After the deed was done, friend and foe alike considered it the greatest blunder of Wilson's presidency. In Paris, Colonel House was "gravely disturbed"; had he been on the scene, he wrote in his diary, he would have counseled against it (although he had kept silent when the subject had come up in September). Even Mrs. Wilson had said to her husband, "I would not send it out. It is not a dignified thing to do." A month after the election, Taft described it as "one of those surprises in a career of a uniformly successful man which comes from losing his bearings because of his political success."[60] Historians have confirmed this collective contemporary judgment. Arthur S. Link, among others, has characterized the appeal as an "egregious mistake."[61]

Yet, taking account of the preponderance of advice that Wilson received beforehand both from party regulars and influential editors, he would have been damned no matter what he did. Then, too, compared with the fiercely partisan statements of the Republicans, Wilson's tone was comparatively restrained; neither was he personally abusive, nor did he impugn the opposition's loyalty. The initial private reactions of leading Republicans also suggest that they apprehended that the appeal, however dramatic, was not quite a response in kind and that it might prove more effective than their own. Roosevelt, for instance, did not seem to think that his nemesis had necessarily made a fatal error. "I have no idea how successful he will be," he confessed over the weekend to his son Kermit.[62] According to Will Hays, the appeal dispirited most of his colleagues, including Lodge and Knox. Not until Monday morning—after the chairman had hit upon a way to rally a party—did it become apparent that Wilson had, indeed, hurled a brick into a beehive.[63]

"A more ungracious, more unjust, more wanton, more mendacious accusation never was made by the most reckless stump orator, much less by a President of the United States," Hays declared in his official capacity. The real motivation behind Wilson's appeal was actually "to reconstruct in peace time the great industrial affairs of the nation . . . in unimpeded conformity with whatever socialistic doctrines . . . may happen to possess him at the time."[64] That evening at Carnegie Hall, some twenty thousand additional words of scorn were heaped upon the President. "He asks only for support of himself," Roosevelt bristled, apparently forgetting the prerogative that McKinley had exercised twenty years before. The Fourteen Points, he also reminded his audience of 5,000, had been "greeted with enthusiasm by Germany and by all the pro-Germans on this side of the water, especially by the Germanized Socialists and the Bolshevists of every grade." He ended his three-hour-long tirade by reaffirming the Republican party's commitment to unconditional surrender and by exalting "the triumph of the war spirit of America."[65]

Three days later, the nation's two surviving ex-presidents met ceremoniously at the Union Club of New York to draft a joint statement. "[T]he work of reconstruction must not be done by one man or finally formulated according to his academic theories and ideals," they declared. "We urge all Americans who are Americans first to vote for a Republican Congress."[66] Taft then set out on a swing through three Northeastern states to denounce the Fourteen Points and to warn the people of the horrendous consequences of a Democratic victory—a presidential dictatorship.[67]

To counter the final Republican assault, Tumulty put together a full-page advertisement for publication in the country's major newspapers on the eve and morning of the election. The text traced the issues broadly and, unlike the appeal of October 25, singled out Roosevelt and Lodge: "The people have to decide whether they will follow President Wilson or Colonel Roosevelt, whether they want a peace of liberalism and justice or a peace of imperialism, standpatism, militarism that leaves the old causes of war exactly where they were before we undertook to root out militarism and the rule of force and war itself." Figuratively and literally, it ended boldly: "The President stands for a LEAGUE OF NATIONS. . . . EVERYBODY WANTS THIS EXCEPT THOSE WHO WILL PROFIT BY THE OLD ORDER. . . .

BACK UP YOUR PRESIDENT WHO IS RECOGNIZED EVERYWHERE AS THE TRUE SPOKESMAN OF LIBERALS AND PROGRESSIVES THROUGHOUT THE WORLD. DO NOT VOTE TO EMBARRASS THE PRESIDENT. . . . VOTE TO SUSTAIN HIM BY ELECTING DEMOCRATIC SENATORS AND REPRESENTATIVES TO SPEAK FOR YOU."[68]

For the first and only time since the Fourth Liberty Loan address, the White House had invoked the progressive internationalist spirit of Wilson's campaign of 1916. The most striking thing for readers to respond to, however, was now a partisan appeal of a far more blatant sort than its immediate predecessor, and one that lent credence to the Republicans' eleventh-hour charges that Wilson had sullied the dignity of his office. By this juncture, things were at white heat.

Shortly before the polls opened, the *New York Times* stated that Wilson's belated intervention had "vested the fight with a new and deeper meaning and rendered it momentous and epochal beyond any fight for control of the Congress that has been staged since the Civil War."[69] The *New Republic* offered other insights into the campaigns that both parties had conducted. If the Democrats met defeat as a result of the Republican strategy, it would be but another symptom of "the unwholesome condition of American public opinion which results from the suppression during the war of living political discussion." For this, the administration shared responsibility. It had "encouraged intellectual stagnation in relation to the issues of the war" and had worked "against the popular appreciation of a daring and lofty political innovation."[70] The *Nation* had even blunter words for Wilson: "At the very moment of his extremest trial our liberal forces are by his own act, scattered, silenced, disorganized, some in prison. If he loses his great fight for humanity, it will be because he was deliberately silent when freedom of speech and the right of conscience were struck down in America."[71]

During these cheerless closing days of the campaign, Colonel House, too, was waging the "great fight for humanity," from an ornate salon in the Trianon Palace at Versailles.[72] Into this, the most exacting test of his career, he carried no specific instructions. "I feel you will know what to do," the President had said as his emissary departed.[73] Indeed, the Colonel well understood his paramount task—to get the Allied governments formally to adopt the Fourteen Points. "If this is done," his diary entry for October 28 reads, "the basis for the peace will already have been made."[74] The Allied prime ministers and foreign secretaries also understood this to be the case. None of them was unmindful of the plain fact that Germany was suing for peace based on the Fourteen Points; should they fail now to obtain specific reservations, they would be bound permanently to Wilson's program.

On October 27, Clemenceau presented House with a draft armistice prepared by Marshal Foch. It included the following recommendations: the surrender by Germany of 35,000 pieces of heavy artillery and machine guns, 5,000 locomotives and 150,000 railroad cars, and 160 submarines; the internment of her entire surface fleet; the evacuation of all invaded countries; and the occupation by Allied and American forces of the left bank of the Rhine and the establishment of bridgeheads on the right bank.[75]

The ensuing discussions often resembled confrontations. The main source of acrimony, in keeping with American priorities, proved to be the President's famous address, rather than the military conditions of the armistice *per se*. During House's first meeting with the Allied statesmen, on October 29, Clemenceau claimed unfamiliarity with the Fourteen Points, and that Wilson had never solicited his opinion of them. "I have never been asked either," Lloyd George added disingenuously.[76] House then produced a detailed commentary on the address, which Walter Lippmann had prepared the night before.[77] Lloyd George stopped at Point Two. In no circumstances, he declared, could Great Britain accept "freedom of the seas," a doctrine that impinged upon his country's chief means of defense. When the French and Italians compounded this objection by voicing skepticism about the League of Nations, House warned that President Wilson might be compelled to conclude a separate peace.[78]

House had not misspoken. Wilson, upon receiving his report of the day's interchange, cabled that the exclusion of "freedom of the seas" would mean the substitution of British navalism for German militarism. "Neither could I participate in a settlement which did not include league of nations," he went on, "because peace would be without any guarantee except universal armament which would be intolerable. I hope I shall not be obliged to make this decision public."[79]

Lloyd George had meanwhile worked out a solution, couched in the language of compromise, and showed a draft of it to House moments before their meeting with Clemenceau on the following morning. The British government would make peace with the enemy on the President's terms, subject to two reservations. First, the question of "freedom of the seas" must be deferred until the peace conference. (Should he herein concede more, he claimed, he would be forced to resign "in a week's time.") And, second, Germany must make compensation for all damage she had inflicted upon Allied civilians and their property.[80]

The revised British position, though hardly a retreat, struck House as reasonable. It soon appeared, however, that the French and the Italians were preparing their own list of reservations. If they persisted, House announced, he would have to advise the President to lay before Congress all of their conditions, not to mention the prospect of having to continue the war in order to fulfill them. Unlike the previous threat, Lloyd George and Clemenceau seemed to take this one seriously. With amazing sudden-ness, the French premier yielded, ostensibly because of the prevailing Anglo-American unity as well as House's ultimatum. That evening, House notified Wilson of the breakthrough and recommended that he accept the British proposal together with Foch's terms for the military settlement.[81]

By virtue of their dissent, House believed that the Allies had under-cut their own ability to challenge Wilson any further. "I am glad the exceptions were made, for it emphasizes the acceptance of the Fourteen Points," he wrote in his diary.[82] With the final draft of the armistice in hand, he sent word on November 5 that "a great diplomatic victory" had been won, telling his chief that he doubted whether the Allies "realize how far they are now committed to the American peace programme."[83]

House's contribution to the so-called Pre-Armistice Agreement re-mains a historical ambiguity. Two European scholars, Klaus Schwabe and Inga Floto, have argued that he won Allied acceptance of the League and the remaining eleven points only at considerable cost—that is, in the trade-off with Lloyd George and, more important, in his endorsement of Foch's plan to occupy of the Rhineland. (Floto speculates that Clemenceau had secretly offered to abandon opposition to American war aims in exchange for House's support of French security interests—in particular, Allied oc-cupation of the Rhineland. The theory is certainly plausible, and it per-haps best explains Clemenceau's sudden turnabout.[84]) Consequently, the Allies gained a stranglehold on Germany that weakened Wilson's future bargaining position. Schwabe has characterized House's "victory" as "at best, a partial one," while Floto maintains that he "failed miserably."[85]

Without question, House paid too little attention to the military as-pects of the negotiations. Even so, it was not House's alleged bungling, but the unanticipated collapse of the German state and the onset of revo-lution after the Armistice, which snapped the diplomatic lever Wilson hoped to use against accelerating Allied demands. Moreover, Wilson him-self, in his determination to make the Fourteen Points the basis of peace, pursued a strategy that emphasized the political over the military dimen-sions of the armistice. To be sure, on October 28 he had cautioned House that "too much success or security on the part of the Allies will make a genuine peace settlement exceedingly difficult if not impossible." And in a dispatch to General Pershing on the same day, he had doubted the advisability of taking up positions east of the Rhine, "as that is practically an invasion of German soil."[86] But never again in his ten subsequent cablegrams to House did the President question Foch's terms, much less make an issue out of them.

In considering the efficacy of both Wilson's and House's diplomacy, it is also important to note that Great Britain and France had suffered, respectively, some 900,000 and 1.4 million battle deaths in the war—or forty-seven times as many as the United States. Unlike Roosevelt and Lodge, who yearned to spill blood on German soil, the Allied statesmen were acutely sensitive to the hazards of confronting a wounded animal, of demanding unconditional surrender from a flagging enemy perhaps still capable of a *levée en masse*.[87] On this issue (albeit for different reasons), the Allies were as one with Wilson, and he quickly discerned it once the negotiations got under way.

Only in the provision for bridgeheads east of the Rhine did Foch expand the general scope of Wilson's third note to Berlin. Of all the subjects that he addressed in his cables, however, Wilson maintained comparative silence on the Rhineland occupation. (Even Lloyd George worried over the severity of this condition.) But then, as House reported, Clemenceau had given "his word of honor that France would withdraw after the peace conditions had been fulfilled."[88] In these circumstances, Wilson evidently did not consider a *temporary* occupation unwarranted, not if the Allies were willing to comply in the main with the Fourteen Points and the League. All things considered—not the least his domestic difficulties—Wilson, and House in his stead, had not, perhaps, done so badly.

On the day of House's "great diplomatic victory" at Versailles, Wilson had apparently managed a great political defeat at home. November fifth transformed Democratic majorities in the House and Senate into Republican majorities by forty-five and two seats, respectively. By the end of the week there were as many explanations of the reversal as there were politicians and newspaper editors. Republicans, almost reflexively, embraced Wilson's *a priori* interpretation. "In no other free government would he at this moment be in office," Roosevelt wrote to Viscount Bryce. Inasmuch as "the entire pro-German and peace vote was behind the Wilson Democratic ticket," he told the *New York Times,* the verdict was "really extraordinary."[89] Taft, too, seized upon Wilson's appeal and its implications. "The news is too good to be true," he wrote to a relative. "The President can thank himself and his crass egotism." To the Philadelphia *Public Ledger* he offered a somewhat different analysis: Wilson's notes to Germany had "alarmed the people, lest he might make peace by negotiations."[90]

Among Democratic and independent newspapers, the New York *World* considered the decisive factor to be the heavy wartime taxation imposed on the Republican North by the Democratic South. The *New York Times* and the New York *Evening Post* contended that the President's call for a Democratic Congress probably "saved the situation from being a landslide." Many Republican editors, of course, agreed with Roosevelt and Taft. "In a single American sentence," said the the *Rocky Mountain News,* "the American Voice" had demanded " 'Unconditional Surrender!' " Other anti-Wilson publications, however, read the returns with less certitude. The New York *Tribune,* the New York *Globe,* and the Cincinnati *Commercial Tribune,* for instance, referred to the outcome as a "rebuke" to Wilson's interposition, though not necessarily as a repudiation of his leadership.[91]

There was good reason for the Republican editors' circumspection, for one of the most dramatic aspects of the election was the slim margin by which so many candidates stood or fell. Senator George H. Moses, who would become one of the so-called Irreconcilables in the battle against the League, beat his opponent by only 500 out of some 73,000 votes in New Hampshire. Albert B. Fall, a corrupt reactionary whom the President had publicly denounced, would have been eliminated if 900 voters had switched to the Democratic senatorial candidate in New Mexico's tally of 46,700. Among defeated Democratic incumbents, Senator John Shafroth of Colorado, a loyal Wilson supporter, lost by 3,330 out of a total of 212,000 votes. A shift of 4,000 among the 432,000 votes cast in Michigan would have sent Henry Ford, the "administration candidate," to the Senate. Willard Saulsbury of Delaware, one of the most capable Democrats in the upper chamber, failed to retain his seat by a similar factor of 600 ballots out of 41,000. A different outcome in just one of these races would have given the Democrats control of the Senate.[92]

Several historians have discounted any national issue as the determining factor in the election. The prevailing scholarly consensus approximates what one might call the "Wheat Thesis." Selig Adler, David Burner, and Seward Livermore have aptly pointed out that the Democrats sustained their worst casualties in the Middle West and Far West (traditionally Republican regions where "Progressive Democracy" had made significant inroads in 1916). According to these studies, the GOP captured at least twenty-two seats in the House (and perhaps a few in the Senate) primarily because the administration had stubbornly maintained a low ceiling on the price of wheat ($2.20 a bushel), yet had posted no such wartime restrictions on Southern cotton.[93] Livermore further attributes the results to the GOP's bigger campaign coffers and to a heavier turnout among Republicans. In all, about five per cent fewer Democrats than Republicans voted on Election Day.[94]

Virtually all scholarly examinations of the event (as well as of the League) have overlooked perhaps the most compelling analysis of Wilson's misfortune, one that enjoyed wide currency among progressive internationalists. It had little to do with the price of wheat or partisan appeals, but a great deal to do with Wilson's failure to nurture the coalition that had constituted the winning majority in 1916.

To the degree that the elections might be construed as *his* defeat, the *New Republic* mourned, Wilson was "himself partly to blame." He had

not encouraged public discourse even on the League of Peace: "In allowing the mind of the country to stagnate, he had played into the hands of
the incorrigible enemy of his own policy." As a result, when he needed
the people's support, "he obtained it only in a half-hearted measure." The
nation had "voted in the dark" and remained "wholly unprepared to deal
with the new responsibilities to which it is committed as the consequence
of its own acts and the convulsions of the world."[95]

Oswald Garrison Villard also echoed the fearful predictions of numerous progressive internationalists during the previous months. "I am
dismayed by the defeat," he wrote to Tumulty, "because you in the White
House have not built up a liberal party and have permitted Burleson and
Gregory to scatter and intimidate such liberal forces as have existed." The
President could at any moment have stopped his subordinates. Because he
did not, "he is today without the liberal support he needs in this trying
hour when the real victory in the war is still to be won." Villard also
referred to the *Nation*'s growing readership as evidence of an untapped
body of advanced progressive opinion waiting to be led. Could the great
coalition be reunited? "That the President himself and no one else will
decide."[96]

Likewise, the *Dial*, the left-liberal fortnightly, was worried that
American public opinion might fail to support the League of Nations, "in
part due to the ban placed by the repressive measures of the Administration itself upon any real discussion, during the war, of the wider issues
involved." The Espionage and Sedition acts had aided the Republican
campaign "to such an extent indeed that they made it a penal offense to
defend the policy which the President was enunciating."[97] On the socialist
left, Max Eastman, like an embittered suitor spurned too many times, now
only saw "an opaque ethical vapor" exuding from the President. "The
forces of imperialism and militarism and industrial reaction are a little
alarmed by it perhaps, the forces of liberty not in the least assisted. The
defeat of the President was an expression of disgust from both sides of
him."[98]

The head of the Committee on Public Information surveyed the ruins,
too. George Creel had no doubts about the veracity of the progressive
internationalist interpretation. "All the radical, or liberal friends of your
anti-imperialist war policy were either silenced or intimidated," he told
the President. "The Department of Justice and the Post Office were allowed to silence and intimidate them. There was no voice left to argue
for your sort of peace. The Nation and the Public got nipped. All the
radical and socialist press was dumb." The situation was not utterly hope-
less, but there was only one way to repair it. "The liberal, radical, labor
and socialist press will have to be rallied to the President's support. You
will have to give out your program for peace and reconstruction and find

friends for it. Otherwise, the reactionary patrioteers will defeat the whole immediate future of reform and progress."[99]

Although the absence of public opinion polls makes it difficult to identify with absolute assurance a single, overarching cause of the Democratic set-back, its consequences and meaning are not unfathomable. To begin with, while the election created new and formidable obstacles to American participation in the League of Nations, it did not necessarily render the League a lost cause. Nor was the campaign responsible for making the League a partisan issue; that had occurred some time ago. The election of 1918 was the tentative resolution (if not the climax) of a sequence of events set in motion in 1915–16, at the very inception of the progressive internationalist movement—in the politics of neutrality and preparedness and in the forging of the Wilsonian victory of 1916. In this respect, the alternative post mortem of the progressive internationalists is as important as any of the more familiar interpretations.

By the touchstone of "Progressive Democracy" and "Peace Without Victory," progressive internationalists—the Woman's Peace party, the American Union Against Militarism, the Socialist party, and liberals in general—had defined the ideological terms of the debate and claimed title to the League, at least until the spring of 1917. Although it did not altogether vitiate their influence, the declaration of war inexorably splintered those groups and organizations. Thereafter, whereas Wilson's ends remained the same as before, coercion frequently superseded persuasion among the means he used to realize them. On a very critical level, Wilson lost sight of the relationship between politics and foreign policy. Growing increasingly singleminded in the desperate struggle against Germany, he took for granted his natural base of support outside the Democratic party and consequently began to lose his grip on it. Many progressive internationalists had foreseen this eventuality and had tried to alert him, but to no avail.

Of all the various counterfactual scenarios, perhaps the most tempting one is what might have happened if Wilson had ground his heel down on Burleson and Gregory from the start and had consistently encouraged a lively public discussion of war aims, the League included. Even in the absence of those initiatives, Roosevelt and company had all but exhausted their inventories of aspersions. How many times could the Republicans have called Wilson a "dictatorial, pacifistic, socialistic, anti-American, pro-German internationalist"—how many more than they had done in the circumstances that actually prevailed? The President's "firm hand of stern repression" held rewards only for conservatives and reactionaries. Unless he was prepared to take steps to revitalize his once-ascendent coalition, the new configurations on Capitol Hill would simply overwhelm him.

None of this is meant to put the entire blame on Wilson. The impact of the opposition's propaganda cannot be dismissed. The Republican strategy, after all, was smartly conceived and executed. Indeed, Roosevelt, Lodge, and Hays had virtually written a textbook on how a political party might, with penetrating effect, brand liberals as incipient socialists, whether they were or not. One might even conclude that they cut the pattern for Republican campaigns for the rest of the century.

At the same time, it should be emphasized that, despite the explosive energy they released, neither Roosevelt, Lodge, nor Hays turned out to be the key Republican player. That distinction must go to Taft. The president of the League to Enforce Peace was the one Republican with sufficient influence and prestige to check the obstructionists. Nevertheless, he exhibited the most peculiar behavior of anyone in the campaign. Even allowing for both a normal degree of party loyalty and Roosevelt's misleading assurances, Taft's attacks on Wilson defied rational explanation. Surely, Roosevelt's public denunciations of all internationalists, in tandem with Wilson's Fourth Liberty Loan address, should have caused Taft to hesitate. Unwittingly or no, he became the anti-League forces' greatest asset in the campaign.

Of course, Taft was not alone in being guilty of poor judgment and bad faith. Wilson had never treated his immediate predecessor with the consideration that he deserved; nor had the LEP ever been able to get so much as a friendly grunt out of the President. In his long silence on the details of the League, Wilson had in essence demanded the same thing from conservative and progressive internationalists alike—to wit, complete and unquestioning faith in his own wisdom. This was not good political leadership in either instance. He had only postponed the reckoning and thus had permitted a disparate opposition to exploit wartime passions, to consolidate itself, and, ultimately, to secure positions of power.

But both Wilson and Taft waived potential opportunities to break the chain reaction. On one hand, Wilson might have tried to reach some kind of understanding with Taft and to use the predominantly Republican LEP to counter the League's detractors. On the other hand, Taft should have been more discerning about Roosevelt. Instead of issuing joint statements with the old Bull Moose, he might have signed one with the President. For the sake of the League, Wilson and Taft together might have agreed to stay out of the partisan arena. Whether such acts of statesmanship would have altered the course of the election is pure speculation; but they could not but have helped to shield the League from injurious constructions of the returns, regardless of which party had won.

There is a final factor to consider—the timing of Germany's request for an armistice—which was beyond anyone's control. The reactions of Democrats as well as Republicans amply demonstrate that, more than any other development, the German overture of October 6 set the American political landscape ablaze. Once again, the counterfactual possibilities are intriguing, especially in the light of the Kaiser's abdication on November 9 and of the solemn occasion that took place at the Capitol on the afternoon of November 11, when Wilson presented the terms of the Armistice to a joint session of Congress.

Tanks, trains, trucks, planes, artillery, battleships and submarines—or, practically all of Germany's machines of war—were to be to be confiscated or interned. Evacuation of invaded territories, a fortified Allied watch on the Rhine, and compensation for civilian damages—to these conditions, also, Germany had agreed. There was no mention of unconditional surrender. The Fourteen Points were to serve as the basis of the peace settlement itself. Yet, as Wilson read out the articles, members of Congress gasped audibly as the completeness of the victory grew more and more apparent. Would greater numbers of voters have shown their appreciation at the polls if this armistice had been hammered out a week sooner? One can only wonder what thoughts went through his mind as he looked out upon the chamber and said, "The war thus comes to an end." [100]

From this point onward Wilson would have no respite from controversy. Within the month, he announced his appointments to the American Commission to Negotiate Peace (ACNP) and his decision to lead the delegation personally. These revelations caused a commotion to match any that had come before. In addition to House and Lansing, the President named General Tasker H. Bliss and Henry White as commissioners. Bliss, former Army Chief of Staff and an amateur classicist, represented Wilson on the Allied Supreme War Council. White, a career diplomat, had previously served Republican presidents as ambassador to France and Italy and had not lived in the United States for years. [101]

Given the composition of the next Congress, the glaring exclusion from the ACNP of any prominent Republican clouded the prospects for Senate ratification of a Wilsonian peace treaty. Like pundits at the time, historians usually place the omission second, after the appeal to the voters, among the President's more serious blunders. [102] The decision was not a lapse in judgment *per se,* however, or an example of Wilson's rigidity—a factor that obtained only in the case of Charles Evans Hughes, one of the three Republicans most often mentioned as a potential commissioner. (On that count, Wilson said, "there is no room big enough for Hughes & me to stay in.") [103]

Wilson was painfully aware that his rejection of the two other contenders, Taft and Root, could prove to be a mistake. But the bitter residue of the election—not to mention Wilson's personal method of conducting diplomacy and, especially, the authentic differences between progressive and conservative internationalism—made their selection unlikely. Was he to assume that Taft and Root had not meant what they had said during the campaign? "Republicans whom one would naturally choose," he explained to Richard Hooker, "are already committed to do everything possible to prevent the Peace Conference from acting upon the peace terms which [the Allies] have already agreed to."[104] More specifically, Wilson considered Root a reactionary. As for Taft (whose exclusion continues to perplex many historians), if his recent public statements did not disqualify him, then his private exchanges with Governor Bickett surely did, for, soon after the election, Bickett sent their correspondence to the White House.[105] "I would not dare take Mr. Taft," Wilson subsequently wrote. "I have lost all confidence in his character." It was, as he lamented, "a distressing situation indeed"—but not one, as he also claimed, that the Republicans had brought about by themselves.[106]

The other post-Armistice controversy—Wilson's decision to attend the peace conference—seems somewhat extreme when one considers how commonplace presidential "summitry" has become since Franklin D. Roosevelt's time. But such a journey was something new in 1918—something one might have expected of Theodore Roosevelt had he held the office—and it exercised members of both parties. Democrats inundated the White House with diverse opinions. There were the pressing problems of domestic reconstruction to attend to, some argued. More important, the President would drain himself, lower his dignity, and mar his prestige by stepping down from his Olympian pedestal to engage in the thrust and parry of the negotiations. He would forfeit his strongest weapon—"the very mystery and uncertainty that attach to him while he remains in Washington." Whereas Colonel House equivocated, the Secretary of State was convinced that the President was "making one of the greatest mistakes of his career and imperiling his reputation."[107]

Other counselors saw the matter quite differently. Diplomacy by cable, they pointed out, was inadequate in view of the magnitude of the task at hand. Because of his international prestige, his presence at the conference was essential to the adoption of his program. "I believe the League of Nations . . . will fail if you do not go," Supreme Court Justice John Hessin Clarke summed it all up. "If this is not obtained, the sacrifices of the great war will have been, in large measure, made in vain."[108]

Such estimations of Wilson's personal influence motivated opposition to the trip among Republican legislators and editors. The New York *Globe* was disturbed about it because he "entertains ideas akin to . . . British Labor and the minority of French Socialists." The *Sacramento Bee* was alarmed about his "leniency to the defeated Hohenzollern."[109] Senator Lawrence Y. Sherman wanted his colleagues to declare the office of President vacant if Wilson went abroad, while Senator Knox introduced a resolution calling for the postponement of a league of nations until after the peace was made.[110]

Many leaders of the GOP, however, soon began to worry that a reaction might set in against "attempts to pin-prick the President"; that the public would perceive Republicans as meddlesome spoilers.[111] The attacks pretty much ceased when Taft, in a surprise move, denounced them as "the poorest kind of politics." Defending Wilson with the same arguments as those who applauded the undertaking, he said that nothing in the Constitution prohibited the President from leaving the country. It was his duty to go; this peace conference was that important. In a conspicuously gracious gesture, he even said that if Wilson aspired to it, he would make "a most fitting head" of the League of Nations. (Privately, Taft continued to doubt Wilson's fidelity. The trip was "a good thing," he explained to Bryce, because "it may bring home to him the demand of the common people of England, France and Italy that we have a League of Nations."[112])

In the end, Wilson's desire to go to Paris was neither unreasonable— when the Allies were sending their own chief statesmen—nor entirely unexpected. It was, in fact, implicit in his rationalization for belligerency. "[A]s the head of a nation participating in the war he would have a seat at the Peace Table," he had said to Jane Addams. "The foreign policies which we so extravagantly admired could have a chance if he were there to push and to defend them, but not otherwise."[113] Although the Allied prime ministers now confidentially disclosed to Colonel House their profound anxiety over Wilson's participation, Lloyd George himself had averred back in February 1917: "The President's presence at the peace conference is necessary for the proper organization of the world."[114]

Moreover, among most of the war-weary peoples of Europe, the Fourteen Points had acquired the status of sacred text, and the word "Wilson" was now becoming something more than simply the name of a president. Three times on November 5, thousands of demonstrators outside the American embassy in Rome beckoned Thomas Nelson Page to come to the window and gratify their wishes by acclaiming the President. "Your name was not only applauded wildly, but continually shouted," the Ambassador reported. Italian soldiers were placing his picture in their barracks. An old woman said she heard that in America "there was a great saint who was making peace for us." Italian politicians feared him, Page went on, but "by the common people you are adored."[115] In an open letter to Wilson, the French Nobel laureate Romain Rolland designated him the greatest "moral authority" in the world, "the only one who can speak alike to both the proletariat and the middle classes of all nations and be listened to by them."[116] All things considered, it *would* have been surprising if Wilson had stayed home, at the very moment when his supreme ambition was on the threshold of accomplishment.

His disciples later attributed to him premonitions almost too felicitous to be credible. "People will endure their tyrants for years, but they tear their deliverers to pieces if a millennium is not created immediately," he said during the interim before the peace conference, according to George Creel. To Tumulty he supposedly said, "[T]his trip will either be the greatest success or the supremest tragedy in all history."[117] Whether or not he actually made these remarks, they convey poetic truth about a potential turning point of singular intensity in the annals of the Republic and the affairs of the world, and, of course, in the modern memory of Woodrow Wilson. As Edith Benham (Mrs. Wilson's secretary) wrote in her diary, "It is to be the final test of his strength—this coming Congress—and if he can force his ideals on the Allies. . . . I cannot help but feel sorry for the defeat he may have."[118]

   Yet, at this juncture, no one could confidently predict failure or success. There were too many imponderables. Although Henry Cabot Lodge would be the next chairman of the Senate Foreign Relations Committee, it was not a foregone conclusion that most Republicans would join the avowed opponents of the League. On November 17, the LEP adopted a resolution that pledged "its hearty support to the President in the establishment of . . . a League of Nations."[119] Providentially, Taft was beginning to realize exactly where Lodge and Knox stood, and publicly admonished them while Wilson was on the high seas: "This treaty at Paris is going to be worth nothing but the paper it is written on unless you have a League to Enforce Peace. . . . Unless you have such a league, your war is a failure, your treaty is a failure, and your peace is a failure."[120] And many progressive internationalists, Max Eastman notwithstanding, showed a willingness (for the time being) to close ranks behind the President and forgive his transgressions against them. On November 30, Paul Kellogg's and Herbert Croly's League of Free Nations Association published a "Statement of Principles" and, despite their differences with the LEP, temporarily united with that organization in a common "Victory Program."[121]

   Then, too, whereas the League was not at the center of their concerns, Lloyd George, Clemenceau, and Orlando, by virtue of the political terms of the Armistice, had all but agreed to make it a priority at the peace conference—this in the face of Roosevelt's repeated reminders that "Mr. Wilson has no authority to speak for the American people at this time."[122] The Allied prime ministers well knew that their countrymen regarded the President—even under the cloud of his political setback, or perhaps because of it—as "our Wilson." Europeans in general were "not impressed at all by the thousands of American ward bosses who feel superior to him," George Bernard Shaw observed, "and that fact must be accepted for the moment unless American democracy wishes to be set down as a political failure which has accidentally produced a greater individual success than it is capable of appreciating." [123]

Indeed, if the League of Nations represented the hopes of millions in Europe and America and now seemed nearer fruition, and if those who condemned it could not ignore the League even in its present abstract form, then it was because of Wilson's incomparable ability to communicate to an international constituency—"to evoke, by open speech, the latent sanity of mankind," as H. N. Brailsford put it. [124] And, as he had done in the past, Wilson would continue (perhaps too much) to rely on the appeal to principle, on the judgment of "the people." It was not without justification that, in his final address to Congress on the eve of his departure, he evinced a feeling of personal responsibility for the creation of the League of Nations: "The gallant men of our armed forces on land and sea have consciously fought for the ideals which they knew to be the ideals of their country; I have sought to express those ideals; they have accepted my statements of them as the substance of their own thought and purpose, as the associated Governments have accepted them; I owe it to them to see to it, so far as in me lies, that no false or mistaken interpretation is put upon them, and no possible effort omitted to realize them. It is now my duty to play my full part in making good what they offered their life's blood to obtain. I can think of no call to service which could transcend this." [125] With this penitential invocation, Wilson joined the ranks of those Americans who went across the sea to fight the war to end all wars.

11

The Stern Covenanter

New York Harbor erupted in splendid pandemonium as the *George Washington,* bearing President Wilson and a small army of advisers and newspaper reporters, began its historic voyage to Europe on the morning of December 4, 1919. Naval vessels fired nineteen-gun salutes, and tugboats and ferries tied down their whistle valves. From the Hoboken waterfront and the tall buildings of Manhattan, tens of thousands of people waved handkerchiefs and threw confetti. As the liner approached the Statue of Liberty, a giant dirigible swung overhead while a squadron of airplanes "looped the loop." Further out, eleven battleships made ready to escort the presidential argosy to its destination.[1]

Almost from the moment the *George Washington* sighted the coast of Brittany nine days later, any remaining doubts about Wilson's decision to attend the peace conference had vanished. The spectacle at Brest—the cheers of the entire population of the city and banners bearing the slogans "Hail the Champion of the Rights of Man" and "Honor to the Founder of the Society of Nations"—was but a prelude. Never before in the history of France had such a demonstration taken place as the one that awaited Wilson in Paris. From the Gare des Invalides to the Arc de Triomphe, down the Champs-Élysées and across the Place de la Concorde, some two million Parisians turned out to hail the President of the United States.

Along the parade route, seats in windows sold for 300 francs and young men and children climbed trees to catch a better glimpse of "Wilson, the Just." Thirty-six thousand French soldiers held back the crowds as the procession of eight horse-drawn carriages, the first one carrying Wilson and President Raymond Poincaré, passed along the avenues. Cannon boomed in the distance. Bouquets of violets rained down on Mrs. Wilson, almost burying her carriage. The cheers were deafening, even frightening. "I saw Foch pass, Clemenceau pass, Lloyd George, generals, returning troops," wrote one American journalist, "but Wilson heard from his carriage something different, inhuman—or superhuman."[2]

The scene virtually repeated itself when the President visited London, Carlisle, and Manchester the following week. After his entrance into Rome in early January—where the streets were sprinkled with golden sand, in accordance with ancient tradition, and the banners read "Welcome to the God of Peace"—it was said that Caesar had never had a grander triumph. In Milan, the ovations verged on hysteria, and Wilson was moved to tears. Enormous throngs choked the streets and inundated his automobile with papers acclaiming him "The Savior of Humanity" and "The Moses from Across the Atlantic." At La Scala people clamored for his autograph, and his doctor saw many of those who received it kiss the signature and press it to their hearts. Throughout the country, Italian families placed sacred candles next to his photograph.[3]

The extraordinary tribute the peoples of Europe paid Wilson was the stuff the Allied prime ministers' nightmares were made of. These unprecedented demonstrations transcended mere pageantry. Indeed, they were an articulate expression of mass political opinion—and one, significantly, set in motion by the liberal, labor, and socialist movements within the Allied countries. In effect, "the people" had presented Wilson with new and imposing credentials to compensate for the majorities denied him in the congressional elections;[4] they also gave him an unexpected opportunity to strike successive blows on behalf of the League of Nations, propitiously before the peace conference convened. Beginning in Great Britain, Wilson issued a series of hard-hitting indictments of militarism, imperialism, and the concept of the balance of power—the most sustained such forensic effort he had undertaken since the campaign of 1916.

At Guildhall on December 28, Wilson said that practically all the soldiers he had spoken with believed that they had "fought to do away with an old order and to establish a new one." At the center of the old order, he explained, was " 'the balance of power'—a thing in which the balance was determined by the sword . . . by the unstable equilibrium of competitive interests." The world could ill afford a reincarnation of this system. When the war began, a league of nations was regarded as "something that men could think about but never get," he said. "Now we find the practical leading minds of the world determined to get it. No such sudden and potent union of purpose has ever been witnessed in the world before."[5]

At Manchester's Free Trade Hall, Wilson told the overflow crowd of British workers: "If the future had nothing for us but to keep the world at a right poise by a balance of power, the United States would take no interest, because she will join no combination of power which is not the combination of all of us." There was "a great compulsion of the common conscience now in existence which if any statesman resist he has gained the most unenviable eminence in history." He cautioned that it was not likely that every problem confronting the peace conference could be settled satisfactorily; but that was all the more reason to provide "a machinery of adjustment in order that we may have a machinery of good will and of friendship."[6]

For Wilson, the cataclysm of the war was evidence enough in support of his conclusions. "We know that there cannot be another balance of power," he declared before the Italian Parliament. "That has been tried and found wanting, for the best of all reasons that it does not stay balanced inside itself, and a weight which does not hold together cannot constitute a makeweight in the affairs of men. Therefore, there must be something substituted for the balance of power. . . ." A league of nations, "once considered theoretical and idealistic[,] turns out to be practical and necessary."[7]

Upon receiving the freedom of the city of Milan from its Socialist mayor, Wilson delivered his most politically radical address of the tour. He was wary of being identified solely with the left, he had recently told House, because "those interested in opposing his principles" had already seized upon "the source of the popular support which he [was] receiving" and continued to use it against him.[8] But this did not seem to bother him in Milan. He was keenly aware, he said to the vast crowd, "that the social structure rests upon the great working classes of the world, and that those working classes . . . have by their conscience of community of interest . . . done perhaps more than any other influence to establish a world opinion, an opinion which is not of a nation . . . but is the opinion, one might say, of mankind." The peacemakers "must think and act and confer in the presence of this opinion." He was touched to have received from some wounded Italian soldiers "a memorial in favor of a league of nations, and to be told by them that that was what they had fought for, . . . some guarantee of justice, some equilibrium for the world . . . [so] that they would never have to fight a war like this again." This was the added obligation. "We can not merely sign a treaty of peace and go home with clear consciences," he concluded. "We must do something more."[9]

Colonel House and Ray Stannard Baker had encouraged the President. They both believed that the tour would enhance popular devotion to the League and impress upon the Allied statesmen that they dare not oppose it.[10] True to their predictions, the response of his massive audiences seemed to certify Wilson "as a sort of Messiah sent to save them from all the ills that the war has brought on the world."[11] Still, it was not quite clear, practically speaking, how the adoration of the masses could be converted into tangible political leverage, and not only with respect to the League of Nations.

Prime Minister Orlando and Foreign Minister Sidney Sonnino, for instance, desired a league of nations about as much as they reveled in the Fourteen Points; which is to say, hardly at all. Their preoccupation—the British and French called it an obsession—was the Treaty of London of 1915, which promised Italy portions of Turkey, the South Tyrol, the Trentino, and the Dalmation islands and littoral.[12] In addition, they now claimed the Croation port city of Fiume as the just rewards for Italy's unexpected victory over the Austrian army in October last.[13]

The popular glorification of "Saint Woodrow" vastly complicated the lives of Orlando and Sonnino and exacerbated the sharp contention between the Italian left and right over imperialist pretensions. As Ray Stannard Baker reported, "The labor and socialist groups are solidly and sincerely behind Mr. Wilson and his program."[14] Accordingly, Wilson pitched his speeches to that constituency. He also held a highly publicized interview with Leonida Bissolati, a Reformist Socialist who had resigned from the government to protest the claims on Dalmatia and Fiume. Bissolati vouchsafed that the majority of his fellow citizens did not covet the Adriatic territories. When Wilson asked if most Italians had confidence in the League of Nations, Bissolati replied, "The Italian people are the most Wilsonian in Europe, the most adapted to your ideals."[15] Wilson's Italian sojourn thus confirmed all of his preconceptions—that Orlando was "a damned reactionary," but that the people of Italy were determined to see the League of Nations through. For his part, Orlando deeply resented Wilson's trespasses, but realized that any overt attempt to forestall the League would not advance his own priorities and might even bring about his political ruin.[16]

In France, too, Wilson received, at best, mixed signals. By all reports, Clemenceau was both amazed and disturbed by the magnitude of his fellow citizens' salute to the President.[17] After his entrance into Paris, the French government (unlike the British and the Italians) was determined to control Wilson's exposure to mass meetings. Whereas he received an official delegation from the French Socialist party on the day of his arrival,[18] he later complained about two instances in which the government prevented him from addressing other groups representing

labor. One scheduled gathering of working women was cancelled because Clemenceau "objected to any more demonstrations in favor of
the President." The Premier permitted a small group of women to
meet with Wilson only on condition that they would make "no laudatory remarks about him" and would "not speak of the League of
Nations."[19]

Clemenceau paid the President a personal call on December 15. Their
hour-long exchange, orchestrated by Colonel House, "was felicitous from
start to finish." Clemenceau even swore his "eternal friendship" when
Wilson returned the courtesy the next day. At a third meeting, however,
Wilson broached the controversial subject. Clemenceau said he doubted
whether the League was "workable," but agreed, "in a mild way," that it
was a worthy endeavor.[20] In fact, "mild" was an exaggeration. Just after
Wilson left for London, the pro-Wilsonian Socialist minority in the Chamber
of Deputies forced the Premier to answer criticisms that his government
had no peace program of its own; in his response, on December 29, he
chose to rebut Wilson's Guildhall address. "There is an old system which
appears to be discredited today, but to which . . . I am still faithful," he
declared. "Here in this system of alliance . . . is the thought which will
guide me at the conference." As for a league of nations, America was far
away from Germany. He was loath to raise extravagant hopes. If France
remained mistress of her own defense, he would gladly accept "any sup-
plemental guarantees which may be given." President Wilson, he added,
"is a man who inspires respect by the frankness of his speech and the
noble candeur of his spirit."[21]

Clemenceau's comments on the balance of power were not well received anywhere outside of France, least of all in the United States.[22]
Within France, the remark about Wilson's *"noble candeur"* incensed the
Socialists; depending on the context, the phrase could mean either "well
intentioned naïveté" or "candor." Clemenceau explained that he had certainly meant the latter and afterward assured Colonel House that he was
for the League of Nations.[23] Even so, he was dedicated heart and soul to
his country's security and therefore to the reduction of Germany to military impotence and something approaching economic vassalage—a view
one member of the ACNP privately described as "little less than one of
insanity."[24]

Clemenceau's pronouncement gave Wilson no reason to change his
earlier characterization of the seventy-seven-year-old partisan as "an old
man, too old to comprehend new ideas."[25] The incident in the Chamber,
compounded by the overwhelming vote of confidence Clemenceau's coalition subsequently won, contributed to a shift in Wilson's strategy; both
he and House now firmly regarded the British as their key ally in the
task confronting them.[26] It also marked the beginning of an intermittently

antagonistic relationship between Wilson and "the Tiger." The President complained that Clemenceau was "unreliable" and "tricky," while the latter once quipped that "talking to Wilson is something like talking to Jesus Christ." Neither one tried "to understand the other's best qualities," Lloyd George observed. "When Wilson talks of idealism, Clemenceau . . . touches his forehead, as much as to say, 'A good man, but not quite all there!' "[27] The Prime Minister later remarked that he sometimes felt as if he were seated between Jesus and Napoleon.[28]

Wilson found the political climate comparatively agreeable on the other side of the Channel, where a well-organized national consensus on the League prevailed. In October, the two leading British league societies had merged into one organization—the League of Nations Union—with Viscount Grey of Fallodon as president and Lloyd George and Balfour as honorary presidents. (The LNU also had declared that the League must be created at the peace conference.) The organization then began to disseminate pamphlet literature and to hold mass meetings throughout the country. With the cooperation of hundreds of churches, December 22 was designated "League of Nations Sunday."

The good works of the LNU were somewhat blunted, however, by the results of the so-called Khaki Election of December 14, the first held in Great Britain since 1910. On one hand, the LNU's propaganda proved so effective that some form of lip service to the League became a basic requirement for the winning candidate. On the other hand, whereas early in the campaign he stressed issues pertaining to postwar domestic reconstruction, Lloyd George soon succumbed to expedience and exploited the more popular issues of extracting huge indemnities from Germany and of prosecuting the Kaiser. When the votes were counted (two days after Wilson's arrival in London), the Prime Minister's predominantly Conservative coalition had scored a smashing victory over the Labour and Liberal parties. Many of the League's friends—including H. N. Brailsford, Arthur Ponsonby, Charles and Noel Buxton, as well as former Prime Minister Asquith and Arthur Henderson, the leader of British Labour—were among the casualties.[29]

Lloyd George still was not wont to read too much into the returns. The Imperial War Cabinet could not help but be impressed, for instance, by the distinguished deputation from the LNU—Grey, Asquith, Bryce, and the Archbishop of Canterbury—that called on Wilson at the American embassy to wish him godspeed; nor by the publication, on the same day, of the Trades Union Congress and Labour party's declaration in support of the League. And, of course, there were the phenomenal public outpourings wherever the President went.[30]

The Imperial War Cabinet was apprised of Wilson's outlook on the League even before he started making speeches. "He considers that almost

all the difficult questions . . . can only be satisfactorily settled on the basis
of a LEAGUE OF NATIONS," Sir William Wiseman reported from Paris.[31]
The Prime Minister and the Foreign Secretary soon gathered as much on
their own in extended conversations with Wilson at Buckingham Palace
and 10 Downing Street on December 27. Wilson, following House's advice, listened sympathetically to their concerns as well (in particular, about
the issues of freedom of the seas, indemnities, and the disposition of former enemy colonies), but did not commit himself. When he raised his
glass to the King and Queen that evening he spoke of finding himself "in
the company of a body of men united in ideal and in purpose"—for Lloyd
George and Balfour had expressed a willingness to make the League the
first subject of the peace conference.[32]

The discussions with Wilson provoked heated debate in the Imperial
War Cabinet on December 30 and 31. Prime Minister William Hughes of
Australia disputed Lloyd George's assumption that the interests of the
British Empire and of the United States overlapped in compelling ways.
If they were not careful, he warned, they would discover themselves chained
"behind the wheels of President Wilson's chariot." Citing the good professor's positions on colonial claims, disarmament, indemnities, and freedom of the seas, and belittling the American contribution to the war,
Hughes considered it "intolerable" that Wilson should tell them what to
do. Lord Curzon reminded the Prime Minister of the implications of the
recent British and American elections. England and France, Hughes added,
rightfully "could settle the peace of the world as they liked." The League,
alas, was to Wilson "what a toy was to a child—he would not be happy
till he got it."[33]

Hughes spoke for a minority in the War Cabinet. The majority—
including Lloyd George, Robert Cecil, Ambassador Reading, Canadian
prime minister Robert Borden, and George Barnes of the Labour party—
beheld the future as well as the past and present. The principle of the
balance of power no doubt would continue to obtain in many ways, even
with a league of nations. But, as Barnes implied, Clemenceau's pledge of
allegiance to the old diplomacy was surely de trop; his claims against Germany jingoistic. The long age of the primacy of Europe in world politics
was at an end. Would the welfare of the British Empire be advanced by
another alliance with the French, or by cooperation with the Americans?
Good relations with the latter, Borden argued, was "the best asset we
could bring home from the war." As against France, Barnes was "entirely
in favor of supporting America for all we were worth."[34]

Lloyd George was presently inclined to agree. Only on the question
of indemnities had Wilson shown "really hard resistance," and on the
essentials of the League of Nations "he had been by no means extreme."
The League "was a matter of life and death" to Wilson; if they gave him

that, he could be induced to consent, "though possibly under protest, to the things to which we attached importance." No, the case for cooperation—for an Atlantic, rather than a Continental, strategy—was compelling. Lloyd George also referred to a trump card. Should Wilson prove obstinate, nothing prevented them from reviewing the situation.[35]

There was an additional cogent reason why the Prime Minister should strive to accommodate the most insistent manifestation of the New Diplomacy. Second only to Wilson among all the peacemakers, the League's two most stalwart advocates—Robert Cecil and Jan Christiaan Smuts, the celebrated scholar-statesman of the Union of South Africa—held important positions in the War Cabinet. Also, Cecil and Smuts had recently written and circulated papers on the subject. Smuts' composition, in particular, was already having a substantial impact on public opinion; both documents would influence the course of events surrounding the drafting of the Covenant of the League of Nations.

Lord Robert's contribution thereon contained few surprises. Essentially a shorter version of the Phillimore Report, it called for regular conferences ("the pivot of the League") of all the prime ministers and foreign secretaries of the five great powers (Great Britain, France, Italy, Japan, and the United States). Qualifications for membership need not be too rigid, "since the smaller powers will in any case not exercise any considerable influence." (Cecil singled out only the Bolshevik government, an "untrustworthy and hostile state," for exclusion.) A permanent secretariat, located in Geneva, would perform administrative functions.

As for the prevention of armed conflict, potential belligerents would be obliged not to go to war before submitting their dispute to a court of arbitration or conciliation. Only a unanimous vote of the judges would make their decision binding. Any member state that violated this covenant would be regarded "as, *ipso facto,* at war" with the rest, and subject to appropriate sanctions. Like the Phillimore Report, Cecil's did not specify what the League might do if neither of the "litigants" refrained from hostilities once the foregoing process had taken place. The emphasis was on ensuring a delay of hostilities and a public discussion of the threat to peace.[36]

By far the more comprehensive (and progressive) British formulation was General Smuts' *The League of Nations: A Practical Suggestion,* published in late December.[37] It is frequently maintained that the most original feature of this document was the so-called mandate system, Smuts' answer to the problem of what to do about the breakup of Russia and the Ottoman and Hapsburg empires. Citing the famous slogan of progressive internationalists and revolutionary socialists, "No annexations and the self-determination of nations," Smuts deemed the spoils system "incorrigible madness." The only acceptable alternative was to entrust the peoples and territories in question to the care and tutelage of the League. The "successor to empires" would appoint individual mandatary states to supervise or control each of the incipient states, the object being (ostensibly) to guide them along the path to self-government.

On resolving conflicts, the "Practical Suggestions" were virtually identical to the Phillimore and Cecil texts.[38] In other respects, however, they bore a resemblance to the Covenant that Wilson and House had hammered out at Magnolia in August 1918. For instance, Smuts (unlike Cecil) included a major section requiring the reduction of armaments, the nationalization of the manufacture of the weapons of war, and the abolition of conscription.[39] He also addressed the controversial issue of the comparative status of great and small powers—again, a question Wilson and House had debated at Magnolia. The Practical Suggestions provided for a General Conference of nations in which all states would have an equal vote. Executive authority, however, would repose in a Council of the League. In this body, the five great powers would enjoy a majority, but just barely; four other powers, chosen by the General Conference, would represent the "middle" and "minor" states. A minority of three could veto any action of the Council.[40] This arrangement did not conform categorically to the principle of the equality of states; but, in giving the smaller powers substantial representation on the Council, it clearly leaned toward Wilson's position, in contrast to Cecil's scheme, which would deny those states the "exercise [of] any considerable influence."

The sixty-page tract ended in high meditation. The League was destined to become "to the peoples the guarantee of peace, to the workers of all races the great international, and to all the embodiment and living expression of the moral and spiritual unity of the human race."[41] Smuts' employment of the Wilsonian idiom, here and elsewhere, was bound to gratify the President's constituency. In the drawing rooms of British Labour and Liberalism, the South African's round blend of noble sentiments and practicality was savored like fine sherry. Several members of the Imperial War Cabinet, however, found it far too heady and "dangerously overelaborated," and advised against an official endorsement. For his part, Lloyd George told Smuts that it was "one of the ablest state papers he had ever read."[42]

No one was more pleased with the sketch than President Wilson.[43] When he sat down to revise his original Covenant during the first week of January 1919, he incorporated, verbatim, whole paragraphs from Smuts— in particular, the recommendations for a bicameral organization and for mandates; he even substituted sizable portions of Smuts' provisions for arbitration for his own. For these reasons, scholarly studies of the drafting process almost invariably have concluded that the President was "greatly influenced" by, or "fell under the spell of Smuts." One historian has argued that Wilson thus lost the initiative and exerted "very little influence on the actual provisions and structure of the Covenant."[44]

To be sure, Wilson described the Smuts document as "thoroughly statesmanlike in character."[45] Yet the foregoing deductions are not well founded. Among other things, they fail to reckon fully with either the synthetic nature of Smuts' proposal or its pervasive acknowledgements to Wilson. Nor do they take account of the entire range of Smuts' motivations. Whereas the former Boer leader was dedicated to the broad principles of the League, he was equally devoted to the British Empire. Like Lloyd George, Smuts recognized the importance of satisfying Wilson, if only to get the President "to drop some of the other contentious points he has unfortunately raised."[46] Then, too, new evidence suggests that Wilson's motivation in adopting a good deal of Smuts' language amounted to a deliberate calculation.

To begin, it must be pointed out that the mandate system had had currency for some time. As early as 1915, J. A. Hobson, in *Towards International Government,* had contemplated some form of international trusteeship as a first step toward phasing out colonialism.[47] The Inter-Allied Labour and Socialist Conference of February 1918 also had called for the same sort of policy for colonial regions.[48] On the American side, George Louis Beer, the famous Columbia University professor and The Inquiry's expert on colonies, had written detailed memoranda on a mandate system for Africa and Mesopotamia in 1917–18.[49]

Wilson himself anticipated the idea in the fifth of the Fourteen Points—"a free, open-minded, and absolutely impartial adjustment of colonial claims," taking care that "the interests of the populations concerned . . . have equal weight with the equitable claims of the government whose title is to be determined." In more specific terms, he articulated the principle in an interview with Wiseman in October 1918. The German colonies, he had said, must not revert to Germany; neither could they be handed over to the British Empire. (Smuts did not mention Germany's colonial possessions because he intended for them to be parceled out among the Dominions.) Wilson "wondered whether . . . they could be administered in trust," Wiseman recorded. " 'In trust,' I asked, 'for whom?' 'Well, for the League of Nations, for instance,' he said."[50] To Ambassador Jusserand, as well, Wilson revealed his thoughts, in November, with regard to former colonial areas in the Near East. Jusserand "gathered the firm impression that the President [would] propound such a scheme . . . at the Peace Conference."[51] Finally, it should be mentioned that Wilson discussed the idea with members of The Inquiry on board the *George Washington.* The League should appoint mandataries, he said, though (as distinct from Smuts) not from among the great powers.[52] The mandate system, then, was the work of many minds.

Wilson held a high opinion of the Practical Suggestions, but mainly because of the central role that they envisioned for the League in the overall peace settlement and because they duplicated much of the tone and substance of the Magnolia draft. In other words, Wilson saw a fair measure of convergence between Smuts' terms and many of the precepts of progressive internationalism. He was surprised, he said to Tasker Bliss, by "the extraordinary resemblance of General Smuts' views" to his own.[53] Suddenly, the prospects for substantial agreement on the League were "more encouraging than I had dared to hope."[54]

At the same time, through the Practical Suggestions, Wilson had chanced upon a strategy for ensuring the inclusion of the League in the peace treaty. "[I]t would be good politics to play the British game 'more or less' in formulating the league covenant," he said to Dr. Grayson two days before completing his "First Paris Draft," so that "England might feel her views were chiefly to be embodied in the final draft, thus gaining British support that [might otherwise] be withheld."[55] Wilson also explained his long silence on the details of the League. He had been criticized for not taking anyone into his confidence, he noted in conversation with A. G. Gardiner, Dr. Grayson, and Edith Benham. But he had felt constrained from doing so until he had personally "familiarized himself with the European state of mind." After all of the mystery, this was "the real reason" why he had not disclosed his plans to Congress.[56]

Whether or not this reasoning was sound with respect to domestic politics, it did serve Wilson's purposes to promote Smuts' work, which mirrored his own views more closely than any of the other British proposals. He had heard no criticism of the Practical Suggestions, and he "hoped that [these] views might be more or less the [British] governmental views."[57] If this was the case—and he would proceed on the assumption that the report enjoyed official license—then the outlook for a league bearing the stamp of progressive internationalism perhaps *was* greater than he had "dared to hope."

Wilson wrote two constitutions for the League of Nations in January 1919. The opening paragraphs of his First Paris Draft registered his greatest debt to the Practical Suggestions—that is, his recommendation for the administrative framework of the League. This was perhaps inevitable. If there was a single brilliant stroke in Smuts' blueprint, it was not the mandate system, but his attempt to balance certain unavoidable realities of great-power politics with a meaningful application of the principle of the equality of states—a matter of major concern to all progressive internationalists. Of somewhat less importance, Wilson also borrowed the British provisions on arbitration, but retained his own procedure for appealing decisions. To his original article on the reduction of armaments and the prohibition of the manufacture of the implements of war by private enterprise, he added Smuts' terms for the abolition of all forms of compulsory military service. As for mandates, the First Paris Draft extended the reach of Smuts' plan by including Germany's former colonies.

A provision for the mutual guarantee of political independence and territorial integrity of all members of the League was Wilson's own most important supplement. It had, of course, figured prominently in his thoughts ever since the Pan-American Pact, but, like the "Magnolia draft," now explicitly recognized that future territorial readjustments would be accommodated "pursuant to the principle of self-determination." Finally, Wilson wrote two entirely new articles, rather modest in scope, that embraced other progressive internationalist goals. The first of these articles would oblige all signatories "to establish and maintain fair hours and humane conditions of labour"; the second would require new member states to guarantee to their "racial or national minorities" the same rights enjoyed by their national majorities.[58]

Colonel House considered the President's new draft "much improved over the Magnolia document" and apprised Robert Cecil of its contents.[59] Within the American peace delegation, however, markedly different perspectives now surfaced—mainly because Wilson had thus far kept his subordinates pretty much in the dark. On December 23, Secretary of State Lansing had sent Wilson a brief sketch of the League, but had received no reply.[60] Apparently without Wilson's knowledge, but with House's encouragement, Lansing and David Hunter Miller then drew up a more detailed proposal some time in late December.[61] Citing the arguments of many Republicans, Lansing believed that compulsory arbitration and collective security constituted infringements upon the Monroe Doctrine, the war-making powers of Congress, and upon the American tradition of abstaining from entangling alliances. Instead of "the positive guaranty," Lansing counseled a self-denying clause, or "negative covenant," in which members of the League would simply pledge not to violate one another's territorial integrity and political independence.[62]

"I don't want lawyers drafting this treaty," Wilson said archly, during a meeting of the ACNP on January 10, when Tasker Bliss mentioned this plan.[63] The President rarely took Lansing's advice on anything. (By all accounts, neither did anyone else. Lloyd George regarded the Secretary as "insolent," whereas Cecil deemed him "merely rather stupid."[64]) Yet, in fairness to Lansing, Wilson might have sat down with him and explained his views. Short of that, if he held his Secretary of State in such low esteem, he should have left him behind in Washington (or asked him to resign long ago). Instead, Wilson only permitted Lansing's resentment to fester, as his private papers pathetically demonstrate.[65] Time would reveal a measure of political astuteness in Lansing's approach to the League.

When he appeared before the Senate Foreign Relations Committee in
August 1919, he would not hesitate to seek vindication and revenge.

His contempt for Lansing notwithstanding, Wilson was not imper-
vious to criticism from within his own ranks. General Bliss offered a full
list of suggestions, prompting the President to return to the drawing board.[66]
The result was his "Second Paris Draft," completed on January 18. Among
other changes inspired by Bliss, Wilson omitted the establishment of "orderly government" (a phrase in the preamble to the previous draft) as one
of the goals of the League; and to the collective security article he added
the proviso that League members would guarantee each other's political
independence and territorial integrity only "as against external aggression." As Bliss pointed out, these changes would clarify the main purpose
of the League—to prevent international war, not to put down internal
uprisings.

Like Lansing, Bliss worried that American opponents of the League
would blanch at provisions that appeared to surrender certain powers vested
in the Congress. For example, one of the articles on arbitration stipulated
that any nation that defied the "cooling off" procedures would "thereby
ipso facto become at war" with the League. Wilson rewrote this article to
read that such violators would "be *deemed to have committed* an act of
war"—a subtle change of wording, but one Bliss believed would render
the article less likely to provoke Constitutional objections at home, while
leaving its central purpose intact.[67]

Bliss offered criticisms of the mandate system, too. Inasmuch as Wilson intended the smaller powers to play the major role in this plan, the
General observed that mandatary responsibilities would involve financial
obligations too onerous for them to bear. Accordingly, the Second Paris
Draft specified that those expenses would be defrayed by assessments imposed on the League's wealthier signatories. Of far greater importance,
however, he also remarked that "the sole object" of Smuts' original proposition was, in fact, "to bring the United States into line with Great Britain in exercising supervisory control over certain areas of the earth." In
response to this perception of the real intentions of the British, Wilson
inserted, for the sake of emphasis, a statement that the object of the mandate system was "to build up in as short a time as possible . . . a political
unit which can take charge of its own affairs." Finally, with the Bliss
memorandum in hand, Wilson added declarations against secret treaties
and exclusive economic agreements among members of the League. On
his own, he wrote still other supplementary articles—to prohibit religious
persecution and to assert the League's right to close the seas in order to
enforce the peacekeeping covenants.[68]

Tasker Bliss never receives due credit for his contribution to the
League. On one hand, he persuaded Wilson to modify particular details,

at least in a tentative way, with an eye focused on domestic politics. On the other hand, because of the stress he placed on the right to revolution and on certain pitfalls inherent in the mandate system, his critique enhanced the progressive internationalist character of Wilson's design. (It is interesting to note, also, that no one believed more deeply in the absolute necessity of disarmament than this old soldier who loved the classics.[69])

The Second Paris Draft was Wilson's most important formulation for the League. On one level, by methodically plotting out common ground with the British, Wilson demonstrated an awareness of what was possible. Yet, insofar as it constituted his final composition before a drafting committee was appointed, we may safely conclude that the document also approximated Wilson's ideal League—a peacekeeping organization designed, not to maintain the postwar status quo, but to insure both peace and change in international relations. For example, while providing machinery for the peaceful settlement of disputes and for protection against foreign invasion, the document also recognized that future political conditions would require territorial adjustments pursuant to the principle of self-determination. The recommendation for the administrative structure of the League comprehended the need to observe the principle of equality in relations between small and great powers. Moreover, this League would not only carry out a sweeping program for the reduction of armaments; it would also endeavor, through the mandate system, to dam up and reverse the swift current of colonialism and other cruder forms of imperialism that had helped steer the nations onto the rocks of catastrophe. And by undertaking other responsibilities, such as the establishment of basic rights for working people around the world, Wilson would have the League fulfill purposes that went beyond what most people understood its proper mission to be.

Even so, Wilson intended the League to serve as a *guide* for the conduct of international relations. Some two years earlier, he had admitted to Ambassador Jusserand that he was not sure exactly how, or even whether, the League would work. Just five days after writing the Second Paris Draft, he said to the President of Switzerland that he could not hide the fact "that only the essential lines could be immediately traced and that the rest will be the fruit of long labor and repeated experiences."[70] Thus, to the extent that the League was a constitution—one embodying covenants both specific and general—its practical meaning would depend upon what its executors, in the course of decades, would have it mean.

During his tour of Great Britain, Wilson told an audience at Mansion House that it rather distressed him that people seemed to perceive him as "a perfectly bloodless thinking machine." He wanted them to know that, despite the self-restraint that came of his Scotch ancestry, he had within

him "all the insurgent elements of the human race." Yet, he was obliged
to say, "The stern Covenanter tradition that is behind me sends many an
echo down the years."[71] Robert Cecil, for one, would have readily vouched
for that, if his diary entries after January 19, 1919, are a dependable compass. On that evening, the two statesmen, accompanied by General Smuts,
had their first significant face-to-face encounter. For nearly three hours,
they pored over the Second Paris Draft and discussed their respective
approaches the League.

Wilson, Cecil noted, was possessed of "a quick businesslike mind,
and undoubtedly a broad outlook"; he was also "a vain man" and "a trifle
of a bully [who] must be dealt with firmly." Cecil was somewhat surprised, however, to learn that the President did not seem to mind that the
League was becoming "very largely the production of others."[72] Still, he
considered Wilson's Covenant "badly expressed, badly arranged, and very
incomplete," despite its many references to British proposals.[73] (It is probable that this reaction was owed in part to the document's obvious slant
toward the Smuts proposal rather than toward Cecil's latest "Draft Convention," which he had transmitted to Wilson only that morning.[74]) Neither was Smuts altogether pleased with Wilson's new composition. "Even
my mistakes are appropriated," he complained to a friend. But what really
disturbed him was the President's progressive reformulation of the mandate system: "He is entirely opposed to our annexing a little German
colony here and there which pains me deeply and will move Billy Hughes
to great explosions of righteous wrath."[75]

Several scholars have suggested that, at this juncture, Wilson, Cecil,
and Smuts actually were not very far apart in their views on the League.[76]
For instance, on the peaceful settlement of disputes, Wilson had already
moved closer to the British position, which emphasized the efficacy of
simply delaying hostilities as opposed to an insistence on compulsory arbitration. Nevertheless, "the British case on the subject," as Cecil touted
his Draft Convention,[77] scarcely evidenced any distinctly Wilsonian traces.
Whereas, in deference to Wilson, Cecil now included a discrete article on
collective security, in his version contracting powers would "undertake to
respect the territorial integrity" of others, rather than guarantee it.[78] Of
equal importance, Cecil's administrative structure would make the League
the exclusive domain of the five great powers, ruling out utterly the participation of small powers on the executive council. At the same time, the
document provided for separate representation for the British dominions
in the Conference (or general assembly) of the League.[79] Moreover, the
Draft Convention contained but a single, vague sentence on mandates.
Disarmament, alas, was not even mentioned. These were hardly insignif-
icant differences; how they would be resolved would determine the fun-

damental nature of the League. To Cecil and David Hunter Miller fell the task of reconciling the British and American documents.

In the meantime, on January 18 the peace conference had officially begun. Four days later, Lloyd George agreed to introduce resolutions calling for the creation of the League and its inclusion "as an integral part of the general treaty of peace."[80] Then, on January 25, during a plenary session at the Quai d'Orsay, the so-called Council of Ten appointed a commission to draft the Covenant—the occasion for speeches not only by Wilson but by the others as well, all affirming the dawn of a new age in the life of the world.[81] These were notable preliminary victories, and a large portion of the credit belonged to Lord Robert. Yet, in the end, they were more palpably the consequence of other things: the steadfast emphasis that Wilson had placed on the League and the Fourteen Points during the Armistice negotiations; the collective voice of the millions of reinforcements who had flooded the streets and piazzas and made his arrival in Europe a moment in the conscience of humankind; and, the words he had chosen to speak to his mass following—an interpretation of those demonstrations that none of his fellow peacemakers had as yet dared to gainsay. Still, there were nagging doubts. Even Lloyd George's gesture had its darker side, for it registered his intention to make acceptance of the League the basis of his strategy in dealing with other potent issues. Wilson, ever mindful of the risks that he ran, could not quite shake off his own sense of foreboding. "The hungry expect us to feed them, the roofless look to us for shelter, and the sick of heart and of body depend upon us for a cure," he had said bleakly to Creel. "What I seem to see—with all my heart I hope I am wrong—is a tragedy of disappointment."[82]

12

"A Practical Document and a Humane Document"

A cordial, almost informal atmosphere prevailed during the opening days of the Paris peace conference. "Everything reminded me of a faculty committee meeting, rather than a gathering of statesmen," the young Yale professor Charles Seymour wrote to his family. Clemenceau often looked bored, his face expressionless, his eyes half closed.[1] Nearly everyone fell asleep at one session or another—except, apparently, Wilson, who took some pleasure in needling slumberers such as Cecil.[2] The members of the Council of Ten (in particular, Lloyd George and Orlando) frequently betrayed gross ignorance of the subjects under discussion, an affliction that rarely inhibited the voicing of strong opinions.[3] But the President, Seymour observed, "appears absolutely at home and seems to get on very well with the Europeans, speaking naturally, almost colloquially . . . and likes to make a humorous allusion." Indeed, it was Wilson who set the initial tone by the graciousness of a speech in which he nominated Clemenceau as presiding officer of the conference. "You are much too good, Mr. President," said the French premier, flushed and enormously pleased. "You cover me with confusion."[4]

But the air of geniality did not stay long. Once the League commission was set up, the conference turned to the difficult problem of determining the fate of Germany's former colonies. The Allies' position on these captured territories not only challenged the principle of "no annexations," but also had disturbing implications for their regard for progressive internationalism. Of all of the unpleasant episodes at the conference, none had a more direct impact on the League.

In December, Lord Derby had told Colonel House that the President's notions about colonies and the League "rather horrified" him.[5] Wilson, too, was no doubt rather horrified when, on the afternoon of January 24, the representatives of the British dominions staked their claims. Prime Minister William Massey of New Zealand wanted Samoa, Hughes demanded New Guinea for Australia, and Smuts himself presented South Africa's brief on German Southwest Africa. All three based their arguments on humanitarian and strategic grounds. Before the week was out, the French revealed their designs on Togoland and the Cameroons, and the Japanese theirs on Kiaochow, in the Chinese province of Shantung. Lloyd George initiated these discussions; while he had no territorial levies to impose and repeatedly affirmed Great Britain's acceptance of the idea of international trusteeship, the Dominions' case for annexation, he said, constituted a legitimate exception to the rule. Privately, to Cecil, he "chortled greatly" over the delicious irony of Smuts' (the "father of the mandate system") crossing Wilson. Lord Robert "listened grimly."[6]

Wilson unburdened himself on the afternoon of the twenty-seventh. To most of his colleagues, his discourse sounded something like the Sermon on the Mount, updated by Lenin. "The world [was] against any further annexations," he declared. The only alternative was trusteeship through League-appointed mandatories. Such a program was not intended to exploit or to exercise arbitrary sovereignty over the inhabitants of the territories in question; rather, it was meant to protect them and assure their proper development, under the full view of the world, until they were able to take charge of their own affairs.[7] The Dominions' rationale for annexation, he went on, if it was sincerely based on concerns for their own security, indicated "a fundamental lack of faith in the League of Nations." Should any nation threaten, say, Australia, by attempting to seize New Guinea, the members of the League would rise up against the aggressor. He would admit to some imprecision about the exact method of putting both collective security and the mandate system into practice, but it was really only a matter of their willingness to try something new. "[I]f all the delegates in the room decided that it must succeed, it would succeed"; but "if the process of annexation went on, the League of Nations would be discredited from the beginning."[8]

German Southwest Africa was "a piece of land cut out of the Union," rejoined Prime Minister Louis Botha. Very few white people lived there, and the natives were "quite happy" under South African rule.[9] Mandatories were an inefficient, or "indirect," form of government, Hughes added.

New Guinea was essential to Australia's security, and Australia was a democracy. The world might favor Wilson's proposal because it was against annexations, "but annexation was only bad when it made for Imperialism[!]"[10]

Wilson's demeanor stiffened after listening to the French and Japanese on the following day. What it all came down to, he said, was "a negation in detail—case by case—of the whole principle of mandatories." Everyone present had professed agreement with the idea of trusteeship but then proceeded to claim permanent sovereignty over individual territories. "The world would say that the Great Powers first portioned out the helpless parts of the world, and then formed a League of Nations." They would make the League "a laughing stock." Could the delegates not see that world opinion would regard this matter "as a test"? Despite the difficulties, they *must* agree on the principle of mandatories "and leave its application to the League."[11]

After only a few days of deliberations, then, the Council of Ten, as Wilson gravely intoned, was approaching "a point where it looked as if their roads diverged."[12] To avoid a fatal rupture, Lloyd George and General Smuts hastened to construct a detour over which both Wilson and the Dominions might pass. This could be done, Smuts reasoned, by yielding to Wilson on the general principle, while differentiating between the character of mandated territories according to their stage of development. On January 29, the British Empire Delegation adopted a plan devised by Smuts for so-called A-, B-, and C-type mandates. The last referred to those areas that might be entrusted to the Dominions—territories that, because of their remoteness, sparse population, and the like, could "be best administered under the laws of the mandatory state as integral portions thereof." When Lloyd George finally cajoled the fuming Billy Hughes into going along with the compromise, the situation seemed neatly composed.[13]

At the next morning's session of the Council, however, Wilson was willing to approve the plan only as "a precursor of an agreement." Actual mandatories, he said, could not be assigned until the details of the League were worked out.[14] Hearing this, Lloyd George could no longer conceal his irritation. The President must understand what he, Lloyd George, had achieved by persuading the Dominions (and especially Hughes) to swallow even the principle of mandates. In refusing to assign mandatories now, Wilson was essentially proposing that the conference adjourn until the League was created. This, said Lloyd George, "filled him with despair." Clemenceau did not want the President to miss the point, either; if Wilson presumed to write a "constitution for the whole world . . . in eight days he was bound to feel some anxiety." Then Hughes declared that the Council of Ten was a *de facto* League of Nations that had every right to appoint mandates straightaway.[15] At the afternoon session, the unhappy Australian demanded Wilson's complete compliance—a virtual ultimatum, which gave vent to a ripping exchange between the two antagonists and ended in a riposte from Wilson so severe that he later asked to have it expunged from the *procès-verbal*.[16] Later in the day, the Council provisionally adopted the Smuts scheme.[17] Eventually, the territories would be mandated on the basis of military occupation.

The quarrel over colonies collided with the League of Nations with perhaps greater force than any other issue at the peace conference. First, as Wilson no doubt privately believed, the Smuts compromise was just so much subterfuge for dividing the swag among the Allies and then having the League legitimate their title.[18] But, whereas the controversy occasioned one of Wilson's heroic moments at Paris, his complicity in its resolution opened him up to charges of hypocrisy. Even before the drama had begun, many individuals who shared his convictions had anticipated such an outcome. T. E. Lawrence, the legendary champion of Arab self-determination, had commented to a member of The Inquiry about the President's beautiful wartime rhetoric: " 'Yes, when we read those speeches we chuckled in the desert.' "[19] Indeed, because of Wilson's identification with self-determination and the impartial adjustment of colonial claims, the Allied division of the spoils would be rendered in the boldest of relief. The League of Nations was "making a lovely beginning," the Socialist *Vorwarts* of Berlin wrote in early February. "It appears more and more as if . . . the Western imperialists [intend] to leave to Mr. Wilson the merely musical declamatory roles of the performance and to reserve to themselves the business end of the show."[20] This editorial prefigured the sort of criticism which many American progressive internationalists would level against the League, months later, in the context of the treaty as a whole—exactly as Wilson had predicted.

Second, the mandate controversy underscored Wilson's fundamental negotiating problem at the Paris conclave. At this and subsequent critical junctures, he found himself in an absolute minority of one. A public protest, which he briefly considered, might have been effective; but such a step at this early stage carried the risk of wrecking the conference even before the League was created. Conversely, the episode yielded alternative solutions to the Allies' problem in dealing with Wilson. They could, for example, wrest from him something of the practical substance of an issue in exchange for formal recognition of the finer principle involved; or, in certain circumstances, they could deflect his sermons with menacing references to the League. Clemenceau may have had these debates in mind when he made the remark, "Wilson talked like Jesus Christ but acted like Lloyd George."[21]

Finally, as we shall see, the confrontation set in motion a scheme by

Lloyd George to sidetrack the League—this at the precise moment that Robert Cecil and David Hunter Miller were completing their amalgamation of the President's Second Paris Draft and the British Draft Convention. Let us, then, examine in brief compass the work the two draftsmen had accomplished during the last week of January 1919, as the battle over mandates was reaching its climax.

The "Cecil-Miller Draft," though it retained Wilson's provision for the mutual guarantee of territorial integrity, bore a closer resemblance to the British Draft Convention than to the President's. To begin, it should be noted that Miller, a highly competent legal adviser, did not possess outstanding credentials as a progressive internationalist. When Cecil asserted that "the Great Powers must run the League and that it was just as well to recognize it flatly as not," Miller agreed unequivocally.[22] Hence the Cecil-Miller Draft eliminated the four small powers from the League's executive council. In addition, Cecil prevailed in obtaining for each of the Dominions separate representation in the Body of Delegates. Of slightly less gravity, Miller also assented to placing in the "reserved" category Wilson's supplementary articles on mandates, freedom of the seas, protection of minorities, economic equality, and his procedures for appealing arbitration decisions. (Cecil's counter-recommendation for a Permanent Court of International Justice was held in abeyance, too.)[23] Finally, the Cecil-Miller Draft deleted from Wilson's article on disarmament the prohibition against the manufacture of the implements of war by private enterprise. In all, then, the document represented a comparatively conservative approach to the League and a provisional victory for Lord Robert.[24]

Cecil had entered into discussions with the Americans with no firm guidelines from his superiors. Repeatedly he had tried to discern Lloyd George's exact position on the League—a subject "in which he takes no real interest," Cecil lamented after several attempts to engage him.[25] But Lloyd George became quite interested during the storm over mandates. He at last gave Cecil and Smuts his full attention on January 31, only hours before they were scheduled to present the Cecil-Miller Draft to Wilson. To their shock and dismay, the Prime Minister suddenly proposed that the entire project be postponed until after the peace conference. Armed with a memorandum hastily prepared by skeptics within his coalition (and perhaps instigated by Lansing as well), he went on to denounce collective security in any form. To require nations to go to war under certain stated conditions, he argued, would prevent them from joining it in the first place and would end "in the destruction of the League itself." The organization's "paper obligations" should be kept to "an absolute minimum"; it should serve primarily as a medium of counsel among the great powers.[26]

Precisely what motivated Lloyd George remains unclear. On one hand, his criticisms reflected the views of the French; on the other hand, they took into account many of the objections likely to be raised in the United States Senate. Even so, the Prime Minister's turnabout was too well timed, to say the least, and rather unseemly. He was, after all, the honorary president of the League of Nations Union; only the week before he had declared that the League should be "an integral part of the general treaty of peace." It is inconceivable that he would have launched such a bolt if Wilson, instead of kicking up a row over the mandate principle, had helped expedite the division of the German colonies. Moreover, Wilson's show of temper on the previous day had momentarily diminished his standing among his peers.[27] It would seem, then, that Lloyd George's gambit was less a matter of conviction or political perspicacity than a tactical move to press the advantage—to serve notice to Wilson, presently through Cecil, that the price of the League had yet to be fixed. Lord Robert, however, was not easily taken. Disinclined to convey a message guaranteed to ruin his imminent parlay with Wilson, he decided to keep the mercurial Prime Minister's "thoroughly bad" plan to himself.[28]

At that evening's conference (attended also by Smuts, Miller, and Colonel House), Cecil expounded the Cecil-Miller Draft. Curiously, Wilson did not remonstrate over any of the proposed changes—even those providing for an international court, separate representation for the Dominions, and, most significantly, for an executive council composed exclusively of the great powers. On the last, vital point, one that had serious implications for the basic character of the League, it is important to note that Cecil had the support of both Miller and House, and that the President was probably still distressed about the altercation with Billy Hughes on the previous afternoon. Understandably, he very much wanted to accommodate Cecil. Yet, contrary to most historical accounts of this meeting, Wilson was not in flight; even Cecil's carefully worded diary entry— that Wilson "agreed *to try* my [Cecil's] plan of an executive committee of the Great Powers"—indicates no more than tentative accord on his part.[29] Subsequent developments bear this out in full.

In any case, before adjourning, the caucus decided that Miller and C. J. B. Hurst, the British delegation's chief legal counsel, should write a final summary covenant to serve as the basis for the impending deliberations of the League of Nations Commission.[30] During the next forty-eight hours the two men produced a synthesis known as the "Hurst-Miller Draft." This document adopted most of the features of its immediate predecessor, but diluted the Wilsonian content still further. For example, Hurst and

Miller cut out the "reserved" articles on freedom of the seas and the rights of minorities, and, in lieu of Wilson's articles on mandates, inserted but a brief line on the captured colonies. Their most important alteration affected Wilson's proviso to the collective security article, to accommodate territorial changes in accordance with self-determination; both Hurst and Miller believed that the clause "would simply tend to legalize agitation in Eastern Europe for a future war," so they eliminated it.[31] This would later prove to be an unfortunate deletion.

Wilson read the Hurst-Miller draft on the evening of February 2. He did not like it. Because a considerable part of the document reflected the general drift of his conversation with Cecil, some historians have characterized his dissatisfaction as inexplicable.[32] Yet the negative reaction is fairly easily explained. Up to this point, the most recent British proposal that the President had actually seen and studied was Cecil's original Draft Convention of January 20. As with the later document, Cecil had neglected to provide him with an advance copy of the Cecil-Miller Draft. Until Hurst and Miller put it all down on paper, it would seem that Wilson simply had not grasped just how much of his own contribution had been whittled away.

Even so, with the first meeting of the League Commission set for the next afternoon, the President should have known that it was too late to abjure; regardless of the circumstances, everyone concerned believed him to be a party to the Hurst-Miller Draft to one degree or another. Yet he now retrieved his Second Paris Draft. As Miller and House looked on, the President began to scratch onto the margins those changes from the Hurst-Miller Draft that he was willing to accept, while resurrecting most of his original plans—the inclusion of small powers on the executive council, the strictures against the manufacture of munitions for profit, an elaboration of the mandate principle, and so on. Miller dutifully labored all through the night to recast it in proper form so that, as Wilson hoped, the League Commission might proceed on the basis of this, his Third Paris Draft.[33]

Cecil was incensed when, after breakfast, Sir William Wiseman informed him of Wilson's intention to scrap the Hurst-Miller Draft. At Wiseman's behest, Colonel House immediately telephoned the President to remind him that Cecil was "the only one connected with the British Government who really had the League of Nations at heart." Lloyd George presently supported the League only "because of the pressure of public opinion," whereas Cecil would not hesitate to take his patron to task, even in Parliament, if need be. The President's latest draft was preferable, House granted, but they simply could not afford to alienate Lord Robert.[34]

Wilson readily grasped the point. In a *tête-à-tête* with Cecil fifteen minutes before the inaugural meeting of the League of Nations Commission, he reversed himself and abandoned his draft covenant. Still, he considered the Hurst-Miller Draft but "a skeleton, reserving to himself the right to clothe it with flesh and blood, as he put it," Cecil recorded. As they walked into the meeting room Cecil nonetheless felt that the President had met him "nobly." They were, he added, "except on a few points, all agreed—at least I hope so."[35]

Nineteen delegates served on the League of Nations Commission—two representatives from each of the five great powers and one representative from each of nine smaller allied powers.[36] In addition to Wilson, who served as chairman, the Commission was graced by several other principal players at the peace conference: Orlando of Italy, Baron Makino of Japan, Léon Bourgeois of France, and, of course, Cecil, Smuts, and House.

It may be, as Cecil wrote in his diary on February 3, that the fracas over the Hurst-Miller Draft was "exceedingly characteristic of [Wilson's] . . . incapacity for cooperation resulting from a prolonged period of autocratic power."[37] Yet the Commission itself would vindicate his drafts and repudiate Cecil's, as things turned out. This central fact—that Wilson was able to restore most of the progressive internationalist features of his own drafts of the League, and without exerting himself very much—has been missed in virtually all monographs on the subject. The subtlety of Wilson's game in this development has remained obscure as well.

The possibility that the Commission might reject much of the substance of Cecil's conception was evident at the outset; only with reluctance did the delegates accept the Hurst-Miller Draft as the basis of their deliberations.[38] Wilson, it should be noted, sustained Cecil on this particular point of procedure, but strictly out of expediency; contrary to a commonplace historical inference, it is clear that he did not regard the Hurst-Miller Draft as an Anglo-*American* document, and, more important, neither did most of the others.

During their second meeting, the commissioners subjected Cecil's (i.e., the Hurst-Miller) scheme to intense examination. Their foremost concern was the proposal for the Executive Council. As Smuts observed, "People will perhaps scrutinize the make-up of the Executive Council more closely than any other point."[39] Once this question was out on the table, the delegates began to express a decided preference for Wilson's Paris drafts, all of which had recommended a Council composed of four smaller powers along with the five great powers. One by one, Wellington Koo of China, Pessoa of Brazil, Reis of Portugal, Vesnic of Serbia, Hymans of Belgium, and even Orlando and Bourgeois stressed the virtues of what they all called "the first American plan." The Hurst-Miller draft, they argued, would create too wide a gulf between the two broad classifications of states.[40]

Fur began to fly over the issue during the third meeting. Orlando sought the middle ground between the Cecil and Wilson plans by proposing the inclusion of two small powers instead of four.[41] Paul Hymans described such a quota as little more than a "beau geste." Any more than two, contended General Smuts (with whom the idea for small-power representation had originated), would give those nations too much influence. As for Cecil, he believed that a ratio of four to five was tantamount to "an equality of members," and would run the "real risk of one or two great powers holding out." "What you propose," Hymans rejoined, "is nothing else than the Holy Alliance."[42]

In the face of such a "great and fundamental difference of opinion" (Cecil's words), the Commission agreed to postpone the decision on the precise number.[43] Yet, by virtue of the course of the debate, the principle of small-power representation on the League's Executive Council had been firmly established. On February 13, during its ninth meeting, the Commission decided in favor of the four–five ratio. The small powers had scored an absolute victory.[44]

It was the President's victory, too, although chroniclers of the drafting process have either misunderstood what he was up to, erroneously equated his position with Cecil's, or ignored altogether the significance of the outcome.[45] Wilson surely realized that the main burden of carrying out the League's decisions would fall upon the great powers. Yet, from his Magnolia Draft of August 1918 to this Third Paris Draft of February 1919, he was consistent in the conviction that the League should not become the unshared province of the great powers. Notwithstanding his concession to Cecil on the Hurst-Miller Draft, we now know from the recently published diary of Edith Benham that Wilson considered the second meeting of the League Commission "quite a triumph"—because "the committee called for the original American draft."[46] This was one of those cases, however, as he had explained to Dr. Grayson in early January, when "it would be good politics to play the British game 'more or less' in formulating the league covenant."[47] The need to avoid offense dictated that he keep his sense of triumph to himself and, at least occasionally, lend Lord Robert a little support. At one point, for instance, he stated that, in tandem with the League's territorial guarantee, an augmentation of just two on the Executive Council would probably insure against "any injustice that could be done to the small powers."[48]

Yet such remarks were intended primarily to humor Cecil. For one thing, Wilson actually helped trigger the debate over the Executive Council by suggesting that the Commission might want to consider "what other elements, if any, there should be in it."[49] This seemingly innocuous comment opened the way for the staccato of invocations on behalf of "the first

American plan." Nudging things forward, he also asked Paul Hymans which "system" (Wilson's or Cecil's) he preferred, knowing full well what the answer would be. Then he wondered aloud (again, not without purpose) "whether the French Government would be agreeable to the American scheme." Bourgeois, too, replied in the affirmative.[50] During the next meeting, Smuts defended Cecil's design, pointing out that the Executive Council would call in the small powers whenever issues directly affecting their interest arose. "They only, as the text says, 'attend,'" Wilson noted. "They don't vote."[51] By correcting Smuts, Wilson not only clarified Cecil's aim to subordinate the small powers, but also subtly reminded the others that the first written proposal for small-power representation had come not from "the American plan," but from Smuts' Practical Suggestions. Wilson thereby further undermined Cecil's arguments.

It does not appear that Lord Robert fathomed Wilson's tactic of asking leading questions while the small powers proceeded overtly to expose the weaknesses of a position the President did not believe in. In his diary, Cecil complained only about the "foreigners" (presumably Hymans, Pessoa, Vesnic, Wellington Koo) for their lack of pragmatism and credited the Americans for grasping the necessity of "a much more workable instrument of administration."[52] Nor did he ever seem to realize that the small powers' most powerful weapon was the use of Wilson's drafts, which gave their claims added leverage from the start.

The significance of all of this has largely been lost in the literature on the League. Of all the aspects of the general peace settlement, no greater responsibility, of course, would be attributed to Wilson than that for the Covenant. If Cecil's plan for the Executive Council had prevailed—if Wilson had permitted it to prevail—then Article III arguably would have rivalled Article X as the most controversial of the compact, at least for progressive internationalists. Some meaningful observance of the principle of the equality of states was not only a matter of conviction for Wilson; if he were to keep faith with his constituency, it was an absolute necessity.

During its fourth session, on February 6, the Commission focused on the provision that Wilson called "the key to the whole Covenant." The mutual guarantee of territorial integrity and political independence, he said, would demonstrate that "we mean business and not only discussion."[53] Cecil, mindful of his recent encounter with Lloyd George, cautioned that this sort of "business" meant "war if it means anything," and he proposed to strike the obligation to protect all signatories against invasion; in its stead he would have a self-denying clause (similar to Lansing's) whereby signatories simply pledged not to violate one another's territorial integrity and political independence.[54] The delegates, however, again favored Wilson's approach over Cecil's. Not only the "singularly perverse" (Cecil's words) small powers, but the French and the Italians, too, insisted on a strong collective security article.[55] (Indeed, as we shall see, Bourgeois and Larnaude believed that the guarantee was much too weak as it was.)

Yet again, Wilson granted Cecil an important interposition—a motion to place in the hands of the Executive Council the responsibility of advising and planning the means by which sanctions would be carried out. This amendment, Cecil believed, "softened [the obligation] down a little," and Miller pronounced the revised article constitutional. Wilson himself also made the much-overlooked point that the article was *not* an ironclad guarantee against war in every instance.[56] Indeed, in this regard, the amendment conformed to views that he had maintained from the beginning—that the circumstances of a particular incident should determine whether, or how, military force might be employed, that the method of carrying out the mutual pledge "should be left to develop by itself, case by case."[57]

With the Covenant's most far-reaching proposition permanently (and rather expeditiously) settled, the commission turned to another matter of special concern to Wilson—the article on disarmament. Here the Hurst-Miller Draft had borrowed the President's phraseology—"the maintenance of peace will require the reduction of national armaments to the lowest point consistent with domestic safety"—but had left out the clause prohibiting the manufacture of munitions by private enterprise. Wilson now proposed to restore that restriction. Although Lord Robert was apprehensive about "the difficulties which it may land us in," he did not try to thwart the President.[58]

From there the delegates proceeded to approve, with only minor changes, four of the eight provisions for the arbitration of disputes (Articles IX through XII of the Hurst-Miller Draft), including the creation of a Permanent Court of International Justice.[59] But on this occasion the Belgian delegation initiated a protracted debate that carried over into the next meeting. Their concern was Article XIII, which gave the Executive Council authority to hear disputes not susceptible to normal arbitration. This article, like the related ones, only required members to submit such disputes to the procedure; it did not invest the Council with powers to enforce the judgments it might render, even in the case of unanimity. The Belgians therefore proposed an amendment to put sanctions behind unanimous decisions. This amounted to compulsory arbitration, something that Cecil had never entertained and that Wilson had abandoned, in part because he knew the Senate would reject it.

At length, the Commission's drafting subcommittee worked out a compromise: should a state defy a unanimous decision, the Council would "consider what steps can best be taken to give effect to their recommendation."[60] In settling the immediate question, however, the compromise underscored a serious ambiguity in both the Covenant and Wilson's thinking. Whereas Wilson had joined Cecil in refusing to endow the arbitration articles with provisions for enforcement, those articles, placed alongside the territorial guarantee, nonetheless seemed to denote compulsory arbitration. For the time being, Wilson preferred to finesse the issue rather than face it squarely.

The sixth and seventh meetings of the Commission went comparatively smoothly. The lone Hurst-Miller paragraph on mandates was expanded to several paragraphs, drafted by Smuts, conforming to the Council of Ten's resolution of January 30.[61] To the Hurst-Miller version of Wilson's original article on the basic rights of working people, Cecil proposed an amendment to create a permanent Commission of Labour. And to that article's statement of purpose, "to secure and maintain fair and humane conditions of labour," Wilson added the words, "for men, women, and children." Together with the creation of an international labor bureau, this emendation expressly to include women and children suggested a future League-sponsored endeavor to restrict child labor and to establish standards for the working conditions of women in all member nations.[62]

By the end of the eighth meeting the entire Covenant had been examined. Now, just three days before the Commission would complete its business, Bourgeois and Larnaude unexpectedly set off a bombshell in the form of amendments extracted from their own draft of the League.[63] One of these amendments revived the Belgian proposal on sanctions for unanimous arbitration decisions. Another, aimed at Germany, would make admission to the League contingent upon the sincerity of a prospective member's professions to abide by the Covenant and to accept restrictions on military forces and armaments laid down by the League; new member states would also have to have governments based on representative institutions. By far the most extraordinary of the French amendments embodied a plan to transform the League into a North Atlantic treaty organization—that is, into a union complete with an international army and a general staff. Bourgeois defended these amendments in part by quoting some of the President's own words, which ostensibly corresponded to the latter proposal; he also implied that the Chamber of Deputies might demand their adoption in exchange for its support for the League.[64]

Wilson's response is instructive in light of the impending political struggle in the United States. No nation would consent to the kind of control Monsieur Bourgeois was talking about, he said. "We must make a distinction between what is possible and what is not." Domestic opponents were already claiming that, under the League, the government of the United States would forfeit sovereign command of its own army—

"that American troops would thus be liable to be ordered to fight at any moment for the most remote causes." He was compelled to seek some middle ground compatible with the Constitution. Of course, "unity of command" had been essential to overcome the danger that had threatened civilization; but German militarism had been destroyed. "[I]f we organize from now onwards an international army," he declared, "it would appear that we were substituting international militarism for national militarism."[65]

Bourgeois explained that when he used the word "control," he was referring only to the need for assurances that states were not secretly producing arms and munitions in violation of whatever accords the League might arrange. As for an international army, he was simply advocating the establishment of an administrative organization to facilitate the rapid deployment of joint military force against an aggressor.[66] "Perhaps within a hundred years," Larnaude interjected, the League would become "the guarantee of safety." In the meantime, a league and an international force were two ideas bound together, "unless one is content that the League should be a screen of false security."[67]

On this fundamental issue the French and the Belgians, on one hand, and the Americans and the British, on the other, were not likely to communicate on the same wavelength. From the President's perspective, collective security was but one element of the compound. There was also the process of arbitration, which (even without explicit sanctions) would defuse most problems before they became acute. And a major reduction of armaments, together with the removal of the profit motive from the production of the instruments of war, he believed, would also go a long way toward easing the anxieties of nations. Without question, the mutual guarantee of territorial integrity against aggression was definite; but it was impractical (politically and otherwise) to prescribe in advance the manner in which that guarantee would be effected. For Wilson, mutual security came down to one issue: "The only method by which we can achieve this end lies in our having confidence in the good faith of the nations who belong to the League," he said almost plaintively. "When danger comes, we too will come, and we will help you, but you must trust us."[68]

For the representatives of nations so lately ravaged by Germany and presumably still vulnerable, Wilson's emphasis on "mutual good faith" was not edifying. The French would not let the matter rest, even after the meeting adjourned. Privately, Cecil told them that they could not persist in their demands, "that the League of Nations was their only means of getting the assistance of America and England, and if they destroyed it they would be left without an ally in the world."[69] Nor was Wilson any more sympathetic to Bourgeois and Larnaude—owing as much to the firmness of his views as to his aggravation with Clemenceau and the onset of anti-American propaganda in the Paris newspapers.[70]

The League of Nations Commission held two final meetings on February 13, the day before the Covenant was to be presented to a plenary session of the peace conference. At the morning session, Wilson undertook a systematic oral reading of the reworked articles and called for binding votes. At this time, Larnaude proposed a change in the preamble—language akin to a war-guilt clause aimed at Germany—and it was summarily voted down.[71] The Commission then fixed at three the number of representatives for each state in the Body of Delegates, with one vote per delegation, and at last settled the question of small-power representation on the Executive Council.[72] Then, the French proposal on admission to the League of states not signatories to the Covenant was incorporated into what would become Article VII; whereupon the meeting adjourned.[73]

Because the Council of Ten required Wilson's presence, Cecil assumed the chair during the afternoon. Miller described this session as "tiresome and confused." His characterization was due chiefly to repetitious debate over the idea of an international force and general staff, sparked, once again, by the tenacious Larnaude and Bourgeois.[74] In the end, the only concession that a majority of the delegates would permit was a provision for a permanent commission to advise the League "on military and naval questions generally."[75]

By far the most interesting (and, in some ways, poignant) discussion of the afternoon grew out of the single amendment to the Covenant advanced by the Japanese—an article on racial equality.[76] Baron Makino and Viscount Chinda had first broached this delicate issue, privately, with Colonel House on February 4. The Colonel had told them how much he "deprecated race, religious and other kinds of prejudice," but asked for *two* resolutions—"one which they desired, and another which they would be willing to accept."[77]

On account of their ambitions in Shantung and their expanding naval presence throughout the Pacific, Wilson was highly suspicious of the intentions of the Japanese. "He had trusted them before," he told Miller, but they had broken their agreement on Siberia, and "he would not trust them again."[78] Then, too, despite their service on the League Commission, the fact that Makino's and Chinda's government had yet to approve Lloyd George's resolution of January 22 was hardly reassuring.[79] Nevertheless, Wilson received with equanimity the Japanese resolution of the second category mentioned by House, altering it only slightly.[80]

Perhaps purposefully, Makino's resolution alluded to the controversy over the Executive Council and the small powers: "The equality of nations being a basic principle of the League," it began. He also justified the amendment as complementary to Wilson's article on religious freedom, and spoke of how the war had brought different races together in a common endeavor of "suffering and deliverance." It was only just, he said, that "the principle at least of equality among men should be admitted and be made the basis of future intercourse."[81] For the British Empire, however, Makino's "nobility of thought," as Cecil put it, raised "extremely serious problems." Indeed, when Colonel House had tried to get the British to embrace the amendment that he and Wilson had approved, Balfour derided the proposition that "all men are created equal" as an eighteenth-century notion. Prime Minister Hughes deemed such a declaration unacceptable in any form.[82] In these circumstances, Cecil recommended dropping both Makino's amendment on racial equality and Wilson's article on religious freedom. The majority regarded this as the best solution, at least for now. House, on Wilson's behalf, reserved the right to raise the question at another time, and Makino, without further remonstration, did likewise.[83] With this, Cecil resumed his reading of the remaining articles and ordered them spread upon the minutes. The Commission, he announced, had adopted the Covenant of the League of Nations.[84]

Meanwhile, Wilson had informed the Council of Ten that the work was almost done. Because he was scheduled to leave within two days for a short visit home, he requested the calling of a plenary session for the following afternoon so that the Covenant might be publicly read and explained. It was understood that he would report as chairman of the League Commission, not as a member of the Conference of the Great Powers; the holding of such a ceremony, even one as elaborate as a plenary session, would not mean that the Council of Ten was committed in any way.[85]

Within the province of his own biography, February 14, 1919, would seem to be the climactic day toward which Wilson's life had supremely moved. On the eve of that event, Colonel House wondered just how much of the original Magnolia draft remained in the final Covenant.[86] If he had actually compared them, he would have found more than a fair measure of congruence. This had not been the case when the Commission had convoked, however. As a result of all the preliminary wrangling, the League at that point had been shorn of an Executive Council that adhered reasonably closely to the principle of the equality of states; disarmament would not be emphasized as a central mission of the organization; the first major, if awkward, step toward decolonization was scarcely mentioned as a suitable undertaking for the League; and collective security was interpreted by the authors of the Hurst-Miller Draft primarily as a proposition of self-denial. Yet it seems no exaggeration to say that, in the course of the Commission's deliberations (whether Cecil or anyone else realized it), the Covenant had been thoroughly reconstructed along Wilsonian lines.

As he commented on the text at the gathering at the Quai D'Orsay, Wilson was careful to strike a balance between his own and Cecil's contribution. For instance, he cited the relative simplicity of the document and the parliamentary character of the Body of Delegates as being among the League's chief virtues. International misunderstandings would now become everybody's business; the League would subject them to "the moral force of the public opinion of the world." Certainly armed force was there, "but it is in the background, and if the moral force of the world will not suffice, the physical force of the world shall. But that is the last resort, because this is intended as a constitution of peace, not as a League of War."

Wilson also commented on the open-endedness of the articles on arbitration, again fusing his own views with Cecil's. They had been "unable to plan all the machinery that might be necessary to meet differing and unexpected contingencies." The Covenant, therefore, was "not a straightjacket, but a vehicle of life. A living thing is born," he declared. What, precisely, that living thing would become in maturity would depend on the aspirations of its trustees, "and in accordance with the changing circumstances of the time." But the League was both elastic enough to provide for readjustment and definite enough to guarantee peace.

Wilson outlined other purposes the organization would serve, for the Covenant was at one and the same time "a practical document and a humane document." Through the Bureau of Labour, for example, it would ameliorate the conditions of life and work for men, women, and children and draw them "into the field of international consultation." Every treaty entered into by members of the League would automatically be exposed to the light of international publicity. The mandate system, he said, represented "one of the greatest and most satisfactory advances"; no longer could a great power possess another's territory "for European purposes." The world had expressed "its conscience in law" and had affirmed, " 'We are done with annexations of helpless people.' " He closed on a note of high expectation: "Many terrible things have come out of this war, gentlemen, but some very beautiful things have come out of it. . . . People who were suspicious of one another can now live as friends in a single family, and desire to do so. The miasma of distrust, of intrigue, is cleared away. Men are looking eye to eye and saying: 'We are brothers and have a common purpose. We did not realize it before, but now we do realize it, and this is our Covenant of fraternity and friendship.' "[87]

The day was not Wilson's alone. Cecil, too, made an effective speech. As he saw it, devising a system that would preserve peace and interfere as little as possible with national sovereignty was the main challenge, and it had been met. He underscored the slow and circuitous procedure for imposing sanctions and stressed that any coercive action would require a unanimous vote in the Executive Council. To refrain from war until every other possible means of settling disputes should have been exhausted, then, was the "first and chieftest" principle behind the League. Moreover (though he had previously believed otherwise), if that principle were "really to be acted upon," nations must go one step further and carry into effect a meaningful reduction of armaments, as that was also clearly laid down as a responsibility of the League. They all "must try to substitute for the principle of international competition, that of international cooperation." He concluded with an observation at once Cecilian and Wilsonian: "We are not seeking to produce for the world a building finished and complete in all respects." If those who built on this foundation cultivated "the habit of cooperating with one another," if they really believed "that the interest of one is the interest of all, . . . then and only then, will the finished structure of the League be what it ought to be—a safety and a glory for the humanity of the world."[88]

The presentation of the Covenant was a triumphal event. When it was all over, Wilson and Cecil received high marks all around. From Wilson's vantage point, if this League were incorporated into the general settlement, then he could feel confident that he had kept the faith, that the most important objective of the Great War had been consummated, and that any injustices done by the treaty of peace itself could be redressed later with relative ease. Though far from perfect, this League could become a "temporary shelter from the storm" and help release "some of the more generous forces of mankind" in the course of the next crucial decade.[89] Its contents perhaps pushed things to the limits of what the great powers might accept; but Cecil's heartfelt enthusiasm for the present Covenant (combined with his influence within the British Cabinet) was a good omen.

There were others. Tumulty telegraphed Wilson on the morning of his departure, quoting the Philadelphia *Public Ledger* on the Covenant: "Its superb achievement crowns his home coming with sweeping victory." "Plain people throughout America are for you," Tumulty added. "You have but to ask their support and all opposition will melt away."[90] And, to House's surprise, all of official France turned out with evergreens and red carpets to bid the President adieu. "He looked happy," the Colonel noted to himself as Wilson boarded the train for Brest, "as well indeed he should."[91]

13

"The Thing Reaches the Depth of Tragedy"

The *George Washington* dropped anchor in Boston Harbor on the evening of February 23. That afternoon a dense fog had caused the ship to stray some seventeen miles off course and nearly run aground 300 yards from land. Four days earlier, a wave had swept away two sailors from the decks of an accompanying destroyer. The high seas and strong winds that President Wilson's transport had encountered almost from the start of the voyage home were fitting harbingers of the politics that lay ahead.[1]

It is not the mission of this book to retell, in all of its intricate detail, the familiar story of the Senate's rejection of the Treaty of Versailles, although some aspects of the historiography surrounding it cannot be ignored. The primary emphasis of the final portion of this study will be the stage of inquiry that compelled Wilson to revise the Covenant when he returned to Paris for the second half of the peace conference. For it was during this period—in particular, the first month or so after the publication of the original Covenant—that the deep lines of demarcation were unmistakably drawn. Traces of this development, as we have seen, had first become manifest in the sharp ideological and partisan conflict vented by the recent congressional campaign. But, in light of those sources from which the President had derived his synthesis of the New Diplomacy as well as of the nature of his political base outside the Democratic party, it would be a mistake to focus exclusively upon the consequences of his tactical errors in responding to the Republicans. The state of Wilson's relationship with the progressive internationalists was in many ways just as important for the future of the League as the bitter parliamentary struggle. Although certain potentially remedial options revealed themselves, the series of events set in motion during this crucial period foreclosed any real possibility for launching a Wilsonian League of Nations.

Let us begin with three general observations. First, Wilson's attitude toward the opposition, contrary to the common historical characterization, was not utterly defiant from beginning to end, although this was surely the case by the end of his visit. Rather, it would be more accurate to say that he had returned to Washington with an abiding faith that he would prevail. His sense of confidence was not altogether unjustified in view of the Covenant's initial reception in the press and among leading conservative and progressive internationalists. Before the *George Washington* had eased into its berth at Boston, Taft and Lowell had already set out on nationwide speaking tours on behalf of the League. (Rumor had it that Taft had said he would quit the party if the Republicans opposed American membership.[2]) Regional chapters of the League to Enforce Peace had announced their unqualified support and declared that "the overwhelming public opinion of the United States . . . will sustain the President."[3] The Federal Council of Churches of Christ of America (claiming to represent 33,000,000 people) had passed a resolution of endorsement; by mid-February, several state legislatures, along with the World Court League and the New York Peace Society, had done the same.[4] According to the *Literary Digest,* the majority of the nation's editorial pages regarded the experiment as "tremendously worthwhile." Although many bitterly anti-Wilson newspapers, such as the New York *Sun,* spared no criticism, many other partisan Republican newspapers, such as the *Boston Herald* and the *Los Angeles Times,* gave the Covenant their approval. In the staunchly conservative community of Amherst, Massachusetts, Ray Stannard Baker found "almost unanimous support of the League . . . [and] outspoken disapproval of the obstinate position of Senator Lodge." The President's opponents, stated the *New York Times,* "will contend in vain against an overwhelming public opinion."[5] At least to some extent, then, it was not unreasonable for Wilson to regard the verdict of the press as "splendid" or to believe "that the people are absolutely with the purposes and plan of the thing."[6]

Second, notwithstanding public opinion, the intensity of the political storm about to break over Wilson's head was directly proportionate to the success that he had thus far achieved at Paris. By virtue of their assent to his priorities—from Lloyd George's resolution to make the venture "an integral part" of the treaty, to the triumphal presentation of the Covenant—it appeared that Wilson's European counterparts either had decided to follow his lead in spite of his November setback, or had proved unable to exploit his Achilles' heel. By the end of the first major phase of the peace conference, one might have thought the mid-term elections had gone the other way.

Third, with respect to the more salient objections to the League aired during 1919–20, hardly any of them had not been registered before—either in the abbreviated Senate debates sparked by Wilson's peace moves in December 1916 and January 1917, or in the anti-League themes of the autumn campaign and the contention over the Armistice. It would be misleading, however, to characterize the preponderance of these objections as "isolationist." (That term fit only a small number of opponents, even among the dozen or so "irreconcilables.")[7] No one better captured the essence of the situation than the Democratic leader in the Senate, Gilbert Hitchock. "*Internationalism has come*," he declared in defense of the draft Covenant on February 27, "*and we must choose what form the internationalism is to take.*"[8]

Wilson's harshest critic would not have demurred. In a series of articles after the Armistice, Theodore Roosevelt had written that the United States could never again "completely withdraw into its shell" and that international consultation could help avert war.[9] Yet Roosevelt, like most opponents of a *Wilsonian* league, was ever the ardent nationalist and the champion of universal military training; he could accept a league "only as an addition to, and in no sense as a substitute for the preparedness of our own strength for our own defense."[10] Moreover, he wanted to know if Wilson meant to go to war "every time a Jugoslav wishes to slap a Czechoslav in the face."[11] In his ongoing condemnation of the Fourteen Points, Roosevelt would brook none but a "spheres of influence" partnership with the Allies. "Let civilized Europe and Asia introduce some kind of police system in the weak and disorderly countries at their thresholds," he wrote, and let the United States look after the Western Hemisphere.[12] As for anything else, "let us with deep seriousness ponder every promise we make *so as to be sure our people will fulfill it.*"[13]

Along these lines of battle, he planned to lead his party against "Wilson's Hill," and it would have been the most spectacular charge of his career; but it was not to be. During the early hours of January 6, 1919, the sixty-year-old Bull Moose at last succumbed to the ravages of "the strenuous life."[14] While most Americans mourned, Oswald Garrison Villard remarked that Roosevelt's passing was an act "of divine mercy for the country and another piece of Woodrow Wilson's extraordinary luck."[15]

Perhaps so. However, other prominent Republicans had been raising doubts, too, in anticipation of the kind of league they believed Wilson would bring home. Among the more notable ones was Philander C. Knox's speech to the Senate on December 18. Knox demanded that the League be separated from the peace treaty and went on to articulate his "new American Doctrine," a variation on Roosevelt's spheres-of-influence idea within the context of a limited Allied-American entente.[16] As for the next chairman of the Senate Foreign Relations Committee, Henry Cabot Lodge's thinking had not changed since his attack on the "Peace Without Victory" address two years earlier. Like Roosevelt, he believed that the United States must play its part in the peace settlement and work closely with the Allies in upholding it. Any league of nations, if it were to be more than "an exposition of vague ideals," must, of course, have both "authority to issue decrees and force to sustain them." It was at this point, Lodge emphasized to the Senate on December 21, "that questions of great moment arise."[17] Even though Wilson had yet to make clear what he meant by a "league," his archrival feared the demise of the Monroe Doctrine and the submersion of American sovereignty.[18] Anxious about all the easy talk about "the beauty and necessity of peace," he asked his colleagues: "[A]re you ready to put your soldiers and your sailors at the disposition of other nations?"[19]

As of February 14, it became obvious that Wilson had devised no slender organization. On the same day, he gave his critics even more to digest— a cable to each member of the House and Senate committees on foreign affairs requesting that they refrain from further public comment on the League until he could discuss the Covenant with them, article by article.[20] It is frequently maintained by scholars (as it was at the time) that Wilson thereby tried to muzzle the opposition so that he could fire the opening shot at Boston's Mechanic's Hall, where he told his audience he had "fighting blood" in him. Thus, the argument goes, it was Wilson who set the confrontational tone.[21]

Yet even Wilson's admirers among historians have overlooked several mitigating circumstances surrounding this seemingly partisan offensive. Although he had approved the idea (Tumulty's) for a presidential homecoming in Senator Lodge's own state, Wilson had not intended to make an important speech. En route to America he learned of newspaper announcements to the contrary and exchanged with Tumulty eight radiograms on the subject. He knew his "immediate duty" was to get to Washington; he was worried about the "impression on the hill" if his stopover became "an arrangement for a premeditated address." Could they not forgo an elaborate ceremony and just let him make a few informal comments at the train station?[22] Tumulty plainly had misconstrued Wilson's communications; but by this time he had invited the governors of all the New England states; and, he beseeched the President, the people of Boston looked forward to the event "with splendid and entirely non-partisan enthusiasm."[23] Wilson had no choice but to accept a *fait accompli.*

The speech itself, except for one or two sentences, was not markedly partisan. For half an hour he spoke extemporaneously about the great esteem in which Europeans held Americans. The people of Europe believed that the United States had converted the war to "the cause of human right and justice," and that the world was about to enter a new age when nations would "understand one another" and "unite every moral fiber and physical strength to see that right shall prevail." This imposed a proud burden upon America; if she were to fail, despair would send the nations back into hostile camps and America would forever have to live with a gun in her hand. Anyone who resisted the "present tides," he also declared, would find himself thrown upon a "high and barren" shore. But he had no doubt about the ultimate verdict. The world's peoples were in the saddle and they had "set their heads now to do a great thing."[24]

If any of this was terribly unfair (or impolitic), it should be recalled that, since autumn, a steady rhythm of denunciations of both the League and Wilson had filled the air of the Senate; moreover, three irreconcilables (Borah, Poindexter, and the Democrat James A. Reed of Missouri) ignored the request for a temporary cease-fire and, before Wilson landed, had delivered some of the most vituperative addresses ever heard in the chamber.[25] Taft called them "barking critics." To a friend he bemoaned "the vicious narrowness of Reed, the explosive ignorance of Poindexter, the ponderous Websterian language . . . of Borah, the vanity of Lodge . . . [and] the selfishness . . . of Knox."[26] It is no reflection upon the integrity of his opponents' convictions to say that, as in the case of the 1918 campaign, Wilson was probably more sinned against than sinning. He may nonetheless have erred, but in number rather than degree. In part because of the crush of work confronting him during his ten-day stay, he made no other public addresses on the League until the eve of his return to Europe, and that would be that for almost half a year.

Wilson did, however, engage in significant parlay with his legislative colleagues at a White House dinner on February 26. For several hours he and his thirty-four guests explored most of the substantive issues at stake. Although it seldom receives more than brief scholarly notice, this was the most revealing and decisive encounter that would ever take place between the President and the League's critics.[27]

One of their first questions concerned the disarmament article and the right of Congress to establish the size of the armed forces. That right, Wilson maintained, was safeguarded, more or less. The Executive Council's responsibility for effecting a reduction of armaments was subject to the approval of each of the governments represented on that body; therefore, unanimity was required before any such plan could go into effect. (This was a reasonable interpretation of how the League might well proceed; but Article VIII, which Wilson considered among the Covenant's most important components, contained no such explicit qualifications.)

The League's potential impact on the Monroe Doctrine was in the forefront of the discussion. On at least two previous occasions, Wilson had faulted that shibboleth—because it had never protected Latin America against aggression from the United States—when he had unveiled the Pan-American Pact and in his remarks to a group of Mexican editors in June 1918. Now, he iterated its traditional stated purpose: to insure the Western Hemisphere against foreign aggression. In a sense, he said, the League would make all nations a party to the Monroe Doctrine and broaden its scope to cover the world.

Many senators also asked about the articles on arbitration. Anticipating their objections, Wilson gave a construction that suggested a limited application. Before resorting to arms, of course, League members would be required to submit their disputes to arbitration; if this were unacceptable, the next step would be an inquiry by the Executive Council. Only in the case of unanimity was the Council's decision binding on the disputants, on pain of sanctions. Therefore, the Covenant's provisions for the settlement of international disputes fell somewhat short of compulsory arbitration. (Again, the point was not clarified, but if, after going through the process, one nation invaded the other, then that nation would have violated Article X. While their main purpose was to delay hostilities, these articles, in the context of the whole, were still fairly strong.)

Some of the questions put to Wilson were captious. For instance, one related Senator Borah's recent assertion that, because the British dominions would have separate representation in the Body of Delegates, the Covenant embodied "the greatest triumph for English diplomacy in three centuries."[28] Wilson met this protest by explaining that Great Britain would never be more than one among the five permanent members of the Executive Council; and it was inconceivable that the Body of Delegates, whose right it was to name the other four of the council's nine members, would chose from among any but the smaller powers.

The most heavily stressed issues were Article X and sovereignty. Wilson did not mince words. "[S]ome of our sovereignty would be surrendered," he said. How could an enterprise to eliminate war hope to succeed "without some sacrifice[,] . . . each nation yielding something to accomplish such an end"? But, one senator asked, would the obligation to participate in some concerted action not impair the right of Congress to declare war? Not necessarily, Wilson replied. The United States would be bound to the Covenant, like any other treaty; it was possible, though far more likely under the old order, that a situation might arise that would compel Congress to declare war. But the fact that such a situation *"might* force us to declare war was not a usurpation of the power of Congress to declare war." Even so, he went on, the United States "would willingly relinquish some of its sovereignty . . . for the good of the world"; and, of course, other nations would be doing the same. Wilson's summary comment underscored the central issue: the League "would never be carried out successfully if the objection of sovereignty was insisted upon by the Senate."[29]

Most witnesses gave this signal conference a favorable report shortly after it adjourned. According to a *New York Times* canvas of participants, the session was nothing if not "good humored." Dr. Grayson's record for that day, based on what Wilson told him, described it as "free and easy." Some adversaries remarked that Wilson had gone some distance in allaying charges that he was secretive or imperious. Two senators told the *Times* that the President said he did not expect the charter to go through without some changes (though he hoped otherwise).[30]

Two weeks later, however, Wilson complained bitterly about the way some senators had allegedly treated him. " '*Your* dinner,' " he said to Colonel House upon returning to Paris, " 'was a failure as far as getting together was concerned.' "[31] After initially speaking respectfully about it, one critic later said that he "had had tea with the Mad Hatter."[32] These dramatic changes in perception, as we shall see, owed to subsequent events during the remainder of Wilson's stay—a chain reaction set swiftly in motion within two days of the White House gathering. For, rather than bringing them around, Wilson's forthright explanation of the Covenant— in particular, his comments about Article X and sovereignty—had simply confirmed his opponents' predictions. "I can say that nothing the President said changed my opinion about the League of Nations," Senator Frank Brandegee remarked. "I am against it, as I was before."[33]

There was, of course, another constituency of consequence whose advice and consent Wilson had yet to secure. In light of ongoing developments in early 1919, the disposition of progressive internationalists toward the President had an increasingly significant bearing on the League's prospects. As Norman Hapgood had written to Colonel House in January, "most assuredly, we cannot gain the Senate if, in addition to the opposition of the reactionaries we have the liberals dissatisfied."[34]

A few preliminary observations are in order before we consider the progressive internationalists at this critical juncture. As Wilson had interpreted it at the plenary session, the Covenant was both definite enough to

guarantee peace and elastic enough to provide for readjustment, its powers subject to "those who exercise it and in accordance with the changing
circumstances of the time." Thus, as had been once the case with the
Constitution of the United States, the League of Nations awaited practical
definition. Considering the diplomatic realities that constrained him, Wilson had probably infused the Covenant with as great a progressive internationalist character as possible; but only time could tell in what direction
the tree would actually grow. Under the best of circumstances (perhaps a
third Wilson administration), progressive internationalists could feel reasonably confident that the United States would pursue a progressive construction and not only shoulder new responsibilities but also accept limi-
tations on its own freedom of action in international relations. Yet a highly
conservative, even reactionary, construction could be also put on the Covenant if the task of putting it into operation fell to conservatives and
reactionaries. So the question was not just of the League in itself. Other
matters of politics and foreign policy and perceptions of their relationship
to the League—and, therefore, of what was likely to unfold in the immediate postwar years—shaped the thoughts and actions of progressive
internationalists. (This much could be said, as well, of the thoughts and
actions of Henry Cabot Lodge.)

Despite their dismay over his regrettable contribution to the advers-
ities confronting them at home, Wilson had left for Europe with the blessings of most progressive internationalists upon him. But for one major
exception, their early response to the Covenant was highly favorable, from
Hamilton Holt's *Independent,* to Paul Kellogg's *Survey.* Matching its kindred,
the *New Republic* extolled "the Constitution of 1919," ridiculed references
to a weakened Monroe Doctrine, and dismissed other criticism that the
document did not go far enough in a progressive direction. No one, the
editorial asserted, "can doubt for a moment that if such an organization
had been in existence in 1914 there would have been no war."[35]

As for the socialist press, the *Appeal to Reason* (still circulating in the
hundreds of thousands) hailed the Covenant as a "revolutionary document
. . . designed to preserve the world's peaceful equilibrium." By itself, the
League would not "absolutely wipe out the possibility of war," but it
augured the eventual disappearance of the plague of "belligerent and wholly
selfish nationalism." The President's opponents in the Senate, the *Appeal*
also vigorously submitted, were not isolationists. They were imperialists
and militarists who feared restrictions on "America's armed forces . . .
[and] the commercial and territorial greed of American capitalists." The
League foreshadowed "the internationalism of balanced justice and cooperation," while the Lodge crowd favored "the internationalism of unre-
strained plunder and competition."[36]

Many progressive internationalists held the great hope that the League would become the vehicle for reuniting liberals and socialists. They gave Wilson credit for seeing to the drafting of the Covenant before the conference proceeded to impose a settlement on Germany. This was a significant achievement; and it fueled their hopes that, in the final peace terms, the New Diplomacy would replace the balance of power. Yet (evincing a close reading of Wilson) the Covenant was, as one of them put it, "a blank check—a form which may be signed but will then require filling out with the figures which alone can give it meaning."[37]

Thus the ultimate worthiness of the League depended on the contents of a treaty as yet unwritten, and this made many progressive internationalists somewhat uneasy. As Paul Kellogg once noted, the League of Free Nations Association (LFNA), unlike the League to Enforce Peace, was not "absorbed in the machinery of international control," but rather in "the democratic principles which must shoot through" the League to make the peace settlement "tolerable."[38] Would the organization become merely a league of governments, or one of peoples, as Wilson had often said it should? Did it deal adequately with the economic causes of war? Was the disarmament article strong enough? Could Germany and Russia expect to be invited into the family of nations?

At this point progressive internationalists did not want to put such questions into print, for Wilson seemed to share their concerns. Meeting with representatives of the LFNA on March 1, he explained that some of the provisions they all desired had been impossible to obtain. But most of the important ones were there, including some that were not written out. (For example, his idea of giving each country a three-member delegation in the general assembly, he said, would make it possible for conservative, liberal, and radical groups alike to be represented in the League. And the present requirement for unanimity in the Executive Council in order to amend the Covenant itself would, in time, no doubt be reduced to a two-thirds majority.) Just now, however, he feared that too many proposals to alter the structure would only assist the obstructionists. "[T]he important thing to do is to get behind the covenant as it is," he said. And if changes had to be made, they should be pointed "in a liberal direction [and] not in the direction of the opposition."[39]

In all, Wilson could not have hoped for a more thoughtful reception. And, for the time being—or pending the announcement of the final terms of the peace treaty—most progressive internationalists honored his request. If, in any case, apprehensions seized them during this winter of discontent, they did not center on the Covenant, or even on the arithmetic of the Senate. Far more ominous was the pall that darkened the skies above the national political scene.

By early 1919, "One Hundred Per Cent Americanism" was shifting focus from the German menace to the threat of Bolshevism, although it was hard to tell where one form of hysteria left off and the other began: In February, Scott Nearing of the Rand School of Social Science was tried in federal court for attempting, through his writings, to obstruct the draft. On Capitol Hill, the Senate Judiciary Committee investigated alleged Bolshevik efforts to overthrow the government. In Seattle, when rising prices caused workers to strike for higher wages and the police brutally crushed the movement, Mayor Ole Hanson declared, "We didn't need any more law than we did to stop the red flag. We just stopped it." Later that month, senators Poindexter and Reed attacked the League by equating it with Bolshevism. In March, the Supreme Court, in *Schenck* vs. *the United States,* ruled that some forms of political expression were not protected under the First Amendment. Roger Baldwin, director of the National Civil Liberties Union, was in jail. Rose Pastor Stokes had begun serving a ten-year sentence for making an anti-war speech. Eugene Debs, after losing an appeal, would soon enter prison as well. And, though the fighting was over, the Post Office Department continued to harass or suppress radical publications such as the *Liberator,* the *Milwaukee Leader,* and the New York *Call.* It did not yet have a name, but Wilson's return visit coincided with the opening phase of the "Red Scare."[40]

For progressive internationalists, the fate of the League presently did not hinge on what was in the Covenant, but rather on the persistence of a domestic environment that was discouraging liberals from giving the crusade their full devotion and preventing many influential radicals from participating in it at all. As far as the ultimate peace settlement was concerned, Wilson's performance so far had earned him the benefit of the doubt. Yet, in the circumstances, they needed further reassurance that their confidence in him was not otherwise misplaced. It was now essential that he take extraordinary steps to restore their erstwhile coalition to vitality. Without delay, he simply must put an end to the repression and extend to its past victims a sweeping presidential amnesty.[41]

This was not the counsel of malcontents on the periphery. Wilson received the same message from Democrats and nonpartisan liberals, pacifists and pro-war socialists, journalists across the progressive internationalist spectrum, and from personal friends. This aspect of the story has long been ignored, but it is no exaggeration to say categorically that, until the publication of the Treaty of Versailles, the broad issue of civil liberties rivaled the Covenant as the chief subject of concern among progressive internationalists.

The general question had first been raised in leading liberal publications shortly after the Armistice. For example, the *Dial* wondered: "Can we now look forward to something like normal conditions of freedom of speech and opinion? Will radicals and dissenters now be permitted to have their say, or must we expect more orgies of suppression?" Citing the severe punishment meted out to Rose Pastor Stokes "for a few unimportant remarks," the journal hoped that, at a minimum, "some leniency [would] be now shown to . . . political prisoners."[42] In January, Norman Thomas asked in the *New Republic,* "With what possible grace can we appear before the conference table as a champion of liberty" when so many in America were in prison "for no other crime than loyalty to conviction?" Charles Beard put the matter derisively. "The time has come," he wrote, "[t]o release political prisoners whose offense was to retain Mr. Wilson's pacifist views after he abandoned them."[43]

Once he had arrived back in Washington, progressive internationalists lost no time in pressing the point—that herein the League hung in the balance—in correspondence with Wilson as well as in editorials. John Palmer Gavit was the first. Because of the burdens of peacemaking, the editor of the *New York Evening Post* wrote to him, Wilson probably did not realize the extent of the damage being done. But the administration's policy on civil liberties was "the very reason that you are not having now the liberal backing that is your right." The President had "a golden opportunity." Nothing "would so uplift and electrify" the country's liberal forces or have a more "far-reaching political effect," Gavit affirmed, as an "immediate and unconditional amnesty for all those persons convicted for expression of opinion."[44]

John Nevin Sayre wrote Wilson that labor looked upon the repressive war machinery as a tool used in many instances by selfish capitalist interests to persecute labor leaders—that it tended "to undermine confidence in your proposals for a League." A general amnesty was the "one thing" that could "rally the laboring classes" to his side.[45] (On the broader subject, Ray Stannard Baker considered the recent official statement of the new American Labor party of Greater New York important enough to outline it for the President: The party resolutely supported the Fourteen Points and "a real league of nations." But labor demanded "honest disarmament," "honest self-determination," "open trade," and "open discussion" at home. They would oppose with all their might the Poindexters, the Reeds, and the Lodges. "As between them and Wilson we are for Wilson, but we are not behind Wilson. We are a long way ahead of him."[46])

Dudley Field Malone made the case with a direct reference to 1916. Many radical groups who had supported Wilson then, Malone explained, opposed him now because the government continued to act as if the war had not ended. A "bold and generous stroke," however, could win radical support for the Covenant. The President must urge Congress to repeal the Espionage Act, order the Attorney General to drop all pending cases under it, put a stop to Burleson's activities, and proclaim a general amnesty for all political prisoners. Courageous action was the key to victory.

It would create "a force great and militant enough to crush the opposition to the League."[47]

Of all the anxious warnings, none was more emphatic than an open letter published in the *Appeal to Reason* on March 1. In the battle for the League, the message to Wilson began, "[y]ou will be met by a storm of reactionary opposition." Then, speaking on behalf of its less radical brethren, the socialist weekly asked, "Where in America can you turn for aid and comfort save to the American people?—to American liberals?" It was common knowledge that the President had received both public and personal notice of the gravity with which virtually all progressive internationalists regarded the issue of amnesty. "They cannot accept your leadership in the League of Nations movement so long as . . . you persist in ignoring their single demand," the *Appeal* concluded. "They must lose faith in you— regard your flowering rhetoric as mere 'wind along the waste,' signifying nothing sure or stable."[48]

Wilson's response fell far short of stirring. With some dispatch, he looked into the questions of censorship and amnesty, but once again hesitated to act resolutely. After writing to Burleson on the subject of radical publications—"I cannot believe that it would be wise to do any more suppressing"—he failed to follow through. "Continued to suppress and Courts sustained me every time," Burleson subsequently scratched on the bottom of the President's note.[49] As for the Espionage Act, the Attorney General maintained that no one had been convicted "for *mere expression of opinion.*" In those few cases where punishment had been unusually severe, a warrant of commutation was in order, but in no circumstances could he recommend "an indiscriminate pardon." Tumulty voiced doubts about the Justice Department's assertion that there were no political prisoners; he also pointed out to Wilson that Gregory took on the mien of prosecuting attorney and that, in most cases, the proposed reductions of sentences were "not at all considerable." Wilson should not grant Gregory's request to announce such a compassionless policy. It would be better, Tumulty advised, "if you would keep in mind the idea of a general amnesty and not foreclose yourself from acting along a different line."[50]

Nevertheless, on March 1, Wilson did defer to Gregory's persistent ministrations. His decision could only compound the difficulties should he wish to change the policy later on; though not irrevocable, it certainly reduced the possibilities for an amnesty. "I can only say that it is a matter which I have approached again and again without being able to satisfy myself of a wise conclusion," he wrote to John Nevin Sayre two days later. "I am going to keep on thinking about it."[51] But merely "thinking about it" was a luxury he could ill afford. Progressive internationalists had made it abundantly clear that both principle and political common sense required a long-overdue act of faith, a test of his sincerity in the search for a democratic peace. Wilson needed their unconditional support; he would no longer have it. Soon they would disregard his appeal to refrain from publicly offering criticism of the Covenant. This additional complication, however, was owed as much to new developments on Wilson's right flank (precipitated by the White House dinner of February 26)—to which we now turn.

Few historians have ever doubted that the League, at least until 1920, enjoyed overwhelming public approval. Nor did Henry Cabot Lodge; that fact informed his strategy at every turn. "[T]he people of the country are very naturally fascinated by the idea of eternal preservation of the world's peace," he wrote to ex-senator Beveridge. The problem was that "[t]hey have not examined it; they have not begun to think about it." To an extent, this was probably the case, but the observation also reflected Lodge's contempt for public opinion, especially in foreign policy, whenever it intruded with judgments averse to his own. (His attitude toward the public's regard for progressive taxation and the eight-hour day, it should be noted, was no different.) The remedy was to educate the people, to take every opportunity to bring them to a full understanding of the practical details. "[T]he second thought," Lodge assured Beveridge, "is going to be with us."[52]

At the same time, Lodge knew that it would be counterproductive to confront Wilson "with a blank negative." Even among his own constituents the League idea was popular. Some two hundred thousand Bostonians had turned out to give the President a rousing hero's welcome, and Governor Coolidge had reminded the Senator that "Massachusetts is a pacifist state in a way."[53] If the party adopted the position of the irreconcilables, a minority view among critics, it was bound to backfire. Wilson could easily make capital out of an uncompromising stand against any League at all; moreover, it would alienate Republicans like Taft, who found the Covenant satisfactory, or those others who apparently desired a league but had qualms about its present form. As his most insightful and sympathetic biographer has observed, "we may reasonably assume that Lodge would have swallowed the League had he seen therein the means of securing a Republican victory."[54]

There were other grave concerns—in a sense, the mirror opposite of those of progressive internationalists—at work as well. "Any party which carries out . . . a great progressive and constructive program is sure to bring out a reaction," Wilson said to members of the Democratic National Committee on February 28, in reference to the mid-term elections.[55] He might also have applied that analysis to current circumstances. As the Republicans' recent campaign suggested, his prewar domestic policies and "war socialism," from labor legislation to tariffs and taxation, gave them every cause for alarm over the issue of postwar reconstruction. Since November, Wilson had refused to appoint a formal commission on reconstruction, in order to prevent Republicans from controlling it.[56] And, while he had scarcely begun to consider a program (as progressive internationalists complained), there was talk within administration circles about permanent government ownership of the nation's railroads and telegraph system, the establishment of a permanent federal employment service, and federal coordination of a major public works program. Furthermore, on the day of his arrival in Washington, the President signed into law a new progressive tax bill that sharply increased the previous, high rates on large incomes and corporate profits.[57] From the Republicans' standpoint, then, the triumph of an unmitigated Wilsonian League held profound implications for foreign and domestic policy alike. Here partisanship was imbued with ideological conviction. Their present advantage in the Senate was as slim as could be, perhaps ephemeral. What would become of the party—indeed, of the country—if Wilson got his League, if the Democrats could boast of "the greatest constructive world reform in history"?[58]

With Roosevelt's death, the torch had been passed, and the stakes could not be higher. Wilson's League must be overhauled or, better, defeated; but this could be done, Lodge reasoned, only by holding "such a position that I shall be able to unite the [Republican] senators behind me."[59] To that end, the battle was formally joined two days after the White House dinner. On February 28, Lodge delivered the second most important address of his career.

The President, he began, was unfortunately prone to "enticing generalities" and "shrill shrieks." What was needed were "facts, details, and sharp, clear-cut definitions." The present constitution of the League was crudely expressed and susceptible to diverse interpretations. Rather than promoting harmony, the Covenant itself would become the source of disagreement among those who signed on. One thing was nonetheless definite: Article X would turn American foreign policy upside down. He wanted "very complete proof . . . of the superiority of any new system before we reject the policies of Washington and Monroe." To guarantee the political independence and territorial integrity of all the members of the League was "a very perilous promise to make." And "that guarantee we must maintain at any cost when our word is once given." The question of compulsive force was not a matter of interpretation, he told his fellows. "It is there in article 10 absolutely and entirely by the mere fact of these guarantees." Moreover, dismissing Wilson's attempt to reconcile collective security with the Monroe Doctrine, he asserted that, under the League, domestic questions, including such issues as immigration, would no longer be settled by Americans alone. The United States would also waive the right at all times to take independent action in its foreign affairs, "if there is a majority against us." Wilson would substitute "an international state for pure Americanism." In other words, the country was being asked "to move away from George Washington to . . . the sinister figure of Trotsky the champion of internationalism."

The Senator granted that a league might be advantageous. All he asked was for "consideration, time and thought." As the League stood now, the danger of future collision with Europe was very great. The Covenant required amendments to exclude from its jurisdiction the Monroe Doctrine and immigration, to provide for the right of withdrawal from the organization, and to clarify how international force might be employed. Perhaps it would be wiser, he concluded, to have a league "made up by the European nations whose interests are chiefly concerned, and with which the United States could cooperate fully at any time, whenever cooperation was needed."[60]

Lodge's carefully calibrated assault had the desired effect all around. His catalogue of the troubles that might be visited upon the country garnered the applause of the irreconcilables; his list of "reasonable" suggestions for improving the Covenant impressed the more moderate critics. The performance even had the benefit of provoking Wilson. Later that day, to the Democratic National Committee, he cast aspersions upon the intelligence of his adversaries and declared that they were "going to have the most conspicuously contemptible names in history." Though meant to be off-the-record, the remarks quickly made the rounds and added credence to the Republicans' charges that the President was unreasonable.[61]

Even so, it appeared to Lodge and Brandegee that Wilson still enjoyed the upper hand, at least on the surface of things. Many Republican newspapers remained more or less favorably disposed toward the League. ("We have been almost entirely cut off," Lodge complained to Viscount Bryce.[62]) The LEP was unwavering in its support. Taft and Wilson were scheduled to appear together at New York's Metropolitan Opera House on March 4. It did not occur to Lodge that the President's following among progressive internationalists could possibly be in jeopardy. Most important, because of the dinner at the White House, Wilson could truthfully report to the Peace Conference that he had met and consulted with members of the legislature.

Thus, before Wilson returned to Europe, it was essential to demonstrate the views of a strategic minority. To that end, Lodge, Brandegee, and Knox drew up an appropriate resolution, circulated it strictly among Republicans, and secured some thirty-seven signatures. The document stated that it was the sense of the Senate that a league of nations should be considered only after peace terms with Germany were settled and that the Covenant *"in the form now proposed* . . . should not be accepted by the United States." These rather open-ended words fit Lodge's strategy perfectly, for they were deliberately chosen to attract (in addition to the ir-reconcilables) a good number of senators not on record as diehard oppo-nents of the League. In a daring parliamentary maneuver just before midnight on March 3, Lodge introduced this, his famous "Round Robin," and read off the names of the signatories.[63]

The impact of this simple device was manifold. First, literally over-night, it forced most of the League's supporters to review the entire situ-ation. In his address at the Metropolitan Opera House, Taft, while de-ploring the tactic and insisting that the League must be a part of the treaty, conceded the necessity of amendments to preserve the Monroe Doctrine and to safeguard American control over immigration.[64] Demo-cratic newspapers also soon began to realize that such modifications were inevitable.[65]

Second, as the dispatches from the British Embassy in Washington to the Foreign Office amply demonstrate, the Republicans accomplished their main goal—to serve notice to the Allied leaders that at least one-third of the Senate would probably vote not to ratify the peace treaty, barring certain changes in the Covenant.[66] This would have unending repercussions. The fact that Wilson needed to obtain any important changes would weaken his bargaining position in other areas of contention, and that would have an enormous impact on the peace treaty.

Third, the Round Robin altered the debate in several ways with respect to progressive internationalists. Almost immediately, it under-mined Wilson's argument about getting behind the Covenant as it stood. Now that it was clear that the document was going to be revised, pro-gressive internationalists concluded that those revisions ought to be deter-mined, not by reactionaries like Lodge or even conservatives like Taft, but by the League's real friends. And their concerns had little to do with the Monroe Doctrine, control of immigration, or sovereignty.

Robert Morss Lovett, editor of the *Dial* and a member of the League of Free Nations Association, outlined the progressive internationalist po-sition on March 8. While maintaining that the Covenant should be wel-comed "with such signs of acceptance as the Senate cannot fail to under-stand," he counseled Wilson to provide for Germany's and Russia's entry into the League and to ensure that the mandate system be implemented "in conspicuous good faith." Moreover, the Covenant was too vague on the subject of disarmament, the supreme test of nations, and silent on the subject of the economic causes of war. And, whereas it contained a pro-vision to secure for labor humane conditions of work (Article XX), the League needed some form of direct representation of peoples as well as of governments.[67]

A week later, the *New Republic* asserted that defeat could be avoided only by combining "agitation on behalf of the official draft with candid and thoroughgoing criticism." Noting that radicals and liberals must not imitate their foes and "threaten to upset the whole applecart" if they did not get everything they wanted, the journal added to Lovett's list of short-comings the draft's omission of a guarantee to protect minorities in national states. In this, the first in a series of articles, the *New Republic* also began to raise new doubts about Article X, but not because it "too severely limits sovereign discretion." Rather, it was potentially "dangerous and ambiguous" because it "may mould the League into an agency of international inertia rather than into an agency of international adjustment." The New York *Call,* too, worried about the League's capacity to "subdue the aspirations of sullen subject populations for the very self-determination for which we avowedly fought the war." Walter Lippmann put it this way: Article X constituted "an effort to be wiser than the next generation." There was no question of trusting the President; it was "a matter of the future, when Mr. Wilson will be a private citizen, and when perhaps some other person will be in the White House who needs to be checked by Congress."[68] Here, then, the Round Robin revealed how ineptly Wilson had marshaled the best among his own forces. Although they were judicious enough to leaven their criticisms with appeals to pragmatism, the very fact that progressive internationalists had opened up this entirely new front demonstrated, on one hand, that they expected to be heeded and, on the other hand, that Wilson now exerted little if any control over them.

Finally, in a more comprehensive way, Lodge's resolution also drew back the curtain and exposed both how much Wilson had overestimated his personal powers of persuasion and how inadequately he had played the role of propagandist in general. Only five days before, he had told Breckinridge Long, "I am in doubt whether the time has come for a systematic campaign."[69] But that was precisely what was needed. As Ray Stannard Baker urged, it was of paramount importance for Wilson to explain that *this* League really was the best one obtainable, to "defend the Covenant as adopted by your committee, to convince the people . . . and enforce and re-enforce the Covenant, illustrating how it applies in specific cases."[70]

Lodge's timing left Wilson only one day to respond, in his farewell address at the Metropolitan Opera House. This was an event attended by thousands and scrutinized by millions. (The President looked, according to Baker, "very much worn, his face gray & drawn, showing the strain of his heavy work at Washington.") There were, to be sure, moving insights in his comments about the hopes of suffering Europeans, the sacrifice that tens of thousands of American soldiers had made to a great ideal, and about the dangers of another war if the balance of power were not supplanted by a community of nations. Yet, he maintained, "it is perhaps not

necessary for me to discuss in any particular way the contents of the document." Hence one single, hapless line of defiance reverberated: "And
when that treaty comes back gentlemen on this side will find the Covenant not only in it, but so many threads of the treaty tied to the Covenant
that you cannot dissect the Covenant from the treaty without destroying
the whole vital structure."[71] No matter how otherwise emotionally effective they might have been, Wilson's two addresses in Boston and New
York, about general conditions in Europe and the duty of the United
States to fulfill a historic mission, were hardly enough—not when he would
be absent for another five months and the Republicans would continue to
hammer on the details.

Two paths to the League now lay before Wilson, neither one guaranteeing success. He could undertake some heroic eleventh-hour endeavor to
bring life back to the progressive internationalist coalition, or he could
seek help from sympathetic conservative internationalists. It had been a
long time since the Fourteen Points and the Fourth Liberty Loan addresses; progressive internationalists were in sore need of some tangible
evidence that they still counted for something in the President's book.
Primarily because of obstacles that he apparently did not care to clear
away, the opportunity to take the first path was rapidly receding. The
compliments he paid to Taft at the Metropolitan Opera House, however,
as well as his estimation that the latter's presence there meant that the
League was "not a party issue," seemed to suggest, ironically, that Wilson
now considered the conservative second path as the more practical means
to his own progressive ends.

But this entailed a tremendous gamble, notwithstanding Taft's prestige and willingness to help. Whatever "clarifying amendments" Wilson
and Taft might settle on, there was no assurance that they would satisfy
a sufficient number of the signers of the Round Robin. Nor did this approach take into account that Taft had faltered before—that he was bound,
sooner or later, to come under pressure from fellow Republicans to draw
back from Wilson. And, if after all of this Wilson was left high and dry,
what other conclusion would progressive internationalists come to but that
he had permanently abandoned them?

Then, too, what would the League mean, even if it won adoption on
a decidedly conservative basis? Would the possibilities for a progressive
internationalist League not have been lost forever? To whom would Wilson (or a like-minded successor) turn for understanding and support to
sustain a progressive construction of the Covenant during the first postwar
crisis when, hypothetically, the United States might have to sacrifice its
own short-term interests for the well-being of the fledgling organization?

In this regard, the domestic political circumstances that prevailed would be as important as any other factor.

By March 1919, the events of the previous months had at last acquired an unmistakable meaning as they continued to hurtle out of Wilson's control with seemingly inexorable logic. Just after Wilson returned to Paris, Oswald Garrison Villard reflected upon the recent past and, with great perspicacity, contemplated the future. The Republican opposition was "more or less factitious," he admitted. The President ought now to realize, however, that arrayed against him was "a body of liberal thought" as well as "a body of feudal thought," and that "between them, though there can never be conscious cooperation, there is enough power to wreck his plans." He might well attempt to appease the Senate, but his persistent diffidence toward progressive internationalist concerns would continue to militate against him; "the compromises he has charted with an eye to the conservatives have not placated the latter, while they have chilled the faith of the radicals," Villard concluded. "Honest politics are always good politics, and there is only one method by which the President can win victories—by loyalty to the fourteen points and to the league that he formerly preached."[72]

This was a harsh indictment from someone who, somewhat to the left of Wilson, had become as skeptical of the League as had Lodge, far to the right of Wilson. Yet, Villard had gotten to the crux. "The thing reaches the depth of tragedy," Wilson himself had said to members of the Democratic National Committee on the last day of February.[73] Indeed, the story had taken on that quality, but this was so, as much for any other reason, because Wilson did not seem to realize why.

14

Wilson's Fate

"H e will probably be beaten," Ray Stannard Baker wrote in his diary in early April, during the "dark days" of the peace conference. "He can escape no responsibility & must go to his punishment not only for his own mistakes and weaknesses of temperament but for the greed and selfishness of the world."[1] Indeed, even before Wilson returned to Paris, the Allied statesmen, having closely followed the politics of the Round Robin, had decided to take the League of Nations hostage. Throughout the spring, each of them would present a different ransom note. The first one, appropriately, would be French in origin, and it had at least the partial consent of the British and of Colonel House. Embodied in a short-lived proposal to conclude a preliminary treaty, it presumed to give France perpetual control over the Rhineland by detaching it from Germany, and to uncouple the League from the Treaty itself.

House's explanation—that this procedure would expedite the negotiations—only added to Wilson's mounting labors and distress. The Colonel quickly backtracked, but his complicity in the Allied scheme dealt his relationship with the President a blow it would never recover from. " 'House has given away everything I had won before we left Paris,' " Wilson said bitterly to the First Lady.[2] The comment was not a wholesale exaggeration. Paris now buzzed with rumors about the demise of the

246

League. Even a public announcement by Wilson on March 15—that the Covenant would prevail as an integral part of the peace treaty—did not lay the issue to rest.[3] From this point onward he would find himself, as often as not, in the position of supplicant.

Robert Cecil should not, perhaps, have been surprised to discover Wilson "in a very truculent mood" on the following day, during their first conversation about possible changes in the Covenant. A little persuasion from Senator Hitchcock and William Howard Taft, however, softened his attitude somewhat. On March 4, Hitchcock had written that a "larger number" of Republicans, including several signers of the Round Robin, would vote for the League if certain amendments were made.[4] Taft corroborated this opinion. After digesting the Lodge manifesto and consulting with the LEP, he wrote Wilson the following on March 18:

> If you bring back the treaty with the League of Nations in it, make more specific reservation of the Monroe Doctrine, fix a term for the duration of the League and the limit of armament, require expressly unanimity of action in Executive Council and Body of Delegates, and add to Article XV a provision that where the Executive Council and the Body of Delegates finds the difference to grow out of an exclusively domestic policy, it shall recommend no settlement. . . .

Senator Porter J. McCumber, Republican of North Dakota, sent similar messages, and Taft assured the President that if he followed their advice, "the ground will be completely cut from under the opponents."[5]

That evening Wilson proposed to Cecil general amendments designed to overcome senatorial apprehensions: to eliminate the compulsory nature of the process of arbitration contained in Article XV, to permit withdrawal from the League upon two years' notice, and to exclude domestic issues from the League's jurisdiction. In addition, Cecil suggested an explicit requirement for unanimity in all decisions by the Executive Council and a proviso to make acceptance of a mandatory strictly voluntary. He also offered a provision for the future expansion of the Council with an eye toward the eventual membership of Germany and Russia. This would meet a criticism common to both the American and the British left. Wilson subsequently recommended that neutral states be invited to join the League at its inception.[6] In four fairly uneventful sessions during the last week of March, the League of Nations Commission incorporated all of these changes into the Covenant. Only an amendment on the Monroe Doctrine was still outstanding.[7]

The mere fact that the Commission had agreed to these revisions pulled little weight in the newly constituted Council of Four. With divisive crises escalating on all sides over French security, Italian and Japanese territorial claims, and the question of how properly to punish Germany,

Lloyd George seized the moment to extract a major concession from Wilson with respect to the challenge the United States posed to British naval supremacy. Wilson had been astute enough (though it contradicted his views on disarmament) not to discard the bargaining chip of America's ongoing program of naval construction. Lloyd George, still doubting the efficacy of the League, called the President's hand. In a new "Outline of Peace Terms," the Prime Minister, on March 25, advised that the League become a separate convention and demanded the termination of the American naval program.[8]

Coincidentally, on the same day, Wilson had countered the former threat by inducing the Council of Four to reaffirm that the Covenant would not be thus detached.[9] Lloyd George then collared the Monroe Doctrine; he would withhold support for any such amendment to the Covenant until the Americans promised to give up some un-built ships. Cecil, realizing the potential consequences, seethed with anger. "The President has practically agreed to everything I have asked," he wrote to Balfour; but when the President asked for one thing in return, they refused him.[10]

The "naval battle of Paris" ended in a moratorium. On April 10, Lord Robert and Colonel House worked out a memorandum that expressed the desire on both sides to avoid competition and to hold an Anglo-American naval conference after the treaty with Germany was signed.[11] Lloyd George thereupon reversed himself on the qualification to Article X. In its final form, the discrete amendment stated: "Nothing in this Covenant shall be deemed to affect the validity of . . . regional understandings like the Monroe Doctrine for securing the maintenance of peace." Wilson was "very much cheered" when Taft sent word that the clause was "eminently satisfactory."[12]

Meanwhile, another battle royal was being waged among the "Big Four" over French demands to take over the left bank of the Rhine and to annex the coal-rich Saar valley. For Clemenceau, the survival of France was at stake; for Wilson, the integrity of the Fourteen Points. When Wilson, his jaw firmly set, persisted in challenging Clemenceau's latest claim, the latter denounced his colleague as "the friend of Germany" and stormed out of the room.[13] Growing "grayer and grimmer all the time" and weary of multifarious Allied obstructions (including Lloyd George's attempt to scuttle the League), the President, on April 6, ordered the *George Washington* to make ready to take him home. The distinct possibility that the conference might break up moved Clemenceau to relent in his more extreme requirements. For his part, Wilson agreed to a fifteen-year Allied occupation of the Rhineland and to a special treaty, devised by Lloyd George, which pledged Anglo-American military assistance to France should Germany ever attack her. The separate security pact betokened Clemenceau's fundamental lack of confidence in the League; Wilson, however, saw it as a diplomatic stopgap, or as a reinforcement of Article X, specifically and temporarily applied to France.[14]

In this instance, Wilson had succeeded in curbing the French; yet a passing (and seldom quoted) remark to Clemenceau about the compromise package conveyed an inescapable fact as he continued to resist violations of self-determination. "I am obliged," he said, "to remain faithful to my Fourteen Points, but without inflexibility."[15] That admission obtained in two other crises concerning the imperialist ambitions of the Allies.

In January, Wilson had yielded to certain strategic claims put forth by Orlando and Sonnino pertaining to the Austrian-Italian border; this concession gave Italy jurisdiction over 200,000 Austrians. But Wilson refused to indulge the Italian appetite for the Yugoslav port city of Fiume and the Dalmatian coast, which caused the indignant Orlando to walk out of the peace conference. Wilson then publicly appealed to the Italian people to support him against their own prime minister. He anticipated the applause of Bissolati's social democrats; instead, they pointed to his inconsistency in holding Italy to the principle of self-determination. Why was he not as exacting with the British and the French? one of them asked. Although Orlando eventually returned to the conference, the controversy would never be resolved at Paris.[16]

Wilson's inability to invent a consistent standard for self-determination continued to plague him as he confronted the Japanese; but in this case the issue grazed the League much more directly. When the League Commission met to put the final touches on the Covenant on April 11, Baron Makino offered for inclusion in the preamble a diluted version of his article on racial equality—an "endorsement of the principle of the equality of Nations and the just treatment of their nationals." He defended this emendation in the context of the Covenant's social-reform provisions and of Wilson's aspirations for the mandate system. The President had considered the previous Japanese request "absurdly mild," and favored the new one. Cecil repaired to the objections he had raised in February, however; despite the Commission's majority vote in favor, Wilson obliged Cecil and ruled Makino's motion not adopted.[17]

Amidst all the other compromises, Makino's failure to get the simple statement into the Covenant tended to increase Japan's leverage in the struggle for the Shantung peninsula. No dilemma caused Wilson more sleepless nights than the Japanese ransom note based on their legal rights (won from Germany and recognized by the Allies) to retain sweeping economic concessions over that province.[18] " 'They are not bluffers, & they will go home unless we give them what they should not have,' " he said to Ray Stannard Baker. And if both Japan and Italy bolted the peace

conference, " 'what becomes of the League of Nations?' " [19] Thus Wilson
had come again to Gethsemane. He was, however, able to wring from the
Japanese a verbal pledge (which they would honor in 1922) to restore
Chinese sovereignty in Shantung "through the mediation of the League
of Nations." [20] As he said to Grayson, the deal may have been "the best
that could be accomplished out of a 'dirty past'." [21] But it would make a
terrible impression in the United States and stoke the fires of denunciation
that Wilson had forsaken the Fourteen Points.

His difficulties in keeping faith with his own principles, especially
"no annexations and no indemnities," culminated in the reparations settlement, fought out more or less simultaneously with all the other conflicts.
The Pre-Armistice Agreement had allowed for compensation for civilian
damages; then, in late March, Lloyd George added military pensions to
the already astronomical reparations bill Clemenceau had presented against
Germany. [22] Enormous pressure was brought to bear to gain Wilson's consent. Lloyd George even exploited the President's well-known admiration
for Jan Smuts by recruiting the League commissioner to draw up a brief
to justify Allied pensions (a deed that Smuts later regretted). [23]

On the verge of physical exhaustion, Wilson capitulated on April 5.
When a member of The Inquiry said that these allowances violated both
sound logic and the Fourteen Points, he replied, "Logic! Logic! I don't
give a damn for logic. I am going to include pensions." [24] Actually, Wilson
had never contended that reparations, in principle, were unjust. What he
objected to was the Allies' insistence on binding Germany to an indeterminate obligation. In unharried moments, he cultivated the hope that, in
the more tranquil postwar environment, a League commission would establish a reasonable sum and fix a schedule of payments. But then came
Article 231 of the treaty, an affirmation of Germany's responsibility for
all the losses and damages suffered by the Allied peoples "as a consequence of the war imposed upon them by the aggression of Germany.
. . ." The reparations agreement, coupled with the "war-guilt clause,"
would cause Europe unending grief. [25]

"[W]e are all miserable," Robert Cecil wrote in late May 1919, evincing the feeling that overwhelmed many of the peacemakers once they saw
how all the pieces fit together. [26] Because he alone had promised so much,
Wilson, in his own time and in history, would bear the main burden of
criticism for the punitive qualities of the Treaty of Versailles—although
it is now practically a truism to say that, without his sometimes heroic
strivings, many of its 440 conditions would have been far more severe
than they were. Arthur S. Link and Robert H. Ferrell have maintained,
for example, that the territorial provisions of the treaty were not remotely
as bad as disillusioned contemporaries and revisionist historians of the

interwar years believed them to be.[27] Link has also observed that Wilson labored under a decisive handicap—the collapse of Germany as a stable counterbalance against Allied ambitions.[28] To this we might add the Round Robin. The Allies had always planned to press hard, but that instrument helped significantly to give their demands the strength of an ultimatum. And, like a domino effect, one demand weakened Wilson's defenses in combatting the next. In this sense, Lodge and the Republicans bore some responsibility for the final shape of the overall settlement. In any event, the ceremonious occasion of the signing of the treaty in the Hall of Mirrors on June 28, 1919 (five years to the day after the assassination of Franz Ferdinand), was but a fleeting triumph.

The voyage home afforded the President some much-needed rest. For more than six months he had kept up a killing pace, frequently working twelve and fourteen hours a day. In April, the most arduous and critical month, he came down with a serious illness accompanied by high fever (and complicated by untreated hypertension) that put him in bed for nearly a week. In the mornings "he would appear refreshed and eager to go on with the fight," Ray Stannard Baker wrote; but in the evenings after the meetings of the Council of Four, "he looked utterly beaten, worn out, his face quite haggard and one side of it and the eye twitching painfully." His labors at Paris rendered Wilson medically much older than his sixty-two years.[29] And yet the hardest work still lay before him.

On July 10, two days after Wilson returned to Washington, the Senate assembled to receive the treaty. In the corridors of the Capitol the mood was not altogether somber. As Wilson shook hands with his friends and enemies, Senator Lodge approached and, pointing to the bulky document under his arm, said, "Mr. President, can I carry the treaty for you?" "Not on your life," Wilson replied with a big smile, and everyone roared. Inside the Senate chamber, however, partisanship quickly dispelled the light moment; although the Democrats gave their leader a stirring ovation as he entered, only four or five Republicans deigned to join in.[30]

Wilson spoke for about thirty minutes but dwelt on generalities. The League of Nations, he exclaimed, was "the practical statesman's hope," the "indispensable instrumentality for the maintenance of the new order" to insure against another catastrophe costing millions of lives. "Dare we reject it and break the heart of the world?" The war had established "a new role and a new responsibility" for the American people and nothing but their own mistaken action could alter that fact: "The stage is set, the destiny disclosed. It has come about by no plan of our conceiving, but by the hand of God who led us into this way. We cannot turn back. We can

only go forward, with lifted eyes and freshened spirit, to follow the vision.
It was of this that we dreamed at our birth. America shall in truth show
the way. The light streams upon the path ahead, and nowhere else."[31]

The appeal was "fair and temperate," many commentators said, but
spare on details; one Democratic senator worried that "it did not 'scour.' "
As he chatted with reporters afterwards, Wilson himself seemed untrou-
bled and, despite their questions about reservations, optimistic.[32] To be
sure, at the time of his return to the United States, there was substantial
evidence that the overwhelming majority of the American people favored
the League. Thirty-two state legislatures and thirty-three governors had
endorsed the Covenant; and the results of a *Literary Digest* poll of some
1,377 newspaper editors showed that the vast majority (including a majority of Republican papers) advocated American membership, with only
181 irreconcilably opposed.[33] Even so, Wilson had produced a League that
was politically indefensible—but not only because of the Republicans' in-
curable dissatisfaction with the revised Covenant. Perhaps the most instructive and tragic part of the story is also the least known.

One might charitably argue that the League's final constitution, adopted
unanimously by the peace conference and published on April 28, was a
comparatively progressive document; nonetheless, it was not the same
Covenant of February 14, 1919, described as "revolutionary" by the principal organ of the Socialist Party of America.[34] The changes that Wilson
was forced to secure were designed solely (to paraphrase Taft) to cut the
ground out from under the senatorial opposition; they were not "indicated
in a liberal direction," as Wilson had said to the League of Free Nations
Association in March that they ought to be. Progressive internationalists
were the first in print to say so. Their disappointment with both Wilson
and the Covenant was multiplied a hundredfold by the treaty itself. Whereas
he might have every intention of using the League to right the wrongs
done, many progressives believed that the President had helped to make
a bad peace; and, true to his parting words at the Metropolitan Opera
House, he had engineered it so that "you cannot dissect the Covenant
from the treaty."

The overall settlement (and, to a lesser extent, the amendments imposed by the Republicans) appeared to have divested the Covenant of its
elastic quality, of its potential to provide for readjustment, which Wilson
had touted back in February. Ironically, many progressive internationalists
found Article X more objectionable than did most Republicans, though
for decidedly different reasons. "Defeat Article X," the *New Republic* declared on March 29, even before most of the compromises had become
public knowledge: "to respect and preserve as against external aggression
the territorial integrity and existing political independence" of all members of the League was a dubious proposition. "[F]inal justice cannot pos-

sibly be done at Paris," and "America should not be pledged to uphold injustices." Whereas the arbitration articles, the League's most salutary feature, would guarantee peaceful settlement of disputes, "the result of Article Ten will be to guarantee the mistakes made at Paris."[35]

Article X would compel the dissection of every aspect of the treaty. In countless editorials, beginning in April and May, leading progressive internationalist journals took inventories, quoting Wilson's most famous lines alongside the many provisions that violated the principle of self-determination or imposed harsh terms on Germany. The Covenant, Thorstein Veblen declared in the *Dial,* was "an instrument of realpolitik, created in the image of nineteenth century imperialism." Having used the treaty "to buy off opposition to the League," another editorialist wrote, Wilson had become "the architect who robs his foundation of stone to build on flying buttresses." The chief danger lay in Article X because it seemed "in effect to validate existing empires." The whole settlement contradicted the progressive theory behind the League and would commit it to sustaining "territorial and economic arrangements which are wrong in principle and impossible in practice." Wilson's masterwork would "block the path to a new order." Thus the *Dial* rejected the treaty and demanded "an honest Covenant."[36]

J. A. Hobson, on behalf of the Union of Democratic Control, struck the first blow for the *Nation.* Notwithstanding Wilson's efforts to include four smaller powers on the Executive Council, Hobson pronounced the League "A New Holy Alliance" of the five great powers; likewise, the absence of a specific timetable for the admission of Germany and Russia rendered it a "sham League." While applauding mandates, Hobson wondered why that system should apply only to the enemies' former colonies. Nor could he find an infusion of the principle of "the open door, or equality of economic opportunity." And the League's assigned role in bringing about disarmament appeared now to be merely advisory in nature. Finally, amending the Covenant itself seemed impossible because of the requirement for unanimity in the Executive Council; a single state could paralyze the League.[37]

" 'Try it,' they say, 'and out of it may come something worth while.' " That was how Oswald Garrison Villard characterized the basic (and not unreasonable) argument of the Covenant's innumerable defenders. But could they not see that it was "doomed to failure," not only for the reasons cited by Hobson and others, but also because of the "insincerity" (he spared Wilson that charge) of those at Paris who accepted the League while fashioning a peace of "intrigue, selfish aggression, and naked imperialism"?[38] Week by week, Villard's attacks grew sharper and the *Nation's* readership grew larger. The climax came fairly early in the debate, in "The Madness at Versailles," in which Villard mourned the forcible checking of the "progress of democracy" and declared Wilson "discredited and condemned." A supplement, "Out of His Own Mouth," followed on May 24—a compendium of pertinent extracts from his speeches subtitled, "President Wilson in Opposition to the Peace Treaty."[39]

Any spark of hope that Wilson might be able to resurrect the progressive internationalist coalition and rally it behind the League was probably extinguished when he also lost those individuals who had always bent over backwards to give him the benefit of the doubt. In mid-May, Jane Addams, Florence Kelley, and Lillian Wald publicly denounced the violations of the Fourteen Points and called for a drastic revision of terms.[40] Then, on May 24, after much soul-searching by its editorial board, the *New Republic* published a special issue under the banner, "THIS IS NOT PEACE." The articles described the treaty as an "inhuman monster" and said that liberalism had "committed suicide." On one hand, as for the League, it was "not powerful enough to redeem the treaty"; on the other hand, the treaty was "vicious enough to incriminate the League." The United States was being asked to guarantee a settlement that was unjust and therefore unstable. In the circumstances, the editors concluded momentously, America had but one choice—to "withdraw from all commitments under the Covenant which in any way impair her freedom of action."[41]

Some of the foregoing assessments of the League were incisive; some of them were unfair. In April, Wilson had confided to Norman H. Davis that he did not have enough support "to force just the kind of treaty he wanted." He had considered bolting the conference and going home in protest, but he feared that that "would throw Europe into still greater turmoil." The more honorable course was to try to "get the best treaty possible under the circumstances," and to establish the League in order to improve upon it and adjust the differences growing out of the settlement itself.[42] Clearly, Wilson had thoroughly progressive plans for the League: under the proper guidance, it could become the instrument for the peaceful settlement of disputes, for a significant reduction in armaments, improvements in labor conditions in member states, the gradual liquidation of imperialism, and for protection against invasion. Wilson surely did not conceive of Article X as the agent of the status quo. As he privately explained to one associate and frequently said on his Western tour, he had been "careful *not* to preclude the right revolution";[43] that was why, on General Bliss's advice, he had inserted in the collective-security article the words "as against external aggression." (Apprehensions might not have become so acute if the article had retained the explicit qualification that future political conditions might require territorial adjustments "pursuant to the principle of self-determination," as Wilson's Magnolia draft and First and Second Paris drafts had stated.)

The progressive internationalist critique did not dismiss important questions on Wilson's behalf. What other course could he possibly have followed at Paris? Would it not be best to accept his assumptions and rationale and indulge him this one last, and most crucial, time? After all, what, realistically, was the alternative? But Wilson's own actions (or rather, his inaction) suggested disturbing answers. Not without sound reasons did the *Nation* assert that it was a poor bet to trust "the managers of this bastard League of Nations to right the wrongs the treaty contains."[44] For, irrespective of the peace settlement, Wilson had declined to give progressive internationalists anything else to hold on to: at home he offered no program for reconstruction, while he continued to do nothing to end the repression.

From the Armistice onward, his preoccupation with the League and peacemaking closed out virtually all other concerns; throughout 1919, the absence of any Wilsonian program for postwar domestic reform became a major theme in most liberal and many socialist publications.[45] In June, Tumulty had submitted a memorandum (an advance blueprint for the New Deal, actually) that listed the things that the President ought to put before Congress. It included legislation to recognize collective bargaining; to give labor a meaningful role in the councils of industry; to establish a national minimum wage, health insurance, old age pensions, and the eight-hour day; and to begin federal housing construction.[46] In March, George L. Record had made the case for such sweeping measures, using the same political reasoning as those who were pressing for amnesty. "This program," he told Wilson, "would gather around you at once, as if by magic, the forces of intelligent and orderly radicalism who have been looking in vain to you for leadership." Record heartily approved of the League; but only if Wilson also should take up the leadership "of the radical forces in America, and present to the country a constructive program of fundamental reform" would history mark him "a truly great man."[47]

From the spring of 1916 to the winter of 1917–18, Wilson had built his sponsorship of the League on a sturdy domestic foundation. "Progressive Democracy" and "war socialism" alike had endowed progressive internationalism with legitimacy and the strength of a comprehensive, substantive vision of the future. Now, however, he was apparently unable to see what he had once instinctively seen when the progressive internationalist coalition had come together. The disarray within the ranks over the League and his failure to move forward on the domestic front during the long months of peacemaking were closely intertwined. But he was not simply standing still; if anything, the state of civil liberties in America suggested that he was moving backward. How could he expect to succeed while he abetted "that state of mind, which blocks his own endeavors"? When he "suspended free speech and trampled upon opinion," the *Dial* observed, "he was preparing exactly such a situation" as he presently confronted.[48]

While he was still in Paris, progressive internationalists had continued to implore Wilson to let the political prisoners out of jail (and perhaps throw his Postmaster General in).[49] On June 28, he cabled Tumulty that it was his "earnest desire to grant complete amnesty and pardon" to all who suffered imprisonment for anything they may have said or written against the war or the government—this, as "a just act to accompany the signing of the peace." Nevertheless, he acceded to the recommendation of his new Attorney General, A. Mitchell Palmer, to wait until he returned to the United States.[50]

The amnesty movement naturally focused on Eugene Debs, and Wilson briefly contemplated a "respite" for him, only again to defer to Palmer, who objected in part on the grounds that conservatives would seize on it "in a way that would prejudice many people against the liberal labor provisions of the treaty."[51] As Debs languished in a federal penitentiary, pro-war socialists such as Allen Benson and Charles Edward Russell played a prominent role among the petitioners. The conditions of Debs' confinement, Upton Sinclair wrote to the President, were a "menace to the life of an old man."[52] Clarence Darrow, John Palmer Gavit, Samuel Gompers, Norman Hapgood, and John Nevin Sayre also sent appeals on behalf the man who, said Darrow, had "proclaimed the truth as he saw the truth." (Eventually, the Cabinet, Burleson excepted, encouraged Debs' release, but this act of statesmanship would be left to Warren G. Harding.)[53]

No one tried harder than John Spargo to explain to Wilson the implications of his reticence. "We are being driven by the irresistible compulsion of conscience into a position of opposition to you at the very time we would gladly be upholding you," he wrote in August 1919. Their undivided help in the fight for ratification was needed more than ever, but "[m]any thousands of Liberals and Radicals" were finding it impossible "to argue for the League of Nations in the name of democratic idealism without being at once placed on the defensive." The *"overwhelming majority . . . are in revolt."*[54]

"I believe that Spargo is right," Wilson said to Attorney General Palmer just before embarking upon his Western tour. But his reply to Spargo was too familiar, and it lacked credibility: "I assure you that I am going to deal with the matter as early and in as liberal a spirit as possible."[55] By January 1920 his most loyal supporter among pro-war socialists at last concluded, "the administration has become reactionary, and deserves no support from any of us."[56]

The defection of so many leading lights of progressive internationalism was a severe blow to Wilson's great crusade; their disillusionment was important, intellectually and politically, also because it informed the thinking and the tactics of the League's senatorial opponents. For example, among progressive Republicans, Asle J. Gronna of North Dakota based his opposition on the concern that Article X would freeze the territorial status quo and thereby advance the cause of imperialism. Robert La Follette would vote against the treaty because he believed that it was too punitive toward Germany and that the disarmament provision was too weak; for him, restoration of civil liberties and progressive legislation on the home front were at least as important as the League. Citing the same battery of reasons, George Norris, at once an irreconcilable and a devout believer in the League ideal, stated that Wilson could no longer say anything that would change his mind. On similar grounds, Joseph I. France of Maryland and at least one Democrat, David I. Walsh of Massachusetts (who was not an irreconcilable) also opposed the treaty; and, depending on the mood of a particular debate, William E. Borah and Hiram Johnson, the two leading irreconcilables, made comparable arguments against ratification.[57]

Moreover, the soft spots that progressive internationalists had exposed (including those related to Article X) were cynically exploited by conservatives and reactionaries. For example, whether or not his concern was sincere, Senator Lodge denounced the Shantung settlement as "one of the blackest things in the history of diplomacy," which the League presumably would require the United States to uphold.[58] The defections played into the hands of Wilson's adversaries in other ways as well. Lincoln Colcord (Colonel House's one-time protégé) and Oswald Garrison Villard actually plotted strategy with many progressive Republican irreconcilables, including La Follette and Johnson. Even Walter Lippmann, who had helped draft the Fourteen Points but now regarded the League of Nations as "fundamentally diseased," supplied Senator Borah with inside information with which to combat Wilson.[59] Nothing could have given Lodge greater comfort than the formation of this unholy alliance.

Yet Lodge, unlike Wilson's erstwhile fellow travelers, never doubted the progressive, or "bolshevik," purposes behind the President's internationalism. Nothing that Wilson had done at Paris, including the dearly purchased revisions of the Covenant or his interpretation of Article X throughout the ratification fight, altered Lodge's views. Carthaginian peace or no, the Covenant was still vague (to Wilson, "elastic") enough to have any construction put on it. In this, most Republicans agreed that Wilson's revisions did not meet their requirements; then, too, Article X remained intact. According to Widenor, in dealing with the various blocs of Republican opinion, Lodge "had to be less than forthright in expressing his own views, had often to be all things to all men."[60] It is still a major point of historical contention whether he wished, like the irreconcilables, to kill the League entirely, or merely to make it "safe" for the United States.

Most scholars lean toward the former explanation.[61] In any case, using his prodigious parliamentary skills (and ably assisted by Elihu Root and Will Hays), Lodge eventually consummated a commanding coalition against a Wilsonian League.

Packed with "strong reservationists" (the majority attitude among Republicans) as well as irreconcilables, the Senate Foreign Relations Committee commenced hearings in late July. In a deliberate attempt to dissipate public enthusiasm, Lodge consumed two weeks by reading the treaty aloud. Then the Committee spent six weeks calling upon any and all witnesses who wished to give hostile testimony.[62] The most sensational of these came last. On September 12, William C. Bullitt, a former Wilsonian who had resigned from the peace commission to protest the treaty, testified that Secretary Lansing (whom Wilson at last would fire, for insubordination, five months later) had said to him, " 'the league of nations at present is entirely useless.' " When Bullitt quoted Lansing a second time— " 'if the Senate could only understand what this treaty means . . . it would unquestionably be defeated' "—his listeners could barely conceal their delight.[63]

The reservationist movement had already received its biggest boost, however, in July—this from the nation's second-most-eminent champion of the League. Although he preferred that the Senate ratify the treaty as it was, Taft had confidentially submitted to Will Hays six reservations that, he believed, might persuade a sufficient number of "mild reservationists" to combine with Democratic senators for a two-thirds majority.[64] Taft's reservations corresponded closely to the views of Lodge and Root; but he did not want them circulated prematurely, in part because the LEP officially supported the League without qualification. Then, on July 24, his letter to Hays (which also criticized Wilson personally) somehow found its way into the newspapers. Taft was deeply aggrieved and even offered to resign from the LEP.[65] Nonetheless, his indiscretion seriously undermined Wilson; it also rendered his adoption of Taft's original recommendations worse than an exercise in futility.

After considerable wrangling, the Republicans had by summer's end formulated forty-six amendments as the conditions for ratification; between September and November these evolved into formal reservations, honed down to a total of, curiously, fourteen. Reservation II was the most important: "The United States assumes no obligation to preserve the territorial integrity or political independence of any country . . . unless in any particular case the Congress . . . by act or joint resolution [shall] so provide." Reservation V said that the United States would not submit to arbitration any questions or disputes that related in any way to the Monroe Doctrine and declared the doctrine subject to interpretation "by the United States alone" and "to be wholly outside the jurisdiction" of the

League. Two other reservations further clarified the right of withdrawal and the exclusion of internal affairs from the League's authority, while still others raised doubts about membership in the International Labor Organization, the obligation to contribute financial support, and compliance with disarmament and economic boycotts.[66]

Meanwhile, realizing that forty-two or forty-three loyal Democrats were not enough to carry the day, Wilson held a series of interviews with small groups of Republican senators. These encounters with both mild and strong reservationists were friendly and, without exception, unavailing. All the senators reported that Wilson was "informative and instructive," but not one of them was persuaded that the reservations were not necessary.[67] Then, on August 19, he welcomed the entire Senate Foreign Relations Committee to the White House. This three-hour meeting proved to be the most fruitless of all—though, in view of the circumstances, it was remarkably cordial. Only one of the cross-examiners, Brandegee, behaved aggressively. Wilson himself was not in top form; he made several factual errors and his memory failed him more than once. When he attempted to relate the evolution of the Covenant at Paris, for instance, he could not remember the differences between one draft and another. When Senator Borah asked about the secret Allied treaties (a question inspired by Walter Lippmann) he claimed, inexplicably, that he had had no knowledge of them until the opening of the peace conference.

His comments about Article X, however, were fairly lucid, if too finely shaded in certain distinctions he drew. Presently he did not dwell on the fact, as he had done during the White House dinner of February 26, that the League, to one degree or another, would infringe upon national sovereignty. Although it was "the very backbone of the whole Covenant," he emphasized instead that sanctions under Article X required the Executive Council's unanimous consent, and that this was "only advice in any case." Even so, the collective-security provision constituted "a very grave and solemn obligation." Whereas Congress was "absolutely free to put its own interpretation upon it in all cases that call for action," Article X amounted to "a moral, not a legal obligation." It was "binding in conscience only, not in law"; but, then, a "moral obligation" was "superior to a legal obligation."[68] None of this brought anyone around. The Republicans subsequently resumed work on amendments and reservations, and the President, having for weeks conferred patiently but to no avail with dozens of senators, came to a momentous decision.

From the standpoint of high drama, no episode in the history of the creation of the League of Nations surpasses Wilson's "swing around the circle" of September 1919. In American political culture during the Second World War it would be called up as epic tragedy, with Wilson, his physical reserves nearly spent, cast as the Promethean statesman besieged on every front, undertaking the final exertion to light the flame with which to bring humanity out of the darkness. At the time, however, those closest to him doubted the wisdom of his decision. The chief potential hazards were twofold. First, Dr. Grayson and Mrs. Wilson worried that such an expedition (as strenuous as any presidential campaign) would wreck his health—and then what would become of the treaty?—and they pleaded with him not to go. Second, although there was divided counsel, at least a few advisers questioned how efficacious it would be politically. For example, Thomas W. Lamont warned that a presidential tour inevitably "would be painted as a campaign against the Senate" and thus would merely intensify partisan opposition.[69] On that count many scholars have pointed out that most senators, because of their six-year terms, were not immediately susceptible to the pressures of public opinion that Wilson hoped to raise.[70]

But Wilson also intended to regain the political advantage simply by reviving his long-neglected role as public educator. As he remarked in San Diego, the journey was confirming for him that the people had not been adequately informed about either the contents of the Covenant or "the real meaning of this great human document."[71] Yet the fact that this was so, and that a tour might have been necessary at this stage, verified what progressive internationalists, in their chagrin, had been telling him throughout the war and the peacemaking. (If he had gone out before his broader political base had begun to erode—the summer or fall of 1918 might have been the more propitious time—Wilson would have served both himself and his cause far better.)

Be that as it may, Wilson's tour remains the single greatest effort of its kind in American history. For three weeks, he traveled by train some ten thousand miles across the Middle and Far West and delivered forty addresses. Their content and quality varied, but he expounded details in a way he had not done before; in their entirety, his speeches are the most cogent exposition of the League that Wilson ever offered, either in private or in public. And, it should be added, they constituted, in most respects, an expanded treatise on progressive internationalism.

For example, for the first time since 1916, Wilson strove to connect an issue of foreign policy with social reform. Starting with his opening speech, in Columbus, Ohio, he often highlighted the International Labor Organization, embodied in Part XIII of the treaty—the "Magna Carta" of working people around the world, he called it. To the applause of Coloradans he declared the issue to be "nothing more or less than the problem of the elevation of humanity." Under the auspices of the League, an International Labour Conference would meet annually to establish standards "which ought to have come long ago" in all member states, including the abolition of child labor, protective legislation for women, a minimum wage, and the eight-hour day. "Such a thing as that," he said in Omaha, "was never dreamed of before."[72]

Of course, the cause of labor was not Wilson's main theme; but he was always careful to stress that Article X was just one of twenty-six. Throughout the tour he placed at least as much emphasis on the Covenant's provisions for the *peaceful* settlement of disputes, for the League would substitute arbitration and discussion for war. "This is the center of the document," he told a crowd in St. Louis.[73] A nine months' delay in hostilities between potential belligerents was built into the system—time enough to work out *most* problems.[74]

In addition to arbitration, Wilson concentrated on disarmament. Sounding much like a card-carrying member of the American Union Against Militarism, he posed two alternatives to his audiences—disarmament through the League or the eventuality of a national security state. Should it stand apart, he argued, the United States would have to "be physically ready for whatever comes." The nation would have to maintain a great army; it would have to burden young men with compulsory military service; it would have to keep munitions and hardware constantly up to date; and this would mean exorbitant, never-ending taxation, not to mention "the building of a military class." In time the United States would become a "militaristic organization of government," replete with "a system of intelligence" and "secret agencies planted everywhere." Moreover, the President would be transformed from "a representative of the civil purposes of this country . . . into a commander in chief, ready to fight the world." All of this, Wilson counseled, was "absolutely antidemocratic in its influence." Thus, to go it alone meant an "absolute reversal of all the ideals of American history!"[75] (It would appear that the first president to warn against the dangers of a "military-industrial complex" was not Dwight D. Eisenhower.)

When he spoke of the most controversial issue of all, Wilson usually gave a progressive construction to Article X, in the context of the League as a whole. In the postwar environment, with the existence of such a forum for airing international opinion, with arbitration procedures established, and with disarmament under way, the employment of collective military force really was not very likely. (And, if a nation violated the arbitration procedures, not even then would the League take military action; the next step would be an economic boycott of that nation.) Yet Article X was the heart of the Covenant. It offered protection to the small states and put restraints upon the great. Without it, he said in Salt Lake City, "we have guaranteed that any imperialistic enterprise may revive, we have guaranteed that there is no barrier to the ambition of nations [including the United States] that have the power to dominate, we have

abdicated the whole position of right and substituted the principle of might."
He could not accept the Lodge proviso to collective security because it
was nothing short of "a rejection of the covenant." Such reservations were
not merely interpretive in nature, he added at Cheyenne, Wyoming; they
would "change the entire meaning of the Treaty and exempt the United
States from all responsibility for the preservation of peace."[76]

In the end, the emotional appeal may have eclipsed the intellectual.
Wilson liked to talk about the children who gathered in every station to
greet him and about the little boy in Billings, Montana, who ran up to
him and pressed a dime into his hand. What would happen to their generation? And everywhere he went there were the mothers who had lost
sons in France and who wept upon his hand, saying, "God bless you, Mr.
President."[77] He brought many in his audiences to tears when he related
these incidents and reminded them of the horrors they had just passed
through and of American ideals and the duty of the United States to see
to it that history did not repeat itself. If the League were crippled by
reservations, he said in St. Louis, he would feel obliged to stand "in mor-
tification and shame" before the boys who went across the sea to fight the
war to end all wars and say, " 'You are betrayed. You fought for something that you did not get.' " And there would come, "sometime, in the
vengeful Providence of God, another struggle in which, not a few hundred
thousand fine men from America will have to die, but as many millions
as are necessary to accomplish the final freedom of the peoples of the
world."[78] Passages like these could not fail to move people, but they could
carry the argument only so far; their impact was probably greater on
Americans in 1944–45.

In the days before the trip was called short, the throngs grew larger
and the cheers more enthusiastic. Wilson seemed to be making headway.
But he was trying singlehandedly to recapture too much lost time and to
redeem too many missed opportunities to expand and solidify a political
foundation. The *New Republic* could have been speaking about the Western tour when, in May, it had lamented that Wilson "preferred the lone
hand to the effort of building up an informed and energetic public opinion in America to back him up."[79] Untoward developments on his right
and his left, some of which he could have altered to his advantage, had
perhaps already rendered him politically impotent.

The unremitting strain of the past year had begun to tell on Wilson. In
city after city, he endured endless parades, stood in open cars for hours at
a time, shook hands with hundreds of well-wishers, and spoke to crowds
as large as 40,000 without the aid of an electronic public address system.
Coughing spells plagued him at night and he sometimes had to sleep
propped up in a chair in order to breathe properly. Headaches so excru-

ciating " 'that he could hardly see' " recurred. In Cheyenne a reporter noticed "a look of almost inexpressible weariness" pass over his countenance when he finished his speech. On September 25, at Pueblo, Colorado, though he managed to give an impassioned performance, he stumbled and needed assistance in mounting the speaker's platform. Early the next morning he awakened nauseated, his cheek muscles twitching uncontrollably. "I have never been in a condition like this," he said to Tumulty. "I just feel as if I am going to pieces." Dr. Grayson, sustained by Mrs. Wilson, told him that he simply could not continue. The President turned away so they would not see the tears streaming down his face.[80]

On October 2, four days after returning to Washington, Wilson suffered a massive stroke that paralyzed the left side of his body. For a week it was not certain whether he would live or die. Not until the end of December could he work at all, and then for only a few minutes a day. Because the First Lady overruled Dr. Grayson's plan to make a full disclosure to the press, the extent of Wilson's incapacity would remain the subject of conjecture and wild rumor—although it soon became common knowledge that the affliction was "cerebral thrombosis." Mrs. Wilson also vetoed Grayson's recommendation that her husband resign from office (even when, for a brief interlude, Wilson himself thought he should step down). Throughout the crisis, she served as the principal arbiter of what and whom the President should, or should not, see. Contrary to a popular invention, however, whereas she was the conduit for political communication to and from the White House, the First Lady did not run the executive branch of the government; for all practical purposes, that task, until the end of Wilson's term, was performed by the various departmental heads.[81]

Public apprehensions about the President's condition subsided somewhat after senators Hitchcock and Albert Fall were granted a carefully orchestrated bedside interview on December 5. "He seemed to me to be in excellent trim, both mentally and physically," Fall (a Republican irreconcilable) told reporters.[82] By February 1920, Wilson had in fact recovered enough to assert himself intermittently. Yet he would continue to fade in and out. The palace guard (Mrs. Wilson, Grayson, and Tumulty) in essence practiced a deception upon the American people. As Ike Hoover, head usher at the White House, wrote in an unpublished draft of his memoirs, "Never was a conspiracy so pointedly or artistically formed."[83]

On November 19, during the initial stage of Wilson's illness, the Senate voted the treaty down, both with and without the fourteen reservations. The irreconcilables joined the Democrats in the first ballot to defeat it fifty-five to thirty-nine. On the motion to approve the treaty unconditionally, the irreconcilables voted with the majority of Republicans, fifty-three nays to thirty-eight ayes. Public opinion, mobilized by the LEP and a handful of weary progressive internationalists, forced the Senate to reconsider four months later. But by then the partisan dimension had become magnified beyond correction; on January 8, 1920, Wilson had declared, in his Jackson Day message to fellow Democrats, that the forthcoming national election should take the form of "a great and solemn referendum" on the League.[84] Then, on March 8, eleven days before the scheduled second vote in the Senate, he issued another highly charged, ill-advised set of instructions, through a letter to Hitchcock, making a strong case for ratification without reservations and also declining to see any difference between "a nullifier and a mild nullifier."[85] This time twenty-one Democrats defied the President and voted for the Lodge version; but again, the treaty failed, forty-nine to thirty-five, or seven votes short of a two-thirds majority.[86]

Even sympathetic scholars locate the primary responsibility for the debacle, one way or another, in the White House sickroom.[87] Not without good reason, most of the literature on the ratification fight focuses on a controversy that persists to this day—that is, on the degree to which Wilson's stroke determined the outcome. Without question, the affliction loosened the President's control over his emotions, exaggerated certain unfortunate personality traits, and impaired his political judgment and ability to lead. Many historians, including the editors of *The Papers of Woodrow Wilson,* concur in the conclusions of the pioneering medical biography by Dr. Edwin Weinstein and the more recent studies by the neurosurgeon Dr. Bert E. Park.[88] While differing on several aspects of the genesis of his infirmity, they agree that Wilson suffered from long-standing hypertension, carotid artery disease, and progressive cerebrovascular disease. Weinstein contends that Wilson actually experienced a series of small, undetected strokes throughout his life, particularly in 1896 and 1906; these strokes, he has observed, coincided with, and adversely affected Wilson's behavior in, earlier battles (such as the one over the location and control of the Graduate College at Princeton, which Wilson lost).[89] Based on an analysis of new documentation released by Grayson's family in 1987 and 1990, Dr. Park has diagnosed Wilson's brief illness during the peace conference as probably a minor stroke; and he is "reasonably certain" that yet another occurred on July 19, 1919. (The presence of incipient "organic brain syndrome," he suggests, would account for Wilson's faltering during the meeting with the Foreign Relations Committee.[90]) The implications of their findings are categorical: a healthy Wilson would have realized that "half a League" was better than none and almost certainly would have found a way to accommodate the reservationists.

Other scholars, such as Alexander and Juliette George, have advanced a psychological interpretation, holding that the President's inflexibility on the League was consistent with his past political behavior. According to the Georges, this was primarily a function of feelings of inadequacy ingrained in him by an overly demanding father. Wilson furthermore found compensation through "his quest for political power"; and it was "his manner of exercising it"—his urge to dominate—that had sometimes brought on failure. (The Georges, too, cite the bitter struggle over the Graduate College as an illustration.) While not utterly dismissing the impact of the massive stroke, they maintain that Wilson "did not *want* to reach a compromise agreement with the Senate. He wanted to defeat the Senate, and especially Lodge."[91]

Between the two, the weight of evidence would now appear to favor Weinstein's and Park's medical explanation over the Georges' Freudian-based analysis.[92] It may be, however, that neither is entirely correct or complete. Wilson's personality and the state of his health are of obvious relevance; but the limited focus of the foregoing debate tends to sidetrack and rob the larger issue of its significance. It essentially ignores the political evolution of the League idea (and Wilson's crucial role in it) and the gulf that had consistently separated progressive and conservative internationalism since the neutrality period. Neither does it take adequate account of the all-out assault on progressive internationalism that the Republican reservations embodied, nor of Lodge's own singlemindedness and inexhaustible contempt for *his* rival.

The Lodge reservations were extremely wide-ranging, and they must be put in the context of the previous years' struggles over domestic as well as foreign policy. Along with other purposes, as we have seen, they were designed to deny the President his crowning glory and thereby to prevent a revival of the "Progressive Democracy" of 1916. (Lloyd George commented in 1922 that Wilson had "voiced the cause of the common people against the propertied classes in America in a most courageous and effective way. . . . That was the real cause of his downfall."[93]) In this respect, some of the reservations frequently dismissed by historians as "unimportant" speak volumes about the Republicans' suspicions of Wilson's intentions and about the differences between progressive and conservative internationalism.

For example, many conservative and reactionary opponents considered the worst part of the treaty to be one which Wilson considered among the best—the International Labor Organization, created in Part XIII, in tandem with a corresponding article in the Covenant. Senator Henry L. Myers of Montana called this section "a nursery for the germination . . . of socialistic and bolshevistic doctrines." Burt Fernald of Maine said the I.L.O. "would pose great dangers to American industry," while Senator Reed said it would place "the destiny of the world" in the hands of organized labor.[94] Their reservation to the provision withheld assent in a manner nearly identical in scope to the one attached to Article X.

Then, too, the reservation to the disarmament article—it read, in part, "the United States reserves the right to increase its armament without the consent of the council"—defied one of the elementary tenets of progressive internationalism and harked back to the politics of preparedness. Reservation XI, on behalf of American businessmen, claimed a special dispensation also—the right to continue trading with a Covenant-breaking state in the event of a League-imposed boycott—which would undercut the effect of economic sanctions. Perhaps the most revealing (surely the most ungracious) reservation was the ninth. Declaring that the United States "shall not [necessarily] be obligated to contribute to any of the expenses of the league," it captured the spirit that suffused the whole.[95]

The concerns that the Republicans raised about collective security and national sovereignty demonstrated a more fundamental difference between two kinds of internationalism. And, to quote Lodge, they devolved upon not only "releas[ing] us from obligations which might not be kept," but also preserving "rights which ought not to be infringed."[96] Here, then, the reservation to Article X cannot be fully understood without reference to Lodge's exemption of the Monroe Doctrine (far more emphatic than the one Wilson had inserted). Lodge repeatedly maintained throughout the debates that he could "never assent to any change" in these two explicit qualifications to Wilson's plan.[97] Together they addressed the corollary to collective security: the hindrance to unilateral action by the United States, which Article X also represented. The *Nation* once summarized this issue with regard to reactionaries like Senator Fall of New Mexico. That irreconcilable opposed the League "because at bottom he desires to see the United States free to make war on Mexico, whenever his constituents demand it." This was typical of much of the opposition, the *Nation* went on to say. "[M]any are against the plan, not because it is not good enough, but because they think it is too good."[98]

Wilson's references to the question of sovereignty in relation to both arbitration and Article X compounded the Republicans' worries thereon. "The only way in which you can have impartial determinations in this world is by consenting to something you do not want to do," he had said, for example, to the people of Billings, Montana. The obvious corollary, here, was to consent not to do something that you *want* to do. There might be times "when we lose in court," he continued, "[and] we will take our medicine."[99] Because the Covenant was plainly open to this interpretation, as Wilson occasionally was frank enough to admit—indeed, had he not also once described the Pan-American Pact to a group of Mexican editors as "an arrangement by which you would be protected from us"?—the Lodge Republicans could easily envision situations in which a Wilsonian on the League's council might cast a vote that would set a precedent of interfering with the prerogative of the United States to take independent coercive action. Lodge was dedicated to eliminating that possibility from the start. Wilson described the situation perfectly in his controversial public letter to Hitchcock, on March 8, 1920: "The imperialist wants no League of Nations, but if . . . there is to be one, he is interested to secure one suited to his own purposes."[100]

As early as June 1919 (long before the stroke), he had told Tumulty that additional reservations "would put the United States as clearly out of the concert of nations as a rejection. We ought either to go in or to stay out."[101] Yet, during the second half of the peace conference, Wilson had shown some willingness to accommodate conservative internationalists like Taft who had urged him to try to appease the Republicans. Those tactics had blown up in his face; they contributed to other unfortunate compromises at Paris, offended most progressive internationalists, and impressed nobody in the Senate (as Villard had predicted). And then, to add insult to injury, there was Taft's letter to Will Hays. Wilson believed, and he was probably correct, that he had gone about as far as he could go in that direction without permanently disabling the League or turning it into a wholly different organization from the one he had worked so hard to create.

In the prevailing circumstances, Wilson's illness may have been the decisive factor behind the treaty's defeat. But it does not necessarily follow (all other factors remaining the same) that the absence of the stroke would have produced a different (or happier) outcome. If Wilson had aimed from the start to create a League to serve conservative ends, then there never would have been any question about reaching some middle ground with the conservatives or ratifying the treaty with the Lodge reservations. But he wanted something much different—which brings us back to his leadership in the American progressive internationalist movement from 1915–16 onward.

In a very real sense, Wilsonian, or progressive, internationalism had begun at home, as part of the gathering momentum of the reform impulse during "the age of socialistic inquiry." The movement had flourished in large measure because, from Greenwich Village to the White House, political and intellectual intercourse between liberals and socialists had flourished—because so many American liberals and socialists had been willing to accept the risk of discovering that each could make a contribution, by their respective lights, to a better society. In both domestic and foreign policy they shared many goals: to see social and economic justice (alternately in the form of "social democracy" or "industrial democracy") done at home and to promote the cause of political democracy around the world; to establish instruments for the peaceful settlement of disputes among nations; and to bring an end to the armaments race, to imperialism, and to the balance of power in international politics. Together, they had helped create the domestic political conditions—particularly from the time of his address to the League to Enforce Peace in May 1916, through the "Peace Without Victory" manifesto of January 1917—that had given Wilson his great opportunity to make the idea of the League and a new world order so potent.

Although he continued to be the chief agent of the movement by virtue of the Fourteen Points and the original Covenant of February 1919— and the preponderance of progressive internationalists fully appreciated these outstanding accomplishments—Wilson had made crucial mistakes long before the treaty was in the Senate. He had neglected to play the steady role of propagandist and educator; he had allowed the coalition of 1916 to unravel, primarily by refusing to acknowledge his administration's culpability in the wartime reaction and to take any serious action to combat it; and, from late 1918 onward, he was either unable or unwilling to accept the implications of "Progressive Democracy" and "war socialism" and take the next logical step beyond them. The result was the erosion of the domestic base and the depletion of the political environment essential both to ratification and to American leadership in a progressive, as opposed to a conservative, league movement. By the summer of 1919, Wilson had barely any strategy at all, except to rely upon his own dwindling rhetorical gifts. "The one secure conclusion that history will draw," the *New Republic* observed, "is that a liberal democrat at large is not an adequate instrument of democracy."[102] Thus had the humane cause he personified fallen into the grip of unalterable circumstance: everything depended virtually on his ability alone to persuade enough conservative Republicans to help him bring forth a new world order alien to their own understanding of how the world worked.

Yet Wilson still possessed the soul of a progressive internationalist. Even as the Senate was about to render its final verdict, he publicly defended Article X as "a renunciation of wrong ambition on the part of powerful nations" and as "the bulwark, the only bulwark, of the rising democracy of the world against the forces of imperialism and reaction."[103] If the stroke (to return momentarily to that issue) made him less amenable to compromise, his stubbornness would seem nonetheless to have been grounded firmly in progressive internationalist principles. For, if he permitted the United States to go in under the Lodge reservations, then the nature of the League would no longer be in doubt. It would become a conservative league, an imperialist league, a Lodgian league—the final triumph of reaction. And perhaps no League at all was better than a League that would, as Wilson wrote to Hitchcock, "venture to take part in reviving the old order."[104] In the end, despite their scorn for him, Wilson, in his way, was as one with the progressive internationalists.

For anyone who was not a Republican, 1920 was an interminably funereal year—a stark and dismal contrast to Eugene Debs' 1912, the "year with supreme possibilities," or 1916, "a year of excitement, more profound than the world has ever known," as the President had once exclaimed to Max Eastman and Lillian Wald. The Democratic party, shorn of the dynamic leadership it had grown accustomed to, seemed to be coming apart at the seams. Labor unrest and racial tensions erupted in violence in major cities throughout the country. The cost of living spiraled, while the price of farm commodities plunged. Attorney General Palmer, in an attempt to advance his presidential ambitions, embarked on a campaign to persecute and deport alleged radicals. Wilson himself became as much the object of contempt as of pity. By the autumn of the year, the question of the League had grown so confused and protracted that few Americans knew for certain whether the Republican party officially stood for membership with reservations or against it no matter what. In November, Warren G. Harding buried Democrat James M. Cox in the biggest electoral landslide theretofore in American history—because, Robert H. Ferrell has proffered, "Wilson was as unpopular as he had once been popular."[105] Not surprisingly, the Republicans interpreted the returns (sixteen million votes to nine million) as the "great and solemn referendum" that the President had wanted for the unreserved Covenant. "So far as the United States is concerned," Lodge could now say, "that League is dead."[106]

Wilson's apotheosis began in some quarters almost immediately after the election. In December 1920, he was awarded the Nobel Peace Prize. But a decade would pass before any of his severest critics among progressive internationalists would gain enough perspective to relieve him of some of the burden he was fated to carry to the grave. Not until 1930 did Walter Lippmann, for instance, feel moved to repent for the comfort he had given the enemy. "If I had it to do all over again," he allowed in the *New Republic,* "I would take the other side"; finally, he admitted, "we supplied the Battalion of Death with too much ammunition."[107] Others could never forgive Wilson, because he had failed at Paris to take his case completely out into the open and call the people to his side, in order to resist the forces arrayed against the creation of an international order based on "'universal principles of right and justice.'" The President "did not fight our fight to the finish," William C. Bullitt would always believe.[108] Even Ray Stannard Baker had preferred that he go down fighting at the peace conference and not yield. "It would be better for him & for the principles—for the world—in the long run," he had written in his diary in April 1919.[109]

Whether or not Baker was right, Wilson's response to the disillusionment of fellow progressive internationalists was a cry of anguish. "What more could I have done?" he asked historian William E. Dodd during a private interview in January 1921. "I had to negotiate with my back to the wall. Men thought I had all power. Would to God I had had such power." His voice choking, he added in reference to erstwhile comrades, "The 'great' people at home wrote and wired every day that they were against me."[110]

Perhaps it was too much to expect him also to acknowledge that mutual transgressions had contributed mightily to their mutual historic failure; presently, as he reviewed the causes behind it, he could think of little else but the "heartless talk and receding ideals of October and November 1919." Since that time, for Wilson—no doubt for all progressive internationalists—it had been "one long wilderness of despair and betrayal, even by good men."[111]

Epilogue
Echoes from Pueblo

The final "irony of fate" occurred in the administration's closing hour. On Inauguration Day, 1921, Wilson accompanied his successor to the Capitol but, owing to his frail condition, did not attend the formal ceremony. Instead, he went to the President's Room, where several last-minute bills awaited his signature and friends and members of his Cabinet gathered to say farewell. Just before noon an official delegation entered to inform him that Congress stood ready to adjourn, unless he had "any further communications." Senator Lodge was the committee's designated spokesman. All voices fell quiet as the two statesmen studied each other, briefly, for the last time. Wilson broke the silence: "I have no further communication to make. I would be glad if you would inform both Houses and thank them for their courtesy." A few minutes later the President, clutching Mrs. Wilson's arm, walked out of the room and into history.[1]

History was not immediately kind. During the 1920s and 1930s, scholarly discourse tended to dwell, not on the League, but rather on the nature of American neutrality and Wilson's decision for war. And, in part as a result of this first cycle of revisionism, millions of Americans came to believe that neutrality had been predisposed, unfairly and regrettably, toward the Allies, and that their own involvement as a belligerent in the Great

War had been an egregious mistake. Criticism of the Treaty of Versailles often went hand-in-hand with such views. Notwithstanding the publication of an admiring eight-volume biography by Ray Stannard Baker and memoirs by Mrs. Wilson and several Cabinet members, evaluations of Wilson's presidency remained comparatively low throughout the interwar years of disillusionment and withdrawal.

But then, after 1941, Wilson's stock began an extraordinary recovery; for a season of three or four years, a new wisdom held that the Second World War might have been averted if only the United States had joined the League of Nations. This conviction was implicit in the best-selling book of the period, Wendell L. Willkie's *One World* (1943), and in Thomas A. Bailey's two widely read volumes on the peace conference and the League. From 1943 to 1945, news magazines and journals of opinion published countless features about "The Unforgettable Figure Who Has Come Back to Haunt Us" and his "epic struggle." Hollywood also contributed to the historiography, in Darryl F. Zanuck's spectacular *Wilson* (1944); the climactic reel of this controversial film focused on the League campaign (including the President's prophesy, at Pueblo, of another terrible war) and struck a strong chord in its audiences. The theme was manifest as well in all manner of wartime propaganda on behalf of the United Nations, and it suffused President Roosevelt's rhetoric on the future of American foreign policy in general.[2] In the summer of 1945, President Harry S Truman stated that the Charter of the United Nations had at last vindicated Wilson.[3] By the late 1960s, many scholars, particularly those of the New Left, were prepared go Truman one better, contending, for instance, that "Wilsonian values" had had "their *complete triumph* in the bipartisan Cold War consensus."[4]

Not long before he died in 1924, Wilson confided to his daughter Margaret, "I think it was best after all that the United States did not join the League of Nations. . . . Now, when the American people join the League it will be because they are convinced it is the right thing to do, and then will be the *only right* time for them to do it."[5] Yet it is somewhat doubtful whether Wilson would have accepted Truman's tribute or the verdict of the New Left. For what is frequently overlooked in such analyses is the fact that Wilson's views on world politics set him at odds, not only with his conservative contemporaries, but also with the so-called realists of the post–World War II era—those diplomatists (and not a few diplomatic historians) who frankly advocated the establishment of a new balance of power, advanced the doctrine of "containment," and helped construct the American military-industrial complex.[6] Believing that differences among nations naturally outweighed common interests, Cold War intellectuals and practitioners, from George F. Kennan to Henry Kissinger, were the first to deny kinship with Wilson. Indeed, Kennan, as both foreign-policy planner and historian of the "realist" school, repeatedly condemned what he called Wilson's "legalistic-moralistic approach" to international relations and its "inordinate preoccupation with arbitration treaties, . . . efforts toward world disarmament . . . and illusions about the possibilities of achieving a peaceful world through international organization." Despite the fact that his conception of international order was never systematically implemented, Wilson was reproached, in the late 1940s and early 1950s, for having failed to provide sound foundations for foreign policy and for having made "violence more enduring, more terrible, and more destructive to political stability than did older motives of national interest."[7]

If Wilson was the father of internationalism, then his children—those who fashioned Cold War *globalism,* as distinct from internationalism—were, in the main, illegitimate. What triumphed in the postwar period was at best a mutant form of Wilson's internationalism, and Wilson almost certainly would have denied paternity. For example, even Franklin Roosevelt's concept of postwar internationalism was based overtly on the idea of the "Four Policemen" and hardly conformed to the Wilsonian version.[8] And even at that, after 1945, American foreign policy makers proceeded to undermine the United Nations Organization. Within less than two years of its creation, Truman's advisers had concluded that faith "in the ability of the United Nations . . . to protect, now, or hereafter, the security of the United States . . . could quite possibly lead to results fatal to that strategy," and that the goal of American policy ought to be "the restoration of [the] balance of power in both Europe and Asia and . . . all action would be viewed in light of that objective."[9] "Perhaps the whole idea of world peace," Kennan himself told the State Department's Policy Planning Staff, "has been a premature, unworkable grandiose form of day-dreaming and . . . we should have held up as our goal: 'Peace if possible, and insofar as it effects our interests.' "[10]

It would be difficult to make the case that the American architects of the Cold War attempted, as a matter of either principle or policy, forthrightly to find and employ Wilsonian instruments for the peaceful settlement of international disputes or to reduce the dangers of massive armaments. Despite charter membership in the U.N., the United States reserved the right to act unilaterally, undertook military interventions at will (frequently in direct violation of the U.N. charter and of international law), and went on to develop a military-industrial complex of staggering dimensions. Then, too, whereas both Republican and Democratic administrations promulgated a series of multilateral security pacts—the North Atlantic Treaty Organization being the most striking example—such engagements represented, not an affirmation of Wilsonian internationalism, but rather a negation; for NATO and the Warsaw Pact constituted opposing systems of collective security—that is, a reformulation of the concept of the balance of power, and one rendered by nuclear weapons far more susceptible to calamity than the balance that had obtained prior to 1914. Taken together, these developments would seem to suggest that Lodgian, not Wilsonian, values had triumphed in the Cold War.

The anti-Wilsonian cast of American foreign policy does not end there. In the 1980s, when smaller countries began to assert themselves, the administration of Ronald Reagan pronounced the United Nations "anti-American," and, in the spirit of the Lodge reservations, even threatened to withhold financial support and hinted about the possibility of American withdrawal from the organization. In 1984, Jeane Kirkpatrick, the American Ambassador to the United Nations, affirmed, "Unilateral compliance with the Charter's principles of non-intervention and non-use of force may make sense in some specific, isolated instance, but are hardly a sound basis for either U.S. policy or for international peace and stability."[11] Moreover, as American rhetoric rose to a new fever pitch amidst a revival of the Cold War, leading members of the Reagan administration openly discussed the feasibility and survivability of "limited" nuclear war. For them, Wilson's historical legacy lay as cold as the granite in which his remains are entombed in the National Cathedral in Washington.

In retrospect, it would seem that a reconsideration of Wilson and his work might be in the offing, at least in part because American foreign policy makers had appeared, by the mid-1980s, to have lost a sense of proportion. It is a significant fact that Kennan, having previously abjured the excesses of Cold War containment policy, had already begun to call for the dismantling of the vast military establishments of the great powers. Moved by his perception of impending apocalyptic catastrophe (acutely similar to kind of compulsion that had animated Wilson), he began in the early 1980s to employ a new and distinctly Wilsonian idiom in his writings and speeches. Although he had once used Wilson as a negative point of departure in advancing his strategies for American foreign policy, Kennan now argued: "War itself, as a means of settling disputes among the great industrial powers, will have to be in some way ruled out"; that war was "simply no longer a rational means of affecting the behavior of other governments."[12] By 1989, he was prepared "to correct or modify" many of the impressions he had had about Wilson during an earlier stage. He now characterized Wilson "as ahead of any other statesman of his time," as a man "of broad and acute sensitivities" who "did not live long enough to know what great and commanding relevance many of his ideas would acquire before the century was out."[13]

Mikhail Gorbachev, too, made allusions to Wilson as part of his manifold exertions to bring an end to the Cold War. "Our ideal is a world community of states with political systems and foreign policies based on law," he declared in his celebrated address to the United Nations on December 7, 1988. "As awareness of our common fate grows, every nation would be genuinely interested in confining itself within the limits of international law." Gorbachev went on to exhort his audience about the need for the "demilitarization of international relations" and for "consistent movement" toward disarmament—to "make the world a safer place for all of us."[14] "Perhaps not since Woodrow Wilson presented his Fourteen Points in 1918," observed the *New York Times,* had any world statesman "demonstrated the vision Mikhail Gorbachev displayed yesterday at the United Nations."[15]

The questions that Wilson asked and the solutions that he proposed continued to command attention as the Cold War came to an end. In the early 1990s the United Nations began to overcome the paralysis that had afflicted it since its inception, and a growing recognition began to take hold that any number of critical problems besetting all the nations of the world (including those concerning the global environment) could not be solved except through the concerted action of the international community.[16] And, since President George Bush's address of September 11, 1990, on the crisis in the Persian Gulf, references to the establishment of a "new world order" have become commonplace.[17] (It remains to be seen, however, whether that coinage was meant as anything more than rhetorical effusion to accompany, as it did, a highly selective—in certain ways, distorted—application of but a single internationalist principle; and whether those who momentarily agitated for collective security will work as assiduously as did the "wise men" of the Cold War to put the Wilsonian genie back into the bottle, once it served their transitory purpose.)

If, at a time when the entire system of international relations has reached a state of maximum fluidity, and if, as Senator Daniel Patrick Moynihan has suggested in his book, *On the Law of Nations,* the "Wilsonian project" is still before us, then it is important to remember progressive internationalism for what it was and the good will and humanity with which it was imbued. "We have accepted the truth," Wilson said at Pueblo, Colorado, "and we are going to be led by it, and it is going to lead us, and, through us, the world, out into pastures of quietness and peace such as the world never dreamed of before." This was the conclusion to the final speech of his public career, in which he spoke about endeavors to meet the grievances of labor and the dangers of great standing armies, about the imperative of a massive reduction of armaments and the elimination of their production for profit, about the virtues of refraining from war until every other possible means has been exhausted, and about an experimental approach to international security that would impose on the great powers constraints as well as responsibilities. To his credit, he did not lay claim to ultimate wisdom; for, while assuming that Americans would rise and extend their hand to the enterprise, he also felt compelled to say, "I do not know any *absolute* guarantee against the errors of human judgment or the violence of human passion."[18]

When Wilson told Lodge that he had "no further communication to make," he could not have been more wrong. Upon his retirement from the presidency, his fellow covenanter, Jan Christiaan Smuts, credited Wilson with having actuated "one of the great creative documents in human history" and predicted that "Americans of the future will yet proudly and gratefully rank him with Washington and Lincoln, and his fame will have a more universal significance than theirs."[19] By the last decade of the twentieth century Americans had yet to elevate him to a station comparable to Washington's and Lincoln's, and it seemed unlikely that they would. Nonetheless, his tragic decline and failure notwithstanding, Woodrow Wilson's significance continues to inhere in his inclusive comprehension of the unfolding epoch, in his eloquence, and in the enduring relevance of his vision. In this he remains unique among presidents of the American Century.

Abbreviations and Symbols

Collections and Archives

DLC	Library of Congress
DNA	National Archives
FFM-Ar	French Foreign Ministry Archives
FO	British Foreign Office
IWC	Imperial War Council
HP, CtY	The Papers of Edward M. House, Yale University Library
NjP	Princeton University Library
PRO	Public Record Office
RSB, DLC	Ray Stannard Baker Collection, Library of Congress
SDR	State Department Records
WP, DLC	Woodrow Wilson Papers, Library of Congress

Works

IPCH	*The Intimate Papers of Colonel House*
FR-US	*Papers Relating to the Foreign Relations of the United States*

FR-LP   *Papers Relating to the Foreign Relations of the United States, The Lansing Papers*

FR-PPC   *Papers Relating to the Foreign Relations of the United States, Paris Peace Conference*

FR-WWS   *Papers Relating to the Foreign Relations of the United States, World War Series*

LTR   *The Letters of Theodore Roosevelt*

PWW   *The Papers of Woodrow Wilson*

WWLL   *Woodrow Wilson: Life and Letters*

Notes

This book, while building on and accounting for the capacious secondary literature on the subject, is based on research in both American and European manuscript sources and on a variety of newspapers and journals of the 1910s, including the socialist press (which, in its day, was read on a regular basis by perhaps as many as three million Americans). The reader will notice that there is scarcely a footnote without a citation to *The Papers of Woodrow Wilson (PWW)*. This monumental sixty-eight-volume series has made available to scholars tens of thousands of documents from hundreds of collections around the world. Hence, in most cases, I have made a practice of citing the more accessible *PWW*, rather than the original manuscript source. The *PWW* does not print everything, however. There are sequences of footnotes, for example, in which Colonel House's or Robert Cecil's diaries are cited from an entry published in the *PWW*, but the next footnote may cite the House diary at Yale University, or the Cecil diary at the Public Record Office in London; in these instances, I have referred to the original because it is not available in any published form. I draw attention to this inconsistency for the benefit of those who may be unfamiliar with the Wilson Papers project.

Notes for Chapter 1

1. Woodrow Wilson, "Abraham Lincoln: 'Man of the People,'" Feb. 12, 1909, in Arthur S. Link, David W. Hirst, John E. Little, Manfred F. Boemeke, Denise Thompson,

and Fredrick Aandahl (eds.), *The Papers of Woodrow Wilson,* 67 vols. to date (Princeton, 1966), XIX, 33, hereinafter cited as *PWW.*

2. John M. Mulder, *Woodrow Wilson: The Years of Preparation* (Princeton, 1978), 3–28; see also Ray Stannard Baker, *Woodrow Wilson, Life and Letters,* 8 vols. (Garden City, N.Y., 1927–1939), I, 1–27, and 49–55 (hereinafter cited as *WWLL*); and George C. Osborn, *Woodrow Wilson: The Early Years* (Baton Rouge, 1968), 13–17.

3. "An Address on Robert E. Lee," ca. Jan 19, 1909, *PWW,* XVIII, 635.

4. *Ibid.,* 631.

5. Speech at Mansion House, London, Dec. 28, 1918, *PWW,* LIII, 534.

6. Mulder, *Years of Preparation,* xiii. See also Link, "Woodrow Wilson and His Presbyterian Inheritance," in *The Higher Realism of Woodrow Wilson, and Other Essays* (Nashville, 1971), 3–20. For Wilson's testimony to his father's influence on him, see *PWW,* XXX, 74–75 and 103–108, and *ibid.,* XXXIII, 49–50.

7. Mulder, *Years of Preparation,* 37 and 271.

8. Journal entry, May 3, 1879, *PWW,* I, 639 (Wilson's emphasis); see also "The Ideal Statesman," Jan. 30, 1877, *ibid.,* 245.

9. Mulder, *Years of Preparation,* xiii and 7–8; see also H. Richard Niebuhr, "The Idea of the Covenant and American Democracy," *Church History,* XXIII (1954), 126–135.

10. Wilson to Ellen Louise Axson, Oct. 30, 1883, *PWW,* II, 500.

11. Wilson to Axson, Feb. 2 and July 15, 1884, *ibid.,* III, 3 and 248, respectively.

12. "The Royal United Kingdom Yacht Club," ca. July 1, 1874, *ibid.,* I, 54–56.

13. Constitution of the Liberal Debating Club, ca. Feb. 1–March 15, 1877, *ibid.,* 245.

14. See "A New Constitution for the Jefferson Society," Dec. 4, 1880, *ibid.,* 689–699; "Draft of a Constitution for a 'Georgia House of Commons,'" ca. Jan. 11, 1883, *ibid.,* II, 288–289; Wilson to Axson, Dec. 15, 1884, *ibid.,* III, 544, n. 3; "A Constitution for the Wesleyan House of Commons," ca. Jan. 5, 1889, *ibid.,* VI, 39–46; see also Mulder, *Years of Preparation,* 82–83 and 102.

15. *Congressional Government* is printed in its entirety in *PWW,* IV, 13–179; for analyses, see Arthur S. Link, *Wilson: The Road to the White House* (Princeton, 1947), 12–19; and Henry W. Bragdon, *Woodrow Wilson: The Academic Years* (Cambridge, Mass., 1967), 124–140. For Wilson's appreciation of Bagehot, see his lectures, "A Literary Politician," July 20, 1889, *PWW,* VI, 335–354; and "Walter Bagehot—A Lecture," Feb. 24, 1898, *ibid.,* X, 423–442.

16. *Congressional Government,* printed in *PWW,* IV, 39, 130, and 133 (emphasis added).

17. "The Modern Democratic State," ca. Dec. 1–20, 1885, *ibid.,* V, 61–92; see also "Editorial Note," 54–58.

18. *Ibid.,* 92, 59, 84.

19. *Ibid.,* 92.

20. *Ibid.,* 63, 71–75.

21. See, for instance, *The State* (1889), his widely used text on comparative government (portions printed in *PWW,* VI, 244–311), 261.

22. "The Modern Democratic State," *PWW,* V, 90. Wilson struck very similar themes in "The Study of Administration," *Political Science Quarterly* (July 1887), printed in *PWW,* V, 359–380; a review of James Bryce's *American Commonwealth,* Jan. 31, 1889, *ibid.,* VI, 75–76; "The Nature of Democracy in the United States," May 10–16, 1889, *ibid.,* 221–239; "Political Sovereignty," Nov. 9, 1891, *ibid.,* VII, 325–341; "Democracy," c. Dec. 5, 1891, *ibid.,* 345–369; "The True American Spirit," Oct. 27, 1892, *ibid.,* VIII, 37–40; "Government Under the Constitution," ca., June 26, 1893, *ibid.,* 254–270; "University Training and Citizenship," ca. June 20, 1894, *ibid.,* 587–596; and notes for a series of lectures at Johns Hopkins from 1891 to 1894, *ibid.,* VII, 114–158.

23. Important exceptions are Bragdon, *Woodrow Wilson: The Academic Years,* (Cam-

bridge, Mass., 1967), 114–116, 177–178, and 183–184; John Milton Cooper, Jr., *The Warrior and the Priest: Woodrow Wilson and Theodore Roosevelt* (Cambridge, Mass., 1983), 209–219; and Niels A. Thorsen, *The Political Thought of Woodrow Wilson, 1875–1910* (Princeton, N.J., 1988).

24. "Socialism and Democracy," ca. Aug. 22, 1887, *PWW*, V, 559–563.

25. *Ibid.*, 561 (emphasis added).

26. *Ibid.*, 562.

27. *Ibid.*, 561–62.

28. *The State,* printed in *PWW*, VI, 304.

29. *Ibid.*, 303–304 (Wilson's emphasis).

30. *Ibid.*, 307–308.

31. See Wilson's notes for the course, ca. January 1891, in the Woodrow Wilson Papers, Library of Congress (hereinafter cited as WP, DLC). Topics covered under the general heading of "Socialism" included: "Its Nature, Foundations, Opportunities, Tendencies, and Status"; "Theoretical Basis of Socialism"; "Saint-Simon: Bazard"; and "Views of Rodbertus, Marx, and Lassalle Constrasted."

32. "Edmund Burke: The Man and His Times," ca. Aug. 31, 1893, *PWW*, VIII, 318–343 (341). For the provenance of this lecture, see Editorial Note in *ibid.*, pp. 313–318; and Mulder, *Years of Preparation,* 126–129. See also "Edmund Burke: A Lecture," Feb. 23, 1898, *PWW*, X, 408–428.

33. "Edmund Burke: The Man and His Times," *PWW*, VIII, 343.

34. See two news reports of an address at Pittsburgh, April 17, 1910, *ibid.*, XX, 363–368; the *Pittsburgh Dispatch* said of Wilson's address, "A more unsparing denunciation of the churches of the country could scarcely have come from the lips of the most radical Socialist leader" (p. 366).

35. See Wilson's extensive notes for lectures, July 2–10, 1894, *PWW*, VIII, 597–599; and for lectures on public law, ca. Sept. 22, 1894–Jan. 20, 1895, *ibid.*, IX, 5–106.

36. "Democracy," ca. Dec. 5, 1891, *ibid.*, VII, 348.

37. The information on these lectures comes from the detailed set of notes taken by Andrew Clarke Imbrie (Princeton, Class of 1895), who took the course in 1894. Imbrie's papers are in the Manuscript Division at the Princeton University Library (hereinafter cited as NjP). See also Wilson's notes for the course, March 8, 1892–May 1, 1894, and notes for a classroom lecture, March 8, 1892, in *PWW*, VII, 453–457.

38. Imbrie notes, Lecture One, March 5, 1894, Imbrie Papers.

39. *Ibid.*, Lecture Two, March 6, 1894. For Wilson's lectures on Roman law, see the notes from his course on the History of Law (recast and offered again in 1894 and 1895), in which he traced the history of Roman law in detail (*PWW*, IX, 50–93).

40. Imbrie notes, Lecture Four, March 19, 1894, Imbrie Papers.

41. *Ibid.*, Lecture Two, March 6, 1894; Lecture Seven, April 2; and Lecture Eight, April 3, 1894, Imbrie Papers.

42. *Ibid.*, Lecture Two.

43. As Wilson had put it in *The State* (*PWW*, VI, 261) and in "The Modern Democratic State" (*ibid.*, V, 90).

44. "What Ought We to Do?" ca. August 1, 1898, *PWW*, X, 574; see also "The Ideals of America," Dec. 26, 1901, *ibid.*, XII, 208–227; and "The Statesmanship of Letters," Nov. 5, 1903, *ibid.*, XV, 33–46.

45. *A History of the American People,* 5 vols. (New York, 1902), IV, 122.

46. Important studies on American imperialism include William Appleman Williams' seminal *Tragedy of American Diplomacy* (New York, 1959); Walter La Feber, *The New Empire: An Interpretation of American Expansion* (New York, 1963); Robert L. Beisner, *From the Old Diplomacy to the New, 1865–1900* (Arlington Heights, Mich., 1975), and

Twelve Against Empire: The Anti-imperialists, 1898–1900 (New York, 1969); Ernest R. May, *Imperial Democracy* (Boston, 1961); and Margaret Leech, *In the Days of McKinley* (New York, 1959). The connection between progressivism and imperialism was first explored by William E. Leuchtenburg in a famous article, "Progressivism and Imperialism: The Progressive Movement and American Foreign Policy, 1898–1916," *Mississippi Valley Historical Review,* XXXIX (December 1952), 483–504. Two of the best of many responses to Leuchtenburg are John Milton Cooper, Jr., "Progressivism and American Policy: A Reconsideration," *Mid-America,* LI (October 1969), 260–277; and Gerald E. Markowitz, "Progressivism and Imperialism: A Return to First Principles," *The Historian,* XXXVII (February 1975), 257–275. See also Emily Rosenberg, *Spreading the American Dream* (New York, 1982); and Michael H. Hunt, *Ideology and U.S. Foreign Policy* (New Haven, Conn., 1987).

47. Quoted in Nick Salvatore, *Eugene V. Debs, Citizen and Socialist* (Urbana, Ill., 1982), 107, 227.

48. The platform stated: "We assert that no nation can long endure half republic and half empire, and we warn the American people that imperialism abroad will lead quickly and inevitably to despotism at home." *National Party Platforms,* compiled by Kirk H. Porter and Donald Bruce Johnson (Urbana, Ill., 1961), 112.

49. Report of a speech on patriotism, Waterbury, Conn., Dec. 14, 1899, *PWW,* XI, 298.

50. "Democracy and Efficiency" (published in the *Atlantic Monthly,* LXXXVII, March 1901, pp. 289–299), printed in *PWW,* XII, 11–19.

51. News report of an address on patriotism in Syracuse, Feb. 17, 1904, *PWW,* XV, 172.

52. "What Ought We to Do?" *ibid.,* X, 576.

53. Wilson and Turner had been good friends since 1889, when they had met at Johns Hopkins and roomed in the same boardinghouse. Turner had sought Wilson's opinion of a draft of "The Significance of the Frontier upon American History" (1893) during the latter's visit to Madison, Wisconsin, in December 1892. (See "The Course of American History," May 17, 1895, *ibid.* IX, 257–274, n. 3.)

54. News report of an address in Monclair, N.J., Jan. 28, 1904, *ibid.,* XV, 143.

55. *Ibid.,* XII, 18.

56. Address in Montclair, N.J., Jan. 28, 1904, *ibid.,* XV, 143; news report of an address on patriotism in Syracuse, Feb. 17, 1904, *ibid.,* 171; address to the Lotus Club of New York, Feb. 3, 1906, *ibid.,* XVI, 297–298.

57. "Democracy and Efficiency," *ibid.,* XII, 11, 18.

58. "The Statesmanship of Letters," Nov. 5, 1903, *ibid.,* XV, 41.

59. Speech to the Sons of St. Patrick, March 17, 1909, *ibid.,* XXIV, 107.

60. Campaign address, May 26, 1912, *ibid.,* XXIV, 443.

61. The definitive studies are Calvin Davis, *The First Hague Peace Conference* (Ithaca, N.Y., 1962), and *The Second Hague Peace Conference: American Diplomacy and International Organization, 1899–1914* (Durham, N.C., 1975). Among the best surveys of the period under discussion is David S. Patterson, *Toward a Warless World: The Travail of the American Peace Movement, 1887–1914* (Bloomington, Ind., 1976). For a more extensive listing, see notes to Chapter 4.

62. Patterson, *Toward a Warless World,* 137–147, 166–170, and 181–204.

63. Most studies on the subject stress this quality of the movement in one way or another. See, in particular, Patterson, *Toward a Warless World,* 48–91, 130–132; and C. Roland Marchand, *The American Peace Movement and Social Reform* (Princeton, 1972), *passim.*

64. "The Study of Administration," *PWW,* V, 380, originally published in *Political Science Quarterly,* II (July 1887), 197–222.

65. See Robert Erskine Ely to Wilson, March 25, 1907, *PWW*, XVII, 92–93, n. 2; Benjamin Trueblood to Wilson, Sept. 9, 1908, *ibid.*, XVIII, 419–420; Wilson to Melancthon W. Jacobus, Feb. 11, 1910, *ibid.*, XX, 119–120; Andrew Carnegie to Wilson, March 21, 1911, *ibid.*, XXII, 514–515; and Wilson to Joseph Hodges Choate, Nov. 1, 1911, *ibid.*, XXIII, 520.

66. Henry Kissinger, *The White House Years* (Boston, 1979), 54.

67. Address of Jan. 28, 1838, in Roy P. Basler (ed.), *The Collected Works of Abraham Lincoln*, 8 vols. (New Brunswick, N.J., 1953), I, 114.

68. Confidential Journal, Dec. 28, 1889, *PWW*, VI, 463 (Wilson's emphasis).

69. All of these essays are published in *PWW*..

70. "Leaders of Men," June 17, 1890, *ibid.*, VI, 664.

71. Wilson to Ellen Louise Axson, Feb. 24, 1885, *ibid.*, IV, 287.

72. See "Leaderless Government," ca. Aug. 5, 1897, and "The Making of a Nation," ca. April 15, 1897, *ibid.* X, 288–304 and 217–236, respectively; see also "The Modern Democratic State," *ibid.*, V, 86–87; and "The Real Idea of Democracy," Aug. 31, 1901, *ibid.*, XII, 178–179.

73. Preface to the fifteenth edition of *Congressional Government*, Aug. 15, 1900, *ibid.*, XI, 570.

74. *Constitutional Government in the United States*, printed in *ibid.*, XVIII, 108.

75. Commemorative Address at the First Presbyterian Church of Schenectady, New York, Sept. 29, 1904, *ibid.*, XV, 497.

76. Sept. 9, 1901, *ibid.*, XII, 184.

Notes for Chapter 2

1. Quoted in Nick Salvatore, *Eugene V. Debs*, 264.

2. For the breakup of the Republican party, see George E. Mowry, *Theodore Roosevelt and the Progressive Movement* (Madison, Wisc., 1946); William H. Harbaugh, *Power and Responsibility: The Life and Times of Theodore Roosevelt* (New York, 1961), 355–409; Paolo E. Coletta, *The Presidency of William Howard Taft* (Lawrence, Kansas, 1973), 88–255; John Allen Gable, *The Bull Moose Years: Theodore Roosevelt and the Progressive Party* (Port Washington, N.Y., 1978), 3–130; and John Milton Cooper, Jr., *The Warrior and the Priest: Woodrow Wilson and Theodore Roosevelt* (Cambridge, Mass., 1983), 143–163.

3. For the Progressive party convention, see Mowry, *Theodore Roosevelt and the Progressive Movement*, 256–283; and Gable, *Bull Moose Years*, 75–110.

4. For Wilson's governorship, see James Kerney, *The Political Education of Woodrow Wilson* (New York, 1926); Baker, *WWLL*, III; and Link, *Road to the White House*, 140–174 and 205–307.

5. The definitive study of the Baltimore convention remains Link, *Road to the White House*, 348–465.

6. Cooper, *The Warrior and the Priest*, 141.

7. For examinations of the New Nationalism, see *ibid.*, 143–163; Mowry, *Theodore Roosevelt and the Progressive Movement*, 256–283; Gable, *Bull Moose Years*, 130–174.

8. A campaign address at Buffalo, Sept. 2, 1912, *PWW*, XXV, 25.

9. For the development of Wilson's campaign, see Link, *Road to the White House*, 467–510.

10. See addresses at Sea Girt, N.J., Aug. 7, 1912, *PWW*, XXV, 8–11, and at Scranton, Pa., Sept. 23, 1912, *ibid.*, 222. The most recent, and one of the best, analyses of New Nationalism and the New Freedom is Cooper, *Warrior and the Priest*, 164–221.

11. Wilson's Inaugural Address, Mar. 4, 1913, *PWW*, XXVII, 148–152.

12. For the growth of the Socialist Party of America, see Ira Kipnis, *The American Socialist Movement, 1897–1912* (New York, 1952); David A. Shannon, *The Socialist Party of America* (New York, 1955); James A. Weinstein, *The Decline of Socialism in America* (New York, 1967; reprinted 1984). In addition to Salvatore, the principal works on Debs are Ray Ginger, *The Bending Cross: A Biography of Eugene Victor Debs* (New Brunswick, N.J., 1949) and H. Wayne Morgan, *Eugene V. Debs, Socialist for President* (Syracuse, N.Y., 1962).

13. For a contemporary analysis, see reports in the *Appeal to Reason,* Nov. 16 and Dec. 21, 1912. See also Kipnis, *American Socialist Movement,* 362; Salvatore, *Debs,* 220–221; Weinstein, *Decline of Socialism,* 102–103; John P. Diggins, *The American Left in the Twentieth Century* (New York, 1973), p. 60.

14. Of the countless socialist dailies, the *Milwaukee Leader* and the New York *Call* each boasted a circulation of 35,000; at one time, eleven socialist weeklies were published in Oklahoma. See Weinstein, *Decline of Socialism,* 90.

15. See Turner's "The Significance of History" (1891), in Fritz Stern (ed.), *The Varieties of History: From Voltaire to the Present* (New York, 1957), 197–208.

16. See Kipnis, *American Socialist Movement,* 116–122, 216, and 220–221; and Weinstein, *Decline of Socialism in America,* 4–7.

17. Debs, quoted in Weinstein, *Decline of Socialism,* p. 11.

18. Hillquit, quoted in Kipnis, *American Socialist Movement,* 220. For critical comment on the center-right-wing approach, see *ibid.,* 427–429; and Salvatore, *Debs,* 265, 268–269.

19. See Salvatore, *Debs,* 60–61, 148–154, 186–187, and 343–344; and Weinstein, *Decline of American Socialism,* 12.

20. See Morgan, *Debs,* 129–138 and 141–142; and Svend Petersen, *A Statistical History of American Presidential Elections* (Westport, Conn., 1981), 78–79. The most thorough analysis is Jun Furuya, "The Socialist Party of America and Eugene V. Debs' Campaign in the 1912 Election," *The Hokkaido Law Review,* XXVIII and XXIX, No. 4 and No. 1 (1978), 1–50.

21. Salons and seminars, in which leading socialists and liberals exchanged ideas, thrived. At such gatherings, particularly in Greenwich Village, one was likely to encounter such luminaries as Morris Hillquit, Lincoln Steffens, Victor Berger, Charles Beard, Finley Peter Dunne, Norman Hapgood, Helen Keller, Margaret Sanger, John Reed, and Hamilton Holt. (See Shannon, *Socialist Party of America,* 55–56; and Weinstein, *Decline of Socialism,* 80–84.) Walter Lippmann, in explaining the quality of the *New Republic*'s liberalism, wrote to Van Wyck Brooks in early 1914: "We have no party axe or propaganda to grind. We shall be socialistic in direction, but not in method, or phrase or allegiance." Quoted in Ronald Steel, *Walter Lippmann and the American Century* (Boston, 1980), 62.

22. See, for instance, a news report of remarks to the New Jersey Consumers' League in Trenton, Feb. 25, 1911, *PWW,* XXII, 452–453; and Max Eastman, *Enjoyment of Living* (New York, 1948), 385–387. (Wilson gave Eastman permission to quote in publicity material a compliment he had paid to the latter's public lectures in 1912; according to Eastman, it "yielded me income in future years as though he had handed me a jewel.")

23. News report of an address in Buffalo, April 10, 1912, *PWW,* XXIV, 313. For other examples, see address at the University of North Carolina, May 30, 1911, *ibid.,* XXIII, 105 and 107; to the South Carolina Press Association, June 2, 1911, *ibid.,* 116; interview in the New York *World,* Dec. 24, 1911, printed in *ibid.,* 609; address at Savannah, April 20, 1912, *ibid.,* XXIV, 351; and in Boston, April 27, 1912, *ibid.,* 366.

24. New York *Call,* September 10, 1912, quoted in Furuya, "The Socialist Party and Debs' Campaign," 37.

25. Allan L. Benson, "Our New President," *The Masses,* IV, no. 7 (May 1913), 3.

26. For a convenient summary of these issues, see Coletta, *Taft,* 143–146; and John P. Campbell, "Taft, Roosevelt, and the Arbitration Treaties of 1911," *Journal of American History,* LIII, 2 (September 1966), 279–298.

27. See Kipnis, *The American Socialist Movement,* 95–96. In 1900, Debs' platform contained one phrase on foreign policy—calling for "the abolition of war and the introduction of international arbitration"—but said nothing on the subject in 1912 (Porter and Johnson, *National Party Platforms,* 128 and 188–191).

28. *National Party Platforms,* 180, 181, and 174.

29. Report of an address to the Universal Peace Union, Feb. 9, 1912, *PWW,* XXIV, 182.

30. A Message to Democratic Rallies, Nov. 2, 1912, *ibid.,* XXV, 502–503.

31. See, for example, Wilson's speech accepting the Democratic presidential nomination, Aug. 7, 1912, *ibid.,* 16; an address to farmers in New Jersey, Aug. 15, 1912, *ibid.,* 38; and an address to the Commercial Club of Omaha, Oct. 5, 1912, *ibid.,* 341, from which the quotation is taken.

32. Wilson to E. G. Conklin, quoted in Baker, *WWLL,* IV, 55.

33. On these points, see also Link, *Woodrow Wilson: Revolution, War, and Peace* (Arlington Heights, Ill., 1979), 1–4; and John Milton Cooper, Jr., " 'An Irony of Fate': Woodrow Wilson's Pre–World War I Diplomacy," *Diplomatic History,* III (Fall 1979), 425–438.

34. For obvious cues to his modus operandus as President, see Wilson's *Constitutional Government in the United States* (1908), printed in *PWW,* XVII, 20.

35. Link, *Woodrow Wilson,* 13–15.

36. Fourth of July address, July 4, 1914, *ibid.,* XXX, 255.

37. The principal published source remains Charles Seymour (ed.), *The Intimate Papers of Colonel House,* 4 vols. (Boston, 1926–28), hereinafter cited as *IPCH;* for a succinct analysis see Charles E. Neu, "Woodrow Wilson and Colonel House: The Early Years, 1911–1915," in Cooper and Neu (eds.), *The Wilson Era, Essays in Honor of Arthur S. Link* (Arlington Heights, Mich., 1991), 248–78. See also Rupert Norval Richardson, *Colonel Edward M. House: The Texas Years, 1858–1912* (Abilene, Tex., 1964).

38. Quoted in *IPCH,* I, 114.

39. House did not publicly acknowledge authorship until the publication of *IPCH,* I (152–158), in 1926. See also Billie Barnes Jensen, "Philip Dru, The Blueprint of a Presidential Adviser," *American Studies* (Spring 1971), 49–58; and Matthew Josephson, *The President Makers* (New York, 1940, 1964 ed.), 387–391 and 466–467.

40. Quoted in Link, *Wilson: The New Freedom, 1913–1914* (Princeton, N.J., 1956), 94.

41. The definitive work is Paolo E. Coletta, *William Jennings Bryan,* 3 vols. (Lincoln, Nebr., 1964–69). For commentary on the Wilson–Bryan relationship see Vol. II, pp. 86–95 and 356–359; see also Kendrick A. Clements, *William Jennings Bryan, Missionary Isolationist* (Knoxville, Tenn., 1983).

42. Quoted in Coletta, *Bryan,* II, 358.

43. For details see *ibid.,* 239–249; Coletta, "William Jennings Bryan's Plans for World Peace," *Nebraska History,* 58, (Summer 1977), 193–217; Merle E. Curti, "Bryan and World Peace," *Smith College Studies in History,* XVI (April–July 1931), 113–149.

44. For a survey of responses, see Link, *New Freedom,* 153–156; Coletta, *Bryan,* II, 243–244.

45. *New York Times,* Sept. 17 and 20, Oct. 4, 1914; the London *Times,* Sept. 28, 1914; Spring Rice to Bryan, Oct. 26, 1914, quoted in Coletta, *Bryan,* II, 246–247.

46. The quotation is from Link, *New Freedom,* 283.

47. For example, see Wilson to William J. Stone (chairman of the Senate Foreign Relations Committee), Aug. 13, 1914, *PWW,* XXX, 378; and Sept. 21, 1914, *ibid.,* XXXI, 64; see also press conferences, April 24 and 28, 1913, *ibid.,* XXVIII, 352–353 and 359–360,

respectively, and the diary of Josephus Daniels (Secretary of the Navy), April 8 and 15, 1913, Daniels Papers, Library of Congress.

48. See Wilson's speech at Indianapolis, *New York Times*, Sept. 5, 1919; see also memorandum by Baker of a conversation with Wilson, May 12, 1916, *PWW*, XXXVII, 33.

49. See House diary, Dec. 2 and 12, 1913, *PWW*, XXIX, 12–13 and 33, respectively.

50. House to Wilson, May 29, 1914, *ibid.*, XXX, 109.

51. House to Wilson, June 3, 1914, *ibid.*, 139–140; House diary, June 1, 1914, House Papers, Yale University Library (hereinafter cited as HP, CtY).

52. House diary, June 29, 1914, HP, CtY; House to Wilson, June 17 and 26, July 3, 1914, *PWW*, XXX, 189–190, 214–215, and 247–248, respectively; and House to Wilhelm II, July 8, 1914, printed as "Enclosure with House to Wilson," July 9, 1914, *ibid.*, 266. See also, Link, *New Freedom*, 314–318.

53. House diary, June 21, 1914, HP, CtY; House to Wilson, June 26, 1914, in WP, DLC.

54. House to Wilson, July 4, 1914, *PWW*, XXX, 255–256.

55. House to Wilson, June 24, 1914, *ibid.*, 215; see also Wilson to House, June 16 and 24, July 9, 1914, *ibid.*, 187, 214, and 264, respectively; and House diary, July 3, 1914, HP, CtY.

56. For details see Link, *New Freedom*, 177–197 and 199–240.

57. The most authoritative account of the passage of the Clayton Act and the Federal Trade Commission Act is in *ibid.*, 417–444.

58. Several articles have appeared that deal with each of these issues—for instance, Christine A. Lunardini and Thomas J. Knock, "Woodrow Wilson and Woman Suffrage: A New Look," *Political Science Quarterly*, XCV (Winter 1980–81), 655–671; and Nancy J. Weiss, "The Negro and the New Freedom: Fighting Wilsonian Segregation," *ibid.*, LXXXIV (March 1969), 61–79. For a general overview of all of them, see Link, *New Freedom*, 241–264.

59. See Link, *New Freedom*, 255, 269–274, and 427–432.

60. Major studies include Howard Cline, *The United States and Mexico* (Cambridge, Mass., 1953; rev. ed., New York, 1963); Clarence Clendenen, *The United States and Pancho Villa: A Study in Unconventional Diplomacy* (Ithaca, N.Y., 1961); Peter Calvert, *The Mexican Revolution, 1910–1914: The Diplomacy of Anglo-American Conflict* (Cambridge, England, 1968); P. Edward Haley, *Revolution and Intervention: The Diplomacy of Taft and Wilson with Mexico* (Cambridge, Mass., 1970); Mark T. Gilderhus, *Diplomacy and Revolution: United States–Mexican Relations Under Wilson and Carranza* (Tucson, 1977); and Friedrich Katz, *The Secret War in Mexico: Europe, the United States, and the Mexican Revolution* (Chicago, 1981). See also Lloyd C. Gardner, *Safe for Democracy: The Anglo-American Response to Revolution, 1913–1923* (New York, 1984), 25–69; Gardner's "Woodrow Wilson and the Mexican Revolution," in Link (ed.), *Woodrow Wilson and a Revolutionary World, 1913–1921* (Chapel Hill, N.C., 1982), 3–48; and Kendrick A. Clements, "Woodrow Wilson's Mexican Policy, 1913–15," *Diplomatic History*, IV (Spring 1980), 113–136. My debt to Gardner and Clements will become apparent.

61. Gardner, *Safe for Democracy*, 50, and Gilderhus, *Diplomacy and Revolution*, 1.

62. Quoted in Link, *New Freedom*, 350.

63. For the origins of Wilson's mediation plan, see *ibid.*, 351–361; see also Clements, "Woodrow Wilson's Mexican Policy," 114–116.

64. Link, *New Freedom*, 365–374; Gilderhus, *Diplomacy and Revolution*, 7–8; Gardner, *Safe for Democracy*, 54–56.

65. Printed in *PWW* XXVIII, 448–452. On March 13, Wilson had issued a similar, written statement on relations with Latin America, in part in response to Huerta's regime.

See *ibid.*, XXVII, 172–173. See also Clements, "Woodrow Wilson's Mexican Policy," 116–119.

66. Clements, *ibid.*, 119–121; Gardner, "Woodrow Wilson and the Mexican Revolution," 17–21.

67. Memorandum by Thomas B. Hohler, Feb. 11, 1914, Enclosure II, with Spring Rice to Grey, Feb. 14, 1914, *PWW*, XXIX, 260.

68. Spring Rice to Grey, Feb. 7, 1914 (no. 32), *ibid.*, 229.

69. Spring Rice to Grey, Feb. 6 and 7, 1914, *ibid.*, 228 and 230, respectively (my emphasis). See also Link, *New Freedom*, 374–377 and 384–387.

70. Hohler memorandum, Feb. 11, 1914, *PWW*, XXIX, 255; see also Gardner, "Woodrow Wilson and the Mexican Revolution," 22–23.

71. The definitive study is Robert E. Quirk, *An Affair of Honor* (Lexington, Ky., 1962).

72. Gilderhus, *Diplomacy and Revolution*, 11.

73. *Ibid.*, 12–14; Link, *New Freedom*, 400–416.

74. See, for example, Haley, *Revolution and Intervention*, 108–109; and Cline, *United States and Mexico*, 150. N. Gordon Levin, *Woodrow Wilson and World Politics* (New York, 1968), argues that Wilson intervened to create in Mexico a political economy "basically liberal-capitalist rather than socialist in intent" (20). See also Gilderhus, *Diplomacy and Revolution*, 13–14, for a similar, but subtler interpretation.

75. The interpretations of Kendrick L. Clements and Lloyd C. Gardner are practically unique in this respect; but see also Frederick S. Calhoun, *Power and Principle, Armed Intervention in Wilsonian Foreign Policy* (Kent, Ohio, 1986), 39–51.

76. Quoted in Burton J. Hendrick, *The Life and Letters of Walter Hines Page*, 3 vols. (Garden City, N.Y., 1924–26), I, 204.

77. Wilson to Lindley M. Garrison, Aug. 8, 1914, *PWW*, XXX, 362.

78. Wilson to Edith Bolling Galt, Aug. 18, 1915, *ibid.*, XXXIV, 242.

79. A Fourth of July Address, 1914, ibid., XXX, 251, 252, and 254.

80. See William C. Widenor, *Henry Cabot Lodge and the Search for an American Foreign Policy* (Berkeley, 1980), 176–183 and 210 (quotation, 182); Lodge thought that Huerta would "do sufficient throat cutting to restore peace" (*ibid.*, 178).

81. *Ibid.*, 179 and 183.

82. Roosevelt to Lodge, Sept. 9, 1913, in Elting Morison *et al.* (eds.), *The Letters of Theodore Roosevelt*, 8 vols. (Cambridge, Mass., 1951–1954), VII, 747 (hereinafter cited as *LTR*). For the uproar over Colombia, see Link, *New Freedom*, 321–324; and Mowry, *Theodore Roosevelt and the Progressive Movement*, 307–308.

83. See the *New York Times Magazine*, Dec. 6, 1914; *New Republic*, I (Dec. 12, 1914), 5; David W. Levy, *Herbert Croly of the* New Republic (Princeton, N.J., 1985), 239–241; and Mowry, *Theodore Roosevelt*, 308–309.

84. Link provides an extensive list of editorial and other citations on the reaction to Veracruz in the *New Freedom*, 403–405, n 81–90.

85. Walling, "The World-Wide Battle Line," *Masses*, V, no. 2 (November 1913), 20.

86. See Robert A. Rosenstone, *Romantic Revolutionary; A Biography of John Reed* (New York, 1975).

87. In a letter to Page, May 18, 1914 (*PWW*, XXX, 42), for example, Wilson enclosed Reed's "The Causes Behind the Mexican Revolution" (*New York Times*, April 27, 1914), which described the revolution as a struggle between the masses and the great landowners; it also praised Villa and Emiliano Zapata, raised doubts about Carranza's commitment to agrarian reform, and condemned the American occupation of Veracruz. Wilson wrote Page that Reed "summed up my own conclusions. . . ."

88. Reed to William Phillips, June 4, 1914, enclosure with Phillips to Joseph P. Tumulty (Wilson's private secretary), June 6, 1914, *PWW,* XXX, 156 and 157; Reed to Upton Sinclair, June 18, 1914, quoted in Rosenstone, *Romantic Revolutionary,* 176.

89. Reed's article, based on the interview with Wilson, is published as an enclosure with Reed to Tumulty, June 30, 1914, in *PWW,* XXX, 231–238. The quotations and summaries are from 232–237. See also Reed to Wilson, June 15 and 18, 1914; and Wilson to Reed, June 17, 1914, in *ibid.,* 186–187, 192–193, and 189, respectively.

90. See Tumulty to Wilson, June 22, 1914; Reed to Wilson, June 27, 1914; Wilson to Tumulty, June 29, 1914, in *ibid.,* 202, 219–220, and 223, respectively.

91. *Masses,* VI, no. 3 (December 1914), 4. See also, Reed, "What About Mexico?" *ibid.,* V, no. 9 (June 1914), 11 and 14; and another editorial by Eastman in *ibid.,* 18. These two pieces provide further clarification of their views on both the revolution and Wilson.

Notes for Chapter 3

1. House diary, July 11 and 20, 1914, HP, CtY.

2. See transcripts of Wilson's press conferences, June 29 and July 2, 6, 9, 13, 23, 27, and 30, 1914, all in *PWW,* XXX, 222–223, 243–245, 259–260, 267–271, 279–280, 296–297, 307, and 317–319, respectively.

3. See press release, Aug. 4, 1914, *PWW,* XXX, 342; and *Papers Relating to the Foreign Relations of the United States, 1914, Supplement, The World War* (Washington, D.C., 1928), 547–551 (series hereinafter cited as *FR-WWS*).

4. Quoted in Link, *New Freedom,* 462.

5. Wilson to House, Aug. 3, 1914, *PWW,* XXX, 336.

6. For encyclopedic coverage of American neutrality, see Link, *Wilson: The Struggle for Neutrality* (Princeton, N.J., 1960)ā *Wilson: Confusions and Crises* (Princeton, N.J., 1964); other studies include John Milton Cooper, Jr., *The Vanity of Power: American Isolationism and the First World War, 1914–1917,* (Westport, Conn., 1969); Patrick Devlin, *Too Proud to Fight: Woodrow Wilson's Neutrality* (New York and London, 1975); and Ernest R. May, *The World War and American Isolation, 1914–1917* (Cambridge, Mass., 1959); Ross Gregory, *The Origins of American Intervention in the First World War* (New York, 1971); John W. Coogan, *The End of Neutrality: The United States, Britain, and Maritime Rights, 1899–1915* (Ithaca, N.Y., 1981).

7. Wilson's appeal was carried on the front page of most daily newspapers throughout the United States. It is printed in *PWW,* XXX, 393–394.

8. Wilson's statements were not published until 1931. See F. Fraser Bond, *Mr. Miller of "The Times"* (New York, 1931), 142–143.

9. A memorandum by Herbert Bruce Brougham, December 14, 1914, *PWW,* XXXI, 458–460.

10. Devlin's observations about Wilson's attitude toward the British—*Too Proud to Fight,* 26–29 and 151–155—are particularly astute.

11. See "Dr. Axson—Memorandum of conversations with him on Feb. 8, 10, 11, 1925," Ray Stannard Baker Papers, DLC; Baker, *WWLL,* V, 73–75; and Link, *Struggle for Neutrality,* 56.

12. Long before the Baker interview, Axson had dictated a memorandum (ca. Dec. 6, 1919) that outlined the conversation in question. Axson states that it took place in August 1914, but adds that Wilson also expressed anxiety over Germany's intention to commence submarine warfare. In view of the facts that Wilson, according to Axson, sketched his ideas in fuller detail in subsequent conversations, and that Germany did not announce the submarine policy until February 4, 1915, it seems more likely that the particular con-

versation in which Wilson talked about a league was among the later ones Axson referred to. See typescript, *Mr. Wilson in August 1914, Sketches of the League of Nations Idea,* portion of an unpublished memoir, Stockton Axson Papers, Princeton University Library.

13. See, for example, Neil Thorburn, "A Progressive and the First World War: Frederic C. Howe," *Mid-America,* LI (April 1969), 108–118; and J. A. Thompson, "American Progressive Publicists and the First World War, 1914–1917," *Journal of American History* (September 1971), 364–383.

14. The definitive study is Marvin Swartz, *The Union of Democratic Control in British Politics During the First World War* (London, 1970).

15. For additional background, see Keith Robbins, *The Abolition of War; The 'Peace Movement' in Great Britain, 1914–1919* (Cardiff, 1976), 7–26; Laurence W. Martin, *Peace Without Victory; Woodrow Wilson and the British Liberals* (New Haven, 1958), 1–13; A. J. P. Taylor, *The Troublemakers: Dissent Over Foreign Policy, 1792–1939* (Bloomington, Ind., 1958), 95–131; and Norman Angell, *The Great Illusion* (London, 1910).

16. For the complete text—the foregoing is a paraphrase—see Swartz, *Union of Democratic Control,* 42; see also 28–45; and Arno J. Mayer, *The Political Origins of the New Diplomacy* (New Haven, 1959), 44–48. The UDC's fifth "cardinal point" was not added until May 1916; it was drafted by J. A. Hobson, the author of *Imperialism* (London, 1902).

17. G. Lowes Dickinson, "The War and the Way Out," *Atlantic Monthly,* Vol. 114 (December 1914), 820–837. The quotation is from 837.

18. See Baker to Wilson, Jan. 6, 1915, and Wilson to Baker, Jan. 11, 1915, *PWW,* XXXI, 24 and 53, respectively.

19. Arno J. Mayer's *The Persistence of the Old Regime* (New York, 1981), challenges a long-established interpretation of the origins of the First World War, which holds that Europe's rising middle-class capitalists and industrialists, having supplanted the old régime, initiated the conflict in order to consolidate and expand their influence. Mayer argues that the "feudal elements" throughout Europe, in fact, continued to dominate all aspects of civil, political, and religious society in 1914, and succeeded in imposing their archaic values upon the pliable managerial strata that helped them run the state. Confronted by the fledgling vanguard of liberalism and socialism, these ultraconservatives overreacted to the perceived internal threat to their authority and consciously seized on the external crisis in the Balkans to bring on a general war. This supreme test of fitness would reforge national solidarity, exorcise the degenerate forces of democracy, and secure forever the old régime's privileged position and control. Though somewhat less overarching, Wilson's analysis of the Mexican Revolution and, implicitly, his provisional analysis of the war in Europe bear several striking similarities to Mayer's controversial thesis.

20. The chief studies on the Pan-American Pact are Mark T. Gilderhus, "Pan-American Initiatives: The Wilson Presidency and 'Regional Integration,' 1914–1917," *Diplomatic History,* IV (Fall 1980), 409–423; the same author's *Pan-American Visions, Woodrow Wilson and the Western Hemisphere* (Tucson, 1986); and Thomas J. Knock, "Wings of the Phoenix: The Pan-American Pact and the League of Nations," Chap. 3 in "Woodrow Wilson and the Origins of the League of Nations" (Ph.D. diss., Princeton University, 1982), 140–201. Gilderhus explores the economic ramifications of the Pact with respect to all of Latin America, while I underscore the importance of the Pact as an integral element in the development of Wilson's internationalism in general and his European peace moves in particular. Both studies include extensive bibliographies on Pan-Americanism. See also Alexander Knott, "The Pan-American Policy of Woodrow Wilson, 1913–1921" (Ph.D. diss., University of Colorado, 1968).

21. See Bryan to Wilson, Nov. 6, 1913; and Wilson to Bryan, Nov. 7, 1913, *PWW,* XXVIII, 491 and 505, respectively.

22. See Carnegie to Wilson, ca. Sept. 23, 1914, with enclosure; and Wilson to Carnegie, Sept. 29, 1914, WP, DLC. For a discussion o the peace movement's advocacy of a Pan-American league, see Warren F. Kuehl, *Seeking World Order: The United States and World Organization to 1920* (Nashville, 1968), 223–225 and 275–276; and Patterson, *Toward a Warless World,* 221.

23. House diary, Dec. 16, 1914, *PWW,* XXXI, 469; see also diary entry for Nov. 25, 1914, *ibid.,* 354–355; House to Wilson, Nov. 30, 1914; and Wilson to House, Dec. 2, 1914, *ibid.,* 369–370 and 379, respectively.

24. House diary, Dec. 16, 1914, *ibid.,* 470.

25. In the 1910s, Hiram Bingham proposed a modification of the Monroe Doctrine to curb intervention in Latin American countries. In theory Wilson's first article could be seen as a mutualization of the Doctrine, or as a multilateral, rather than unilateral, defense policy. See Bingham's *The Monroe Doctrine; an Obsolete Shibboleth* (New Haven, Conn., 1916); and Charles S. Sherrill, *Modernizing the Monroe Doctrine* (Boston, 1916); see also Thomas L. Karnes, "Hiram Johnson and His Obsolete Shibboleth," *Diplomatic History,* III (Winter 1979), 39–58; and Gilderhus, "Wilson, Carranza, and the Monroe Doctrine: A Question in Regional Organization," *ibid.,* VII (Spring 1983), 103–115.

26. For a comparison, see Article X of the Covenant, printed in *Papers Relating to the Foreign Relations of the United States; The Paris Peace Conference, 1919,* 13 vols. (Washington, D.C., 1942–1947), III, 233 (series hereinafter cited as *FR-PPC*).

27. House diary, Dec. 19, 1914, *PWW,* XXXI, 497–499.

28. See House to Wilson, Dec. 26, 1914, with enclosures, Da Gama to House, Dec. 24, 1914; and Naón to House, Dec. 26, 1914, *ibid.,* 535–536; House to Wilson, Dec. 27, 1914, *ibid.,* 540; and House diary, Dec. 29, 1914, *ibid.,* 548–549.

29. See House diary, Dec. 30, 1914, *ibid.,* 552 and Jan. 13, 1915, *ibid.,* XXXII, 64; and House to Wilson, Jan. 21, 1915, with enclosure, Suárez–Mujica to House, Jan. 19, 1915, *ibid.,* 98–99.

30. The original articles on collective security and control of munitions remained basically the same. See Wilson to Bryan, Jan. 28, 1915, *ibid.,* 146; and Draft of the Pan-American Pact, enclosure with Wilson to Bryan, Jan. 29, 1915, *ibid.,* 159–160.

31. See Bryan to Suárez, Feb. 1, 1915, in *Papers Relating to the Foreign Relations of the United States, The Lansing Papers, 1914–1920,* 2 vols. (Washington, D.C., 1940), II, 473 (series hereinafter cited as *FR-LP*); Bryan to Wilson, March 8, 1915, *PWW,* XXXII, 338; and Bryan to Wilson, April 3, 1915, with enclosure, telegram from George Summerlin (Secretary of the U.S. Embassy in Santiago), April 12, 1915, *ibid.,* 474–475. See also Bryan to Wilson, April 21, 1915, with enclosure, Confidential Memorandum by the Chilean Ambassador, *ibid.,* XXXIII, 52–60 (counterproposal, 58–60), a copy of which (April 19) is also in the Henry P. Fletcher Papers, Library of Congress.

32. See Wilson to Bryan, April 22 and 26, 1915, *PWW,* XXXIII, 62 and 68; and Bryan to Wilson, April 27, 1915, with enclosure, Suárez-Mujica to Bryan, April 27, 1915, *ibid.,* 77–78. See also Wilson to House, April 22, 1915; and House to Wilson, April 23, 1915, *ibid.,* 62–63 and 65.

33. Quoted in Frederick B. Pike, *Chile and the United States, 1880–1962* (South Bend, Ind., 1963), 151 and 153. See also Gilderhus, *Pan-American Visions,* 53.

34. For the administration's efforts to organize foreign trade, see Burton I. Kaufman, *Efficiency and Expansion; Foreign Trade Organization in the Wilson Administration, 1913–1921* (Westport, Conn., 1974), 63–90; for the ship purchase bill, see Link, *Struggle for Neutrality,* 86–87, 143–158, and 179–186.

35. See Kaufman, *Efficiency and Expansion,* 91–111; and Gilderhus, *Pan-American Visions,* 37–45.

36. Thanksgiving Proclamation, Oct. 28, 1914, *PWW*, XXXI, 242; see also Wilson's annual message, Dec. 8, 1914, *ibid.*, 416 and 418.

37. See McAdoo to Wilson, Oct. 28, 1914; and Wilson to McAdoo, Nov. 3, 1914, *ibid.*, 244 and 258, respectively; see also McAdoo to Wilson, Nov. 28, 1914, enclosing a clipping from the New York *Herald* (Nov. 24, 1914), which quoted Ambassador Naón's call for more ships to increase trade between the United States and Latin America, *ibid.*, 360–361. See, especially, *Proceedings of the First Pan-American Financial Conference, May 24 to 29, 1915* (Washington, D.C., 1915).

38. A Welcome to the Pan-American Financial Conference, May 24, 1915, *PWW*, XXXIII, 245.

39. *Washington Post*, May 30, 1915; *New York Times*, May 27 and 25, 1915 respectively. For further coverage, see *ibid.*, May 22, 23, 24, 26, 28, 29, and 30; and the *Washington Post*, May 25.

40. Quotations from Gilderhus, *Pan-American Visions*, 62.

41. The two most influential of such works are William Appleman Williams, *The Tragedy of American Diplomacy*; and N. Gordon Levin, *Woodrow Wilson and World Politics* (both previously cited).

42. Williams, *Tragedy of American Diplomacy*, 52 and 50; see also 58–89 (Chap. 2, "The Imperialism of Idealism").

43. The quotation is from the final sentence of Wilson's address to the Pan-American Financial Conference, *PWW*, XXXIII, 244–245.

44. See House diary, Oct. 3, 1914, HP, CtY; and House to Wilson, Oct. 6, 1914, WP, DLC. For Wilson's message, see House to Walter Hines Page, Oct. 3, 1914, printed in Burton J. Hendrick (ed.), *The Life and Letters of Walter Hines Page*, 3 vols. (New York, 1922–1923), I, 412–415.

45. Bethmann, quoted in Link, *Struggle for Neutrality*, 209–210.

46. At this time the British Foreign Office was working to bring Italy, Greece, and Rumania into the war by offering them the reward of Austrian and Turkish territories. See Grey to Spring Rice, Dec. 22, 1914, Grey Papers, Foreign Office (F.O.) 800/84, Public Record Office (PRO), London.

47. For the events leading up to this decision, see Link, *Struggle for Neutrality*, 191–217.

48. See Bryan to Wilson, Dec. 17, 1914, *PWW*, XXXI, 480–481; and House diary, Dec. 17, *ibid.*, 481.

49. Wilson to House, Jan. 18 and 29, 1915, *ibid.*, XXXII, 84–85 and 157–158, respectively.

50. The following account deals with the mission only in this context. For a comprehensive exposition see Link, *Struggle for Neutrality*, 217–231; and Devlin, *Too Proud to Fight*, 263–282.

51. House to Wilson, Feb. 9, 1915, *PWW*, XXXII, 204–205. See also Grey to Spring Rice, Dec. 22, 1914, and Jan. 2, 1915; and Spring Rice to Grey, Dec. 24, 1914, and Jan. 14 and 29, 1915, all in the Grey Papers, F.O. 800/84, PRO.

52. See Page to Wilson, Feb. 10, 1915, and House to Wilson, Feb. 11, 1915, *PWW*, XXXII, 211–214 and 220–221, respectively; House diary, Feb. 11, 1915, HP, CtY.

53. House diary, Feb. 11, 1915, HP, CtY.

54. Quoted in Link, *New Freedom*, 94.

55. See, for example, House diary, Nov. 11 and Dec. 3, 1914, *PWW*, XXXI, 282 and 385; see also, Link, *Struggle for Neutrality*, 47–48 and 208.

56. Compare House's diary entry of Feb. 11, 1915 (HP, CtY) with his two dispatches to Wilson of the same date, in *PWW*, XXXII, 220–221. For further comment see Link,

Struggle for Neutrality, 219–227; and Keith Robbins, *Sir Edward Grey; A Biography of Lord Grey of Fallodon,* (London, 1971), 317.

57. See House to Wilson, Feb. 15, 1915, *PWW,* XXXII, 238; and House diary, Feb. 25 and March 4 and 7, 1915, HP, CtY.

58. *Ibid.,* March 27, 1915; House to Wilson, March 20, 23, and 26, 1915, *PWW,* XXXII, 402–403, 423, and 438, respectively.

59. House to Wilson, March 20, 27, and 29, and April 3, 11, and 22, 1915, in *PWW,* XXXII, 402, 441, 456, 475, 504, and *PWW,* XXXIII, 64, respectively. See also House to Wilson, Feb. 28 and March 15, 1915; and Wilson to House, March 18, 1915, in *ibid.,* XXXII, 300, 376–377, and 396, respectively.

60. See House to Wilson, April 22, 1915, *ibid.,* XXXIII, 64; House diary, April 30 and June 3, 1915, HP, CtY; and Link, *Struggle for Neutrality,* 229–231.

61. Quoted in Link, *Struggle for Neutrality,* 231.

Notes for Chapter 4

1. "The Belgian Tragedy," *The Outlook,* 108 (September 23, 1914), 169–178.

2. "Summing Up," *New York Times,* Nov. 29, 1914. See also (all in *ibid.*) TR's "Unwise Peace Treaties a Menace to Righteousness," Oct. 4, 1914; "How to Strive for World Peace," Oct. 18, 1914; and "An International Posse Comitatus," Nov. 8, 1914; and Cooper, *Warrior and the Priest,* 279–282.

3. Roosevelt to Arthur Lee, Aug. 1 and 22, 1914, *LTR,* VII, 790–791 and 809.

4. See Mowry, *Theodore Roosevelt and the Progressive Movement,* 310–314; Harbaugh, *Power and Responsibility,* 466–473; and Cooper, *Warrior and the Priest,* 282–87.

5. Taft to Otto Bannard, Sept. 10, 1911, quoted in *ibid.,* 154.

6. See his *Constitutional Government in the United States,* in *PWW,* XVIII, 116, for an example of this.

7. On the general disarray of the American peace movement in the first months of the war, see Patterson, *Toward a Warless World,* 229–247; and Marchand, *American Peace Movement and Social Reform,* 144–181; for a review of the new interest in world organization before the war, see Kuehl, *Seeking World Order,* 172–220.

8. I employ these two terms only for general descriptive purposes; their finer meaning will soon become evident.

On the subject of early twentieth-century peace movements, pacifism, and internationalism, Sondra R. Herman, *Eleven Against War; Studies in American Internationalist Thought, 1898–1921* (Stanford, 1969); and Charles Chatfield, *For Peace and Justice: Pacifism in America, 1914–1941* (Knoxville, Tenn., 1971); along with Kuehl, *Seeking World Order,* and Marchand, *American Peace Movement and Social Reform,* are pioneering works. The field has expanded in recent years, however. In addition to Patterson's *Toward a Warless World,* see also Chatfield, *International War Resistance Through World War II* (New York, 1975); and his "World War I and the Liberal Pacifist in the United States," *American Historical Review,* LXXV (December 1970), 1,920–1,937; Charles DeBenedetti's *Origins of the Modern American Peace Movement, 1915–1929* (Millwood, N.Y., 1978); and his *Peace Reform in American History* (Bloomington, Ind., 1986); DeBenedetti (ed.), *Peace Heroes in the Twentieth Century* (Bloomington, Ind., 1986); and Chatfield and Peter van den Dungen (eds.), *Peace Movements and Political Culture* (Knoxville, Tenn., 1988). For an excellent collection of documents, see John W. Chambers II (ed.), *The Eagle and the Dove: The American Peace Movement and U.S. Foreign Policy, 1900–1922* (New York, 1976; rev. ed., Syracuse, N.Y., 1992). Two other reference works are Warren Kuehl (ed.), *Biographical Dictionary of Internationalists. (Westport Conn., 1983),* and Harold Josephson *et al.* (eds.), *Biographical Dic-*

tionary of Modern Peace Leaders, 1800–1975 (Westport, Conn., 1985). See also Lawrence S. Wittner, "Peace Movements and Foreign Policy: The Challenge to Diplomatic Historians," *Diplomatic History,* XI (Fall 1987), 355–370; and three groundbreaking dissertations—Michael A. Lutzker, "The 'Practical' Peace Advocates: An Interpretation of the American Peace Movement, 1899–1917" (Rutgers, 1969); Blanche Wiesen Cook, "Woodrow Wilson and the Antimilitarists, 1914–1917" (Johns Hopkins, 1970); and James R. Martin, "The American Peace Movement and the Progressive Era" (Rice, 1975).

9. The definitive work is Marie Louise Degen, *The History of the Woman's Peace Party* (Baltimore, 1939). See also the chapter on Jane Addams in Herman, *Eleven Against War,* 114–149; William L. O'Neill, *Everyone Was Brave, The Rise and Fall of Feminism in America* (Chicago, 1969), 174–184; and Marchand, *American Peace Movement,* 188–189, 197–200, and 204–208.

10. Degen, *Woman's Peace Party,* 38–46; John A. Alyward and Addams to Wilson, March 4, 1915, WP, DLC. See especially David S. Patterson, "Woodrow Wilson and the Mediation Movement," *Historian,* XXXIII, 4 (August 1971), 536–540. For an example of contemporary coverage of the convention, see "A Woman's Peace Party Full Fledged for Action," in *The Survey,* XXXIII (Jan. 16, 1915), 433–434.

11. Degen, *Woman's Peace Party,* 64–126; Jane Addams' memoir, *Peace and Bread in Time of War* (New York, 1922; reprint, 1972) 12–19; Martin, "American Peace Movement," 178–201; and Marchand, *American Peace Movement,* 209–212.

12. Roosevelt to Henry Green, July 2, 1915, quoted in Mowry, *Theodore Roosevelt and the Progressive Movement.* See also Michael A. Lutzker, "Jane Addams: Peacetime Heroine, Wartime Heretic," in DeBenedetti, *Peace Heroes,* 40–42. For Addams's homecoming speech at Carnegie Hall, see "The Revolt Against War," in *Survey,* XXXIV (July 17, 1915), 355–359.

13. See House to Wilson, July 17 and 19, 1915, *PWW,* XXXIII, 516 and 533, respectively; House diary, July 19, 1915, HP, CtY; Balch to Addams, Aug. 19, 1915, *PWW,* XXXIV, 250–252; and Wilson to Galt, Aug. 18, 1915, *ibid.,* 243. See also Patterson, "Wilson and Mediation," 541–542.

14. Lansing to Wilson, Sept. 1, 1915, *PWW,* XXXIV, 398; for a sampling of Wilson administration correspondence on continuous mediation, see Lansing to Wilson, Aug. 6 and 18, 1915, *ibid.,* 110 and 236–237; Wilson to Lansing, Aug. 19 and 30, 1915, *ibid.,* 247–248 and 399; Wilson to Lansing, Aug. 7, 1915, WP, DLC; Charles R. Crane to Wilson, July 2, 1915; and Wilson to Lillian Wald, July 3, 1915, *PWW,* XXXIII, 469 and 472, respectively; and Wilson to Balch, Aug. 28, 1915; and Aletta Jacobs to Addams, Sept. 15, 1915, *ibid.,* XXXIV, 350 and 473, respectively.

15. Addams, quoted in Degen, *Woman's Peace Party,* 115. See also Addams to Wilson, Jan. 29, 1915, *PWW,* XXXII, 162; Wilson to Addams, Dec. 13, 1915, *ibid.,* XXXV, 348–349; and Wilson to Addams, Oct. 17, 1916, ibid., XXXVIII, 460.

16. Wilson, quoted in Degan, *Woman's Peace Party,* 115. See also, Addams, *Peace and Bread,* 59; Patterson, "Wilson and Mediation," 545–549; memorandum by Louis Paul Lochner, Nov. 12, 1915, *PWW,* XXXV, 196; and the *New York Times,* July 22, 1915 (news report and editorial).

17. Shannon, *Socialist Party of America,* 82–86; Weinstein, *Decline of Socialism,* 119–121. As Arno J. Mayer points out in *Political Origins of the New Diplomacy, 1917–1918* (New Haven, 1959), the major socialist parties of the belligerent countries observed domestic political truces until well into 1917. (See *ibid.,* 5–6, 99–109, 143–144, and 152–154.)

18. Ginger, *Bending Cross,* 346.

19. Quotations, respectively, from Salvatore, *Debs,* 274; and Ginger, *Bending Cross,* 346. For similar indictments, see *Appeal to Reason,* Sept. 5 and 12, 1914.

20. See Marchand, *American Peace Movement,* 290–291; Weinstein, *Decline of Social-*

ism, 122–123; Shannon, *Socialist Party of America,* 82 and 86–87; and Milton Cantor, "The Radical Confrontation with Foreign Policy: War and Revolution, 1914–1920," in Alfred F. Young, *Dissent: Explorations in the History of American Radicalism* (DeKalb, Ill., 1968), 223–224. The foregoing text is Hillquit's verbatim summary of the final manifesto as approved by the party, printed in his autobiography, *Loose Leaves from a Busy Life* (New York, 1934), 160. For the earlier "Proposed Manifesto," see *American Socialist* (the party's official periodical), Dec. 26, 1914.

21. Cantor argues that left-wing analyses published in the *Masses* and the *International Socialist Review*—which alternately stressed commercial competition, militarism, feudalism versus capitalism, and autocracy versus democracy in their interpretations of the war— "scarcely differed from that of the reformers" ("Radical Confrontation with Foreign Policy," 225–226).

22. Hillquit, *Loose Leaves,* 161; Weinstein, *Decline of Socialism,* 124. Hillquit and others also claimed as much for the clause on no forcible annexations. However, this principle had previously been advanced not only by the WPP, but also by the Union of Democratic Control as early as November 1914 and by Wilson, privately, in his conversations with Brougham and Axson.

23. See Weinstein, *Decline of Socialism,* 124. Salvatore, *Debs,* 275; and Hillquit, *Loose Leaves,* 161.

24. The foregoing is based on Hillquit, *Loose Leaves,* 161–162; Maurer's autobiography, *It Can Be Done* (New York, 1938), 215–216; and "Wilson Receives Socialists," in *Appeal to Reason* (Feb. 5, 1916). Maurer also records a subsequent session that took place one month later and notes that Wilson delayed his next appointment to give Maurer more time. On his first visit to the White House on August 25, 1915, Mexico was the main topic (*It Can Be Done,* 212–213 and 216–217). See also Walter Lanfersiek (Executive Secretary of the Socialist party) to Wilson, Jan. 15, 1916, *PWW,* XXXV, 487.

25. For an excellent analysis of the different views of Root, Butler, and Taft, see Herman, *Eleven Against War,* 25–43 and 55–77.

26. The standard study is Ruhl J. Bartlett, *The League to Enforce Peace* (Chapel Hill, N.C., 1944); an important documentary source is John H. Latane (ed.), *The Development of the League of Nations Idea: Documents and Correspondence of Theodore Marburg,* 2 vols. (New York, 1932).

27. Named for James Bryce, the former Ambassador to the United States, the Group had put together a small, privately circulated pamphlet, "Proposals for the Avoidance of War," in February 1915. The proposals were laid before the organizers of the League to Enforce Peace on March 30, 1915. For details, see Henry R. Winkler, *The League of Nations Movement in Great Britain, 1914–1919* (New Brunswick, N.J., 1952), 16–23, and George W. Egerton, *Great Britain and the Creation of the League of Nations: Strategy, Politics, and International Organization, 1914–1919* (Chapel Hill, N. C., 1978), 7–9 and 18–19; see also Robbins, *Abolition of War,* 49–50; Leon E. Boothe, "Anglo-American Pro-League Groups Lead Wilson, 1915–1918," *Mid-America,* LI (April 1969), 93–95; and Latane, *Development of the League of Nations Idea,* I, vii–viii.

28. See Bartlett, *League to Enforce Peace,* 40–41, for the complete text.

29. For details about the LEP's various activities, see *ibid.,* 48–62, and Kuehl, *Seeking World Order,* 214–216. See also Egerton, *Great Britain and the Creation of the League of Nations,* 11–13.

30. Press conferences, June 8 and 22, 1915, *PWW,* XXXIII, 369 and 435–436, respectively.

31. For example, when A. Lawrence Lowell sent Wilson copies of the LEP proposals, he explained that he was doing so "in such a way as not to request any expression of

opinion." Lowell to Wilson, June 30, 1915; and Wilson to Lowell, July 5, 1915, *ibid.,* 459 and 476, respectively.

32. Quoted in Marchand, *American Peace Movement,* 157 (the LEP's italics).

33. Although he never joined the LEP, Root was perhaps the paragon of conservative internationalism; the best study of his life is Richard W. Leopold, *Elihu Root and the Conservative Tradition* (Boston, 1954). See also Herman, *Eleven Against War,* 24–33, and 64–65.

34. *New York Times,* Oct. 16, 1914; H.J.R. 372, *Congressional Record,* 63d Cong., 2d sess., 16,694 and 16,745–47.

35. Annual message, Dec. 8, 1914, *PWW,* XXXII, 421–423; see also Link, *Struggle for Neutrality,* 137–143. In 1914, the total number of active military and naval personnel of the United States stood at approximately 164,000; the country ranked eighth among the great powers, after Italy and Japan, each of which had roughly twice that number in their respective armed forces. The United States placed third, however, in warship tonnage, after Great Britain and Germany. (Wright, *Study of War,* 670–671.)

36. See Austrian Naval Attaché to Vienna, Dec. 23, 1913, in Robert C. Walton (ed.), *Over There: European Reaction to America in World War I* (Ithaca, N.Y., 1971), 7–8. See also Spring Rice to Grey, May 11, 1914, commenting on the socialist influence on the Wilson administration and Secretary Daniels' proposal to have officers and enlisted men "mess" together. (F.O. 371/2153/7893, PRO, printed in *ibid.,* 5–6).

37. Sullivan, *Our Times: The United States, 1900–1925* (New York, 1932), V, 120, n. 5., cited in Cooper, *Warrior and the Priest,* 288.

38. See James Morgan Read, *Atrocity Propaganda, 1914–1919* (New Haven, Conn., 1941), 201–209.

39. For an analysis, see John A. Thompson, *Reformers and War, American Progressive Publicists and the First World War* (Cambridge and New York, 1987), 129–133; and Link, *Struggle for Neutrality,* 39, 41, and 375–379. The most exhaustive study on all aspects of the event is Thomas A. Bailey and Paul B. Ryan, *The Lusitania Disaster: An Episode in Modern Warfare and Diplomacy* (New York and London, 1975).

40. Address in Philadelphia to Newly Naturalized Citizens, May 10, 1915, *PWW,* XXXIII, 149.

41. Wilson to Galt, Aug. 19, 1915, *ibid.,* XXXIV, 261; see also 257–259.

42. For the *Arabic* crisis, see Link, *Struggle for Neutrality,* 560–587 and 645–681; and *Confusions and Crises,* 55–100.

43. *New York Evening Post,* Sept. 2, 1915. See also Michael Wreszin, *Oswald Garrison Villard, Pacifist at War* (Bloomington, Ind., 1965), 49–53. On Bryan's resignation and its effect, see Link, *Struggle for Neutrality,* 410–455; for the first round of the complicated negotiations between Wilson and the German foreign office, see *ibid.,* 383–409.

44. Quoted in "Colonel Roosevelt's New Crusade," in *Literary Digest,* LII (June 3, 1916), 1618.

45. For contemporary accounts, see "Labor's Dread of Preparedness," in *ibid.* (April 8, 1916), 957–958; and "A Huge Preparedness Parade" and "Doubling Our Regular Army," *ibid.,* May 27, pp. 1,518–21. See also J. Garry Clifford, *The Citizen Soldiers: The Plattsburg Training Camp Movement* (Lexington, Ky., 1972); Michael Pearlman, *To Make Democracy Safe for America: Patricians and Preparedness in the Progressive Era* (Urbana, Ill., 1984); John Whiteclay Chambers II, *To Raise an Army: The Draft Comes to Modern America* (New York, 1987), 73–124; and John Patrick Finnegan, *Against the Specter of the Dragon: The Campaign for American Military Preparedness* (Westport, Conn., 1974).

46. Quoted in John A. Garraty, *Henry Cabot Lodge: A Biography* (New York, 1953), 315.

47. For background and details, see Link, *Struggle for Neutrality,* 137–143 and 588–593; and *Confusions and Crises,* 15–54 and 327–341. See also Wilson's address on preparedness to the Manhattan Club, Nov. 4, 1915, and his message to Congress, Dec. 7, 1915, *PWW,* XXXV, 168–169 and 297–306.

48. For instance, Lodge wrote to Roosevelt the following on August 5, 1915: "Wilson evidently has come to the conclusion that there is a rising popular feeling for preparedness, and, seeing votes in it, is prepared to take it up. Last winter he did everything he could to stop any improvement in the Army and Navy." (Quoted in Link, *Struggle for Neutrality,* 592.) Taft's views on Wilson's motivations were similar, as he conveyed them to Mabel T. Boardman, Nov. 8, 1915, Taft Papers, Library of Congress. See also Roosevelt to Lodge, Feb. 4, 1916, *LTR,* VIII, 1,011–1,014.

49. Quoted in *Appeal to Reason,* Jan. 15, 1916.

50. Jane Addams and others to Wilson, Oct. 29, 1915, *PWW,* XXXV, 135–136. For Wilson's troubled response, see his letter to Addams, Nov. 2, 1915, *ibid.,* 158. For a similar exchange, see Villard to Wilson, Oct. 30, 1915; and Wilson to Villard, Nov. 2, 1915, *ibid.,* 141–143 and 157, respectively.

51. For details on the founding and activities of the AUAM, see Blanche Wiesen Cook, "Woodrow Wilson and the Antimilitarists, 1914–1917" (Ph.D. diss., Johns Hopkins, 1970); Marchand, *American Peace Movement,* 223–248; Donald Johnson, *The Challenge to American Freedoms; World War I and the Rise of the American Civil Liberties Union* (Lexington, Ky., 1963), 1–9; Chatfield, *For Peace and Justice,* 22–25; and his "World War I and the Liberal Pacifists," 1922–26.

52. For a discussion of the Democratic opposition, see Cooper, *Vanity of Power,* 86–98.

53. See Lillian Wald, *Windows on Henry Street* (Boston, 1934), 289, 290, 293, and 302–304; Wald to Wilson, April 21, 1916, *PWW,* XXXVI, 524–525; Johnson, *Challenge to American Freedoms,* 5–7; Thompson, *Reformers and War,* 128 and 135–138; Thorburn, "A Progressive and the First World War," 110–112; for an excellent contemporary account, see "Swinging Around the Circle," *Survey,* XXXVI (April 22, 1916), 95–96.

54. Quoted in Shannon, *Socialist Party of America,* 89; see also Ginger, *Bending Cross,* 347–351.

55. See, for example, Reed, "At the Throat of the Republic," *Masses,* VIII, no. 2 (July 1916), 7–9; see also Rosenstone, *Romantic Revolutionary,* 244. For a sampling of socialist antipreparedness views, see *Appeal to Reason,* Nov. 27 and Dec. 11, 1915; Jan. 8, Feb. 19, and March 11, 1916.

56. See, as representative, the following articles in the *New Republic:* "Are We Militarists?" II (March 20, 1915), 166–167; " 'Preparedness' for What?" III (June 26, 1915), 188; "The Plattsburgh Idea," IV (Oct. 9, 1915), 248–250; "Preparedness—A Trojan Horse," V (Nov. 6, 1915), 6–7; "The Newer Nationalism," V ((Jan. 26, 1916), 319–321. See also Charles Forcey, *The Crossroads of Liberalism: Croly, Weyl, Lippmann and the Progressive Era, 1900–1925* (New York, 1961), 234–250; Levy, *Herbert Croly of the New Republic,* 224–227; Thompson, "American Progressive Publicists and the First World War," 376–378; and Laura Smith Porter, "The Development of an Internationalist Foreign Policy: *The New Republic* and American Neutrality, 1914–1917," unpublished manuscript in the possession of the author.

57. William Allen White, *The Autobiography of William Allen White* (New York, 1946), 513.

58. See, all in the *New Republic:* "The End of Isolationism," I (Nov. 7, 1914), 9–10; "Pacifism vs. Passivism," I (December 12, 1914), 6–7; two articles under the same title, "A League of Peace," II, (March 20, 1915), 167–169, and III (June 26, 1915), 190–191. See also

Forcey, *Crossroads of Liberalism,* 221–234; Levy, *Herbert Croly,* 218–224; and Steel, *Walter Lippmann,* 88–94.

59. Christopher Lasch, *The New Radicalism in America: The Intellectual as a Social Type, 1889–1963* (New York, 1965), 184; see also 168–188.

60. On House's relationship with Croly and Lippmann, see Levy, *Herbert Croly,* 244–247 and 255; Steel, *Walter Lippmann,* 63 and 113; and Lasch, *New Radicalism,* 220–221.

61. The following account is based primarily upon "A Colloquy with a Group of Antipreparedness Leaders," May 8, 1916, *PWW,* XXXVI, 634–648, from the shorthand notes by Charles L. Swem, White House stenographer; but this transcript should be supplemented by the account in Max Eastman, *"The Masses* at the White House," *Masses,* VIII (July 1916), 16–17, and by a partial account in the *New York Times,* May 9, 1916.

62. A Memorial to the President presented by the AUAM, ca. May 8, 1916, *PWW,* XXXVI, 632–633.

63. A Colloquy, *ibid.,* 641.

64. *Ibid.,* 642 and 643.

65. *Ibid.,* 644 and 645.

66. *Ibid.*

67. *Ibid.,* 645–646.

68. Eastman's opinion was not exaggerated. Describing Wilson's preparedness speech to the Manhattan Club, William Allen White wrote, "I never saw an unhappier face; it was dour. He scarcely spoke to those at his right and left. The gay quips and facile persiflage . . . were missing" (*Autobiography of William Allen White,* 513).

69. Max Eastman, *"The Masses* at the White House," *Masses,* VIII (July 1916), 16. See also Eastman, *Enjoyment of Living,* 544–547; William L. O'Neill, *The Last Romantic; a Life of Max Eastman* (New York, 1978), 60–61; and Wald, *Windows on Henry Street,* 302–304.

70. In mid-1915, the *New Republic* sold around 15,000 copies per issue. After 1916, when rumors of the editors' close ties to the Wilson administration spread, circulation increased dramatically between 1917 and 1920, but was never over 45,000. Eastman's publication, even after it was forced to close down in late 1917 and reopen in early 1918 under the title *The Liberator,* sold some 60,000 copies per monthly issue. See Levy, *Herbert Croly,* 255; and O'Neill, *Last Romantic,* 75.

71. Lutzker, "Jane Addams," 43.

72. For instance, as early as the summer of 1915, E. D. Morel, secretary of the UDC, had issued a dramatic appeal on the front page of the *New York Tribune*'s Sunday feature section (July 4, 1915), entitled "Save the World—An Englishman to Wilson."

73. The foregoing account is based on two memoranda by Lochner (both dated Nov. 12, 1915), printed in *PWW,* XXXV, 195–200.

74. See Link, *Confusion and Crises,* 101–111.

75. Both letters are quoted in *ibid.,* 102 and 103–104.

76. Wilson to House, Dec. 24, 1915, *PWW,* XXXV, 387–388; see also Bernstorff to Bethmann Hollweg, Nov. 23, 1915, *ibid.,* 240–243.

77. Wilson to Axson, Feb. 24, 1915, *ibid.,* IV, 287.

78. A comment to the AUAM at the White House, May 8, 1916, *ibid.,* XXVI, 644–645.

Notes to Chapter 5

1. Bryan to Wilson, May 19, 1915, *PWW,* XXXIII, 220–221; see also Wilson to Bryan, May 20, 1915, *ibid.,* 223.

2. Wilson to Lansing, Oct. 27, 1915, *ibid.,* XXXV, 113–114. The Lansing-Naón draft is printed as an enclosure with Lansing to Wilson, Nov. 11, 1915, *ibid.,* 188–189. For details about these developments, see Knock, "Woodrow Wilson and the Origins of the League of Nations," 168–172.

3. Address to the Pan-American Scientific Congress, Jan. 6, 1916, *PWW,* XXXV, 444–446.

4. *New York Times,* Jan. 7; 1915; *New Republic,* Jan. 15, 1916, 265. For additional comment, see the *Washington Post,* Jan. 7, 1916, and *Literary Digest,* LII, Jan. 8, 1916, 51–53, and Jan. 29, 1916, 216–217.

5. "Mr. Wilson's Policy and the Pact of Peace," London *Daily News and Leader,* Feb. 26, 1916, clipping enclosed with House to Wilson, March 15, 1916, *PWW,* XXXVI, 321–322.

6. House diary, Feb. 10, 11, and 22, 1916, HP, CtY.

7. According to House, Grey "enthused over the idea" and wrote out the statement he would make in Parliament—that "any agreement that was to the advantage of the American States was also to the advantage of the British Colonies in America." (*Ibid.,* Feb. 21, 1916.)

8. See Link, *Confusions and Crises,* 41; and his *Wilson; Revolution, War, and Peace,* 37.

9. For the text, see House to Wilson, Feb. 15, 1916, *PWW,* XXXVI, 180, n. 2. See also David Lloyd George, *War Memoirs of David Lloyd George,* 6 vols. (Boston, 1933–1937), II, 137–139. Wilson added the "probablys" later, as explained below.

10. See House diary, May 3, 1916, *PWW,* XXXVI, 601–602; and House to Wilson, June 18, 1916, WP, DLC.

11. See Egerton, *Great Britain and the Creation of the League of Nations,* 27–30; John Milton Cooper, Jr., "The British Response to the House-Grey Memorandum: New Evidence and New Questions," *Journal of American History,* LIX (March 1973), 958–971; and Link, *Confusions and Crises,* 127–141.

12. For details, see Link, Confusions and Crises, 222–255.

13. See House to Grey, April 6, 1916, *PWW,* XXXVI, 421; and House diary, April 6, 1916, *ibid.,* 421–426. For details on the new problems with Chile, see Knock, "Woodrow Wilson and the Origins of the League of Nations," 186–188.

14. Grey to House, March 23, 1916, printed as Enclosure III with House to Wilson April 8, 1916, *PWW,* XXXVI, 445.

15. Grey to House March 24 and April 8, 1916, printed as Enclosures I and II with Wilson to House, April 8, 1916, *ibid.,* 443–444; and Grey to House, April 7, 1916, enclosure with House to Wilson, April 19, 1916, *ibid.,* 511–512.

16. Wilson's note to Germany, dated April 12, 1916, is printed as an enclosure with Wilson to Lansing, April 17, 1916, in *ibid.,* 491–496. See also an explanatory address to Congress, on April 19, 1916, *ibid.,* 506–510. For a detailed discussion, see Link, *Confusions and Crises,* 256–279.

17. See, for instance, "The Opportunity for Peace," *Springfield Republican,* May 9, 1916; and Simeon Strunsky, "Post: Impressions," New York *Evening Post,* May 13, 1916. See also Wilson to House, May 9, 1916, *PWW,* XXXVII, 3.

18. Wilson and House made only minor changes in the document on May 3 and discussed the appropriate time for Grey to announce Great Britain's accord. The draft that was sent to the embassies of Argentina, Brazil, and Chile, dated May 3, is printed in *PWW,* XXXVI, 595–596; the administration's emendations are in italics. See also House diary, May 3, *ibid.,* 596–597, 600, and 601–602; and Knock, "Woodrow Wilson and the Origins of the League of Nations," 190–192.

19. House to Grey, May 10, 1916, enclosure with Wilson to House, May 9, 1916,

PWW, XXXVII, 6–7; see also House to Wilson, May 7, 1916; and Wilson to House, with enclosure, May 8, 1916, both in *ibid.,* XXXVI, 631–632 and 652–653, respectively; and House to Grey, May 11, 1916, *ibid.,* XXXVII, 21.

20. Grey to House, May 12, 1916, printed as an enclosure with House to Wilson, May 14, 1916, *ibid.,* 42–44.

21. *Ibid.* See also House Diary, May 13, 1916, HP, CtY.

22. Wilson to House, May 16, 1916, *PWW,* XXXVII, 57–58.

23. See Taft to Wilson, April 11; and Wilson to Taft, April 14, 1916, *ibid.,* XXXVI, 458–459 and 481, respectively; and Taft to Wilson, May 9; and Wilson to Taft, May 18, 1916, *ibid.,* XXXVII, 6 and 69, respectively.

24. See (all in *PWW,* XXXVII), a memorandum by Ray Stannard Baker of a conversation with Wilson on May 5, 1916, pp. 36–37; Tumulty to Wilson, May 16, 1916, pp. 58–59; Wilson to Tumulty, May 17 and 19, 1916, pp. 62 and 76; Hamilton Holt to Wilson, May 11, 1916, printed as an enclosure with Tumulty to Wilson, May 19, 1916, p. 75; two letters from House to Wilson on May 19, 1916, pp. 76–77; Lansing to Wilson, May 25, 1916, pp. 106–108; Wilson to Lansing, May 25, 1916, pp. 108–109. See also Baker, *WWLL,* VI, 217–219.

25. See House to Wilson, May 9, 17, 19, and 21, 1916, *PWW,* XXXVII, 6–7, 64, 78, n.1, and 88–91, respectively; see also a Memorandum, May 24, 1916; and House diary, May 24, 1916, *ibid.,* 102 and 103–104, respectively.

26. Lodge never joined the LEP, but maintained regular contact with its leadership, most of whom, of course, were prominent Republicans. In his speech the Senator said, in part: "I do not believe that when Washington warned us against entangling alliances he meant for one moment that we should not join with the other civilized nations of the world if a method could be found to diminish war and encourage peace." See Baker, *WWLL,* VI, 219–220, and Widenor, *Henry Cabot Lodge,* 238–239.

27. An address in Washington to the League to Enforce Peace, May 27, 1916, *PWW,* XXXVII, 113–116.

28. See House to Wilson, May 28, 1916, *ibid.,* 117; Lippmann to Henry Hollis, May 29, 1916, printed as an enclosure with Wilson to Hollis, June 7, 1916, *ibid.,* 166; Harry A. Garfield (president of Williams College) to Wilson, May 30, 1916, *ibid.,* 130; Holt to Wilson, May 29, 1916, *ibid.,* 120; *New Republic,* VII (June 3, 1916), 102–104. See also three editorials by Holt, "The President on the Enforcement of Peace," "A Declaration of Interdependence," and "The League to Enforce Peace," all in *Independent,* LXXXVI (June 5, 1916), 357–358. For a general survey of American press opinion, see "The President's Peace Plan" in *Literary Digest* LII (June 10, 1916), 1,683–85.

29. The *St. Louis Republic,* quoted in *Literary Digest,* LII (June 10, 1916), 1,684.

30. *New York Tribune,* May 29, 1916.

31. *Outlook,* CXIII (June 7, 1916), 303–304. For additional critical comment, see, in particular, the New York *Sun* and the *Pittsburgh Gazette-Times,* May 29, 1916; as well as the *Literary Digest* survey cited above.

32. Quoted in Swartz, *Union of Democratic Control,* 131.

33. Gardiner, "What Does America Stand For?" *London Daily News,* June 17, 1916, synopsis enclosed with House to Wilson, June 18, 1916, *PWW,* XXXVII, 265–266; Plunkett to House, June 7, 1916, printed as an enclosure with House to Wilson, June 25, 1916, *ibid.,* 295–296.

34. Courtney, quoted in Swartz, *Union of Democratic Control,* 132; House to Wilson, June 25 and 27, 1916, *PWW,* XXXVII, 294–295 and 311, respectively.

35. Bryce to House, June 8, 1916, printed as an enclosure with House to Wilson, June 23, 1916, *ibid.,* 289. For additional comment of a similar nature, see "If America Backs the Bill!" and "A Disentangling Alliance," both in the London *Nation,* XIX (June 3, 1916),

276–278; "The League of Peace," *Manchester Guardian,* May 31, 1916; and Norman Angell's "Mr. Wilson's Contribution," *War and Peace,* III (June 1916), 136–138.

36. See, for instance, *New York Tribune*'s front-page report, May 28, 1916.

37. Jusserand to Aristide Briand, June 1, 1916, reporting a conversation with House on May 31, 1916, *PWW,* XXXVII, 136; for the French press response, see Link, *Campaigns for Progressivism and Peace,* 27; and *Literary Digest,* June 10, 1916, 1,685.

38. *Literary Digest,* June 10, 1916, p. 1,685.

39. Link, *Campaigns for Progressivism and Peace,* 28–32.

40. Lord Cromer to the Editor, London *Times,* May 29, 1916. Wilson's comment, "With its causes and objects we are not concerned," worried friends of the administration as well. See (all in *PWW,* XXXVII) Plunkett to House, May 29, 1916, pp. 137–138; Page to Wilson, June 1, 1916, pp. 143–147; Bryce to House, June 8, 1916, printed as an enclosure with Wilson to House, June 23, 1916, pp. 289–290; Bryce to House, June 12, 1916, and Gardiner to House, June 15, 1916, printed as enclosures with House to Wilson, June 27, 1916, pp. 311–313. See also Grey to House, June 28, 1916, printed as an enclosure with House to Wilson, July 12, 1916, pp. 411–413; and a Memorandum by Walter Hines Page, ca. Sept. 23, 1916, WP, DLC.

41. For a detailed discussion of these mixed views, see Egerton, *Great Britain and the Creation of the League of Nations,* 33–39.

42. See Link, *Campaigns for Progressivism and Peace,* 32–35.

43. Grey to House, May 29, 1916, printed as an enclosure with House to Wilson, May 31, 1916, *PWW,* XXXVII, 131–132.

44. Wilson to House, July 2, 1916, *ibid.,* 345.

45. For a discussion of these events and their impact, see Link, *Campaigns for Progressivism and Peace,* 13–15 and 65–80.

46. House to Grey, July 15, 1916, printed as an enclosure with House to Wilson, July 14, *PWW,* XXXVII, 422–424; Grey to House, Aug. 28, 1916, *ibid.,* XXXVIII, 89–92 (emphasis added).

47. Fletcher to House, June 15, 1916, printed as an enclosure with House to Wilson, June 16, 1916, *ibid.,* XXXVII, 238–239, and Fletcher to Lansing, June 16, 1916, enclosure with Lansing to Wilson, June 17, 1916, *ibid.,* 241–244. See also F. L. Polk to the American embassy at Santiago, May 29, 1916, *ibid.,* 122; and Wilson to Lansing, June 21, 1916, *ibid.,* 271.

House had brought in Fletcher to preside over the negotiations in late March. (See House to Wilson, March 31, 1916, *ibid.,* XXXVI, 398, and Wilson to Lansing, April 3, 1916, *ibid.,* 402–403). Fletcher, from the vantage point of Santiago, had provided the State Department with information about Chile's attitude toward the Pact since 1914. For an account of his role until the time of his appointment as Ambassador to Mexico, see Fletcher's handwritten notes, "The Negotiations of the Pan American Treaty—Confidential Memorandum," April 19, 1915; and Fletcher to Lansing, Nov. 1, 1915 ("President's Plan"), in the Fletcher Papers, DLC.

48. See Link, *Confusions and Crises,* 205–206; and Friedrich Katz, "Pancho Villa and the Attack on Columbus, New Mexico," *American Historical Review,* LXXXIII (February 1978), 101–130.

49. See Calhoun, *Power and Principle,* 51–67.

50. For a detailed account of these events, see Link, *Confusions and Crises,* 195–221 and 280–313; Smith, *United States and Revolutionary Nationalism in Mexico,* 43–70; and Gilderhus, *Diplomacy and Revolution,* 32–52.

51. See Link, *Confusions and Crises,* 311–314.

52. See N. D. Baker to Wilson, June 24, 1916, *PWW,* XXXVII, 291, enclosing a news

report from the New York *World,* June 24, 1916. See also Marchand, *American Peace Movement and Social Reform,* 243–244.

53. See the New York *World* and the *New York Times,* June 26, 1916; and *Survey,* XXXVI (July 8, 1916), 379–380.

54. See Addams and others, June 27, 1916, *PWW,* XXXVII, 308, and Wilson to Addams, June 28, 1916, *ibid.,* 316.

55. See remarks to the New York Press Club, June 30, 1916, *ibid.,* 333–334, and a report in the New York *World,* July 1, 1916.

56. See, for instance, Lillian Wald's interpretation in *Window on Henry Street,* 289–298; and Marchand, *American Peace Movement and Social Reform,* 243–244.

57. See Lansing to Wilson, June 21, 1916, State Department Records, Record Group 59, 812.00/18533A, National Archives (hereinafter cited as DNA); and Fletcher to House, June 24, 1916, *PWW,* XXXVII, 292–293.

58. Quoted in "Latin America's View of Mexico," *Literary Digest,* LIII, July 15, 1916, p. 121.

59. Naón to Fletcher, June 27, 1916, enclosure with Fletcher to House, July 10, 1916, *PWW,* XXXVII, 398–400.

60. See Fletcher to House, Aug. 9, 1916, with enclosure, Fletcher to Lansing, Aug. 9, 1916, *ibid.,* XXXVIII, 17–19; and Polk to House, Aug. 8, 1916, Polk Papers, CtY. See also Knock, "Woodrow Wilson and the Origins of the League of Nations," 194–197, for documents pertaining to the administration's attempt to revive the Pact.

61. Remarks to Mexican editors, June 7, 1918, *PWW,* XLVIII, 258.

Notes to Chapter 6

1. House to Wilson, May 29, 1916, *PWW,* XXXVII, 121.

2. Plunkett to House, June 7, 1916, printed as an enclosure with House to Wilson, June 25, 1916, *ibid.,* 294–296; Loreburn to House, June 13, 1916, enclosure with House to Wilson, July 3, 1916, *ibid.,* 351–352; Buxton to House, Aug. 19, 1916, *ibid.,* XXXVIII, 54 (House notes in his diary that he showed this letter to Wilson on Sept. 24, *ibid.,* 258); and Buxton to Franklin K. Lane (Secretary of the Interior), July 5, 1916, enclosure with Lane to Wilson, *ibid.,* XXXVII, 370–372.

3. See Draft of the National Democratic Platform of 1916, ca. June 10, 1916, *ibid.,* 190–201 (for the two planks under discussion, 194–196); and Wilson to House, July 2, 1916, *ibid.,* 345.

4. Pinchot to Norman Hapgood, ca. Jan. 29, 1916, printed as an enclosure with Hapgood to Tumulty, Feb. 2, 1916, *PWW,* XXXVI, 22–23. Pinchot added that the nomination would "pull a strong oar for Wilson" in Wisconsin, Minnesota, and North and South Dakota; see also "Brandeis," *La Follette's Magazine,* VII (February 1916), 2.

5. Taft to G. J. Karger, Jan. 31, 1916, Taft Papers, DLC; Alpheus T. Mason, *Brandeis: A Free Man's Life* (New York, 1946), 470–493; and "Mr. Justice Brandeis," *Literary Digest,* LII (June 17, 1916), 1768, which surveys editorial opinion and the opposition movement.

6. See Link, *Confusions and Crises,* 357–362.

7. The appellation is from the title of an article in the *Literary Digest,* LIII (July 29, 1916), 240–241. Newton D. Baker had brought Clarke to Wilson's attention. See Baker to Wilson, July 10, 1916, *PWW,* XXXVII, 397–398; and Wilson to House, July 23, 1916, *ibid.,* 466–467.

8. The foregoing quotations are taken from "Another Supreme Court Radical," in the *Literary Digest,* cited above.

9. Wilson to Clarke, July 18, 1916, *PWW,* XXXVII, 431. See also Wilson to Norman Hapgood, July 20, 1916, in which Wilson states: "I hope and believe that progressives of all sorts will have reason to approve of my nomination of Mr. Clarke" (*ibid.,* 446).

10. Taft to J. Markham, Oct. 21, 1916, Taft Papers, quoted in Link, *Confusions and Crises,* 141.

11. For an extended analysis, see Mowry, *Theodore Roosevelt and the Progressive Movement,* 284–303 and 320–344; and Cooper, *Warrior and the Priest,* 248–250.

12. Roosevelt to White, Nov. 7, 1914, *LTR,* VIII, 836 and 839. See also *Autobiography of William Allen White,* 512–527.

13. See "Farm Loan Act Under Way," *Literary Digest,* LIII (Aug. 26, 1916), 445–446; and Link, *Confusions and Crises,* 345–350, for a detailed discussion.

14. Roosevelt, quoted in "Colonel Roosevelt's New Crusade," *Literary Digest,* LII (June 3, 1916), 1,618; Wood to E. M. House, April 17, 1916, quoted in Link, *Confusions and Crises,* 332.

15. Maurer, quoted in "Why Labor Is Against Preparedness," *Masses,* VIII (May 1916) 6; Bailey, quoted in Link, *Campaigns for Progressivism and Peace,* 61.

16. For the evolution and culmination of the revenue struggle, see Link, *Confusions and Crises,* 60–65.

17. For the Republican and Socialist party platforms, see Porter and Johnson, *National Party Platforms,* 204–211; see also "A Comparison of the Chicago Platforms," *Literary Digest* LIII (June 17, 1916), 1,762–1,763.

18. The Brooklyn *Eagle* is quoted in "The President and the Mill-Child," *Literary Digest,* LIII (August 5, 1916), 290; for background on the movement for the child labor bill, see Allen F. Davis, *Spearheads for Reform,* 123–147; for specifics on the Keating-Owen and Kern-McGillicuddy bills and reaction to them, see Link, *Campaigns for Progressivism and Peace,* 39–40 and 56–60. See also Wilson's remarks upon signing the Child Labor bill, Sept. 1, *PWW,* XXXVIII, 123–124.

19. An address in Atlantic City to the National American Woman Suffrage Association, September 8, 1916, *PWW,* XXXVIII, 162–163.

20. Dedication address at the American Federation of Labor Building, July 4, 1916, *ibid.,* XXXVII, 355.

21. For a full account, see Link, *Campaigns for Progressivism and Peace,* 83–92.

22. Charles W. Eliot to J. P. Tumulty, Sept. 11, 1916, *PWW,* XXXVIII, 167.

23. Address to a Joint Session of Congress, Aug. 29, 1916, *PWW,* XXXVIII, 97 and 98.

24. See the *New York Times,* Sept. 13, 1916; "Political Effects of the Labor Victory," *Literary Digest,* LIII (Sept. 16, 1916), 651 (see also 652–653 for a survey of editorial opinion); and Link, *Campaigns for Progressivism and Peace,* 103, from which Hughes' statement at Beverly is quoted.

25. See "The Political Effects of the Labor Victory," *Literary Digest,* LIII (September 16, 1916), 651; and the *New Republic,* VIII (Sept. 9, 1916), 100.

26. On Benson's campaign, see Weinstein, *Decline of Socialism,* 106; "Socialism's Stake in the War," *Literary Digest,* LII (March 25, 1916), 807; and "The Case for Benson," *New Republic,* VIII (Oct. 7, 1916), 243–245.

27. Max Eastman, quoted in the *New York Times,* Oct. 16, 1916, and reprinted in Eastman, "Sect or Class," *Masses,* IX (December 1916); the *Weekly People,* quoted in "Paying for the Railroad Men's Victory," *Literary Digest,* LIII (September 9, 1916), 592.

28. Interview in the *Davenport News* (Iowa), ca. October 1916, quoted in Philip S. Foner (ed.), *Mother Jones Speaks; Collected Speeches and Writings* (New York, 1983), 523.

29. Frank Bohn, "The Reelection of Wilson," *Masses,* IX (January 1917), 15.

30. They included Lincoln Steffans, George Creel, Frederick C. Howe, Ben Lindsey, John Dewey, Jane Addams, Amos Pinchot, Norman Thomas, Bainbridge Colby, Edward P. Costigan, and Matthew Hale. For a complete listing, see Link, *Campaigns for Progressivism and Peace,* 124–125.

31. *New York Times,* Oct. 17, 1916.

32. Addams to Arthur Kellogg, Oct. 25, 1916, quoted in Clark A. Chambers, *Paul U. Kellogg and the Survey: Voices for Social Welfare and Social Justice* (Minneapolis, 1971), 55. On October 17 Wilson wrote to Addams the following: "I cannot deny myself the pleasure of telling you how proud I am and how much strengthened I feel like I should have your approval and support" (*PWW,* XXXVIII, 460). See also the *New York Times,* October 15, 1916.

33. See Gus Meyers, "Why Idealists Quit the Socialist Party," the *Nation,* CIV (Feb. 15, 1917), 118–120; and Reed to the National Executive Committee of the Socialist Party of America, Oct. 13, 1916, in Weinstein, *Decline of Socialism in America,* 105–106; see also Shannon, *Socialist Party of America,* 92–93.

34. Interviews in the *Evansville Times* (Illinois), Sept. 4, 1916; and the *Davenport News,* ca. October 1916, in Foner, *Mother Jones Speaks,* 521 and 523.

35. Bohn, "The Reelection of Wilson," *Masses,* IX (January 1917), 15–16; Eastman, "Sect or Class," *Ibid.,* (December 1916); see also Eastman, "To Socialist Party Critics," *ibid.,* (Feb. 1917), 24.

36. See "A Presidential Straw Vote of Union Labor," *Literary Digest,* LIII (Oct. 7, 1916), 871–874 and 919–922.

37. *Ibid.,* p. 872.

38. Quoted in Cantor, "Radical Confrontation with Foreign Policy," in Young (ed.), *Dissent* (previously cited), 227.

39. Eastman, "An Issue at Last," *Masses,* VIII (August 1916), 10 (my emphasis).

40. A Speech in Long Branch, New Jersey, Accepting the Presidential Nomination, Sept. 2, 1916, *PWW,* XXXVIII, 126–139, quotations from 131–132, 135, and 136.

41. Address in Omaha, Oct. 5, 1916, *ibid.,* 346, 347, and 348.

42. An address at Indianapolis, Oct. 12, 1916, *ibid.,* 414, 415, 416–417, and 418.

43. Campaign Address at Shadow Lawn, Oct. 14, 1916, *ibid.,* 437.

44. An Address at Chicago to Nonpartisan Women, Oct. 19, 1916, *ibid.,* 484 and 488.

45. A Luncheon Address to Women in Cincinnati, Oct. 26, 1916, *ibid.,* 531.

46. A Nonpartisan Address in Cincinnati, Oct. 26, 1916, *ibid.,* 541 and 542.

47. Address at Madison Square Garden, Nov. 2, 1916, *ibid.,* 599, 600, and 601.

48. Final Campaign Address, Nov. 4, 1916, *ibid.,* 611–615.

49. House to Grey, July 15, 1916, *ibid.,* XXXVII, 423.

50. *New York Times,* Oct. 14, 1916, and reprinted in the *Masses,* IX (December 1916).

51. See, for instance, Levy, *Herbert Croly of the New Republic,* 242–243; Forcey, *Crossroads of Liberalism,* 258–259; and Link, *Campaigns for Progressivism and Peace,* 129–130, in which foreign policy and Wilson's internationalism—the subjects to which Croly devoted about half of his famous, lengthy editorial—are never mentioned.

52. See Croly, "The Two Parties in 1916," *New Republic,* VIII (Oct. 21, 1916), 289 and 290; and *ibid.,* (Oct. 28, 1916), 1.

53. W. H. Taft to Horace D. Taft, Jan. 8, 1917, quoted in Henry F. Pringle, *The Life and Times of William Howard Taft,* 2 vols. (New York, 1939), II, 931.

54. See Widenor, *Henry Cabot Lodge and the Search for an American Foreign Policy,* 226–231 and 235–241.

55. Lodge to Roosevelt, June 14, 1916, quoted in Link, *Campaigns for Progressivism and Peace,* 142.

56. See Latane (ed.), *The Development of the League of Nations Idea,* I, 138; Bartlett, *League to Enforce Peace,* 56–60; and Widenor, *Henry Cabot Lodge,* 240–243. A plank entitled "Foreign Relations" included the following sentence: "We believe in the pacific settlement of international disputes, and favor the establishment of a world court for that purpose" (Porter and Johnson, *National Party Platforms,* 204).

57. The major study on Hughes is Merlo J. Pusey's Pulitzer Prize–winning *Charles Evans Hughes,* 2 vols. (New York, 1951).

58. Roosevelt to W. A. Wadsworth, June 23, 1916, *LTR,* VIII, 1078; White, quoted in "How the Progressives Voted," *Literary Digest,* LIII (Nov. 25, 1916), 1,393.

59. See "How Labor Voted," *Literary Digest* (Nov. 25, 1916), 1391; "Hughes and Wilson on the Eight-Hour Law," *ibid.* (Oct. 7, 1916), 875–877; "Political Reports from 3,000 Communities," *ibid.* (Oct. 28, 1916), 1114; see also Walter Lippmann, "The Puzzle of Hughes," *New Republic,* VIII (September 30, 1916), 210–213.

60. See "The Hughes-Roosevelt Alliance," *Literary Digest,* LIII (July 8, 1916), 56–57; "He Kept Us Out of War," *ibid.* (Oct. 14, 1916), 933–935; and Link, *Campaigns for Progressivism and Peace,* 110–112.

61. Lodge to Roosevelt, July 15, 1916, quoted in Widenor, *Henry Cabot Lodge,* 243.

62. Taft to C. Cobb, July 19, 1916, Taft Papers, DLC.

63. The analysis which follows is based on election statistics as compiled in Petersen, *Statistical History of the American Presidential Elections,* 78–82.

64. See Link, *Campaigns for Progressivism and Peace,* 127 and 161–163.

65. See Lunardini and Knock, "Woodrow Wilson and Woman Suffrage," 563–65.

66. The California vote went as follows: Wilson, 466,200; Hughes, 462,394; Benson, 43,259 (as contrasted to Debs' 79,201). It is interesting to note that, despite the increase in California's turnout (because woman suffrage was now in effect), the Socialist popular vote came to only 4.33 per cent, whereas in 1912 it reached 11.76 per cent.

67. The vote went as follows: North Dakota—Wilson, 55,206; Hughes, 53,471; Benson, none recorded (vs. Debs' 6,966 in 1912); New Hampshire—Wilson, 43,779; Hughes, 43,723; Benson, 1,318 (vs. Debs' 1,980); Washington—Wilson, 183,388; Hughes, 167, 244; Benson, 22,800 (vs. Debs' 40,134).

68. "Why Wilson Won," *Literary Digest,* LIII (Nov. 18, 1916), 1,315; see also 1,312–1,314. In 1912, Debs had won nearly 90,000 votes in Ohio; whereas in 1916, Benson won about 38,000; Wilson won approximately 604,000 votes to Hughes' 515,000. The Missouri vote went as follows: Wilson, 398,000; Hughes, 369,000; Benson, 14,000 (vs. 28,000 for Debs in 1912).

69. Walling, "Socialists for Wilson," *Masses,* IX (January 1917), 24; the *New York Evening Star* assessment is carried in "How Labor Voted," *Literary Digest,* LIII (Nov. 25, 1916), 1,391.

70. Hopkins to Wilson, Nov. 14, 1916, *PWW,* XXXVIII, 642.

71. Minnesota voted as follows: Wilson, 179,152; Hughes, 179,544; Benson, 20,117 (vs. 27,505 for Debs in 1912). For the turnout in Minneapolis, see "Why Wilson Won," *Literary Digest,* LIII (Nov. 18, 1916), 1,314.

72. See the *New York Times,* Nov. 10, 1916; "The Two Parties After the Election," *New Republic,* IX (Nov. 18, 1916), 63–64; and "How the Progressives Voted," *Literary Digest,* LIII (Nov. 25, 1916), 1,392–1,393.

73. Eastman, "To Socialist Party Critics," *Masses,* IX (February 1917), 24. Despite the decline in the presidential vote, most Socialist party members did not despair. Meyer London was re-elected to Congress, and Grant Miller of Nevada, with thirty per cent of the vote in a three-way race, barely missed winning a seat in the U.S. Senate. Several major cities, including Milwaukee and Minneapolis, elected Socialist mayors. See Weinstein, *De-*

cline of Socialism in America, 106–108, and "How Labor Voted," *Literary Digest,* LIII (Nov. 24, 1916), 1,391.

74. J. A. H. Hopkins to Wilson, with Enclosure (Hopkins to Vance McCormick), both dated Nov. 14, 1916, *PWW,* XXXVIII, 642–643. In response, Wilson agreed that "the fundamental [question] in the next four years" was "How can what has already been accomplished be given unbroken continuity by the use and combination of existing elements?" (Wilson to Hopkins, Nov. 16, 1916, *ibid.,* 663.

75. See Mayer, *Political Origins of the New Diplomacy;* Swartz, *Union of Democratic Control;* and Lawrence W. Martin, *Peace Without Victory: Woodrow Wilson and the British Liberals* (New Haven, Conn., 1958).

76. Pinchot, "What the Election Means," *Masses,* IX (January 1917), 18 and 19.

Notes to Chapter 7

1. Gardiner, "America and the Future," London *Daily News and Leader,* Nov. 18, 1916. See also "The Allies Greet the President," *Literary Digest,* LIII (December 16, 1916), 1,589–1,590.

2. See the *New York Times,* Nov. 10, 1916; and "Opening a Way to Peace," *Literary Digest,* LIII (Nov. 25, 1916), 1,398.

3. "Germany and the League of Peace," *New Republic,* IX (Nov. 18, 1916), 60.

4. See "Opening a Way to Peace" and "Germany's Restive Socialists," *Literary Digest,* LIII (Nov. 25, 1916), 1,398 and 1,399.

5. For details on these developments, see Link, *Campaigns for Progressivism and Peace,* 165–175 and 184–196.

6. See the *New York Times,* Sept. 29, 1916; and Egerton, *Great Britain and the Creation of the League of Nations,* 41–42.

7. House diary, Nov. 14, 1916, *PWW,* XXXVIII, 645–647.

8. Unpublished Prolegomenon to a Peace Note, ca. Nov. 25, 1916, *PWW,* XL, 67–68, and 70.

9. See Draft of a Peace Note, ca. Nov. 25, 1916, *ibid.,* 71–74.

10. House diary, Nov. 26 and 28, 1916, printed in *ibid.,* 85, 96; and Nov. 30 and Dec. 7, 1916, HP, CtY; House to Wilson, with enclosure, Dec. 7, 1916, *PWW,* XL, 185–186.

11. Wilson to House, Dec. 8, 1916, *ibid.,* 189. In September, Wilson had also obtained retaliatory legislation to combat the British blacklist. In October, the British had secretly conducted an investigation that revealed that Wilson, by mid-1917, would be "in a position, if he wishes, to dictate his own terms to us." Wilson of course did not know the extent to which the Allies were dependent upon American money and material. On these matters, see Link, *Campaigns for Progressivism and Peace,* 178–184 and 200–206.

12. Lansing to Wilson, Dec. 10, 1916, *ibid.,* 209. See also "What Will the President Do?" Lansing diary, Dec. 3, 1916, Lansing Papers, DLC.

13. Undated typescript in WP, DLC, probably conveyed by John P. Gavit. See Gavit to Wilson, with enclosure, Dec. 2, 1916, *PWW,* XL, 124–125; and Trevelyan to Wilson, Nov. 23, 1916, enclosure with House to Wilson, Dec. 6, 1916, *ibid.,* 178–180. Trevelyan's article was published in the *Survey,* XXXVII (Dec. 9, 1916), 261–262.

14. Wilson to House, Dec. 8, 1916, *ibid.,* 189.

15. See Egerton, *Great Britain and the Creation of the League of Nations,* 42–43.

16. Bethmann dispatched his formal peace note to Washington and other neutral governments on December 12, and requested that it be transmitted to the Allied powers. The note stated that the German people had proved their invincibility in the field, but

that they did not seek a punitive victory. Rather, they desired to meet their enemies at the conference table and restore the peace. Should the Allies ignore the call, they, the Allies, would be responsible for the consequences. For details, see Link, *Campaigns for Progressivism and Peace,* 212–214.

17. For the complete text, see an Appeal for a Statement of War Aims, *PWW,* XL, 273–276.

18. *Congressional Record,* Senate, 64th Cong., 2nd sess., Dec. 21, 1916, p. 635 (S. Res. 296).

19. *Ibid.,* Jan. 3, 1917, p. 795.

20. *Ibid.,* 794 and 797; see also *ibid.,* Jan. 4, 1917, 830–833.

21. *Ibid.,* Jan. 5, 1917, pp. 883–886 and 897. See also the *New York Times,* Dec. 22, 1916 and Jan. 3, 4, 5, and 6, 1917; Paul Ritter (Swiss Ambassador to the United States) to Arthur Hoffman, Jan. 12, 1917, *PWW,* XL, 460–462. Widenor, *Henry Cabot Lodge,* 248–255; and, for an analysis of other critics' views of the peace note, Cooper, *Vanity of Power,* 133–146.

22. See, for instance, Harry Garfield to Wilson, and W. J. Bryan to Wilson, both Dec. 21, 1916, *PWW,* XL, 314; the Swiss Federal Council to the White House, Dec. 23, 1916, *ibid.,* 325–326; and "Peace Without Victory," and "The Note As Americanism," *New Republic,* IX (December 30, 1916), 201–202 and 228–231, respectively. For a survey of press opinion, see "The President As Peace Pilot," *Literary Digest,* LIII (Dec. 30, 1916), 1,694–1,695.

23. Page to Lansing, Dec. 22, 1916, *PWW,* XL, 319–320. See also Link, *Campaigns for Progressivism and Peace,* 227–231.

24. *Ibid.,* 233–237.

25. For analysis of the response of the Allied governments to Bethmann's peace note, along with a survey of American press opinion, see "The Allies Ask Restitution, Reparation, Security," *Literary Digest,* LIII (Dec. 30, 1916), 1,691–1,693.

26. Lansing diary, Dec. 3, 1916, Lansing Papers, DLC.

27. *New York Times,* Dec. 22, 1916.

28. See *ibid.;* House diary, Jan. 11, 1916, *PWW,* XL, 445–456; and Wilson to Lansing, Dec. 21, 1916, *ibid.,* 307.

29. See J. J. Jusserand to the Foreign Ministry, Dec. 20, 21, and 23, 1916, *Telegrammes Washington,* Vol. 46, pp. 97–98, 99–100, and 101, respectively, French Foreign Ministry Archives (hereafter, FFM-Ar); and Spring Rice to the Foreign Office, Dec. 21, 1916, F.O. 371/2805, pp. 496–497, PRO. See also the lengthy annotation to Wilson to Lansing, Dec. 21, 1916, *PWW,* XL, 307–311.

30. Link, *Woodrow Wilson: Revolution, War and Peace,* 57.

31. The joint note is printed as Ambassador Sharp to the Secretary of State, Jan. 10, 1917, in *FR-WWS, 1917,* I, 5–9. For the minutes of the meetings in which Lansing's suggestions were discussed, see "Conference du 26 Decembre 1916 . . ." and "Conference du 28 Decembre 1916 . . ." in *Guerre, 1914–1918,* Vol. 990, pp. 84–94 and 132–139, FFM-Ar. Sterling Kernek, in "The British Government's Reactions to President Wilson's 'Peace' Note of December 1916," *Historical Journal,* XIII (December 1970), 721–766, argues that Lansing's actions had little practical effect on the joint Allied note.

32. For these developments, see Link, *Campaigns for Progressivism and Peace,* 249–250.

33. House diary, Jan. 3, 11 and 12, 1917, *PWW,* XL, 403–404, 445–446, and 462–463.

34. *New York Times,* Jan. 23, 1917.

35. For the complete text, see Address to the Senate, Jan. 22, 1917, *PWW,* XL, 533–539.

36. *New York Times,* Jan. 23, 1917.

37. Quoted in Cooper, *Vanity of Power,* 156–157. Privately, Taft told an associate that

Wilson had endorsed the league principle "in such a way as to embarrass me, because I don't agree with much of what he says in respect to the kind of peace that ought to be achieved . . . [and] I don't think a just peace can be attained without the victory of the Allies." (Taft to W. Murray Crane, Jan. 23, 1917, quoted in Pringle, *Life and Times of William Howard Taft,* II, 934.)

38. *New York Times,* Jan. 23 and 29, 1917.

39. *New York Times,* Jan. 23, 1917. The *Times'* coverage of the speech and the reactions to it is excellent. See also, Link, *Campaigns for Progressivism and Peace,* 270, n. 162, for a compilation of newspaper citations.

40. See House to Wilson, Jan. 22, 1917, *PWW,* XL, 539, and Croly to Wilson, Jan. 23, 1917, *ibid.,* 559. Wilson wrote to Croly that his letter gave him "the deepest gratification" and noted that a recent *New Republic* editorial ("Peace Without Victory," Vol. IX, Dec. 23, 1916, pp. 201–202) had "served to clarify and strengthen my thought not a little" (Wilson to Croly, Jan. 25, *PWW,* XLI, 13). In fact, however, Wilson's address and the *New Republic* article bore very little substantive resemblance to each other. See also *New Republic* editorial on Wilson's address, "America Speaks," Jan. 27, 1917, pp. 340–342; and Levy, *Herbert Croly,* 229–232.

41. Wald *et al.* (for the AUAM) to Wilson, Jan. 24, 1917, *PWW,* XLI, 7–8.

42. Eastman, "Revolutionary Progress," *Masses,* IX (April 1917), 5. For other interesting responses, see Andrew Carnegie to Wilson, Jan. 23, 1917, *PWW,* XL, 560; and W. J. Bryan to Wilson, Jan. 26, 1917, *ibid.,* XLI, 29.

43. For a wide-ranging survey of British and German responses, see Link, *Campaigns for Progressivism and Peace,* 272–277.

44. Wilson to Gavit, Jan. 29, 1917, *PWW,* XLI, 55; see also House diary, Jan. 11, 1917, *ibid.,* XL, 445.

45. The quotations are from Mayer, *Political Origins of the New Diplomacy,* 159–160 and 161. See also Swartz, *Union of Democratic Control,* 136–137; and Francis Johnson (secretary of the Independent Labour party) to Wilson, Jan. 6, 1917, *PWW,* XLI, 36; Cleveland Dodge to Wilson, Jan. 24, 1917, *ibid.,* 6–7; and Noel Buxton to House, Feb. 8, 1917, HP, CtY.

46. Link, *Campaigns for Progressivism and Peace,* 272. All of the foregoing developments were widely reported and commented on in the American press; see, for example, the *New York Times,* Jan. 27, 1916.

47. Wilson to House, Jan. 24, 1917, *PWW,* XLI, 3 (Wilson's emphasis).

48. Germany's terms, which could not be construed as anything less than terms of conquest by the Allies, included the restitution of French-occupied Alsace and all German colonies; establishment of a buffer state between Germany and Russia; the return of French territories now occupied by Germany, but with compensation to Germany; restoration of Belgium; indemnities for losses incurred by German citizens; commercial agreements to insure Germany's economic well-being; and freedom of the seas. See Fritz Fischer, *Germany's Aims in the First World War* (New York, 1967, English trans.), *passim.*

49. See House diary, Feb. 1, 1917, *PWW,* XLI, 86–89; and Link, *Campaigns for Progressivism and Peace,* 290–302. For an account of the vicissitudes of armed neutrality and Wilson's last peace drive, see *ibid.,* 340–359 and 314–325, respectively.

50. On the Zimmermann Note, see Link, *Campaigns for Progressivism and Peace,* 342–346, 353–359, and 433–436; on the sinkings, 347, 350, 351, and 396–397.

51. F. K. Lane to G. W. Lane, April 1, 1917, *PWW,* XLI, 517.

52. *Outlook,* CXV (March 14, 1917), 452. For a review of pro-war sentiment in most of the American press by mid- to late March, see "A 'State of War' with Germany," *Literary Digest,* LIV (March 31, 1917), 881–882.

53. "In Defense of the Atlantic World," *New Republic,* X (Feb. 17, 1917), 59–61; see

also "Justification," *ibid.,* (Feb. 10, 1917), 36–38. (Walter Lippmann had written both editorials.) For an extended discussion, see Forcey, *Crossroads of Liberalism,* 273–276; and Steel, *Walter Lippmann,* 110–111.

54. See Kellogg, "The Fighting Issue," *Survey,* XXXVII (Feb. 17, 1917), 572–577, for the complete text.

55. See Marchand, *American Peace Movement,* 249–253; Chambers, *Paul U. Kellogg and the Survey,* 58–61; and Link, *Campaigns for Progressivism and Peace,* 416–417. See also the *New York Times,* Feb. 2, 5, and 13, and March 28 and 29, 1917, for particularly interesting coverage of the anti-interventionists' activities.

56. "A Visit to the President," *Friends' Intelligencer,* LXXIV (March 10, 1917), 147–148, printed in *PWW,* XLI, 302–304; an address to the President by Max Eastman, Feb. 28, 1917, *ibid.,* 305–308; New York *Evening Post,* Feb. 28, 1917.

57. See Chatfield, "World War I and the Liberal Pacifists," 1924; Ginger, *Bending Cross,* 360–361; Marchand, *American Peace Movement,* 252; *New York Times,* March 24, 1917; and Wald to J. P. Tumulty, Feb. 8, 1917, *PWW,* XLI, 167.

58. See Link, *Campaigns for Progressivism and Peace,* 409–415; and *Woodrow Wilson: Revolution, War and Peace,* 68–71. For a different interpretation, see Cooper, *Warrior and the Priest,* 318–323.

59. The message was conveyed by Page to Lansing on Feb. 11 (printed in *PWW,* XLI, 210–214).

60. A Memorandum by Norman Angell, ca. Nov. 20, 1916, *PWW,* XL, 10–19. Wilson kept this document in his personal files.

61. Trevelyan, "Open Letter to Americans," cited above; Noel Buxton, quoted in W. H. Buckler to House, Feb. 23, 1917, enclosure with House to Wilson, March 9, 1917, *PWW,* XLI, 373–375.

62. Lippmann to Wilson, with enclosure, March 11, 1917, *ibid.,* 388–389. See also, Steel, *Walter Lippmann,* 111–112.

63. Addams, *Peace and Bread in Time of War,* 63–64.

64. Robert Bridges, *The Spirit of Man* (London, 1916), i–ii and iii–iv; see also, Paul Fussell, *The Great War in Modern Memory* (New York, 1975), 10–13, for a discussion of Bridges' volume.

65. An Address in Omaha, Oct. 5, 1916, *PWW,* XXXVIII, 348.

66. An Address to a Joint Session of Congress, April 2, 1917, *ibid.,* XLI, 519–527.

67. "The Great Decision," *New Republic,* X (April 7, 1917), 279–280.

68. Max Eastman, *Enjoyment of Living* (New York, 1948), 586.

Notes to Chapter 8

1. *Congressional Record,* Senate, 64th Cong., 2nd sess., Jan. 23, 1917, p. 1808. Sherman spoke on January 24 (*ibid.,* 1,884).

2. See Senate Res. 329 and McCumber's speech of February 1 in *ibid.,* 1,950 and 2,361–2,364, respectively.

3. *Ibid.,* 2,364–2,370; see also 2,370–2,373.

4. Widenor, *Henry Cabot Lodge,* 256–258.

5. Lodge to Lowell, Jan. 30, 1917, quoted in *ibid.,* 258. See also Lodge to Taft, Jan. 23, 1917, quoted in *ibid.,* 258, n. 134.

6. Quoted in Ralph Stone, *The Irreconcilables: The Fight Against the League of Nations* (Lexington, Ky., 1970), 14. Borah had also invoked the tradition of "no alliances, no leagues, no entanglements" in his objections to the "Peace Without Victory" address, on February 7. "What this passion-torn world needs and will need are not more leagues and alliances,

but a great untrammeled, courageous neutral power, representing not bias, not prejudice, not hate, not conflict, but order and law and justice." (See *Congressional Record,* 64th Cong., 2nd sess., Feb. 7, 1917, p. 2,749.)

7. Wilson to C. H. Dodge, Jan. 25, 1917, *PWW,* XLI, 11.

8. See Croly to Wilson, Jan. 23, 1917, *ibid.,* XL, 559; and Wilson to Croly, Jan. 25, 1917, *ibid.,* XLI, 13.

9. *New Republic,* X (Feb. 3, 1917), 1–2.

10. Lochner memorandum of an interview with Wilson, Feb. 1, 1917, *PWW,* XLI, 91.

11. Remarks at a press conference, Jan. 30, 1917, *ibid.,* 64.

12. Wilson to Filene, Jan. 30, 1917, *ibid.,* 68.

13. "Bases of Peace," Enclosure II, with Wilson to Lansing, Feb. 9, 1917, *ibid.,* 173–174. See also Wilson's draft of this document, Enclosure I, in Wilson to Lansing, Feb. 8, 1917, *ibid.,* 160–161.

14. J. J. Jusserand to the French Foreign Ministry, March 7, 1917, *ibid.,* 356–357; F. L. Polk to Jusserand, Aug. 3, 1917, *ibid.,* XLIII, 360.

15. Memorandum by William E. Rappard of an interview with Wilson, Nov. 1, 1917, *ibid.,* XLIV, 488.

16. See Lippmann, *The Stakes of Diplomacy,* 2nd ed. (New York, 1917), xxii; and Lippmann to Wilson, Jan. 3, 1917, WP, DLC; and Wilson to Lippmann, Feb. 3, 1917, *PWW,* XLI, 113.

17. Jusserand to the Foreign Ministry, March 7, 1917, *ibid.,* 356–357.

18. See, for example, Theodore Marburg to Wilson, March 5, 1918; and Wilson to Marburg, March 8, 1917, *ibid.,* XLVI, 549 and 572, respectively; Marburg to Wilson, May 3, 1918; and Wilson to Marburg, May 6, 1918, *ibid.,* XLVII, 507–508 and 535, respectively; A. Lawrence Lowell to Wilson, July 10, 1918; and Wilson to Lowell, July 11, 1918, *ibid.,* XLVIII, 586 and 590–591, respectively.

19. Wilson to B. D. Gibson, May 5, 1917, *ibid.,* XLII, 221.

20. Wilson to House, March 20, 1918, *ibid.,* XLVII, 85–86; House diary, June 1, 1918, HP, CtY.

21. House diary, Apr. 11, 1918, *PWW,* XLVII, 324. For an appreciation of the range of House's work with the LEP, see House to Wilson, Feb. 19, 1917, *ibid.,* XVI, 250–251; House to Wilson, March 8, 1918, *ibid.,* XLVI, 574–575; House to Wilson, March 21, 1918 (with enclosures from Lowell and Robert Cecil, *ibid.,* XLVII, 101–104; House diary, April 11 and 12, May 14, July 27, and Aug. 25, 1917; Jan. 3, March 7, June 24, July 22, and Sept. 21, 1918, HP, CtY.

22. For details, see Bartlett, *League to Enforce Peace,* 88–91.

23. Lasch, *New Radicalism in America,* 202.

24. "A War Program for Liberals," *New Republic,* X (March 31, 1917), 249–250. See also Noble, *"New Republic* and the Idea of Progress," 395–398; Forcey, *Crossroads of Liberalism,* 276–281; and Levy, *Herbert Croly,* 249–250.

25. Lippmann to J. G. Phelps Stokes, May 1, 1917, quoted in Weinstein, *Decline of Socialism in America,* 132.

26. Croly to Willard Straight, n.d., quoted in Levy, *Herbert Croly,* 249.

27. Allen F. Davis, "Welfare, Reform, and World War I," *American Quarterly,* XIX (Fall 1967), 516–533, and reprinted under the title "The Flowering of Progressivism," in Arthur S. Link (ed.), *The Impact of World War I* (New York, 1969). See also Ronald Shaffer, *America in the Great War: The Rise of the War Welfare State* (New York, 1991).

28. See Robert D. Cuff, *The War Industries Board: Business–Government Relations During World War I* (Baltimore, 1973); see also William E. Leuchtenburg's "The New Deal and the Analogue of War," in John Braeman (ed.), *Change and Continuity in Twentieth-Century America* (Columbus, Ohio, 1964), 88–144.

29. See David M. Kennedy, *Over Here: The First World War and American Society* (New York, 1980), 253–257, for a discussion; and Grenville Macfarland to Wilson, Dec. 11, 1917, *PWW,* XLV, 271.

30. For a discussion, see Kennedy, *Over Here,* 98–113. (Lodge is quoted on 109.)

31. Howe, quoted in Thompson, *Reformers and War,* 214.

32. See, Kennedy, *Over Here,* 257–272; Davis, "Welfare, Reform, and World War I," *passim;* see also Robert H. Ferrell, *Woodrow Wilson and World War I* (New York, 1985), 91–97 and 114–117.

33. Seward Livermore's *Politics Is Adjourned: Woodrow Wilson and the War Congress, 1916–1918* (Seattle, 1968 ed.) was the first study to provide an accurate appraisal of the war Congress of 1916–18 and Wilson's relationship with it.

34. Baker Notebook (15), Jan. 21, 1918, pp. 60–61, quoted in Thompson, *Reformers and War,* 216.

35. See H. C. Peterson and Gilbert C. Fite, *Opponents of War, 1917–1918* (Madison, Wisc., 1957), 5–8; and Kennedy, *Over Here,* 20–24.

36. Weinstein, *Decline of Socialism in America,* 125–129; and Shannon, *Socialist Party of America,* 93–101.

37. See Wald, *Windows on Henry Street,* 308–311; Johnson, *Challenge to American Freedoms,* 14–25; Chambers, *Paul U. Kellogg and the Survey,* 62–63; Marchand, *American Peace Movement,* 253–259; and Chatfield, "World War I and the Liberal Pacifists," 1,925–34.

38. See Shannon, *Socialist Party of America,* 99–104 and Weinstein, *Decline of Socialism in America,* 129–133.

39. Reported in the *New York Times,* June 2, 1917.

40. Myers, quoted in Shannon, *Socialist Party of America,* 100.

41. Walling to W. B. Wilson, May 2, 1917, printed as an enclosure with W. B. Wilson to the President, May 3, 1917, *PWW,* XLII, 197–198.

42. Quoted in John L. Heaton, *Cobb of "The World",* (New York, 1924), 270.

43. An Address to a Joint Session of Congress, April 2, 1917, *PWW,* XLI, 526.

44. Flag Day Address, June 14, 1917, *ibid.,* XLII, 504.

45. The definitive study is Stephen Vaughn, *Holding Fast the Inner Lines: Democracy, Nationalism, and the Committee on Public Information* (Chapel Hill, N.C., 1980); for Creel's own account, see his *How We Advertised the War* (New York, 1920).

46. See Peterson and Fite, *Opponents of War,* 194–207.

47. *Ibid.,* 53–56; and Kennedy, *Over Here,* 263–264.

48. Peterson and Fite, *Opponents of War,* 57–59.

49. Paul L. Murphy, *World War I and the Origin of Civil Liberties in the United States* (New York, 1979), 164–166.

50. *Ibid.,* 196–197, 92–93, and 102–112. For a truly classic contemporary account of some of the foregoing and other incidents, see John Reed, "One Solid Month of Liberty," *Masses,* IX (September 1917), 5–6.

51. Wald *et al.* to Wilson, April 14, 1917, *PWW,* XLII, 119; see also Wald, *Windows on Henry Street,* 308–310.

52. Wald to Wilson, April 13, 1917, Wald Papers, New York Public Library, reel 1.

53. For a discussion, see Harry N. Scheiber, *The Wilson Administration and Civil Liberties, 1917–1921* (Ithaca, N.Y., 1960), 11–28.

54. See *ibid.,* 17–20; and Murphy, *World War I and the Origins of Civil Liberties,* 76–79.

55. See House diary, Feb. 11, 1918, *PWW,* XLVI, 327; Burleson to Wilson, Aug. 8, 1917, *ibid.,* XLIII, 395; and George P. West, "A Talk with Mr. Burleson," New York *Public,* XX (Oct. 12, 1917), 985–987, excerpt in *PWW,* XLIV, 470.

56. *New York Times,* Oct. 10, 1917, quoted in Scheiber, *Wilson Administration and Civil Liberties,* 33.

57. Sinclair to Wilson, Oct. 30, 1917, *PWW,* XLIV, 469–470.

58. For a general discussions, see Shannon, *American Socialist Party,* 110–114; Weinstein, *Decline of Socialism,* 143–145; and Scheiber, *Wilson Administration and Civil Liberties,* 29–41.

59. Eastman, Pinchot, and Reed, to Wilson, July 12, 1917, *PWW,* XLIII, 165.

60. Wilson to Tumulty, July 14, 1917, *ibid.,* 176; Wilson to Burleson, July 13, 1917, *ibid.,* 164, enclosing the letter from Eastman, Pinchot, and Reed. See also Wilson to Pinchot, July 13, 1917, *ibid.,* 164; and Pinchot to Tumulty, July 14, 1917, *ibid.,* 175–176. See also "What Happened to the August *Masses,*" *Masses* IX (September 1917), 3; and *New York Times,* July 22, 1917.

61. Burleson to Wilson, July 16, 1917, *PWW,* XLIII, 188.

62. Eastman to Wilson, Sept. 8, 1917, *ibid.,* XLIV, 169–172. Judge Learned Hand granted a preliminary injunction against the postal service on November 2, 1917. See *New York Times,* Nov. 3, 1917.

63. Wilson to Eastman, Sept. 18, 1917, *PWW,* XLIV, 210–211.

64. Wilson to Burleson, Sept. 4, 1917, *ibid.,* 147.

65. The *Milwaukee Leader* case, in particular, sparked protests to Wilson from Villard, Mayor Daniel Hoan of Milwaukee, and Grenville Mcfarland, as well as demands from such newspapers as the *Springfield Republican* that Burleson be relieved of his powers of censorship. See Villard to Tumulty, Sept. 27, 1917, *PWW,* XLIV, 271–273; Hoan to the White House, Oct. 8, 1917, *ibid.,* 338–340; McFarland to Wilson, Oct. 12, 1917, *ibid.,* 366; and "The Washington Censors," *Springfield Republican,* Oct. 9, 1917, which Wilson sent to Burleson, Oct. 10, 1917, *PWW,* XLIV, 358.

66. House to Wilson, Oct. 17, 1917, *PWW,* XLIV, 393.

67. Lippmann to House, Oct. 17, 1917, enclosure with House to Wilson, Oct. 17, 1917, *ibid.* (House had encouraged Lippmann to formulate his thoughts on the problem so that he could forward them to Wilson.)

68. Wilson to Croly, Oct. 22, 1917, *ibid.,* 420; in reply to Croly to Wilson, Oct. 19, 1917, *ibid.,* 408–410.

69. Wilson to Burleson, Oct. 18, 1917, *ibid.,* 396–397.

70. Sinclair to Wilson, Oct. 30, 1917, *ibid.,* 467–472.

71. Spargo to Wilson, Nov. 1, 1917, *ibid.,* 491–492.

72. See, for example, "Bases of Peace," ca. Feb. 9, 1917, *ibid.,* XLI, 1974; and Wilson to House, March 22, 1918, *ibid.,* XLVII, 105.

73. The principal studies on Allied wartime relations include: Wilton B. Fowler, *British American Relations, 1917–1918: The Role of Sir William Wiseman* (Princeton, N.J., 1969); Seth P. Tillman, *Anglo-American Relations at the Paris Peace Conference of 1919* (Princeton, N.J., 1961); as well as the works, previously cited, by Mayer, *Political Origins of the New Diplomacy;* Egerton, *Great Britain and the Creation of the League of Nations;* Martin, *Peace Without Victory;* and the most recent of such contributions, Gardner, *Safe for Democracy* (especially chaps. 6–10).

74. House to Wilson, April 22, 1917, *PWW,* XLII, 120.

75. These included the Treaty of London, which awarded to Italy portions of Turkey, the South Tyrol, and the Trentino; the Sykes-Picot Agreement, which provided for British and French dismemberment of the Ottoman Empire; and yet another treaty, which promised Constantinople to Russia. See Balfour to Wilson, May 18, 1917, with enclosures, *ibid.,* 327–328 (and WP, DLC for the treaties themselves); Wilson to Balfour, May 19, 1917, *PWW,* XLII, 346; and Tillman, *Anglo-American Relations,* 8–14.

76. Wilson to House, July 21, 1917, *PWW,* XLIII, 238 (Wilson's emphasis).

77. For additional background, see George F. Kennan, *Russia Leaves the War* (Princeton, N.J., 1956), 16–26; and Mayer, *Political Origins of the New Diplomacy,* 167–168. For a comprehensive study on American reaction to the Russian Revolution, see Christopher Lasch, *The American Liberals and the Russian Revolution* (New York, 1962).

78. Mayer, *Political Origins of the New Diplomacy,* 78–80; Gardner, *Safe for Democracy,* 133–135.

79. See the *New Republic,* XI (May 19, 1917), 62 and 65–67. (Tumulty sent a copy of this piece to Wilson on May 21; see *PWW,* XLII, 360–363.)

80. Dated May 29, the signers of the UDC letter included Norman Angell, J. A. Hobson, E. D. Morel, Charles Trevelyan, and J. Ramsay MacDonald. Colonel House withheld it from Wilson until June 28 because he, House, did not agree "altogether" with its purpose. See MacDonald *et al.* to Wilson, May 29, 1917, *ibid.,* 420–422; and House diary, June 28, 1917, HP, CtY.

81. See the Flag Day address, June 14, 1917, *PWW,* XLII, 498–504.

82. For the reaction of the British radicals, see Martin, *Peace Without Victory,* 136–137.

83. See Lansing to Wilson, Aug. 13, 1917, with enclosure, *PWW,* XLIII, 438–439; Mayer, *Political Origins of the New Diplomacy,* 229–236.

84. Wilson to House, Aug. 23, 1917, *PWW,* XLIV, 33.

85. For the complete text, see Wilson to Walter Hines Page, Aug. 27, 1917, with enclosure, *ibid.,* 57–59.

86. For the response of the British radicals, see Martin, *Peace Without Victory,* 144–145.

87. *Appeal to Reason,* Sept. 8, 1917.

88. Eastman to Wilson, Sept. 8, 1917, *PWW,* XLIV, 170; see also Sinclair to Wilson, Oct. 22, 1917, *ibid.,* 468.

89. This staff included George Louis Beer, Isaiah Bowman, Walter Lippmann, David Hunter Miller, Samuel Eliot Morison, Charles Seymour, James T. Shotwell, and Sidney Mezes (House's brother-in-law) as chairman. The definitive study is Lawrence E. Gelfand, *The Inquiry: American Preparation for Peace, 1917–1919* (New Haven, Conn., 1963).

90. See House diary, Oct. 13 and 24, 1917, *PWW,* XLIV, 378–379 and 437–439. The main purpose of this conference was to establish badly needed economic, military, and strategic coordination between the United States and the Allies.

91. For these events, see Kennan, *Russia Leaves the War,* 71–84 and 92–93; Mayer, *Political Origins of the New Diplomacy,* 245–266 and 278–280; and Gardner, *Safe for Democracy,* 148–150. The most exhaustive study is E. H. Carr, *The Bolshevik Revolution, 1917–1923,* 3 vols. (London, 1953).

92. See House to Wilson, Nov. 30, 1917; Wilson to House, Dec. 1, 1917; and House to Wilson, Dec. 2, 1917, *PWW,* XLV, 166, 176, and 184, respectively; and House diary, Nov. 16, 21, and 30, and Dec. 1, 1917, HP, CtY.

93. See Annual Message on the State of the Union, Dec. 4, 1917, *PWW,* XLV, 194–202.

94. See Martin, *Peace Without Victory,* 154–155.

95. See Peabody to Wilson, Dec. 4, 1917, *PWW,* XLV, 203–204; Philadelphia *Public Ledger,* Dec. 5, 1917; *New York American,* Dec. 6, 1917.

96. Kopelin to Wilson, Dec. 4, 1917, *PWW,* XLV, 203; and *Appeal to Reason,* Dec. 15, 1917.

97. See Mayer, *Political Origins of the New Diplomacy,* 295–298. It is important to note that Joffe's Six Points did not include disarmament or a league of nations; thus, the Bolshevik peace program was not as comprehensive as Wilson's.

98. House diary, Dec. 18, 1917, *PWW,* XLV, 323–324.

99. See Memorandum by Sidney Mezes, David Hunter Miller, and Walter Lippmann, "The Present Situation: The War Aims and Peace Terms It Suggests," ca. Dec. 22, 1917, in *ibid.*, 459–475; for a discussion of The Inquiry's work, see Gelfand, *The Inquiry*, 134–153; and Steel, *Walter Lippmann*, 133–134.

100. See House diary, Jan. 9, 1917, *PWW*, XLV, 550–559; First Versions of the Fourteen Points, Jan. 5, 1917, *ibid.*, 476–485; Wilson's shorthand draft and typescript of the draft, Jan. 6, 1917, *ibid.*, 493–518; and the final draft, Jan. 7, 1917, *ibid.*, 519–531.

101. See Mayer, *Political Origins of the New Diplomacy*, 315–323; and Egerton, *Great Britain and the Creation of the League of Nations*, 54–57.

102. See Egerton, *Great Britain and the Creation of the League of Nations*, 57–61; Mayer, *Political Origins of the New Diplomacy*, 323–328; and David R. Woodward, "The Origins and Intent of David Lloyd George's January 5 War Aims Speech," *Historian*, XXIV (November 1971), 22–39.

103. House diary, Jan. 9, 1918, *PWW*, XLV, 556–557.

104. An Address to a Joint Session of Congress, Jan. 8, 1918, *ibid.*, 534–539.

105. *New York Herald Tribune*, Jan. 9, 1918.

106. A frequent point of departure for the interpretation that Wilson was hostile from the start toward the Bolsheviks is Robert Lansing. Wilson's views are often erroneously assimilated with those of Lansing. Yet, when it came to Russia, as in so many other matters, Wilson virtually ignored the advice of his Secretary of State. Moreover, Wilson complained to House on several occasions about the company that Lansing kept— "society folk and reactionaries"; every time that he, Wilson, put out a statement, "Lansing followed it up with a conservative construction." See House diary, Sept. 9, 1917, *ibid.*, XLIV, 176; and Sept. 27, 1918, *ibid.*, LI, 144.

107. Mayer, *Political Origins of the New Diplomacy*, 373.

108. N. D. Baker to Wilson, with enclosure, Jan. 15, 1918, *PWW*, XLV, 594–595; Jusserand to Stephen Pichon, Jan. 9, 1918, *ibid.*, 550; see also Mayer, *Political Origins of the New Diplomacy*, 383–387.

109. See Swartz, *Union of Democratic Control*, 183–139. The London *Times* and the *Star* are quoted in the *New York Times*, Jan. 10, 1918. Balfour's made his comment in a speech at Edinburgh on January 10, summarized in *ibid.*, Jan. 11, 1918. Lloyd George's sentiments were conveyed in Sir Eric Drummond to Spring Rice, Jan. 12, 1918, *PWW*, XLV, 577–578. For additional commentary, see Tillman, *Anglo-American Relations*, 30–32; and Mayer, *Political Origins of the New Diplomacy*, 387–388.

110. The *New York Times*, Jan. 9, 1918, contains excellent coverage of congressional reaction.

111. *Ibid.*, Jan. 11, 1918; *Independent*, XCIII (Jan. 19, 1918), 89–92. For a survey of press opinion, see *Literary Digest*, LVI (Jan. 19, 1918), 11–14.

112. Wald to Wilson, Jan. 8, 1918, *PWW*, XLV, 541–542; Addams to Wilson, Jan. 14, 1918, *ibid.*, 586; Spargo to Wilson, Jan. 8, 1918, *ibid.*, 542. See also Bryan to Wilson, Jan. 15, 1917, *ibid.*, 599.

113. "A World's Peace," *Liberator*, I (March 1918), 10.

114. *Appeal to Reason*, Jan. 12 and May 25, 1918.

115. Debs is quoted in Weinstein, *Decline of Socialism*, 119 (see also 164–166); Jones in *Mother Jones Speaks*, 296; London in *Appeal to Reason*, May 25, 1918.

116. "Wilson and the World's Future," *Liberator*, I (May 1918), 19 and 21.

117. Randolph S. Bourne, *War and the Intellectual: Collected Essays, 1915–1919*, edited by Carl Resek (New York, 1964), 57. See also Kennedy, *Over Here*, 51–52.

Notes to Chapter 9

1. Wilson to Addams, Jan. 15, 1918, *PWW,* XLV, 593.

2. See Winkler, *League of Nations Movement in Great Britain,* Chap. 3, "Propaganda for the League," 50–83.

3. See Cecil to House, Sept. 3, 1917, *IPCH,* IV, 6–7; and House Diary, Nov. 13, 1917, HP, CtY. See also Drummond to Balfour, Nov. 15, 1917, *PWW,* XLV, 68.

4. Cecil to House, Feb. 16, 1918, *ibid.,* XLVII, 103–104; for a discussion, see Egerton, *Great Britain and the Creation of the League of Nations,* 65–66.

5. See Kuehl, *Seeking World Order,* 241–246.

6. For the LEP's "Tentative Draft," see Latane (ed.), *Development of the League,* II, 791–794; see also Bartlett, *League to Enforce Peace,* 92–94.

7. See, for example, Marburg to Wilson, March 3, 1917; and Wilson to Marburg, March 8, 1918, *PWW,* XLVI, 549 and 572, respectively; House to Wilson, March 21, 1918, with enclosure, Lowell to House, March 13, 1918, *ibid.,* XLVII, 101–103; Marburg to Wilson, May 3, 1918, with enclosure, Bryce to Marburg, ca. May 1, 1918, *ibid.,* 507–508.

8. Wilson to House, March 22, 1918, *ibid.,* 105.

9. *Ibid.,* 105. See also House to Wilson, March 21, 1918, with enclosures, *ibid.,* 101–104.

10. See Bainbridge Colby (who acted as Wilson's intermediary in setting up the meeting) to Wilson, March 15 and 22, 1917, *ibid.,* 42 and 119; and Wilson to Colby, March 16 and 25, 1917, *ibid.,* 43 and 137.

11. Memorandum by Taft, ca. March 29, 1918, *ibid.,* 198–202.

12. See Grayson diary, Feb. 22, 1919, *ibid.,* LV, 225.

13. See Taft to T. W. Bickett, Oct. 30, 1918, enclosure with Burleson to Wilson, Nov. 10, 1918, *ibid.,* LIII, 29–30.

14. Lowell to Wilson, July 10, 1918, and Wilson to Lowell, July 11, 1918, *ibid.,* XLVIII, 586 and 590–591.

15. The suggestion came from Lippmann and Mezes. See House diary, Jan. 10, 1918, HP, CtY.

16. Sir William Wiseman gave House a copy of the report on June 20. (See Wiseman to Cecil, July 17, 1918, *PWW,* XLVIII, 647.) Wilson received a copy from Lord Reading, the new British Ambassador to the United States, on July 3. (Reading to Wilson, with enclosure, July 3, 1918, *ibid.,* 501–502.)

17. The Phillimore Report is printed in David Hunter Miller, *Drafting the Covenant,* 2 vols. (New York, 1928), II, 3–6. For an analysis, see Egerton, *Great Britain and the Creation of the League of Nations,* 66–69.

18. Egerton, *Great Britain and the Creation of the League of Nations,* 68.

19. *Ibid.,* 73.

20. House to Wilson, June 25, 1918, *PWW,* XLVIII, 424.

21. The letter stated that any war was of concern to the League. Disputes should be settled through arbitration, but the arbitrators should be selected by both the League and the parties to the dispute. This could be done on an *ad hoc* basis; the arbitration decision, however, would be subject to appeal, but the appeal was the last resort; should a disputant afterward defy the final judgment by going to war, every member of the League would break off diplomatic relations and exert economic and perhaps even physical force against the offender until it relented. The method of doing this would be dictated by the circumstances surrounding the incident. See House to Cecil, June 24, 1918, enclosure with House to Wilson, June 25, 1918, *PWW,* XLVIII, 425–426; and House diary, June 24, 1918, HP, CtY.

22. Wiseman to Reading, Aug. 16, 1918, *PWW*, XLIX, 273.

23. Wilson to House, with enclosure (Wilson's copy of the Phillimore Report), July 8, 1918, *ibid.*, XLVIII, 549–550.

24. See House diary, July 9, 14, 15, and 16, 1918, HP, CtY.

25. These included the creation of a Body of Delegates; the obligation of signatories to abrogate treaties inconsistent with the terms of the League; and the provision that empowered the delegates of charter members to grant or deny membership to other nations in the future.

26. The document is printed as an enclosure with House to Wilson, July 16, 1918, *PWW*, XLVIII, 630–637.

27. House to Wilson, July 14, 1918, *ibid.*, 608.

28. Wilson apparently made only two final copies, one for himself and one that he sent to House on September 7, printed in *PWW*, XLIX, pp. 467–471. It should be noted that the LEP's "Tentative Draft" offered no absolute guarantee of territorial integrity, made no provisions for territorial adjustments pursuant to self-determination, and said nothing about disarmament or its desirability. It also outlined three classes of league membership; the first group, presumably the great powers, would always enjoy a majority control over the two lesser groups. See Latane, *Development of the League of Nations Idea*, II, 791–795.

29. See House diary, Aug. 15, 1918, *PWW*, XLIX, 265–267.

30. See Wiseman to Reading, Aug. 16, 1918, *ibid.*, 273–274; and Egerton, *Great Britain and the Creation of the League of Nations*, 74–80.

31. Mayer, *Political Origins of the New Diplomacy*, 387–380.

32. The historiography on this controversial subject is quite large, but see Betty Miller Unterberger, *America's Siberian Expedition, 1918–1920* (Durham, N.C., 1956); and her "Woodrow Wilson and the Bolsheviks: The 'Acid Test' of Soviet-American Relations," *Diplomatic History*, XI (Spring 1987), 71–90; George F. Kennan, *The Decision to Intervene* (Princeton, N.J., 1958); William Appleman Williams, *American–Russian Relations, 1781–1947* (New York, 1971, reprint). Two excellent surveys of the literature are Eugene C. Trani, "Woodrow Wilson and the Decision to Intervene in Russia: A Reconsideration," *Journal of Modern History*, XLVIII (September 1976), 440–461; and John W. Long, "American Intervention in Russia: The North Russian Expedition, 1918–1919," *Diplomatic History*, VI (Winter 1982), 45–67.

33. See, for example, F. L. Polk to AmEmbassy, Tokio, Jan. 20, 1918, *PWW*, XLVI, 35; W. G. Sharp to Lansing, Feb. 19, 1918, *ibid.*, 388–389; Tasker Bliss to H. P. McCain, Feb. 19, 1918, *ibid.*, 391–392; two memoranda by W. V. Judson, Feb. 26 and March 4, 1918, enclosures with Benedict Crowell to Wilson, March 5, 1918, *ibid.*, 532–540; memorandum by William C. Bullitt for the State Department, March 2, 1918, *ibid.*, 510–513; memorandum by Wiseman for the Foreign Office, March 9, 1918, *ibid.*, 590–591.

34. Conveyed in Polk to Roland S. Morris, March 5, 1918, *ibid.*, 545.

35. See Wilson to Lansing, April 4, 1918, with Enclosure IV (telegram from Mr. Lockhart, April 2, on conversation with Trotsky) *ibid.*, XLVII 241 and 245–246; Balfour to Reading, April 15, 1918 (conveyed to Wilson by Lansing on April 19), *ibid.*, 355–357; Balfour to Reading, April 18, 1918, *ibid.*, 366–369; House to Wilson, April 24, 1918, *ibid.*, 417–418; and House diary, April 24, 1918, HP, CtY.

36. Foch to Wilson, June 27, 1918, *PWW*, XLVIII, 446; Wilson to House, July 8, 1918, *ibid.*, 550.

37. See David R. Woodward, "The British Government and Japanese Intervention in Russia During World War I," *Journal of Modern History*, XLVI (December 1974), 680–681; Reading to Lloyd George and Lord Milner, June 22, 1918, *PWW*, XLVIII, 395–397; and Lansing to Wilson, June 23, 1918, with enclosure, *ibid.*, 398–399.

38. Reading to Lloyd George, July 12, 1918, *ibid.,* 603.

39. Memorandum by Wiseman of an interview with Wilson, Oct. 16, 1918, *PWW,* LI, 350.

40. Minutes of War Cabinet Meeting 601, July 29, 1919, PRO, quoted in Trani, "Wilson and the Decision to Intervene in Russia," 459.

41. Reading to Lloyd George, July 12, 1918, *PWW,* XLVIII, 603.

42. Thomas to Wald, March 1, 1918, quoted in Shannon, *American Socialist Party,* 120.

43. Eastman, "Wilson and the World's Future," *The Liberator,* I (May 1918), 19 and 21.

44. Wilson to Masaryk, Aug. 7, 1918, *PWW,* XLIX, 203.

45. See, for a comparative example, *New Republic,* XVI (Aug. 31, 1918), 120; *ibid.,* XVI (Oct. 12, 1918), 301–304; *ibid.,* XVII (Dec. 21, 1918), 208; and William Hard, "Anti-Bolshevik: Mr. Sack," *ibid.,* XIX (July 23, 1919), 385–387. See also Christopher Lasch, *The American Liberals and the Russian Revolution* (New York, 1962), 109–118.

46. *Nation,* CVII (August 10 and 17, 1918), 135 and 159, quoted in Wreszin, *Oswald Garrison Villard,* 96.

47. Lasch, *New Radicalism in America,* 248.

48. See Norman Thomas, "The Acid Test of Our Democracy," *World Tomorrow,* I (October 1918), 219–226.

49. Eastman, "The Campaign Issue," *Liberator,* I (October 1918), 23.

50. For accounts of the *Masses* trials, see O'Neill, *Last Romantic,* 65–66, and Rosenstone, *Romantic Revolutionary,* 330–333.

51. Pinchot to Wilson, May 24, 1918, *PWW,* XLVIII, 146 and 147.

52. Sinclair to Wilson, May 18, 1918, *ibid.,* 59–60.

53. Costigan to Wilson, May 29, 1918, *ibid.,* 197–198.

54. Kent to Wilson, June 3, 1918, *ibid.,* 235.

55. Wilson sent all of these appeals to Gregory for his consideration. See Gregory to Wilson, June 6, 1918, *ibid.,* 251, n. 2. For coverage of the second *Masses* trial, see the *New York Times,* Oct. 1–6, 1918.

56. Wilson to Gregory, June 24, 1918, *PWW,* XLVIII, 405. For a discussion of the Stokes case, see Shannon, *American Socialist Party,* 112–113.

57. See *ibid.,* 115–117; Salvatore, *Citizen Debs,* 290–296; and Ginger, *Debs,* 372–378 and 384–386.

58. See W. A. Swanberg, *Norman Thomas, The Last Idealist* (New York, 1976), 60–64 (Burleson is quoted on 63); Wilson to Burleson, Sept. 16, 1918, *PWW,* LI, 12; and J. N. Sayre to Wilson, Sept. 19, 1918, *ibid.,* 77.

59. *Nation,* CVII (Sept. 14, 1918).

60. See Villard to Wilson and Villard to Tumulty, Sept. 17, 1918, *PWW,* LI, 56 and 57; Wilson to Tumulty, Sept. 18, 1918, *ibid.,* 55; and Villard to Tumulty, Sept. 18, 1918, *ibid.,* 57.

61. New York *World,* Sept. 22, 1918. For additional comment and discussion, see the *New York Times,* Sept. 20, 1918; Wreszin, *Oswald Garrison Villard,* 96–98; and Villard, *Fighting Years: Memoirs of a Liberal Editor* (New York, 1939), 355–356.

62. Villard to House, Feb. 14, 1918, quoted in Wreszin, *Oswald Garrison Villard,* 94.

63. Quoted in *ibid.,* 95.

64. "Memorandum by Paul Kellogg," ca. April 1918, quoted in Thompson, *Reformers and War,* 197.

65. There is no monograph on the LFNA, but see Wald, *Window on Henry Street,* 311–317; Chambers, *Paul U. Kellogg,* 72–77; DeBenedetti, *Origins of the Modern American Peace Movement,* 7–10; Thompson, *Reformers and War,* 1997–198; and, especially, Wolf-

gang J. Helbich, "American Liberals in the League of Nations Controversy," *Public Opinion Quarterly,* XXXI (Winter 1967–1968), 568–577.

66. The LFNA's "Statement of Principles" was published as an eight-page pamphlet on November 27, 1918. The *New Republic,* the *Nation,* and the *Survey* published it in their issues of November 30, 1918, and the *Independent* on Dec. 14, 1918.

67. Kellogg to Frankfurter, June 20, 1918, quoted in Chambers, *Paul U. Kellogg,* 68.

68. Quoted in Baker, *WWLL,* VIII, 253. Crosby's conversation with Wilson took place on July 5, 1918.

69. Baker to House, Aug. 19, 1918, HP, CtY.

70. House to Wilson, Sept. 3, 1918, *PWW,* XLIX, 428–429.

71. Quoted in Baker, *WWLL,* VIII, 253.

72. House diary, Sept. 24, 1918, *PWW,* LI, 103–104.

73. An Address at the Metropolitan Opera House, Sept. 27, 1918, *ibid.,* 127–133 (all italics are Wilson's).

74. See *Literary Digest,* LIX (Oct. 12, 1918), 11; "A Victory of Justice vs. a Victory of Power," *New Republic,* XVI (Oct. 5, 1918), 271; and *New York Times,* Sept. 28, 1918.

75. This editorial commentary is quoted in the *New York Times,* in the second of two compilations, Sept. 29 and 30, 1918. For another sampling, see "Shall the Peace League Include Germany," in *Literary Digest,* LIX (Oct. 12, 1918), 11–12.

76. Quoted in the survey by the *New York Times,* Sept. 30, 1918.

77. *New York Times,* Sept. 28, 1918.

78. *Ibid.,* Sept. 29, 1918.

79. *Ibid.*

80. *Ibid.,* Sept. 28, 1918.

81. See Martin, *Peace Without Victory,* 182.

82. Cecil's letter was conveyed in Gordon Auchincloss to Wilson, Sept. 30, 1918, *PWW,* LI, 164.

83. See Egerton, *Great Britain and the Creation of the League of Nations,* 90.

84. Quoted in the *Literary Digest,* LIX (Oct. 19, 1918), 12.

85. Both French sources are quoted in *ibid.,* 17–18.

86. See W. G. Sharp to Lansing, Sept. 28, 1918; and T. N. Page to Lansing, Sept. 29, 1918, in *FR-WWS, 1918,* Supp. 1, Vol. I, 328–329 and 331–334, respectively. On the blackout, see Henry F. Hollis (in Paris) to Wilson, Oct. 2, 1918, *PWW,* LI, 182–183. The French and British editorial commentary did not appear until the middle of October.

87. For the complete text, see Friedrich Oederlin, with Enclosure, to Wilson, Oct. 6, 1918, *PWW,* LI, 252–253. For details on the German decision and the gradual reconstitution of the government in light of the crisis, see Harry R. Rudin, *Armistice 1918* (New Haven, Conn., 1944), 1–88; and Klaus Schwabe, *Woodrow Wilson, Revolutionary Germany, and Peacemaking, 1918–1919* (Chapel Hill, N.C., 1985; translation of Schwabe's *Deutsche Revolution und Wilsons Frieden* (Dusseldorf, 1971), 30–39.

Notes to Chapter 10

1. See the *New York Times,* July 19 and 20, 1918.

2. Lodge, in the *Boston Evening Transcript,* Sept. 17, 1918, quoted in Livermore, *Politics Is Adjourned,* 212–213.

3. *New York Times,* Sept. 13 and 14, 1918.

4. As Herbert Croly had written to Wilson on Oct. 19, 1917 (*PWW,* XLIV, 410).

5. Hays' exposition of the Republican party platform of 1918, printed in *Forum* mag-

azine (August 1918), quoted in Hays, *The Autobiography of Will H. Hays* (New York, 1955), 167–168.

6. *American Economist,* Oct. 4, 1918, pp. 190–191, quoted in Arno J. Mayer, *Politics and Diplomacy of the Peacemaking: Containment and Counterrevolution at Versailles, 1918–1919* (New York, 1967), 122; see also *ibid.,* 121–123.

7. See *Congressional Record,* 65th Cong., 2d sess., 9,393–9,394; see also Widenor, *Henry Cabot Lodge,* 280–287.

8. Roosevelt to Anna Roosevelt Cowles, May 17, 1917, *LTR,* VIII, 1,192.

9. *Chicago Tribune,* Aug. 27, 1918, quoted in Livermore, *Politics Is Adjourned,* 212.

10. *New York Times,* Sept. 7, 1918.

11. Wilson to House, Oct. 28, 1918, *PWW,* LI, 473.

12. See *Congressional Record,* 65th Cong., 2d sess., 11,155–11,158.

13. *Ibid.,* pp. 11,158–11,163.

14. House diary, Oct. 9, 1918, *PWW,* LI, 278.

15. For the text, see Lansing to Oederlin, Oct. 8, 1918, *ibid.,* 268–269.

16. See *Congressional Record,* 65th Cong., 2d sess., Oct. 10, 1918, pp. 11,171–11,172; *New York Times,* Oct. 12, 1918; and "The President's Reply and the People's Reply," *Literary Digest,* LIX (Oct. 19, 1918), 7–8.

17. *Congressional Record,* 65th Cong., 2d sess., Oct. 10, 1918, p. 11,167; see also *New York Times,* Oct. 11, 1918.

18. See *Congressional Record,* 65th Cong., 2d sess., Oct. 14, 1918, pp. 11,229–11,231.

19. Quoted in *Literary Digest,* LIX (Oct. 19, 1918), 8–9.

20. Quoted in *ibid.,* 10.

21. Henry F. Hollis to Wilson, Oct. 11, 1918, *PWW,* LI, 298.

22. Reading to Wiseman, Oct. 10, 1918, *ibid.,* 295.

23. For the text of Germany's response to Wilson, see Wilhelm Solf to Lansing, Oct. 14, 1918, State Dept. Records, RG 59, 763.72119/2313, DNA. See also Schwabe, *Wilson, Revolutionary Germany, and Peacemaking,* 47–50.

24. Ashurst diary, Oct. 14, 1918, *PWW,* LI, 338–340. See also David Lawrence to Wilson, Oct. 13, 1918, *ibid.,* 320–324, for a similar opinion.

25. See, for example, Cecil's three telegrams (all on October 9) to the British Embassy in Washington, printed in *ibid.,* 288–290; Lloyd George to Sir Eric Geddes, Oct. 12, 1918, *ibid.,* 313; Reading to Wiseman, Oct. 12 and 13, 1918, *ibid.,* 313–314 and 324–325; Balfour to the British Chargé (two telegrams), Oct. 14, 1918, printed as enclosures with Lansing to Wilson, Oct. 14, 1918, *ibid.,* 334–336.

26. See Jusserand's account of this interview, printed as an enclosure with J. J. Jusserand to C. A. de R. Barclay, Oct. 11, 1918, *ibid.,* 307–309.

27. Geddes to Lloyd George, Oct. 13, 1918, *ibid.,* 325. See also Wiseman to Reading and Drummond, Oct. 13, 1918, *ibid.,* 328.

28. The note was sent as Lansing to Oederlin, Oct. 14, 1918, in SDR, RG 59, 763.72119/2313, DNA; the penultimate draft is printed in *PWW,* LI, 333–334. For a discussion of the drafting process, see House diary, Oct. 15, 1918, *ibid.,* 340–342. See also, Schwabe, *Wilson, Revolutionary Germany, and Peacemaking,* 50–55.

29. Memorandum by Homer S. Cummings, Oct. 20, 1918, *PWW,* LI, 392. For a review of opinion in the American and Allied press, see *New York Times,* Oct. 15, 1918; and "Passing Sentence on the Kaiser and His People," *Literary Digest,* LIX (Oct. 26, 1918), 14–16; see also *New Republic,* XVI (Oct. 19, 1918), 324–325.

30. The complete text is printed in *Correspondence between the Governments of the United States and Germany, October 23, 1918* (Washington, D.C.), SDR, RG 59, 763.72119/2377A, DNA, 5–6. For a discussion of the German decision, see Rudin, *Armistice 1918,* 133–165; and Schwabe, *Wilson, Revolutionary Germany, and Peacemaking,* 55–58.

31. Cummings to Wilson, Oct. 22, 1918, *PWW*, LI, 408–409.

32. Telegram from Balfour, Oct. 21, 1918, conveyed to Wilson on Oct. 22, printed in *ibid.*, 411–412; see also Rudin, *Armistice 1918*, 168–170.

33. Memorandum by Franklin K. Lane, Oct. 23, 1918, printed in *PWW*, LI, 413–414.

34. *Ibid.*, 415.

35. David F. Houston, *Eight Years with Wilson's Cabinet, 1913–1920*, 2 vols. (New York, 1926), I, 316.

36. Daniels diary, Oct. 23, 1918, *PWW*, LI, 416. Wilson held an informal meeting of other advisers on October 23.

37. See Wilson to Lansing, with enclosures, Oct. 23, 1918, *ibid.*, 416–419. For the German government's reaction, see Schwabe, *Wilson, Revolutionary Germany, and Peacemaking*, 95–117.

38. Quoted in Livermore, *Politics Is Adjourned*, 216.

39. Poindexter, quoted in *New York Times*, Oct. 22, 1918; the resolution is printed in *Congressional Record*, 65th Cong., 2nd sess., Oct. 21, 1918, p. 11,402.

40. Roosevelt to Lodge, Oct. 24, 1918, *LTR*, VIII, 1,380–1,381, and printed in *New York Times*, Oct. 25, 1918.

41. See the Philadelphia *Public Ledger*, Oct. 25, 1918; *New York Times*, Oct. 23, 26, and 28, 1918; and Bartlett, *League to Enforce Peace*, 108–110.

42. Bickett to Taft, Oct. 25, 1918, enclosure with Burleson to Wilson, Nov. 10, 1918, *PWW*, LIII, 28–29.

43. Taft to Bickett, Oct. 30, 1918, *ibid.*, 29–30.

44. Bickett to Taft, Nov. 2, 1918, *ibid.*, 30–31.

45. For the details of this interesting story, see Pringle, *Life and Times of William Howard Taft*, 912–914.

46. See Taft to Roosevelt, Aug. 20, 1918, quoted in *ibid.*, 931–932; and Roosevelt to Taft, Aug. 15, 1918, *LTR*, VIII, 1,362; see also Roosevelt to Taft, Aug. 26, 1918, Taft Papers, DLC; and an article by Roosevelt, "Sound Nationalism and Sound Internationalism," *Kansas City Star*, Aug. 4, 1918.

47. Roosevelt to Beveridge, Oct. 31, 1918, *LTR*, VIII, 1,385.

48. Taft to Bickett, Oct. 30, 1918, *PWW*, LIII, 29–30.

49. Throughout the summer and fall, Democratic candidates who faced particularly tight races had solicited White House endorsements for local consumption and had, in most cases, received them.

50. Quoted in "War and the New Congress," *Literary Digest* LIX (Oct. 26, 1918), 18.

51. Quoted in *ibid.*, 15.

52. New York *World*, Oct. 6, 1918.

53. "An Election in a Fog," *New Republic*, XVI (October 26, 1918), 364; see also "The President's Responsibility," *ibid.*, 360–361.

54. Lane wrote two accounts of this meeting, on November 1 and 6, 1918, printed in *PWW*, LI, 548 and 604–605.

55. House diary, Sept. 24, 1918, *ibid.*, 105.

56. Memorandum of a conversation by Lamont, Oct. 4, 1918, *ibid.*, 225.

57. See Tumulty's draft of Oct. 11, 1918, *ibid.*, 304–306; a fragment of a draft, ca. Oct. 13, 1918, *ibid.*, 317–318; a Second Draft, ca. Oct. 15, 1918, *ibid.*, 343–344; Wilson to Tumulty, with Enclosure, ca. Oct. 17, *ibid.*, 353–355; a Memorandum by Homer S. Cummings, Oct. 18, 1918, *ibid.*, 380–381; see also a Cummings Memorandum, Oct. 20, 1918, *ibid.*, 389–393.

58. David Lawrence also advances this thesis in *The True Story of Woodrow Wilson* (New York, 1924) 236; see also Joseph P. Tumulty, *Woodrow Wilson As I Know Him* (New York, 1921), 322–334.

59. An Appeal for a Democratic Congress, *PWW*, LI, 381–382.

60. According to Ray Stannard Baker's subsequent interviews with Cabinet members (including Burleson) as well as with other Democrats, the appeal came as a surprise, Wilson supposedly having made the decision on his own. See Baker, *WWLL*, VIII, 513–514, n. 1. Mrs. Wilson is quoted in *ibid.*, 510. See also House diary, Sept. 24, 1918, *PWW*, LI, 105; and Oct. 25, 1918, HP, CtY; and Taft to Bryce, Dec. 5, 1918, quoted in Pringle, *Life and Times of William Howard Taft*, 913.

61. See, for example, Link, *Woodrow Wilson, Revolution, War and Peace*, 88; and *American Epoch: A History of the United States Since 1900*, 2 vols. (New York, 1980, 5th ed.), I, 210; Livermore, *Politics Is Adjourned*, 220–223; and Thomas A. Bailey, *Woodrow Wilson and the Lost Peace* (New York, 1944; Chicago, 1963), 58–59 and 66–70.

62. Roosevelt to Kermit Roosevelt, Oct. 27, 1918, *LTR*, VIII, 1,382–1,383.

63. See Hays, *Memoirs*, 175–180.

64. See *ibid.*, 176; and the *New York Times*, Oct. 28, 1918; see also *ibid.*, Oct. 27, 1918.

65. *Ibid.*, Oct. 29, 1918.

66. Printed in the *New York Times*, Nov. 1, 1918.

67. *Ibid.*, Nov. 1, 2, and 5, 1918. Taft delivered major addresses at Wilmington, Delaware; Boston; and Portsmouth, New Hampshire, before coming home to Ohio.

68. Tumulty to Wilson, with Enclosure, Nov. 3, 1918, *PWW*, LI, 572–574.

69. *New York Times*, Nov. 3, 1918, quoted in Selig Adler, "The Congressional Election of 1918," *South Atlantic Quarterly*, XXXVI (October 1917), 459.

70. "An Election in a Fog," *New Republic*, XVI (Oct. 26, 1918), 363, 364 and 365.

71. Villard, "The German Collapse," *Nation*, CVII (November 2, 1918), 502, quoted in Wreszin, *Oswald Garrison Villard*, 101.

72. The most detailed studies of these negotiations are Inga Floto, *Colonel House in Paris: A Study of American Policy at the Paris Peace Conference, 1919* (Copenhagen, 1973; reprinted by Princeton University Press, 1980), 38–60; Schwabe, *Wilson, Revolutionary Germany, and Peacemaking*, 81–94; Arthur Walworth, *America's Moment: 1918, American Diplomacy at the End of World War I* (New York, 1977), 32–73; and Rudin, *Armistice*, 177–192 and 266–319. *IPCH*, IV, 89–200, remains an indispensable published source.

73. *Ibid.*, 88.

74. House diary, Oct. 28, 1918, quoted in *ibid.*, 150–151.

75. See House to Wilson, Oct. 27, 1918 (no. 2), *PWW*, LI, 463. Foch's memorandum, dated Oct. 26, 1918, is printed in *IPCH*, IV, 143–145; all of his conditions would be incorporated into the armistice, virtually without alteration.

76. Lloyd George is quoted in *ibid.*, 162. It will be recalled that the Prime Minister had sent word that he was "grateful" that his and Wilson's peace policies were "so entirely in harmony." (See *New York Times*, Jan. 11, 1918; and Sir Eric Drummond to Spring Rice, Jan. 12, 1918, *PWW*, XLV, 577–578.)

77. The so-called Cobb-Lippmann Memorandum is in House to Wilson, Oct. 29, 1918, *ibid.*, LI, 495–504. See also Steel, *Walter Lippmann*, 149–150.

78. See House to Wilson, Oct. 30, 1918 (no. 8), *PWW*, LI, 511–513; see also Rudin, *Armistice*, 266–271; and Floto, *Colonel House in Paris*, 50–51.

79. Wilson to House, Oct. 30, 1918, *PWW*, LI, 513. See also Wilson to House, Oct. 29, 1918, *ibid.*, 504–505.

80. The British memorandum is in House to Wilson, Oct. 30, 1918 (no. 12), *ibid.*, 515–516. See also Wilson to House, Oct. 31, 1918; and House to Wilson, with enclosure, Nov. 4, 1918, (no. 41) *ibid.*, 533 and 569–570.

81. House to Wilson, Oct. 30, 1918 (no. 12), *ibid.*, 515–517. See also Tillman, *Anglo-American Relations*, 44–51.

82. House diary, Nov. 4, 1918, *IPCH*, IV, 188.

83. House to Wilson, Nov. 5, 1918, *PWW,* LI, 594. For a detailed discussion of the actual drafting of the armistice terms, see Rudin, *Armistice 1918,* 285–319. The Germans were notified that they should send a representative to Marshal Foch, who would communicate to them the terms of the armistice (see Lansing to Sulzer, the Swiss foreign minister, Nov. 5, 1918, in *FRUS, 1918,* Supp. 1, Vol. I, 468–469).

84. See Schwabe, *Wilson, Revolutionary Germany, and Peace Making,* 90–92; and Floto, *Colonel House in Paris,* 44–47 and 53. Keith L. Nelson, however, was the first scholar to analyze House's performance along these lines, in "What Colonel House Overlooked in the Armistice," *Mid-America,* LI (April 1969), 75–91, expanded in Nelson's *Victors Divided: America and the Allies in Germany 1918–1923* (Berkeley, 1975).

85. Schwabe, *Wilson, Revolutionary Germany, and Peace Making,* 92 (see also 94); and Floto, *Colonel House in Paris,* 60. Link, *Woodrow Wilson, Revolution, War and Peace* (87–88); and Walworth, *America's Moment* (51 and 71–73) basically agree, but are not nearly so harsh in their assessments.

86. Wilson to House, Oct. 28, 1918; and Peyton C. March (Army Chief of Staff) to Pershing, Oct. 27, 1918, enclosure with N. D. Baker to Wilson, Oct. 28, 1918, *PWW,* LI, 473 and 471–472, respectively.

87. For instance, Foch said to House, "Fighting means struggling for certain results. If the Germans now sign an armistice under the general conditions we have just determined, . . . no man has the right to cause another drop of blood to be shed." (Quoted in *IPCH,* IV, 91.)

88. See House to Wilson, Oct. 30, 1918, *PWW,* LI, 516.

89. Roosevelt to Bryce, Nov. 11, 1918, Bryce Papers, Vol. 7, Bodleian Library, Oxford University; and *New York Times,* Nov. 7, 1918. Lodge wrote similar letters to Bryce, dated Dec. 14, 1918 and Jan. 16, 1919, in the Bryce Papers.

90. Taft to Horace Taft, Nov. 9, 1918, quoted in Pringle, *Life and Times of William Howard Taft,* 913; and *Public Ledger,* Nov. 7, 1918.

91. For a wide sampling and analysis of editorial opinion, see *New York Times,* Nov. 7, 1918; "President Wilson to Face a Republican Congress," *Literary Digest,* LIX (Nov. 16, 1918), 14–15; and "The Republican Opportunity," *ibid.,* Nov. 23, pp. 14–15.

92. See Livermore, *Politics Is Adjourned,* 227–237.

93. See Adler, "The Congressional Elections of 1918," 450–451; Burner, "The Breakup of the Wilson Coalition of 1916," *Mid-America,* XLV (January 1963), 19–23; and his *The Politics of Provincialism, The Democratic Party in Transition, 1918–1932* (New York, 1975, paper ed.) 34–40; and Livermore, *Politics Is Adjourned,* 169–175.

94. *Ibid.,* 227–238.

95. *New Republic,* XVII (Nov. 9, 1918), 26. An accompanying article, "The Foes of American Unity," condemned the administration's suppression of freedom of speech and of the press (27).

96. Villard to Tumulty, Nov. 8, 1918, *PWW,* LI, 646. See also "Woodrow Wilson, Politician," and "Why Is Roosevelt Unjailed?" *Nation,* CVII (Nov. 2, 1918), 503 and 546.

97. "Why the Wilson Peace Policy May Fail," *Dial,* LXV (Nov. 30, 1918), 459–463.

98. Eastman, "The Twilight of Liberalism," *Liberator,* I (February 1918), 5. See also Eastman's "The Campaign Issue," *ibid.,* October 1918, p. 24; "The League of Nations," *ibid.,* December 1918, pp. 5–6; and "Which League of Nations?" *ibid.,* February 1919, pp. 7–8.

99. Creel to Wilson, Nov. 8, 1918, *PWW,* LI, 645–646. Two years later, in his memoir, Creel reprinted this letter but omitted the sentences about "the liberal, radical, progressive, labor and socialist press." See *The War, The World and Wilson* (New York, 1920), 145–146.

100. Wilson's address is printed in *PWW,* LIII, 35–43. See also H. F. Ashurst diary,

Nov. 11, 1918, *ibid.,* 35; *New York Times,* Nov. 9 and 12, 1918; "The German Collapse," *Literary Digest,* LIX (Nov. 16, 1918), 9–10; and "An 'Unconditional Surrender'," *ibid.,* Nov. 23, 1918, pp. 12–13.

101. House's estimation of Wilson's selection, except for Bliss, was extremely negative. (House diary, Dec. 16, 1918, *PWW,* LIII, 401–402). For background on Bliss and White, see Frederick C. Palmer, *Bliss, Peacemaker* (New York, 1934); David F. Trask, *The United States and the Supreme War Council, 1917–1918* (Middletown, Conn., 1961); and Allan Nevins, *Henry White: Thirty Years of American Diplomacy* (New York, 1930).

102. For example, Bailey, *Woodrow Wilson and the Lost Peace,* 87–105; and Ferrell, *Woodrow Wilson and World War I,* 137–138.

103. For references within the administration to possible commissioners, see House diary, Sept. 24, 1918, *PWW,* LI, 109; House to Wilson, Nov. 10 and 14, 1918, *ibid.,* LIII, 25 and 72, respectively. Wilson's comment on Hughes is quoted in the Daniels diary, Nov. 19, 1918, *ibid.,* 135.

104. Wilson to Richard Hooker, Nov. 29, 1918, *ibid.,* 243–244.

105. Burleson to Wilson, with enclosures, Nov. 10, 1918, *ibid.,* 28–31.

106. Wilson to Hooker, Nov. 29, 1918, *ibid.,* 243. See also Creel, *The War, The World, and Wilson,* 153–156.

107. Cobb memorandum, Nov. 8, 1918, *ibid.,* LI, 590–591; Lansing memorandum, Nov. 18, 1918, *ibid.,* LIII, 127–128 (see also Lansing memorandum, Nov. 12, 1918, *ibid.,* 65–66); House diary, Oct. 13, 1918, *ibid.,* LI, 315; and House to Wilson, Nov. 14, 1918, *ibid.,* LIII, 71–72. For additional "anti" opinion of a friendly nature, see Pittman to Wilson, Nov. 15, 1918, *ibid.,* 93–95.

108. Clarke to Wilson, Nov. 18, 1918, *ibid.,* 120. For an additional sampling, see also Bryan to Wilson, Nov. 20, 1918, *ibid.,* 150; and E. P. Davis to Wilson, Nov. 28, 1918, *ibid.,* 243.

109. Quoted in "The President at the Peace Table," and "Making War on Our Chief Peacemaker," *Literary Digest,* LIX (Nov. 30 and Dec. 14, 1918), 14 and 10, respectively.

110. See *Congressional Record,* 65th Cong., 3rd sess., 23–31.

111. The quote is from James R. Mann, Republican floor leader, in *New York Times,* Dec. 4, 1918. For similar Republican editorial sentiment, see "Making War on Our Chief Peacemaker," *Literary Digest* (Dec. 14, 1918), 9–12.

112. "Taft Defends Wilson Trip; Says Advantages Are Clear; Constitution Confers the Right," Philadelphia *Public Ledger,* Dec. 5, 1918, clipping enclosed with Baker to Wilson, Dec. 5, 1918, *PWW,* LIII, 322–323; and Taft to Bryce, Dec. 5, 1918, quoted in Pringle, *Life and Times of William Howard Taft,* 939.

113. Addams, *Peace and Bread in Time of War,* 63–64.

114. Lansing to Wilson, Feb. 13, 1917 (with enclosure, Page to Lansing on Feb. 11, 1917), *PWW,* XLI, 210–214). For Lloyd George and Clemenceau's efforts to dissuade Wilson, see House to Wilson, Oct. 30, 1918 (no. 10), and Wilson to House, Oct. 31, 1918, *ibid.,* LI, 515 and 533, respectively; and (all in *ibid.,* LIII) House to Wilson, Nov. 14 and 15, 1918 (two cables), 71–72 and 84–85, respectively; Wilson to House, Nov. 16, 1918, p. 97.

115. Page to Wilson, Nov. 5, 1918, *ibid.,* LI, 601.

116. Quoted in *Literary Digest,* Dec. 14, 1918, p. 11.

117. Creel, *The War, the World, and Wilson,* 163; Tumulty, *Woodrow Wilson As I Know Him,* 335.

118. Benham diary, Dec. 5, 1918, *PWW,* LIII, 321.

119. *New York Times,* Nov. 17, 1918.

120. *New York Times,* Dec. 7, 1918; see also Taft's address to the Commercial Congress in New York, *ibid.,* Dec. 10, 1918; and Bartlett, *League to Enforce Peace,* 110.

121. See Bartlett, *League to Enforce Peace,* 111–112 and 220–222; DeBenedetti, *Origins*

of the Modern American Peace Movement, 7–11; "America and the League of Nations," *New Republic,* XVII (Nov. 30, 1918), 116–118; and the LFNA's "Statement of Principles," in *ibid.,* 134–137. Taft noted that the LFNA had "some very radical adherents and some who are more moderate," but was "glad to have their support." (*New York Times,* Dec. 7, 1918).

122. Quoted in *New York Times,* Nov. 27, 1918.

123. Bernard Shaw, *Peace Conference Hints* (London, 1919), 49–50.

124. Brailsford in the *Herald* of London, Jan. 4, 1919, quoted in Mayer, *Politics and Diplomacy of the Peacemaking,* 193.

125. State of the Union address, Dec. 2, 1918, *PWW,* LIII, 285.

Notes to Chapter 11

1. See *New York Times,* Dec. 5, 1918; Grayson diary, Dec. 4, 1918, *PWW,* LIII, 315; and Charles Seymour, *Letters from the Paris Peace Conference,* ed. by Harold B. Whiteman, Jr. (New Haven, Conn., 1965), 8.

2. Seymour, *Letters from the Paris Peace Conference,* 36–39; Raymond B. Fosdick diary, Dec. 14, 1918, *PWW,* LIII, 384–385; the reporter, William Bolitho, is quoted in Gene Smith, *When the Cheering Stopped: The Last Years of Woodrow Wilson* (New York, 1964), 39.

3. Grayson diary, Dec. 26–31, 1918, and Jan. 2–6, 1919, *PWW,* LIII: 508–512, 519–522, 526–529, 537–541, 543–547, 569–570, 589, 595–597, 605–607, 613–614, and 620–622, respectively.

4. "The attitude of the whole country toward trip has changed," Tumulty cabled Wilson on Jan. 6. "Feeling universal that . . . [your] prestige and influence greatly enhanced here and abroad. The criticisms of the cloakroom statesmen have lost their force" (*ibid.,* 625). See also R. S. Baker to Wilson, Dec. 18, 1918, *ibid.,* 435; *New York Times,* Dec. 19, 1918; and London *Times,* Dec. 21, 1918.

5. Address at Guildhall, Dec. 28, 1918, *PWW,* LIII, 532.

6. Address at Free Trade Hall, Dec. 30, 1918, *ibid.,* 550–551.

7. Address to the Italian Parliament, Jan. 3, 1919, *ibid.,* 599.

8. Wilson to House, Dec. 10, 1918, *ibid.,* 359.

9. Address at the City Hall of Milan, Jan. 5, 1919, *ibid.,* 618.

10. House diary, Dec. 17, 1918, *ibid.,* 418; Baker memorandum for Wilson, Dec. 18, 1918, *ibid.,* 435.

11. T. N. Page to Wilson, Dec. 24, 1918, *ibid.,* 496.

12. The Treaty of London was the main inducement the British government had contrived to persuade Italy to switch sides from the Central Powers to the Allies in 1915.

13. For background, see Rene Albrecht-Carrie, *Italy at the Paris Peace Conference* (New York, 1938); Mayer, *Politics and Diplomacy of the Peacemaking,* 194–226; and David F. Schmitz, "Woodrow Wilson and the Liberal Peace: The Problem of Italy and Imperialism," *Peace and Change,* XII (December 1987), 29–44.

14. Baker to Wilson, Dec. 18, 1919, *PWW,* LIII, 435; see also Baker to House, Nov. 22, 1918, HP, CtY.

15. See transcript of the Wilson-Bissolati conference, Jan. 4, 1919, enclosure with T. N. Page to Wilson, Jan. 7, 1919, *PWW,* LIII, 641–644.

16. For Wilson's attitude toward Orlando and Sonnino, see Bullitt diary, Dec. 11, 1918, *ibid.,* 367; and Lord Derby to Balfour, Dec. 22, 1918, *ibid.,* 472; see also Bliss to N. D. Baker, Jan. 4, 1919, *ibid.,* 609–610.

17. See House diary, Dec. 15, 1918, *ibid.,* LIII, 401; Lord Derby to Balfour, Dec. 16, 1918, *ibid.,* 409–410; Eric Drummond to Wiseman, Dec. 17, 1918, *ibid.,* 414.

18. See remarks to French Socialists, Dec. 14, 1918, *ibid.,* 387–388.

19. Benham diary, Jan. 27, 1918, *ibid.,* LIV, 307.

20. House diary, Dec. 15 and 19, 1918, *ibid.,* LIII, 400–401 and 448; and Grayson diary, Dec. 16, 1918, *ibid.,* 403.

21. See *London Times,* Dec. 31, 1918; and Seymour, *Letters,* 83–86; for a detailed account, see Mayer, *Political Origins of the New Diplomacy,* 177–187.

22. See "Clash of French and American Peace Plans," *Literary Digest,* LX (Jan. 11, 1919), 9–11.

23. House diary, Dec. 31, 1918, and Jan. 1 and 7, 1919, *PWW,* LIII, 577, 586–587, and 652–653, respectively.

24. Bliss to N. D. Baker, Jan. 4, 1918, *ibid.,* 610.

25. William C. Bullitt diary, Dec. 11, 1918, *ibid.,* 367.

26. See House diary, Dec. 31, 1918, and Jan. 1, 1919, *ibid.,* 577 and 586–587, respectively.

27. Wilson, quoted in Grayson diary, Feb. 8, 1919, *ibid.,* LV, 3; Clemenceau and Lloyd George, in George Allardice Riddell, *Lord Riddell's Intimate Diary of the Peace Conference and After, 1918–1923* (New York, 1934), 78 and 34, respectively.

28. Paul F. Boller, Jr., *Presidential Anecdotes* (New York, 1981), 220.

29. See J. A. Thompson, "The League of Nations Union and the Promotion of the League Idea in Great Britain, *Australian Journal of Politics and History,* XVIII (April 1972), 52–61; A. Lentin, *Lloyd George, Woodrow Wilson, and the Guilt of Germany: An Essay in the Pre-History of Appeasement* (Baton Rouge, 1985), 16–27; and Mayer, *Politics and Diplomacy of the Peacemaking,* 133–166; see also Harold Nicolson, *Peacemaking 1919* (New York, 1965 ed.), 19–24.

30. See Remarks to the League of Nations Union, Dec. 28, 1918, *PWW,* LIII, 530–531; and Grayson Diary, Dec. 28, 1918, *ibid.,* 527; published statement by the Trades Union Congress and Executive Committee of the Labour Party, Dec. 28, 1918, *ibid.,* 535–536. See also Wilson to Arthur Henderson, Jan. 24, 1919, *ibid.,* LIV, 257.

31. Wiseman to Foreign Office, Dec. 15, 1918, *ibid.,* LIII, 394–395; see also Derby to Balfour, Dec. 14, 1918, Derby Papers, House of Lords Record Office, F/52/2/52.

32. See Imperial War Cabinet (IWC) memorandum 47, draft minutes, Dec. 30, 1918, *PWW,* LIII, 558–559; House diary, Dec. 27, 1918, and Jan. 1, 1919, *ibid.,* 525 and 586–587; Grayson diary, Dec. 27, 1918, *ibid.,* 520–521; and Wilson's after-dinner remarks at Buckingham Palace, Dec. 27, 1918, *ibid.,* 523–524.

33. IWC memorandum, draft minutes, Dec. 30, 1918, *ibid.,* 565–566.

34. See *ibid.,* 567; and IWC memorandum 48, draft minutes, Dec. 31, 1918, pp. 5–6, Cab. 23/42, PRO.

35. IWC memorandum 48, draft minutes, Dec. 31, 1918, pp. 6–7, Cab. 23/42, PRO. See also, Egerton, *Great Britain and the Creation of the League of Nations,* 83–90 and 103–109. For Lloyd George's somewhat doctored account, see his *The Truth About the Peace Treaties,* 2 vols. (London, 1938), I, 184–201.

36. Cecil submitted this memorandum to the War Cabinet on Dec. 17 and to Wilson on Dec. 26, 1918. See *PWW,* LIII, 415–417.

37. The best exegesis of the document is Egerton, *Great Britain and the Creation of the League of Nations,* 83–88 and 101–103; see also W. K. Hancock, *Smuts: The Sanguine Years, 1870–1919* (London, 1962), 496–501; and George Curry, "Woodrow Wilson, Jan Smuts, and the Versailles Settlement," *American Historical Review,* LXVI (July 1961), 968–986. The pamphlet itself is a rare item; but it is printed in full in David Hunter Miller,

Drafting the Covenant, 2 vols. (New York, 1928), II, 23–60. All citations are to this source unless otherwise indicated.

38. Miller, *Drafting the Covenant,* II, 52–59.

39. *Ibid.,* pp. 48–52. Wilson's Covenant did not mention the abolition of conscription.

40. *Ibid.,* 39–46.

41. *Ibid.,* 60.

42. Smuts to M. C. Gillett, Dec. 27, 1918, in W. K. Hancock and Jean van der Poel (eds.), *Selections from the Smuts Papers* (Cambridge, 1966) IV, 34; Egerton, *Great Britain and the Creation of the League of Nations,* 102–103.

43. Wilson received the Smuts document, along with Cecil's memorandum, on December 26. See Memorandum, Dec. 26, 1918, *PWW,* LIII, 515 n. 1.

44. The quotations, respectively, are from Lloyd E. Ambrosius, *Woodrow Wilson and the American Diplomatic Tradition: The Treaty Fight in Perspective* (Cambridge, England, 1987), 56–57; Curry, "Woodrow Wilson, Jan Smuts, and the Versailles Settlement," 971; and Peter Raffo, "The Anglo-American Preliminary Negotiations for a League of Nations," *Journal of Contemporary History,* IX (October 1974), 154 (see also 153 and 176).

45. See Bliss to N. D. Baker, Jan. 4, 1919, *PWW,* LIII, 609; and Benham diary, Jan. 18, 1919, *ibid.,* LIV, 149.

46. Smuts, quoted in a somewhat different context, in Curry, "Woodrow Wilson, Jan Smuts, and the Versailles Settlement," 971.

47. J. A. Hobson, *Towards International Government* (New York, 1915), 139–142.

48. For a discussion of the conference, see Mayer, *Politics and Diplomacy of the Peacemaking,* 46–52.

49. See Gelfand, *Inquiry,* 229–240.

50. Memorandum by Wiseman, Oct. 16, 1918, *PWW,* LI, 350.

51. C. A. de R. Barclay to the British Foreign Office, Nov. 3, 1918, *ibid.,* 574; see also Cecil to Barclay, Oct. 31, 1918, *ibid.,* 539–540, nn. 1 and 2.

52. See Bullitt diary, Dec. 10, 1918, *ibid.,* LIII, 351; memorandum by Isaiah Bowman, Dec. 10, 1918, *ibid.,* 355. The most comprehensive study is James M. Carr, "A Sacred Trust of Civilization: Woodrow Wilson and the Genesis of the Mandate System," unpublished senior thesis, Princeton University, 1982.

53. Bliss to N. D. Baker, Jan. 4, 1919, *ibid.,* LIII, 609.

54. Wilson to Bryce, Jan. 16, 1919, *ibid.,* LIV, 104.

55. Grayson diary, Jan. 6, 1919, *ibid.,* LIII, 622.

56. Benham diary, Jan. 21, 1919, *ibid.,* LIV, 197; Grayson diary, Jan. 21, 1919, *ibid.,* 177.

57. Bliss to N. D. Baker, Jan. 4, 1919, *ibid.,* LIII, 609.

58. Draft of a Covenant, ca. Jan. 8, 1919, *ibid.,* 678–686. Wilson had earlier discussed the idea for a plank on labor with House, Bullitt, and Raymond Fosdick, among others; see Bullitt diary, Dec. 11, 1918, *ibid.,* 367; and House diary, Dec. 16, 1918, *ibid.,* 402.

59. See Cecil diary, Jan. 8, 1919, Papers of Lord Robert Cecil, PRO, copy in Wilson Papers Archive, NjP (portions of which are printed in *PWW*); Cecil's "Very Secret Record of an interview with Colonel House at Paris, Thursday, January 9, 1919," Jan. 10, 1919, in Cecil Papers, Additional Mss; and House diary, Jan. 8, 1919, *PWW,* LIII, 693.

60. Lansing to Wilson, with Enclosure, Dec. 23, 1918, *ibid.,* 474–476; see also Lansing's *The Peace Negotiations* (Boston, 1921), 50–68.

61. House diary, Jan. 8, 1918, *PWW,* LIII, 694–695; Miller, *Drafting the Covenant,* I, 28–33; see also *FR-PPC,* I, 298–315.

62. See Miller, *Drafting the Covenant,* I, 29–30, and II, 61–64. Miller shared Lansing's negative views on Wilson's basic approach; see, for instance, his massive *My Diary at the*

Conference of Paris, with Documents, 21 vols. (New York, 1924), I, 72. For Lansing's labors, see Ambrosius, *Woodrow Wilson and the American Diplomatic Tradition,* 59–62.

63. Lansing Memorandum, Jan. 11, 1919, *PWW,* LIV, 4.

64. Cecil diary, Jan. 13 and 15, 1919, Cecil Papers.

65. See, for example, Lansing's account of this incident, printed in *PWW,* LIV, 3–4; see also Bliss to N. D. Baker, Jan. 11, 1919, *ibid.,* LIII, 720–721.

66. Bliss to Wilson, with Enclosure, Jan. 15, 1919, *ibid.,* LIV, 84–88.

67. Emphasis added.

68. See Wilson's "Second Paris Draft," Jan. 18, 1919, *ibid.,* 138–148; see also, Wilson to Bliss, Jan. 17, 1919, *ibid.,* 123.

69. See, for example, Bliss to N. D. Baker, Oct. 23, 1918, *ibid.,* LI, 585: "If the President's idea of rational disarmament can only be realized it will simplify the whole problem. . . . there will be no necessity of taking away this or that or the other part of the defeated nation."

70. Memorandum by Gustave Ador, Jan. 23, 1919, *ibid.,* LIV, 233.

71. Speech at Mansion House, London, Dec. 28, 1918, *ibid.,* LIII, 534.

72. Cecil diary, Jan. 19, 1919, *ibid.,* LIV, 152.

73. Cecil diary, Jan. 22, 1919, Cecil Papers.

74. See House to Wilson, Jan. 19, 1919, with enclosure, WP, DLC, and Cecil to Wilson, Jan. 20, 1919, with enclosure, *PWW,* LIV, 160–170; see also Wiseman diary, Jan. 19, 1919, *ibid.,* 151, and Miller, *Drafting the Covenant,* I, 51–64. For background on Cecil's "Draft Convention," see Egerton, *Great Britain and the Creation of the League of Nations,* 114–117.

75. Smuts to M. C. Gilbert, Jan. 20, 1919, *Smuts Papers,* IV, 50.

76. See Tillman, *Anglo-American Relations,* 119; Egerton, *Great Britain and the Creation of the League of Nations,* 118; and Ambrosius, *Woodrow Wilson and the American Diplomatic Tradition,* 64.

77. Quoted in Egerton, *Great Britain and the Creation of the League of Nations,* 117.

78. Cecil's "Draft Convention," Jan. 20, 1919, *PWW,* LIV, 161.

79. *Ibid.,* 161–163.

80. Maurice Hankey's notes of a meeting of the Council of Ten, Jan. 22, 1919, *ibid.,* 206 (see also, 207–211). About the composition of these resolutions, see House to Wilson, Jan. 19, 1919, *ibid.,* 150 and Wiseman diary, Jan. 19, 1919, *ibid.,* 151.

81. Protocol of a Plenary Session of the Inter-Allied Peace Conference, Jan 25, 1919, *ibid.,* 264–271. (The Council of Ten, consisting of representatives of the five great powers, was the main decision-making body at Paris during the initial phase of the peace conference.)

82. Quoted in Creel, *The War, the World, and Wilson,* 163.

Notes to Chapter 12

1. Seymour to his family, Jan. 30, 1919, *Letters from the Paris Peace Conference,* 134–135. According to Wilson, the first meeting of the conference resembled "an old ladies' tea party" (Benham diary, Jan. 12, 1919, *PWW,* LIV, 34).

2. Cecil diary, Feb. 10, 1919, Cecil Papers.

3. Seymour to his family, Jan. 30 and Feb. 8, 1919, *Letters from the Paris Peace Conference,* 137 and 155.

4. *Ibid.,* 135; Clemenceau is quoted in Grayson diary, Jan. 18, 1919, *PWW,* LIV, 127. See also Herbert Bayard Swope, "Personal Cordiality Wins Colleagues to President," New York *World,* Jan. 15, 1919.

5. Derby to Balfour, Dec. 24, 1918, *PWW*, LIII, 498.

6. See Hankey's notes, Council of Ten, BC-10, Jan. 24, 1919 (3 P.M.), and Jan. 27, 1919 (3 P.M.) *ibid.*, LIV, 249–254 and 291–301, respectively; and Cecil diary, Jan. 25, 1919, Cecil Papers. For a detailed study of the dominions' position, see William Roger Louis, *Great Britain and Germany's Lost Colonies, 1914–1919* (London, 1967).

7. Hankey's notes, Council of Ten, BC-12, Jan. 27, 1919 (3 P.M.), *PWW*, LIV, 293–294.

8. *Ibid.*, 295–296.

9. *Ibid.*, 296–297.

10. *Ibid.*, 298–299.

11. Hankey's notes, Council of Ten, BC-14, Jan. 28, 1919 (4 P.M.), *ibid.*, 323 and 325.

12. *Ibid.*, 323.

13. See British Empire Delegation minutes, Jan. 27 and Jan. 29, 1919, Cab. 28/29, PRO. The quotation is from the annex attached to Hankey's notes of the Council of Ten, BC-17, Jan. 30, 1919 (11 A.M.), *PWW*, LIV, 361. See also House diary, Jan. 29, 1919, *ibid.*, 347; House to Wilson, Jan. 29, 1919; and Wilson to House, Jan. 29, 1919, HP, CtY.

14. Hankey's Notes of Council of Ten, BC-17, Jan. 30, 1919 (11 A.M.), *PWW*, LIV, 353–54.

15. *Ibid.*, 354 and 357–358.

16. See *ibid.* (BC-18, 3:30 P.M.), 363–364; Riddell, *Intimate Diary of the Peace Conference*, 19; and Arthur Walworth, *Wilson and His Peacemakers, American Diplomacy at the Paris Peace Conference, 1919* (New York, 1986), 76–79.

17. See Hankey's Notes of Council of Ten, BC-17, Jan. 30, 1919 (3:30 P.M.), *PWW*, LIV, 365–371.

18. See Grayson diary, Jan. 28, 1919, *ibid.*, 308.

19. William L. Westerman diary, Jan. 12, 1919, Columbia University Library.

20. Quoted in "The Future of Germany's Colonies," *Literary Digest*, LX (Feb. 15, 1919), 21.

21. Quoted in Ferrell, *Woodrow Wilson and World War I*, 152.

22. Miller, *Drafting the Covenant*, I, 53.

23. See Miller, *ibid.*, I, 51–64; Cecil diary, Jan. 21, 25, and 27, 1919, Cecil Papers; and House diary, Jan. 30, 1919, *PWW*, LIV, 386–387.

24. The Cecil-Miller Draft is printed in *Drafting the Covenant*, II, 131–141.

25. Cecil diary, Jan. 20, 1919, Cecil Papers.

26. For a detailed discussion, see Egerton, *Great Britain and the Creation of the League of Nations*, 120–125. Quotations from a memorandum prepared by Philip Kerr, which Lloyd George read aloud to Cecil (*ibid.*, 122 and 123). The evidence that Lansing had a hand in all of this is only circumstantial, but see Lansing to Wilson, with enclosure, Jan. 31, 1919, *PWW*, LIV, 400–402.

27. See House diary, Jan. 30, 1919, *PWW*, LIV, 386.

28. Cecil diary, Jan. 31, 1919, Cecil Papers.

29. Cecil diary, Jan. 31, 1919, extract in *PWW*, LIV, 408 (emphasis added). See also House diary, Jan. 31, 1919, in *ibid.*, 407; and Miller, *Drafting the Covenant*, I, 65–67.

30. According to Sir William Wiseman's diary (Feb. 3, 1919), Wilson was less than enthusiastic about this decision: "After much difficulty CECIL persuaded the PRESIDENT to let HURST and MILLER re-write the President's draft treaty . . ." (*PWW*, LIV, 461).

31. The Hurst-Miller Draft is printed in *ibid.*, 433–439. For an account of their discussions, see Miller, *Drafting the Covenant* I, 67–71 and 52–53. The new article on collective security, which would become Article X of the final covenant, now read as follows: "The High Contracting Parties undertake to respect and preserve as against external

aggression the territorial integrity and political independence of all States members of the League."

32. See, for example, Ambrosius, *Woodrow Wilson and the American Diplomatic Tradition*, 70; and Raffo, "Anglo-American Preliminary Negotiations for a League of Nations," 171–172.

33. The first version of Wilson's Third Paris Draft is printed *in camera*, in *PWW*, LIV, 441–448; Miller's recasting is enclosed with Miller to Wilson, Feb. 3, 1919, *ibid.*, 449–458. See also Miller diary, Feb. 2–3, 1919, *ibid.*, 439–440; House diary, Feb. 3, 1919, *ibid.*, 459; and Feb. 2, 1919, in HP, CtY.

34. See House diary, Feb. 3, 1919, *PWW*, LIV, 459; Wiseman diary, Feb. 3, 1919, *ibid.*, 461; and Cecil diary, Feb. 3, 1919, *ibid.*, 460–461.

35. Cecil diary, *ibid.*, 460–461.

36. The delegations to the Commission went as follows: the United States—Wilson and House; the British Empire—Cecil and Smuts; France—Léon Bourgeois and Fernand Larnaude; Italy—Orlando and Vittorio Scialoja; Japan—Sutemi Chinda and Nobuaki Makino; China—Ku Wei-chun (V. K. Wellington Koo); Belgium—Paul Hymans; Brazil—Epitacio Pessoa; Portugal—Jayne Batalha Reis; Serbia—Melinko R. Vesnic; Greece—Eleutherios Veniselos; Poland—Roman Dmowski; Romania—Constantin J. Diamandy; Czechoslovakia—Karel Kramar. The last four delegates were not original members; the decision to invite them was made during the Commission's second meeting. See Hankey's Notes, Council of Ten, Feb. 3, 1919, (11 A.M.) *PWW*, LIV, 461–463; and Miller, *Drafting the Covenant*, I, 134, 138, and 156.

37. Cecil diary, Feb. 3, 1919, *PWW*, LIV, 460.

38. See Miller, *Drafting the Covenant*, I, 130–136; and House diary, Feb. 3, 1919, *PWW*, LIV, 460.

39. Quoted in Miller, *Drafting the Covenant*, I, 161.

40. Miller, *Drafting the Covenant*, I, 140, 146–148, and 151–152.

41. The article had been referred to the Commission's drafting committee (House, Cecil, Wellington, Koo, Orlando, Bourgeois, and Smuts). House presented a version, inspired by Wilson, setting the number of small powers at four; however, House and Cecil agreed on a draft providing for only two small powers. See House to Wilson, Feb. 5, 1919, *PWW*, LIV, 494–495; Cecil diary, Feb. 5, 1919, Cecil Papers; and Miller, *Drafting the Covenant*, I, 154–155.

42. See *Drafting the Covenant*, I, 160–162.

43. *Ibid.*, 162–163; House diary, Feb. 5, 1919, in *IPCH*, IV, 311.

44. See Miller, *Drafting the Covenant*, II, 301–302.

45. See, for example, Egerton, *Great Britain and the Creation of the League of Nations*, 129–131; Tillman, *Anglo-American Relations*, 124; Ambrosius, *Woodrow Wilson and American Diplomatic Tradition*, 73; and Walworth, *Wilson and His Peacemakers*, 117–118.

46. Benham diary, Feb. 6, 1919, *PWW*, LIV, 522, n. 1.

47. Grayson diary, Jan. 6, 1919, *ibid.*, LIII, 622.

48. Quoted in Miller, *Drafting the Covenant*, I, 162–163; for two other examples, see *ibid.*, 146 and 161.

49. *Ibid.*, 146.

50. *Ibid.*, 147 and 148.

51. *Ibid.*, 161 and 163.

52. Cecil diary, Feb. 4, 1919.

53. Miller, *Drafting the Covenant*, I, 168.

54. *Ibid.*, 168–169.

55. Cecil diary, Feb. 6, 1919, *PWW*, LIV, 514.

56. *Ibid.*; and Miller, *Drafting the Covenant*, I, 170.

57. As he had phrased it in Wilson to House, March 22, 1918, *PWW*, XLVII, 105.

58. See Miller, *Drafting the Covenant*, I, 172–174; and Cecil diary, Feb. 6, 1919, *PWW*, LIV, 514.

59. Miller, *Drafting the Covenant*, I, 173–178.

60. *Ibid.*, 179, 181–182; see also *ibid.*, II, 265–266 and 268–270. The subcommittee's amendment was accepted during the Commission's seventh meeting, on February 10. For details, see *ibid.*, I, 192–195, and II, 283.

61. See *ibid.*, I, 185–188, and II, 272–273.

62. See *ibid.*, I, 191, and II, 272.

63. The French draft is printed in *ibid.*, II, 238–246.

64. See *ibid.*, I, 206–210, and II, 290–293.

65. *Ibid.*, II, 293–294.

66. *Ibid.*, 294–295.

67. *Ibid.*, 296.

68. *Ibid.*, 297.

69. Cecil diary, Feb. 11, 1919, *PWW*, LV, 80. See also Miller, *My Diary at the Peace Conference*, I, 119 (Feb. 12, 1919), printed in *PWW*, LV, 118; and Miller, *Drafting the Covenant*, I, 216–217.

70. Grayson diary, Feb. 10, 1919, *PWW*, LV, 41; see also House diary, Feb. 11, 1919, *ibid.*, 88–89; and Florence Haskell Corliss Lamont diary, Feb. 12, 1919, *ibid.*, 120.

71. *Drafting the Covenant*, I, 225 and 229–230, and II, 298–299.

72. *Ibid.*, I, 231–236, and II, 300–302.

73. *Ibid.*, I, 236–240, and II, 303–304. (New members would be admitted upon a two-thirds vote of the Body of Delegates.)

74. See *ibid.*, I, 243 and 244–267.

75. An expanded clause to this effect became Article IX of the Covenant, with explicit reference to Article VIII, on disarmament. See *ibid.*, I, 243 and 251–252, and II, 296 and 317–321.

76. It read as follows: "The equality of states being a basic principle of the League of Nations, the High Contracting Parties agree to accord, as soon as possible, to all alien nationals of States members of the League, equal and just treatment in every respect, making no distinction, either in law or fact, on account of their race or nationality" (*ibid.*, II, 324).

77. House diary, Feb. 4, 1919, *PWW*, LIV, 485.

78. Miller diary, Jan. 30, 1919, *ibid.*, 379.

79. See Hankey's notes of a meeting of the Council of Ten, Jan. 22, 1919, *ibid.*, 206–208.

80. See Draft Article, Feb. 5, 1919, *ibid.*, 500.

81. See Miller, *Drafting the Covenant*, I, 269, and especially II, 324–325.

82. See *ibid.*, 325; Miller, *My Diary*, I, 116; and House diary, Feb. 9, 1919, *IPCH*, IV, 313, and Feb. 13, 1919, *PWW*, LV, 155.

83. See *Drafting the Covenant*, I, 267–269, and II, 325–326; Miller, *My Diary*, I, Feb. 13, 1919, printed in *PWW*, LV, 154; and House diary, Feb. 13, 1919, *ibid.*, 155–156.

84. Miller, *Drafting the Covenant*, II, 325–327.

85. *Ibid.*, 240–242.

86. House diary, Feb. 13, 1919, *PWW*, LV, 156.

87. Wilson's address, along with the entire Covenant, is printed in *ibid.*, 164–178.

88. Cecil's speech is printed in *FR-PPC*, III, 215–217.

89. As Walter Lippmann had put it in 1917 in *The Stakes of Diplomacy*, xxii.

90. Tumulty to Wilson, Feb. 15, 1919, *PWW*, LV, 198.

91. House diary, Feb. 15, 1919, *ibid.*, 196.

Notes to Chapter 13

1. For these untoward events, see Grayson diary, Feb. 19 and 23, 1919, *PWW,* LV, 207 and 229, respectively.

2. T. W. Gregory to Wilson, Jan. 14, 1919, *ibid.,* LIV, 58, and Wilson to Taft, Feb. 26, 1919, *ibid.,* LV, 281–282; see also Bartlett, *League to Enforce Peace,* 118–121.

3. Statement by the Great Lakes Congress of the LEP, Feb. 10, 1919, copy in WP, DLC; see also W. H. Short to Wilson, Feb. 9, 1919, reporting on the Atlantic Congress of the LEP, and Wilson to Short, Feb. 14, 1919, *PWW,* LV, 37–38 and 186.

4. See, for example, Joint Resolution of the Wisconsin legislature, copy in Merlin Hull to Wilson, Feb. 13, 1919, *ibid.,* 158; F. H. Lynch to Wilson, Jan. 25, 1919, *ibid.,* LIV, 277; and T. E. Burton to Wilson, Feb. 24, 1919, WP, DLC.

5. See McAdoo to Wilson, Feb. 17, 1919, *PWW,* LV, 205; Baker memo to Wilson, March 6, 1919, *ibid.,* 449–450; "Will the Peace League Prevent War?" *Literary Digest,* LX (March 1, 1919), 11–13, for a summary of opinion; *New York Times,* Feb. 18, 1919; New York *Sun,* Feb. 15, 1919. See also *New York Tribune,* Feb. 15 and 18, 1919; New York *World,* Feb. 15, 1919; and Philadelphia *Public Ledger,* Feb. 24, 1919.

6. As Wilson wrote to Edward Bok, Feb. 27, 1919, *PWW,* LV, 303.

7. Since the 1950s, most writers on the subject—Link, Mayer, Stone, Levin, Widenor, Ferrell, and Ambrosius, to name a few—have dismissed "isolationism" as a serious factor. The major exceptions are Adler's *The Isolationist Impulse* (New York, 1957) and John Chalmers Vinson's *Referendum for Isolation: Defeat of Article Ten of the League of Nations Covenant* (Athens: University of Georgia Press, 1961).

8. See *Congressional Record,* 65th Cong., 3rd sess, (Feb. 27, 1919), 4,414–4,418 (emphasis added).

9. Quoted in Cooper, *Warrior and the Priest,* 333.

10. Roosevelt to Balfour, Dec. 10, 1918, *LTR,* VIII, 1,415.

11. Roosevelt to his physician, quoted in Harbaugh, *Power and Responsibility,* 486.

12. Quoted in Cooper, *Warrior and the Priest,* 334. See also Ralph Stout (ed.) *Roosevelt in the Kansas City Star,* 188–196, 277–281, and 292–295.

13. Quoted in Widenor, *Henry Cabot Lodge,* 295.

14. For a discussion, see Cooper, *Warrior and the Priest,* 332–335; and Harbaugh's moving account of TR's last days in *Power and Responsibility,* 479–490.

15. Quoted in Wreszin, *Oswald Garrison Villard,* 110.

16. For the "Knox Resolution," see Stone, *Irreconcilables,* 44–46; for other preliminary criticism in the Senate, 24–51.

17. *Congressional Record,* 65th Cong., 3rd sess., Dec. 21, 1918, pp. 723–728 and 972–972 (quotation on 727).

18. Lodge to Bryce, Jan. 16, 1918, Bryce papers, Vol. 7, Bodleian Library.

19. *Congressional Record,* 65th Cong., 3rd sess., Dec. 21, 1918, 728.

20. See Wilson to Tumulty, Feb. 14, 1919; and House diary, Feb. 14, 1919, *PWW,* LV, 184 and 194, respectively.

21. See, for example, Ambrosius, *Wilson and the American Diplomatic Tradition,* 82–83; Widenor, *Henry Cabot Lodge,* 307–308; Bailey, *Woodrow Wilson and the Lost Peace,* 197–198; see also *New York Times,* Feb. 16, 1919.

22. See Wilson to Tumulty, Feb. 20, 21, 22 (2), and 23, 1919, *PWW,* LV, 218–219, 222, 225, 226, 231, respectively. See also Tumulty to Wilson, Jan. 6, 1919, *ibid.,* LIII, 625–626; Wilson to Tumulty, Feb. 14, 1919, and House to Wilson, Feb. 20, 1919, *ibid.,* LV, 185 and 221.

23. See Tumulty to Wilson, Jan. 18, 21 and 22, 1919, *ibid.,* 205–206, 223, and 226, respectively.

24. Address in Boston, Feb. 24, 1919, *PWW,* LV, 238–245.

25. See Stone, *Irreconcilables,* 55–58.

26. Taft to Karger, Feb. 22, 1919, quoted in Pringle, *Taft,* II, 943.

27. Stone's *Irreconcilables* (60–61 and 63) is the exception to the rule, although my sources and interpretation are different. (Wilson's subsequent conference with the Senate Foreign Relations Committee, on August 19, 1919, is often characterized as momentous; but by then his physical capacities were rapidly dwindling and his performance was erratic.)

28. Borah declined to accept Wilson's invitation to the White House. For his speech on the Covenant, see the *New York Times,* Feb. 22, 1919.

29. The foregoing is based on a lengthy story in the *New York Times,* Feb. 27, 1919, printed in *PWW,* LV, 268–276.

30. Grayson diary, Feb. 26, 1919, *ibid.,* 267; *New York Times,* Feb. 27, 1919.

31. House diary, March 14, 1919, *PWW,* LV, 499 (emphasis added). Wilson called it "your dinner" because the idea for it came from House.

32. Brandegee, to *New York Sun,* Feb. 28, 1919, quoted in Stone, *Irreconcilables,* 63.

33. Quoted in the *New York Times,* Feb. 27, 1919.

34. Hapgood to House, Jan. 23, 1919, HP, CtY.

35. *New Republic,* XVIII (Feb. 22, 1919), 100–102; see also the *Survey,* XLI (Feb. 22, 1919), 724–726. For the exception, see Oswald Garrison Villard's editorial, "The Net Result," in the *Nation,* CVIII (Feb. 22, 1919), 268.

36. *Appeal to Reason,* March 1, 1919.

37. Robert Morss Lovett, "The Covenant—and After," *Dial,* LXVI (March 8, 1919), 219.

38. "Memorandum by Paul Kellogg," ca, April 1918, quoted in Thompson, *Reformers and War,* 197.

39. Report by Norman Hapgood and Stephen Duggan to the LFNA executive committee, March 4, 1919, quoted in Helbich, "American Liberals in the League of Nations Controversy," 579.

40. The standard study is Robert F. Murray, *The Red Scare: A Study in National Hysteria, 1919–1920* (Minneapolis, 1955). For Wilson's personal knowledge of most of these incidents, see D. F. Malone to Wilson, Feb. 28, 1919, *PWW,* LV, 337–338 (on the Nearing case); T. W. Gregory to Wilson Nov. 9, 1918 *ibid.,* LIII, 12–13 (on Baldwin); Charles W. Ervin (editor of the *Call*) to Wilson, Feb. 1, 1919, *ibid.,* LIV, 430; and Wilson to Burleson, Feb. 28, 1919, *ibid.,* LV, 327. See also "Bolsheviki in the United States," *Literary Digest,* LX (Feb. 22, 1919), 11–13; Scott Nearing, *The Making of a Radical: A Political Autobiography* (New York, 1972), 115–120; Hanson is quoted in the *Dial,* LXVI (March 22, 1919), 311; Poindexter's and Reed's statements are reported in the *New York Times,* Feb. 13 and 23, 1919.

41. There is no published monograph on the subject, but see Ernest Ray Closser's excellent "Some Day a Silent Guard: Political Prisoners and the Amnesty Issue in post–World War I America," senior thesis, Princeton University, 1984.

42. *Dial,* LXV (Nov. 30, 1919), 497–498.

43. *New Republic,* XVII (Jan. 4 and 18, 1919), 282 and 343; see also *Dial,* LXVI (Jan. 11, 1919), 6.

44. Gavit to Wilson, Feb. 24, 1919, enclosure with Tumulty to Wilson, Feb. 25, 1919, *PWW,* LV, 255.

45. Sayre to Wilson, March 1, 1919, *ibid.,* 365–366.

46. Memorandum by Baker, March 6, 1919, *ibid.,* 450.

47. Malone to Wilson, Feb. 28, 1919, *ibid.,* 337–338.

48. "Mr. President, We Demand Peace and Democracy at Home as Well as Abroad," *Appeal to Reason,* March 1, 1919; see also *(ibid.)* "Public Opinion for Amnesty, As Reflected in Liberal Press."

49. Wilson to Burleson, Feb. 28, 1919, *PWW,* LV, 327.

50. See, all in *PWW,* Wilson to Tumulty, Feb. 25, 1919, with enclosure, 254–255; Gregory to Tumulty, March 1, 1919, p. 344; Tumulty to Wilson, March 1, 1919, with two enclosures from Gregory to Wilson, March 1, 1919, pp. 344–347.

51. Wilson to Sayre, March 3, 1919, *ibid.,* 395.

52. Lodge to Beveridge, Feb. 18, 1919, quoted in Widenor, *Henry Cabot Lodge,* 313. Lodge repeated this message time and again to his colleagues *(ibid.,* 301, 302, 308, 310).

53. Lodge to Beveridge, Feb. 18, 1919, and Coolidge to Lodge, Feb. 22, 1919, quoted in *ibid.,* 308. For the Boston reception, see the *New York Times,* Feb. 25, 1919.

54. Widenor, *Henry Cabot Lodge,* 309.

55. Remarks to Members of the Democratic National Committee, Feb. 28, 1919, *PWW,* LV, 309.

56. For a discussion of the reconstruction commission, see Kennedy, *Over Here,* 248–250.

57. On these subjects, see Tumulty to Wilson, Jan. 30 and Feb. 6, 1919, *PWW,* LIV, 390–393 and 520–521; W. D. Hines to Wilson, Feb. 24 and 25, 1919, *ibid.,* LV, 246–250 and 257–258; McAdoo to Wilson, Feb. 25, 1919, with enclosure, *ibid.,* 258–261; W. B. Wilson to Wilson, Feb. 26, 1919, *ibid.,* 291–292. See also Wilson's address to a conference of governors and mayors, March 3, 1919, *ibid.,* 389–390; and Stanley Shapiro, "The Twilight of Reform: Advanced Progressives After the Armistice," *Historian,* XXXIII (May 1971), 349–364.

58. Beveridge to Lodge, Jan. 28, 1919, quoted in Widenor, *Henry Cabot Lodge,* 301.

59. Quoted in Ambrosius, *Wilson and the American Diplomatic Tradition,* 105.

60. *Congressional Record,* 65th Cong., 3rd sess., 4,520–4,528.

61. Remarks to the Democratic National Committee, Feb. 28, 1919, *PWW,* LV, 323.

62. Lodge to Bryce, March 4, 1919, Bryce Papers, Vol. 7, Bodleian Library.

63. *Congressional Record,* 65th Cong., 3rd sess., 4,974 (emphasis added). For further discussion, see Stone, *Irreconcilables,* 70–74, and Widenor, *Henry Cabot Lodge,* 315–316.

64. For Taft's address, see the *New York Times,* March 5, 1919.

65. For a survey, see "The Kind of League the Republicans Want," *Literary Digest,* LX (March 15, 1919), 13–16.

66. See Barclay to Balfour, March 9, 10, and 16, 1919; and Reading to Balfour and Lloyd George, March 17 and 20, 1919, in F.O. files 800 and 608 (09533), nos. 222 and 244, PRO.

67. "The Covenant—and After," *Dial,* LXVI (March 8, 1919), 219–220; see also unsigned editorial, *ibid.,* March 22, 1919, pp. 309–310.

68. See "Agitation for a League of Nations without Criticism," *New Republic,* XVIII (March 15, 1919), 200–202; New York *Call,* March 28, 1919; Lippmann, *New Republic* (Supplement), XVIII (March 22, 1919), 10 and 11. See also William Hard, "Article Ten of the League," in *ibid.,* 237–240. (It will be recalled that Wilson's Second Paris Draft contained a provision on minorities that he had been forced to drop.)

69. Wilson to Breckinridge Long, Feb. 26, 1919, *PWW,* LV, 279.

70. Memorandum by Baker, March 6, 1919, and Baker diary, March 8, 1919, *ibid.,* 451 and 463–464.

71. Address at the Metropolitan Opera House, March 4, 1919, *ibid.,* 413–421. For the description of Wilson's appearance, see Baker's diary, March 8, 1919, *ibid.,* 463.

72. *Nation,* CVIII (March 15, 1919), 382.

73. Remarks to members of the Democratic National Committee, Feb. 28, 1919, *PWW,* LV, 313.

Notes to Chapter 14

1. Baker diary, April 3, 1919, *PWW,* LVI, 577 and 578.

2. Edith Bolling Wilson, *My Memoir* (Indianapolis and New York, 1938), 245–246; see also Grayson diary, March 13, 1919, *PWW,* LV, 487–488; about the break with House, see Floto, *Colonel House in Paris,* 164–170; and Weinstein, *Woodrow Wilson,* 347–348.

3. Wilson's statement is printed in note 1 to Baker diary, March 15, 1919, *PWW,* LV, 531; see also Tumulty to Wilson, March 13, 1919, *ibid.,* 493.

4. Cecil diary, March 16, 1919, *ibid.,* 539; Hitchcock to Wilson, March 4, 1919, *ibid.,* 437; see also T. J. Walsh to Wilson, Feb. 25; and Wilson to Walsh, Feb. 26, 1919, *ibid.,* 262–263 and 280; and Grayson diary and House diary, March 16, 1919, *ibid.,* 538 and 539.

5. Taft to Wilson, March 18, 1919, *ibid.,* LVI, 83; and McCumber to Wilson, March 13, 1919, *ibid.,* LV, 491–492.

6. The Miller diary, March 18, 1919, printed in *ibid.,* LVI, 75–81, gives the most complete account of the meeting; but see, also on that date, Cecil diary and House diary, *ibid.,* 81–83.

7. See Miller, *Drafting the Covenant,* I, 322–353 and 390–418; and II, 336–360.

8. These conditions were embodied in Lloyd George's famous "Foutainbleau Memorandum," drafted March 22–24 and sent to both Wilson and Clemenceau on March 25, 1919; it is printed in *PWW,* LVI, 259–270. For a detailed discussion, see Egerton, *Great Britain and the Creation of the League of Nations,* 156–161. (The Council of Ten had been reduced in size to the so-called Big Four on the previous day.)

9. See Mantoux's Notes of a Meeting of the Council of Four, March 25, 1919 (11 A.M.) *PWW,* LVI, 249–250.

10. Cecil to Balfour, March 27, 1919, F.O. 800, 215, 09533, PRO.

11. See Cecil to Lloyd George, April 10, 1919, F.O. 800, 216, 09533, PRO; and Egerton, *Great Britain and the Creation of the League of Nations,* 161–162.

12. See Article XXI, printed in *PWW,* LVIII, 195; Oscar Straus to Wilson, April 17 and Wilson to Straus, April 18, 1919, *ibid.,* LVII, 445 and 469. Miller, *Drafting the Covenant,* I, 442–450 and 453–461, provides the fullest documentary coverage.

13. See House diary and Lansing memo, both March 28, 1919, *PWW,* LVI, 349 and 351; and Mantoux's Notes of a Meeting of the Council of Four, March 28, 1919 (4 P.M.), *ibid.,* 360–371; see also Clemenceau to Wilson, March 17, 1919, with memorandum, March 17, 1919, *ibid.,* 9–14.

14. The description of Wilson is in Baker diary, April 3, 1919, *ibid.,* 577. For details, see Ambrosius, *Wilson and the American Diplomatic Tradition,* 108–113; Louis A. R. Yates, *United States and French Security* (New York, 1957), 44–50; and Walworth, *Wilson and His Peacemakers,* pp. 322–328. See also Mantoux's Notes of a Meeting of the Council of Four, April 9, 1919 (3:30 P.M.), *PWW,* LVII, 161–164. The French security treaty was never ratified.

15. *PWW,* LVII, 163–164.

16. For a discussion, see Schmitz, "Woodrow Wilson and the Liberal Peace," 29–44; and Mayer, *Politics and Diplomacy of the Peacemaking,* 112–139.

17. See Miller, *Drafting the Covenant,* I, 461–466 and II, 387–394; House diary, April 12, 1919, *PWW,* LVII, 285; Baker diary, March 8, 1919 (Wilson quotation), *ibid.,* LV, 464;

Egerton, *Great Britain and the Creation of the League of Nations,* 163–164; and Birdsall, *Versailles, Twenty Years After* (New York, 1941), 89–115.

18. See Hankey's Notes of a Meeting of the Council of Four, April 28 (11 A.M.), and April 30, 1919 (12:30 A.M.), *PWW,* LVIII, 178–182, and 257–261.

19. Baker diary, April 25, 1919, *PWW,* LVIII, 143; see also Baker's memorandum on Sino-Japanese relations, April 29, 1919, *ibid.,* 229–232; and Bliss to Wilson, April 29, 1919, *ibid.,* 232–234.

20. See Wilson to Tumulty, April 30, 1919, *ibid.,* 273.

21. Grayson diary, April 30, 1919, *ibid.,* 244–245; see also Tillman, *Anglo-American Relations,* 333–343; and Walworth, *Wilson and His Peacemakers,* 372–375.

22. See, in particular, Mantoux's Notes of a Meeting of the Council of Four, March 25 and March 28 (both 11 A.M.), 1919, *PWW,* LVI, 249–252 and 355–360, respectively.

23. See Memorandum by Smuts, March 31, 1919, *ibid.,* LVI, 480–482; Smuts to M. C. Gilbert, March 31, 1919, in Hancock and van der Poel, *Smuts Papers,* IV, 94–95.

24. Quoted in Lentin, *Lloyd George, Woodrow Wilson, and the Guilt of Germany,* 58.

25. For a recent critical analysis, see *ibid.,* 54–58, 66–68, and 82–141; for an interesting defense of Wilson in this controversy, see Birdsall, *Versailles, Twenty Years After,* 251–253; and Tillman, *Anglo-American Relations,* 245–246. See also Marc Trachtenberg's "Versailles after Sixty Years," *Journal of Contemporary History,* XVII (1982), 487–506; and his *Reparations in World Politics: France and European Economic Diplomacy, 1916–1923* (New York, 1980), 1–154.

26. Quoted in Lentin, *Lloyd George, Woodrow Wilson, and the Guilt of Germany,* x. See also Cecil to Lloyd George, May 24, 1919, F.O. 800, 216, 09533, PRO.

27. See, for example, Ferrell, *Woodrow Wilson and World War I,* 151–155; and Link, *Wilson, Revolution, War and Peace,* 100–103.

28. Link, *Wilson, Revolution, War and Peace,* 101.

29. Baker, quoted in Weinstein, *Woodrow Wilson,* 335. The state of Wilson's health during this period (as well as at other times) continues to generate much discussion among scholars and a number of historically trained medical practitioners. See *ibid.,* 333–348, and the following essays in the appendix to *PWW,* LVIII: Bert E. Park, M.D., M.A., "The Impact of Wilson's Neurologic Disease During the Paris Peace Conference," 611–630; Weinstein, M.D., "Woodrow Wilson's Neuropsychological Impairment and the Paris Peace Conference," 630–635; James F. Toole, M.D., "Some Observations on Wilson's Neurologic Illness," 635–638; and "Editors' Commentary," 638–640.

30. See *New York Times,* July 11, 1919; and Grayson diary, July 10, 1919, *PWW,* LXI, 416–417.

31. Address to the Senate, July 10, 1919, *ibid.,* 426–436.

32. W. A. White, "The President and the Peace," *Emporia* [Kansas] *Daily Gazette,* July 11, 1919; H. F. Ashurst diary, July 11, 1919, *PWW,* LXI, 445; and *New York Times,* July 11, 1919.

33. "Nation-wide Press-Poll on the League of Nations," *Literary Digest,* LXI (April 5, 1919), 13–16 and 120–128. The response to the question, "Do you favor the proposed League of Nations," went as follows: Yes—718, No—181, Conditional—478. For an insightful regional analysis, see Ralph B. Levering, "Public Culture and Public Opinion: The League of Nations Controversy in New Jersey and North Carolina," in Cooper and Neu, *Wilson Era,* 159–197.

34. The Covenant, as it appeared in the final peace treaty, is printed in *PWW,* LVIII, 188–199; see also Wilson's remarks upon its adoption, April 28, 1919, *ibid.,* 199–202.

35. "Defeat Article Ten," *New Republic,* XVIII (March 29, 1919), 263–265.

36. See, all in the *Dial,* LXVI, Veblen's "Peace" and an unsigned editorial, May 17,

1919, pp. 485–486 and 511–513; and "Keep the Faith" and an unsigned editorial May 31, 1919, 533 and 565–566.

37. Hobson, "The New Holy Alliance," *Nation,* CVIII (April 19, 1919), 626–628.

38. Villard, "The Truth About the Peace Conference," *ibid.,* 646–647.

39. See, all in *ibid.,* unsigned editorial, May 10, 1919, p. 721; Villard, "The Madness at Versailles," May 17, 1919, pp. 778–779; "Out of His Own Mouth," May 24, 1919, pp. 845–851. See also articles by H. W. Massingham and Felix Adler, May 24, 1919 (regular edition), 826 and 827; and "Defeat the Treaty!" (June 21, 1919), 972.

40. They issued their statement at the Women's International Conference for Permanent Peace in Zurich; see *New York Times,* May 15 and 16, 1919.

41. *New Republic,* XIX (May 24, 1919), 100, 101, 102, and 110. See also Levy, *Herbert Croly,* 262–266; and Steel, *Walter Lippmann,* 158–162.

42. A Memorandum by Norman H. Davis, August 23, 1921, *PWW,* LXVII, 375–378.

43. Wilson to Homer H. Johnson, March 20, 1919, *PWW,* LVI, 120 (Wilson's emphasis).

44. "The Growing Revolt Against the Treaty," *Nation,* CVIII (May 31, 1919), 856–857.

45. See, for example, editorials in the *New Republic,* XVII (Dec. 7, 1918), 146–147; XVIII (March 8 and 15, 1919), 162 and 196; "The Deeper Uneasiness," *Nation,* CVIII (March 15, 1919), 385. For extended discussion, see Shapiro, "The Twilight of Reform," 349–364; and Thompson, *Reformers and War,* 247–258.

46. Memorandum by Tumulty and Tumulty to Wilson, June 4, 1919, *PWW,* LX, 150–153 and 153–154.

47. Record to Wilson, March 31, 1919, quoted at length in James Kerney, *Political Education of Woodrow Wilson,* 438–446.

48. *Dial,* LXVI (June 14, 1919), 607.

49. See "Government and Propaganda," *Nation,* CVIII (March 1, 1919), 318; and a series of articles about Burleson in the *New Republic,* XIX (May 10, 17, and 24, 1919), 42–45, 76–78, and 111–114.

50. Wilson to Tumulty and Tumulty to Wilson, June 28, 1919, *PWW,* LXI, 352.

51. Palmer to Wilson, July 30, 1919, *ibid.,* XLII, 58.

52. See, all in *PWW,* LVI, Francis P. Walsh and others to Wilson, March 24, 1919; Charles E. Russell and others to Wilson, March 25, 1919; Wilson to Tumulty, March 26, 1919; and Tumulty to Wilson, April 4, 1919, 245, 282–283, 310, and 618; Sinclair to Wilson, July 21, 1919, *ibid.,* LXI, 577; and Palmer to Wilson, July 30, 1919 and Wilson to Palmer, August 1, 1919, *ibid.,* LXII, 58–59 and 98.

53. For a detailed discussion, see Shannon, *Socialist Party of America,* 115–117 and 159–161; but see Darrow to Wilson, July 29, 1919; and Sayre to Wilson, Aug. 1, 1919, *PWW,* LXII, 58–59 and 126–128.

54. Spargo to Wilson, Aug. 25, 1919, enclosure with Wilson to Palmer, Aug. 29, 1919, *ibid.,* 555–559 (Spargo's emphasis).

55. Wilson to Palmer, Aug. 29, 1919; and Wilson to Spargo, August 29, 1919, *ibid.,* 555 and 559.

56. Spargo to Stokes, Jan. 29, 1920, quoted in Ronald Radosh, *American Labor and Foreign Policy* (New York, 1969), 51.

57. See Stone, *Irreconcilables, passim,* but especially 105, 119–120, 134–135, 136–137; and John H. Flannagan, Jr., "The Disillusionment of a Progressive: U.S. Senator David I. Walsh and the League of Nations Issue," *New England Quarterly,* XLI (December 1968), 491.

58. See Widenor, *Henry Cabot Lodge,* 327–328; see also 324–325.

59. See Adler, *Isolationist Impulse,* 60 and 65; and Steel, *Walter Lippmann,* 160 and 163.

60. Widenor, *Henry Cabot Lodge,* 322.

61. Bailey, *Woodrow Wilson and the Great Betrayal;* Garraty, *Henry Cabot Lodge;* and Denna Frank Fleming, *The United States and the League of Nations, 1918–1920* (New York, 1932), have no doubt that he wanted to destroy both the League and Wilson; Ambrosius, *Woodrow Wilson and the American Diplomatic Tradition;* and Widenor, *Henry Cabot Lodge,* suggest that there is room for argument.

62. See Stone, *Irreconcilables,* 94–99 and 123–125; and Ambrosius, *Woodrow Wilson and the American Diplomatic Tradition,* 163–164.

63. See the *New York Times,* Sept 13, 1919, and Lansing to Wilson, Sept. 17, 1919, *PWW,* LXIII, 337–338, n. 1. Wilson dismissed Lansing ostensibly for holding unauthorized Cabinet meetings during the President's long illness; previous acts of disloyalty, along with the Secretary's scarcely concealed lack of confidence in the Covenant, no doubt contributed to the termination as well. See documents in *PWW,* LXIV. The press responded negatively to the decision. See "President Wilson 'Comes Back'," *Literary Digest,* LXIV (Feb. 28, 1920)' 13–15.

64. See Herbert F. Margulies, *The Mild Reservationists and the League of Nations Controversy in the Senate* (Columbia, Mo., 1989) for a thorough discussion of these "middle-grounders."

65. See Tumulty to Wilson, with enclosure, July 23, 1919, and a memorandum by Taft, *PWW,* LXI, 605–608; and Bartlett, *League to Enforce Peace,* 142–148.

66. The reservations are printed in Bailey, *Woodrow Wilson and the Great Betrayal,* 387–394. For a detailed exegesis, see Ambrosius, *Woodrow Wilson and the American Diplomatic Tradition,* 172–175 and 180–206; but also see Widenor, *Henry Cabot Lodge,* 316–324; and Stone, *Irreconcilables,* 100–127.

67. For excellent reports on these meetings, see the *New York Times,* July 23, 24, 31 and August 1, 1919; and the *Washington Post,* July 18, 19, 26, 27, and August 1 and 2, 1919. See also, Margulies, *Mild Reservationists,* 50–58; and Kurt Wimer, "Woodrow Wilson Tries Conciliation: An Effort That Failed," *Historian,* XXV (August 1963), 419–438.

68. The transcript of the meeting is printed in *PWW,* LXII, 339–411. For differing analyses, see Vinson, *Referendum for Isolation,* 91–93; Stone, *Irreconcilables,* 124–127; and Ambrosius, *Woodrow Wilson and the American Diplomatic Tradition,* 164–167.

69. See Grayson, *Woodrow Wilson: An Intimate Memoir* (New York, 1960), 94–95; E. B. Wilson, *My Memoir,* 272; and Lamont to Wilson, July 25, 1919, *PWW,* LXI, 641–642.

70. See Bailey, *Woodrow Wilson and the Great Betrayal,* 90–101; and Link, editorial note, *PWW,* LXII, 507. The most evenhanded analysis is John Milton Cooper, Jr., "Fool's Errand or Finest Hour? Woodrow Wilson's Speaking Tour in September 1919," in *Wilson Era,* 198–220. For other accounts of the tour, see Bailey, *Woodrow Wilson and the Great Betrayal,* 105–122; Smith, *When the Cheering Stopped,* 60–83; and Link, *Wilson, Revolution, War and Peace,* 113–121.

71. Address in San Diego, Sept. 19, 1919, *PWW,* LXIII, 371.

72. The quotations are from Wilson's addresses in Columbus; Pueblo, Colorado; and Omaha, *ibid.,* 15, 99, 502; for other examples, see addresses in Des Moines, St. Paul (two), Minneapolis, Tacoma, Oakland, and Denver, 78, 127–128 and 147, 137, 246, 356–357, and 497, respectively.

73. *Ibid.,* 49.

74. For examples, see addresses in Indianapolis, Kansas City, Minneapolis, Helena, Coeur D'Alene, San Francisco, Los Angeles, *ibid.,* 20–22, 67–68, 135, 194–195, 218, 345, 409.

75. The quotations are from addresses in St. Louis, Kansas City, Sioux Falls, Port-

land, and Billings, in *ibid.,* 46–47, 69, 112, 279, and 173; for other examples, see addresses in Columbus, Denver, and Pueblo, 11, 495, and 511.

76. *Ibid.,* 452 and 480.

77. For examples, see addresses in Billings, Tacoma, San Francisco, San Diego, and Pueblo, *ibid.,* 179, 249, 312 and 335, 386–387, and 511.

78. Address in St. Louis, *ibid.,* 42.

79. *New Republic,* XIX (May 24), 103.

80. See Grayson diary, Sept. 10, 13, 17, 24, 25, and 26, 1919, *PWW,* LXIII, 152, 240, 308–309, 467, 488–489, and 518–519; news report in the [Cheyenne] *Wyoming State Tribune,* Sept. 25, 1919, in *PWW,* LXIII, 489.

81. For a description of the stroke, see Weinstein, *Woodrow Wilson,* 355–357. For an evaluation of Wilson's condition by the principal specialist attending him, see Dr. Francis X. Dercum to Grayson, Oct. 20, 1919, with enclosure (published for the first time in 1991, with extensive commentary by Park and Dr. James F. Toole), in *PWW,* LXIV, 500–507. For Grayson's report on Wilson's true condition, which Mrs. Wilson refused to release to the press, see undated memo, *ibid.,* 507–511. Grayson's attempt to persuade Wilson to resign, and Mrs. Wilson's opposition, is related in R. S. Baker diary, Feb. 4, 1919, and notes thereto, *ibid.,* 362–363. For Mrs. Wilson's own account of her role, see *My Memoir,* 283–289.

82. *New York Times,* Dec. 6, 1919. Hitchcock had twice met with Wilson to discuss the status of the treaty in the Senate in November.

83. "The Facts About President Wilson's Illness," undated, *PWW,* LXIII, 634.

84. A Jackson Day Message, Jan. 8, 1920, *PWW,* LXIV, 258.

85. Wilson to Hitchcock, March 8, 1920, *ibid.,* LXV, 67–71.

86. Ambrosius, *Woodrow Wilson and the American Diplomatic Tradition,* 172–250; and Margulies, *Mild Reservationists,* 185–260, provide excellent, highly detailed accounts of these events.

87. See, for example, the previously cited works by Ambrosius, Bailey, Cooper, Clements, Ferrell, and Link.

88. See Park, *The Impact of Illness on World Leaders* (Philadelphia, 1986), 3–76.

89. Weinstein, *Woodrow Wilson,* 165–180 and 195–216. For a somewhat different account of this bitter controversy in Wilson's academic career, see Cooper, *Warrior and the Priest,* 89–108.

90. In addition to his works cited above, see Park, "Wilson's Neurologic Illness During the Summer of 1919," appendix of *PWW,* LXII, 628–638, and "Woodrow Wilson's Stroke of October 2, 1919," *ibid.,* LXIII, 639–646.

91. Alexander L. and Juliette L. George, *Woodrow Wilson and Colonel House: A Personality Study* (New York, 1956), 114 and 311. See also the scathing *Thomas Woodrow Wilson, Twenty-eighth President of the United States: A Psychological Study* (New York, 1967), by Sigmund Freud and William C. Bullitt. This book, written thirty-five years before it appeared in print, was principally the work of Bullitt; Freud's family claimed that the father of modern psychoanalysis had little or nothing to do with its composition.

92. Practically all historians who have written on the question cite a body of evidence—either the coincidence of previous serious illness with outbursts of erratic behavior in an otherwise highly successful career, or a seemingly pathological stubbornness mixed with a bit of meanness that sometimes brought on failure. From this, they proceed to interpretations of the League controversy, counterfactual in nature and, in their own right, not unreasonable. Link and Weinstein on one side and the Georges on the other have previously disputed each others' research and conclusions. See, for example, Weinstein, Link, and James W. Anderson, "Woodrow Wilson's Political Personality: A Reappraisal," *Political Science Quarterly,* XCIII (Winter 1978), 585–598, and George, George, and Mi-

chael F. Marmor, M.D., "Issues in Wilsonian Scholarship: References to Early 'Strokes' in the Papers of Woodrow Wilson," *Journal of American History*, LXX (March 1984), 845–853. The literature on this subject has grown quite large in recent years; an extensive bibliography is printed in *PWW*, LIV, ix–xi, and in the notes to Ambrosius, "Woodrow Wilson's Health and the Treaty Fight," *International History Review*, IX (February 1987), 73–84; see also Thomas T. Lewis, "Alternative Psychological Interpretations of Woodrow Wilson," *Mid-America*, LXII (April–July 1983), 71–85.

93. Quoted in *Lord Riddell's Intimate Diary*, 397.

94. Quoted in Ambrosius, *Woodrow Wilson and the American Diplomatic Tradition*, 197; and Stone, *Irreconcilables*, 137.

95. These reservations are printed in Bailey, *Woodrow Wilson and the Great Betrayal*, 387–394.

96. Lodge to J. T. Morse, Aug. 19, 1919, quoted in Widenor, *Henry Cabot Lodge*, 321.

97. Quoted in *ibid.*, 340.

98. *Nation*, CVIII (March 1, 1919), 309.

99. Address in Billings, Sept. 11, 1919, *PWW*, LXIII, 177.

100. Wilson to Hitchcock, March 8, 1920, *ibid.*, LXV, 67–71.

101. Wilson to Tumulty, June 23, 1919, *ibid.*, LXI, 115.

102. *New Republic*, XIX (May 24, 1919), 103.

103. Wilson to Hitchcock, March 8, 1920, *PWW*, LXV, 67–71.

104. *ibid.*

105. Ferrell, *Woodrow Wilson and World War I*, 229.

106. Quoted in Fleming, *United States and the League of Nations*, 487.

107. Quoted in Steel, *Walter Lippmann*, 166.

108. Bullitt to Wilson, May 17, 1919, *PWW*, LIX, 232–233.

109. Baker diary, April 3, 1919, *ibid.*, LVI, 577.

110. Quoted in W. E. Dodd, *Woodrow Wilson and His Work* (New York, 1932), 434.

111. As Dodd put it in a letter to Virginia Le Roy, ca, Jan. 7, 1921, *PWW*, LXVII, 39–40.

Notes for Epilogue

1. Tumulty, *Woodrow Wilson As I Know Him*, 509–510; Smith, *When the Cheering Stopped*, 185–186.

2. See Robert A. Divine, *Second Chance: The Triumph of Internationalism in America During World War II* (New York, 1967); and Thomas J. Knock, " 'History With Lightning': The Forgotten Film *Wilson*," *American Quarterly* XXVII (Winter 1976–77), 523–43.

3. Harry S Truman, *Memoirs: The Years of Decision* (New York, 1955; Signet ed., 1965), 326.

4. Levin, *Woodrow Wilson and World Politics*, 260 (emphasis added).

5. Quoted in Edith Giddings Reed, *Woodrow Wilson: The Caricature, the Myth, and the Man* (New York, 1934), 236.

6. The historiography on the "realist" critique of Wilsonian idealism is enormous; among the best examples are Robert E. Osgood, *Ideals and Self-Interest in American Foreign Relations* (Chicago, 1953); and Roland N. Stromberg, *Collective Security and American Foreign Policy: From the League of Nations to NATO* (New York, 1963). For an interpretive discussion of this historical contention, see Thomas J. Knock, "Kennan vs. Wilson," in Cooper and Neu, *Wilson Era*, 302–326.

7. Kennan, *Memoirs, 1950–1963* (Boston, 1972), 71; and *American Diplomacy, 1900–1950* (Chicago, 1951; 1984 ed.), 101.

8. Widenor reviews contending interpretations of Roosevelt's approach in "American Planning for the United Nations: Have We Been Asking the Right Questions?" *Diplomatic History,* VI (Summer 1982), 245–264.

9. Memoranda of the Joint Chiefs of Staff, April 1947, and of George C. Marshall to Truman, November 1947, quoted in John L Gaddis, *Strategies of Containment: A Critical Appraisal of Postwar American National Security Policy* (New York, 1982), 57.

10. Naval War College lecture, June 18, 1947, quoted in *ibid.,* 29.

11. Kirkpatrick, "Law and Reciprocity," quoted in Daniel P. Moynihan, *On the Law of Nations* (Cambridge, Mass., 1990), 133.

12. See, for example, Kennan, *The Nuclear Delusion: Soviet–American Relations in the Atomic Age* (New York, 1982), xxvii and 246. For a discussion, see Knock, "Kennan vs. Wilson," 317–320.

13. Kennan, "Comments on a Paper Entitled 'Kennan versus Wilson' by Professor Thomas J. Knock," in Cooper and Neu, *Wilson Era,* 330.

14. *New York Times,* Dec. 8, 1988. For a discussion, see Moynihan, *On the Law of Nations,* 80–82 and 97–100.

15. *New York Times,* Dec. 8, 1988.

16. On the latter point, see Kennan, "Comments on a Paper entitled 'Kennan versus Wilson,' " 329–230.

17. *New York Times,* Sept. 12, 1990.

18. Address at Pueblo, Colorado, Sept. 25, 1919, *PWW,* LXIII, 513 and 512 (emphasis added).

19. See Smuts to Wilson, Jan 4, 1921, with enclosure, memo, "Woodrow Wilson's Place in History," *ibid.,* LXVII, 26–27.

Bibliography

Manuscript Collections

France

The Papers of Jean Jules Jusserand, French Foreign Ministry Archives.

Germany

Politisches Archiv, Auswartiges Amt, Bonn.

Great Britain

The Papers of Arthur James Balfour, British Museum.
The Papers of James Bryce, Bodleian Library, Oxford University.
The Papers of Robert Cecil, Public Record Office.
Foreign Office Records, Public Record Office.
The Papers of Grey of Fallodon, Public Record Office.
The Papers of David Lloyd George, House of Lords Record Office.

Switzerland

The Swiss Federal Archives.

United States

The Papers of Stockton Axson, Princeton University Library.
The Papers of Ray Stannard Baker, Library of Congress.
The Ray Stannard Baker Collection of Wilsoniana, Library of Congress.
The Diary of Thomas W. Brahany, photographic copy in the Papers of Woodrow Wilson, Princeton University Library.
The Papers of Albert Sidney Burleson, Library of Congress.
The Papers of Josephus Daniels, Library of Congress.
The Papers of Henry Prather Fletcher, Library of Congress.
The Diary and Papers of Edward Mandell House, Yale University Library.
The Papers of Andrew Clark Imbrie, Princeton University Library.
The Desk Diary and Papers of Robert Lansing, Library of Congress.
The Papers of Frank Lyon Polk, Yale University Library.
The State Department Records, National Archives.
The Charles L. Swem Collection, Princeton University Library.
The Papers of Robert A. Taft, Library of Congress.
The Papers of William Howard Taft, Library of Congress.
The Papers of Lillian D. Wald, New York Public Library.
The Papers of William L. Westerman, Columbia University Library.
The Papers of Woodrow Wilson, Library of Congress.
The Papers of Sir William Wiseman, Yale University Library.

Public Documents

Publications of the United States Government

Department of State. *Papers Relating to the Foreign Relations of the United States, The Lansing Papers, 1914–1920.* 2 vols., Washington, D.C., 1939–1940.
———. *Papers Relating to the Foreign Relations of the United States, 1914, Supplement, The World War.* Washington, D.C., 1928.
———. *Papers Relating to the Foreign Relations of the United States, 1916, Supplement, The World War.* Washington, D.C., 1929.
———. *Papers Relating to the Foreign Relations of the United States, 1917, Supplement I, The World War.* 2 vols., Washington, D.C., 1931.
———. *Papers Relating to the Foreign Relations of the United States, 1918, Supplement I, The World War.* 2 vols., Washington, D.C., 1933.
———. *Papers Relating to the Foreign Relations of the United States, The Paris Peace Conference, 1919.* 13 vols., Washington, D.C., 1942–1947.
United States Congress. *Congressional Record,* 61st Cong., 3rd sess. Washington, D.C., 1911.
———. *Congressional Record,* 63rd Cong., 2nd sess., through 65th Cong., 3rd sess. Washington, D.C., 1914–1919.
Proceedings of the first Pan-American Financial Conference . . . May 24 to 29, 1915. Washington, D.C., 1915.
Report to the Secretary General. Second Pan-American Scientific Congress, Washington, D.C., 1917.

Correspondence and Collected Works

Baker, Ray Stannard, and William E. Dodds, eds. *The Public Papers of Woodrow Wilson,* 6 vols. New York: Harper and Brothers, 1925–1927.

Basler, Roy P. (ed.). *The Collected Works of Abraham Lincoln,* 8 vols. New Brunswick, N.J., 1953.

Foner, Philip S. (ed.). *Mother Jones Speaks, Collected Speeches and Writings.* New York, 1983.

Hancock, W. K., and Jean van der Poel (eds.). *Selections from the Smuts Papers,* 6 vols. Cambridge, 1966.

Hendrick, Burton, J., ed. *The Life and Letters of Walter Hines Page,* 3 vols. New York: Doubleday, Page and Co., 1922–1923.

Lane, Anne Wintermute, and Louis Herrick Wall, eds. *The Letters of Franklin K. Lane.* Boston and New York: Houghton Mifflin Co., 1922.

Latane, John H., ed. *The Development of the League of Nations Idea, Documents and Correspondence of Theodore Marburg,* 2 vols. New York: Macmillan Co., 1932.

Link, Arthur S., David W. Hirst, John E. Little, Manfred F. Boemeke, *et al.* (eds.). *The Papers of Woodrow Wilson,* 67 vols. to date. Princeton, N.J.: Princeton University Press, 1966–.

Miller, David Hunter. *Drafting the Covenant,* 2 vols. New York, 1928.

———. *My Diary at the Conference of Paris, With Documents,* 21 vols. New York, 1924.

Morison, Elting E., *et al.* (eds.). *The Letters of Theodore Roosevelt,* 8 vols. Cambridge, Mass., 1951–1954.

Porter, Kirk H., and Donald Bruce Johnson. *National Party Platforms.* Urbana, Ill., 1961.

Seymour, Charles. *Letters from the Paris Peace Conference.* Harold B. Whiteman, Jr. (ed.). New Haven, Conn., 1965.

——— (ed.). *The Intimate Papers of Colonel House,* 4 vols. Boston: Houghton Mifflin Co., 1926–1928.

Walton, Robert C. (ed.). *Over There: European Reaction to America in World War I.* Ithaca, N.Y., 1971.

Memoirs

Addams, Jane. *Peace and Bread in Time of War.* New York, 1922; reprinted by Garland Pub., 1972.

Eastman, Max. *Enjoyment of Living.* New York, 1948.

Grayson, Cary T. *Woodrow Wilson: An Intimate Memoir.* New York: Holt, Rinehart, and Winston, 1960.

Hays, Will. *The Autobiography of Will H. Hays.* New York, 1955.

Hillquit, Morris. *Loose Leaves from a Busy Life.* New York, 1934.

Houston, David F. *Eight Years with Wilson's Cabinet, 1913–1920,* 2 vols. New York, 1926.

Kennan, George F. *Memoirs, 1950–1963.* Boston, 1972.

Lloyd George, David. *The Truth About the Peace Treaties,* 2 vols. London, 1938.

———. *War Memoirs,* 6 vols. Boston, 1933–1937.

Maurer, James. *It Can Be Done.* New York, 1938.

Nearing, Scott. *The Making of a Radical: A Political Autobiography.* New York, 1972.

Reed, Edith Giddings. *Woodrow Wilson: The Caricature, the Myth and the Man.* New York, 1934.

Riddell, George Allardice. *Lord Riddell's Intimate Diary of the Peace Conference and After, 1918–1923.* New York, 1934.

Truman, Harry S. *Memoirs, The Years of Decision.* New York, 1955.
Tumulty, Joseph P. *Woodrow Wilson As I Know Him.* New York: Doubleday, Page and
    Co., 1921.
Villard, Oswald Garrison. *Fighting Years: Memoirs of a Liberal Editor.* New York, 1939.
Wald, Lillian. *Windows on Henry Street.* Boston, 1934.
White, William Allen. *The Autobiography of William Allen White.* New York, 1946.
Wilson, Edith Bolling. *My Memoir.* Indianapolis and New York, 1938.

Works by Woodrow Wilson

Wilson, Woodrow. *A History of the American People,* 5 vols. New York: Harper and Bros.,
    1902. Not printed in *The Papers of Woodrow Wilson.*

Miscellaneous Contemporary Works

Angell, Norman. *The Great Illusion.* London, 1910.
Bernstein, Eduard. *Evolutionary Socialism.* London, 1899.
Bingham, Hiram. *The Monroe Doctrine, An Obsolete Shibboleth.* New Haven, Conn., 1913.
Bourne, Randolph S. *War and the Intellectual: Collected Essays, 1915–1919.* Carl Resek, ed.
    New York, 1964.
Bridges, Robert. *The Spirit of Man.* London, 1916.
Creel, George. *How We Advertised the War.* New York, 1920.
————.*The War, the World and Wilson.* New York, 1920.
Croly, Herbert. *The Promise of American Life.* New York, 1902.
Hobson, J. A. *Imperialism.* London, 1902.
————.*Towards International Government.* New York, 1915.
House, Edward M. *Philip Dru: Administrator.* New York, 1912.
Lippmann, Walter. *The Stakes of Diplomacy,* 2nd. ed. New York, 1917.
Shaw, Bernard. *Peace Conference Hints.* London, 1919.
Sherrill, Charles S. *Modernizing the Monroe Doctrine.* Boston, 1916.
Smuts, Jan C. *The League of Nations: A Practical Suggestion.* London, 1918.

Newspapers

American

Albany [N.Y.] *Knickerbocker Press,* 1918.
Boston Evening Transcript, 1918.
[Cheyenne] *Wyoming State Tribune,* 1919.
Chicago Tribune, 1918.
Cincinnati Commercial Tribune, 1918.
Emporia [Kansas] *Daily Gazette,* 1919.
Kansas City Star, 1918.
Milwaukee Leader, 1916–1918.
New York *Call,* 1912–1919.
New York *Globe,* 1918.
New York Evening Post, 1915–1921.
New York *Herald,* 1916–1917.
New York *Sun,* 1916–1919.

New York Times, 1914–1919.
New York *Tribune,* 1915–1917.
New York *World,* 1913–1920.
Philadelphia *Public Ledger,* 1916–1918.
Pittsburgh *Dispatch,* 1918.
Pittsburgh Gazette-Times, 1916 and 1918.
Portland [Ore.] *Press,* 1918.
Richmond *Times-Dispatch,* 1918.
Rocky Mountain News, 1918–1919.
St. Louis Republic, 1918.
Springfield [Mass.] *Republican,* 1916–1919.
Washington Post, 1915–1918.

Foreign

Berliner Tagblatt, 1916.
London *Daily News and Leader,* 1916–1918.
London *Times,* 1914–1918.
Manchester Guardian, 1916 and 1918.
Paris *Journal des Débats,* 1918.

Periodicals

Appeal to Reason, 1912–1919.
Atlantic Monthly, 1914.
The Dial, 1918–1919.
The Independent, 1916–1920.
Literary Digest, 1916–1921.
The Liberator, 1918–1919.
London Nation, 1916–1918.
The Masses, 1914–1918.
The Nation, 1916–1920.
New Republic, 1914–1921.
New Statesman, 1918.
New York *Public,* 1917.
The Outlook, 1916 and 1918.
The Survey, 1916–1921.
War and Peace, 1916.
The World Tomorrow, 1918.

Signed Contemporary Articles

Angell, Norman. "Mr. Wilson's Contribution." *War and Peace,* III (June 1916), 136–138.
Benson, Allan L. "Our New President." *The Masses,* IV (May 1913), 3.
Bohn, Frank. "The Reelection of Wilson." *The Masses,* IX (January 1917), 15–16.
Colcord, Lincoln. "Message May Swing Russians into Line." Philadelphia *Public Ledger,* December 5, 1917.
Croly, Herbert. "Peace Without Victory." *New Republic,* IX (December 23, 1916), 201–202.
———. "The Structure of Peace." *New Republic,* IX (January 6, 1917), 287–291.

―――. "The Two Parties in 1916." *New Republic,* VIII (Oct. 21, 1916), 289–290.

Dickinson, G. Lowes. "The War and the Way Out." *Atlantic Monthly,* CXIV (December 1916), 820–837.

Eastman, Max. "A World's Peace." *The Liberator,* I (March 1918), 10.

―――. "An Issue at Last." *The Masses,* VIII (August 1916), 10.

―――. "Revolutionary Progress." *The Masses,* IX (April 1917), 5.

―――. "Sect or Class." *The Masses,* IX (December 1916).

―――. "The Campaign Issue." *The Liberator,* I (October 1918), 23.

―――. "The Masses at the White House." *The Masses,* VIII, (July 1916), 16–17.

―――. "The Twilight of Liberalism," *The Liberator,* I (February 1919), 5.

―――. "To Socialist Party Critics," *The Masses,* IX (February 1917), 24.

―――. "Wilson and the World's Future," *The Liberator,* I (May 1918), 19–21.

Gardiner, A. G. "America and the Future." London *Daily News and Leader,* November 18, 1916.

―――. "Mr. Wilson's Policy and the Pact of Peace." London *Daily News and Leader,* February 26, 1916.

―――. "What Does America Stand For?" London *Daily News and Leader,* June 17, 1916.

Hard, William. "Anti-Bolshevik: Mr. Sack." *New Republic,* XIX, (July 23, 1919), 385–387.

―――. "Article Ten of the League." Supplement to *New Republic,* XVIII (March 22, 1919), 237–240.

Hobson, J. A. "The New Holy Alliance." *The Nation,* CVIII (April 19, 1919), 626–628.

Holt, Hamilton. "The President on the Enforcement of Peace." *The Independent,* LXXXVI (June 5, 1916), 356.

―――. "A Declaration of Interdependence." *The Independent,* LXXXVI (June 5, 1916), 357.

―――. "The League to Enforce Peace." *The Independent,* LXXXVI (June 5, 1916), 358.

Kellogg, Paul. "The Fighting Issue." *The Survey,* XXXVII (Feb. 17, 1917), 572–577.

Lippmann, Walter. "The Puzzle of Hughes." *New Republic,* VIII (September 30, 1916), 210–213.

Lovett, Robert Morss. "The Covenant—and After." *The Dial,* LXVI (March 8, 1919), 219.

Maurer, James. "Why Labor Is Against Preparedness." *The Masses,* VIII (July 1916), 10.

Meyers, Gus. "Why Idealists Quit the Socialist Party." *The Nation,* CIV (Feb. 15, 1917), 118–120.

Morel, E. D.. "Save the World—An Englishman to Wilson." *New York Tribune,* July 4, 1915.

Pinchot, Gifford. "What the Election Means." *The Masses,* IX (January 1917), 18–19.

Reed, John. "At the Throat of the Republic." *The Masses,* VIII, (July 1916), 7–9.

―――. "One Solid Month of Liberty." *The Masses,* IX (September 1917), 5–6.

―――. "What About Mexico?" *The Masses,* V (June 1914), 11–14.

Roosevelt, Theodore. "Sound Nationalism and Sound Internationalism." *Kansas City Star,* Aug. 4, 1918.

Strunsky, Simeon. "Post: Impressions." *New York Evening Post,* May 13, 1916.

Thomas, Norman. "The Acid Test of Our Democracy." *The World Tomorrow,* I (October 1918), 219–226.

Trevelyan, Charles P. "An Open Letter to Americans." *The Survey,* XXXVII (December 9, 1916), 261–262.

Veblen, Thorstein. "Peace." *The Dial,* LXVI (May 17, 1919), 485–486.

Villard, Oswald Garrison. "The Madness at Versailles." *The Nation,* CVIII (May 17, 1919), 778–779.

―――. "The Net Result." *The Nation,* CVIII (February 22, 1919), 268.

————. "The Truth About the Peace Conference." *The Nation,* CVIII (April 19, 1919), 646–647.

Walling, William E. "Socialists for Wilson." *The Masses,* IX (January 1917), 24.

————. "The World-Wide Battle Line." *The Masses,* V (November 1913).

West, George P. "A Talk with Mr. Burleson." New York *Public,* XX (October 12, 1917), 985–987.

White, William Allen. "The President and the Peace." *Emporia* [Kansas] *Daily Gazette,* July 11, 1919.

Unsigned Contemporary Articles

"Agitation for a League of Nations Without Criticism." *New Republic,* XVIII (March 15, 1919), 200–202.

"The Allies Ask Restitution, Reparation, Security." *Literary Digest,* LIII (December 30, 1916), 1,691–1,693.

"The Allies Greet the President." *Literary Digest,* LIII (December 16, 1916), 1,589–1,590.

"America and the League of Nations." *New Republic,* XVII (November 30, 1918), 116–118.

"America Speaks." *New Republic,* IX (January 27, 1917), 340–342.

"An Election in a Fog." *New Republic,* XVI (October 26, 1918), 363–365.

"An 'Unconditional Surrender.'" *Literary Digest,* LIX (November 23, 1918), 12–13.

"Another Supreme Court Radical." *Literary Digest,* LIII (July 29, 1916), 240–241.

"Are We Militarists?" *New Republic,* II (March 20, 1915), 166–167.

"Bolsheviki in the United States." *Literary Digest,* LX (February 22, 1919), 11–13.

"The Case for Benson." *New Republic,* VIII (October 7, 1916), 243–245.

"Clash of French and American Peace Plans." *Literary Digest,* LX (January 11, 1919), 9–11.

"Colonel Roosevelt's New Crusade." *Literary Digest,* LII (June 3, 1916), 1,618.

"A Comparison of the Chicago Platforms." *Literary Digest,* LIII (June 17, 1916), 1,762–1,763.

"A Disentangling Alliance." London *Nation,* XIX (June 3, 1916), 277–278.

"Defeat Article Ten." *New Republic,* XVIII (March 29, 1919), 263–265.

"Defeat the Treaty!" *The Nation,* CVIII (June 21, 1919), 972.

"The Deeper Uneasiness." *The Nation,* CVIII (March 15, 1919), 385.

"Doubling Our Regular Army." *Literary Digest,* LII (May 27, 1916), 1,518–1,521.

"The End of Isolationism." *New Republic,* I (November 7, 1914), 9–10.

"Farm Loan Act Under Way." *Literary Digest,* LIII (August 26, 1916), 445–446.

"The Foes of American Unity." *New Republic,* XVII (November 9, 1918), 27.

"Germany and the League of Peace." *New Republic,* IX (November 18, 1916), 60.

"The German Collapse." *Literary Digest,* LIX (November 16, 1918), 9–10.

"Germany's Restive Socialists." *Literary Digest,* LIII (November 25, 1916), 1,399.

"Government and Propaganda." *The Nation,* CVIII (March 1, 1919), 318.

"The Great Decision." *New Republic,* X (April 7, 1917), 279–280.

"The Growing Revolt Against the Treaty." *The Nation,* CVIII (May 31, 1919), 856–857.

"He Kept Us Out of War." *Literary Digest,* LIII (October 14, 1916), 933–935.

"How the Progressives Voted." *Literary Digest,* LIII (November 25, 1926), 1,393.

"Hughes and Wilson on the Eight-Hour Law." *Literary Digest,* LIII (October 7, 1916), 875–877.

"The Hughes-Roosevelt Alliance." *Literary Digest,* LIII (July 8, 1916), 56–57.

"If America Backs the Bill." London *Nation*, XIX (June 3, 1916), 276–278.

"In Defense of the Atlantic World." *New Republic*, X (February 17, 1917), 59–61.

"Justification." *New Republic*, X (February 17, 1917), 59–61.

"The Kind of League the Republicans Want." *Literary Digest*, LX (March 15, 1919), 13–16.

"Labor's Dread of Preparedness." *Literary Digest*, LII (April 8, 1916), 957–958.

"Latin America's View of Mexico." *Literary Digest*, LIII (July 15, 1916), 121.

"The League of Nations." *The Liberator* (December 1918), 5–6.

"The League of Peace." *Manchester Guardian*, May 31, 1916.

"A League of Peace." *New Republic*, II, (March 20, 1914), 167–169.

"Making War on Our Chief Peacemaker." *Literary Digest*, LIX (December 14, 1918), 9–12.

"Mr. Justice Brandeis." *Literary Digest*, LII (June 17, 1916), 1,768.

"Mr. President, We Demand Peace and Democracy at Home as Well as Abroad." *Appeal to Reason* March 1, 1919.

"Nation-wide Press-Poll on the League of Nations." *Literary Digest*, LXI (April 5, 1919), 13–16 and 120–128.

"The Newer Nationalism." *New Republic*, V (January 26, 1916), 319–321.

"The Note as Americanism." *New Republic*, IX (December 23, 1916), 201–202.

"Opening a Way to Peace." *Literary Digest*, LIII (November 25, 1916), 1,398.

"The Opportunity for Peace." *Springfield Republican*, May 9, 1916.

"Pacifism *vs.* Passivism." *New Republic*, I (December 12, 1914), 6–7.

"Passing Sentence on the Kaiser and His People." *Literary Digest*, LIX (October 26, 1918), 14–16.

"Paying for the Railroad Men's Victory." *Literary Digest*, LIII (September 9, 1916), 592.

"The Plattsburgh Idea." *New Republic*, IV (October 9, 1915), 248–250.

"Political Effects of the Labor Victory." *Literary Digest*, LIII (September 16, 1916), 651.

"Political Reports from 3,000 Communities." *Literary Digest*, LIII (October 28, 1916), 1,114.

"Preparedness—A Trojan Horse." *New Republic*, V (November 6, 1915), 6–7.

" 'Preparedness' for What?" *New Republic*, III (June 26, 1915), 188.

"The President and the Mill-Child." *Literary Digest*, LIII (August 5, 1916), 290.

"The President as Peace Pilot." *Literary Digest*, LIII (December 30, 1916), 1,694–1,695.

"The President at the Peace Table." *Literary Digest*, LIX (November 30, 1918), 14.

"President Wilson to Face a Republican Congress." *Literary Digest*, LIX (November 16, 1918), 14–15.

"President Wilson's Peace Plan." *Literary Digest*, LII (June 10, 1916), 1,683–1,685.

"A Presidential Straw Vote of Union Labor." *Literary Digest*, LIII (October 7, 1916), 872–874 and 919–922.

"The President's Reply and the People's Reply." *Literary Digest*, LIX (October 19, 1918), 7–9.

"The President's Responsibility." *New Republic*, XVI (October 26, 1918), 360–361.

"Public Opinion for Amnesty, As Reflected in Liberal Press." *Appeal to Reason* (March 1, 1919).

"The Republican Opportunity." *Literary Digest*, LIX (November 16, 1918), 14–15.

"Republicans Plan an Early Campaign." *New York Times*, December 21, 1917.

"Shall the Peace League Include Germany." *Literary Digest*, LIX (October 12, 1918), 11–12.

"Socialism's Stake in the War." *Literary Digest*, LII (March 25, 1916), 807.

"A 'State of War' with Germany." *Literary Digest*, LIV (March 31, 1917), pp. 881–882.

"Swinging Around the Circle." *The Survey*, XXXVI (April 22, 1916), 95–96.

"The Two Parties After the Election." *New Republic*, IX (November 18, 1916), 63–64.

"A Victory of Justice *vs.* a Victory of Power." *New Republic,* XVI (October 5, 1918), 271.

"War and the New Congress." *Literary Digest,* LIX (October 26, 1918), 18.

"A War Program for Liberals." *New Republic,* X (March 31, 1917), 249–250.

"The Washington Censors." Springfield *Republican,* October 9, 1917.

"What Happened to the August *Masses." The Masses,* IX (September 1917), 3.

"Which League of Nations?" *The Liberator,* February 1919, 7–8.

"Why Is Roosevelt Unjailed?" *The Nation,* CVII (November 2, 1918), 546.

"Why Wilson Won." *Literary Digest,* LIII (November 18, 1916), 1,315.

"Will the Peace League Prevent War?" *Literary Digest,* LX (March 1, 1919), 11–13.

"A Woman's Peace Party Full Fledged for Action." *The Survey,* XXXIII (January 16, 1915), 433–434.

"Woodrow Wilson, Politician." *The Nation,* CVII (November 2, 1918), 503.

Secondary Works, Articles, and Theses

Adler, Selig. "The Congressional Election of 1918." *South Atlantic Quarterly,* XXXVI (October 1937), 447–465.

———. *The Isolationist Impulse: Its Twentieth-Century Reaction.* New York, 1957.

Albrecht-Carrie, Rene. *Italy at the Paris Peace Conference.* New York, 1938.

Ambrosius, Lloyd E. *Wilsonian Statecraft: Theory and Liberal Practice of Internationalism during World War I.* Wilmington, Delaware, 1991.

———. *Woodrow Wilson and the American Diplomatic Tradition, The Treaty Fight in Perspective.* Cambridge, England, 1987.

———. "Woodrow Wilson's Health and the Treaty Fight," *International History Review,* IX (February 1987), 73–84.

Bailey, Thomas A. *Woodrow Wilson and the Great Betrayal.* New York, 1945.

———. *Woodrow Wilson and the Lost Peace.* New York, 1944.

Baker, Ray Stannard. *Woodrow Wilson, Life and Letters,* 8 vols. Garden City, New York, 1927–1939.

———. *Woodrow Wilson and World Settlement,* 3 vols. Garden City, New York, 1922.

Bartlett, Ruhl J. *The League to Enforce Peace.* Chapel Hill, N.C., 1944.

Beisner, Robert L. *From the Old Diplomacy to the New, 1865–1900.* Arlington Heights, Mich., 1975.

———. *Twelve Against Empire: The Antiimperialists, 1898–1900.* New York, 1969.

Bemis, Samuel Flagg. *The Latin American Policy of the United States.* New York, 1943.

Birdsall, Paul. *Versailles Twenty Years After.* New York, 1941.

Bond, F. Fraser. *Mr. Miller of "The Times."* New York, 1931.

Boothe, Leon E. "Anglo-American Pro-League Groups Lead Wilson, 1915–1918." *Mid-America,* Vol. 51 (April 1969), 93–95.

Bragdon, Henry W. *Woodrow Wilson: The Academic Years.* Cambridge, Mass., 1967.

Burner, David. "The Break-up of the Wilson Coalition of 1916." *Mid-America,* XLV (January 1963), 18–33.

———. *The Politics of Provincialism: The Democratic Party in Transition, 1918–1932.* New York, 1967; 1975 ed.

Burr, Robert. *By Reason of Force: Chile and the Balance of Power in South America, 1830–1905.* Berkeley, 1965.

Calhoun, Frederick S. *Power and Principle, Armed Intervention in Wilsonian Foreign Policy.* Kent, Ohio, 1986.

Calvert, Peter. *The Mexican Revolution, 1910–1914: The Diplomacy of Anglo-American Conflict.* Cambridge, England, 1968.

Campbell, John P. "Taft, Roosevelt, and the Arbitration Treaties of 1911." *Journal of American History,* LIII (September 1966).

Cantor, Milton. "The Radical Confrontation with Foreign Policy: War and Revolution, 1914–1920," in Alfred F. Young, *Dissent: Exploration in the History of American Radicalism.* DeKalb, Ill., 1968, 217–249.

Carr, James M. "A Sacred Trust of Civilization: Woodrow Wilson and the Genesis of the Mandate System." Senior thesis, Princeton University, 1982.

Chambers, Clark A. *Paul U. Kellogg and the Survey: Voices for Social Welfare and Social Justice.* Minneapolis, 1971.

Chambers II, John W. (ed.). *The Eagle and the Dove: The American Peace Movement and U.S. Foreign Policy, 1900–1922.* New York, 1976 and 1992.

———. *To Raise an Army: The Draft Comes to Modern America.* New York, 1987.

Chatfield, Charles. *For Peace and Justice: Pacifism in America, 1914–1941.* Knoxville, Tenn., 1971.

———. (ed.). *International War Resistance Through World War II.* New York, 1975.

———. "World War I and the Liberal Pacifist in the United States." *American Historical Review,* LXXV (December, 1970), 1920–1937.

Chatfield, Charles, and Peter van den Dungen (eds.). *Peace Movements and Political Culture.* Knoxville, Tenn., 1988.

Clements, Kenrick A. *William Jennings Bryan, Missionary Isolationist.* Knoxville, Tenn., 1982.

———. "Woodrow Wilson's Mexican Policy, 1913–1915." *Diplomatic History,* Vol. IV, No. 2 (Spring 1980).

———. *Woodrow Wilson, World Statesman.* Boston, 1987.

Clendenen, Clarence. *The United States and Pancho Villa: A Study in Unconventional Diplomacy.* Ithaca, N.Y., 1961.

Clifford, J. Garry. *The Citizen Soldiers: The Plattsburg Training Camp Movement.* Lexington, Ky., 1972.

Cline, Howard. *The United States and Mexico.* Cambridge, Mass., 1953.

Closser III, Ernest Ray. "Some Day a Silent Guard: Political Prisoners and the Amnesty Issue in Post–World War I America." Senior thesis, Princeton University, 1984.

Coffman, Edward M. *The War to End All Wars: The American Military Experience in World War I.* New York, 1968.

Coletta, Paolo E. *The Presidency of William Howard Taft.* Lawrence, Kansas, 1973.

———. *William Jennings Bryan,* 3 vols. Lincoln, Neb., 1964–1969.

———. "William Jennings Bryan's Plan for World Peace." *Nebraska History,* LVIII (Summer 1977).

Coogan, John W. *The End of Neutrality: The United States, Britain, and Maritime Rights, 1899–1915.* Ithaca, N.Y., 1981.

Cook, Blanche W. "Woodrow Wilson and the Antimilitarists, 1914–1917." Ph. D. dissertation, Johns Hopkins University, 1970.

Cooper, Jr., John M. " 'An Irony of Fate': Woodrow Wilson's Pre–World War I Diplomacy." *Diplomatic History,* III (Fall 1979), 425–438.

———. "The British Response to the House-Grey Memorandum: New Evidence and New Questions." *Journal of American History,* LIX (March 1973), 958–971.

———. "Fool's Errand or Finest Hour? Woodrow Wilson's Speaking Tour in September 1919." Cooper and Charles E. Neu (eds.), *The Wilson Era, Essays in Honor of Arthur S. Link.* Arlington Heights, Mich., 1991, pp. 198–220.

———. "Progressivism and American Policy: A Reconsideration." *Mid-American,* 51 (October 1969), 260–277.

————. *The Vanity of Power: American Isolationism and the First World War, 1914–1917.* Westport, Conn., 1969.

————. *The Warrior and the Priest: Woodrow Wilson and Theodore Roosevelt.* Cambridge, Mass., 1983.

Cuff, Robert D. *The War Industries Board: Business–Government Relations During World War I.* Baltimore, 1973.

Curry, George. 'Woodrow Wilson, Jan Smuts, and the Versailles Settlement." *American Historical Review.* LXVI (July 1961), 968–986.

Curti, Merle. "Bryan and World Peace." *Smith College Studies in History,* XVI (April–July 1931), 113–149.

————. *Peace or War: The American Struggle, 1636–1936.* Boston, 1936.

Davis, Allen F. *Spearheads for Reform.* New York, 1967.

Davis, Calvin. *The First Hague Peace Conference.* Ithaca, N.Y., 1962.

————. *The Second Hague Peace Conference: American Diplomacy and International Organization, 1899–1914.* Durham, N.C., 1975.

DeBenedetti, Charles. *Origins of the Modern American Peace Movement, 1915–1929.* Millwood, N.Y., 1978.

————. (ed.). *Peace Heroes in the Twentieth Century.* Bloomington, Ind., 1986.

————. *The Peace Reform in American History.* Bloomington, Ind., 1980.

Devlin, Patrick. *Too Proud to Fight: Woodrow Wilson's Neutrality.* New York, London, 1975.

Degen, Mary Louise. *The History of the Woman's Peace Party.* Baltimore, 1939.

Diggins, John P. *The American Left in the Twentieth Century.* New York, 1973.

Divine, Robert A. *Second Chance: The Triumph of Internationalism in America During World War II.* New York, 1967.

Dodd, William E. *Woodrow Wilson and His Work.* New York, 1932.

Egerton, George W. *Great Britain and the Creation of the League of Nations: Strategy, Politics, and International Organization, 1914–1919.* Chapel Hill, N.C., 1978.

————. "The Lloyd George Government and the Creation of the League of Nations." *American Historical Review,* LXXIX (April 1974), 419–444.

Ekirch, Walter. *The Decline of American Liberalism.* New York, 1955.

Ferrell, Robert H. *Woodrow Wilson and World War I.* New York, 1985.

Finnegan, John Patrick. *Against the Spector of the Dragon: The Campaign for American Military Preparedness.* Westport, Conn., 1974.

Fischer, Fritz. *Die Kriegszielpolitik des Kaiserlichen Deutschland, 1914–1918.* Dusseldorf: Droste Verlag, 1961; English trans., *Germany's Aims in the First World War.* New York, 1967.

Flannagan, Jr., John H. "The Disillusionment of a Progressive: U.S. Senator David I. Walsh and the League of Nations Issue." *New England Quarterly,* XLI (December 1968).

Fleming, Denna Frank. *The United States and the League of Nations, 1918–1920.* New York, 1932.

Floto, Inga. *Colonel House in Paris: A Study in American Policy at Paris, 1919.* Copenhagen: Universitetsforlaget I Aurhus, 1973; reprinted by Princeton University Press, 1980.

Forcey, Charles. *The Crossroads of Liberalism: Croly, Weyl, Lippmann and the Progressive Era, 1900–1925.* New York, 1961.

Fowler, Wilton B. *British-American Relations, 1917–1918: The Role of Sir William Wiseman.* Princeton, N.J., 1969.

Freud, Sigmund, and William C. Bullitt. *Thomas Woodrow Wilson, Twenty-eighth President of the United States: A Psychological Study.* New York, 1967.

Furuya, Jun. "The Socialist Party of America and Eugene V. Debs' Campaign in the 1912 Election." *The Hokkaido Law Review,* XXVIII and XXIX, No. 4 and No. 1, 1978.

Fussell, Paul. *The Great War in Modern Memory.* London, 1975.

Gable, John Allen. *The Bull Moose Years: Theodore Roosevelt and the Progressive Party.* Port Washington, N.Y., 1978.

Gaddis, John Lewis. *Strategies of Containment: A Critical Appraisal of Postwar American National Security Policy.* New York, 1982.

Gardner, Lloyd C. *Safe for Democracy: The Anglo-American Response to Revolution, 1913– 1923.* New York, 1984.

―――. "Woodrow Wilson and the Mexican Revolution." Arthur S. Link (ed.), *Woodrow Wilson and a Revolutionary World, 1913–1921.* Chapel Hill, N.C., 1982.

Garraty, John A. *Henry Cabot Lodge: A Biography.* New York, 1953.

Gelfand, Lawrence E. *The Inquiry: American Preparations for Peace, 1917–1919.* New Haven, Conn., 1963.

George, Alexander L., and Juliette L. George. *Woodrow Wilson and Colonel House: A Personality Study.* New York, 1956.

George, Alexander L., Juliette L. George. and Michael F. Marmor. "Issues in Wilsonian Scholarship: References to Early Strokes in *The Papers of Woodrow Wilson.*" *Journal of American History,* LXX (March 1984), 845–853.

Gilbert, Charles. *American Financing of World War I.* Westport, Conn., 1970.

Gilderhus, Mark T. *Diplomacy and Revolution, U.S.–Mexican Relations under Wilson and Carranza.* Tucson, 1977.

―――. "Pan-American Initiatives: The Wilson Presidency and 'Regional Integration,' 1914–1917," *Diplomatic History,* IV (Fall 1980), 409–423.

―――. *Pan-American Visions: Woodrow Wilson and the Western Hemisphere.* Tucson, 1986.

―――. "Wilson, Carranza, and the Monroe Doctrine: A Question in Regional Organization." *Diplomatic History,* VII, (Spring 1983), 103–115.

Ginger, Ray. *The Bending Cross: A Biography of Eugene Victor Debs.* New Brunswick, N.J., 1949.

Gregory, Ross. *The Origins of American Intervention in the First World War.* New York, 1971.

Haley, P. Edward. *Revolution and Intervention: The Diplomacy of Taft and Wilson with Mexico.* Cambridge, Mass., 1970.

Heaton, John L. *Cobb of "The World."* New York, 1924.

Hancock, W. K. *Smuts: The Sanguine Years, 1870–1919.* London, 1962.

Harbaugh, William H. *Power and Responsibility: The Life and Times of Theodore Roosevelt.* New York, 1961.

Hecksher, August. *Woodrow Wilson.* New York, 1991.

Helbich, Wolfgang J. "American Liberals in the League of Nations Controversy." *Public Opinion Quarterly,* XXXI (Winter 1967–1968), 568–596.

Hemleben, Sylvester J. *Plans for World Peace Through Six Centuries.* Chicago: University of Chicago Press, 1943.

Herman, Sondra R. *Eleven Against War: Studies in American Internationalist Thought, 1898– 1921.* Standford, Calif., 1969.

Hunt, Michael H. *Ideology and U.S. Foreign Policy.* New Haven, Conn., 1987.

Inman, Samuel Guy. *Inter-American Conferences, 1826–1954: History and Problems.* Harold E. Davis (ed.). Washington, D.C., 1965.

―――. *Problems in Pan-Americanism.* New York, 1921.

Jensen, Billie Barnes. "Philip Dru: The Blueprint of a Presidential Adviser." *American Studies* (Spring 1971), 49–58.

Johnson, Donald. *The Challenge to American Freedoms: World War I and the Rise of the American Civil Liberties Union.* Lexington, Ky., 1963.

Josephson, Harold, *et al.* (eds.). *Biographical Dictionary of Modern Peace Leaders, 1800–1975.* Westport, Conn., 1985.

Josephson, Matthew. *The President Makers.* New York, 1940.

Karnes, Thomas L. "Hiram Johnson and His Obsolete Shibboleth," *Diplomatic History,* III (Winter 1979), 39–58.

Katz, Friedrich. "Pancho Villa and the Attack on Columbus, New Mexico." *American Historical Review,* LXXXIII (February 1978), 101–130.

———. *The Secret War in Mexico: Europe, the United States and the Mexican Revolution.* Chicago, 1981.

Kaufman, Burton I. *Efficiency and Expansion: Foreign Trade Organization in the Wilson Administration, 1913–1921.* Westport, Conn., 1974.

Kennan, George F. *American Diplomacy, 1900–1950.* Chicago, 1951; 1982.

———. "Comments on a Paper Entitled 'Kennan versus Wilson' by Professor Thomas J. Knock." Cooper and Neu (eds.). *The Wilson Era, Essays in Honor of Arthur S. Link.* Arlington Heights, Ill., 1991, pp. 327–330.

———. *The Decision to Intervene.* Princeton, N.J., 1958.

———. *The Nuclear Delusion: Soviet–American Relations in the Atomic Age.* New York, 1982.

———. *Russia Leaves the War.* Princeton, N.J., 1956.

Kennedy, David M. *Over Here: The First World War and American Society.* New York, 1980.

Kernek, Sterling. "The British Government's Reactions to President Wilson's 'Peace Note' of December 1916." *The Historical Journal,* XIII (December 1970), 721–766.

Kerney, James. *The Political Education of Woodrow Wilson.* New York, 1926.

Kipnis, Ira. *The American Socialist Movement, 1897–1912.* New York, 1952.

Kissinger, Henry. *The White House Years.* Boston, 1979.

Knock, Thomas J. "'History with Lightning': The Forgotten Film, *Wilson.*" *American Quarterly,* XXVII (Winter 1976–77), 523-43.

———. "Kennan vs. Wilson." Cooper and Neu (eds.). *The Wilson Era, Essays in Honor of Arthur S. Link.* Arlington Heights, Ill., 1991, pp. 302–326.

———. "Woodrow Wilson and the Origins of the League of Nations." Ph. D. dissertation, Princeton University, 1982.

Knott, Alexander W. "The Pan-American Policy of Woodrow Wilson, 1913–1921." Ph. D. dissertation, University of Colorado, 1968.

Kuehl, Warren F. (ed.). *Biographical Dictionary of Internationalists.* Westport, Conn., 1983.

———. *Seeking World Order: The United States and World Organization to 1920.* Nashville, 1968.

La Feber, Walter. *The New Empire: An Interpretation of American Expansion.* New York, 1963.

Lasch, Christopher. *The American Liberals and the Russian Revolution.* New York, 1962.

———. *The New Radicalism in America: The Intellectual as a Social Type, 1889–1963.*

Lawrence, David. *The True Story of Woodrow Wilson.* New York, 1924.

Leech, Margaret. *In the Days of McKinley.* New York, 1959.

Lentin, A. *Lloyd George, Woodrow Wilson, and the Guilt of Germany: An Essay in the Pre-History of Appeasement.* Baton Rouge, 1985.

Leopold, Richard W. *Elihu Root and the Conservative Tradition.* Boston, 1954.

Leuchtenburg, William E. "The New Deal and the Analogue of War." John Braeman (ed.). *Change and Continuity in Twentieth-Century America.* Columbus, 1964.

——. "Progressivism and Imperialism: The Progressive Movement and American Foreign Policy, 1898–1916." *Mississippi Valley Historical Review*, XXXIX (December 1952), 483–504.

Levering, Ralph B. *The Public and American Foreign Policy, 1918–1978*. New York, 1978.

——. "Public Culture and Public Opinion: The League of Nations Controversy in New Jersey and North Carolina." Cooper and Neu (eds.). *The Wilson Era, Essays in Honor of Arthur S. Link*. Arlington Heights, Ill., 1991, pp. 159–197.

Levin, N. Gordon. *Woodrow Wilson and World Politics: America's Response to War and Revolution*. Oxford, England, 1968.

Levy, David W. *Herbert Croly of the New Republic*. Princeton, N.J., 1985.

Lewis, Thomas T. "Alternative Psychological Interpretations of Woodrow Wilson." *Mid-America*, LXII (April–July 1983), 71–85.

Link, Arthur S. *American Epoch, A History of the United States Since 1900*, 2 vols., 5th ed. New York, 1980.

——. *The Higher Realism of Woodrow Wilson, and Other Essays*. Nashville, 1971.

——. (ed.). *The Impact of World War I*. New York, 1969.

——. *Wilson: Campaigns for Progressivism and Peace*. Princeton, N.J., 1965.

——. *Wilson: Confusions and Crises*. Princeton, N.J., 1964.

——. *Wilson the Diplomatist: A Look at His Major Foreign Policies*. New York, 1957.

——. *Wilson: The New Freedom*. Princeton, N.J., 1956.

——. *Wilson: The Road to the White House*. Princeton, N.J., 1947.

——. *Wilson: The Struggle for Neutrality*. Princeton, N.J., 1960.

——. (ed.). *Woodrow Wilson and a Revolutionary World*. Chapel Hill, N.C., 1981.

——. *Woodrow Wilson and the Progressive Era, 1910–1917*. New York, 1954.

——. *Woodrow Wilson: Revolution, War, and Peace*. Arlington Heights, Ill., 1979.

Livermore, Seward W. *Politics Is Adjourned: Woodrow Wilson and the War Congress, 1916–1918*. Middletown, Conn., 1966.

——. "The Sectional Issue in the 1918 Congressional Elections." *Mississippi Valley Historical Review*, XXXV (June 1948), 29–60.

Long, John W. "American Intervention in Russia: The North Russian Expedition, 1918–19." *Diplomatic History*, VI (Winter 1982), 45–67.

Louis, William Roger. *Great Britain and Germany's Lost Colonies, 1914–1919*. London, 1967.

Lunardini, Christine A., and Thomas J. Knock. "Woodrow Wilson and Woman Suffrage: A New Look." *Political Science Quarterly*, XCV (Winter 1980–81), 655–667.

Lutzker, Michael A. "The 'Practical' Peace Advocates: An Interpretation of the American Peace Movement, 1899–1917." Ph. D. dissertation, Rutgers University, 1969.

——. "Jane Addams: Peacetime Heroine, Wartime Heretic," in DeBenedetti (ed.), *Peace Heroes in the Twentieth Century*, 29–55.

Marchand, C. Roland. *The American Peace Movement and Social Reform, 1898–1918*. Princeton, N.J., 1972.

Margulies, Herbert F. *The Mild Reservationists and the League of Nations Controversy in the Senate*. Columbia, Mo., 1989.

Markowitz, Gerald E. "Progressivism and Imperialism: A Return to First Principles." *The Historian*, XXXVII (February 1975), 257–275.

Martin, James R. "The American Peace Movement and the Progressive Era." Ph. D. dissertation, Rice University, 1975.

Martin, Lawrence W. *Peace Without Victory: Woodrow Wilson and the British Liberals*. New Haven, Conn., 1958.

Mason, Alpheus T. *Brandeis: A Free Man's Life*. New York, 1946.

May, Ernest R. *Imperial Democracy*. Boston, 1961.

——. *The World War and American Isolation, 1914–1917*. Cambridge, Mass., 1959.

May, Henry F. *The End of American Innocence*. New York, 1959.

Mayer, Arno J. *Political Origins of the New Diplomacy, 1917–1918*. New Haven Conn., 1959.

————. *Politics and Diplomacy of the Peacemaking: Containment and Counterrevolution at Versailles, 1918–1919*. New York, 1967.

————. *The Persistence of the Old Regime*. New York, 1981.

Morgan, H. Wayne. *Eugene V. Debs, Socialist for President*. Syracuse, N.Y., 1962.

Morland, Robert L. *Political Prairie Fire: The Nonpartisan League, 1915–1922*. Minneapolis, 1935.

Mowry, George E. *Theodore Roosevelt and the Progressive Movement*. Madison, Wisc., 1946.

Moynihan, Daniel P. *On the Law of Nations*. Cambridge, Mass., 1990.

Mulder, John M. *Woodrow Wilson: The Years of Preparation*. Princeton, N.J., 1978.

Murphy, Paul L. *World War I and the Origin of Civil Liberties in the United States*. New York, 1979.

Murray, Robert F. *The Red Scare: A Study in National Hysteria, 1919–1920*. Minneapolis, 1955.

Nelson, Keith L. "What Colonel House Overlooked in the Armistice." *Mid-America,* LI (April 1969), 75–91.

————. *Victors Divided: America and the Allies in Germany, 1918–1923*. Berkeley, 1975.

Neu, Charles E. "Woodrow Wilson and Colonel House: The Early Years, 1911–1915." Cooper and Neu (eds.), *The Wilson Era, Essays in Honor of Arthur S. Link*. Arlington Heights, Mich., 1991, pp. 248–278.

Nevins, Allan. *Henry White: Thirty Years of American Diplomacy*. New York, 1930.

Nicolson, Harold. *Peacemaking 1919*. New York, 1965 ed.

Niebur, Richard. "The Idea of the Covenant and American Democracy." *Church History,* XXIII (1954), 126–135.

Noble, David W. *"The New Republic* and the Idea of Progress, 1914–1920." *Mississippi Valley Historical Review,* XXXVIII (1951), 387–402.

Notter, Harley. *The Origins of the Foreign Policy of Woodrow Wilson*. Baltimore, 1937.

O'Neill, William L. *Everyone Was Brave: The Rise and Fall of Feminism in America*. Chicago, 1969.

————. *The Last Romantic; A Life of Max Eastman*. New York, 1978.

Osborn, George C. *Woodrow Wilson: The Early Years*. Baton Rouge, 1968.

Osgood, Robert E. *Ideals and Self-Interest in American Foreign Relations: The Great Transformation of the Twentieth Century*. Chicago, 1953.

Palmer, Frederick C. *Bliss, Peacemaker*. New York, 1934.

Park, Bert E. *The Impact of Illness upon World Leaders*. Philadelphia, 1986.

Patterson, David S. *Toward a Warless World: The Travail of the American Peace Movement, 1887–1914*. Bloomington, Ind., 1976.

————. "Woodrow Wilson and the Mediation Movement." *The Historian,* XXXIII (August 1971), 535–556.

Pearlman, Michael. *To Make Democracy Safe for America: Patricians and Preparedness in the Progressive Era*. Urbana, Ill., 1984.

Petersen, Svend. *A Statistical History of American Presidential Elections*. Westport, Conn., 1981.

Peterson, Horace C., and Gilbert C. Fite. *Opponents of War, 1917–1918*. Madison, Wisc., 1957.

Pike, Frederick C. *Chile and the United States, 1880–1962*. South Bend, Ind., 1963.

Porter, Laura Smith. "The Development of an Internationalist Foreign Policy: *The New Republic* and American Neutrality, 1914–1917." Unpublished manuscript in the possession of the author.

Pringle, Henry F. *The Life and Times of William Howard Taft,* 2 vols. New York, 1939.

Pusey, Merlo J. *Charles Evans Hughes,* 2 vols. New York, 1951.

Quirk, Robert E. *An Affair of Honor.* Lexington, Ky., 1962.

Radosh, Ronald. *American Labor and Foreign Policy.* New York, 1969.

Raffo, Peter. "Anglo-American Preliminary Negotiations for a League of Nations." *Journal of Contemporary History,* IX (October 1974), 153–176.

Read, James Morgan. *Atrocity Propaganda, 1914–1919.* New Haven, Conn., 1941.

Richardson, Rupert Norval. *Colonel Edward M. House: The Texas Years, 1858–1912.* Abilene, Tex., 1964.

Robbins, Keith. *The Abolition of War: The 'Peace Movement' in Great Britain, 1914–1919.* Cardiff, 1976.

———. *Sir Edward Grey; A Biography of Lord Grey of Fallodon.* London, 1971.

Rosenberg, Emily. *Spreading the American Dream.* New York, 1982.

Rosenstone, Robert A. *Romantic Revolutionary; A Biography of John Reed.* New York, 1975.

Rudin, Harry R. *Armistice 1918.* New Haven, Conn., 1944.

Salvatore, Nick. *Eugene V. Debs, Citizen and Socialist.* Urbana, Ill., 1982.

Saunders, Frances. *Ellen Axson Wilson.* Chapel Hill, N.C., 1986.

Schaffer, Ronald. *America in the Great War: The Rise of the War Welfare State.* New York, 1991.

Schwabe, Klaus. *Woodrow Wilson, Revolutionary Germany, and Peacemaking, 1918–1919.* Chapel Hill, N.C., 1985.

Scheiber, Harry N. *The Wilson Administration and Civil Liberties.* Ithaca, N.Y., 1960.

Schmitz, David F. "Woodrow Wilson and the Liberal Peace: The Problem of Italy and Imperialism." *Peace and Change,* XII (December 1987, 29–44).

Shannon, David A. *The Socialist Party of America.* New York, 1955.

Shapiro, Stanley. "The Twilight of Reform: Advanced Progressivism After the Armistice." *The Historian,* XXXIII (May 1971), 349–364.

Smith, Gene. *When the Cheering Stopped; The Last Years of Woodrow Wilson.* New York, 1964.

Smith, Robert Freeman. *The United States and Revolutionary Nationalism in Mexico, 1916–1932.* Chicago, 1972.

Soder, John P. "The Impact of the Tacna-Arica Dispute on the Pan-American Movement." Ph. D. dissertation, Georgetown University, 1970.

Steel, Ronald. *Walter Lippmann and the American Century.* Boston, 1980.

Stern, Fritz (ed.). *The Varieties of History: From Voltaire to the Present.* New York, 1957.

Stone, Ralph. *The Irreconcilables: The Fight Against the League of Nations.* Lexington, Ky. 1970.

Stromberg, Roland N. *Collective Security and American Foreign Policy: From the League of Nations to NATO.* New York, 1963.

Swanberg, W. A. *Norman Thomas; The Last Idealist.* New York, 1976.

Swartz, Marvin. *The Union of Democratic Control in British Politics in the First World War.* Oxford, England, 1971.

Taylor, A. J. P. *The Troublemakers: Dissent Over Foreign Policy, 1792–1939.* Bloomington, Ind., 1958.

J.A. "The League of Nations Union and the Promotion of the League Idea in Great Britain." *The Australian Journal of Politics and History,* XVIII (April 1972), 52–61.

Thompson, John A. "American Progressive Publicists and the First World War, 1914–1917." *Journal of American History* (September 1971), 364–383.

———. *Reformers and War: American Progressive Publicists and the First World War.* Cambridge and New York, 1987.

Thorburn, Neil. "A Progressive and the First World War: Frederic C. Howe." *Mid-America,* LI (April 1969) 108–118.

Thorsen, Niels A. *The Political Thought of Woodrow Wilson, 1875–1910.* Princeton, N.J., 1988.

Tillman, Seth P. *Anglo-American Relations at the Paris Peace Conference of 1919.* Princeton, N.J., 1961.

Trachtenberg, Marc. *Reparations in World Politics: France and European Economic Diplomacy, 1916–1923.* New York, 1980.

———. "Versailles After Sixty Years." *Journal of Contemporary History,* XVII (1982), 487–506.

Trani, Eugene C. "Woodrow Wilson and the Decision to Intervene in Russia: A Reconsideration." *Journal of Modern History,* XLVIII (September 1976), 440–461.

Trask, David F. *The United States and the Supreme War Council.* Middletown, Conn., 1961.

———. *World War I at Home: Readings on American Life, 1914–1920.* New York: John Wiley, 1970.

Unterberger, Betty Miller. *America's Siberian Expedition, 1918–1920.* Durham, N.C., 1956.

———. *The United States, Revolutionary Russia, and the Rise of Czechoslovakia.* Chapel Hill, N.C., 1989.

———. "Woodrow Wilson and the Bolsheviks: The 'Acid Test" of Soviet-American Relations." *Diplomatic History,* XI (Spring 1987), 71–90.

Vaughn, Stephen. *Holding Fast the Inner Lines: Democracy, Nationalism, and the Committee on Public Information.* Chapel Hill, N.C., 1980.

Vinson, John Chalmers. *Referendum on Isolation: Defeat of Article Ten of the League of Nations Covenant.* Athens, Ga., 1961.

Walworth, Arthur. *America's Moment, 1918: American Diplomacy at the End of World War I.* New York, 1977.

———. *Wilson and His Peacemakers: American Diplomacy at the Paris Peace Conference, 1919.* New York, 1986.

Walters, Frank P. *A History of the League of Nations.* London, 1960.

Weinstein, Edwin A. *Woodrow Wilson: A Medical and Psychological Biography.* Princeton, N.J., 1981.

———, Arthur S. Link, and James W. Anderson. "Woodrow Wilson's Political Personality: A Reappraisal." *Political Science Quarterly,* XCIII (Winter 1978), 585–598.

Weinstein, James A. *The Decline of Socialism in America.* New York, 1967.

Weiss, Nancy J. "The Negro and the New Freedom: Fighting Wilsonian Segregation." *Political Science Quarterly,* LXXXIV (March 1969), 61–79.

Wheeler-Bennett, John W. *Brest-Litovsk: The Forgotten Peace, March 1918.* New York, 1939.

Widenor, William C. "American Planning for the United Nations: Have We Been Asking the Right Questions?" *Diplomatic History,* VI (Summer 1982), 243–264.

———. *Henry Cabot Lodge and the Search for an American Foreign Policy.* Berkeley, 1980.

Wiebe, Robert H. *The Search for Order, 1877–1920.* New York, 1967.

Williams, William Appleman. *American-Russian Relations, 1781–1947.* New York, 1971.

———. *The Tragedy of American Diplomacy.* New York, 1959.

Wimer, Kurt. "Woodrow Wilson and World Order." Unpublished manuscript in the possession of the author.

———. "Woodrow Wilson Tries Conciliation: An Effort That Failed." *The Historian,* XXV (August 1963).

Winkler, Henry R. *The League of Nations Movement in Great Britain, 1914–1919.* New Brunswick, N.J., 1952.

Wittner, Lawrence S. "Peace Movements and Foreign Policy: The Challenge to Diplomatic Historians." *Diplomatic History,* XI (Fall 1987), 355–370.

Woodward, David R. "The British Government and Japanese Intervention in Russia during World War I." *Journal of Modern History,* XLVI (December 1974), 680–681.

―――. "The Origins and Intent of David Lloyd George's January 5 War Aims Speech." *The Historian,* XXXIV (November 1971), 22–39.

Wreszin, Michael. *Oswald Garrison Villard, Pacifist at War.* Bloomington, Ind., 1965.

Yates, Louis A. R. *United States and French Security.* New York, 1957.

Index

"Acid Test of Our Democracy, The" (Thomas), 157

ACNP. *See* American Commission to Negotiate Peace

Adams, John Quincy, 20

Adamson Act, 92–93, 94, 95, 100

Addams, Jane, 161, 191; her hopes for Woodrow Wilson, viii, 50–52, 67, 82, 94, 118, 146, 148; her disappointment in Wilson, 63; on her 1917 meeting with Wilson, 120; withdraws from Board of AUAM, 131–32; and wartime political repression, 134, 135; denounces Versailles Treaty, 254. *See also* Woman's Peace party

Adler, Selig, 185

Allies: Wilson's problems with, 80, 154; reaction to Wilson's peace note, 110–11; war aims of, 137–38, 139, 141; intervention, in Russia, 154–58; and League of Nations idea, 160–65; reactions to German peace overtures to Wilson, 172–75, 184; take League of Nations hostage, 246. *See also* Great Britain; France; House, Colonel Edward Mandell: and Allies; Italy; Treaties: secret Allied; War aims

Alsace-Lorraine, 144

American Commission to Negotiate Peace (ACNP), 187, 198, 205

American Defense Society, 61

American Economist, 169

American Federation of Labor, 91, 93, 129, 130

American intervention: in Great War, encouragements to, 73, 80, 115–17; growing support for, 117–22, and progressive internationalists, 128–40; in Russia, 154–58; in international affairs, 273. *See also* Latin America; Mexican Revolution

American Labor Party of Greater New York, 237

American Peace Society (Boston), 11, 12

American Protective League, 133

American School Peace League, 149

American Socialist, 135

American Society for the Judicial Settlement of International Disputes, 55

American Union Against Militarism (AUAM), viii, 76, 94, 112, 187, 261; founding of, 63–67; 1916 meeting with Wilson, 66–67, 75, 86, 87; role of, in averting war with Mexico, 82–83; on "Peace Without Victory" speech, 114; opposition to U.S. intervention in Great War, 117, 118, 131–32; Burleson on, 135. *See also names of members*

Amnesty: Wilson's response to progressive internationalists' calls for, 236–39, 255–56

Angell, Norman, 36, 37, 119, 160

Annexation. *See* Colonies; Mandate system

Anti-Bolshevik sentiments, 235–36, 241, 265, 269

Anti-German sentiments, 133–34, 139; Roosevelt's, 169, 180, 184, 187

Anti-imperialism. *See* Imperialism

Antitrust legislation, 17, 24, 88

Antiwar rallies: in U.S., 118

"Appeal for a Democratic Congress": Wilson's, 179–80, 189

Appeal to Reason, 17, 55, 139–42, 146; censorship of, 135; and the League of Nations, 234, 238

Arabic (ship), 60–61, 73

Arbitration: UDC's position on, 38; in Pan-American Pact, 40; WPP's position on, 51; Taft's views on, 56; Wilson's views on, 57, 152, 153; in 1916 Republican platform, 100; Phillimore Report on, 151; in Wilson's First Paris Draft, 201, 204; Lansing's views of, 205; in Wilson's Second Paris Draft, 206; in Cecil-Miller Draft, 214; in Covenant of the League of Nations, 220–22, 232, 247, 261–62; Kennan's view of, 273

Archangel, 155, 156

Argentina: offers to mediate in Mexican Revolution, 27; and Pan-American Pact, 40, 74, 81, 83–84

Arica (Chile), 40–41, 74

Arizona: Mexican designs on, 117. *See also* Bisbee (Ariz.)

Armaments: manufacture of, 35–36, 37, 39, 152, 205, 216, 220, 222, 275; WPP's position on manufacture of, 51. *See also* Disarmament

Armed neutrality, 116–17

Armies. *See* Army; Force; Navy; Standing armies

Armistice: WPP's call for, 51; draft of, by Foch, 181–82; terms of, 189, 192, 209; debate over, 229. *See also* Pre-Armistice Agreement

Arms race, 36. *See also* Armaments; Military-industrial complex

Army: expansion of U.S., 89–90; notion of a League of Nations, 221–22; Congress's right to establish size of, 232. *See also* Force; League of Nations: enforcement of decisions of; Standing armies

Article X. *See* Covenant of the League of Nations: Article X

Ashurst, Henry F., 170, 171, 172, 174

Asquith, Herbert Henry, 22, 51, 72, 76, 108, 110, 199

Atlantic Monthly, 10, 11, 37–38

Attorney General. *See* Gregory, Thomas Watt; Palmer, A. Mitchell

AUAM. *See* American Union Against Militarism

Augusta (Ga.), 3

Australia. *See* Hughes, William

Austria-Hungary, 32, 144

Axson, Ellen Louise, 4, 13, 69. *See also* Wilson, Ellen Axson

Axson, Stockton, 35–36, 38, 39, 44

Baden, Max von, 166, 167, 173

Bagehot, Walter, 5

Bailey, Thomas A., 272

Bailey, Warren Worth, 90

Baker, Newton D., 28, 38, 134, 178

Baker, Ray Stannard, 21, 35, 94, 131, 161, 197, 228, 237, 243, 246, 249, 251, 269, 272

Balance of power: advocates of, ix; Wilson's criticism of, ix, 36, 97, 107, 112, 115, 195–96; House's concerns about European, 22; UDC's position on, 37; Roosevelt's views on, 49, 229, 230; WPP's position on, 51; Clemenceau's views on, 198, 200; British views on, 200; progressive internationalists' views on, 235, 268; "realist" views on, 272, 273, 274

Balch, Emily Greene, 50, 51–52, 118

Baldwin, Roger, 131–32, 236

Balfour, Arthur James, 79–80, 146, 174, 175, 224; on League of Nations, 108, 149, 199–200, 248; on war aims, 138

Balkan states: Wilson's proposals for, 144

Barnes, George, 200

"Bases of Peace" (Wilson), 126–27

Battle of the Marne, 31

Beard, Charles A., 160, 237

Beer, George Louis, 203

Belgium: Germany's invasion of, 48, 49; Wilson calls for evacuation of, 144; delegation from, at League of Nations Commission, 217, 220, 221, 222

Benedict XV, Pope, 51, 139–40

Benham, Edith, 192, 204, 218

Benson, Allan L., 18, 93–95, 132, 256

Berger, Victor, 18, 95, 132

Bergson, Henri, 147

Berkman, Alexander, 135

Berle, Adolf, Jr., 66

Bethmann Hollweg, Theobald von, 44, 46, 51, 106–7, 108, 110–11, 116

Beveridge, Albert J., 177, 239

Bickett, Thomas W., 176–77, 190

Bigelow, Herbert, 134

"Big Stick" policy, 26

Billings (Mont.): Wilson's address in, 262

Bingham, Hiram, 290 n.25

Bisbee (Ariz.): miners' strike at, 133–34

Bismarck, Otto von, 13

Bissolati, Leonida, 197, 249

Bliss, General Tasker H., 189, 204, 205; contributions to League of Nations, 206–7, 254

Bluntschli, Johann Kaspar, 8

Bohn, Frank, 93, 94, 132

Bolsheviks: and the Great War, 140–42, 143, 145; excluded from League of Nations, in Cecil's draft, 201. *See also* Anti-Bolshevik sentiments; Russia

Borah, William E., 109, 124, 125, 231, 232, 257, 259

Borden, Sir Robert, 72, 74, 200

Bork, Robert, 87

Bosnia, 32

Boston: Wilson's address at Mechanic's Hall in, 230–31, 239, 244

Boston Common: attacks on Socialists on, 133

Boston Herald, 228

Botha, Louis, 211

Bourgeois, Léon, 217, 219–23

Bourne, Randolph, 147, 157

Brailsford, H. N., 36, 193, 199

Brain Trusts. *See* Inquiry, The

Brandegee, Frank, 233, 241, 259

Brandeis, Louis D., 17, 87, 88, 160

Brazil, 217; offers to mediate in Mexican Revolution, 27; and Pan-American Pact, 40, 74, 81, 83–84

Brest-Litovsk armistice, 142, 143, 145; and Allied war aims, 154–55

Bridges, Robert, 120

Britain. *See* Great Britain

British Dominions. *See* Dominions (British)

British Empire, 71, 73; and amendment on racial equality, 224

British Trades Union Congress, 199

British Trades Union League: Lloyd George's speech to, 143, 154

Brooklyn *Eagle,* 91

Brougham, Herbert Bruce, 34–36, 38, 44

Bryan, William Jennings, 102; his candidacy for President, 10, 16; as Wilson's Secretary of State, 21–22, 23, 40, 44, 45, 46; Roosevelt's attacks on, 49, 61; antimilitary stance of, 59, 63, 70, 82, 151; resignation of, 60. *See also* Cooling-off treaties

Bryce, Viscount James, 60, 76, 78, 110, 114, 149, 184, 191, 199, 241

Bryce Group: similarities of LEP to, 56; and League of Nations idea, 79, 151

Bryce Report, 60

Buchanan, James, 100, 169

Bullitt, William C., 258, 269

Burke, Edmund, 7, 8, 9, 13, 26

Burleson, Albert Sidney: political repression of radicals by, 134–37, 140, 158–60, 186, 237–38, 255, 256; counsels unconditional surrender, 174; criticizes Wilson, 178; counterfactual speculations about, 187–88

Burner, David, 185

Bush, George, 275

Business: Republican appeals to big, 168–69; opposition to Wilson, 130-31, 265; regulation of, 15-16, 23, 24; and exemption from League sanction (Reservation XI), 266

Butler, Nicholas Murray, 55

Buxton, Charles, 199
Buxton, Noel, 78, 86, 119, 199

Calhoun, Frederick S., 287 n.75
California, 134; support for Wilson in, 101–2
Call, The (New York), 18, 88, 136, 236, 243
Cambon, Jules, 72
Cameroon, 211
Canada. *See* Borden, Robert
Canterbury, Archbishop of, 165, 199
Caporetto battle, 140
Carabao Club, 21, 59
Carnegie, Andrew, 39
Carnegie Endowment for International Peace, 51, 55
Carranza, Venustiana, 26–29, 81–83
Carrizal (Mexico). *See* "Punitive Expedition"
Catholic Church, 28
Cecil, Lord Robert, 148–49, 151–52, 154, 160, 164, 172, 200, 210, 211; and League of Nations Covenant, 201, 202, 205, 208–9, 216–17, 247–48; at League of Nations Commission, 217, 218, 222–26, 249, 250. *See also* "Cecil-Miller Draft"; "Draft Convention"
"Cecil-Miller Draft," 214–15, 216, 219–20
Censorship. *See* Burleson, Albert Sidney
Central Powers: designs of, on Russia, 143, 155–58
Cheyenne (Wyo.): Wilson's address in, 262, 263
Chicago (Ill.): Wilson's campaign speech at, 97
Chicago *Daily News,* 178
Chicago Peace Society, 50, 67
Chicago Tribune, 172
Child labor: Roosevelt's proposals for, 16; and Wilson, 24, 90–91, 94, 95; and foreign policy, 50; and League of Nations Covenant, 221, 261
Chile: offers to mediate in Mexican Revolution, 27; and Pan-American Pact, 40–41, 70, 74, 81, 83–84
China, 217. *See also* Shantung
Chinda, Viscount Sutemi, 223
Christianity: and international law, 8, 14, 33; and war, 11–12; and socialism, 18;

as influence on Bryan, 21. *See also* Missionaries; Presbyterianism
Cincinnati (Oh.): Wilson's campaign speech at, 97, 106
Cincinnati *Commercial Tribune,* 164, 185
Cincinnati *Times-Star,* 102
City of Memphis (ship), 117
Civil liberties: in wartime, under Wilson, x, 134–37, 158–60, 168, 181, 236–39, 255, 256, 257. *See also* Amnesty; Espionage Act; Repression
Civil War, 169, 181; effects of, on Wilson, 3–4; compared to Great War, 31–32
Clark, Champ, 16
Clarke, John Hessin, 87–88, 190
Clayton Act, 24, 93
Clemenceau, Georges, 140–41, 145, 154, 161, 162, 170, 175, 181, 183, 184, 195, 197, 210, 213, 248; and League of Nations, 192, 198–99, 212, 223, 250
Clements, Kendrick L., 287 n.75
Coalition of 1916: Wilson's failure to nurture, x, 185–87, 236, 244–45, 255, 260, 267–68; development of, 86–103. *See also* Progressive internationalists
Cobb, Frank, 132
Cobb-Lippmann Memorandum, 320 n.77
Colcord, Lincoln, 141, 157, 257
Cold Harbor battle, 31
Cold War: and internationalism, x, 272–75
Collective security, 56; Wilson's position on, 35, 39, 57, 75, 78, 95, 97, 106, 112, 115, 119, 206, 211, 220, 222, 224, 259; elimination of, 216; in Pan-American Pact, 39, 70; Lansing's views of, 205; Cecil's position on, 208; Lloyd George opposes, 214–15; reservations on, 266; and NATO, 273–74
Colombia, 28, 49
Colonialism: Wilson's distinction between imperialism and, 11, 43. *See also* Colonies; Imperialism; Mandate system
Colonies: postwar disposition of former, 200, 203, 205, 208, 210–16, 224. *See also* Imperialism; Mandate system
Columbia University, 55
Columbus (Oh.): Wilson's address in, 260
"Committee on Nothing at All," 161
Committee on Public Information (CPI), 133, 186

Community (of nations): Wilson's beliefs about, 8–9, 14, 33, 115. *See also* Covenantal tradition; League of Nations

"Confession of Faith" (Roosevelt), 15–16

"Confidential Journal" (Wilson), 13

Congress: declares war on Germany, 121–22, 131; questions about role of, in League of Nations, 124, 149, 205, 206, 221–22, 232–33, 259; Wilson presents Fourteen Points to, 143–44; hears Armistice terms, 189; Wilson's address to, before leaving for peace negotiations, 193; Wilson asks, to refrain from discussion of League of Nations, 230. *See also* Congressional campaign of 1918; Espionage Act; Senate; Wilson, Woodrow: his wartime refusal to discuss the League of Nations; White House dinner; *names of legislators*

Congressional campaign of 1918, pp. 167–69, 176–89, 229; and Wilson's popularity in Europe, 195

Congressional Government (Wilson), 5, 13

Conquest. *See* Imperialism

Conscription: Smuts' proposals against, 202, 205

Conservative internationalism, viii, 55–58, 78. *See also* Conservative internationalists

Conservative internationalists: support of, for League of Nations, 68, 69, 99, 160; opposition to Wilson, 87–88, 127–28; Wilson tries to appeal to, 244–45, 247, 267; gulf between progressive internationalists and, 265–67. *See also* Conservative internationalism; League to Enforce Peace; Nationalism; Republican Party; Taft, William Howard

Constitution (United States), 5, 234

Constitutional Government in the United States (Wilson), 13

Constitutions: Wilson's interest in, 4–5, 10, 13–14. *See also* Covenant of the League of Nations

"Containment," 272, 274

Coolidge, Calvin, 239

Cooling-off treaties: Bryan's, 21–22, 36, 39, 57, 151, 153

Cooper, John Milton, Jr., 16

Corporations: and Wilson, 6, 7, 23, 24. *See also* Business; Lobbyists; Monopolies

Costigan, Edward P., 158

Council of Four, 247–48, 251

Council of Ten (peace conference), 209, 210, 212, 221, 223, 224

Courtney, Kate, 78

Covenant: Wilson's Magnolia, 153–54, 162, 202–4, 205, 218, 224–25, 254, Cecil's criticisms of, 208

Covenantal tradition: of Presbyterianism, 4–6, 10, 207–8

Covenant of the League of Nations: provisions of, 22; Wilson's early views of, 127; drafting of, 201–4, 210–26, 268; revising of, 227, 246–51, 252; American criticism of, 239–43; Article III, 219; Article VII, 223; Article VIII, 232; Article X, 39, 127, 219, 232–33, 240–41, 243, 248, 249, 252–54, 257, 259, 261–62, 266, 268; Article XV, 247; Article XX, 242. *See also* "Negative covenant"; Reservationist movement; *names of various drafts for*

Cox, James M., 269

CPI. *See* Committee on Public Information

Creel, George, 133, 186, 192, 209

Croly, Herbert, 64, 65, 99, 114, 125–26, 129, 160, 192; on wartime political repression, 134, 136

Cromer, Lord, 79

Crosby, Oscar T., 161, 162

Cuba: and Spanish-American War, 9

Cummings, Homer S., 174, 178, 179

Curzon, Lord, 200

Czechs: rescue operation for, in Russia, 156, 157

da Gama, Domicio, 40, 81, 83

Dalmation Islands: Italy's desire for, 197, 249

Daniels, Josephus, 59, 175

Darrow, Clarence, 256

Davis, Allen F., 129

Davis, Jefferson, 3

Davis, Norman H., 254

Debs, Eugene V., 87, 101–2; political stance of, 7, 10, 19; on 1912, pp. 15, 269; as candidate for President, 17–18; his support for neutrality, 53, 64, 132; on

Debs, Eugene V. (*continued*)
Fourteen Points, 146; wartime political repression of, 159, 236, 255
Declaration of Independence, 77, 97, 113, 130
Defeat. *See* Victory
Democracy: Wilson's belief in, 5–7, 14, 33, 121, 267; UDC's position on, 37; progressive internationalists' concerns about wartime suppression of, 134–37, 158–60; Wilson's insistence on German, 171, 172, 173, 175
Democratic National Committee, 241, 245
Democratic party: and imperialism, 10; nominates Wilson for President, 14, 16; and Bryan, 21; and Republican charges of lack of patriotism, 62, 168, 176, 187–88, 256; and 1916 presidential campaign, 86, 90, 100–101, 134; decline of, in 1914 House of Representatives, 88–89; opposition to American involvement in Great War by, 117; during congressional elections of 1918, pp. 178–81, 184–89; and amnesty, 236; 1920 disarray of, 269. *See also* Democratic National Committee; Liberals; Progressive internationalists
Derby, Lord, 211
Dewey, Admiral George, 9
Dewey, John, 94, 147, 160
Dial, 160, 186, 236–37, 242, 253, 255
Díaz, Porfirio, 25, 29
Disarmament: Wilson's advocacy of, 22, 23, 57, 68, 113, 115, 126, 127, 144, 152, 153, 204–5, 207, 222, 261, 268; UDC's position on, 37, 38; WPP's position on, 51; SPA's position on, 54; LEP's position on, 57; Phillimore Report's silence on, 151; Roosevelt on, 177; Smuts' proposals for, 202; Bliss's views of, 207; British position on, 208; in Covenant of League of Nations, 220, 224, 235, 242, 253, 266; Congress's questions about, 231–32; Kennan on, 273, 274; Gorbachev on, 275
Disney, Walt, 168
Dodd, William E., 269–70
"Dollar Diplomacy," 19, 26, 29
Domestic policy: and foreign policy, vii, ix, 30, 50, 57, 75, 87, 88, 96–98, 131–32,

136, 159, 255–57, 260–61, 267, gap in, 187, 236–39; Wilson's reform measures for, ix, 16–17, 19, 23–24, 86–87, 129–30, opponents of, ix, 62, 104, 130–31; Roosevelt's, 16–17; and 1916 reelection campaign, 100; Republican fears about foreign policy and, 240. *See also* Civil liberties; Economic policies; Coalition of 1916; Labor; Nationalization; Progressive internationalism; Reconstruction commission; Socialism; Socialists
Dominican Republic, 84
Dominions (British): representation in League of Nations, 208, 214, 215, 232; interest in former German colonies, 210–13
"Draft Convention" (Cecil), 208–9, 214, 216
Dru, Philip. *See Philip Dru: Administrator* (House); House, Colonel Edward Mandell
Du Pont, Pierre S., 130

Eastman, Crystal, 50, 63, 66
Eastman, Max, 63, 122, 269; his support for Wilson, viii, 18, 30, 50, 66–67, 93, 94, 95, 98, 102–3, 114, 118, 140, 146–47; and wartime political repression, 135–36; and Russian Revolution, 157–58; wartime political repression of, 158, 165; his disappointment with Wilson, 186, 192
Economic policies: Republican criticism of Wilson's, 168–69. *See also* Corporations; Domestic policy; Labor; Tax policy; Trade
Egerton, George, 151
Eight-hour day, 90–93, 130, 239, 261
Eisenhower, Dwight D., 261
Elections: Wilson's insistence on fair, 26, 39, 40–41, 73, 112
El Mercurio (Santiago), 42–43
Ely, Richard T., 6
Emancipation Proclamation, 130
Emergency Peace Federation, 118, 120
Enforcement. *See* League of Nations: enforcement of decisions of
English Constitution, The (Bagehot), 5

Entangling foreign alliances: Wilson's distrust of, 5; Lansing's concerns about, 205. *See also* Balance of power; Washington, George: his Farewell Address

Equality of states: relationships between different-size nations, 35–36, 71, 77, 112, 153, 202, 204, 206, 207, 214, 223–24; Reagan on, 274. *See also* League of Nations: administrative structure of

Espionage Act, 135; progressive internationalists charged under, 158–59, 186; calls to repeal, 237, 238

Ethnic equality. *See* Minorities

Executive Council (of the League of Nations), 217–20, 223–25, 232, 235, 247, 259. *See also* League of Nations: administrative structure of

Fall, Albert B., 185, 263, 266

Farewell Address. *See* Washington, George

Farm legislation, 24, 89, 94

Farm vote: in 1916 election, 101

Federal Council of Churches of Christ of America, 228

Federal Farm Loan Act, 89

Federal Reserve Act, 23, 41, 93

Federal Reserve Board, 23; and loans to Allies, 108

Federal Trade Commission Act, 24, 93

Fernald, Burt, 265

Ferrell, Robert H., 250, 269

Feudal thought: *vs.* liberal thought, 245, 289 n.19

Filene, Edward A., 126

First Amendment. *See* Civil liberties

"First Paris Draft" (of League of Nations Covenant): Wilson's, 202–5, 254

Flag Day address: Wilson's, 139–40

Fletcher, Henry P., 81, 83

Floto, Inga, 183

Foch, Marshal Ferdinand, 156, 181, 183, 184, 195

Force: relation of, to peace, 48, 66, 112. *See also* Armaments; League of Nations: enforcement of decisions of; Sanctions; Standing armies

Ford, Henry, 185

Foreign policy: Wilson's views of, 9–11, 32–33; in 1912 presidential campaign, 19–23; U.S.A.'s goal in, 43; "democratic control" of, 57; anti-Wilsonian cast of American, 273–76. *See also* Balance of power; Cold War; Domestic policy: and foreign policy; Imperialism; League of Nations; Militarism; Monroe Doctrine; Pan-American Pact; *specific foreign policy issues*

"Fountainbleau Memorandum" (Lloyd George), 333 n.8

"Four-Minute Men," 133

"Four Policemen," 273

Fourteen Points: as possible basis of peace negotiations, 166, 170–73, 175, 184, 189, 191, 209; Republican denunciation of, 176–77, 179, 180, 229; House's efforts to get Allied support for, 181–83; Italy's lack of enthusiasm for, 197; and colonialism, 203, 248, 249, 250; Covenant's violation of, 253–54; progressive internationalists' support for, 268. *See also* Fourteen Points address

Fourteen Points address, ix, 142–47, 153, 154, 165, 244, 245, 275. *See also* Fourteen Points

Fourth Liberty Loan, 169

Fourth Liberty Loan address: Wilson's, 162–66, 172, 181, 188, 244

France, 22, 23, 71; casualties of, in Great War, 31–32, 183–84; Germany declares war on, 32; blamed for Great War, 37; reluctance of, to participate in peace talks, 72, 74; reaction in, to Wilson's speeches, 79, 114–15, 145, 165; war aims of, 138, 155; Wilson's proposals for, 144; concerns of, over German peace overtures to Wilson, 173; suggestions of, for peace terms, 182; imperial interests of, 184, 211, 248–49; Wilson's popularity in, 194–95, 197–98, 226; and peace negotiations, 200; suggestions by, for League of Nations, 220–23, 246. *See also* Alsace-Lorraine; Clemenceau, Georges; French Socialist party; Rhineland; Saar valley

France, Joseph I., 257

Frankfurter, Felix, 161

Franz Ferdinand, Archduke, 32

"Freedom of the seas": American insistence on, 34, 51, 68, 75, 113, 115, 143, 182, 200; omission of, 214, 216

French Revolution, 8, 28
French Socialist party, 53, 115, 197

Gallinger, Jacob H., 109
Galt, Edith Bolling, 28, 61, 68. *See also* Wilson, Edith Bolling Galt
Gardiner, A. G., 71–72, 78, 105, 106, 204
Gardner, Augustus Peabody, 59
Gardner, Lloyd C., 144, 287 n.75
Gavit, John Palmer, 114, 161, 237, 256
George, Alexander and Juliette, 264–65
George V (King of Great Britain), 110
George Washington (ship), 194, 203, 227, 228, 248
German Social Democratic party, 53
German Southwest Africa, 211, 212
Germany, 22, 23, 71; casualties of, in Great War, 31–32; declares war on Russia, 32; blamed for Great War, 35, 37, 223, 250; its invasion of Belgium, 36; Wilson's concerns about imperialist motivations of, 38, 144; House meets with representatives from, 46; propaganda campaign against, 60; and possible peace talks, 72, 78, 107, 145; Wilson's negotiations with, 74, 106, 110, 141, 165–66, 171–75, 188–89; reaction to Wilson's speeches, 79, 114; role in Wilson's reelection, 106; accusations of Wilson's partiality toward, 109–10, 165, 248; U.S. severs diplomatic relations with, 116–20; U.S. declares war on, 121–22; its armistice with the Bolsheviks, 142; indemnities against, 182, 250; collapse of, 183, 251; colonies of, 203, 205, 208, 210–15; question of membership of, in League of Nations, 221, 235, 242, 247, 253. *See also* Anti-German sentiments; Central Powers; Indemnities; Peace note(s); Submarine warfare
Gettysburg Address, 77, 114
Gettysburg battle, 31
Gilderhus, Mark, 27
Gladstone, William Ewart, 13
Globalism: *vs.* internationalism, x, 273
Goldman, Emma, 135
Gompers, Samuel, 256
Gorbachev, Mikhail, 274–75

Grant, Ulysses S., 31, 171
Grayson, Dr. Cary T., 150, 195, 204, 218, 233, 250, 260, 263
Grayson family, 264
"Great Adventure": House's, 22–23
Great Britain: Wilson's relationship with radicals in, viii, 34, 36–38, 104, 139, 141, 143, 146; and the Mexican Revolution, 25, 26–27; casualties of, in Great War, 31–32, 183–84; declares war on Germany, 32; its blockade of American trade, 33–34, 41, 49, 59, 72, 75, 80; blamed for Great War, 37; war aims of, 38, 138, 142–43, 155; its lack of candor with Wilson, 44, 73; on territorial integrity and victory, 45–46; reaction to Wilson's speeches, 78, 79–81, 114, 115, 146, 165; on mediation, 107–8; concerns about German peace overtures to Wilson, 173; suggestions of, for peace terms, 182–83; Wilson's popularity in, 195–96, 199; and the League of Nations, 198, 199–200, 201, 207, 242. *See also* British Empire; Cecil, Robert; Dominions; Executive Council; Grey, Edward; Imperialism; Imperial War Cabinet; Labor Party; Lloyd George, David; Union of Democratic Control
Great Illusion, The (Angell), 36
Great War: possible averting of, 22; 234; casualties in, 31–32, 183–84; Wilson's attempts to mediate, 44–47, 57; Wilson's analysis of causes of, 112; progressives' hopes for, 129, 131; debate about causes of, 289 n.19. *See also* American intervention; Antiwar rallies; Great Britain: its blockade of American trade; Mediation; Neutrality; Peace conference; Peace movement; Progressive internationalism; Repression; Submarine warfare; Treaty of Versailles; Victory; Wilson, Woodrow: his desire for peace without victory
Gregory, Thomas Watt, 134; political repression by, 158–60, 186, 237, 238; counterfactual speculations about, 187–88
Grey, Sir Edward, 51, 68, 76, 108, 148, 164–65; House's negotiations with, 45–

47, 72, 74–75, 80–81, 98; and League of
  Nations Union, 199
Gronna, Asle J., 256–57

Hague Congress (International Congress of
  Women), 51
Hague Convention (1899), 11
Haiti, 84
Haldane, Lord Chancellor, 79
Hamilton, Alexander, 17
Hand, Learned, 161
Hankey, Maurice, 79
Hanna, Mark, 87
Hanson, Ole, 236
Hapgood, Norman, 160, 233, 256
Hapsburg Empire, 71, 201
Harding, Warren G., 256, 269, 271
Harper's Encyclopedia of the United States,
  14
Harvard University, 56
Hawaii, 10
Hay, John, 43
Hays, Will H., 168–69, 176, 177, 180, 188,
  258, 267
"He Kept Us Out of War," 106
Henderson, Arthur, 199
Henry V (King of England), 129
Henry Street Settlement (N.Y.C.), 50, 63,
  91
Hillquit, Morris, viii, 18, 53–55, 132
History: assessment of Wilson's
  contributions by, 271–76
History of the American People (Wilson), 9
Hitchcock, Gilbert M., 109, 170–71, 229,
  247, 263, 264, 267, 268
Hobson, J. A., 38, 203, 253
Holt, Hamilton, 56, 63, 76, 77, 78, 146,
  160, 234
Hooker, Richard, 190
Hoover, Ike, 263
Hopkins, J. A. H., 102
House, Colonel Edward Mandell, 32, 52,
  76, 78, 83, 98, 100, 120, 138, 139, 143,
  144, 149, 160, 164, 190, 196, 226, 233;
  power of, 20–21; and Allies, 22, 23, 32,
  72–74, 140–42, 155–56, 161–62, 175,
  181–84, 191, 205, 211, 216, 224, 246–48;
  and disarmament, 22–23; and Pan-
  American Pact, 39, 40; and U.S.

mediation of Great War, 44–47, 68–69,
  72–75, 80–81, 107–8, 111, 116; his lack
  of candor with Wilson, 45–47, 72, 246–
  47, 311 n.80; and the *New Republic,* 65,
  114, 119, 157; on Wilson's address to
  LEP, 77, 95; and Wilson's reelection
  campaign, 85–86; and LEP, 128, 150–
  51; on wartime censorship, 136; and
  Inter-Allied Conference, 140–42; and
  the Phillimore Report, 150–51; urges
  Wilson to draw up plans for League of
  Nations, 151–54; views on League of
  Nations membership, 152, 153; urges
  Wilson to join Allies in commitment to
  League of Nations, 161–62; meets with
  Allies in Paris, 175, 181–84; on Wilson's
  "Appeal for a Democratic Congress,"
  179; and peace negotiations, 189, 191,
  198, 200, 215; urges Wilson's European
  tour, 197; at League of Nations
  Commission, 217, 223; and break with
  Wilson, 246. *See also Philip Dru:
  Administrator;* Pre-Armistice Agreement
House-Grey Memorandum, 72–74, 80,
  107–8
Houston, David F., 174–75
Howe, Frederick C., 63, 130, 161
Huerta, General Victoriano, 25, 27, 29, 30
Hughes, Charles Evans, 92–95, 99–101,
  189
Hughes, William, 200, 208, 212–13, 215,
  224
Hull House, 50, 91
Hurst, C. J. B., 215–17
"Hurst-Miller Draft," 215–17, 218, 220,
  221, 224
Hymans, Paul, 217–18, 219

"I Didn't Raise My Boy to Be a Soldier,"
  63
Illinois (ship), 117
Imbrie, Andrew Clarke, 281 n.37
Immigration: and the League of Nations,
  240, 241, 242
Impeachment. *See* Poindexter, Miles
Imperialism: Wilson's beliefs about, ix, 9–
  11, 25–26, 35–36, 77, 115, 138, 145, 155,
  157, 180, 195, 206, 261–62, 266–68;
  advocates of, ix, 9; UDC's position on,

Imperialism (*continued*)
37; Latin American fears of U.S.'s
economic, 42–43; among conservative
internationalists, 55; Joffe's proposals on,
142; in the Senate, 234; Allies' ambitions
of, 248–50; in Covenant, 253, 268. *See
also* Colonialism; Latin America;
Mandate system; Monroe Doctrine
Imperialism (Hobson), 38
Imperial War Cabinet (Great Britain),
199–201, 202
Indemnities: Socialists' position on, 53, 54;
Joffe's proposals on, 142; Armistice
terms on, 189; Lloyd George's position
on, 199, 200; Wilson capitulates on, 250
Independent, 56, 76, 146, 160, 234
Independent Labour Party (Great Britain),
115
Indianapolis (Ind.): Wilson's campaign
speech at, 96
Indianapolis *Star,* 164
Inquiry, The (brain trust), 203, 213, 250;
founding of, 140; work of, 142, 145, 150,
152
Inter-Allied Conference (Paris), 140–41,
161
Inter-Allied Labour and Socialist
Conference, 203
International Association of Machinists, 95
International Congress of Women, 51
International Court: proposals concerning,
152, 153, 215, 220
Internationalism. *See* Conservative
internationalism; Progressive
internationalism; Wilson, Woodrow:
uniqueness of his internationalism
International Labor Organization, 259–61,
265–66
International Labour Conference, 260
International law: Wilson's belief in, 8–9,
13, 14
International Socialist Review, 95, 135
Irish Rebellion, 80
Irreconcilables, 185, 229, 231, 241, 242, 252,
256–57, 258, 263, 266. *See also*
Reservationist movement
Isolationism: American, 64, 78, 125, 229,
234
Italy, 71, 140; Wilson's proposals for, 144;
and the League of Nations, 197;

response of, to Wilson's Fourth Liberty
Loan address, 165; reaction of, to
German peace overtures to Wilson, 173;
suggestions of, for peace terms, 182;
Wilson's popularity in, 195, 196;
imperialist desires of, 197, 249; and
collective security idea, 220. *See also*
Orlando, Vittorio; Sonnino, Sidney
Izvestiya, 145

James, William, 147, 158
Japan: its imperialist interests, 155–57, 211,
212, 249–50; its suggestion for Covenant
of the League of Nations, 223–24
Jefferson, Thomas, 16, 17
Jesus Christ: Wilson compared to, 199, 213
Jewish Daily Forward, 136
"Jingo" (AUAM mascot), 63
Joffe, Adolf, 142
Johns Hopkins University, 5
Johnson, Hiram, 176, 257
Johnson, Tom, 87
Jones, Mary Harris ("Mother"), 93, 94,
146–47
Jordon, David Starr, 50, 67–68, 82
Journal des Débats (Paris), 165, 172
Jusserand, Jean Jules, 79, 127, 173, 203, 207
Justice Department, 186, 238; wartime
political repression by, 134. *See also*
Gregory, Thomas Watt

Kaiser. *See* Wilhelm II, Kaiser
Katz, Friedrich, 81
Keating-Owen child labor bill, 90
Keller, Helen, 63, 94
Kelley, Florence, 18, 63, 94, 254
Kellogg, Paul, 50–51, 63, 66, 94, 114, 117,
160–61, 192, 234, 235; withdraws from
AUAM's board, 131–32; and wartime
political repression, 134
Kennan, George F., 272–73, 274
Kent, William, 158
Kerensky, Alexander, 138, 140
Kern-McGillicuddy bill, 90
"Khaki Election" (Great Britain), 199
Kirkpatrick, Jeane, 274
Kissinger, Henry, 12, 272
Kitchin, Claude, 63
Kjaochaw. *See* Shantung
Knickerbocker Press (Albany, N.Y.), 164

Knox, Philander C., 180, 191, 192, 230, 231, 241
Kopelin, Louis, 141–42

Labor: Wilson's attitudes concerning, 7, 24, 90–93, 97–98, 169, 260–61, 275; Roosevelt's proposals for legislation regarding, 16; progressive internationalists' agenda for, 50, 54; support of, for Wilson's reelection, 94–95, 101; during the Great War, 130; in League of Nations drafts, 205, 207, 221, 225, 242; and the "Red Scare," 237; 1920 unrest among, 269. *See also* International Labor Organization; *specific issues relating to*
Labor Forum of New York, 63
Labor Movement in America, The (Ely), 6
Labour party (Great Britain), 157, 161, 199, 202; and League of Nations idea, 115, 142, 148; and war aims, 142–43
Laconia (passenger liner), 116
Ladies' Garment-Cutters' Union (Boston), 95
La Follette, Robert M., 24, 88, 113, 131, 257
Lamont, Thomas W., 161, 179, 260
Lane, Franklin K., 86, 117, 174, 178
Lansing, Robert, 52, 73, 80, 116, 190; and Pan-American Pact, 68, 70, 81, 83; and peace notes, 107–8, 110–11; treachery of, 110–11, 313 n.106; anti-Bolshevism of, 155; and peace negotiations, 189, 214, 219; Wilson's treatment of, 205–6, 313 n.106; and Senate Foreign Relations Committee, 206, 258; Wilson's firing of, 258, 335 n.63. *See also* "Negative covenant"
La Prensa (Buenos Aires), 42, 83
Larnaude, Fernand, 220, 221, 222, 223
Lasch, Christopher, 65, 129
Latin America: Wilson's views on imperialism in, 25–26; Wilson's intervention in, 84. *See also* Mexican Revolution; Monroe Doctrine; Pan-American Pact; *names of Latin American countries*
Lawrence, David, 164, 178
Lawrence, T. E., 213
Leadership: Wilson's desire for, 13

League of Free Nations Association (LFNA), 161, 192, 235, 242, 252
League of Nations: American origins of idea of, vi, 45, 47, 49–69; Wilson's conception of, ix, 44, 126–27, 149, 152–53, 207; influence of progressive internationalists on, ix, 204–7, 217, 219; as a partisan issue, ix, 86, 95–101, 103, 123–31, 187, 192–93, 227–31, 239–45, 250, 256–60, 263–67; origins of Wilson's interest in, 3–14, 34–36; coining of the term, 33, 37; Roosevelt's initial support for, 48–49; British interest in, 68–69, 75, 76; as one of Wilson's reelection campaign themes, 85–86, 95–103; connection to negotiated peace, 106–17, 190, 195, 199–200, 204, 209; Lloyd George's references to, 143; Wilson calls for, in Fourteen Points, 144, 145; wartime proposals concerning, 148–54, 160–65, 182, 184; enforcement of decisions of, 151–53, 201, 220–21, 225; membership of, 152, 153, 201, 202, 232; in congressional campaign of 1918, pp. 180, 186, 187; administrative structure of, 204, 207, 208, 214–19, 222–24, 226, 232, 235, 247; accused of Bolshevism, 236; support for, 239, 252; death of, 269; and possible averting of World War II, 272. *See also* American Union Against Militarism; Community (of nations); Covenant of the League of Nations; Equality: between different-size nations; Force; Germany; Irreconcilables; League to Enforce Peace; Minorities; Monroe Doctrine; Russia; Sanctions; Union of Democratic Control; Wilson, Woodrow; World federation; Woman's Peace party
League of Nations, The: A Practical Suggestion (Smuts), 201–4, 219
League of Nations Commission, 215–26, 247–48
League of Nations Society (Great Britain), 56, 148
League of Nations Union (Great Britain), 199, 215
League to Enforce Peace (LEP), 113: and conservative internationalism, viii, 62, 128; and the British government, ix–x; founding of, 56–57; and military

League to Enforce Peace (*cont.*)
preparedness, 61; connections to
Republican party, 62; Wilson's
knowledge of, 65; Wilson's address to,
75–78, 84, 95, 110, 113, 268, and his
reelection campaign, 79, 85–87, 99–101;
differences between its program and
Wilson's, 114, 125, 151, 153, 235;
Lodge's resignation from, 124–25;
recommends establishment of League of
Nations commission, 128; wartime
student debate on, cancelled, 134;
Wilson's relations with, 148–50, 160,
161, 176–77, 188; its draft constitutions
for a League of Nations, 149–51;
endorses League of Nations, 192, 228,
241, 258, 264; recommends changes in
League of Nations Covenant, 247. *See
also* House, Colonel Edward Mandell:
and LEP; Taft, William Howard
Lee, Robert E., 3, 31
Legalists, 55–56
Lenin, V. I., 140, 145
LEP. *See* League to Enforce Peace
Levin, N. Gordon, 144
LFNA. *See* League of Free Nations
Association
Liberal Debating Club (Princeton), 5
Liberals: Wilson's relationship with, viii-x,
18–19, 146–47; pro-war, 139; and
wartime political repression, 158–60,
186, 187, 256; 20th-century Republican
attacks on, 187–88; European, 195; and
the League of Nations, 233, 238; and
amnesty, 236. *See also* Coalition of 1916;
Feudal thought: *vs.* liberal thought;
Progressive internationalism; Repression
Liberator (formerly *The Masses*), 147, 158,
236
Liberty Loans, 130, 133, 147
Lincoln, Abraham, 3, 12, 13, 98, 141, 146,
276. *See also* Gettysburg Address
Link, Arthur S., 20, 86, 111, 118, 179,
250–51
Lippmann, Walter, 77, 94, 127, 259; and
military preparedness, 64, 65; and U.S.'s
entry into Great War, 119–20, 129; on
wartime repression, 136; and The
Inquiry, 145, 182; criticism of League of
Nations Covenant by, 243, 257, 269

Literary Digest, 94, 95, 228, 252
Little, Frank, 134
Livermore, Seward, 185
Lloyd George, David, 146, 170, 172, 175,
178, 184, 195, 205, 213, 219; on
mediation, 107, 110, 118–19; on League
of Nations, 108, 151; and Inter-Allied
Conference, 140; and British war aims,
142–43, 154; on American intervention
in Russia, 156–57; on League of
Nations, 161, 162, 192, 199–203, 209,
210, 212, 216, 223, 229, 248, 250; on the
Fourteen Points, 182, 183; on Wilson's
presence at peace negotiations, 191, 199;
on postwar disposition of colonies, 211;
efforts to sidetrack League of Nations,
214–15, 246; on Wilson's downfall, 265
LNU. *See* League of Nations Union
Lobbyists: Wilson's attack on, 23
Lochner, Louis Paul, 50, 63, 67–68, 118,
126
Lodge, Henry Cabot, 76, 113, 122, 127,
130, 184, 234, 237, 262, 271, 276;
opposition to League of Nations, ix, 99–
100, 109, 124–25, 152, 153, 228, 230, 231,
239–43, 245, 247, 257–59, 269, 271, 274,
276; political strategy in League fight,
239–42, 257–58; on military intervention
in Mexican Revolution, 28; on military
preparedness, 59, 62; and Wilson's
reelection, 106; and congressional
elections of 1918, pp. 167–69, 173, 176,
178, 180; role in establishing enduring
Republican campaign strategy, 188; as
chairman of Senate Foreign Relations
Committee, 192, 251; contempt of, for
Wilson, 265–67; declares League a dead
issue, 269; sees Wilson on last day in
office, 271. *See also* Republican Party;
"Reservationist movement"; "Round
Robin resolution"; Senate Foreign
Relations Committee
London, Jack, 94
London, Meyer, 54–55, 147
London *Daily News,* 71, 78, 164
London *Nation,* 164
London *Outlook,* 165
London *Star,* 146
London *Times,* 21–22, 79, 146, 165
Long, Breckinridge, 243

Long Branch (N.J.): Wilson's speech at, 95–96

Loreburn, Lord, 86

Los Angeles Board of Education, 134

Los Angeles Times, 228

Lovett, Robert Morss, 242, 243

Lowell, Abbot Lawrence, 56, 58, 62, 76, 87, 125, 128, 149, 150, 177, 228

Lowes Dickinson, Goldsworthy, 37–38

Ludlow County, 88

Lusitania (ship), 45; sinking of, 47, 60, 61, 65, 117

McAdoo, William Gibbs, 41–42, 174

McCormick, Vance, 178, 179

McCumber, Porter J., 124, 247

MacDonald, J. Ramsay, 37

Mcfarland, Grenville, 141

McKinley, William, 9, 13, 55, 178, 180

Madero, Francisco I., 25

Madison Square Garden (N.Y.C.): Wilson's campaign speech at, 97–98

"Madness at Versailles, The" (Villard), 253

Magnolia (Mass.): Wilson's covenant draft at, 153–54, 162, 202, 204, 205, 208, 218, 224–25, 254

Mahan, Alfred Thayer, 10

Makino, Nobuaki (Baron): at League of Nations Commission, 217, 223–24, 249

Malone, Dudley Field, 237

Mandate system, 201–3, 205–8, 210–16, 221, 225, 242, 253

Manila Bay (Philippines), 9

Marburg, Theodore, 56, 128, 149

Marshall, Thomas Riley, 111

Masaryk, Thomas, 157

Massachusetts, 239. *See also* Boston; Magnolia

Masses, The, 29, 30, 50, 93, 114; on Wilson in 1912, p. 18; readership of, 67; censorship of, 135–37; cessation of, 158. *See also Liberator*

Massey, William, 211, 212

Maurer, James H., viii, 54–55, 63, 90, 118

Mayer, Arno J., 144, 289n.19

Mayo, Henry T., 27

Mediation: U.S. attempts at, in Great War, 44–47, 57, 65, 68–69, 72–76, 85, 116; Addams' support for continuous, 51–52, 67–68; Socialists' support for continuous,

54, 55; German interest in, 106–7, 111, 116

"Memorandum on War Aims" (British Labour Party), 142–43

Metropolitan Opera House (N.Y.C.): Wilson's mid–peace conference address at, 241–44, 252. *See also* Fourth Liberty Loan address

Mexican Revolution, 43, 44, 91, 155, 157; Wilson's intervention in, viii, 24–30, 49, 81–84; influence on Wilson, 7, 38, 39, 145, 289 n.19

Mexican War: Wilson's opposition to U.S. imperialism in, 9

Mexico, 232, 266; and Germany in Great War, 81, 116–17. *See also* Mexican Revolution; Mexican War; Zimmermann Note

Militarism: advocates of, ix, 229, 234; Wilson's criticism of, ix, 115, 121, 180, 195, 221–22. *See also* Roosevelt, Theodore

Military-industrial complex, 261, 272, 273. *See also* Armaments; Arms race

Military intervention. *See* American intervention

Military preparedness, 187, 229; and Wilson, ix, 58–67, 78, 86, 89–90, 93, 95; Lodge's views on, 99

Miller, David Hunter, 152, 205, 209, 214–17, 220, 223. *See also* "Cecil-Miller Draft"

Mild reservationists. *See* Reservationist movement

Milwaukee Leader, 136, 236

Miners' strike: at Bisbee (Ariz.), 133–34

Minimum wage, 16, 130. *See also* Labor: Wilson's attitudes concerning

Minnesota: 1916 election in, 102

Minorities: racial and ethnic, in League of Nations drafts, 205, 214, 215, 223–24, 243, 249

Missionaries: and imperialism, 9–10

Missouri: 1916 election in, 102

"Mr. Wilson's Great Utterance," 77

Mobile (Ala.): Wilson's address in, 25–26, 36, 40

"Modern Democratic State, The" (Wilson), 5–6

Monopolies, 16–17, 24. *See also* Antitrust legislation; Corporations

Monroe Doctrine, 77, 111; extension of, in Pan-American Pact, 39, 40; Wilson's criticism of, 71, 84; extension of, in League of Nations, 113, 232; Lansing's views of, 205; Republican fear of effects of League of Nations on, 109, 124, 230, 232, 240–42, 247–48, 258, 266–67; Republican and British pressures on, 247–48

Morel, E. D., 37

Morgan, J. P., 135

Moses, George H., 185

Moynihan, Daniel Patrick, 275

Mulder, John M., 4

Munitions. *See* Armaments

Murmansk, 155–56

"Mutual good faith": Wilson's belief in, 222–23

Myers, Gus, 94, 132

Myers, Henry L., 265

Naón, Rómulo Sebastian, 40, 68, 70, 81, 83

Napoleon Bonaparte, 199

Nation, 50, 157, 159, 160, 181, 186, 253, 255, 266

National Cathedral (Washington, D.C.), 274

National Civil Liberties Union, 236

National Committee on the Moral Aims of the War, 149

National Executive Committee (SPA), 54

National Guard, 59

Nationalism: of European Socialist parties, 52–53; of conservative internationalists, 58, 169, 177, 229; Clemenceau's, 198

Nationalization: of industry, 129–30; Republican fears of, 169, 180, 240

National Rip-Saw, 135

National Security League, 61, 64, 133

National sovereignty, 226, 259; Republican concerns about, 230, 232–33, 240–41, 266

National War Labor Board, 130

NATO. *See* North Atlantic Treaty Organization

Navy: expansion of American, 89–90, 248

Nearing, Scott, 236

"Negative covenant": Lansing's ideas about, 205, 219; and Cecil, 219–20

Neutrality: American, in Great War, viii, 32–34, 47, 49, 86, 93, 95–97, 100, 105–6, 187, 271–72; Roosevelt's criticism of, 49; WPP's position on, 51; propaganda campaign opposing, 60; strains on, 64–65. *See also* Armed neutrality; Military preparedness

"New American Doctrine": Knox's, 230

New Diplomacy, 129, 143, 227, 235; progressive internationalists as advance guard of, viii, ix, 104; Wilsonian origins of, 3–9, 103–4; British contributions to, 37; Addams' contribution to, 51, 52; description of, 112–13; embodied in the Brest-Litovsk armistice, 142; and Allies, 154. *See also* "Peace Without Victory"; Fourteen Points address

New Freedom: Wilson's proposals for, 17, 21–24, 30, 43, 86; and international trade, 41–42; accomplishment of, 64; Brandeis' role in, 80, 88

New Guinea, 211, 212

New Hampshire: 1916 election in, 101, 102

New Jersey: 1916 election in, 102

New Left: interpretations of history by, viii, 43; on Wilson, 144, 272

New Mexico: Mexican designs on, 117

New Nationalism, 86; Roosevelt's, 16; and Wilson, 16–17; Wilson's movement toward, 24, 86–88. *See also* "Progressive Democracy"

New Republic, 29, 106, 114, 117, 126, 160; and Wilson, viii, 67, 76–78, 92–94, 99, 122; on military preparedness, 64–65; on Pan-American Pact, 71; its wartime views, 129, 139, 157, 164, 178, 181, 185; and the League of Nations, 234, 237, 242–43, 252, 254, 262, 269; on Wilson, 268; readership of, 297 n.70

New Review, 53

New Statesman, 29

New Willard Hotel (Washington, D.C.). *See* League to Enforce Peace (LEP): Wilson's address to

"New World Order," x, 275

New York *American,* 141

New York *Call. See Call, The*

New York City, 97–98; 1916 election in, 102

New York Evening Post, 50, 61, 164, 184, 237
New York *Evening Sun,* 102
New York *Globe,* 185, 190
New York *Herald,* 144
New York Peace Society, 56, 228
New York Press Club, 18, 83
New York State: preparedness bills passed in, 61
New York *Sun,* 21, 228
New York Times, 21, 34, 67, 87, 92, 132, 164, 172, 181, 184, 228, 233, 275; Roosevelt in, 28–29, 49; on Pan-American Pact, 42, 71; concedes 1916 election to Hughes, 101; on Wilson's "Peace Without Victory" speech, 111, 113–14; on Fourteen Points address, 146
New York *Tribune,* 78, 185
New York *World,* 87–88, 132, 159–60, 172, 179, 184
Nicaragua, 84
Nicholas II (Tsar of all Russias), 138
Nobel Peace Prize: recipients of, 48, 50; Wilson awarded, 269
"No Divided Government" (Pulitzer), 178
Norris, George, 131, 257
North Atlantic Treaty Organization, 273
North Dakota, 102
Nuclear war, 274

Ohio: 1916 election in, 101, 102
Omaha (Nebr.): Wilson's campaign speech at, 96; on League, 261
"One Hundred Percent Americanism," 132, 139, 147, 235–36. *See also* Anti-Bolshevik sentiments; Anti-German sentiments; Un-Americanism
One World (Willkie), 272
On the Law of Nations (Moynihan), 275
Open diplomacy. *See* Secret diplomacy
"Open Door" policy, 43
"Open Letter to Americans, An" (Trevelyan), 108, 119
Oregon: in 1916 election, 101
Orlando, Vittorio, 154, 175, 192, 197, 210; at League of Nations Commission, 217–18, 249
Ottoman Empire: Wilson's proposals for, 144; Italy's designs on, 197; postwar

breakup of, 201. *See also* Mandate system
"Outline of Peace Terms" (Lloyd George), 248
Outlook, 48, 78, 117
"Out of His Own Mouth" (Villard), 253

Page, Thomas Nelson, 191
Page, Walter Hines, 29, 47, 110, 119
Painters Union (Tenn.), 95
Palmer, A. Mitchell, 256, 269
Panama Canal, 19, 28, 41
Pan-American Financial Conference, 42–43
Pan-American Pact, 112, 153, 205, 232, 266; efforts to achieve, 39–45, 65, 68, 70, 81–84, 105; and Great Britain, 72, 73–74, 81
Pan-American Scientific Congress (1916): Wilson at, 70–71
Papers of Woodrow Wilson, The, 264, 279
Paris Peace Conference, vii, 153, 154. *See also* Peace conference
Park, Dr. Bert E., 264, 265
Patriotism. *See* "One Hundred Percent Americanism"
Peabody, George Foster, 141
Peace: debate over kind of, 169–84; Kennan's views on, 273. *See also* Force; League of Nations; Mediation; Peace conference; Peace movement; Peace note(s); Treaty of Versailles; Victory; War; War aims
Peace conference: British enthusiasm for, 80; Wilson's determination to participate in, 118–20; Wilson's terms for, 139–41; Wilson's proposals for, 162–63, 165; workings of first half, 209–26, second half, 227, 246–51, 254, 267. *See also* Armistice; League of Nations; Paris Peace Conference; Pre-Armistice Agreement; Treaty of Versailles
Peace movement: and Wilson, 11–12, 21, 22, 50; and Pan-American Pact, 39; Roosevelt on, 184. *See also* Great Britain: Wilson's relations with radicals in
Peace note(s), ix; Wilson's first, 107–10, 113, 115, 125, 137, 171–72; second, 173, 174; third, 175, 184

Peace treaty: partisan approach to, 189–91
"Peace Without Victory" address, ix, 111–15, 129, 137, 138, 139, 141, 153, 268; Republican responses to, 124–26, 230; embodied in Brest-Litovsk armistice, 142. *See also* Wilson, Woodrow: his desire for peace without victory

Pennsylvania State Federation of Labor, 54

Permanent Court of International Arbitration, 11

Pershing, General John J., 82, 83, 162, 183

Persistence of the Old Regime, The (Mayer), 289 n.19

Peru: its boundary dispute with Chile, 40–41

Pessoa, Epitacio, 217, 219

Petrograd formula (of war aims), 138–39

Phelps-Dodge Corporation, 133–34

Philadelphia *Public Ledger,* 141, 176, 184, 226

Philip Dru: Administrator (House), 20, 22, 23

Philippines: Wilson's views of American annexation of, 9–11; 1912 Democratic party position on, 19

Phillimore, Sir Walter G. F., 149, 150

Phillimore Report, 150–54, 201, 202

Pinchot, Amos, 63; and Wilson, viii, 66, 67, 87, 94, 104, 114, 118, 158, 160; and wartime political repression, 134, 135, 158, 160

Pittman, Key, 171, 179

Pittsburgh *Dispatch,* 164

Plunkett, Sir Horace, 78, 85

Poincaré, Raymond, 195

Poindexter, Miles, 170, 171, 176, 179, 231, 236, 237

Poland: Wilson's proposals for, 144

Political campaigns: 1912 presidential, 15–18. *See also* Coalition of 1916; Congressional campaign of 1918

Political independence: for countries. *See* Territorial integrity

Political prisoners. *See* Repression

Polk, Frank L., 83–84

Ponsonby, Arthur, 199

Portugal, 217

Postmaster General. *See* Burleson, Albert Sidney

Post Office Department, 24, 159, 160, 186, 236. *See also* Burleson, Albert Sidney

Practical Suggestions. See League of Nations, The: A Practical Suggestion

Pre-Armistice Agreement (Paris), 175, 181–84, 250

Preparedness. *See* Military preparedness

Presbyterianism: and Wilson, 3–4. *See also* Covenantal tradition

Presidential campaigns. *See* Political campaigns

Princeton University: Wilson at, 5, 7–9, 16; battle over Graduate College at, 264, 265

"Progressive Democracy," 92, 103, 168, 185, 187, 255, 268. *See also* Coalition of 1916

Progressive Era: socialism in, viii. *See also* Progressive internationalists; Progressive party

Progressive internationalism: and the League of Nations, vii–ix, 68, 69, 78; dissolution of, and 20th-century foreign policy, x; and Wilson, 50–55, 57, 61, 66–68, 75–76, 82–83, 95, 104, 106, 114, 115, 228, 260–61; and military preparedness issue, 62–67; in 1916 coalition, 86–98; opposition to American participation in Great War, 117, 118; wartime dissolution of, 128–41, 157–60, 165, 235–39, 245, 255–56; and the Fourteen Points, 145–48; and Wilson's Covenant, 153–54; goals of, 275–76. *See also* Domestic policy; Liberals; New Diplomacy; Progressive internationalists; Socialists

Progressive internationalists: Wilson appeals to, for support, 180–81; failure to support Wilson in 1918 congressional campaign, 185–87; on Wilson's peace negotiations, 192; influence on League of Nations, 204–7, 217, 219; criticism of League of Nations and peace treaty by, 213, 233–35, 242–43, 252–56; cooperation with anti-League Republicans, 256–59, 269; gulf between conservative internationalists and, 265–67; Wilson's leadership of, 267–68; on Wilson's achievements, 269–70. *See also*

Coalition of 1916; Liberals; Progressive internationalism; Repression; Socialists; *names of particular progressive internationalists*

Progressive party, 15–17, 19, 88–89, 93–94, 103; support for Wilson among former members of, 101

Progressivism. *See* Domestic policy

Propaganda campaigns: American, 60, 133, results of, 170

"Proposed Manifesto and Program of the Socialist Party of America on Disarmament and World Peace," 53–54

Public, 160

Pueblo (Colo.): Wilson's address in, 263, 275–76

Pulitzer, Joseph, 178

Pullman strike (1894), 7

"Punitive Expedition," 81–84

Racial equality. *See* Minorities

Racial segregation: and Wilson, 24

Railroad workers' strike, 91–92, 94

Rand School of Social Science, 236

Rappard, William E., 127

Reading, Lord, 154, 156, 157, 172, 200

Reagan, Ronald, 87, 274

Realists (post–World War II): views of, 272–73

Reconstruction commission, 240, 255, 257

Record, George L., 255

"Red scare," 235–37, 269

Reed, James A., 231, 236, 237, 265

Reed, John: and Wilson, viii, 29–30, 94; and military preparedness campaign, 64; opposes American intervention in Great War, 132; and wartime political repression, 135; wartime political repression of, 158

Reis, Jayne Batalha, 217

Religious freedom: and the League of Nations, 206, 224

Reparations. *See* Indemnities

Repression: of progressive internationalists under Wilson, x, 132–34, 158–60, 165, 168, 181, 186–88, 235–39, 255–57, 268, 269. *See also* Amnesty; Civil liberties; Coalition of 1916; Domestic policy: and foreign policy; Espionage Act

Republican party: and imperialism, 9–11; disruption in, in 1912, pp. 15–17; and Wilson, 29; and conservative internationalists, 57; and military preparedness, 59, 62; pulls itself together in 1916, pp. 88–89; and 1916 presidential campaign, 99–101; and League of Nations, 109, 124–26; and the Fourteen Points address, 146; and the congressional elections of 1918, pp. 167–68, 177–79, 184–86; enduring campaign strategies of, 187–88; absence of representatives from, in peace negotiations, 189–91; on Wilson's presence at peace negotiations, 191; progressive internationalists' aid to, 256–59. *See also* League of Nations: as a partisan issue; Lodge, Henry Cabot; Monroe Doctrine; Nationalization; "Reservationist movement"

"Reservationist movement," 258–59, 262, 264, 265–67, 268, 269; mild reservationists, role of in, 241, 259; strong reservationists, role of in, 258, 259. *See also* Irreconcilables; Lodge, H.C.

Revenue Act of 1916, pp. 90, 93, 130

Revenue Act of 1917, p. 130

Revenue Act of 1918, p. 130

Revolution: Wilson's attitudes concerning, 7–8, 44, 145; and League of Nations, 206–7, 254. *See also* Mexican Revolution; Russian Revolution

Rhineland: occupation of, by Allies, 182, 183, 184, 189, 246, 248–49

Richmond *Times-Dispatch,* 164

Rockefeller, John D., 88

Rocky Mountain News, 176, 184

Rolland, Romain, 191

Roman law, 8

Roosevelt, Franklin D., 20, 190, 272, 273

Roosevelt, Kermit, 180

Roosevelt, Theodore, 13, 55, 67, 78, 80, 101, 117, 164, 171, 178, 190; opposition to League of Nations, ix, 99–100, 169, 192; militarism of, 10, 28–30, 49, 177, 183, 229; as 1912 presidential candidate, 15–18; his initial support for League of Nations, 48–49; on Wilson, 49, 61, 113,

Roosevelt, Theodore (*continued*)
122; on Addams, 51; and militry
preparedness crusade, 61–62, 64;
abandons Progressive party, 88–90, 93;
and Wilson's reelection, 106; "100
percent Americanism" of, 133; and
congressional elections of 1918, 167–68,
177, 180, 184, 187–88; on Fourteen
Points, 176–77, 179, 180; death of, 229–
30. *See also Outlook*
Root, Elihu, 55–56, 58, 87, 149, 150; and
military preparedness, 62; and
congressional elections of 1918, pp. 167–
68; Wilson's exclusion of, from peace
negotiations, 189–90; opposition of, to
Wilsonian League of Nations, 258
"Round Robin resolution": Lodge's, 241–
44, 246, 247, 251
"Royal United Kingdom Yacht Club," 4–5
Russell, Bertrand, 37
Russell, Charles Edward, 94, 118, 132, 256
Russia, 71, 115; casualties in Great War,
32; Germany declares war on, 32;
blamed for Great War, 37; changes in
war aims of, 138–41; Wilson calls for
German withdrawal from, 144;
imperialist designs on, 154–58; postwar
breakup of, 201; question of
membership of, in League of Nations,
235, 242, 247, 253. *See also* Bolsheviks;
Russian Revolution
Russian Council of Workers and Soldiers,
54
Russian Revolution, ix, x, 7, 138, 139, 140,
145, 154–59, 170; and Wilson's Fourteen
Points, 144–45, 241; Wilson's attitude
toward, 155–57. *See also* Bolsheviks
Russo-Japanese War, 48

Saar valley: French desire to annex, 248–
49
Sacramento Bee, 190
St. Louis (Mo.): Wilson's address in, 261,
262
St. Louis Proclamation (of the Socialist
party), 131–32, 146
St. Louis Republic, 164
St. Mihiel, 162
Salt Lake City (Utah): Wilson's address in,
261

Samoa, 211
Sanctions: LEP's position on, 57; Wilson's
position on, 152–53, 163, 222; Cecil's
suggestions for, 201, 220; Belgians'
suggestions for, 221; in League of
Nations Covenant, 226, 261; reservations
on, 266
Saulsbury, Willard, 185
Sayre, Francis B., 159
Sayre, John Nevin, 159, 237, 238, 256
Schenck v. *the United States,* 236
Schwabe, Klaus, 183
Seaman's Act, 24, 88
"Second Paris Draft": Wilson's, 206–7,
214, 216, 254
Secretary of Labor. *See* Wilson, William B.
Secretary of State. *See* Bryan, William
Jennings; Lansing, Robert
Secretary of the Interior. *See* Lane,
Franklin K.
Secretary of War. *See* Baker, Newton D.
Secret diplomacy: SPA's opposition to,
53; Wilson's stand against, 157, 163,
206; in League of Nations Covenant,
225
Self-determination: Wilson's beliefs about,
35, 43–44, 57, 77, 86, 103, 113, 115, 138,
144, 152, 153, 155, 156, 205, 207, 213;
UDC's position on, 37; WPP's position
on, 51; Socialist Party of America's
position on, 53; LEP's positions on, 57;
opposition to, 78; Lodge's questions
about, 124; Joffe's proposals on, 142;
Lloyd George's proposals on, 143; Smuts'
views of, 201–2; Wilson's inconsistent
standards on, 249–50; progressive
internationalists' criticism of Covenant's
stand on, 253
Senate, 229, 233, 245; Wilson's "Peace
Without Victory" address to, ix, 111–13,
121; League of Nations debates in, 109;
Wilson's views of its role in League of
Nations, 149; its rejection of the Treaty
of Versailles, 227, 251–52, 263–64;
denunciations of the League and of
Wilson by, 231; its reluctance to sign
peace treaty that included League of
Nations, 242. *See also* Congress; Senate
Foreign Relations Committee; White
House dinner

Senate Foreign Relations Committee, 206, 258–59, 264. *See also* Lodge, Henry Cabot

Serbia, 32, 217

Seven Arts, The, 147

Seymour, Charles, 210

Shadow Lawn (N.J.): Wilson's speech at, 96, 98

Shafroth, John F., 113, 185

Shakespeare, William, 121

Shantung: Japanese interest in, 211, 223, 249–50, 257

Shaw, George Bernard, 29, 193

Sherman, Lawrence Y., 124, 191

Sherman, William Tecumseh, 3

Siberia: imperialist designs on, 155–56, 223

Simons, Algie M., 94, 132

Sinclair, Upton, viii, 94, 118, 132, 135–37, 147; and wartime political repression, 158, 256

Slayden, James, 39

Smuts, Jan Christiaan: and League of Nations, 201–4, 206, 208, 212–15; imperialist aims of, 211; at League of Nations Commission, 217–19, 221, 250; on Wilson, 276

Snowden, Philip, 78

Social Darwinism: and conservative internationalists, 58

Social democracy: proponents of, in America, viii–ix, 104, 267. *See also* Domestic policy: and foreign policy; "Progressive Democracy"; Progressive internationalism; Progressive internationalists

Socialism: Wilson's view of, 6–7, 9. *See also* Socialist Party of America; Socialists; "War socialism"

"Socialism and Democracy" (Wilson), 6–7, 9

Socialist Party of America (SPA), viii, 147, 187, 252; significance of, 17–19; and progressive internationalism, 52–55, 57, 65; dilemma about American participation in Great War by, 117–18, 131–32, 146. *See also* St. Louis Proclamation; Socialism; Socialists

Socialists: in the Progressive Era, viii, ix; on intervention in Mexican Revolution, 29–30; their 1916 support for Wilson's

reelection, 93–96, 101–3; attacks on, 133; pro-war, 139; and Wilson, 146–47; and wartime political repression, 158–60, 186–87; Republican slurs about, 168–69; European, 195–98. *See also* Coalition of 1916; Nationalization; Progressive internationalism; Repression; Socialist Party of America; Socialism

Social reform. *See* Domestic policy

Social Revolution, 135

Social Workers for Wilson, 94

Somme battle, 32, 80

Sonnino, Baron Sidney, 140–41, 197, 249

Sophie, Archduchess, 32

South Dakota: in 1916 election, 101

Southern Commercial Congress (Mobile, Ala.): Wilson's address to, 25–26, 36, 40

Sovereignty. *See* National sovereignty; Territorial integrity

SPA. *See* Socialist Party of America

Spanish-American War, 178; Wilson's views of, 9, 13. *See also* "Open Door" policy

Spargo, John, 131, 132; and Wilson, viii, 18, 94, 137, 146, 256

"Spheres of influence." *See* Balance of power

Spirit of Man, The (Bridges), 120

Spirit of '76, The (film), 134

Springfield Republican, 172

Spring Rice, Sir Cecil Arthur, 22, 26–27, 44

Stalemate (in the Great War): and League of Nations, 80. *See also* "Peace Without Victory" address; Victory

Standing armies: Wilson's beliefs about, 5–6, 275; U.S. debate over, 59, 61

Stanford University, 50

State, The (Wilson), 7

State Department's policy planning staff, 273

"Statement of Principles" (LFNA), 161, 192

State of the Union address (1917): Wilson's, 141

Staunton (Va.), 3

Stokes, Rose Pastor, 159, 236, 237

Strong reservationists. *See* Reservationist movement

Stone, William J., 63

"Study of Administration, The" (Wilson), 12

Suárez-Mujica, Eduardo, 40–41

Submarine warfare (German), 34, 41, 49, 51, 59–61, 70; abatement of, 58, 73–74; and possible American intervention, 73, 107, 111; preparations for, 108; resumption of, 115–18, 125

Sullivan, Mark, 60

Supreme Court: Wilson's nominations to, 87–88, 93

Survey, 50, 117, 160, 234

Sussex (steamer), 73–74, 75

Tacna (Chile), 40–41, 74

Taft, Charles T., 102

Taft, William Howard, 18, 49, 97, 128, 134, 171, 252, 267; as conservative internationalist, viii, 56, 58; and the League of Nations, x, 164, 228, 239, 248, 258; his arbitration treaties with England and France, 12; as President, 15, 16, 19; and military preparedness, 62; invites Wilson to address LEP, 75–78, 85; as president of LEP, 75–78, 85, 113, 149–50, 176–77, 188, 228, 241–42, 244, 247, 258; opposition to Wilson's Supreme Court nominees, 87, 88; on the Adamson Act, 92; and 1916 presidential campaign issues, 99–101; and congressional elections of 1918, pp. 167–68, 176–77, 179, 180, 184; and Roosevelt, 15, 49, 99, 178, 180, 188; Wilson's exclusion of, from peace negotiations, 189–90; on Wilson's presence at peace negotiations, 191, 192; on Wilson's critics, 231; and cooperation with Wilson in revising Covenant, 241, 242, 244, 247, 248, 267. *See also* "Dollar Diplomacy"; League to Enforce Peace

Talcott, Charles A., 4

Tampico (Mexico), 27, 29

Tariffs, 23, 41, 143, 169. *See also* Trade

Tax policy: Wilson's, 90, 93, 130, 240; Lodge's views of, 239

Ten Days That Shook the World (Reed), 29

"Tentative Draft" (LEP), 149, 150, 151, 153

Territorial integrity: Wilson's views about, 39–41, 57, 71, 75, 77, 126, 127, 150, 152, 153, 211; and the British, 45; Lansing's

views of, 205; in First Paris Draft, 205; in Second Paris Draft, 206; Cecil's position on, 208; in Cecil-Miller Draft, 214; Lodge's concerns about, 240; progressive internationalists' criticism of Covenant's stand on, 252. *See also* "Negative covenant"

Texas: Mexican designs on, 117

"Theology of politics," 4

"Third Paris Draft": Wilson's, 216, 217–18

Thomas, Norman, 131–32, 134, 157, 159, 237

Togoland, 211

Towards International Government (Hobson), 203

Trade: House's views on, 23; UDC's position on, 37; Wilson's policies on, 41–42, 57, 88; Wilson's goals for, in League of Nations, 126, 143; Joffe's proposals on, 142; Republican fears of free trade, 169. *See also* Great Britain: its blockade of American trade

Treasury Department, 24. *See also* McAdoo, William Gibbs

Treaties: secret Allied, 138, 140, 143, 145, 259; Lloyd George's call for sanctity of, 143. *See also* Cooling-off treaties; Secret diplomacy; *names of specific treaties*

Treaty of London of 1915, p. 197

Treaty of Paris, 9

Treaty of Versailles, vii, 58; progressives' dismay with, x, 236, 252–54; Senate rejection of, 227, 256–57; Wilson's blame for, 250; scholarly criticism of, 272. *See also* Peace conference

Trevelyan, Charles P., 37, 108, 119

Trotsky, Leon, 140, 155, 241

Truman, Harry S, 272, 273

Trusts. *See* Antitrust legislation; Monopolies

Tumulty, Joseph P., 179–81, 186, 192, 226, 230–31, 238, 263, 267; postwar domestic reform proposals of, 255

Turkey. *See* Ottoman Empire

Turner, Frederick Jackson, viii, 10, 17

"Twilight of Idols" (Bourne), 147, 157

UDC. *See* Union of Democratic Control

Un-Americanism: Republican slurs about Democratic Party's alleged, 168, 169,

176, 187. *See also* "One Hundred Percent Americanism"

Unconditional surrender: American calls for Germany's, 169–72, 174–76, 180, 184. *See also* Victory

Underwood-Simmons bill, 23, 41, 93, 169

Union Club of New York, 180

Union of Democratic Control (Great Britain), 36–38, 50, 51, 57, 65, 76, 78, 108, 110, 115, 119, 139, 146, 164, 253. *See also* Great Britain: Wilson's relations with British radicals in

United Mine Workers, 93

United Nations, 272, 273–75

United States: its special relationship with Providence, 4, 6, 8, 10–12, 14; Wilson's views of role of, 20; trade, disarmament, and the, 22, 23; its intervention in Mexican Revolution, 24–30; and the Great War, 32; and League of Nations, 165; European postwar economic alliance with, 200–201, 222; its anti-Wilsonian actions, 273–74. *See also* American intervention

United States Court of Appeals: and wartime censorship, 136

United States Railroad Administration, 129

United States Shipping Board, 41

Universal Peace Union (Philadelphia), 19

University of Virginia, 5, 13

Veblen, Thorstein, 253

Veracruz (Mexico), 27

Verdun battle, 32, 74, 107

Vesnic, Melinko R., 217, 219

Victory (in the Great War), 189; conservative internationalists' support for, 58, 78; progressive internationalists' concerns about, 65, 78; and creation of League of Nations, 80; Allies' insistence on, 107; Lansing's insistence on, 110; Lodge's insistence on, 124–25. *See also* Unconditional surrender; Wilson, Woodrow: his desire for peace without victory

Vigilancia (ship), 117

Villa, Francisco ("Pancho"), 26–29, 81–83

Villard, Oswald Garrison, viii, 50, 61, 63, 114, 157, 245, 253, 257, 267; and wartime political repression, 134, 159–60, 186; on Roosevelt's death, 230

Villegas, Enrique, 41, 43

Vladivostok: Japan's designs on, 155–56

von Bernstorff, Count Johann, 44, 107, 111, 116

von Jagow, Gottlieb, 44, 46, 51

Vorwarts (Berlin), 213

Wald, Lillian, viii, 50–51, 94, 146, 157, 160, 269; and the AUAM, 63, 66, 114, 118, 131–32; and wartime political repression, 134, 135; denounces Versailles treaty, 254

Walling, William English, 29, 30, 53, 54, 94, 102, 118, 132

Walsh, David I., 257

Walsh, Frank P., 82

War: causes of, in Wilson's view, ix; and Christianity, 11–12; economic causes of, 38, 51, 57, 235, 242; Kennan's growing opposition to, 274–75. *See also* Peace; War aims

War aims: British, 44, 47, 119; German, 44, 47; debate over, 137–47, 154, 162–66, 170; and agitation for League of Nations plan, 148–66. *See also* Imperialism

"War and the Way Out, The" (Lowes Dickinson), 37–38

War bonds. *See* Liberty Loans

"War-guilt clause," 250

War Industries Board, 129

"War Program for Liberals, A," 129

"Warrant from History" (LEP), 56

Warsaw Pact, 273

"War socialism," 239–40, 255, 268. *See also* Nationalization

Washington, George, 13, 111, 241, 276; his Farewell Address, 76, 124, 163, 240

Washington Post, 42

Washington (State), 102

Wayland, Julius, 17

Weapons. *See* Armaments

Webb, Sidney, 29

Weekly People, 93

Weinstein, Dr. Edwin, 264, 265

Wellesley College, 50

Wellington Koo, V. K., 217, 219

Wesleyan University, 5

Westenhaver, Judge D. C., 159

Western Federation of Miners, 94–95

West Virginia Federation of Labor, 147

Weyl, Walter, 64, 94

"What Ought We to Do?" (Wilson), 9

"Wheat Thesis" (of 1918 congressional elections), 185

White, Henry, 189

White, William Allen, 64, 89, 100

White House dinner: Wilson's congressional, 231–33, 239, 241

Widenor, William C., 28, 99, 124, 239, 257

Wilhelm II (Kaiser), 22, 108, 110, 116, 141, 172, 173, 174; abdication of, 189

Williams, William Appleman, 43, 144

Willkie, Wendell L., 272

Wilson, Edith Bolling Galt (second Mrs. Wilson), 162, 179, 195, 246, 260, 263, 271, 272; marriage of, 70–71. *See also* Galt, Edith Bolling

Wilson, Ellen Axson (first Mrs. Wilson): death of, 32, 35. *See also* Axson, Ellen Louise

Wilson, Henry Lane, 25

Wilson, Dr. Joseph Ruggles, 3, 4, 9, 265

Wilson, Margaret, 272

Wilson, Thomas Woodrow. *See* Wilson, Woodrow

Wilson, William B., 132, 174

Wilson, Woodrow: background and early political development of, 3–14; religious beliefs of, 3–4, 8, 14, 33; belief in democracy, 5–7, 14, 33, 121, 267; belief in covenants, 4–6, 10, 13–14, 22; as professor of international law, 8–9, 19–20; his views on socialism, 6–7, 9, 18; as President of Princeton, 16; enunciates New Freedom, 17; enacts New Freedom legislation, 23–24; as growing progressive, 15–30; 1912 presidential campaign of, 13–17; as New Jersey governor, 20; on role of U.S. in world affairs, 20; as diplomatist, 20, 74; views on imperialism, ix, 9–11, 25–26, 35–36, 77, 115, 138, 145, 155, 157, 180, 195, 206, 261–62, 266–68; attitudes toward war and revolution, ix, 3–4, 7–8, 44, 145; his analysis of causes of the Great War, 34–35, 36, 37–38, 112; relations with House, 20, 21, 46–47, 72, 73, 246; relations with Bryan, 21–22, 45, 60, 61; and the Mexican Revolution, 24–30, 81–84; and Tampico and Veracruz, 27–29; relations

with Roosevelt, 28–29, 49, 169; and American neutrality in Great War, 32–34, 47, 49, 60–61, 64, 81, 86, 119, 120; and Anglo-American relations, 33–34, 44–47, 49, 68–69, 73–75, 79–81, 107–10; and harsher attitude toward Britain, 79–81; and German submarine warfare, 34, 49, 59–61, 73–74, 108, 111, 115–17, 121; and *Lusitania* crisis, 61–62; and Preparedness controversy, 58–67, 78, 89–90, 93, 95; launches independent peace moves, 34–35, 44–47, 65, 72, 74–75; his desire for peace without victory, 34–36, 57, 106, 109, 111–16, 155, 170, 175; and Pan-American Pact, 39–44, 65, 68, 70–74, 81–84, 105; other countries' lack of candor with, 44, 46, 73, 182; and European war aims, 44, 137–38, 140–43, 170; and early development of League of Nations idea, 49–50, 65, 68, 74–79; his relations with progressive internationalists, 51–52, 54–55, 62–63, 158, 160; his relations with conservative internationalists, 55–58, 189–91, 244–45, 247, 267; and the *Arabic* pledge, 60–61, 73; and House-Grey Memorandum, 72–74, 80, 107–8; and *Sussex* pledge, 74; as leader of American League of Nations movement, 78, 105–6, 109, 112–15, 119, 150–54, 165; his intervention in Latin American countries, 81–84; drafts 1916 platform based on "Progressive Democracy," 86; League becomes a partisan issue in 1916 reelection campaign of, 85–86, 95–103, 105–6, 123, 187; social-justice legislation passed during 1916 reelection campaign of, 86–95; appearance on Capitol Hill to push for social-justice legislation, 90–91; his insistence on League's link to peace negotiations, 106–17, 162–63, 190, 195, 199–200, 204, 209; relations with Lansing, 108, 110–11, 205–6, 214; Senate debates proposals of, 109–13; severs diplomatic relations with Germany and pursues "armed neutrality," 116–17, 121; receives emergency peace delegation, 118; his despair over impending war, 116–17; his desire to play a role in peace negotiations a motivation for entering the Great War, 45, 118–20, 189–93; asks Congress to declare war on Germany, 121–22; his wartime refusal to discuss the League linked to Republican opposition to his ideas, ix, 124–28, 148–54, 160–61, 165, 185–86, 188, 204; failure to educate public about League after U.S. enters the war, 127–28, 165, 243–44, 260–62, 268; blunders of, 127–28, 160, 187, 189, 268; relations with Taft, 128, 149, 177, 188, 192, 244; criticism of, by business community, 130–31; criticism of, by progressive internationalists, 131–32; his determination to prosecute the Great War, 132–33, 139; political repression of progressive internationalists permitted under, x, 132–37, 158–60, 165, 168, 181, 186–88, 235–39, 255–57, 268, 269; warned by progressive internationalists of loss of their support, 158, 160; and secret Allied treaties, 138–39, 145; responds to Pope's peace appeal, 139–40; opposes allied intervention in Russia, 154–56; agrees under protest to participate in intervention in Russia, 156–58; his appeal to "the people," 162; and armistice negotiations, 166–75, 181–84, 189, 192, 209; and congressional campaign of 1918, pp. 167–69, 176–81, 184–89, 229; heads American delegation to peace conference, 189–92; popularity of, in Europe, 191–92, 194–201, 209; and Clemenceau, 198–99, 210, 213; effect of Smuts' report on, 202–3; at Paris Peace Conference, 204–26, 246–51; relations with Cecil, 208; as chairman of League of Nations Commission, 217; homecoming of, and efforts to persuade Americans to support the League, 230–44; and the League as an issue in the 1920 elections, 239–43; on his Republican critics, 241; response to Lodge's "Round Robin" and reservationist movement, 241–47, 251, 258–59, 262, 264–69; health of, 250, 251, 259–60; his Western tour on behalf of ratification, 259–62; his refusal to accept Lodge reservations to League Covenant,

260–62, 265–67, 268; his stroke, 262–65, 267; Senate rejects treaty, 263–64; his last day in office, 271; legacy of, x, 105–6, 108, 271–76. *See also* "Appeal for a Democratic Congress"; Covenant; "First Paris Draft"; Flag Day address; Fourteen Points address; Fourth Liberty Loan address; League to Enforce Peace: Wilson's address to; Peace note(s); "Peace Without Victory" address; "Second Paris Draft"; State of the Union address

Wilson (movie), 272

"Wilson and the World's Future" (Eastman), 147

"Wilsonism," 168

Wise, Rabbi Stephen S., viii, 63, 66, 94, 118

Wiseman, Sir William, 152, 154, 156, 200, 203, 216

Woman's Peace party (WPP), xiii, 76, 187; its "Proposal for a Constructive Peace," 51, 52; positions taken by, 50–52, 54, 55, 57, 63, 65, 146, 148; influence of, on Wilson, 52; and averting of war with Mexico, 82–83; opposition to American participation in Great War by, 117. *See also* Addams, Jane; Wald, Lillian

Woman suffrage: and Wilson, 24, 50

Women: their support for Wilson in 1916 reelection campaign, 101

Wood, General Leonard, 62

Woodrow Wilson Independent League, 93, 98

Workers' compensation: Roosevelt's proposals for, 16; 90–91

World Court League, 228

World federation: ideas about, 12

World Peace Foundation, 51

"World's Peace, A" (Eastman), 146

World Tomorrow, 157, 159

World War I. *See* Great War.

World War II: possible averting of, 272; Wilson's prophesy of, 262, 272

WPP. *See* Woman's Peace party

Zanuck, Darryl F., 272

Zimmermann, Arthur, 46, 116–17, 118

Zimmermann Note, 116–17, 118